CompTIA® Security+
Guide to Network
Security Fundamentals

Fifth Edition

Mark Ciampa, Ph.D.

CENGAGE
Learning·

Australia • Brazil • Japan • Korea • Mexico • Singapore • Spain • United Kingdom • United States

CENGAGE Learning®

CompTIA® Security+ Guide to Network Security Fundamentals, Fifth Edition

Mark Ciampa, Ph.D.

Senior Vice President, GM Skills & Global Product Management: Dawn Gerrain

Product Director: Kathleen McMahon

Product Manager: Nick Lombardi

Senior Director, Development: Marah Bellegarde

Product Development Manager: Leigh Hefferon

Managing Content Developer: Emma Newsom

Senior Content Developer: Michelle Ruelos Cannistraci

Developmental Editor: Deb Kaufmann

Product Assistant: Scott Finger

Marketing Manager: Eric LaScola

Senior Director, Production: Wendy A. Troeger

Production Director: Patty Stephan

Senior Content Project Manager: Kara A. DiCaterino

Art Director: GEX

Cover and Interior Design Images: ©Sergey Nivens/Shutterstock.com

> For product information and technology assistance, contact us at
> **Cengage Learning Customer & Sales Support, 1-800-354-9706**
>
> For permission to use material from this text or product,
> submit all requests online at **cengage.com/permissions**
> Further permissions questions can be emailed to
> **permissionrequest@cengage.com**

Library of Congress Control Number: 2014940611

Book Only ISBN: 978-1-305-09394-2

Package ISBN: 978-1-305-09391-1

Cengage Learning
20 Channel Center Street
Boston, MA 02210
USA

Cengage Learning is a leading provider of customized learning solutions with office locations around the globe, including Singapore, the United Kingdom, Australia, Mexico, Brazil, and Japan. Locate your local office at: **www.cengage.com/global**

Cengage Learning products are represented in Canada by Nelson Education, Ltd.

To learn more about Cengage Learning, visit **www.cengage.com**

Purchase any of our products at your local college store or at our preferred online store **www.cengagebrain.com**

Printed in the United States of America
Print Number: 02 Print Year: 2015

Brief Contents

PART VI   Access Control and Identity Management   439

CHAPTER 11
Access Control Fundamentals **441**

CHAPTER 12
Authentication and Account Management **477**

Table of Contents

PART VII   **Compliance and Operational Security**   **521**

CHAPTER 13
Business Continuity **523**

CHAPTER 14
Risk Mitigation **565**

Introduction

The number one concern of computer professionals today continues to be information security, and with good reason. Consider the evidence: a computer cluster for cracking passwords can generate 350 billion password guesses *per second* and could break any eight-character password in a maximum of 5.5 hours. Internet web servers must resist thousands of attacks every day, and an unprotected computer connected to the Internet can be infected in fewer than 60 seconds. From 2005 through early 2014, more than 666 million electronic data records in the U.S. had been breached, exposing to attackers a range of personal electronic data, such as address, Social Security numbers, health records, and credit card numbers.[i] Attackers who penetrated the network of a credit card processing company that handles prepaid debit cards manipulated the balances and limits on just *five* prepaid cards. These cards were then used to withdraw almost $5 million cash from automated teller machines (ATMs) in *one month*.

As attacks continue to escalate, the need for trained security personnel also increases. According to the U.S. Bureau of Labor Statistics (BLS) "Occupational Outlook Handbook," the job outlook for information security analysts through the end of the decade is expected to grow by 22 percent, faster than the average growth rate. The increase in employment will add 65,700 positions to the more than 300,000 already in this field.[ii] And unlike some information technology (IT) positions, security is rarely offshored or outsourced: because security is such a critical element in an organization, security positions generally remain within the organization. In addition, security jobs typically do not involve "on-the-job training" where employees can learn as they go; the risk is simply too great. IT employers want and pay a premium for certified security personnel.

To verify security competency, a vast majority of organizations use the Computing Technology Industry Association (CompTIA) Security+ certification, a vendor-neutral credential. Security+ is one of the most widely recognized security certifications and has become the security foundation for today's IT professionals. It is internationally recognized as validating a foundation level of security skills and knowledge. A successful Security+ candidate has the knowledge and skills required to identify risks and participate in risk mitigation activities; provide infrastructure, application, operational, and information security; apply security controls to maintain confidentiality, integrity, and availability; identify appropriate technologies and products; troubleshoot security events and incidents; and operate with an awareness of applicable policies, laws, and regulations.

CompTIA® Security+ Guide to Network Security Fundamentals, Fifth Edition is designed to equip learners with the knowledge and skills needed to be secure IT professionals. Yet it is more than merely an "exam prep" book. While teaching the fundamentals of information security by using the CompTIA Security+ exam objectives as its framework, it takes an in-depth and comprehensive view of security by examining the attacks that are launched against networks and computer systems, the necessary defense mechanisms, and even offers end-user practical tools, tips, and techniques to counter attackers. *CompTIA® Security+ Guide to Network Security Fundamentals, Fifth Edition* is a valuable tool for those who want to learn about security and who desire to enter the field of information security by providing the foundation that will help prepare for the CompTIA Security+ certification exam.

Intended Audience

This book is designed to meet the needs of students and professionals who want to master basic information security. A fundamental knowledge of computers and networks is all that is required to use this book. Those seeking to pass the CompTIA Security+ certification exam will find the text's approach and content especially helpful; all Security+ SY0-401 exam objectives are covered in the text (see Appendix A). *CompTIA® Security+ Guide to Network Security Fundamentals, Fifth Edition* covers all aspects of network and computer security while satisfying the Security+ objectives.

The book's pedagogical features are designed to provide a truly interactive learning experience to help prepare you for the challenges of network and computer security. In addition to the information presented in the text, each chapter includes Hands-On Projects that guide you through implementing practical hardware, software, network, and Internet security configurations step by step. Each chapter also contains case studies that place you in the role of problem solver, requiring you to apply concepts presented in the chapter to achieve successful solutions.

Chapter Descriptions

Here is a summary of the topics covered in each chapter of this book:

Chapter 1, "Introduction to Security," introduces the network security fundamentals that form the basis of the Security+ certification. It begins by examining the current challenges in computer security and why security is so difficult to achieve. It then defines information security in detail and explores why it is important. Finally, the chapter looks at the fundamental attacks, including who is responsible for them, and defenses.

Chapter 2, "Malware and Social Engineering Attacks," examines attacks that use different types of malware, such as viruses, worms, Trojans, and botnets. It also looks at the different types of social engineering attacks.

Chapter 3, "Application and Networking-Based Attacks," continues the discussion of threats and vulnerabilities from the previous chapter's coverage of malware and social engineering. First the chapter looks at attacks that target server-side and client-side web applications; then it explores some of the common attacks that are launched against networks today.

Chapter 4, "Host, Application, and Data Security," looks at security for host systems achieved through both physical means and technology. It also examines devices beyond common general-purpose computers, followed by an exploration of application security. Finally, it looks at how securing the data itself can provide necessary protections.

Chapter 5, "Basic Cryptography," explores how encryption can be used to protect data. It covers what cryptography is and how it can be used for protection, and then examines how to protect data using three common types of encryption algorithms: hashing, symmetric encryption, and asymmetric encryption. It also covers how to use cryptography on files and disks to keep data secure.

Chapter 6, "Advanced Cryptography," examines digital certificates and how they can be used. It also looks at public key infrastructure and key management. This chapter covers different transport cryptographic algorithms to see how cryptography is used on data that is being transported.

Chapter 7, "Network Security Fundamentals," explores how to secure a network through standard network devices, through network technologies, and by network design elements.

Chapter 8, "Administering a Secure Network," looks at the techniques for administering a network. This includes understanding common network protocols and employing network design principles. It also looks at securing three popular types of network applications: IP telephony, virtualization, and cloud computing.

Chapter 9, "Wireless Network Security," investigates the attacks on wireless devices that are common today and explores different wireless security mechanisms that have proven to be vulnerable. It also covers several secure wireless protections.

Chapter 10, "Mobile Device Security," looks at the different types of mobile devices and the risks associated with these devices. It also explores how to secure these devices and the applications running on them. Finally, it examines how users can bring their own personal mobile devices to work and connect them to the secure corporate network without compromising that network.

Chapter 11, "Access Control Fundamentals," introduces the principles and practices of access control by examining access control terminology, the standard control models, and their best practices. It also covers authentication services, which are used to verify approved users.

Chapter 12, "Authentication and Account Management," looks at authentication and the secure management of user accounts that enforces authentication. It covers the different types of authentication credentials that can be used to verify a user's identity and how a single sign-on might be used. It also examines the techniques and technology used to manage user accounts in a secure fashion.

Chapter 13, "Business Continuity," covers the importance of keeping business processes and communications operating normally in the face of threats and disruptions. It explores disaster recovery, environmental controls, incident response procedures, and forensics.

Chapter 14, "Risk Mitigation," looks at how organizations can establish and maintain security in the face of risk. It defines risk and the steps to control it. This chapter also covers security policies and the different types of policies that are used to reduce risk. Finally, it explores how training and awareness can help provide the user with the tools to maintain a secure environment within the organization.

Chapter 15, "Vulnerability Assessment," explains what vulnerability assessment is and examines the tools and techniques associated with it. It also explores the differences between vulnerability scanning and penetration testing. The risks associated with third-party integration into a system are examined as well, as are controls to mitigate and deter attacks.

Appendix A, "CompTIA SY0-401 Certification Examination Objectives," provides a complete listing of the latest CompTIA Security+ certification exam objectives and shows the chapters and headings in the book that cover material associated with each objective.

Appendix B, "Downloads and Tools for Hands-On Projects," lists the websites used in the chapter Hands-On Projects.

Appendix C, "Security Websites," offers a listing of several important websites that contain security-related information.

Appendix D, "Selected TCP/IP Ports and Their Threats," lists common TCP/IP ports and their security vulnerabilities.

Appendix E, "Information Security Community Site," lists the features of the companion website for this textbook.

Features

To aid you in fully understanding computer and network security, this book includes many features designed to enhance your learning experience.

- **Maps to CompTIA Objectives.** The material in this text covers all of the CompTIA Security+ SY0-401 exam objectives.

- **Chapter Objectives.** Each chapter begins with a detailed list of the concepts to be mastered in that chapter. This list provides you with both a quick reference to the chapter's contents and a useful study aid.

- **Today's Attacks and Defenses.** Each chapter opens with a vignette of an actual security attack or defense mechanism that helps to introduce the material covered in that chapter.

- **Illustrations and Tables.** Numerous illustrations of security vulnerabilities, attacks, and defenses help you visualize security elements, theories, and concepts. In addition, the many tables provide details and comparisons of practical and theoretical information.

- **Chapter Summaries.** Each chapter's text is followed by a summary of the concepts introduced in that chapter. These summaries provide a helpful way to review the ideas covered in each chapter.

- **Key Terms.** All of the terms in each chapter that were introduced with bold text are gathered in a Key Terms list with definitions at the end of the chapter, providing additional review and highlighting key concepts.

- **Review Questions.** The end-of-chapter assessment begins with a set of review questions that reinforce the ideas introduced in each chapter. These questions help you evaluate and apply the material you have learned. Answering these questions will ensure that you have mastered the important concepts and provide valuable practice for taking CompTIA's Security+ exam.

- **Hands-On Projects.** Although it is important to understand the theory behind network security, nothing can improve on real-world experience. To this end, each chapter provides several Hands-On Projects aimed at providing you with practical security software and hardware implementation experience. These projects use the Windows 8.1 or 7 operating system, as well as software downloaded from the Internet.

- **Case Projects.** Located at the end of each chapter are several Case Projects. In these extensive exercises, you implement the skills and knowledge gained in the chapter through real design and implementation scenarios.

New to This Edition

- Fully maps to the latest CompTIA Security+ exam SY0-401

- All new chapter on mobile device security

- Chapters grouped by major domains: Threats, Basic Security, Cryptography, Network Security, Mobile Security, Access Control and Identity Management, and Compliance and Operational Security

- Earlier coverage of cryptography and advanced cryptography

- All new "Today's Attacks and Defenses" opener in each chapter

- Completely revised and updated with expanded coverage on attacks and defenses

- Additional Hands-On Projects in each chapter covering some of the latest security software

- More Case Projects in each chapter

- Information Security Community Site activity in each chapter allows learners to interact with other learners and security professionals from around the world

Text and Graphic Conventions

Wherever appropriate, additional information and exercises have been added to this book to help you better understand the topic at hand. Icons throughout the text alert you to additional materials. The icons used in this textbook are described below.

The Note icon draws your attention to additional helpful material related to the subject being described.

Tips based on the author's experience provide extra information about how to attack a problem or what to do in real-world situations.

The Caution icons warn you about potential mistakes or problems, and explain how to avoid them.

Each Hands-On Project in this book is preceded by the Hands-On icon and a description of the exercise that follows.

Case Project icons mark Case Projects, which are scenario-based assignments. In these extensive case examples, you are asked to implement independently what you have learned.

CertBlaster Test Prep Resources

CompTIA® Security+ Guide to Network Security Fundamentals includes CertBlaster test preparation questions that mirror the look and feel of the CompTIA Security+ certification exam.

To log in and access the CertBlaster test preparation questions for *CompTIA® Security+ Guide to Network Security Fundamentals, Fifth Edition*, go to *www.certblaster.com/login/*.

Activate your CertBlaster license by entering your name, email address, and access code (found on the card bound in this book) in their fields, and then click Submit.

The CertBlaster user's online manual describes features and gives navigation instructions. CertBlaster offers three practice modes and all the types of questions required to simulate the exams:

- *Assessment mode*—Used to determine the student's baseline level. In this mode, the timer is on, answers are not available, and the student gets a list of questions answered incorrectly, along with a Personal Training Plan.

- *Study mode*—Helps the student understand questions and the logic behind answers by giving immediate feedback both during and after the test. Answers and explanations are available. The timer is optional, and the student gets a list of questions answered incorrectly, along with a Personal Training Plan.

- *Certification mode*—A simulation of the actual exam environment. The timer as well as the number and format of questions from the exam objectives are set according to the exam's format.

For more information about dti test prep products, visit the website at *www.dtipublishing.com*.

Instructor's Materials

Everything you need for your course in one place! This collection of book-specific lecture and class tools is available online. Please visit *login.cengage.com* and log in to access instructor-specific resources on the Instructor Companion Site, which includes the Instructor's Manual, Solutions Manual, test creation tools, PowerPoint Presentations, Syllabus, and figure files.

Electronic Instructor's Manual. The Instructor's Manual that accompanies this textbook includes the following items: additional instructional material to assist in class preparation, including suggestions for lecture topics.

Solutions Manual. The instructor's resources include solutions to all end-of-chapter material, including review questions and case projects.

Cengage Learning Testing Powered by Cognero. This flexible, online system allows you to do the following:

- Author, edit, and manage test bank content from multiple Cengage Learning solutions.

- Create multiple test versions in an instant.

- Deliver tests from your LMS, your classroom, or wherever you want.

PowerPoint Presentations. This book comes with a set of Microsoft PowerPoint slides for each chapter. These slides are meant to be used as a teaching aid for classroom presentations, to be made available to students on the network for chapter review, or to be printed for classroom distribution. Instructors are also at liberty to add their own slides for other topics introduced.

Figure Files. All of the figures and tables in the book are reproduced. Similar to PowerPoint presentations, these are included as a teaching aid for classroom presentation, to make available to students for review, or to be printed for classroom distribution.

Total Solutions for Security

To access additional course materials, please visit *www.cengagebrain.com*. At the *CengageBrain.com* home page, search for the ISBN of your title (from the back cover of your book) using the search box at the top of the page. This will take you to the product page where these resources can be found. Additional resources include a Lab Manual, CourseMate, CourseNotes, assessment, and digital labs.

Information Security Community Site

Stay secure with the Information Security Community Site! Connect with students, professors, and professionals from around the world, and stay on top of this ever-changing field.

Visit *www.community.cengage.com/infosec* to:

- **Download** resources such as instructional videos and labs.
- **Ask** authors, professors, and students the questions that are on your mind in our Discussion Forums.
- **See** up-to-date news, videos, and articles.
- **Read** weekly blogs from author Mark Ciampa.
- **Listen** to podcasts on the latest Information Security topics.

Each chapter's Case Projects include information on a current security topic and ask the learner to post reactions and comments to the Information Security Community Site. This allows users from around the world to interact and learn from other users as well as security professionals and researchers.

Additional information can be found in Appendix E, *Information Security Community Site*.

What's New with CompTIA Security+ Certification

The CompTIA Security+ SY0-401 exam was updated in May 2014. Several significant changes have been made to the exam objectives. The exam objectives have been significantly expanded to more accurately reflect current security issues and knowledge requirements. These exam objectives place more importance on knowing "how to" rather than just knowing or recognizing security concepts.

Here are the domains covered on the new Security+ exam:

Domain	Percentage of examination
1.0 Network Security	20%
2.0 Compliance and Operational Security	18%
3.0 Threats and Vulnerabilities	20%
4.0 Application, Data, and Host Security	15%
5.0 Access Control and Identity Management	15%
6.0 Cryptography	12%

CompTIA.

It Pays to Get Certified

In a digital world, digital literacy is an essential survival skill.

Certification demonstrates that you have the knowledge and skill to solve technical or business problems in virtually any business environment. CompTIA certifications are highly- valued credentials that qualify you for jobs, increased compensation and promotion.

LEARN ⟶ **CERTIFY** ⟶ **WORK**

IT is Everywhere	IT Knowledge and Skills Get Jobs	Job Retention	New Opportunities	High Pay-High Growth Jobs
IT is mission critical to almost all organizations and its importance is increasing. • 79% of U.S. businesses report IT is either important or very important to the success of their company	Certifications verify your knowledge and skills that qualifies you for: • Jobs in the high growth IT career field • Increased compensation • Challenging assignments and promotions • 60% report that being certified is an employer or job requirement	Competence is noticed and valued in organizations. • Increased knowledge of new or complex technologies • Enhanced productivity • More insightful problem solving • Better project management and communication skills • 47% report being certified helped improve their probelm solving skills	Certifications qualify you for new opportunities in your current job or when you want to change careers. • 31% report certification improved their career advancement opportunities	Hiring managers demand the strongest skill set. • There is a widening IT skills gap with over 300,000 jobs open • 88% report being certified enhanced their resume

- **Security is one of the highest demand job categories** – growing in importance as the frequency and severity of security threats continues to be a major concern for organizations around the world.

- **Jobs for security administrators are expected to increase by 18%** -the skill set required for these types of jobs maps to the CompTIA Security+ certification.

- **Network Security Administrators -** can earn as much as $106,000 per year.

- **CompTIA Security+ is the first step -** in starting your career as a Network Security Administrator or Systems Security Administrator.

- **More than ¼ million** – individuals worldwide are CompTIA Security+ certified.

- **CompTIA Security+ is regularly used in organizations -** such as Hitachi Systems, Fuji Xerox, HP, Dell, and a variety of major U.S. government contractors.

- **Approved by the U.S. Department of Defense (DoD) -** as one of the required certification options in the DoD 8570.01-M directive, for Information Assurance Technical Level II and Management Level I job roles.

Security+

Certification Helps Your Career

Steps to Getting Certified and Staying Certified	
Review Exam Objectives	Review the Certification objectives to make sure you know what is covered in the exam http://certification.comptia.org/examobjectives.aspx
Practice for the Exam	After you have studied for the certification, review and answer the sample questions to get an idea what type of questions might be on the exam. http://certification.comptia.org/samplequestions.aspx
Purchase an Exam Voucher	Purchase exam vouchers on the CompTIA Marketplace. www.comptiastore.com
Take the Test!	Go to the Pearson VUE website and schedule a time to take your exam. http://www.pearsonvue.com/comptia/
Stay Certified! **Continuing Education**	Effective January 1, 2011, new CompTIA Security+ certifications are valid for three years from the date of certification. There are a number of ways the certification can be renewed. For more information go to: http://certification.comptia.org/ce

How to obtain more information

- **Visit CompTIA online** - http://certification.comptia.org/home.aspx to learn more about getting CompTIA certified.
- **Contact CompTIA** - call 866-835-8020 and choose Option 2 or email questions@comptia.org.
- **Connect with us :**

CompTIA is a nonprofit information technology (IT) trade association.

The Computing Technology Industry Association (CompTIA) is the voice of the world's information technology (IT) industry. Its members are the companies at the forefront of innovation and the professionals responsible for maximizing the benefits organizations receive from their investments in technology.

CompTIA is dedicated to advancing industry growth through its educational programs, market research, networking events, professional certifications, and public policy advocacy.

CompTIA is a not-for-profit trade information technology (IT) trade association. CompTIA's certifications are designed by subject matter experts from across the IT industry. Each CompTIA certification is vendor-neutral, covers multiple technologies, and requires demonstration of skills and knowledge widely sought after by the IT industry.

The CompTIA Marks are the proprietary trademarks and/or service marks of CompTIA Properties, LLC used under license from CompTIA Certifications, LLC through participation in the CompTIA Authorized Partner Program. More information about the program can be found at: http://www.comptia.org/certifications/capp/login.aspx.

About the Author

Mark Ciampa, Ph.D., Security+, is Associate Professor of Information Systems at Western Kentucky University in Bowling Green, Kentucky. Previously, he served as Associate Professor and Director of Academic Computing for 20 years at Volunteer State Community College in Gallatin, Tennessee. Dr. Ciampa has worked in the IT industry as a computer consultant for the U.S. Postal Service, the Tennessee Municipal Technical Advisory Service, and the University of Tennessee. He is also the author of many Cengage Learning textbooks, including *CWNA Guide to Wireless LANs, Third Edition*; *Guide to Wireless Communications*; *Security Awareness: Applying Practical Security in Your World, Fourth Edition*; and *Networking BASICS*. He holds a Ph.D. in technology management with a specialization in digital communication systems from Indiana State University.

Acknowledgments

A large team of dedicated professionals all contributed to the creation of this book. I am honored to be part of such an outstanding group of professionals, and to everyone on the team I extend my sincere thanks. A special thanks goes to Product Manager Nick Lombardi for giving me the opportunity to work on this project and for providing his continual support. Also thanks to Senior Content Developer Michelle Ruelos Cannistraci who was very supportive and helped keep this fast-moving project on track, and to Serge Palladino and Danielle Shaw, Technical Editors, as well as the excellent production and permissions teams at Cengage Learning, including Kara DiCaterino, Ashley Maynard, and Kathy Kucharek. And a big Thank-You to the team of peer reviewers who evaluated each chapter and provided very helpful suggestions and contributions: Angela Herring, Wilson Community College; Dan Hutcherson, Forsyth Technical Community College; Ahmad Nasraty, Heald College; and Deanne Wesley, Forsyth Technical Community College.

Special recognition again goes to the best developmental editor any author could wish for, Deb Kaufmann. First and foremost, Deb is a true professional in every sense of the word. She made many helpful suggestions, found all of my errors, watched every small detail, and even took on additional responsibilities so that this project could meet its deadlines. But even more, Deb is a joy to work with. Without question, Deb is simply the very best there is.

And finally, I want to thank my wonderful wife, Susan. Once again her patience, support, and love helped me through this project. I could not have written this book without her.

Dedication

To Braden, Mia, Abby, Gabe, and Cora.

To the User

This book should be read in sequence, from beginning to end. Each chapter builds on those that precede it to provide a solid understanding of networking security fundamentals. The book may also be used to prepare for CompTIA's Security+ certification exam. Appendix A pinpoints the chapters and sections in which specific Security+ exam objectives are located.

Hardware and Software Requirements

Following are the hardware and software requirements needed to perform the end-of-chapter Hands-On Projects.

- Microsoft Windows 8.1 or 7
- An Internet connection and web browser
- Microsoft Office
- Microsoft Office Outlook 2013

Free Downloadable Software Requirements

Free, downloadable software is required for the Hands-On Projects in the following chapters. Appendix B lists the websites where these can be downloaded.

Chapter 1:

- Oracle VirtualBox

Chapter 2:

- Irongeek Thumbscrew
- Kaspersky TDSSKiller
- GMER
- Spyrix Keylogger

Chapter 3:

- GRC Securable

Chapter 4:

- EICAR AntiVirus Test File

Chapter 5:

- OpenPuff Steganography
- MD5DEEP
- HASHDEEP
- HashTab
- TrueCrypt

Chapter 6:

- Comodo Digital Certificate

Chapter 7:

- ThreatFire
- K9 Web Protection

Chapter 8:

- Sandboxie
- VMware vCenter
- VMware Player

Chapter 9:

- Vistumbler
- SMAC

Chapter 10:

- Prey
- Bluestacks

Chapter 12:

- GreyC Keystroke
- KeePass

Chapter 13:

- Macrium Reflect
- Briggs Software Directory Snoop

Chapter 15:

- Secunia Personal Software Inspector
- Nmap

References

i. "Chronology of data breaches: Security breaches 2005–present," *Privacy Rights Clearinghouse*, updated Dec. 4, 2013, accessed Dec. 4, 2013, www.privacyrights.org/data-breach.

ii. "Network and computer systems administrators: Occupational outlook handbook," *Bureau of Labor Statistics*, Mar. 29, 2012, accessed Mar. 30, 2013, www.bls.gov/ooh/Computer-and-Information-Technology/Network-and-computer-systems-administrators.htm.

## chapter 1

Introduction to Security

After completing this chapter, you should be able to do the following:

- Describe the challenges of securing information
- Define information security and explain why it is important
- Identify the types of attackers that are common today
- List the basic steps of an attack
- Describe the five basic principles of defense

Today's Attacks and Defenses

What is the deadliest security attack that you can imagine? A virus that erases all the contents of a hard disk drive? A malicious program that locks up files until the user pays a "ransom" to have them released? The theft of millions of user passwords? Although each of these attacks can be extremely harmful, the *deadliest* attacks could result in the actual *death* of the victim. These deadly attacks are directed against medical devices that sick patients rely upon to live.

An insulin pump is a small medical device worn by diabetics that administers insulin as an alternative to multiple daily injections with an insulin syringe or pen. One security researcher, himself a diabetic, demonstrated at a security conference a wireless attack on an insulin pump that could secretly change the delivery dosage of insulin to the patient.[1] By scanning for wireless devices in a public space up to 300 feet (91 meters), this researcher could locate vulnerable insulin pumps made by a specific medical device manufacturer, and then force these devices to dispense fatal insulin doses—just as an attacker could.[2] Another security researcher "hacked" into a defibrillator used to stabilize heartbeats and reprogrammed it, and also disabled its power-save mode so the battery ran down in hours instead of years. It is estimated that there are more than 3 million pacemakers and 1.7 million Implantable Cardioverter Defibrillators (ICDs) in use today that are vulnerable to these types of wireless attacks.[3] This threat was so real that a former vice president of the U.S. had his defibrillator removed and replaced with one that lacked capabilities that an attacker might exploit.

Other serious concerns regarding medical devices have also surfaced. A vendor that manufactures medical ventilators maintains a website from which software updates to the ventilators can be downloaded and installed. A security researcher discovered that the website was infected with 48 viruses that could be installed on a user's computer, and 20 of the 347 pages of this website contained infections.[4] And spreading medical device malware is not limited to infecting websites. Today devices that perform medical imaging like computerized tomography (CT) scans automatically send scan results as PDF file attachments to email accounts. This email capability can be highly vulnerable and make an ideal entry point for an attacker to install medical device malware.

The U.S. Department of Homeland Security (DHS) has issued a report entitled "Attack Surface: Healthcare and Public Health Sector." This report says these attacks are "now becoming a major concern…. In a world in which communication networks and medical devices can dictate life or death, these systems, if compromised, pose a significant threat to the public and private sector."[5] The national Information Security and Privacy Advisory Board (ISPAB) said that the United States Computer Emergency Readiness Team (US-CERT) should create "defined reporting categories for medical device cybersecurity incidents."[6]

(continued)

Until recently the Food and Drug Administration (FDA), which regulates the design and manufacture of medical devices, did not have any regulations regarding how these devices should be configured and connected to a network. Now the FDA is taking notice. It has issued an "FDA Safety Communication" document recommending that medical device manufacturers and health care facilities should "take steps to assure that appropriate safeguards are in place to reduce the risk of failure due to cyberattack, which could be initiated by the introduction of malware into the medical equipment or unauthorized access to configuration settings in medical devices and hospital networks." And to make sure that these recommendations are followed, the FDA has stated that for any medical devices that do not "appropriately address" security risks, the FDA "might consider" withholding its approval of the device.[7]

Our world today is one in which all citizens been forced to continually protect themselves, their families, and their property from attacks by invisible foes. Random shootings, suicide car bombings, airplane hijackings, and other types of physical violence occur around the world with increasing frequency. To counteract this violence, new types of security defenses have been implemented. Passengers using public transportation are routinely searched. Fences are erected across borders. Telephone calls are monitored. These attacks and the security defenses against them have impacted almost every element of our daily lives and significantly affect how all of us work, play, and live.

Yet these attacks are not just physical. One area that has also been an especially frequent target of attacks is information technology (IT). A seemingly endless array of attacks is directed at individuals, schools, businesses, and governments through desktop computers, laptops, smartphones, and tablet computers. Internet web servers must resist thousands of attacks every day. Identity theft using stolen electronic data has skyrocketed. An unprotected computer connected to the Internet can be infected in fewer than 60 seconds. Phishing, rootkits, worms, zombies, and botnets—virtually unheard of just a few years ago—are now part of our everyday security technology vocabulary.

The need to defend against these attacks directed toward our technology devices has created an element of IT that is now at the very core of the industry. Known as *information security*, it is focused on protecting the electronic information of organizations and users.

Two broad categories of information security personnel are responsible for this protection. Information security managerial personnel administer and manage plans, policies, and people. Information security technical personnel are concerned with designing, configuring, installing, and maintaining technical security equipment. Within these two broad categories are four generally recognized security positions:

- *Chief information security officer (CISO)*. This person reports directly to the chief information officer (CIO) (large organizations may have more layers of management between this person and the CIO). This person is responsible for assessing, managing, and implementing security.

- *Security manager*. The security manager reports to the CISO and supervises technicians, administrators, and security staff. Typically, a security manager works on tasks identified by the CISO and resolves issues identified by technicians.

This position requires an understanding of configuration and operation but not necessarily technical mastery.

- *Security administrator.* The security administrator has both technical knowledge and managerial skills. A security administrator manages daily operations of security technology, and may analyze and design security solutions within a specific entity as well as identifying users' needs.

- *Security technician.* This position is generally an entry-level position for a person who has the necessary technical skills. Technicians provide technical support to configure security hardware, implement security software, and diagnose and troubleshoot problems.

Individuals in these positions are not the only ones responsible for security. It is the job of every employee—both IT and non-IT—to know and practice basic security defenses.

Employment trends indicate that employees with certifications in security are in high demand. As attacks continue to escalate, the need for trained and certified security personnel also increases. Unlike some IT positions, security is rarely offshored or outsourced: because security is such a critical element in an organization, security positions generally remain within the organization. In addition, security jobs typically do not involve "on-the-job training" where employees can learn as they go; the risk is simply too great. IT employers want and pay a premium for certified security personnel.

The job outlook for security professionals is exceptionally strong. According to the U.S. Bureau of Labor Statistics (BLS) "Occupational Outlook Handbook," the job outlook for information security analysts through the end of the decade is expected to grow by 22 percent, faster than the average growth rate. The increase in employment will add 65,700 positions to the more than 300,000 already in this field.[8]

To verify security competency, a vast majority of organizations use the Computing Technology Industry Association (CompTIA) Security+ certification. Of the more than 250 security certifications currently available, Security+ is one of the most widely recognized security certifications and has become the security foundation for today's IT professionals. It is internationally recognized as validating a foundation level of security skills and knowledge.

The CompTIA Security+ certification is a vendor-neutral credential that requires passing the current certification exam SY0-401. A successful candidate has the knowledge and skills required to identify risks and participate in risk mitigation activities; provide infrastructure, application, operational and information security; apply security controls to maintain confidentiality, integrity, and availability; identify appropriate technologies and products; troubleshoot security events and incidents; and operate with an awareness of applicable policies, laws, and regulations.

The CompTIA Security+ certification is aimed at an IT security professional who has a recommended background of a minimum of two years' experience in IT administration with a focus on security, has technical information security experience on a daily basis, and possesses a broad knowledge of security concerns and implementation.

This chapter introduces the network security fundamentals that form the basis of the Security+ certification. It begins by examining the current challenges in computer security and why it is so difficult to achieve. It then defines information security in detail and explores why it is important. Finally, the chapter looks at who is responsible for these attacks and what are the fundamental attacks and defenses.

Challenges of Securing Information

A *silver bullet* is a specific and fail-safe solution that very quickly and easily solves a serious problem. To a casual observer it may seem that there should be such a silver bullet for securing computers, such as installing a better hardware device or using a more secure software application. But in reality, no single and simple solution to securing devices in order to protect the information contained on them is available. This can be illustrated through looking at the different types of attacks that users face today as well as the difficulties in defending against these attacks.

Today's Security Attacks

Despite the fact that information security continues to rank as the number one concern of IT managers and tens of billions of dollars are spent annually on computer security, the number of successful attacks continues to increase. Recent attacks include the following:

- Attackers penetrated the network of a credit card processing company that handles prepaid debit cards. They then manipulated the balances and limits on just *five* prepaid cards. These cards were then distributed to "cell managers" in different countries who were responsible for using the cards to withdraw cash from automated teller machines (ATMs). In one month almost $5 million was fraudulently withdrawn from ATM machines around the world in 5700 transactions. A cell in New York City was responsible for withdrawing $400,000 in 750 fraudulent transactions at 140 ATM locations in the city in only 2.5 hours. A similar attack manipulated account balances and withdrawal limits on 12 more cards that were distributed to cell members to withdraw an additional $40 million from ATM machines around the world. The New York City cell withdrew $2.4 million in 3000 ATM transactions in just 10 hours.

- Marc G. was in the kitchen when he began to hear strange sounds coming from the nursery of his two-year-old daughter Allyson. Marc and his wife entered the nursery and heard a stranger's voice calling out Allyson's name, cursing at her and calling her vile names. The parents discovered that the voice was coming from the electronic baby monitor in Allyson's room that contained a camera, microphone, and speaker connected to their home Wi-Fi network. Because they did not have any security set on their wireless network, the attacker had been able to take control of the baby monitor from an unknown remote location. When Marc and his wife stepped in front of the camera, the attacker turned his verbal attack toward them. They quickly unplugged the device. The parents surmised that the attacker knew their daughter's name because he saw "Allyson" spelled out on the wall in her room. This situation is not unique: it is estimated that there are more than 100,000 wireless cameras that can easily be exploited because they have virtually no security.

- The Twitter account of the Associated Press (AP) was broken into and a fictitious tweet was posted claiming there were "two explosions in the White House and [the U.S. President] is injured." Even though the tweet was only visible for a matter of minutes before it was removed, because of this fictitious tweet the Dow Jones industrial average dropped immediately (it recovered later in the day). AP now joins the ranks of many large corporate brands—including CBS television websites *60 Minutes* and *48 Hours*, the *New York Times*, the *Wall Street Journal*, the *Washington Post*, Burger King, and Jeep—who have been victims of recent Twitter break-ins. And these attacks will likely only escalate as social media sites become more frequently used for distributing information. The U.S. Securities and Exchange Commission (SEC) recently said that it would allow public companies to disclose corporate information on social media sites like Twitter.

- Malware called Ploutus that infects a bank's ATM demonstrates how vulnerable these cash-dispensing machines can be. The infection begins with the attacker inserting a CD-ROM disc that contains malware into the ATM computer's disc drive (on some ATMs the disc drive is actually accessible from the outside). The malware then installs a "backdoor" so that the attackers can manipulate the machine via the ATM's keypad. After entering the code *123456789ABCDEFG* to access the malware, instructions can be given through entering a series of numbers on the keypad. The latest version of Ploutus malware can be instructed to print the entire ATM configuration (if a USB printer is connected to an exposed USB port), display information about the money currently available in the ATM, and instruct the machine to dispense money.[9]

- A serial server is a device that connects to a remote system through the Internet (technically it provides remote access to serial ports over TCP/IP) so that administrators can access the remote system as if it were connected to the local network. The remote systems that use serial servers include not only traffic stoplight systems but also a wide variety of industrial control applications, point of sale (POS) terminals in retail stores, energy management devices, fueling stations, hospital medical device monitors, and oil and gas monitoring stations. Serial servers are highly vulnerable and can thus expose the remote systems that are connected to them. It is estimated that there are 114,000 serial servers accessible from the Internet that expose more than 13,000 serial ports and their connected remote systems.[10]

- Indonesia has now overtaken China as the number one source of attack traffic. About 38 percent of all attacks now come from Indonesia. China has fallen to second place with about 33 percent of all attacks coming from there, while the U.S. is at a distant third place (6.9 percent but down from 8.3 percent). These three countries, combined with seven others, now account for 89 percent of all attack traffic. The rapid ascent of Indonesia to the top of the list is even more significant given that previously this country accounted for only 1 percent of all attack traffic. The surge is evidently related to the increase in the average Internet connection speed in Indonesia: broadband access has increased 125 percent in one year.[11]

- A security researcher demonstrated how easy it would be to manipulate any aircraft in the sky. This is because the computers that control today's airplanes are not protected from attacks. The researcher, who both works in IT and is a trained commercial pilot, demonstrated how an attacker can easily upload bogus flight plans and give detailed commands to these systems. In one demonstration he showed how to manipulate the steering of a Boeing jet while the aircraft was in autopilot mode. He could also take control of most of the airplane's systems so that, for example, he could send panic throughout the aircraft cabin by making the oxygen masks drop down. And he could even make the plane crash by setting it on a collision course with another airplane in the vicinity.[12]

- Researchers have found similar weaknesses in the systems used by ocean vessels. Ships share information about their current position and course with other ships in the area as well as with offshore installations like harbors, and this information can be tracked via the Internet. Because this software is not protected, an attacker could easily modify every detail of the vessel, such as its position, course, speed, name, and status number. Attackers could also send fake alerts that a person has fallen overboard, that a storm is approaching, or that a collision is imminent with another ship. They could also create a fictitious "ghost" ship that does not even exist or change information about the type of ship or cargo it is carrying (in their test the researchers took a ship that was physically located on the Mississippi River in Missouri but made it appear as if the ship were on a lake in Dallas). An attacker could also alter a system that identifies buoys and lighthouses, causing ships to wreck.[13]

- Web browsers typically send User Agent Strings to a web server that identify such items as the browser type and the underlying operating system so that the web server can respond appropriately (for example, the web server can send different formats of the requested webpage based on what the browser can display). Attackers can use a web browser to send the User Agent String "xmlset_roodkcableoj28840ybtide" to specific wireless routers in order to access the router's settings through a "backdoor" and bypass all security. As an interesting note, it appears that this backdoor was actually implanted by the manufacturer: if the second half of the User Agent String is reversed and the number in the middle is removed, it reads *edit by joel backdoor*.[14]

- Online sites like Craigslist and eBay are very popular for buyers and sellers of items from electronics to automobiles. However, the Federal Bureau of Investigation (FBI) is warning buyers to beware. Attackers masquerading as legitimate sellers frequently advertise items at "too-good-to-be-true" prices to entice a large number of victims; however, the attackers do not post photos of the item for sale but instead offer to send a photo as an email attachment or as a link upon request. Increasingly these attachments contain malware: when the recipients open the attachment their computers become infected. Potential buyers are encouraged to not ask to be sent a photo but instead request that the original posting be modified so that it includes a photo.

- A computer cluster for cracking passwords was configured that comprised five servers and 25 graphics cards that can generate 350 billion password guesses (candidates) *per second*. This cluster could break any eight-character password in a maximum of 5.5 hours.

- Apple has admitted that Mac computers on its own campus became infected. Apple employees visited an infected website for software developers and their computers then became infected. The infection was successful because Apple's own computers were not updated with the latest security patches. Once the attack was identified by Apple it released a tool that patched 30 vulnerabilities and defects and disinfected malware on Apple Mac computers.

The number of security breaches that have exposed users' digital data to attackers continues to rise. From 2005 through early 2014 over 666 million electronic data records in the U.S. had been breached, exposing to attackers a range of personal electronic data, such as address, Social Security numbers, health records, and credit card numbers.[15] Table 1-1 lists some of the major security breaches that occurred during a one-month period, according to the Privacy Rights Clearinghouse.

Organization	Description of security breach	Number of identities exposed
University of Washington Medicine, WA	An employee opened an email attachment containing malicious software that infected the employee's computer and compromised the information on it. Patient names, Social Security numbers, phone numbers, addresses, and medical record numbers dating back five years may have been affected.	90,000
Maricopa County Community College District, AZ	An unspecified data breach may have exposed the information of current and former students, employees, and vendors. Names, Social Security numbers, bank account information, and dates of birth, as well as student academic information, may have been viewed by unauthorized parties.	2.49 million
University of California, San Francisco, CA	The theft of a physician's laptop from a car may have resulted in the exposure of patient information, including patient names, Social Security numbers, dates of birth, and medical record numbers.	8294
Redwood Memorial Hospital, CA	A USB flash drive was discovered missing that contained patient names, report ID numbers, test indications, ages, heights, weights, and clinical summaries of test findings for patients who were seen over a period of 12 years.	1039
Anthem Blue Cross, CA	The Social Security numbers and tax identification numbers of California doctors were posted in the online provider directory.	24,500
New York City Police Department, NY	A former police detective pleaded guilty to paying attackers to steal passwords associated with the email accounts of other officers. At least 43 email accounts and one cellular phone account were hacked.	30
Adobe Systems, San Jose, CA	The email addresses, encrypted passwords and password hints from Adobe Systems customers were stolen from a backup system about to be decommissioned.	152 million
Target Corporation, Minneapolis, MN	The credit and debit card numbers, expiration dates, and 3-digit CVV ("Card Verification Value") numbers of customers who made purchases during a 3-week period were stolen.	110 million

Table 1-1   Selected security breaches involving personal information in a one-month period

Difficulties in Defending Against Attacks

The challenge of keeping computers secure has never been greater, not only because of the number of attacks but also because of the difficulties faced in defending against these attacks. These difficulties include the following:

- *Universally connected devices.* It is unthinkable today for any technology device—desktop computer, tablet, laptop, or smartphone—not to be connected to the Internet. Although this provides enormous benefits, it also makes it easy for an attacker halfway around world to silently launch an attack against a connected device.

- *Increased speed of attacks.* With modern tools at their disposal, attackers can quickly scan millions of devices to find weaknesses and launch attacks with unprecedented speed. Most attack tools initiate new attacks without any human participation, thus increasing the speed at which systems are attacked.

- *Greater sophistication of attacks.* Attacks are becoming more complex, making it more difficult to detect and defend against them. Attackers today use common Internet protocols and applications to perform attacks, making it more difficult to distinguish an attack from legitimate traffic. Other attack tools vary their behavior so the same attack appears differently each time, further complicating detection.

- *Availability and simplicity of attack tools.* Whereas in the past an attacker needed to have an extensive technical knowledge of networks and computers as well as the ability to write a program to generate the attack, that is no longer the case. Today's software attack tools do not require any sophisticated knowledge on the part of the attacker. In fact, many of the tools, such as the Kali Linux interface shown in Figure 1-1, have a graphical user interface (GUI) that allows the user to easily select options from a menu. These tools are freely available or can be purchased from other attackers at a surprisingly low cost.

Figure 1-1 Menu of attack tools
Source: Kali Linux

- *Faster detection of vulnerabilities.* Weakness in hardware and software can be more quickly uncovered and exploited with new software tools and techniques.

- *Delays in security updating.* Hardware and software vendors are overwhelmed trying to keep pace with updating their products against attacks. One antivirus software security institute receives more than 200,000 submissions of potential malware *each day.*[16] At this rate the antivirus vendors would have to create and distribute updates *every few seconds* to keep users fully protected. This delay in distributing security updates adds to the difficulties in defending against attacks.

- *Weak security update distribution.* While vendors of mainstream products, such as Microsoft, Apple, and Adobe, have a system for notifying users of security updates for many of their products and distributing them on a regular basis, few other software vendors have invested in these costly distribution systems. Users are generally unaware that a security update even exists for a product because there is no reliable means for the vendor to alert the user. Also, these vendors often do not create small security updates that "patch" the existing software, but instead they fix the problem in an entirely new version of the software—and then require the user to pay for the updated version that contains the patch. Attackers today are focusing more on uncovering and exploiting vulnerabilities in these products.

 Vendors of smartphone operating systems are particularly well-known for not providing security updates on a timely basis, if at all. Most vendors and wireless carriers do not attempt to provide users with significant updates (such as from version 5.6 to 5.7), instead hoping that users will purchase an entirely new smartphone—and service contract—to have the latest and most secure device.

- *Distributed attacks.* Attackers can use hundreds of thousands of computers under their control in an attack against a single server or network. This "many against one" approach makes it virtually impossible to stop an attack by identifying and blocking a single source.

- *Introduction of BYOD.* Until recently IT departments were "autocratic": they established technology standards for users by specifying which devices could be purchased by a department for its employees and would refuse to allow unauthorized personal devices to be connected to the corporate networks. However, coinciding with the introduction of modern tablet computers in 2010 and the widespread usage of smartphones, users began to pressure IT departments to allow them to use and connect their personal devices to the company's network (called **BYOD** or **bring your own device**). This trend of allowing employees to use their own personal devices to connect to the corporate network has made it difficult for IT departments to provide adequate security for an almost endless array of devices that they do not own.

- *User confusion.* Increasingly, users are called upon to make difficult security decisions regarding their computer systems, sometimes with little or no information to guide them. It is not uncommon for a user to be asked security questions such as *Do you want to view only the content that was delivered securely?* or *Is it safe to quarantine this attachment?* or *Do you want to install this add-on?* With little or no direction, users are inclined to provide answers to questions without understanding the security risks.

Table 1-2 summarizes the reasons why it is difficult to defend against today's attacks.

Reason	Description
Universally connected devices	Attackers from anywhere in the world can send attacks.
Increased speed of attacks	Attackers can launch attacks against millions of computers within minutes.
Greater sophistication of attacks	Attack tools vary their behavior so the same attack appears differently each time.
Availability and simplicity of attack tools	Attacks are no longer limited to highly skilled attackers.
Faster detection of vulnerabilities	Attackers can discover security holes in hardware or software more quickly.
Delays security updating	Vendors are overwhelmed trying to keep pace updating their products against the latest attacks.
Weak security update distribution	Many software products lack a means to distribute security updates in a timely fashion.
Distributed attacks	Attackers use thousands of computers in an attack against a single computer or network.
Introduction of BYOD	Organizations are having difficulty providing security for a wide array of personal devices.
User confusion	Users are required to make difficult security decisions with little or no instruction.

Table 1-2   Difficulties in defending against attacks

What Is Information Security?

2.1 Explain the importance of risk related concepts.

3.2 Summarize various types of attacks.

Before it is possible to defend against attacks, it is necessary to understand exactly what security is and how it relates to information security. Also knowing the terminology used can be helpful when creating defenses for computers. Understanding the importance of information security is also critical.

Understanding Security

A search of the Internet to define the word *security* will result in a variety of definitions. Sometimes security is defined as *the state of being free from danger*, while at other times security is said to be *the protection of property*. And another interpretation of security is *the degree of resistance from harm*. The difference in these definitions actually hinges upon whether the focus is on the *process* (how to achieve security) or the *goal* (what it means to have security). In reality security is both: it is the goal to be free from danger as well as the process that achieves that freedom.

Yet because complete security can never be fully achieved, most often security is viewed as a process. In this light security may be defined as *the necessary steps to protect a person or property from harm*. This harm may come from one of two sources: either from a direct action that is intended to inflict damage or from an indirect and unintentional action. Consider a typical house: it is necessary to provide security for the house and its inhabitants from these two different sources. For example, the house and its occupants must be secure from the direct attack of a criminal who wants to inflict bodily harm to someone inside or a burglar who wants to steal a television. This security may be provided by locked doors, a fence, or a strong police presence. In addition, the house must also be protected from indirect acts that are not exclusively directed against it. That is, the house needs to be protected from a hurricane (by being built with strong materials and installing hurricane shutters) or a storm surge (by being built off the ground).

Security usually includes both preventive measures and rapid response. An individual who wants to be secure would take the preventive measures of keeping the doors to the house locked and leaving outside lights turned on at night. An example of a rapid response could include the homeowner programming *911* into his phone so that if anything suspicious begins to occur around the house an emergency call can be made quickly to the police.

It is also important to understand the relationship between *security* and *convenience*. As security is increased, convenience is often decreased. That is, the more secure something is, the less convenient it may become to use (security is said to be "inversely proportional" to convenience). This is illustrated in Figure 1-2. Consider again a typical house. A homeowner might install an automated alarm system that requires a code to be entered on a keypad within 30 seconds of entering the house. Although the alarm system makes the house more secure, it is less convenient than just walking into the house. Thus, security may be understood as *sacrificing convenience for safety*. Another way to think of security is *giving up short-term comfort for long-term protection*. In any case, security usually requires forgoing convenience to achieve a greater level of safety or protection.

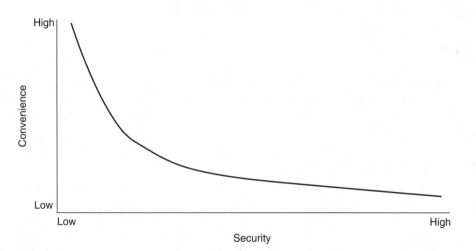

Figure 1-2   Relationship of security to convenience

Defining Information Security

The term **information security** is frequently used to describe the tasks of securing information that is in a digital format. This digital information is manipulated by a microprocessor (such as on a personal computer), stored on a storage device (like a hard drive or USB flash drive), and transmitted over a network (such as a local area network or the Internet).

Just as security can be viewed as both a goal and a process, the same is true with information security. Information security can be best understood by examining its goals and the process of how it is accomplished. Together these can help create a solid definition of information security.

Information security cannot completely prevent successful attacks or guarantee that a system is totally secure, just as the security measures taken for a house can never guarantee complete safety from a burglar or a hurricane. The goal of information security is to ensure that protective measures are properly implemented to ward off attacks and prevent the total collapse of the system when a successful attack does occur. Thus, information security is first *protection*.

 Information security should not be viewed as a war to be won or lost. Just as crime such as burglary can never be completely eradicated, neither can attacks against technology devices. The goal is not a complete victory but instead maintaining equilibrium: as attackers take advantage of a weakness in a defense, defenders must respond with an improved defense. Information security is an endless cycle between attacker and defender.

Second, information security is intended to protect *information* that provides value to people and organizations. There are three protections that must be extended over information: confidentiality, integrity, and availability—or *CIA*:

1. *Confidentiality.* It is important that only approved individuals are able to access important information. For example, the credit card number used to make an online purchase must be kept secure and not made available to other parties. **Confidentiality** ensures that only authorized parties can view the information. Providing confidentiality can involve several different security tools, ranging from software to "scramble" the credit card number stored on the web server to door locks to prevent access to those servers.

2. *Integrity.* **Integrity** ensures that the information is correct and no unauthorized person or malicious software has altered the data. In the example of the online purchase, an attacker who could change the amount of a purchase from $10,000.00 to $1.00 would violate the integrity of the information.

3. *Availability.* Information has value if the authorized parties who are assured of its integrity can access the information. **Availability** ensures that data is accessible to authorized users. This means that the information cannot be "locked up" so tight that no one can access it. It also means that attackers have not performed an attack so that the data cannot be reached. In this example the total number of items ordered as the result of an online purchase must be made available to an employee in a warehouse so that the correct items can be shipped to the customer.

In addition to CIA, another set of protections must be implemented to secure information. These are authentication, authorization, and accounting—or *AAA*:

1. *Authentication.* **Authentication** ensures that the individual is who she claims to be (the authentic or genuine person) and not an imposter. A person accessing the web server that contains a user's credit card number must prove that she is indeed who she claims to be and not a fraudulent attacker. One way in which authentication can be performed is by the person providing a password that only she knows.

2. *Authorization.* **Authorization** is providing permission or approval to specific technology resources. After a person has provided authentication she may have the authority to access the credit card number or enter a room that contains the web server, provided she has been given prior authorization.

3. *Accounting.* **Accounting** provides tracking of events. This may include a record of who accessed the web server, from what location, and at what specific time.

Yet information security involves more than protecting the information itself. Because this information is stored on computer hardware, manipulated by software, and transmitted by communications, each of these areas must also be protected. The third objective of information security is to protect the integrity, confidentiality, and availability of information *on the devices that store, manipulate, and transmit the information.*

Information security is achieved through a process that is a combination of three entities. As shown in Figure 1-3 and Table 1-3, information and the hardware, software, and communications are protected in three layers: products, people, and policies and procedures. These three layers interact with each other: procedures enable people to understand how to use products to protect information.

A comprehensive definition of information security involves both the goals and process. Information security may be defined as *that which protects the integrity, confidentiality, and availability of information on the devices that store, manipulate, and transmit the information through products, people, and procedures.*

Information Security Terminology

As with many advanced subjects, information security has its own set of terminology. The following scenario helps to illustrate information security terms and how they are used.

Suppose that Ellie wants to purchase a new motorized Italian scooter to ride from her apartment to school and work. However, because several scooters have been stolen near her apartment she is concerned about its protection. Although she parks the scooter in the gated parking lot in front of her apartment, a hole in the fence surrounding the apartment complex makes it possible for someone to access the parking lot without restriction. Ellie's scooter and the threat to it are illustrated in Figure 1-4.

Ellie's new scooter is an **asset**, which is defined as an item that has value. In an organization, assets have the following qualities: they provide value to the organization; they cannot easily be replaced without a significant investment in expense, time, worker skill, and/or resources; and they can form part of the organization's corporate identity. Based on these qualities not all elements of an organization's information technology infrastructure may be classified as an asset. For example, a faulty desktop computer that can easily be replaced would generally not be considered an asset, yet the information contained on that computer can be an asset. Table 1-4 lists a description of the elements of an organization's information technology infrastructure and whether or not they would normally be considered as an asset.

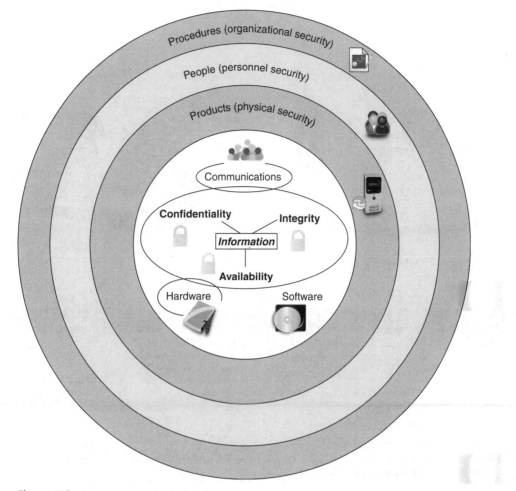

Figure 1-3 Information security layers

Layer	Description
Products	Form the security around the data. May be as basic as door locks or as complicated as network security equipment.
People	Those who implement and properly use security products to protect data.
Policies and procedures	Plans and policies established by an organization to ensure that people correctly use the products.

Table 1-3 Information security layers

What Ellie is trying to protect her scooter from is a **threat,** which is a type of action that has the potential to cause harm. Information security threats are events or actions that represent a danger to information assets. A threat by itself does not mean that security has been compromised; rather, it simply means that the potential for creating a loss is real. For Ellie the

Figure 1-4 Information security components analogy

Element name	Description	Example	Critical asset?
Information	Data that has been collected, classified, organized, and stored in various forms	Customer, personnel, production, sales, marketing, and finance databases	Yes: Extremely difficult to replace
Customized business software	Software that supports the business processes of the organization	Customized order transaction application	Yes: Unique and customized for the organization
System software	Software that provides the foundation for application software	Operating system	No: Can be easily replaced
Physical items	Computers equipment, communications equipment, storage media, furniture, and fixtures	Servers, routers, DVDs, and power supplies	No: Can be easily replaced
Services	Outsourced computing services	Voice and data communications	No: Can be easily replaced

Table 1-4 Information technology assets

threat could result in the theft of her scooter; in information security a threat can result in the corruption or theft of information, a delay in information being transmitted, or even the loss of good will or reputation.

A **threat agent** is a person or element that has the power to carry out a threat. For Ellie the threat agent is a thief. In information security, a threat agent could be a person attempting to break into a secure computer network. It could also be a force of nature such as a hurricane that could damage computer equipment and thus destroy information, or it could be malicious software that attacks the computer network.

Ellie wants to protect her scooter and is concerned about a hole in the fencing around her apartment. The hole in the fencing is a **vulnerability,** which is a flaw or weakness that allows a threat agent to bypass security. An example of a vulnerability that information security must deal with is a software defect in an operating system that allows an unauthorized user to gain control of a computer without the user's knowledge or permission.

If a thief can get to Ellie's scooter because of the hole in the fence, then that thief is taking advantage of the vulnerability. This is known as exploiting the vulnerability through a **threat vector,** or the means by which an attack can occur. An attacker, knowing that a flaw in a web server's operating system has not been patched, is using the threat vector (exploiting the vulnerability) to steal user passwords.

Ellie must make a decision: what is the probability (**threat likelihood**) that the threat will come to fruition and her scooter stolen? This can be understood in terms of risk. A **risk** is a situation that involves exposure to some type of danger.

 Sometimes risk is illustrated by the calculation:
Risk = Consequence × Vulnerability × Threat Likelihood.

There are different options available when dealing with risks:

- *Risk avoidance.* **Risk avoidance** involves identifying the risk but making the decision to not engage in the activity. Ellie could decide based on the risk of the scooter being stolen that she will not purchase the new scooter.

- *Acceptance.* **Acceptance** simply means that the risk is acknowledged but no steps are taken to address it. In Ellie's case, she could accept the risk and buy the new scooter, knowing there is the chance of it being stolen by a thief entering through a hole in the fence.

- *Mitigation.* Risk **mitigation** is the attempt to address the risks by making risk less serious. Ellie could complain to the apartment manager about the hole in the fence in order to have it repaired.

- *Deterrence.* If the apartment manager posted signs in the area that said "Trespassers will be punished to the full extent of the law" this would be an example of risk **deterrence**. Risk deterrence involves understanding something about the attacker and then informing him of the harm that may come his way if he attacks an asset.

- *Transference.* Ellie could transfer the risk to a third party. She can do this by purchasing insurance so that the insurance company absorbs the loss and pays if the scooter is stolen. This is known as risk **transference.**

Table 1-5 summarizes these information security terms.

Understanding the Importance of Information Security

Information security is important to organizations as well as to individuals. That is because information security can be helpful in preventing data theft, thwarting identity theft, avoiding the legal consequences of not securing information, maintaining productivity, and foiling cyberterrorism.

Term	Example in Ellie's scenario	Example in information security
Asset	Scooter	Employee database
Threat	Steal scooter	Steal data
Threat agent	Thief	Attacker, hurricane
Vulnerability	Hole in fence	Software defect
Threat vector	Climb through hole in fence	Access web server passwords through flaw in operating system
Threat likelihood	Probability of scooter stolen	Likelihood of virus infection
Risk	Not purchase scooter	Not install wireless network

Table 1-5   Information security terminology

Preventing Data Theft Security is often associated with theft prevention: Ellie could park her scooter in a locked garage in order to prevent it from being stolen. The same is true with information security: preventing data from being stolen is often cited by organizations as a primary objective of their information security. Business data theft involves stealing proprietary business information, such as research for a new drug or a list of customers that competitors would be eager to acquire.

Yet data theft is not limited to businesses. Individuals are often victims of data thievery. One type of personal data that is a prime target of attackers is credit card numbers. These can be used to purchase thousands of dollars of merchandise online—without having the actual card—before the victim is even aware the number has been stolen.

The extent to which stolen credit card numbers are available can be seen in the price that online thieves charge each other for stolen card numbers. Because credit card numbers are so readily available, 1000 stolen card numbers can be purchased for as little as $6.[17]

Thwarting Identity Theft Identity theft involves stealing another person's personal information, such as a Social Security number, and then using the information to impersonate the victim, generally for financial gain. The thieves often create new bank or credit card accounts under the victim's name and then large purchases are charged to these accounts, leaving the victim responsible for the debts and ruining her credit rating.

In some instances, thieves have bought cars and even houses by taking out loans in someone else's name.

One rapidly growing area of identity theft involves identity thieves filing fictitious income tax returns with the U.S. Internal Revenue Service (IRS). According to the IRS, in one year it delivered more than $5 billion in refund checks to identity thieves who filed fraudulent tax returns. Although the IRS detected and stopped about 940,000 fraudulent returns for that year, claiming $6.5 billion in refunds, 1.5 million undetected false returns were processed. These were filed by thieves seeking refunds after assuming the identity of a dead person, child, or someone else who normally would not file a tax return. It is estimated that identity theft based on tax returns could increase by another $21 billion through 2017.

IRS investigators found that a single address in Lansing, Michigan, was used to file 2137 separate tax returns, and the IRS issued more than $3.3 million in refunds to that address. In another instance the IRS deposited 590 refunds totaling more than $900,000 into a single bank account.[18]

Avoiding Legal Consequences Several federal and state laws have been enacted to protect the privacy of electronic data. Businesses that fail to protect data they possess may face serious financial penalties. Some of these laws include the following:

- *The Health Insurance Portability and Accountability Act of 1996 (HIPAA).* Under the **Health Insurance Portability and Accountability Act (HIPAA)**, health care enterprises must guard protected health care information and implement policies and procedures to safeguard it, whether it be in paper or electronic format. Those who wrongfully disclose individually identifiable health information can be fined up to $50,000 for each violation up to a maximum of $1.5 million per calendar year and sentenced up to 10 years in prison.

In 2013 the HIPAA regulations were expanded to include all third-party "business associate" organizations that handle protected health care information. Business associates are defined as any subcontractor that creates, receives, maintains, or transmits protected health information on behalf of a covered HIPAA entity. These associates must now comply with the same HIPAA security and privacy procedures.

- *The Sarbanes-Oxley Act of 2002 (Sarbox).* As a reaction to a rash of corporate fraud, the **Sarbanes-Oxley Act (Sarbox)** is an attempt to fight corporate corruption. Sarbox covers the corporate officers, auditors, and attorneys of publicly traded companies. Stringent reporting requirements and internal controls on electronic financial reporting systems are required. Corporate officers who willfully and knowingly certify a false financial report can be fined up to $5 million and serve 20 years in prison.

- *The Gramm-Leach-Bliley Act (GLBA).* Like HIPAA, the **Gramm-Leach-Bliley Act (GLBA)** passed in 1999 protects private data. GLBA requires banks and financial institutions to alert customers of their policies and practices in disclosing customer information. All electronic and paper data containing personally identifiable financial information must be protected. The penalty for noncompliance for a class of individuals is up to $500,000.

- *Payment Card Industry Data Security Standard (PCI DSS).* The **Payment Card Industry Data Security Standard (PCI DSS)** is a set of security standards that all companies that process, store, or transmit credit card information must follow. PCI applies to any organization or merchant, regardless of its size or number of card transactions, that processes transactions either online or in person. The maximum penalty for not complying is $100,000 per month.

- *California's Database Security Breach Notification Act (2003).* **California's Database Security Breach Notification Act** was the first state electronic privacy law that covers any state agency, person, or company that does business in California. It requires businesses to inform California residents within 48 hours if a breach of personal information has or is believed to have occurred. Personal information is defined as a name with a Social Security number, driver's license number, state ID card, account number, credit card number, or debit card number and required security access codes. Since this act was passed by California in 2003, all other states now have similar laws with the exception of Alabama, Kentucky, New Mexico, and South Dakota.

The penalties for violating these laws can be sizeable. Businesses must make every effort to keep electronic data secure from hostile outside forces to ensure compliance with these laws and avoid serious legal consequences.

Maintaining Productivity Cleaning up after an attack diverts time, money, and other resources away from normal activities. Employees cannot be productive and complete important tasks during or after an attack because computers and networks cannot function properly. Table 1-6 provides a sample estimate of the lost wages and productivity during an attack and the subsequent cleanup.

Number of total employees	Average hourly salary	Number of employees to combat attack	Hours required to stop attack and clean up	Total lost salaries	Total lost hours of productivity
100	$25	1	48	$4066	81
250	$25	3	72	$17,050	300
500	$30	5	80	$28,333	483
1000	$30	10	96	$220,000	1293

Table 1-6   Cost of attacks

The single most expensive malicious attack was the Love Bug in 2000, which cost an estimated $8.7 billion.[19]

Foiling Cyberterrorism The FBI defines **cyberterrorism** as any "premeditated, politically motivated attack against information, computer systems, computer programs, and data which results in violence against noncombatant targets by subnational groups or clandestine agents."[20] Unlike an attack that is designed to steal information or erase a user's hard disk drive, cyberterrorism attacks are intended to cause panic or provoke violence among citizens. Attacks are directed at targets such as the banking industry, power plants, air traffic control centers, and water systems. These are desirable targets because they can significantly disrupt the normal activities of a large population. For example, disabling an electrical power plant could cripple businesses, homes, transportation services, and communications over a wide area. Yet one of the challenges in combatting cyberterrorism is that many of the prime targets are not owned and managed by the federal government. Because these are not centrally controlled, it is difficult to coordinate and maintain security.

The Department of Homeland Security has identified 7200 key industrial control systems that are part of the critical infrastructure and are directly connected to the Internet, making them vulnerable to cyberterrorism attacks. In one year a 52 percent increase in attacks resulted in 198 directed attacks against these systems, resulting in several successful break-ins.[21]

Who Are the Attackers?

In the past the term *hacker* referred to a person who used advanced computer skills to attack computers. Yet because that title often carried with it a negative connotation, it was qualified in an attempt to distinguish between different types of the attackers. *Black hat hackers* were those attackers who violated computer security for personal gain (such as to steal credit card numbers) or to inflict malicious damage (corrupt a hard drive). *White hat hackers* were described as "ethical attackers": with an organization's permission they would attempt to probe a system for any weaknesses and then privately provide information back to that organization about any uncovered vulnerabilities. In between were *gray hat hackers* who would attempt to break into a computer system without the organization's permission (an illegal activity) but not for their own advantage; instead, they would publically disclose the vulnerability in order to shame the organization into taking action.

However, these "hat" titles did not always accurately reflect the different motives and goals of the attackers and are not widely used in the security community. Instead, more descriptive categories of attackers are used, including cybercriminals, script kiddies, brokers, insiders, cyberterrorists, hactivists, and state-sponsored attackers.

Cybercriminals

The generic term **cybercriminals** is often used to describe individuals who launch attacks against other users and their computers (another generic word is simply *attackers*). However, strictly speaking cybercriminals are a loose network of attackers, identity thieves, and financial fraudsters who are highly motivated, less risk-averse, well-funded, and tenacious. Some security experts believe that many cybercriminals belong to organized gangs of young attackers, often clustered in Eastern European, Asian, and Third World regions.

Cybercriminals often meet in online "underground" forums to trade information and coordinate attacks.

Instead of attacking a computer to show off their technology skills (*fame*), cybercriminals have a more focused goal of financial gain (*fortune*): cybercriminals exploit vulnerabilities to steal information or launch attacks that can generate income. This difference makes the new attackers more dangerous and their attacks more threatening. These targeted attacks against financial networks and the theft of personal information are sometimes known as **cybercrime**.

Financial cybercrime is often divided into two categories. The first category focuses on individuals and businesses. Cybercriminals steal and use stolen data, credit card numbers, online financial account information, or Social Security numbers to profit from its victims or send millions of spam emails to peddle counterfeit drugs, pirated software, fake watches, and pornography.

The second category focuses on businesses and governments. Cybercriminals attempt to steal research on a new product from a business so that they can sell it to an unscrupulous foreign supplier who will then build an imitation model of the product to sell worldwide. This deprives the legitimate business of profits after investing hundreds of millions of dollars in product development, and because these foreign suppliers are in a different country they are beyond the reach of domestic enforcement agencies and courts. Governments are also the targets of cybercriminals: if the latest information on a new missile defense system can be stolen it can be sold—at a high price—to that government's enemies.

Some security experts maintain that East European cybercriminals are mostly focused on activities to steal money from individuals and businesses, whereas cybercriminals from East Asia are more interested in stealing data from governments or businesses. This results in different approaches to their attacks. East European cybercriminals tend to use custom-built, highly complex malware while East Asian attackers use off-the-shelf malware and simpler techniques. Also East European attackers work in small, tightly knit teams that directly profit from their attacks. East Asian cybercriminals usually are part of a larger group of attackers who work at the direction of large institutions from which they receive instructions and financial backing.

The attacks by these well-resourced and trained cybercriminals often result in multiyear intrusion campaigns targeting highly sensitive economic, proprietary, or national security information. This has created a new class of attacks called **Advanced Persistent Threat (APT)**. Cybercriminals are successful with APTs because they use advanced tools and techniques that can defeat many conventional computer defenses.

Script Kiddies

Script kiddies are individuals who want to attack computers yet they lack the knowledge of computers and networks needed to do so. Script kiddies instead do their work by downloading automated attack software (scripts) from websites and using it to perform malicious acts. Figure 1-5 illustrates the skills needed for creating attacks. Over 40 percent of attacks require low or no skills and are frequently conducted by script kiddies.

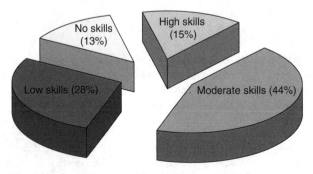

Figure 1-5 Skills needed for creating attacks

Today script kiddies can acquire entire **exploit kits** from other attackers to easily craft an attack. Script kiddies can either rent or purchase the kit from its authors and then specify various options to customize their attacks.

It is estimated that three out of every four Internet-based attacks originate from exploit kits.[22]

Brokers

In recent years several software vendors have started financially rewarding individuals who uncover vulnerabilities in their software and then privately report it back to the vendors so that the weaknesses can be addressed. Some vendors even sponsor annual competitive contests and handsomely pay those who can successfully attack their software.

One security researcher earned over $31,000 in a "bug bounty" program for uncovering three vulnerabilities.[23]

However, other individuals who uncover vulnerabilities do not report it to the software vendor but instead sell them to the highest bidder. Known as **brokers**, these attackers sell their knowledge of a vulnerability to other attackers or even governments. These buyers are generally willing to pay a high price because this vulnerability is unknown to the software vendor and thus is unlikely to be "patched" until after new attacks based on it are already widespread.

Insiders

Another serious threat to an organization actually comes from an unlikely source: its employees, contractors, and business partners, often called **insiders**. For example, a health care worker disgruntled over an upcoming job termination might illegally gather health records on celebrities and sell them to the media, or a securities trader who loses billions of dollars on bad stock bets could use her knowledge of the bank's computer security system to conceal the losses through fake transactions. In one study of 900 cases of business "data leakage," over 48 percent of the breaches were attributed to insiders who abused their right to access corporate information.[24] These attacks are harder to recognize because they come from within the organization yet may be more costly than attacks from the outside.

Most malicious insider attacks consist of the sabotage or theft of intellectual property. One study revealed that most cases of sabotage come from employees who have announced their resignation or have been formally reprimanded, demoted, or fired. When theft is involved, the offenders are usually salespeople, engineers, computer programmers, or scientists who actually believe that the accumulated data is owned by them and not the organization (most of these thefts occur within 30 days of the employee resigning). In some instances the employees are moving to a new job and want to take "their work" with them, while in other cases the employees have been bribed or coerced into stealing the data. In about 8 percent of the incidences of theft, employees have been pressured into stealing from their employer through blackmail or the threat of violence.[25]

In recent years insiders who worked either directly or indirectly for a government have stolen large volumes of sensitive information and then published it. The purpose is to alert its citizens of clandestine governmental actions and to pressure the government to change its policies.

Cyberterrorists

Many security experts fear that terrorists will turn their attacks to a nation's network and computer infrastructure to cause disruption and panic among citizens. Known as **cyberterrorists**, their motivation is ideological, attacking for the sake of their principles or beliefs. Cyberterrorists may be the attackers that are most feared, for it is almost impossible to predict when or where an attack may occur. Unlike cybercriminals who continuously probe systems or create attacks, cyberterrorists can be inactive for several years and then suddenly strike in a new way. Their targets may include a small group of computers or networks that can affect the largest number of users, such as the computers that control the electrical power grid of a state or region.

One cyberterrorist attack directed at three broadcast networks and four major banks in South Korea resulted in disruptions that were designated as "moderate to severe." The source behind the attacks may have been from North Korea as retaliation for a significant and prolonged Internet outage that North Korea suffered, which was blamed on South Korea.

Hactivists

Another group motivated by ideology is **hactivists**. Unlike cyberterrorists who launch attacks against foreign nations to incite panic, hactivists (a combination of the words *hack* and *activism*) are generally not as well-defined. Attacks by hactivists can involve breaking into a website and changing the contents on the site as a means of making a political statement against those who oppose their beliefs. In addition to attacks as a means of protest or to promote a political agenda, other attacks can be retaliatory. For example, hactivists may disable the website belonging to a bank because that bank stopped accepting online payments that were deposited into accounts belonging to the hactivists.

State-Sponsored Attackers

Instead of using an army to march across the battlefield to strike an adversary, governments are using **state-sponsored attackers** for launching computer attacks against their foes. In recent years the work of some attackers appears to have been sponsored by different governments. These attackers target foreign governments or even citizens of the government who are considered hostile or threatening. The following are several examples of these attacks:

- The malware known as Flame appears to target computers in Middle Eastern countries. One of Flame's most ingenious tricks, which had many security researchers in awe, created a fake Microsoft electronic document so that Flame appeared to be an update from Microsoft and was easily distributed to any Windows computer.

- Perhaps the most infamous government-backed malware to date was called Stuxnet. This malware actively targeted Windows computers that managed large-scale industrial-control systems used at military installations, oil pipeline control systems, manufacturing environments, and nuclear power plants. At first it was thought that Stuxnet took advantage of a single previously unknown software vulnerability. Upon closer inspection, it was found that Stuxnet exploited four unknown vulnerabilities, something never seen before.

- It is estimated that more than 300,000 Iranian citizens were having their email messages read without their knowledge by the Iranian government seeking to locate and crack down on dissidents. It appears that the government used stolen electronic documents to permit its spies to log in directly to the email mailboxes of the victims and read any stored emails. In addition, another program could pinpoint the exact location of the victim.

Table 1-7 lists several characteristics of these different attackers.

Attacker category	Objective	Typical target	Sample attack
Cybercriminals	Fortune over fame	Users, businesses, governments	Steal credit card information
Script kiddies	Thrills, notoriety	Businesses, users	Erase data
Brokers	Sell vulnerability to highest bidder	Any	Find vulnerability in operating system
Insiders	Retaliate against employer, shame government	Governments, businesses	Steal documents to publish sensitive information
Cyberterrorists	Cause disruption and panic	Businesses	Cripple computers that control water treatment
Hactivists	To right a perceived wrong against them	Governments, businesses	Disrupt financial website
State-sponsored attackers	Spy on citizens, disrupt foreign government	Users, governments	Read user's email messages

Table 1-7   **Characteristics of attackers**

Attacks and Defenses

Although a wide variety of attacks can be launched against a computer or network, the same basic steps are used in most attacks. Protecting computers against these steps in an attack calls for following five fundamental security principles.

Steps of an Attack

A *kill chain* is a military term used to describe the systematic process to target and engage an enemy. An attacker who attempts to break into a web server or computer network actually follows these same steps. Known as the **Cyber Kill Chain**® it outlines these steps of an attack:

 The Cyber Kill Chain was first introduced by researchers at Lockheed Martin in 2011. The company later trademarked the term "Cyber Kill Chain."

1. *Reconnaissance.* The first step in an attack is to probe for any information about the system: the type of hardware used, version of operating system software, and even personal information about the users. This can reveal if the system is a viable target for an attack and how it could be attacked.

2. *Weaponization.* The attacker creates an exploit (like a virus) and packages it into a deliverable payload (like a Microsoft Excel spreadsheet) that can be used against the target.

3. *Delivery.* At this step the weapon is transmitted to the target, such as by an email attachment or through an infected web server.

4. *Exploitation.* After the weapon is delivered to the victim, the exploitation stage triggers the intruders' exploit. Generally the exploitation targets an application or operating system vulnerability, but it also could involve tricking the user into taking a specific action.

5. *Installation.* At this step the weapon is installed to either attack the computer or install a remote "backdoor" so the attacker can access the system.

6. *Command and Control.* Many times the compromised system connects back to the attacker so that the system can be remotely controlled by the attacker and receive future instructions.

7. *Actions on Objectives.* Now the attackers can start to take actions to achieve their original objectives, such as stealing user passwords or launching attacks against other computers.

These steps of an attack are illustrated in Figure 1-6.

 The underlying purpose of the Cyber Kill Chain is to illustrate that attacks are an integrated and end-to-end process like a "chain." Disrupting any one of the steps will interrupt the entire attack process, but the ability to disrupt the early steps of the chain is the most effective and least costly.

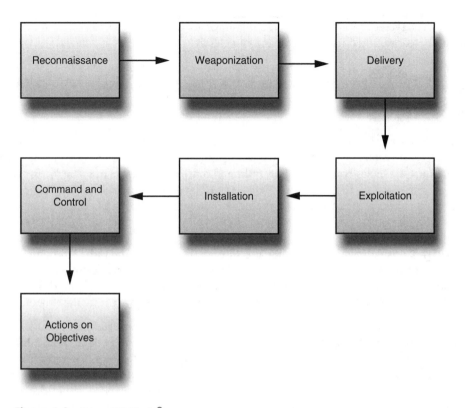

Figure 1-6 Cyber Kill Chain®
Cyber Kill Chain is a registered trademark of Lockheed Martin Corporation.

Defenses Against Attacks

Although multiple defenses may be necessary to withstand an attack, these defenses should be based on five fundamental security principles: layering, limiting, diversity, obscurity, and simplicity. These principles provide a foundation for building a secure system.

Layering The Crown Jewels of England, which are worn during coronations and important state functions, have a dollar value of over $32 million yet are virtually priceless as symbols of English culture. How are precious stones like the Crown Jewels protected from theft? They are not openly displayed on a table for anyone to pick up. Instead, they are enclosed in protective cases with 2-inch thick glass that is bullet-proof, smash-proof, and resistant to almost any outside force. The cases are located in a special room with massive walls and sensors that can detect slight movements or vibrations. The doors to the room are monitored around the clock by remote security cameras, and the video images from each camera are recorded. The room itself is in the Tower of London, surrounded by roaming guards and fences. In short, these precious stones are protected by *layers* of security. If one layer is penetrated—such as the thief getting into the building—several more layers must still be breached, and each layer is often more difficult or complicated than the previous. A layered approach has the advantage of creating a barrier of multiple defenses that can be coordinated to thwart a variety of attacks.

The Jewel House, which holds the Crown Jewels in the Tower of London, is actually located inside an Army barracks that is staffed with soldiers.

Likewise, information security must be created in layers. If only one defense mechanism is in place, an attacker only has to circumvent that single defense. Instead, a security system must have layers, making it unlikely that an attacker has the tools and skills to break through *all* the layers of defenses. A layered approach also can be useful in resisting a variety of attacks. Layered security provides the most comprehensive protection.

Limiting Consider again protecting the Crown Jewels of England. Although the jewels may be on display for the general public to view, permitting anyone to touch them increases the chances that they will be stolen. Only approved personnel should be authorized to handle the jewels. Limiting who can access the jewels reduces the threat against them.

The same is true with information security. Limiting access to information reduces the threat against it. This means that only those personnel who must use the data should have access to it. In addition, the type of access they have should be limited to what those people need to perform their jobs. For example, access to the human resource database for an organization should be limited to only employees who have a genuine need to access it, such as human resource personnel or vice presidents. And, the type of access also should be restricted: human resource employees may be able to view employee salaries but not change them.

What level of access should users have? The correct answer is the *least amount necessary* to do their jobs, and no more.

Some ways to limit access are technology-based (such as assigning file permissions so that a user can only read but not modify a file), while others are procedural (prohibiting an employee from removing a sensitive document from the premises). The key is that access must be restricted to the bare minimum.

Diversity Diversity is closely related to layering. Just as it is important to protect data with layers of security, the layers also must be different (diverse). This means that if attackers penetrate one layer, they cannot use the *same* techniques to break through all other layers. A jewel thief, for instance, might be able to foil the security camera by dressing in black clothing but should not be able to use the same technique to trick the motion detection system. Using diverse layers of defense means that breaching one security layer does not compromise the whole system.

Information security diversity may be achieved in several ways. For example, some organizations use security products provided by different manufacturers. An attacker who can circumvent a security device from Manufacturer A could then use those same skills and knowledge to defeat all of the same devices used by the organization. However, if devices from Manufacturer A and similar devices from Manufacturer B were both used by the same organization, the attacker would have more difficulty trying to break through both types of devices because they would be different.

Obscurity Suppose a thief plans to steal the Crown Jewels during a shift change of the security guards. When the thief observes the guards, however, she finds that the guards do not change shifts at the same time each night. On a given Monday they rotate shifts at 2:13 AM, while on Tuesday they rotate at 1:51 AM, and the following Monday at 2:24 AM. Because the shift changes cannot be known for certain in advance, the planned attack cannot be carried out. This technique is sometimes called *security by obscurity*: obscuring to the outside world what is on the inside makes attacks that much more difficult.

An example of obscurity in information security would be not revealing the type of computer, version of operating system, or brand of software that is used. An attacker who knows that information could use it to determine the vulnerabilities of the system to attack it. However, if this information is concealed it is more difficult to attack the system, since nothing is known about it and it is hidden from the outside. Obscuring information can be an important means of protection.

Although obscurity is an important element of defense, it is not the only element. Sometimes the design or implementation of a device is kept secret with the thinking that if attackers do not know how it works, then it is secure. This attempt at "security through obscurity" is flawed because it depends solely on secrecy as a defense.

Simplicity Because attacks can come from a variety of sources and in many ways, information security is by its very nature complex. Yet the more complex it becomes, the more difficult it is to understand. A security guard who does not understand how motion detectors interact with infrared trip lights may not know what to do when one system alarm shows an intruder but the other does not. In addition, complex systems allow many opportunities for something to go wrong. In short, complex systems can be a thief's ally.

The same is true with information security. Complex security systems can be hard to understand, troubleshoot, and even feel secure about. As much as possible, a secure system should be simple for those on the inside to understand and use. Complex security schemes are often compromised to make them easier for trusted users to work with, yet this can also make it easier for the attackers. In short, keeping a system simple from the inside, but complex on the outside, can sometimes be difficult but reaps a major benefit.

Chapter Summary

- Attacks against information security have grown exponentially in recent years, despite the fact that billions of dollars are spent annually on security. No computer system is immune from attacks or can be considered completely secure.

- It is difficult to defend against today's attacks for several reasons. These reasons include the fact that virtually all devices are connected to the Internet, the speed of the attacks, greater sophistication of attacks, the availability and simplicity of attack tools, faster detection of vulnerabilities by attackers, delays in security updating, weak security update distribution, distributed attacks coming from multiple sources, and user confusion.

- Information security may be defined as that which protects the integrity, confidentiality, and availability of information on the devices that store, manipulate, and transmit the information through products, people, and procedures. As with many advanced subjects, information security has its own set of terminology. A threat is an event or action that represents a danger to information assets, which is something that has value. A threat agent is a person or element that has the power to carry out a threat, usually by exploiting a vulnerability, which is a flaw or weakness, through a threat vector. A risk is the likelihood that a threat agent will exploit the vulnerability.

- The main goals of information security are to prevent data theft, thwart identify theft, avoid the legal consequences of not securing information, maintain productivity, and foil cyberterrorism.

- The types of people behind computer attacks fall into several categories. The generic term cybercriminals describes individuals who launch attacks against other users and their computers. Script kiddies do their work by downloading automated attack software from websites and then using it to break into computers. A broker uncovers a vulnerability and then sells this knowledge to other attackers or governments. One of the largest information security threats to a business actually comes from its employees, contractors, and business partners, known as insiders. Cyberterrorists are motivated by their principles and beliefs, and turn their attacks to the network and computer infrastructure to cause panic among citizens. Another group motivated by ideology is hactivists, although they are generally not as well-defined. Governments are using state-sponsored attackers for launching computer attacks against their foes.

- There are a variety of types of attacks. Seven general steps make up an attack: reconnaissance, weaponization, delivery, exploitation, installation, command and control, and actions on objectives. Although multiple defenses may be necessary to withstand the steps of an attack, these defenses should be based on five fundamental security principles: layering, limiting, diversity, obscurity, and simplicity.

Key Terms

acceptance Acknowledging a risk but taking no action to address it.

accounting The ability that provides tracking of events.

Advanced Persistent Threat (APT)   Multiyear intrusion campaign that targets highly sensitive economic, proprietary, or national security information.

asset   An item that has value.

authentication   The steps that ensure that the individual is who he or she claims to be.

authorization   The act of providing permission or approval to technology resources.

availability   Security actions that ensure that data is accessible to authorized users.

broker   Attacker who sells knowledge of a vulnerability to other attackers or governments.

BYOD (bring your own device)   The practice of allowing users to use their own personal devices to connect to an organizational network.

California's Database Security Breach Notification Act   The first state electronic privacy law, which covers any state agency, person, or company that does business in California.

confidentiality   Security actions that ensure that only authorized parties can view the information.

Cyber Kill Chain®   A systematic outline of the steps of a cyberattack, introduced at Lockheed Martin in 2011.

cybercrime   Targeted attacks against financial networks, unauthorized access to information, and the theft of personal information.

cybercriminals   A network of attackers, identity thieves, spammers, and financial fraudsters.

cyberterrorism   A premeditated, politically motivated attack against information, computer systems, computer programs, and data, which often results in violence.

cyberterrorist   Attacker whose motivation may be defined as ideological, or attacking for the sake of principles or beliefs.

deterrence   Understanding the attacker and then informing him of the consequences of the action.

exploit kit   Automated attack package that can be used without an advanced knowledge of computers.

Gramm-Leach-Bliley Act (GLBA)   A U.S. law that requires banks and financial institutions to alert customers of their policies and practices in disclosing customer information.

hactivist   Attacker who attacks for ideological reasons that are generally not as well-defined as a cyberterrorist's motivation.

Health Insurance Portability and Accountability Act (HIPAA)   A U.S. law designed to guard protected health information and implement policies and procedures to safeguard it.

identity theft   Stealing another person's personal information, such as a Social Security number, and then using the information to impersonate the victim, generally for financial gain.

information security   The tasks of protecting the integrity, confidentiality, and availability of information on the devices that store, manipulate, and transmit the information through products, people, and procedures.

insiders   Employees, contractors, and business partners who can be responsible for an attack.

integrity   Security actions that ensure that the information is correct and no unauthorized person or malicious software has altered the data.

mitigation   Addressing a risk by making it less serious.

Payment Card Industry Data Security Standard (PCI DSS)   A set of security standards that all U.S. companies processing, storing, or transmitting credit card information must follow.

risk   A situation that involves exposure to danger.

risk avoidance   Identifying the risk but making the decision to not engage in the activity.

Sarbanes-Oxley Act (Sarbox)   A U.S. law designed to fight corporate corruption.

script kiddie   Individual who lacks advanced knowledge of computers and networks and so uses downloaded automated attack software to attack information systems.

state-sponsored attacker   Attacker commissioned by governments to attack enemies' information systems.

threat   A type of action that has the potential to cause harm.

threat agent   A person or element that has the power to carry out a threat.

threat likelihood   The probability that a threat will actually occur.

threat vector   The means by which an attack could occur.

transference   Transferring the risk to a third party.

vulnerability   A flaw or weakness that allows a threat agent to bypass security.

Review Questions

1. Which of the following is NOT a characteristic of Advanced Persistent Threat (APT)?

    a. can span several years

    b. targets sensitive proprietary information

    c. uses advanced tools and techniques

    d. is only used by hactivists against foreign enemies

2. Which of the following was used to describe attackers who would break into a computer system without the owner's permission and publicly disclose the vulnerability?

    a. white hat hackers

    b. black hat hackers

    c. blue hat hackers

    d. gray hat hackers

3. Which the following is NOT a reason why it is difficult to defend against today's attackers?

    a. increased speed of attacks

    b. simplicity of attack tools

    c. greater sophistication of defense tools

    d. delays in security updating

4. Why can brokers command such a high price for what they sell?

   a. Brokers are licensed professionals.

   b. The attack targets are always wealthy corporations.

   c. The vulnerability was previously unknown and is unlikely to be patched quickly.

   d. Brokers work in teams and all the members must be compensated.

5. Which phrase describes the term "security" in a general sense?

   a. protection from only direct actions

   b. using reverse attack vectors (RAV) for protection

   c. only available on hardened computers and systems

   d. the necessary steps to protect a person or property from harm

6. _____ ensures that only authorized parties can view the information.

   a. Confidentiality

   b. Availability

   c. Authorization

   d. Integrity

7. Each of the following is a successive layer in which information security is achieved EXCEPT _____.

   a. products

   b. purposes

   c. procedures

   d. people

8. What is a person or element that has the power to carry out a threat?

   a. threat agent

   b. exploiter

   c. risk agent

   d. vulnerability

9. _____ ensures that individuals are who they claim to be.

   a. Demonstration

   b. Accounting

   c. Authentication

   d. Certification

10. What is the difference between a hactivist and a cyberterrorist?

    a. A hactivist is motivated by ideology while a cyberterrorists is not.

    b. Cyberterrorists always work in groups while hactivists work alone.

    c. The aim of a hactivist is not to incite panic like cyberterrorists.

    d. Cyberterrorists are better funded than hactivists.

11. Each of the following is a goal of information security EXCEPT _____.
    a. avoid legal consequences
    b. foil cyberterrorism
    c. prevent data theft
    d. limit access control

12. Which act requires enterprises to guard protected health information and implement policies and procedures to safeguard it?
    a. Hospital Protection and Insurance Association Agreement (HPIAA)
    b. Sarbanes-Oxley Act (Sarbox)
    c. Gramm-Leach-Bliley Act (GLBA)
    d. Health Insurance Portability and Accountability Act (HIPAA)

13. Why do cyberterrorists target power plants, air traffic control centers, and water systems?
    a. These targets have notoriously weak security and are easy to penetrate.
    b. They can cause significant disruption by destroying only a few targets.
    c. These targets are government-regulated and any successful attack would be considered a major victory.
    d. The targets are privately owned and cannot afford high levels of security.

14. What is the first step in the Cyber Kill Chain®?
    a. weaponization
    b. exploitation
    c. actions on objectives
    d. reconnaissance

15. An organization that purchased security products from different vendors is demonstrating which security principle?
    a. obscurity
    b. diversity
    c. limiting
    d. layering

16. Each of the following can be classified as an "insider" EXCEPT _____.
    a. business partners
    b. contractors
    c. stockholders
    d. employees

17. What are attackers called who belong to a network of identity thieves and financial fraudsters?

    a. cybercriminals

    b. script kiddies

    c. hackers

    d. brokers

18. What is an objective of state-sponsored attackers?

    a. to right a perceived wrong

    b. to spy on citizens

    c. to sell vulnerabilities to the highest bidder

    d. fortune instead of fame

19. An example of _____ is not revealing the type of computer, operating system, software, and network connection a computer uses.

    a. layering

    b. diversity

    c. obscurity

    d. limiting

20. The _____ is primarily responsible for assessing, managing, and implementing security.

    a. security administrator

    b. security manager

    c. security technician

    d. chief information security officer (CISO)

Hands-On Projects

Enter

HANDS-ON PROJECTS

Project 1-1: Examine Data Breaches

The Privacy Rights Clearinghouse (PRC) is a nonprofit organization whose goals are to raise consumers' awareness of how technology affects personal privacy and empower consumers to take action to control their own personal information. The PRC maintains a searchable database of security breaches that impact consumer's privacy. In this project you will gather information from the PRC website.

   1. Open a web browser and enter the URL **www.privacyrights.org/ data-breach**.

NOTE

The location of content on the Internet may change without warning. If you are no longer able to access the site through the above web address, use a search engine to search for "Privacy Rights Clearinghouse data breach".

2. First spend time reading about the PRC. Click **About Us** in the toolbar.

3. Scroll down to the content under Mission and Goals and also under Services. Spend a few minutes reading about the PRC.

4. Click your browser's **Back** button to return to the previous page.

5. On the **Chronology of Data Breaches** page scroll down and observe the different breaches listed in chronological order.

6. Now create a customized list of the data that will only list data breaches of educational institutions. Scroll back to the top of the page.

7. Under **Select organization type(s)**, uncheck all organizations except **EDU-Educational Institutions**.

8. Click **GO!**.

9. Scroll down to **Breach Subtotal** if necessary. How many breaches that were made public pertain to educational institutions?

10. Scroll down and observe the breaches for educational institutions.

11. Scroll back to the top of the page. Click **New Search**, located beneath the **GO!** button.

12. Now search for breaches that were a result of lost, discarded, or stolen equipment that belonged to the government and military. Under **Choose the type of breaches to display**, uncheck all types except **Portable device (PORT) - Lost, discarded or stolen laptop, PDA, smartphone, portable memory device, CD, hard drive, data tape, etc.**

13. Under Select organization type(s), uncheck all organizations except **GOV – Government and Military**.

14. Click **GO!**.

15. Scroll down to Breach Subtotal, if necessary. How many breaches that were made public pertain to this type?

16. Scroll down and observe the breaches for governmental institutions.

17. Scroll back to the top of the page.

18. Now create a search based on criteria that you are interested in, such as the Payment Card Fraud against Retail/Merchants during the current year.

19. When finished, close all windows.

Project 1-2: Scan for Malware Using the Microsoft Safety Scanner

In this project you will download and run the Microsoft Safety Scanner to determine if there is any malware on the computer.

1. Determine which system type of Windows you are running. Click **Start, Control Panel, System and Security**, and then **System**. Look under System type for the description.

2. Open your web browser and enter the URL **www.microsoft.com/security/scanner/en-us/default.asp**.

The location of content on the Internet may change without warning. If you are no longer able to access the site through the above web address, use a search engine to search for "Microsoft Safety Scanner".

3. Click **Download Now.**

4. Select either **32-bit** or **64-bit,** depending upon which system type of Windows you are running.

5. When the program finishes downloading, right-click **Start** and click **Open Windows Explorer.**

6. Click the **Downloads** icon in the left pane.

7. Double-click the **msert.exe** file.

8. Click **Run.** If the **User Account Control** dialog box appears, click **Yes.**

9. Click the check box to accept the license terms for this software. Click **Next.**

10. Click **Next.**

11. Select **Quick scan** if necessary.

12. Click **Next.**

13. Depending on your computer this scan may take several minutes. Analyze the results of the scan to determine if there is any malicious software found in your computer.

14. If you have problems you can click **View detailed results of the scan.** After reviewing the results, click **OK.** If you do not find any problems, click **Finish.**

15. If any malicious software was found on your computer run the scan again and select **Full scan.** After the scan is complete, click **Finish** to close the dialog box.

16. Close all windows.

Project 1-3: Create a Virtual Machine of Windows 8.1 for Security Testing—Part 1

Many users are reluctant to use their normal "production" computer for installing and testing new security applications. As an alternative, a virtual machine can be created on the "host" computer that runs a "guest" operating system. Security programs and testing can be conducted within this guest operating system without any impact on the regular host operating system. In this project you will create a virtual machine using Oracle VirtualBox.

The operating system of the host computer is not required to be different from that of the new guest operating system. That is, a computer that already has installed Windows 8.1 as its host operating system can still create a virtual machine of Windows 8.1 that is used for testing.

The location of content on the Internet may change without warning. If you are no longer able to access the site through the above web address, then use a search engine to search for "Oracle VirtualBox download".

1. Open a web browser and enter the URL **www.virtualbox.org**.

2. Click **Downloads**.

3. Under **VirtualBox platform packages** select the latest version of Virtual-Box for your host operating system to download that program. For example, if you are running Windows 7, select the version for "Virtual-Box x.x.x for Windows hosts."

4. Under **VirtualBox x.x.x Oracle VM VirtualBox Extension Pack** click **All supported platforms** to download the extension package.

5. Navigate to the folder that contains the downloads and launch the VirtualBox installation program **VirtualBox-xxx-nnnn-hhh.exe**.

6. Accept the default configurations from the installation Wizard to install the program.

7. If you are asked "Would you like to install this device software?" on one or more occasions, click **Install**.

8. When completed click **Finish** to launch VirtualBox, as seen in Figure 1-7.

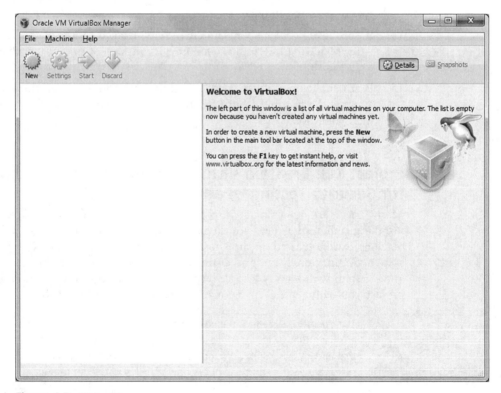

Figure 1-7 VirtualBox
Source: VirtualBox software developed by Oracle Corporation

9. Now install the VirtualBox extensions. Click **File** and **Preferences**.

10. Click **Extensions**.

11. Click the **Add a package** icon on the right side of the screen.

12. Navigate to the folder that contains the extension pack downloaded earlier to select that file. Click **Open**.

13. Click **Install.** Follow the necessary steps to complete the default installation.

14. Click **File** and **Close** to close VirtualBox. Complete the next project to configure VirtualBox and install the guest operating system.

Project 1-4: Create a Virtual Machine of Windows 8.1 for Security Testing—Part 2

After installing VirtualBox the next step is to create the guest operating system. For this project Windows 8.1 will be installed. Different options are available for obtaining a copy of Windows 8.1:

- A retail version of the software can be purchased.

- If your school is a member of the Microsoft DreamSpark program the operating system software and a license can be downloaded (www.dreamspark.com). See your instructor or lab supervisor for more information.

- A 90-day evaluation copy can be downloaded and installed from the Microsoft TechNet Evaluation Center (technet.microsoft.com/en-us/evalcenter/hh699156.aspx).

1. Obtain the ISO image of Windows 8.1 using one of the options above and save it on the hard drive of the computer.

2. Launch VirtualBox.

3. Click **New**.

4. In **Name:** enter **Windows 8.1** as the name of the virtual machine.

5. Be sure that **Type:** changes to **Microsoft Windows** and **Version:** changes to **Windows 8.1**. Click **Next**.

6. Under **Memory size** accept the recommended size or increase the allocation if you have sufficient RAM on your computer. Click **Next**.

7. Under **Hard drive** accept **Create a virtual hard drive now**. Click **Create**.

8. Under **Hard drive file type** accept the default **VID (VirtualBox Disk Image)**. Click **Next**.

9. Under **Storage on physical hard drive** accept the default **Dynamically allocated**. Click **Next**.

10. Under **File location and size** accept **Windows 8.1**. Click **Create**.

11. Now the configuration settings for the virtual machine are set, as seen in Figure 1-8.

Figure 1-8   VirtualBox virtual machine settings
Source: VirtualBox software developed by Oracle Corporation

12. Next you will load the Windows 8.1 ISO image. Click **Settings**.

13. In the left pane click **Storage**.

14. Under **Controller: IDE** click **Empty**.

15. In the right page under **Attributes** click the icon of the optical disc.

16. Click **Choose a virtual CD/DVD disc file...**

17. Navigate to the location of the Windows 8.1 ISO file and click **Open**.

18. Click **OK**.

19. Click **Start** to launch the Windows 8.1 ISO.

20. Follow the Windows 8.1 installation wizard to complete the installation.

21. To close the Windows 8.1 guest operating system in VirtualBox click **File** and then **Exit**.

22. Close all windows.

Case Projects

CASE PROJECTS

Case Project 1-1 Research Cyber Kill Chain®

The Cyber Kill Chain approach to security is increasing in popularity. Research the background of the Cyber Kill Chain and how it is being used today. Begin by reading the original article "Intelligence-Driven Computer Network Defense Informed by Analysis of Adversary Campaigns and Intrusion Kill Chains" by Eric M. Hutchins, Michael J. Clopperty, and Rohan M. Aminot at *www.lockheedmartin.com/content/dam/lockheed/data/corporate/documents/LM-White-Paper-Intel-Driven-Defense.pdf*. Next, search the Internet for additional information and how this approach can help improve security. Write a one-page paper of your research.

Case Project 1-2 Attack Experiences

Based on your own personal experiences or those of someone you know (you may have to interview other students or a friend), write a paragraph regarding a computer attack that occurred. When did it happen? What was the attack? What type of damage did it inflict? Using the information in Table 1-2, list the reason or reasons you think that the attack was successful. How was the computer fixed after the attack? What could have prevented it? Write a one-page paper about these experiences.

Case Project 1-3 Security Podcasts

Many security vendors and security researchers now post regular online podcasts on security. Using a search engine, locate three different podcasts about computer security. Download them to your media player or computer and listen to them. Then, write a summary of what was discussed and a critique of the podcasts. Were they beneficial to you? Would you recommend them to someone else? Write a one-page paper on your research.

Case Project 1-4 What Are Your Layers?

Security defenses should be based on five fundamental security principles: layering, limiting, diversity, obscurity, and simplicity. Analyze these principles for the computers that you use. Create a table that lists the five fundamental security principles across the top, and then list down the side at least three computers that you commonly use at school, your place of employment, home, a friend's house, etc. Then enter the security element of each principle for each of the computers (such as, for *Limiting* you may indicate the number of people who have keys to the door of the office or apartment that contains the computer). Leave blank any box for which that security layer does not exist. Based on your analysis, what can you say regarding the security of these computers? Finally, for each of the elements that you think is inadequate or missing, add what you believe would improve security. Write an analysis of your findings that is at least two paragraphs in length.

Case Project 1-5 Information Security Terminology in Your World

The scenario of Ellie protecting her scooter was used in this chapter to introduce the six key terms used in information security: asset, threat, threat agent, vulnerability, exploit, and risk. Create your own one-paragraph scenario with those six key terms using something that requires protection with which you are familiar, such as protecting a television in a home from being stolen. Also, create a table similar to Table 1-5 that lists these terms and how they are used in your scenario.

Case Project 1-6 Security+ Certification Jobs

What types of jobs require a Security+ certification? Using online career sites such as monster.com, careerbuilder.com, jobfactory.com, and others, research the types of security positions that require a Security+ certification. Create a table that lists the employer, the job title, a description of the job, and the starting salary (if these items are provided).

Case Project 1-7 Bay Pointe Security Consulting

Bay Pointe Security Consulting (BPSC) provides security consulting services to a wide range of businesses, individuals, schools, and organizations. Because of its reputation and increasing demand for its services, BPSC has partnered with a local college to hire technology students close to graduation to assist them on specific projects. This not only helps BPSC with their projects but also provides real-world experience to students who are interested in the security field.

As part of National Cybersecurity Awareness Month a local business organization is conducting a series of "Lunch-and-Learn" meetings during the month for citizens and small business owners to learn more about security. BPSC has been asked to present an introductory session on the fundamentals of security: what it is, why it is important today, who are the attackers, what types of attacks do they launch, etc. Because you are completing your degree, BPSC has asked you to make the presentation to the class.

1. Create a PowerPoint presentation that explains what IT security is and why it is important today. Also include who is responsible for attacks and their attack techniques. Your presentation should be 7 to 10 slides in length.

2. As a follow-up to your presentation, create a Frequently Asked Questions (FAQ) sheet that outlines general principles that can be used to protect valuable assets. Write a one-page FAQ about security protections.

Case Project 1-8 Community Site Activity

The Information Security Community Site is an online companion to this textbook. It contains a wide variety of tools, information, discussion boards, and other features to assist learners. In order to gain the most benefit from the site you will need to set up a free account.

Go to **community.cengage.com/infosec**. Click JOIN THE COMMUNITY. On the Join the Community page, enter the requested information. For your sign-in name, use the first letter of your first name followed by an underscore (_) and then your last name. For example, John Smith would create the sign-in name as J_Smith.

Your instructor may have a different naming convention that you should use, such as the name of your course followed by your initials. Check with your instructor before creating your sign-in name.

Explore the various features of the Information Security Community Site and become familiar with it. Visit the blog section and read the blog postings to learn about some of the latest events in IT security.

References

1. Radcliffe, Jerome, "Hacking medical devices for fun and insulin: Breaking the Human SCADA System," *Blackhat Briefings & Training USA + 2011*, accessed Nov. 16, 2013, www.blackhat.com/html/bh-us-11/bh-us-11-briefings.html.

2. Finkle, Jim, "Exclusive: Medtronic probes insulin pump risks," *Reuters*, Oct. 26, 2011, accessed Nov. 16, 2013, www.reuters.com/article/2011/10/26/us-medtronic-idUSTRE79P52620111026.

3. Shchetko, Nick, "Pacemakers, cars, energy grids: The tech that should not be hackable, is," *Minyanville*, Jul. 31, 2013, accessed Nov. 16, 2013, www.minyanville.com/sectors/technology/articles/The-2527Hackable2527-Devices-We-Wish-Weren2527t253A/7/31/2013/id/51050.

4. Fu, Kevin, "Click here to download your AVEA ventilator software update. Trust me," *Ann Arbor Research Center for Medical Device Security (blog)*, Jun. 8, 2012, accessed Nov. 16, 2013, http://blog.secure-medicine.org/2012/06/click-here-to-download-your-avea.html.

5. "DHS wireless medical devices/healthcare cyberattacks report," *Public Intelligence*, May 15, 2012, accessed Nov. 16, 2013, http://publicintelligence.net/nccic-medical-device-cyberattacks/.

6. Chenok, Daniel, "Information Security Resource Center," *National Institute of Standards and Technology*, Mar. 30, 2012, accessed Nov. 16, 2013, http://csrc.nist.gov/groups/SMA/ispab/documents/correspondence/ispab-ltr-to-omb_med_device.pdf.

7. "FDA safety communication: Cybersecurity for medical devices and hospital networks," *U.S. Food and Drug Administration*, Jun. 13, 2013, accessed Nov. 16, 2013, www.fda.gov/MedicalDevices/Safety/AlertsandNotices/ucm356423.htm.

8. "Network and computer systems administrators: Occupational outlook handbook," *Bureau of Labor Statistics*, Mar. 29, 2012, accessed Mar. 30, 2013, www.bls.gov/ooh/Computer-and-Information-Technology/Network-and-computer-systems-administrators.htm.

9. Regalado, Daniel, "Backdoor.Ploutus reloaded—Ploutus leaves Mexico," *Symantec (blog)*, Oct. 25, 2013, accessed Nov. 16, 2013, www.symantec.com/connect/blogs/backdoorploutus-reloaded-ploutus-leaves-mexico.

10. Moore, H., "Serial offenders: Widespread flaws in serial port servers," *Security Street Rapid*, Apr. 23, 2013, accessed Nov. 16, 2013, https://community.rapid7.com/community/metasploit/blog/2013/04/23/serial-offenders-widespread-flaws-in-serial-port-servers.

11. "Akamai releases second quarter 2013 'State of the Internet' report," *Akamai*, Oct. 16, 2013, accessed Nov. 16, 2013, www.akamai.com/html/about/press/releases/2013/press_101613.html.

12. Teso, Hug, "Aircraft hacking: Practical aero series," *Fourth Annual HITB Security Conference in Europe*, Apr. 10, 2013, accessed Nov. 16, 2013, http://conference.hitb.org/hitbsecconf2013ams/.

13. Balduzzi, Marco, et al., "Hey captain, where's your ship? Attacking vessel tracking systems for fun and profit," *Eleventh Annual HITB Security Conference in Asia*, accessed Nov. 16, 2013, http://conference.hitb.org/hitbsecconf2013kul/materials/D1T1%20-%20Marco%20Balduzzi,%20Kyle%20Wilhoit%20Alessandro%20Pasta%20-%20Attacking%20Vessel%20Tracking%20Systems%20for%20Fun%20and%20Profit.pdf.

14. "Reverse engineering a D-Link backdoor," *Embedded Device Hacking*, Oct. 12, 2013, accessed Nov. 16, 2013, www.devttys0.com/2013/10/reverse-engineering-a-d-link-backdoor/.

15. "Chronology of data breaches: Security breaches 2005–present," *Privacy Rights Clearinghouse*, updated Dec. 4, 2013, accessed Dec. 4, 2013, www.privacyrights.org/data-breach.

16. "Malware," *AVTest*, Dec. 1, 2013, accessed Dec. 5, 2013, www.av-test.org/en/statistics/malware/.

17. Finkle, Jim, "Hackers are creating and selling fake 'likes' on Facebook, Instagram," *Reuters*, Aug. 16, 2013, accessed Dec. 6, 2013, www.huffingtonpost.com/2013/08/16/fake-instagram-likes_n_3769247.html?utm_hp_ref=technology.

18. "IRS missing billions in ID theft," *Chron.com*, accessed Aug. 4, 2012, www.chron.com/business/article/IRS-missing-billions-in-ID-theft-3757389.php.

19. "The cost of 'Code Red': $1.2 billion," *USA Today*, Aug. 1, 2001, accessed Feb. 28, 2011, www.usatoday.com/tech/news/2001-08-01-code-red-costs.htm.

20. Reed, John, "Cyber terrorism now at the top of the list of security concerns," *Defensetech*, accessed Jan. 27, 2013, http://defensetech.org/2011/09/12/cyber-terrorism-now-at-the-top-of-the-list-of-security-concerns/.

21. Goldman, David, "Hacker hits on U.S. power and nuclear targets spiked in 2012," *CNN Money*, Jan. 9, 2013, accessed Jan. 27, 2014, http://money.cnn.com/2013/01/09/technology/security/infrastructure-cyberattacks/.

22. Sweeney, Patrick, "Defending against exploit kits," *Network World*, Jun. 3, 2013, accessed Dec. 7, 2013, www.networkworld.com/news/tech/2013/060313-exploit-kits-270404.html.

23. Keizer, Gregg, "Google pays record $31K bounty for Chrome bugs," *Computerworld*, Apr. 29, 2013, accessed Dec. 7, 2013, www.computerworld.com/s/article/9238753/ Google_pays_record_31K_bounty_for_Chrome_bugs.

24. Cappelli, Dawn, "Internal review: The insider threat risk." *SC Magazine*, Feb. 2, 2011, accessed Feb. 28, 2011, http://inform.com/government-and-politics/internal-review -insider-threat-risk-4737197a.

25. *Ibid.*

## part I

Threats

The security of the data and information contained on computers and digital devices today is threatened by more different types of attacks than ever before, and the threats and attacks are escalating on a daily basis. The chapters in this part outline these threats. The chapters in later parts will give you the network security concepts and tools you need to prevent or defend against these types of attacks.

## chapter 2

Malware and Social Engineering Attacks

After completing this chapter, you should be able to do the following:

- Define malware
- List the different types of malware
- Identify payloads of malware
- Describe the types of social engineering psychological attacks
- Explain physical social engineering attacks

Today's Attacks and Defenses

A security test was recently conducted at a U.S. federal government agency that specializes in "offensive cybersecurity" and is charged with protecting national secrets. Previous security tests indicated that this agency was resistant to technology-based attacks. However, this time the testers used a completely different approach: they created a fake online profile of an attractive and intelligent young female in the security industry, and used it to trick several males in the organization into compromising security in order to help her.

The testers started by creating a fake online profile of "Emily Williams," an attractive 28-year-old who graduated from MIT and had several years of security experience. The profile of "Emily" was posted on the social networking sites Facebook and LinkedIn, along with a photo (in a touch of irony, the photo was actually that of a server from a local restaurant frequented by many of the employees of this same government agency, used with her permission). To make sure her story was complete, the testers also posted on several of MIT's university forums using the name Emily Williams. After only 15 hours, Emily had 60 Facebook and 55 LinkedIn connections with employees from the targeted government agency and its contractors (and after 24 hours she already had three job offers from other companies). Emily then started receiving LinkedIn endorsements for her skills, and males who worked at the government agency offered to help her get a jump-start on a new job within the agency. These men said they would assist her in bypassing the normal procedures for receiving a laptop computer and network access, giving her higher levels of security access than a new hire would normally have.

The next step was to leverage the attention directed toward Emily to actually break into the agency's computers. During the Christmas holidays the testers created a website with a Christmas card and posted a link to it on Emily's social media profiles. Anyone who visited Emily's site was prompted to execute a program to display the card, which actually also contained code that exploited a vulnerability on the victim's computer. The end result was that the testers were able to gain administrative rights over these agency computers and capture user passwords, install applications, and steal sensitive documents, which, in more irony, contained information about state-sponsored attacks on foreign governments.

One of the contractors for this agency who fell for this ploy worked as a developer for an antivirus vendor and had access to the antivirus source code, which the testers were able to see. Later the testing team observed that two of the agency's employees had exchanged information on Facebook about the upcoming birthday of the agency's head of information security. Because the head did not have a Facebook or LinkedIn account (perhaps for security reasons), the testers sent him an email with a birthday card that pretended to come from one of the agency's employees.

(continued)

The head of security fell victim by opening the card and infecting his computer, thus exposing the "crown jewels" of the entire system.

The testers accomplished in just one week all of their goals using "Emily Williams," although they extended it for three more months just to see how far they could go. This test validated what is widely known: because attractive females often receive special treatment in the male-dominated IT industry, attacks using this type of trickery can be very successful. The testing team also tried a similar test by planting a fake male social media profile to see if any of the females at the agency would likewise provide assistance and circumvent security. None of them did.

Successful attacks on computers today generally consist of two elements. One element is malicious software programs that are created by attackers to silently infiltrate computers with the intent to do harm. This software may intercept data, steal information, launch other attacks, or damage a computer's hard drive so that it no longer properly functions. According to a major security vendor, one of these malicious software "events" occurs at an organization on average once every three minutes.[1]

The other element of a successful attack is often overlooked but is equally deadly: tricking users into performing a compromising action or providing sensitive information. Defeating security through a person instead of technology is actually the most cost-effective approach and can also generate some of the highest success rates. These attacks take advantage of user apathy or confusion about good security practices and deceive users into opening the door for the malicious software programs to enter.

This chapter examines attacks using these two elements, malicious software programs and tricking users. It begins by looking at attacks that utilize malicious software. Then it explores how attacks through users are being conducted today.

This chapter explores the background of various malware and social engineering attacks and how attackers use them. Later chapters cover defenses against specific attacks.

Attacks Using Malware

3.1 Explain types of malware.

Malware is software that enters a computer system without the user's knowledge or consent and then performs an unwanted and usually harmful action. Strictly speaking, malware uses a threat vector to deliver a malicious "payload" that performs a harmful function once it is invoked. However, *malware* is most often used as a general term that refers to a wide variety of damaging software programs.

In order to detect malware on an infected computer, a software scanning tool can search for the malware, looking to match it against a known pattern of malware. In order to circumvent this detection of their software, attackers can mask the presence of their malware by having it "mutate" or change. Three types of mutating malware are:

- *Oligomorphic malware.* **Oligomorphic malware** changes its internal code to one of a set number of predefined mutations whenever it is executed. However, because oligomorphic malware has only a limited number of mutations, it will eventually change back into a previous version that may then be detected by a scanner.

- *Polymorphic malware.* Malware code that completely changes from its original form whenever it is executed is known as **polymorphic malware**. This is usually accomplished by the malware containing "scrambled" code that, when the malware is activated, is "unscrambled" before it is executed.

- *Metamorphic malware.* **Metamorphic malware** can actually rewrite its own code and thus appears different each time it is executed. It does this by creating a logical equivalent of its code whenever it is run.

Different types of malware have emerged over time as a result of security defenses becoming more sophisticated and the corresponding attacks becoming progressively more complex. However, there has been no standard established for the classification of the different types of malware. As a result the definitions of the different types of malware are often confusing and may overlap. One method of classifying the various types of malware is by using the primary trait that the malware possesses. These traits are circulation, infection, concealment, and payload capabilities.

- *Circulation.* Some malware has as its primary trait spreading rapidly to other systems in order to impact a large number of users. Malware can circulate through a variety of means: by using the network to which all the devices are connected, through USB flash drives that are shared among users, or by sending the malware as an email attachment. Malware can be circulated automatically or it may require an action by the user.

- *Infection.* Once the malware reaches a system through circulation, then it must "infect" or embed itself into that system. The malware might run only one time and then store itself in the computer's memory, or it might remain on the system and be launched an infinite number of times through an auto-run feature. Some malware attaches itself to a benign program while other malware functions as a stand-alone process.

- *Concealment.* Some malware has as its primary trait avoiding detection by concealing its presence from scanners. Polymorphic malware attempts to avoid detection by changing itself, while other malware can embed itself within existing processes or modify the underlying host operating system.

- *Payload capabilities.* When payload capabilities are the primary focus of malware, the focus is on what nefarious action(s) the malware performs. Does it steal passwords and other valuable data from the user's system? Does it delete programs so the computer can no longer function properly? Or does the malware modify the system's security settings? In some cases the purpose of the malware is to use the infected system to launch attacks against other computers.

The sections that follow give more details and examples of malware classified by circulation/ infection, concealment, and payload capabilities.

Many types of malware have more than one of these traits: that is, the malware both circulates and carries a payload. However, in terms of classification the *primary* trait of the malware is used here.

Circulation/Infection

Three types of malware have the primary traits of circulation and/or infection. These are viruses, worms, and Trojans.

Viruses A *biological virus* is an agent that reproduces inside a cell. When a cell is infected by a virus, the virus takes over the operation of that cell, converting it into a virtual factory to make more copies of it. The cell is forced to produce thousands or hundreds of thousands of identical copies of the original virus very rapidly (the polio virus can make more than *one million* copies of itself inside one single infected human cell). Biologists often say that viruses exist only to make more viruses. A **computer virus** (**virus**) is malicious computer code that, like its biological counterpart, reproduces itself on the same computer. Strictly speaking a computer virus replicates itself (or an evolved copy of itself) without any human intervention.

Sometimes *virus* and *malware* are used synonymously, especially by the general news media when reporting on a security incident. However, this is incorrect: a virus is only one type of malware.

Almost all viruses "infect" by inserting themselves into a computer file. A virus that infects an executable program file is simply called a **program virus**. When the program is launched the virus is activated. A virus can also infect a data file. One of the most common data file viruses is a **macro virus** that is written in a script known as a macro. A **macro** is a series of instructions that can be grouped together as a single command. Often macros are used to automate a complex set of tasks or a repeated series of tasks. Macros can be written by using a macro language, such as Visual Basic for Applications (VBA), and are stored within the user document (such as in an Excel .XLSX worksheet or Word .DOCX file). Once the document is opened, the macro instructions then execute, whether those instructions are benign or a macro virus. A very large number of different file types can contain a virus. Table 2-1 lists some of the 70 different Microsoft Windows file types can be infected with a virus.

One of the first viruses found on a microcomputer was written for the Apple II in 1982. Rich Skrenta, a ninth-grade student in Pittsburgh, wrote "Elk Cloner," which displayed his poem on the screen after every 50th use of the infected floppy disk. Unfortunately, the virus leaked out and found its way onto the computer used by Skrenta's math teacher.[2] In 1984, the mathematician Dr. Frederick Cohen introduced the term *virus* based on a recommendation from his advisor, who came up with the name from reading science fiction novels.

Early viruses were relatively straightforward in how they infected files. One basic type of infection is the *appender infection*. The virus first attaches or appends itself to the end of the infected file. It then inserts at the beginning of the file a "jump" instruction that points to the end of the file, which is the beginning of the virus code. When the program is launched, the jump instruction redirects control to the virus. Figure 2-1 shows how an appender infection works.

File extension	Description
.DOCX, .XLSX	Microsoft Office user documents
.EXE	Executable program file
.MSI	Microsoft installer file
.MSP	Windows installer patch file
.SCR	Windows screen saver
.CPL	Windows Control Panel file
.MSC	Microsoft Management Console file
.WSF	Windows script file
.REG	Windows registry file
.PS1	Windows PowerShell script

Table 2-1 Windows file types that can be infected

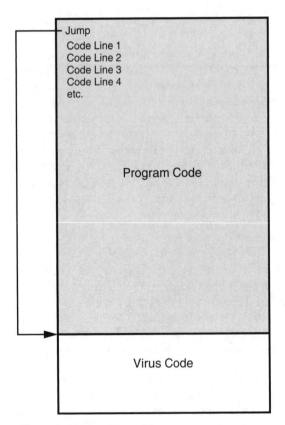

Figure 2-1 Appender infection

However, these types of viruses could easily by detected by virus scanners. Most viruses today go to great lengths to avoid detection; this type of virus is called an **armored virus**. Some of the armored virus infection techniques include:

- *Swiss cheese infection.* Instead of having a single "jump" instruction to the "plain" virus code, some armored viruses perform two actions to make detection more difficult. First they "scramble" (encrypt) the virus code to make it more difficult to detect. Then they divide the engine to "unscramble" (decrypt) the virus code into different pieces and inject these pieces throughout the infected program code. When the program is launched the different pieces are then tied together and unscramble the virus code. A Swiss cheese infection is shown in Figure 2-2.

- *Split infection.* Instead of inserting pieces of the decryption engine throughout the program code, some viruses split the malicious code itself into several parts (along with one main body of code), and then these parts are placed at random positions throughout the program code. To make detection even more difficult these parts may contain unnecessary "garbage" code to mask their true purpose. A split infection virus is shown in Figure 2-3.

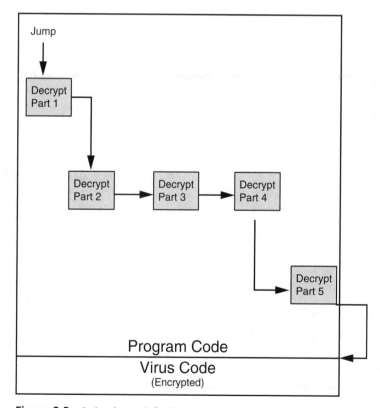

Figure 2-2 Swiss cheese infection

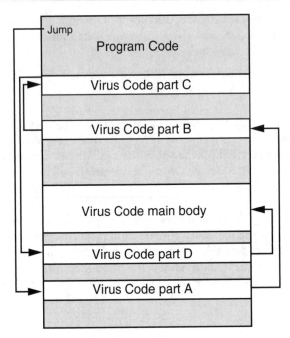

Figure 2-3 Split infection

Some armored viruses scan for the presence of files that security researchers typically use. If those files are present, then it is assumed that the virus is being examined for weaknesses and the virus will then automatically self-destruct by deleting itself.

Each time the infected program is launched or the file is opened—either by the user or the computer's operating system—the virus performs two actions. First, it unloads a payload to perform a malicious action. Although early viruses often did nothing more than display an annoying message, viruses today are much more harmful. Viruses have performed the following actions:

- Caused a computer to crash repeatedly
- Erased files from a hard drive
- Turned off the computer's security settings
- Reformatted the hard disk drive

Sometimes a virus will remain dormant for a period of time before unleashing its payload.

The second action a virus takes when executed is to reproduce itself by inserting its code into another file on the same computer. A virus can only replicate itself on the host computer on which it is located; it cannot automatically spread to another computer by itself.

2

Instead, it must rely on the actions of users to spread to other computers. Because viruses are generally attached to files, viruses are spread by a user transferring those files to other devices. For example, a user may send an infected file as an email attachment or copy an infected file to a USB flash drive and give the drive to another user. Once the virus reaches a new computer it begins to infect it. This means that a virus must have two "carriers": a file to which it attaches and a human to transport it to other computers.

 Several similarities between biological and computer viruses exist: both must enter their host passively (by relying on the action of an outside agent), both must be on the correct host (a horse virus cannot make a human sick, just as an Apple Mac virus cannot infect a Windows computer), both can only replicate when inside the host, both may remain dormant for a period of time, and both types of viruses replicate at the expense of the host.

Worms A second type of malware that has as its primary purpose to spread is a worm. A **worm** is a malicious program that uses a computer network to replicate (worms are sometimes called *network viruses*). A worm is designed to enter a computer through the network and then take advantage of vulnerability in an application or an operating system on the host computer. Once the worm has exploited the vulnerability on one system, it immediately searches for another computer on the network that has the same vulnerability.

 One of the first wide-scale worms occurred in 1988. This worm exploited a misconfiguration in a program that allowed commands emailed to a remote system to be executed on that system, and it also carried a payload that contained a program that attempted to determine user passwords. Almost 6000 computers, or 10 percent of the devices connected to the Internet at that time, were affected. The worm was attributed to Robert T. Morris, Jr., who was later convicted of federal crimes in connection with this incident.

Early worms were relatively benign and designed simply to spread quickly and not corrupt the systems they infected. These worms slowed down the network through which they were transmitted by replicating so quickly that they consumed all network resources. Today's worms can leave behind a payload on the systems they infect and cause harm, much like a virus. Actions that worms have performed include deleting files on the computer or allowing the computer to be remotely controlled by an attacker.

 Although viruses and worms are said to be automatically self-replicating, *where* they replicate is different. A virus will self-replicate *on* the host computer but not to other computers. A worm will self-replicate *between* computers (from one computer to another).

Trojans According to ancient legend, the Greeks won the Trojan War by hiding soldiers in a large hollow wooden horse that was presented as a gift to the city of Troy. Once the horse was wheeled into the fortified city, the soldiers crept out of the horse during the night and attacked the unsuspecting defenders.

A computer **Trojan horse** (or just **Trojan**) is an executable program that masquerades as performing a benign activity but also does something malicious. For example, a user may download what is advertised as a calendar program, yet when it is installed, in addition to installing the calendar it also installs malware that scans the system for credit card numbers and passwords, connects through the network to a remote system, and then transmits that information to the attacker.

Unlike a virus that infects a system without the user's knowledge or consent, a Trojan program is installed on the computer system with the user's knowledge. What the Trojan conceals is its malicious payload.

Table 2-2 lists the differences between viruses, worms, and Trojans.

Action	Virus	Worm	Trojan
What does it do?	Inserts malicious code into a program or data file	Exploits a vulnerability in an application or operating system	Masquerades as performing a benign action but also does something malicious
How does it spread to other computers?	User transfers infected files to other devices	Uses a network to travel from one computer to another	User transfers Trojan file to other computers
Does it infect a file?	Yes	No	It can
Does there need to be user action for it to spread?	Yes	No	Yes

Table 2-2   Difference between viruses, worms, and Trojans

Concealment

Some types of malware have avoiding detection as a primary trait. The most common type of concealment malware first captured the public's attention through music CDs.

In late 2005, Sony BMG Music Entertainment shocked the computer world by secretly installing hidden software on any computer that played one of 50 Sony music CDs. The software that Sony installed was intended to prevent the music CDs from being copied. These CDs created a hidden directory, installed their own device driver software on the computer, and then rerouted normal functions away from Microsoft Windows to Sony's own routines. Finally, the Sony software disguised its presence from both users and the operating system. Once this nefarious behavior was exposed Sony was forced to backpedal and withdraw the CDs from the market.

What Sony did was install a rootkit on computers on which the CD was played. A **rootkit** is a set of software tools used to hide the actions or presence of other types of software. This software can be benign, like playing music CDs, or it can be malicious, such as Trojans, viruses, or worms. Rootkits do this by changing the operating system to force it to ignore their malicious files or activity. Rootkits also hide or remove all traces of evidence that may reveal the malware, such as log entries.

Originally the term *rootkit* referred to a set of modified and recompiled tools for the UNIX operating system. Root is the highest level of privileges available in UNIX, so a *rootkit* described programs that an attacker used to gain root privileges and to hide the malicious software. Today rootkits are not limited to UNIX computers; similar tools are available for other operating systems.

One approach used by rootkits is to alter or replace operating system files with modified versions that are specifically designed to ignore malicious evidence. For example, scanning software may be instructed to scan all files in a specific directory. In order to do this, the scanning software will receive a list of those files from the operating system. A rootkit will replace the operating system's accurate list of files with the rootkit's own routine that will not display malicious files. This is illustrated in Figure 2-4. The scanning software assumes that the operating system will willingly carry out those instructions and retrieve all files; it does not know that the computer is only providing files that the rootkit has approved. In essence, users can no longer trust their computer that contains a rootkit: the rootkit is in charge and hides what is occurring on the computer.

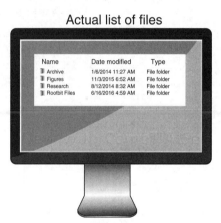
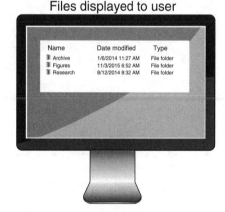

Figure 2-4   Computer infected with rootkit

Because a rootkit often substitutes its own files and routines in the operating system with malicious copies, it can be very difficult to detect the presence of a rootkit; the operating system cannot be trusted to provide accurate information. In addition, these files and routines typically operate at a very low level in the operating system and cannot easily be repaired. Ultimately, the only safe and foolproof way to handle a rootkit infection is to reformat the hard drive and reinstall the operating system.

Payload Capabilities

The destructive power of malware is to be found in its payload capabilities. The primary payload capabilities are to collect data, delete data, modify system security settings, and launch attacks.

Collect Data Different types of malware are designed to collect important data from the user's computer and make it available at the attacker. This malware includes spyware, adware, and ransomware.

Spyware **Spyware** is a general term used to describe software that secretly spies on users by collecting information without their consent. The Anti-Spyware Coalition defines spyware as tracking software that is deployed without adequate notice, consent, or control by the user.[3] This software uses the computer's resources, including programs already installed on the computer, for the purpose of collecting and distributing personal or sensitive information. Table 2-3 lists different technologies used by spyware.

Technology	Description	Impact
Automatic download software	Used to download and install software without the user's interaction	May be used to install unauthorized applications
Passive tracking technologies	Used to gather information about user activities without installing any software	May collect private information such as websites a user has visited
System modifying software	Modifies or changes user configurations, such as the web browser home page or search page, default media player, or lower-level system functions	Changes configurations to settings that the user did not approve
Tracking software	Used to monitor user behavior or gather information about the user, sometimes including personally identifiable or other sensitive information	May collect personal information that can be shared widely or stolen, resulting in fraud or identity theft

Table 2-3   **Technologies used by spyware**

Not all spyware is necessarily malicious. For example, spyware monitoring tools can help parents keep track of the online activities of their children while the children are surfing the Web.

One type of nefarious spyware is a **keylogger** that silently captures and stores each keystroke that a user types on the computer's keyboard. The attacker then searches the captured text for any useful information such as passwords, credit card numbers, or personal information.

A keylogger can be a small hardware device or a software program. As a hardware device, the keylogger is inserted between the computer keyboard connection and USB port, as shown in Figure 2-5. Because the device resembles an ordinary keyboard plug and the computer keyboard USB port is often on the back of the computer, a hardware keylogger can easily go undetected. In addition, the device is beyond the reach of the computer's antimalware scanning software and thus raises no alarms. The attacker who installed the hardware keylogger returns at a later time and physically removes the device in order to access the information it has gathered.

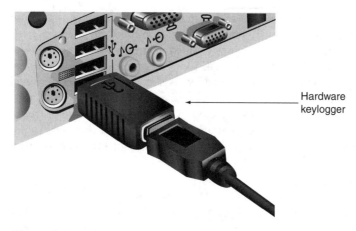

Figure 2-5 Hardware keylogger

Hardware keyloggers are often installed on public access computers, such as those in a school's open computer lab or a public library. If a sensitive password must be entered on one of these computers, almost all operating systems offer an on-screen "virtual" keyboard through which the keys are clicked with a mouse or touch screen, thus defeating a keylogger. For Windows computers it is found by clicking on Accessories and then Ease of Use.

Software keyloggers are programs installed on the computer that silently capture sensitive information. Software keylogger programs act like rootkits and conceal themselves so that they cannot be detected by the user. An advantage of software keyloggers is that they do not require physical access to the user's computer as with a hardware keylogger. The software, often installed as a Trojan or by a virus, can routinely send captured information back to the attacker through the computer's Internet connection.

Today software keyloggers go far beyond just capturing a user's keystrokes. These programs can also make screen captures of everything that is on the user's screen and silently turn on the computer's web camera to record images of the user.

Adware **Adware** delivers advertising content in a manner that is unexpected and unwanted by the user. Once the adware malware becomes installed, it typically displays advertising banners, popup ads, or opens new web browser windows at random intervals. Users generally reject adware because:

- Adware may display objectionable content, such as gambling sites or pornography.
- Frequent popup ads can interfere with a user's productivity.
- Popup ads can slow a computer or even cause crashes and the loss of data.
- Unwanted advertisements can be a nuisance.

Some adware goes beyond affecting the user's computer experience. This is because adware programs can also perform a tracking function, which monitors and tracks a user's online activities and then sends a log of these activities to third parties without the user's authorization or knowledge. For example, a user who visits online automobile sites to view specific types of cars can be tracked by adware and classified as someone interested in buying a new car. Based on the sequence and type of websites visited, the adware can also determine whether the surfers' behavior suggests they are close to making a purchase or are also looking at competitors' cars. This information is gathered by adware and then sold to automobile advertisers, who send the users regular mail advertisements about their cars or even call the user on the telephone.

Ransomware One of the newest and fastest-growing types of malware is ransomware. **Ransomware** prevents a user's device from properly operating until a fee is paid. One type of ransomware locks up a user's computer and then displays a message that purports to come from a law enforcement agency. This message, using official-looking imagery, states that the user has performed an illegal action such as downloading pornography and must immediately pay a fine online by entering a credit card number. The computer remains "held hostage" and locked (except for the numeric keys on the keyboard) until the ransom payment is made. Figure 2-6 shows a ransomware message from the Symantec website in its Security Response Center.

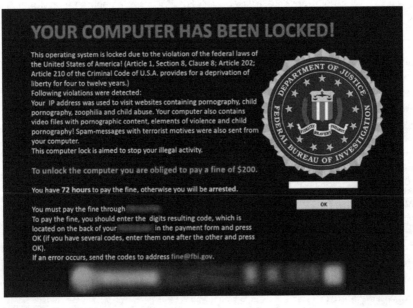

Figure 2-6 Ransomware message
Source: Symantec Security Response

Widespread ransomware first starting appearing about 2010.

2

Ransomware malware is highly profitable. By one estimate nearly 3 percent of those users who have been infected pay the ransom without question, generating almost $5 million annually from extorted victims.[4] Due to its high success rate attackers have started expanding the capabilities of this malware. Instead of just showing a message on the screen, one new variant of ransomware plays a recorded message through the computer's speakers using a regionalized and semipersonalized voice message.

Another variation displays a fictitious warning that there is a problem with the computer such as (in a touch of irony) a malware infection or imminent hard drive failure. No matter what the condition of the computer, the ransomware always reports that there is a problem. This ransomware variation tells users that they must immediately purchase additional software online to fix the problem that in fact does not exist. The warning appears to be legitimate because it mimics the appearance of genuine software and—unlawfully—uses legitimate trademarks or icons. The ransomware example in Figure 2-7 uses color schemes and icons similar to those found on legitimate Windows software. Users who provide their credit card number to make the purchase find that the attackers simply capture that information and then use the card number for their own purposes.

Win 7 Internet Security - Unregistred Version		

Win 7 Internet Security   Support   Registration

Main	**Current PC State: Infected!**	
	None	**Total: 9,460**
Perform Scan	Malware database status: Up to date	
Internet Security	**File**	**Malware Name**
	C:\Windows\assembly\NativeImages_v2.05...\xA756007.rt	Trojan-Spy.HTML.Bankfraud
Personal Security	C:\Windows\assembly\NativeImages_v2...\2A6ppmMoJ.rt	Trojan-Proxy.Win32.Agent.x
	C:\Windows\assembly\NativeImages_v2.0....\2IP5B7Bx.cab	Email-Worm.VBS.Peach
Proactive Defense	C:\Windows\Branding\ImM4y1o6J.sys	Virus.Boot-DOS.V.1536
	C:\Windows\Globalization\X.n76	Macro.PPoint.ShapeShift
Firewall	C:\Windows\inf\MSDTC\8y0mo6L.dl	Backdoor.Perl.AEI.16
	C:\Windows\inf\rdyboost\2L0M8Pxj1B.cab	Trojan-SMS.J2ME.RedBrows
Configuration	C:\Windows\Microsoft.NET\Framework\v3.0\Wn...\xMN.dl	Trojan-Clicker.Win32.Stixo.d
	C:\Windows\PolicyDefinitions\en-US\A88N6.dl	Trojan-Proxy.Win32.Agent.q
	C:\Windows\Prefetch\784j5Y1Y5Aak.m	Trojan-Downloader.BAT.Ftp.
	C:\Windows\servicing\Sessions\LbmxY.J55	Trojan-SMS.SymbOS.Viver.a
	C:\Windows\System32\catroot2\y35alJ.cab	Backdoor.Rbot.gen

Activate your copy right now and get full real-time protection with Win 7 Internet Security!

Scan Process: 100%   Infections found: 32

Remove All

Figure 2-7   Ransomware computer infection
Source: Microsoft Security Intelligence Report

In most instances, the ransomware embeds itself into the computer so that the message cannot be closed and rebooting the computer has no effect.

Delete Data   The payload of other types of malware deletes data on the computer. This may involve deleting important user data files, such as documents or photos, or erasing vital operating system files so that the computer will no longer properly function.

One type of malware that is frequently used to delete data is a logic bomb. A **logic bomb** is computer code that is typically added to a legitimate program but lies dormant until it is triggered by a specific logical event. Once it is triggered, the program then deletes data or performs other malicious activities. In one example, a Maryland government employee tried to destroy the contents of more than 4000 servers by planting a logic bomb script that was scheduled to activate 90 days after he was terminated.[5] Other recent high-profile logic bombs are listed in Table 2-4.

Description	Reason for attack	Results
A logic bomb was planted in a financial services computer network that caused 1000 computers to delete critical data.	A disgruntled employee had counted on this to cause the company's stock price to drop; he planned to use that event to earn money.	The logic bomb detonated but the employee was caught and sentenced to 8 years in prison and ordered to pay $3.1 million in restitution.[6]
A logic bomb at a defense contractor was designed to delete important rocket project data.	The employee's plan was to be hired as a highly paid consultant to fix the problem.	The logic bomb was discovered and disabled before it triggered. The employee was charged with computer tampering and attempted fraud and was fined $5000.[7]
A logic bomb at a health services firm was set to go off on the employee's birthday.	The employee was angered that he might be laid off (although he was not).	The employee was sentenced to 30 months in a federal prison and paid $81,200 in restitution to the company.[8]

Table 2-4   **Famous logic bombs**

NOTE   Logic bombs have sometimes been used by legitimate software companies to ensure payment for their software. If a payment is not made by the due date, the logic bomb activates and prevents the software from being used again. In some instances, logic bombs even erase the software and the accompanying payroll or customer files from the computer.

Logic bombs are difficult to detect before they are triggered. This is because logic bombs are often embedded in very large computer programs, some containing tens of thousands of lines of code, and a trusted employee can easily insert a few lines of computer code into a long program without anyone detecting it. In addition, these programs are not routinely scanned for containing malicious actions.

NOTE   Logic bombs should not be confused with an *Easter egg*, which refers to an undocumented, yet benign hidden feature that launches by entering a set of special commands, key combinations, or mouse clicks. Usually programmers insert Easter eggs for their own recreation or notoriety during the software's development. For example, in Microsoft Excel 95 there was actually an entire game called "The Hall of Tortured Souls" that was embedded as an Easter egg. Microsoft ended the practice of including Easter eggs in 2002 as part of its Trustworthy Computing initiative.

2

Modify System Security The payload of some types of malware attempts to modify the system's security settings so that more insidious attacks can be made. One type of malware in this category is called a backdoor. A **backdoor** gives access to a computer, program, or service that circumvents any normal security protections. Backdoors that are installed on a computer allow the attacker to return at a later time and bypass security settings.

 Creating a legitimate backdoor is a common practice by developers, who may need to access a program or device on a regular basis, yet do not want to be hindered by continual requests for passwords or other security approvals. The intent is for the backdoor to be removed once the application is finalized. However, in some instances backdoors have been left installed, and attackers have used them to bypass security.

Launch Attacks One of the most popular payloads of malware today carried by Trojans, worms, and viruses is software that will allow the infected computer to be placed under the remote control of an attacker. This infected robot (*bot*) computer is known as a **zombie**. When hundreds, thousands, or even hundreds of thousands of zombie computers are gathered into a logical computer network, they create a **botnet** under the control of the attacker (**bot herder**).

 Due to the multitasking capabilities of modern computers, a computer can act as a zombie while at the same time carrying out the tasks of its regular user. The user is completely unaware that his or her computer is being used for malicious activities.

Infected zombie computers wait for instructions through a **command and control** (C&C or C2) structure from the bot herders regarding which computers to attack and how. A common botnet C&C mechanism used today is the Hypertext Transport Protocol (HTTP), which is the standard protocol for Internet usage. For example, a zombie can receive its instructions by automatically signing in to a website that the bot herder operates or to a third-party website on which information has been placed that the zombie knows how to interpret as commands (this latter technique has an advantage in that the bot herder does not need to have an affiliation with that website). By using HTTP, botnet traffic may be more difficult to detect and block. Some botnets even use blogs or send specially coded attack commands through posts on the Twitter social networking service or notes posted in Facebook.

 Some bot herders are using a "dead drop" C&C mechanism. First a bogus Google Gmail email account is set up and the zombie malware has the account username and password coded into it. The bot herder then creates a draft email message in Gmail but never sends it. At set times the zombie logs in to Gmail and reads the draft to receive its instructions. The benefits of this dead drop are that the email message is never sent so there is no record of it and all Gmail transmissions are protected so that they cannot be viewed by outsiders.

Table 2-5 lists some of the attacks that can be generated through botnets.

Type of attack	Description
Spamming	Botnets are widely recognized as the primary source of spam email. A botnet consisting of thousands of zombies enables an attacker to send massive amounts of spam.
Spreading malware	Botnets can be used to spread malware and create new zombies and botnets. Zombies have the ability to download and execute a file sent by the attacker.
Manipulating online polls	Because each zombie has a unique Internet Protocol (IP) address, each "vote" by a zombie will have the same credibility as a vote cast by a real person. Online games can be manipulated in a similar way.
Denying services	Botnets can flood a web server with thousands of requests and overwhelm it to the point that it cannot respond to legitimate requests.

Table 2-5   Uses of botnets

In many ways a botnet is the ideal base of operations for attackers. Zombies are designed to operate in the background, often without any visible evidence of their existence. By keeping a low profile, botnets are sometimes able to remain active and operational for years. The ubiquitous always-on Internet service provided by residential broadband ensures that a large percentage of zombies in a botnet are accessible at any given time. This has resulted in a staggering number of botnets. One botnet contained more than 1.9 million zombies, and botnets of 100,000 zombies are not uncommon.[9] Some security experts estimate that between 7 and 25 percent of all computers on the Internet belong to a botnet.[10]

Social Engineering Attacks

3.2 Summarize various types of attacks.

3.3 Summarize social engineering attacks and the associated effectiveness of each attack.

One morning a small group of strangers walked into the corporate offices of a large shipping firm and soon walked out with access to the firm's entire computer network, which contained valuable and highly sensitive information. They were able to accomplish this feat with no technical tools or skills:

1. Before entering the building, one person of the group called the company's Human Resource (HR) office and asked for the names of key employees. The office willingly gave out the information without asking any questions.

2. As the group walked up to the building, one of them pretended to have lost the key code to the door, so a friendly employee let them in. When they entered a secured area on the third floor, they claimed to have misplaced their identity badges, so another smiling employee opened the door for them.

3. Because these strangers knew that the chief financial officer (CFO) was out of town because of his voicemail greeting message, they walked unchallenged into his office

and gathered information from his unprotected computer. They also dug through trash receptacles and retrieved useful documents. A custodian was even stopped and asked for a box in which to place these documents so they could be carried out of the building.

4. One of the group's members then called the company's help desk from the CFO's office and pretended to be the CFO (they had listened to his voice from his voicemail greeting message and knew how he spoke). The imposter CFO claimed that he desperately needed his password because he had forgotten it and was on his way to an important meeting. The help desk gave out the password, and the group left the building with complete access to the network.

This true story illustrates that technology is not always needed for attacks on IT.[11] **Social engineering** is a means of gathering information for an attack by relying on the weaknesses of individuals. Social engineering attacks can involve psychological approaches as well as physical procedures.

Psychological Approaches

Many social engineering attacks rely on psychology, which is the mental and emotional approach rather than the physical. At its core, social engineering relies on an attacker's clever manipulation of human nature in order to persuade the victim to provide information or take actions. Several basic "principles" or reasons make psychological social engineering effective. These are listed in Table 2-6 with the example of an attacker pretending to be the chief executive officer (CEO) calling the organization's help desk to have a password reset.

Principle	Description	Example
Authority	Directed by someone impersonating authority figure or falsely citing their authority	"I'm the CEO calling."
Intimidation	To frighten and coerce by threat	"If you don't reset my password, I will call your supervisor."
Consensus/social proof	Influenced by what others do	"I called last week and your colleague reset my password."
Scarcity	Something is in short supply	"I can't waste time here."
Urgency	Immediate action is needed	"My meeting with the board starts in 5 minutes."
Familiarity/liking	Victim is well-known and well-received	"I remember reading a good evaluation on you."
Trust	Confidence	"You know who I am."

Table 2-6   Social engineering effectiveness

Social media sites such as Facebook are popular with attackers to create a trust relationship with a user and then gather information.

Because many of the psychological approaches involve person-to-person contact, attackers use a variety of techniques to gain trust without moving quickly so as to become suspicious. For example:

- An attacker will not ask for too much information at one time, but instead will gather small amounts—even from several different victims—in order to maintain the appearance of credibility.

- The request from the attacker needs to be believable. Asking a victim to go into the CFO's office to retrieve a document may raise suspicion, yet asking if the CFO is on vacation would not.

- Slight flattery or flirtation can be helpful to "soften up" the victim to cooperate.

- An attacker works to "push the envelope" just far enough when probing for information before the victim suspects anything unusual.

- A smile and a simple question such as "I'm confused, can you please help me?" or a "Thanks" can usually "clinch the deal."

Social engineering psychological approaches often involve impersonation, phishing, spam, hoaxes, typo squatting, and watering hole attacks.

Impersonation Social engineering **impersonation** means to masquerade as a real or ficti-tious character and then play out the role of that person on a victim. For example, an attacker could impersonate a help desk support technician who calls the victim, pretends that there is a problem with the network, and asks her for her user name and password to reset the account.

Common roles that are often impersonated include a repairperson, IT support, a manager, a trusted third party, or a fellow employee. Often attackers will impersonate individuals whose roles are authoritative because victims generally resist saying "no" to anyone in power.

Phishing One of the most common forms of social engineering is phishing. **Phishing** is sending an email or displaying a web announcement that falsely claims to be from a legitimate enterprise in an attempt to trick the user into surrendering private informa-tion. Users are asked to respond to an email or are directed to a website where they are requested to update personal information, such as passwords, credit card numbers, Social Security numbers, bank account numbers, or other information. However, the email or website is actually an imposter and is set up to steal what information the user enters.

The word *phishing* is a variation on the word "fishing," with the idea being that bait is thrown out knowing that while most will ignore it, some will "bite."

One of the reasons that phishing succeeds is that the emails and the fake websites appear to be legitimate. Figure 2-8 illustrates an actual phishing email message that claims the victim has recently made a large payment to an individual. The message contains the logos, color schemes, and wording used by the legitimate site so that it appears to be genuine. The victim would naturally be puzzled by this message and click the links, which would then ask for a username and password to log in, but instead of accessing a legitimate site, this information is captured by the attacker.

PayPal™

You sent a payment

Transaction ID:
5Y544235VM010428T

Dear PayPal User,
You sent a payment for $1297.20 USD to Morris Cope.
Please note that it may take a little while for this payment to appear in the Recent Activity list on your Account Overview.
View the details of this transaction online

This payment was sent using your bank account.

By using your bank account to send money, you just:

- Paid easily and securely

- Sent money faster than writing and mailing paper checks

- Paid instantly -- your purchase won't show up on bills at the end of the month.

Thanks for using your bank account!

Your monthly account statement is available anytime; just log in to your account at https://www.paypal.com/us/cgi-bin/webscr?cmd=_history. To correct any errors, please contact us through our Help Center at https://www.paypal.com/us/cgi-bin/webscr?cmd=_contact_us.

Amount:	$1297.20 USD	
Sent on:	August 22, 2012	
Payment method:	Bank account	

Sincerely,
PayPal

Figure 2-8 Phishing email message
Source: Email sent to Dr. Mark Revels

The average phishing site only exists for 3.8 days to prevent law enforcement agencies from tracking the attackers. In that short period, a phishing attack can net more than $50,000.[12]

Many phishing attacks have these common features:

- *Deceptive web links.* Phishers like to use variations of a legitimate address, such as *www.ebay_secure.com, www.e—bay.com,* or *www.e-baynet.com.*

- *Logos.* Phishers often include the logo of the vendor and try to make the email look like the vendor's website as a way to convince the recipient that it is genuine.

- *Urgent request.* Many phishing emails include an instruction for the recipient to act immediately or else their account will be unavailable or a large amount of money will be deducted from their account.

Phishing is also used to validate email addresses. A phishing email can display an image retrieved from a website that is requested when the user opens the email message. A unique code is used to link the image to the recipient's email address, which then tells the phisher that the email address is active and valid. This is the reason why most email today does not automatically display images that are received in emails.

Several variations on phishing attacks are:

- *Pharming.* Instead of asking the user to visit a fraudulent website, **pharming** automatically redirects the user to the fake site. This is accomplished by attackers penetrating the servers on the Internet that direct traffic or altering a file on the host computer.

- *Spear phishing.* Whereas phishing involves sending millions of generic email messages to users, **spear phishing** targets only specific users. The emails used in spear phishing are customized to the recipients, including their names and personal information, in order to make the message appear legitimate.

- *Whaling.* One type of spear phishing is **whaling**. Instead of going after the "smaller fish," whaling targets the "big fish," namely, wealthy individuals or senior executives within a business who typically would have larger sums of money in a bank account that an attacker could access if the attack is successful. By focusing upon this smaller group, the attacker can invest more time in the attack and finely tune the message to achieve the highest likelihood of success.

- *Vishing.* Instead of using email to contact the potential victim, a telephone call can be used instead. Known as **vishing** (*voice phishing*), an attacker calls a victim who, upon answering, hears a recorded message that pretends to be from the user's bank stating that her credit card has experienced fraudulent activity or that her bank account has had unusual activity. The victim is instructed to call a specific phone number immediately (which has been set up by the attacker). When the victim calls, it is answered by automated instructions telling her to enter her credit card number, bank account number, Social Security number, or other information on the telephone's key pad.

Phishing attacks are increasing almost 60 percent annually with global annual losses about $1.5 billion.[13]

Spam   The amount of **spam**, or unsolicited email, that goes through the Internet continues to escalate. Google estimates that 9 out of every 10 email messages are spam.[14] The reason why users receive so many spam messages that advertise drugs, cheap mortgage rates, and items for sale is because sending spam is a lucrative business. It costs spammers very little to send millions of spam email messages. In the past, spammers would purchase a list of valid email addresses ($100 for 10 million addresses) and rent a motel room with a high-speed Internet connection ($85 per day) as a base for launching attacks. Today, however, almost all spam is sent from botnets: a spammer who does not own his own botnet can lease time from other attackers ($40 per hour) to use a botnet of up to 100,000 infected computers to launch a spam attack. Even if spammers receive only a very small percentage of responses, they still make a large profit. For example, if a spammer sent spam to 6 million users for a product with a sale price of $50 that cost only $5 to make, and if only 0.001 percent of the recipients responded and bought the product (a typical response rate), the spammer would still make more than $270,000 in profit.

A Russian-owned network was widely believed to be the hosting C&C center for five major botnets. When this network was disconnected from the Internet, all of their botnets stopped functioning and spam volumes worldwide immediately fell by 75 percent.

Text-based spam messages that include words such as *Viagra* or *investments* can easily be trapped by filters that look for these words and block the email. Because of the increased use of these filters, spammers have turned to *image spam*, which uses graphical images of text in order to circumvent text-based filters. Image spam cannot be filtered based on the textual content of the message because it appears as an image instead of text. These spam messages often include nonsense text so that it appears the email message is legitimate (an email with no text can prompt the spam filter to block it). Figure 2-9 shows an example of an image spam.

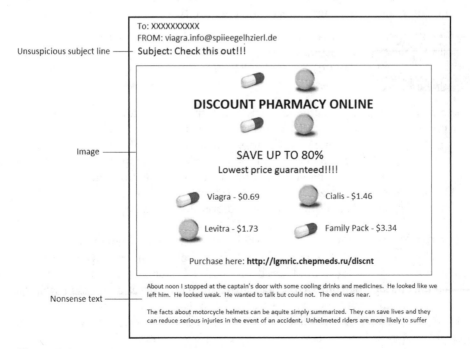

Figure 2-9   Image spam

Beyond just being annoying, spam significantly reduces work productivity as users spend time reading and deleting spam messages. One report estimates that spam email, on average, costs U.S. organizations $874 per person annually in lost productivity.[15] Spam is also costly to organizations that must install and monitor technology to block spam. However, one of the greatest risks of spam is that it is used to widely distribute malware. A variation of spam is **spim**, which targets instant messaging users instead of email users.

Hoaxes Attackers can use hoaxes as a first step in an attack. A **hoax** is a false warning, often contained in an email message claiming to come from the IT department. The hoax purports that there is a "deadly virus" circulating through the Internet and that the recipient should erase specific files or change security configurations, and then forward the message to other users. However, changing configurations allow an attacker to compromise the system. Or, erasing files may make the computer unstable, prompting the victim to call the telephone number in the hoax email message for help, which is actually the phone number of the attacker.

Typo Squatting What happens when a user makes a typing error when entering a uniform resource locator (URL) address in a web browser, such as typing *goggle.com* (a misspelling) or *google.net* (incorrect domain) instead of the correct *google.com*? Most often today the user will be directed to a fake look-alike site. This site may contain a visitor survey that promises a chance to win prizes (but the attacker actually captures the entered email addresses to sell to spammers) or be filled with ads (for which the attacker receives money for traffic generated to the site). These fake sites exist because attackers purchase the domain names of sites that are spelled similarly to actual sites. This is called **typo squatting** or **URL hijacking**. A well-known site like *google.com* may have to deal with more than 1000 typo squatting domains. Over 62 percent of the active domain names based on common misspellings of *facebook.com* are typo squatting sites.

 In one month the typo squatting site *goggle.com* received almost 825,000 unique visitors. It is estimated that typo squatting costs the 250 top websites $285 million annually in lost sales and other expenses.[16]

While a typing error when entering a URL to visit a webpage can be a problem, an even larger problem is the fact that attackers also receive all private email messages that had similar typing errors (such as an email sent to *finances@goggle.com*). Security researchers set up fake domains based on the names of the 500 largest U.S. companies that only omitted the period between the domain name and subdomain. In six months they received more than 120,000 private emails (or 20 gigabytes worth of email) based on this one typing error, many containing confidential information and even lists of passwords.[17]

Watering Hole Attack In many regions similar types of animals are known to congregate around a pool of water for refreshment. In a similar manner a **watering hole attack** is directed toward a smaller group of specific individuals, such as the major executives working for a manufacturing company. These executives all tend to visit a common website, such as that of a parts supplier to the manufacturer. An attacker who wants to target this group of executives will attempt to determine the common website that they frequent and then infect it with malware that will make its way onto the group's computers.

A recent watering hole attack resulted in Mac computers located on Apple's main campus becoming infected. Several Apple employees visited the same website for Apple software developers that was infected.

Physical Procedures

Just as some social engineering attacks rely on psychological manipulation, other attacks rely on physical acts. These attacks take advantage of user actions that can result in compromised security. Two of the most common physical procedures are dumpster diving and tailgating.

Dumpster Diving Dumpster diving involves digging through trash receptacles to find information that can be useful in an attack. Table 2-7 lists the different items that can be retrieved—many of which appear to be useless—and how they can be used.

Item retrieved	Why useful
Calendars	A calendar can reveal which employees are out of town at a particular time.
Inexpensive computer hardware, such as USB flash drives or portable hard drives	These devices are often improperly disposed of and may contain valuable information.
Memos	Seemingly unimportant memos can often provide small bits of useful information for an attacker who is building an impersonation.
Organizational charts	These identify individuals within the organization who are in positions of authority.
Phone directories	A phone directory can provide the names and telephone numbers of individuals in the organization to target or impersonate.
Policy manuals	These may reveal the true level of security within the organization.
System manuals	A system manual can tell an attacker the type of computer system that is being used so that other research can be conducted to pinpoint vulnerabilities.

Table 2-7   **Dumpster diving items and their usefulness**

Tailgating Organizations can invest tens of thousands of dollars to install specialized doors that only permit access to authorized users who possess a special card or who can enter a specific code. These automated access control systems are designed to restrict entry into an area. However, a weakness of these systems is that they cannot always control *how many* people enter the building when access is allowed; once an authorized person opens the door, virtually any number of individuals can follow behind and also enter. This is known as **tailgating**.

Several ways in which tailgating may occur are:

- A tailgater waits at the end of the sidewalk until an authorized user opens the door. She then calls out to him to "Please hold the door!" as she hurries up to the door.

In most cases, good etiquette wins out over good security practices, and the door is held open for the tailgater.

- A tailgater waits near the outside of the door and then quickly enters once the authorized employee leaves the area. This technique is used most commonly during weekends and at nights, where the actions of the more overt tailgater would be suspicious.

- A tailgater stands outside the door and waits until an employee exits the building. He then slips behind the person as he is walking away and grabs the door just before it closes to gain access to the building.

- An employee conspires with an unauthorized person to allow him to walk in with him through the open door (called *piggybacking*).

If an attacker cannot enter a building as a tailgater without raising suspicion, an alternative is to watch an individual entering the security code on a keypad. Known as **shoulder surfing**, it can be used in any setting in which a user "casually observes" someone entering an authorized code on a keypad.

A new defense against shoulder surfing is an application that uses the computer's web cam to watch if anyone nearby is looking at the computer screen. If someone is detected, the user can be alerted with a popup window message or the screen will automatically blur so that it cannot be read.

Chapter Summary

- Malware is malicious software that enters a computer system without the owner's knowledge or consent and includes a wide variety of damaging actions. In order to avoid detection by scanning software, attackers mask the presence of their malware by having it "mutate" or change. One method of classifying the various types of malware is by using the primary trait that the malware possesses. These traits are circulation, infection, concealment, and payload capabilities.

- One of the types of malware that has the primary trait of circulation is a computer virus. A virus is malicious computer code that reproduces itself on the same computer. A virus inserts itself into a computer file (a data file or program) and then looks to reproduce itself on the same computer as well as unload its malicious payload. Another type of such malware is a worm, which travels through a network and is designed to take advantage of vulnerability in an application or an operating system in order to enter a user's computer. Once the worm has exploited the vulnerability on one system, it immediately searches for another computer that has the same vulnerability. A Trojan is a program advertised as performing one activity but in addition does something malicious. Some malware has as its primary trait avoiding detection. A rootkit is a set of software tools used to hide the actions or presence of other types of software.

- The destructive power of malware is to be found in its payload capabilities. Different types of malware are designed to collect important data from the user's computer and make it available at the attacker. Spyware is a general term used to describe software that secretly spies on users by collecting information without their consent. One type of spyware is a keylogger, which silently captures and stores each keystroke that a user types on the computer's keyboard. A keylogger can be a small hardware device or a software program. Adware is a software program that delivers advertising content in a manner that is unexpected and unwanted by the user. Ransomware locks up a user's computer and then displays a message that purports to come from a law enforcement agency or security software company and demands payment of a fine online before the computer is released.

- The payload of other types of malware deletes data on the computer. A logic bomb is computer code that is typically added to a legitimate program but lies dormant until it is triggered by a specific logical event. Once it is triggered, the program then deletes data or performs other malicious activities. The payload of some types of malware attempts to modify the system's security settings so that more insidious attacks can be made. One type of malware in this category is called a backdoor. A backdoor gives access to a computer, program, or service that circumvents any normal security protections.

- One of the most popular payloads of malware today carried by Trojans, worms, and viruses is software that will allow the infected computer to be placed under the remote control of an attacker. This infected computer is known as a zombie. When zombie computers are gathered into a logical computer network, they create a botnet.

- Social engineering is a means of gathering information for an attack by relying on the weaknesses of individuals. Many social engineering attacks rely on psychology, which is the mental and emotional approach rather than the physical. At its core, social engineering relies on an attacker's clever manipulation of human nature in order to persuade the victim to provide information or take actions. Several basic "principles" or reasons make psychological social engineering effective. Social engineering impersonation means to masquerade as a real or fictitious character and then play out the role of that person on a victim. Phishing is sending an email or displaying a web announcement that falsely claims to be from a legitimate enterprise in an attempt to trick the user into surrendering private information. Several variations on phishing attacks exist. Beyond just being annoying, spam significantly reduces work productivity as users spend time reading and deleting spam messages, which are a means for distributing malware as well.

- Attackers can use hoaxes as a first step in an attack, which is a false warning, often contained in an email message claiming to come from the IT department. Recipients are told that they should erase specific files or change security configurations, and then forward the message to other users. Typo squatting (URL hijacking) takes advantage of user misspellings to direct them to fake websites. A watering hole attack is directed toward a smaller group of specific individuals, such as the major executives working for a manufacturing company.

- Social engineering is a means of gathering information for an attack by relying on the weaknesses of individuals. Social engineering attacks can involve psychological approaches as well as physical procedures. One of the most common forms of social engineering is phishing. Phishing is sending an email, displaying a web announcement, or recording a phone call that falsely claims to be from a legitimate enterprise in an attempt to trick the user into surrendering private information. Phishing is most often accomplished by sending spam, which is unsolicited email that is annoying, disruptive, and can also pose a serious security risk.

- Some social engineering attacks rely on physical acts. Dumpster diving involves digging through trash receptacles to find information that can be useful in an attack. Organizations invest large sums of money to install specialized doors that only permit access to authorized users who possess a special card or who can enter a specific code, yet they do not always control how many people enter the building when access is allowed. Following an authorized person through an open door is known as tailgating. If an attacker cannot enter a building as a tailgater without raising suspicion, an alternative is to watch an individual entering the security code on a keypad. This is known as shoulder surfing, and it can be used in any setting in which a user spies on a person entering an authorized code on a keypad.

Key Terms

adware   A software program that delivers advertising content in a manner that is unexpected and unwanted by the user.

armored virus   A virus that goes to great lengths in order to avoid detection.

backdoor   Software code that gives access to a program or a service that circumvents normal security protections.

bot herder   An attacker who controls a botnet.

botnet   A logical computer network of zombies under the control of an attacker.

command and control (C&C or **C2)**   The structure by which a bot herder gives instructions to zombies in a botnet.

computer virus (virus)   Malicious computer code that, like its biological counterpart, reproduces itself on the same computer.

dumpster diving   The act of digging through trash receptacles to find information that can be useful in an attack.

hoax   A false warning designed to trick users into changing security settings on their computer.

impersonation   A social engineering attack that involves masquerading as a real or fictitious character and then playing out the role of that person on a victim.

keylogger   Software or a hardware device that captures and stores each keystroke that a user types on the computer's keyboard.

logic bomb   Computer code that lies dormant until it is triggered by a specific logical event.

macro   A series of instructions that can be grouped together as a single command, often used to automate a complex set of tasks or a repeated series of tasks.

macro virus   A computer virus that is written in a script known as a macro.

malware   Software that enters a computer system without the user's knowledge or consent and then performs an unwanted and usually harmful action.

metamorphic malware   Malware that rewrites its own code and thus appears different each time it is executed.

oligomorphic malware   Malware that changes its internal code to one of a set number of predefined mutations whenever it is executed.

pharming   A phishing attack that automatically redirects the user to a fake site.

phishing   Sending an email or displaying a web announcement that falsely claims to be from a legitimate enterprise in an attempt to trick the user into surrendering private information.

polymorphic malware   Malware code that completely changes from its original form whenever it is executed.

program virus   A computer virus that infects executable program files.

ransomware   Malware that prevents a user's device from properly operating until a fee is paid.

rootkit   A set of software tools used by an attacker to hide the actions or presence of other types of malicious software.

shoulder surfing   Watching an authorized user enter a security code on a keypad.

social engineering   A means of gathering information for an attack by relying on the weaknesses of individuals.

spam   Unsolicited email.

spear phishing   A phishing attack that targets only specific users.

spim   A variation of spam, which targets instant messaging users instead of email users.

spyware   A general term used to describe software that spies on users by gathering information without consent.

tailgating   When an unauthorized individual enters a restricted-access building by following an authorized user.

Trojan horse (Trojan)   An executable program that is advertised as performing one activity but which actually performs a malicious activity.

typo squatting   Redirecting a user to a fictitious website based on a misspelling of the URL. Also called *URL hijacking*.

URL hijacking   Redirecting a user to a fictitious website based on a misspelling of the URL. Also called *typo squatting*.

vishing   A phishing attack uses telephone calls instead of emails.

watering hole attack   A malicious attack that is directed toward a small group of specific individuals who visit the same website.

whaling   A phishing attack that targets only wealthy individuals.

worm   A malicious program designed to enter a computer via a network to take advantage of a vulnerability in an application or an operating system.

zombie   An infected computer that is under the remote control of an attacker.

Review Questions

1. A(n) _____ requires a user to transport it from one computer to another.

   a. worm

   b. rootkit

   c. virus

   d. adware

2. Which of these is NOT an action that a virus can take?

   a. transport itself through the network to another device

   b. cause a computer to crash

   c. erase files from a hard drive

   d. reformat the hard disk drive

3. Which malware locks up a user's computer and then displays a message that purports to come from a law enforcement agency?

   a. virus

   b. ransomware

   c. worm

   d. Trojan

4. Which of the following is an attempt to influence a user by coercion?

   a. authority

   b. social proof

   c. intimidation

   d. familiarity

5. A user who installs a program that prints out coupons but in the background silently collects her passwords has installed a _____.

   a. virus

   b. worm

   c. Trojan

   d. logic bomb

6. What should you do to completely remove a rootkit from a computer?

   a. Flash the ROM BIOS.

   b. Erase and reinstall all files in the WINDOWS folder.

   c. Expand the Master Boot Record.

   d. Reformat the hard drive and reinstall the operating system.

2

7. Which of these could NOT be defined as a logic bomb?

    a. Erase all data if John Smith's name is removed from the list of employees.

    b. Reformat the hard drive three months after Susan Jones left the company.

    c. Send spam email to all users in the company on Tuesday.

    d. If the company's stock price drops below $10, then credit Jeff Brown with 10 additional years of retirement credit.

8. What is it called when a user makes a typing error when entering a URL that takes him to an imposter website?

    a. URL variance

    b. typo squatting

    c. spell scraping

    d. work hijacking

9. Which of these is a general term used for describing software that gathers information without the user's consent?

    a. adware

    b. spyware

    c. scrapeware

    d. pullware

10. Which statement regarding a keylogger is NOT true?

    a. Hardware keyloggers are installed between the keyboard connector and computer keyboard USB port.

    b. Software keyloggers are easy to detect.

    c. Keyloggers can be used to capture passwords, credit card numbers, or personal information.

    d. Software keyloggers can be designed to send captured information automatically back to the attacker through the Internet.

11. The preferred method today of bot herders for command and control of zombies is _____.

    a. Internet Relay Chat (IRC)

    b. botnets

    c. Hypertext Transport Protocol (HTTP)

    d. spam

12. A watering hole attack is directed against _____.

    a. wealthy individuals

    b. attackers who send spam

    c. all users of a large corporation

    d. users who access a common website

13. _____ sends phishing messages only to wealthy individuals.

   a. Spear phishing

   b. Target phishing

   c. Microing

   d. Whaling

14. What is unsolicited instant messaging called?

   a. spim

   b. spam

   c. vishing

   d. SMS phishing

15. Michelle pretends to be the help desk manager and calls Steve to trick him into giving her his password. What social engineering attack has Michelle performed?

   a. aliasing

   b. impersonation

   c. luring

   d. duplicity

16. How can an attacker use a hoax?

   a. By sending out a hoax, an attacker can convince a user to read his email more often.

   b. A hoax could convince a user that a bad Trojan is circulating and that he should change his security settings.

   c. A user who receives multiple hoaxes could contact his supervisor for help.

   d. Hoaxes are not used by attackers today.

17. Which of these items retrieved through dumpster diving would NOT provide useful information?

   a. calendars

   b. memos

   c. organizational charts

   d. books

18. _____ is following an authorized person through a secure door.

   a. Tagging

   b. Backpacking

   c. Tailgating

   d. Caboosing

19. Each of these is a reason why adware is scorned EXCEPT _____.

    a. it displays the attacker's programming skills

    b. it can interfere with a user's productivity

    c. it displays objectionable content

    d. it can cause a computer to crash or slow down

20. What is the term used for an attacker who controls multiple zombies in a botnet?

    a. zombie shepherd

    b. rogue IRC

    c. bot herder

    d. cyber-robot

Hands-On Projects

If you are concerned about installing any of the software in these projects on your regular computer, you can instead install the software in the Windows virtual machine created in the Chapter 1 Hands-On Projects 1-3 and 1-4. Software installed within the virtual machine will not impact the host computer.

Project 2-1: Write-Protecting and Disabling a USB Flash Drive

Viruses and other malware are often spread from one computer to another by infected USB flash drives. This can be controlled by either disabling the USB port or by write-protecting the drive so that no malware can be copied to it. Disabling the port can be accomplished through changing a Windows registry setting while write-protecting the drive can be done through third-party software that can control USB device permissions. In this project, you will download and install a software-based USB write blocker to prevent data from being written to a USB device and also disable the USB port. You will need a USB flash drive for this project.

1. Open your web browser and enter the URL **www.irongeek.com/i.php ?page=security/thumbscrew-software-usb-write-blocker**

The location of content on the Internet may change without warning. If you are no longer able to access the program through the above URL, use a search engine to search for "Irongeek Thumbscrew".

2. Click **Download Thumbscrew.**

3. If the File Download dialog box appears, click **Save** and follow the instructions to save this file in a location such as your desktop or a folder designated by your instructor.

4. When the file finishes downloading, extract the files in a location such as your desktop or a folder designated by your instructor. Navigate to that location and double-click **thumbscrew.exe** and follow the default installation procedures.

5. After installation, notice that a new icon appears in the system tray in the lower right corner of the screen.

6. Insert a USB flash drive into the computer.

7. Navigate to a document on the computer.

8. Right-click the document and then select **Send to**.

9. Click the appropriate **Removable Disk** icon of the USB flash drive to copy the file to the flash drive.

10. Now make the USB flash drive write protected so it cannot be written to. Click the icon in the system tray.

11. Click **Make USB Read Only**. Notice that a red circle now appears over the icon to indicate that the flash drive is write protected.

12. Navigate to a document on the computer.

13. Right-click the document and then select **Send to**.

14. Click the appropriate **Removable Disk** icon of the USB flash drive to copy the file to the flash drive. What happens?

15. Click the icon in the system tray to change the permissions so that the USB drive is no longer read only.

16. Now disable the USB port entirely. First remove the flash drive from the USB port.

17. In the Windows **Run** dialog box enter **regedit**.

18. In the left pane double-click **HKEY_LOCAL_MACHINE** to expand it.

19. Double-click **SYSTEM**.

20. Double-click **ControlSet001**.

21. Double-click **USBSTOR** as shown in Figure 2-10.

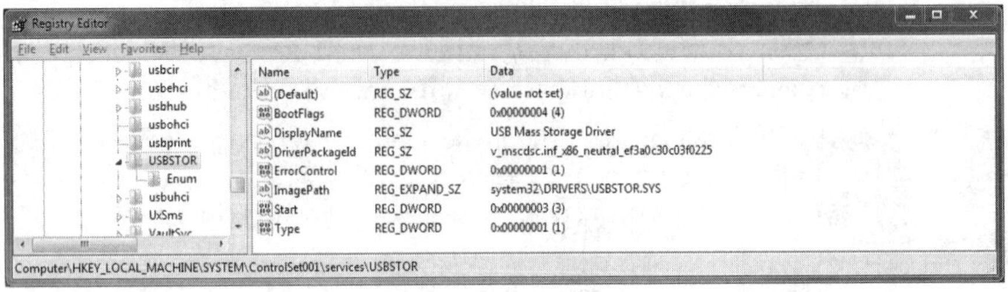

Figure 2-10 Windows Registry Editor
Source: Microsoft Windows

22. In the right pane double-click **Start.**

23. In **Value data:** change the number of 3 to **4.** Be sure that **Hexadecimal** under **Base** is selected.

24. Click **OK.**

25. Now insert a USB flash drive into the USB port. What happens?

26. To reactivate the port, change the **Value data:** back to 3 and click **OK.**

27. Close all windows.

Project 2-2: Scan for Rootkits Using a Basic Tool

Scanning for rootkits can help identify malware on a system. In this project, you will download the basic rootkit scanner Kaspersky TDSSKiller.

1. Open your web browser and enter the URL **support.kaspersky.com/viruses/disinfection/5350**

 The location of content on the Internet may change without warning. If you are no longer able to access the program through the above URL, use a search engine to search for "Kaspersky TDSSKiller".

2. Click each plus sign to expand the information **How to disinfect a compromised system, Operating systems supported by the utility,** and **List of malicious programs the utility fights.** Read through this material.

3. Under the section **How to disinfect a compromised system** click **TDSSKiller.exe** and download it.

4. After the download is complete launch TDSSKiller.

5. Click **Accept** on the **End User License Agreement.**

6. Click **Accept** on the **KSN Statement.**

7. Click **Change parameters** to see the elements that will be scanned.

8. Click **Loaded modules.** The system will need to reboot. Click **Reboot now.**

9. Click **OK.**

10. After the system reboots, it will automatically load the necessary features for TDSSKiller to run.

11. Click **Start scan.**

12. After the scan is completed, click **details.** If nothing malicious is identified this will be empty. Click **Close.**

13. Click **Report** and maximize the screen. This provides a detailed analysis of the scan. After looking through this report, click **Close.**

14. Close Kaspersky TDSSKiller.

Project 2-3: Scan for Rootkits Using an Advanced Tool

In this project, you will download and use the advanced rootkit scanner GMER.

1. Open your web browser and enter the URL www.gmer.net

The location of content on the Internet may change without warning. If you are no longer able to access the program through the above URL, use a search engine to search for "GMER".

2. Click **Download EXE.**

Because GMER reaches deep into the operating system, some anti-malware is triggered thinking that this scanner software is about to do something malicious, while some rootkits check for the presence of GMER and prevent it from running. Clicking the *Download EXE* link will download the program with a different filename instead of *GMER.EXE* in order to reduce the risk of the software being flagged.

3. Launch GMER.

4. GMER will by default run a quick scan on the system. Any hidden items on the system that may indicate the presence of a rootkit will be displayed, although hidden items do not necessary mean that a rootkit is present. GMER will display a warning about a potential rootkit. To compare a listing of hidden items against known rootkits, go to **www2.gmer.net/rootkits.php.**

5. Click **>>>** to display the main menu.

6. Click **Processes** to scan all of the running processes on the computer. If any hidden processes are detected they are listed in red.

7. Click **Modules** to list all of the device drives loaded.

8. Click **Services** to see all of the Windows services that are present. Any hidden services will be listed in red.

9. Now do a full scan of the system. Click **Rootkit/Malware.**

10. In the right pane click **C:\.**

11. Click **Scan.**

12. Note that this scan may take up to 30 minutes depending upon the system. Any hidden resources will be displayed after the scan is completed.

13. Close all windows.

Project 2-4: Use a Software Keylogger

A keylogger program captures everything that a user enters on a computer keyboard. In this project, you will download and use a software keylogger.

The purpose of this activity is to provide information regarding how these programs function in order that adequate defenses can be designed and implemented. These programs should never be used in a malicious fashion against another user.

1. Open your web browser and enter the URL: **www.spyrix.com**

   The location of content on the Internet may change without warning. If you are no longer able to access the program through the above URL, use a search engine to search for "Spyrix Personal Monitor".

2. Click **products** and compare the features of the different Spyrix products.

3. Click **download**.

4. Under **Spyrix Free Keylogger** click **Free Download**.

5. When the file finishes downloading, install Spyrix and follow the default installation procedures.

6. Click **Finish** to launch Spyrix.

7. Click **Next** to use the wizard to set the program settings.

8. The **Hide everywhere** is not available on the Free Keylogger version but for the other versions this would allow Spyrix to act like a rootkit with no traces available. Click **Next**.

9. Create a strong password and enter it under **Password** to protect access to the program. Click **Next**.

10. Change **Screenshot Quality** to **Medium Quality – Medium Size**. Click **Next**.

11. Check **Online Monitoring (via any web-browser)** to set up the ability to view activity online. Click **OK**.

12. Enter your email address and create another strong password. Click **Create NEW Online Monitoring Account**. When the account is set up a message will appear. Click **OK**.

13. Click **Test secure connection**.

14. Click **Try to send log**.

15. Click **Enter your online monitoring account**.

16. Enter your username and password.

17. Click **Remote computer settings**.

18. Under **Delivery Interval** change the time to **2** minutes. Click **Apply**.

19. Close the web browser to return to the Spyrix

20. Under **Delivery Interval** change the time to **2** minutes. Click **Next**.

21. If prompted enter your Spyrix password.

22. Click the Spyrix icon in your system tray and enter the password.

23. Click **Start**.

24. Click **Minimize**.

25. Now use your computer for several minutes as you normally would.

26. Open your web browser and go to **spyrix.net** and enter your username and password.

27. Under **Events** click **ALL EVENTS** to view everything that has been done on the computer.

28. Click **Screenshots**. In the **Value** column click a screenshot.

29. Click **Program Activity** to view the programs that you were using.

30. Select several other options to view the keylogging and spy features of this program.

31. Close the web browser.

32. Click the Spyrix icon in your system tray and enter the password.

33. Click **Stop** and then **Exit**.

34. Enter your password and click **OK**.

35. Close all windows.

Case Projects

Case Project 2-1: Researching Trojan Attacks

Trojans continue to be a highly favored means of attack today and pose a serious threat to users. Use the Internet to search for the latest information regarding current Trojans. You may want to visit security vendor sites, like Symantec or McAfee, or security research sites such as sans.org to find the latest information. What are the latest attacks? What type of damage can they do? What platforms are the most vulnerable? Write a one-page paper on your research.

Case Project 2-2: Social Engineering Psychological Approaches

Several basic "principles" or reasons make psychological social engineering effective. These include authority, intimidation, consensus/social proof, scarcity, urgency, familiarity/liking, and trust. Table 2-6 uses these principles in a scenario of an attacker pretending to be the chief executive officer (CEO) calling the organization's help desk to have a password reset. Create two additional scenarios, such as an attacker impersonating a help desk employee who wants access to an employee's protected information, and create a dialog example for each of the seven principles.

Case Project 2-3: Social Engineering Attack

The opening *Today's Attacks and Defenses* illustrated how attackers used a fictitious attractive and intelligent young female to trick males into compromising security. If you were to create your own social engineering attack, what would it be? Using your place of employment or school, first determine exactly what your goal would be in the attack, and then craft a detailed description of how you would carry out the attack using only social engineering to achieve your goal. You may want to search the Internet for

2

examples of previously successful attacks that used social engineering. Why do you think your attack would be successful? Who would be involved? What would be the problems in achieving your goal? Why? Write a one-page paper on your research.

Case Project 2-4: Comparing Keyloggers

Use the Internet to research different keyloggers. Create a table that lists five different hardware keyloggers, their available memory, specific features, and their cost. Then create another table of five different software keyloggers with their features. Are you surprised at the functionality of these devices? Write a summary of your findings.

Case Project 2-5: Ransomware Attacks

Use the Internet to research some of the different ransomware attacks that have occurred recently. Identify at least three attacks that are current. What do they do? Why are they so successful? How are they being spread? What can users do to protect themselves? How can ransomware be removed from a computer? Write a one-page summary of your research.

Case Project 2-6: Phishing Test

Detecting phishing emails can often be difficult. Point your web browser to *survey.mailfrontier.com/survey/quiztest.cgi*, and then click *The MailFrontier Phishing IQ Test v 2.0*. Click each hyperlink to display an email message or website, and then decide whether or not it is phishing. When you are finished your score will be displayed along with an explanation regarding why the example is or is not phishing. Then, click *The MailFrontier Phishing IQ Test* and take another phishing test. Did what you learn on the first test help? Did your score on this test improve? Write a one-paragraph summary on what you learned about phishing in this test.

Case Project 2-7: Combating Typo Squatting

What can organizations do to fight back against typo squatting? Research the Internet to find out how companies are combating this growing problem. How can these typo squatting sites be taken down? What must a company do in order to stop these sites? And why has it been so difficult to do this? What proactive steps can a company take? Write a one-page report on your research.

Case Project 2-8: Bay Pointe Security Consulting

Bay Pointe Security Consulting (BPSC) provides security consulting services to a wide range of businesses, individuals, schools, and organizations. BPSC has hired you as a technology student to help them with a new project and provide real-world experience to students who are interested in the security field.

P&T Heating and Cooling installs and services residential and commercial air conditioning and heating units in a large metropolitan area. Recently P&T has been the victim of several different successful attacks that have caused significant problems. P&T has contacted BPSC for assistance. Because you are close to completing your degree, BPSC has asked for your help.

1. Create a PowerPoint presentation that lists 15 different types of malware and defines each type in detail regarding what the malware can do, how it spreads, its dangers, etc. Your presentation should contain at least 10 slides.

2. After the presentation and more investigation, it appears that some of the attacks were the result of social engineering. P&T has asked you to create a one-page paper that describes social engineering attacks and how they may be performed, including a list of practical tips for their employees to resist these attacks. Create the paper for P&T.

Case Project 2-9: Community Site Activity 1

The Information Security Community Site is an online companion to this textbook. It contains a wide variety of tools, information, discussion boards, and other features to assist learners. Go to **community.cengage.com/infosec** and click JOIN THE COMMUNITY, using the login name and password that you created in Chapter 1. Visit the **Discussions** section, and then read the following case study.

An auditor was hired to determine if he could gain access to the network servers of a printing company that contained important proprietary information. The chief executive officer (CEO) of the printing company boldly proclaimed that breaking into the servers by the auditor would be "next to impossible" because the CEO "guarded his secrets with his life." The auditor was able to gather information about the servers, such as the locations of the servers in different printing plants and their IP addresses, along with employee names and titles, their email addresses, phone numbers, physical addresses, and other information.

The auditor also learned that the CEO had a family member who had battled through cancer and lived. As a result the CEO became involved in cancer fundraising. By viewing the CEO's entry on Facebook, he was also able to determine his favorite restaurant and sports team.

The auditor then called the CEO and impersonated a fundraiser from a cancer charity that the CEO had been involved with before. The auditor said that those individuals who made donations to this year's charity event would be entered into a drawing for prizes, which included tickets to a game played by the CEO's favorite sports team and gift certificates to area restaurants, one of which was the CEO's favorite.

After stoking the interest of the CEO in the fake charity event, the auditor said that he would email him a PDF document that contained more information. When the CEO received the attachment he opened it, and a backdoor was installed on his computer without his knowledge. The auditor was then able to retrieve the company's sensitive material. (When the CEO was later informed of what happened, he called it "unfair"; the auditor responded by saying, "A malicious hacker would not think twice about using that information against you.")

Now pretend that you are an employee of that company and that it is your job to speak with the CEO about the security breach. What would you say to him? Why? What recommendations would you make for training and awareness for the company? Enter your answers on the InfoSec Community Server discussion board.

Case Project 2-10: Community Site Activity 2

The Information Security Community Site is an online companion to this textbook. It contains a wide variety of tools, information, discussion boards, and other features to assist learners. Go to **community.cengage.com/infosec** and click JOIN THE COMMUNITY, using the login name and password that you created in Chapter 1. Visit the **Discussions** section, and then read the following case study.

A recent attack used both social engineering and basic "detective work" to erase journalist Mat Honan's online Google account along with his personal iPhone, iPad, and MacBook computer data. It all started with the attackers following a link on Mat's Twitter account to his personal website, which listed his Gmail address. The attackers entered his Gmail address on Google's password recovery page and were able to see his partially obscured alternate email address. They correctly guessed that *m****n@me.com* was actually *mhonan@me.com*. The site *me.com* was an Apple service (now called iCloud) so the attackers now knew Mat's Apple ID. Using a basic web search of his website's domain name they uncovered his billing address.

With this information they contacted Amazon.com by telephone and were able to convince the customer service representative that it was Mat who was calling; they tricked the representative into asking if the last four digits of his credit number on file were *1954* (of course, the attackers said it was). With Mat's Apple ID, billing address, and last four digits of his credit card number, the attackers called AppleCare by phone and convinced the representative to issue a temporary password for Mat's Apple account. They then reset the password, locking Mat out, and with the *mhonan@me.com* name and new password, they reset the password on his Gmail account—and then promptly erased more than 6 GB of Google email messages. They also used iCloud's remote wipe service to completely erase all the data on his iPhone, iPad, and MacBook.

What went wrong? What policies should Google, Amazon.com, and AppleCare have had in place to prevent this? What recommendations would you make for the employees who were tricked into giving out information over the phone? Enter your answers on the InfoSec Community Server discussion board.

References

1. "FireEye advanced threat report—2H 2012," *FireEye*, Apr. 3, 2013, accessed Jan. 3, 2014, www2.fireeye.com/rs/fireye/images/fireeye-advanced-threat-report-2h2012.pdf.

2. "The first computer virus," accessed Mar. 3, 2011, www.worldhistorysite.com/virus.html.

3. "Anti-Spyware Coalition definitions document," *Anti-Spyware Coalition*, Nov. 12, 2007, accessed Mar. 3, 2011, www.antispywarecoalition.org/documents/definitions.htm.

4. Gorman, Gavin, and McDonald, Geoff, "Ransomware: A growing menace," *Symantec Security Response*, Nov. 8, 2012, accessed Jan. 6, 2014, www.symantec.com/connect/blogs/ransomware-growing-menace.

5. Cluley, Graham, "Fannie Mae worker accused of planting malware timebomb," *Naked Security Sophos Blog*, accessed Mar. 3, 2011, http://nakedsecurity.sophos.com/2009/01/29/fannie-mae-worker-accused-planting-malware-timebomb/.

6. "History and milestones," *About RSA Conference*, accessed Mar. 3, 2011, www.rsaconference.com/about-rsa-conference/history-and-milestones.htm.

7. "Logic bombs," *Computer Knowledge*, accessed Mar. 3, 2011, www.cknow.com/cms/vtutor/logic-bombs.html.

8. Vijayan, Jaikumar, "Unix admin pleads guilty to planting logic bomb," *Computerworld*, Sep. 21, 2007, accessed Mar. 3, 2011, www.pcworld.com/article/137479/unix_admin_pleads_guilty_to_planting_logic_bomb.html.

9. "Grappling with the ZeroAccess botnet," *Symantec*, Sep. 30, 2013, accessed Jan. 6, 2013, www.symantec.com/connect/blogs/grappling-zeroaccess-botnet.

10. Weber, Tim, "Criminals 'may overwhelm the web,'" *BBC News*, Jan. 25, 2007, accessed Mar. 3, 2011, http://news.bbc.co.uk/2/hi/business/6298641.stm.

11. Granger, Sarah, "Social engineering fundamentals, part 1: Hacker tactics," *Symantec*, Dec. 18, 2001, accessed Mar. 3, 2011, www.symantec.com/connect/articles/social-engineering-fundamentals-part-i-hacker-tactics.

12. Danchev, Dancho, "Average online time for phishing sites," *Dancho Danchev's Blog—Mind Streams of Information Security Knowledge*, Jul. 31, 2007, accessed Mar. 3, 2011, http://ddanchev.blogspot.com/2007/07/average-online-time-for-phishing-sites.html.

13. "The year in phishing," *RSA Online Fraud Report*, Jan. 2013, accessed Jan. 7, 2014, www.emc.com/collateral/fraud-report/online-rsa-fraud-report-012013.pdf.

14. "What percentage of total Internet traffic is spam?" *Skeptics*, Apr. 15, 2011, accessed Aug. 28, 2012, http://skeptics.stackexchange.com/questions/2175/what-percentage-of-total-internet-traffic-is-spam.

15. "Spam costs US employers an average of $874 per employee per year," *OUT-LAW News*, Feb. 7, 2003, accessed Mar. 3, 2011, www.out-law.com/page-3688.

16. McNichol, Tom, "Friend me on Faecbook," *Bloomberg Businessweek*, Nov. 7, 2011.

17. Gee, Garrett, and Kim, Peter, "Doppelganger domains," *GodaiGroup*, Sep. 6, 2011, accessed Jan. 7, 2014, http://files.godaigroup.net/wp-content/uploads/doppelganger/Doppelganger.Domains.pdf.

## chapter 3

Application and Networking-Based Attacks

After completing this chapter, you should be able to do the following:

- List and explain the different types of server-side web application attacks
- Define client-side attacks
- Explain how overflow attacks work
- List different types of networking-based attacks

Today's Attacks and Defenses

Many attacks today are developed by script kiddies, individuals who want to attack computers yet lack the knowledge of computers and networks needed to do so. Script kiddies do their work by downloading automated attack software (scripts) from websites and using it to perform malicious acts. It is estimated that three out of every four Internet-based attacks originate from these exploit kits.

But what about the other 25 percent of attacks? Where do they come from? Skilled attackers are now creating training courses to instruct novice attackers on how to create and launch sophisticated web application and networking attacks. And what is interesting is that these "cybercrime professors" are modeling their training after that typically found in today's colleges.

It has long been common for seasoned criminals to offer advice to newcomers, whether the crime is stealing cars or attacking a web server. Whereas that advice was at one time free, today's cybercriminals are likely to charge a fee to pass on their knowledge. These attacker instructors are not just providing tips and tricks that they have learned; they are delivering a comprehensive education on attacking. Entire cybercrime courses, tutoring lessons, and counseling are being offered and paid for by students' tuition. Most of these courses, advertised in various attacker underground sites, are taught using videoconferencing sessions to help encourage interactivity between teacher and students.

One such course for novice attackers could be called "The Business of Fraud." Students learn how debit and credit cards work and the merchant infrastructure behind them, how to avoid being caught by authorities, and what can be used against the attackers in a court of law if they are caught. The course also covers how to find victims and even how to avoid being scammed by other attackers. The basic cost per lecture is about $75.

Another course, which could be entitled "Anonymity 101," covers how attackers can remain anonymous by avoiding detection and erasing any trace of evidence. Students learn about configuring and using anonymity tools by turning off browser logging features on victims' computers, eliminating traces of an attack, setting up disposable email accounts, and remotely "liquidating" a victim's hard drive. This course also covers what evidence law enforcement personnel will search for and what can be used against attackers who are caught. The cost is about $100.

Taking a page from college courses, these cybercrime professors often post strict policies for online attendance. One course requires students to give a two-hour notice if they cannot attend the session. Students who fail to do this forfeit half of the course fees before being permitted to reschedule a makeup class. In addition, some of these schools even advertise "job placement" for their graduates: instructors will vouch for star pupils in order to help them join advanced underground attacker communities that otherwise would be difficult to access.

It is virtually unimaginable to think of the world today without the Internet. Perhaps no technology over the last 50 years has impacted our lives more than this "international network of networks." Internet users can surf the Web for an untold wealth of information, send text messages and check email, download electronic books, and watch online videos from virtually anywhere. Free wireless Internet connections are available for customers in coffee shops and restaurants across the country. Students use Internet services on their school's campus in order to access instructional material as well as remain connected to friends. Travelers can have wireless Internet access while waiting in airports, traveling on airplanes and trains, and working in their hotel rooms. At work, employees can access remote data during meetings and in conference rooms, thus significantly increasing their productivity. The Internet has also spurred the growth of many other new technologies, such as tablets and smartphones. Our world today is truly shaped by the Internet.

Yet the Internet also has opened the door for attackers to invisibly and instantaneously reach around the world to launch attacks on devices connected to it. And just as users can surf the Web without openly identifying themselves, attackers can use anonymity to cloak their identity and prevent authorities from finding and prosecuting them.

This chapter continues the discussion of threats and vulnerabilities from the previous chapter's coverage of malware and social engineering. First the chapter looks at attacks that target server-side web applications and client-side applications; then it explores some of the common attacks that are launched against networks today.

Application Attacks

3.2 Summarize various types of attacks.

3.5 Explain types of application attacks.

Figure 3-1 illustrates the conceptual view of a networked computer system. A *network* is used to connect different *clients* and *servers* together. These clients and servers run an *operating system* that controls *applications* that in turn manipulate *data*. Each of these represents an attack vector for attackers to exploit. Attacks on the applications in a networked computer system can be directed toward the server, the client, or both.

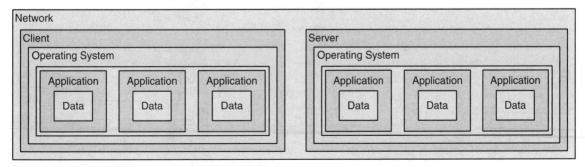

Figure 3-1   Conceptual networked computer system

Server-Side Web Application Attacks

As its name implies, a server provides services to clients. On the Internet, a web server provides services that are implemented as *web applications*. That is, the content provided for users who are "surfing the Web" is generated by a software application running on a server.

 In providing web services to clients, web servers also *expose* those same services to attackers.

An important characteristic of server-side web applications is that they create dynamic content based on inputs from the user. For example, a webpage might ask a user to enter her zip code in order to receive the latest weather forecast for that area. Thus the dynamic operations of a web application depend heavily upon inputs provided by users.

A typical dynamic web application infrastructure is shown in Figure 3-2. The client's web browser makes a request using the Hypertext Transport Protocol (HTTP) to a web server, which may be connected to one or more web application servers. These application servers run the specific "web apps," which in turn are directly connected to databases on the internal network. Information from these databases is retrieved and returned to the web server so that the dynamic information can be sent back to the user's web browser.

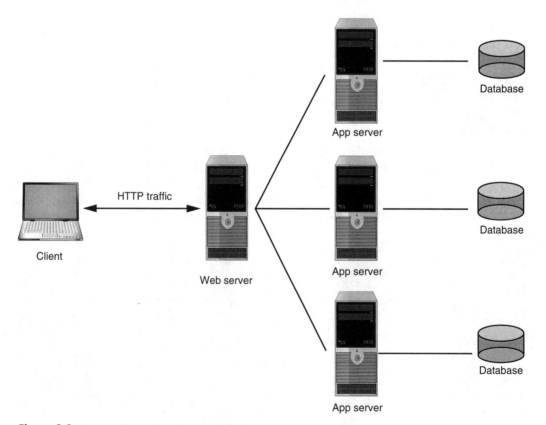

Figure 3-2 Server-side web application infrastructure

3

Securing server-side web applications is often considered more difficult than protecting other systems. First, although traditional network security devices can block traditional network attacks, they cannot always block web application attacks. This is because many traditional network security devices ignore the *content* of HTTP traffic, which is the vehicle of web application attacks. Second, many web application attacks (as well as other application attacks) exploit previously unknown vulnerabilities. Known as **zero-day attacks**, these attacks give victims no time—zero days—to defend against the attacks. Finally, by design the dynamic server-side web applications accept user input, such as the zip code of the region for which a weather forecast is needed. Most other systems would categorically reject any user input as potentially dangerous, not knowing if the user is a friend or foe.

Many server-side web application attacks target the input that the applications accept from users. Such common web application attacks are cross-site scripting, SQL injection, XML injection, and command injection/directory traversal.

Cross-Site Scripting (XSS) Not all attacks on websites are designed to steal content or deface it. Instead, some attacks use the web server as a platform to launch attacks on other computers that access it. One such attack is a **cross-site scripting (XSS)** attack. XSS injects scripts into a web application server to direct attacks at unsuspecting clients.

Many web applications are designed to customize content for the user by taking what the user enters and then displaying that input back to the user. Typical customized responses are listed in Table 3-1.

User input	Variable that contains input	Web application response	Coding example
Search term	*search_term*	Search term provided in output	"Search results for *search_term*"
Incorrect input	*user_input*	Error message that contains incorrect input	"*user_input* is not valid"
User's name	*name*	Personalized response	"Welcome back *name*"

Table 3-1 Customized responses

Figure 3-3 illustrates a fictitious web application that allows friends to share their favorite bookmarks with each other online. Users can enter their name, a description, and the URL of the bookmark, and then receive a personalized "Thank You" screen. In Figure 3-4 the code that generates the "Thank You" screen is illustrated.

XSS attacks occur when an attacker takes advantage of web applications that accept user input without validating it and then present it back to the user. In the previous example, the input that the user enters for *Name* is not verified but instead is automatically added to a code segment that becomes part of an automated response. An attacker can use this vulnerability in an XSS attack by tricking a valid website into feeding a malicious script to another user's web browser, which will then execute it.

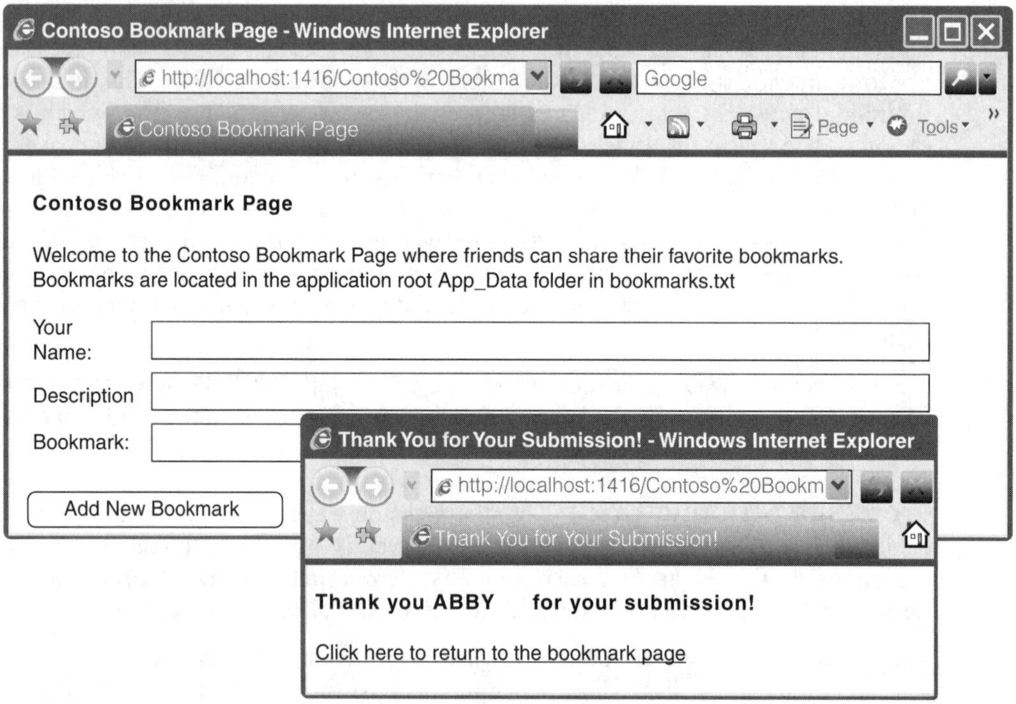

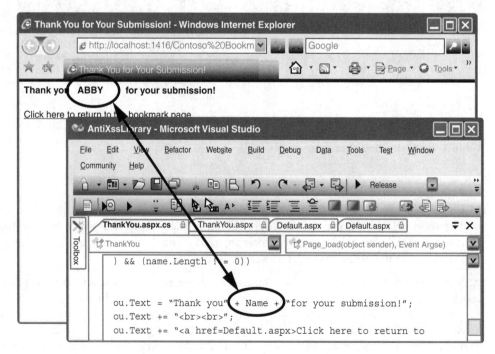

Figure 3-3 Bookmark page that accepts user input
Source: Microsoft Inc.

Figure 3-4 Input used in response
Source: Microsoft Inc.

Although the term *cross-site scripting* can be confusing, it refers to an attack using scripting that originates on one site (the web server) to impact another site (the user's computer).

A typical XSS attack may take advantage of a blogger's website that asks for user comments. The attack begins by the attacker posting a comment. However, within the comment the attacker crafts a script that performs a malicious action or even redirects the user to the attacker's website. When an unsuspecting victim visits the blogger's site and clicks on the attacker's comment, the malicious script is downloaded to the victim's web browser where it is executed. Besides redirecting the victim to a malicious site, other XSS attacks are designed to steal sensitive information that was retained by the browser when visiting specific sites, such as an online site to purchase merchandise. The XSS attack can steal this information and allow it to be used by an attacker to impersonate the legitimate user.

Some security experts note that XSS is like a phishing attack but without needing to trick the user into visiting a malicious website. Instead, the user starts at a legitimate website and XSS automatically directs her to the malicious site.

An XSS attack requires a website that meets two criteria: it accepts user input without validating it, and it uses that input in a response. Despite the fact that XSS is a widely known type of attack, the number of websites that are vulnerable remains very large. Users can turn off active scripting in their browsers to reduce the risk of XSS, but this limits their ability to use dynamic websites.

The malicious content of an XSS URL is not confined to material posted on a website; it can be embedded into virtually any hyperlink, such as one in an email or instant message. That is why users should not blindly click on a URL that they receive.

SQL Injection Another server-side web application attack that manipulates user responses is **SQL injection**. SQL stands for *Structured Query Language*, a language used to view and manipulate data that is stored in a relational database. SQL injection targets SQL servers by introducing malicious commands into them.

Most webpages that require users to log in by entering a user name and password typically offer a solution for the user who has forgotten his password by providing an online form, as shown in Figure 3-5. The user enters a valid email address that is already on file. The submitted email address is compared to the stored email address, and if they match, a reset URL is emailed to that address.

If the email address entered by the user into the form is stored in the variable *$EMAIL*, then the underlying SQL statement to retrieve the stored email address from the database would be similar to:

SELECT fieldlist FROM table WHERE field = '$EMAIL'

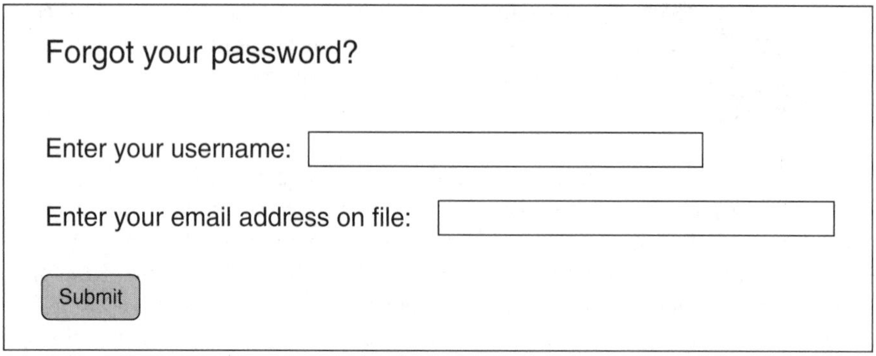

Figure 3-5   Request form for forgotten password

The *WHERE* clause is meant to limit the database query to only display information when the condition is considered true (that is, when the email address in *$EMAIL* matches an address in the database).

An attacker using an SQL attack would begin by first entering a fictitious email address on this webpage that included a single quotation mark as part of the data, such as *braden.thomas@fakemail.com'*. If the message *E-mail Address Unknown* is displayed, it indicates that user input is being properly filtered and an SQL attack cannot be rendered on the site. However, if the error message *Server Failure* is displayed, it means that the user input is not being filtered and all user input is sent directly to the database. This is because the *Server Failure* message is due to a syntax error created by the additional single quotation mark: the fictitious email address entered would be processed as *braden.thomas@fakemail.com'* ' (with two single quotation marks) and generate the *Server Failure* error message.

Armed with the knowledge that input is sent unfiltered to the database, the attacker knows that anything he enters into the *Enter your username:* field on the *Forgot your password?* form would be sent to and then processed by the SQL database. Now, instead of entering a user name, the attacker would enter this command, which would let him view all the email addresses in the database: *whatever' or 'a'='a*. This command is stored in the variable *$EMAIL*. The expanded SQL statement would read:

SELECT fieldlist FROM table WHERE field = 'whatever' or 'a'='a

These values are:

- *'whatever'*. This can be anything meaningless.
- *or*. The SQL *or* means that as long as either of the conditions are true, the entire statement is true and will be executed.
- *'a'='a'*. This is a statement that will always be true.

Because *'a'='a'* is always true, the *WHERE* clause is also true. It is not limited as it was when searching for a single email address before it would become true. The result can be that *all* user email addresses will then be displayed.

Whereas this example shows how an attacker may retrieve all email addresses, a more catastrophic attack would be if user passwords were stored as plaintext and the attacker were able to use SQL injection to extract all of these values. This type of attack has been often used to steal millions of user passwords. Plaintext passwords should *never* be stored in a database.

By entering crafted SQL statements as user input, information from the database can be extracted or the existing data can be manipulated. SQL injection statements that can be entered and stored in *$EMAIL* and their pending results are shown in Table 3-2.

SQL injection statement	Result
whatever' AND email IS NULL; --	Determine the names of different fields in the database
whatever' AND 1=(SELECT COUNT(*) FROM tabname); --	Discover the name of the table
whatever' OR full_name LIKE '%Mia%'	Find specific users
whatever'; DROP TABLE members; --	Erase the database table
whatever'; UPDATE members SET email = 'attacker-email@evil.net' WHERE email = 'Mia@good.com';	Mail password to attacker's email account

Table 3-2   SQL injection statements

XML Injection   A *markup language* is a method for adding annotations to the text so that the additions can be distinguished from the text itself. Hypertext Markup Language (HTML) is such a markup language that uses specific words (*tags*) embedded in brackets (< >) that a web browser then uses to display text in a specific format.

Another markup language is **XML (Extensible Markup Language)**. Several significant differences between XML and HTML exist. First, XML is designed to *carry* data instead of indicating how to display it. Also, XML does not have a predefined set of tags; instead, users define their own tags. An example of a partial XML file is:

<?xml version="1.0" encoding="utf-8"?>

<Employees>

<Employee ID="1000">

<FirstName>James</FirstName>

<LastName>Crockett</LastName>

<UserName>James_Crockett</UserName>

<Password>19mv85sb</Password>

<Type>Administrator</Type>

</Employee>

<Employee ID="1001">

<FirstName>Richard</FirstName>

<LastName>Tubbs</LastName>

<UserName>Richard_TubbsPPan</UserName>

<Password>cbn8919</Password>

<Type>Staff</Type>

</Employee>

</Employees>

 HTML is designed to display data, with the primary focus on how the data looks. XML is for the transport and storage of data, with the focus on what the data is.

An **XML injection** attack is similar to an SQL injection attack; an attacker who discovers a website that does not filter input user data can inject XML tags and data into the database. A specific type of XML injection attack is an *XPath injection,* which attempts to exploit the XML Path Language (XPath) queries that are built from user input.

Directory Traversal/Command Injection
The *root directory* is a specific directory on a web server's file system. Users who access the server are usually restricted to the root directory or directories beneath the root directory; however, they cannot access other directories. For example, the default root directory of Microsoft's Internet Information Services (IIS) web server is *C:\Inetpub\wwwroot*. Users have access to this directory and subdirectories beneath this root (*C:\Inetpub\wwwroot\news*) if given permission, but do not have access to other directories in the file system, such as *C:\Windows\System32*.

 Do not confuse *root directory* with the root user account, root password, rootkits, or root user's home directory.

A **directory traversal** uses malformed input or takes advantage of a vulnerability to move from the root directory to restricted directories. Once the attacker has accessed a restricted directory, she can enter (inject) commands to execute on a server (called **command injection**) or view confidential files. A directory traversal attack is illustrated in Figure 3-6.

A directory traversal attack can be launched through a vulnerability in the web application program that accepts user input, a vulnerability in the web server operating system software, or a security misconfiguration on the server itself. When using input from the user as the attack vector, a long string of characters may be entered, such as *http://../../../../../../../../*, where *../* traverses up one directory level. For example, a browser requesting a compiled dynamic webpage (*dynamic.asp*) from a web server (*www.server.net*) to retrieve a file (*display.html*) in order to display it would generate the request using the URL

http://www.server.net/dynamic.asp?view=display.html

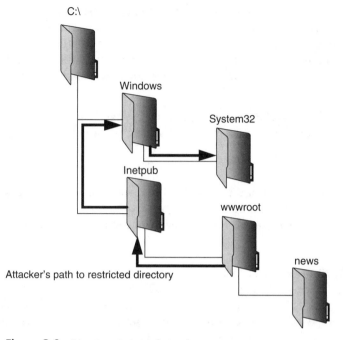

Figure 3-6 Directory traversal attack

However, if user input were permitted and not properly validated, the attacker could create the input *http://www.server.net/dynamic.asp?view=../../../../../TopSecret.docx* which could display the contents of a document.

Client-Side Application Attacks

Whereas server-side web application attacks target web applications on servers, **client-side attacks** target vulnerabilities in client applications that interact with a compromised server or process malicious data. Generally the client initiates the connection with the server that results in an attack.

 Client-side attacks are not limited to the Web; they can occur on any client/server pair, such as email, File Transfer Protocol (FTP), instant messaging (IM), or multimedia streaming.

One example of a client-side attack results in a user's computer becoming compromised just by *viewing* a webpage and not even clicking on any content. This type of attack, known as a *drive-by download*, is a serious threat. Attackers first identify a vulnerable web server and inject content by exploiting the server through vulnerable scripting applications. These vulnerabilities permit the attacker to gain direct access to the server's underlying operating system and then inject new content into the compromised website. To avoid visual detection, the attackers often craft a zero-pixel IFrame. IFrame (short for *inline frame*) is an HTML element that allows for embedding another HTML document inside the main document. A zero-pixel IFrame is virtually invisible to the naked eye; when unsuspecting users visit an infected website, their browsers download the initial exploit script that targets a vulnerability in the browser through an IFrame. If the script can run successfully on the user's computer, it will instruct the browser to connect to the attacker's web server to download malware, which is then automatically installed and executed on the client.

Many successful drive-by downloads sites target older web browsers; these attacks often are not as effective against newer browsers.

Client-side attacks are a favorite with attackers. Much like web application defenses, traditional network security tools cannot always effectively block client-side attacks. Common client-side attacks include header manipulation, cookies, attachments, session hijacking, and malicious add-ons.

Header Manipulation The **HTTP header** consists of fields that contain information about the characteristics of the data being transmitted. The header fields are comprised of a field name, a colon, and the field value, such as *Content-length: 49*. Although HTTP header field names and values may be any application-specific strings, a core set of fields has been standardized by the Internet Engineering Task Force (IETF). Table 3-3 lists some common HTTP header fields.

HTTP field name	Source	Explanation	Example
Server	Web server	Type of web server	*Server: Apache*
Referer or Referrer	Web browser	The address of the previous webpage from which a link to the currently requested page was followed	*Referer: http://www.askapache.com/show-error-502/*
Accept-Language	Web browser	Lists of acceptable languages for content	*Accept-Language:en-us,en;q=0.5*
Set-Cookie	Web server	Parameters for setting a cookie on the local computer	*Set-Cookie: UserID=ThomasTrain; Max-Age=3600; Version=1*

Table 3-3   HTTP header fields

HTTP headers are the result of an HTTP request by a web browser to a web server or the response back to the browser by the web server. Usually HTTP headers are used only by the web browser and the web server software because many web applications choose to ignore them.

An attacker can modify the HTTP headers to create an attack using **HTTP header manipulation**. Strictly speaking, HTTP header manipulation is not an actual attack, but rather the vehicle through which other attacks, such as XSS, can be launched. HTTP header manipulation allows an attacker to pass malicious instructions from her own malicious website or through an infected site to the web browser via HTTP headers. Examples of HTTP header attacks include:

- *Referer.* Because some websites check the Referer field to ensure that the request came from a page generated by that site, an attacker can bypass this security by modifying the Referer field to hide the fact that it came from another site.

- *Accept-Language.* Some web applications pass the contents of this field directly to the database. An attacker can inject an SQL command by modifying this header. In addition, if the web application used the *Accept-Language* field contents to build a filename from which to look up the correct language text, an attacker could generate a directory traversal attack.

- *Response splitting.* One of the most common HTTP header manipulation attacks is response splitting. First, the application on the client computer must allow input that contains carriage return (*CR* using %0d or \r) and line feed (*LF* using %0a or \n) characters in the header. By inserting a *CRLF* in an HTTP header (%0d%0a), these characters can not only give attackers control of the remaining HTTP headers and body of the response but also allow them to create additional responses via HTTP headers that are entirely under their control.

Cookies HTTP does not have a mechanism for a website to track whether a user has previously visited that site. Any information that was entered on a previous visit, such as site preferences or the contents of an electronic shopping cart, is not retained in order for the web server to identify repeat customers. Instead of the web server asking the user for the same information each time the site is visited, the server can store user-specific information in a file on the user's local computer and then retrieve it later. This file is called a **cookie.**

A cookie can contain a variety of information based on the user's preferences when visiting a website. For example, if a user inquired about a rental car at a car agency's website, that site might create a cookie that contained the user's travel itinerary. In addition, it might record the pages visited on a site to help the site customize the view for any future visits. Cookies also can store any personally identifiable information (name, email address, work address, telephone number, and so on) that was provided when visiting the site; however, a website cannot gain access to private information stored on the local computer.

Once a cookie is created on a client computer, only the website that created that cookie can read it.

Several different types of cookies exist:

- *First-party cookie.* A **first-party cookie** is created from the website that a user is currently viewing. For example, when viewing the website *www.cengage.com*, the cookie *CENGAGE* could be created and saved on the user's hard drive. Whenever the user returns to this site, that cookie would be used by the site to view the user's preferences and better customize the browsing experience.

- *Third-party cookie.* Some websites attempt to place additional cookies on the local hard drive. These cookies often come from third parties that advertise on the site and want to record the user's preferences. This is intended to tailor advertising to that user. These cookies are called **third-party cookies** because they are created by a third party (such as DoubleClick) that is different from the primary site.

- *Session cookie.* A **session cookie** is stored in random access memory (RAM), instead of on the hard drive, and lasts only for the duration of the visit to the website. A session cookie expires when the user closes the browser or has not interacted with the site after a set period of time.

- *Persistent cookie.* The opposite of a session cookie is a **persistent cookie**, also called a tracking cookie. A persistent cookie is recorded on the hard drive of the computer and does not expire when the browser closes.

- *Locally shared objects.* A **locally shared object (LSO)** is also called a **Flash cookie**, named after the Adobe Flash player. These cookies are significantly different from regular cookies in that they can store data more complex than the simple text that is typically found in a regular cookie. By default, LSOs can store up to 100 KB of data from a website, about 25 times as much as a regular cookie.

LSOs cannot be deleted through the browser's normal configuration settings as regular cookies can. Typically they are saved in multiple locations on the hard drive and also can be used to reinstate regular cookies that a user has deleted or blocked. In mid-2011, Adobe, after much criticism, released an online tool to delete LSOs.

Cookies can pose both security and privacy risks. First-party cookies can be stolen and used to impersonate the user, while third-party cookies can be used to track the browsing or buying habits of a user. When multiple websites are serviced by a single marketing organization, cookies can be used to track browsing habits on all the client's sites. These organizations can track browsing habits from page to page within all their client sites and know which pages are being viewed, how often they are viewed, and the Internet Protocol (IP) address of the viewing computer. This information can be used to infer what items the user may be interested in, and to target advertising to the user.

Many websites use advertising and tracking features to watch what sites are visited in order to create a profile of user interests. When you visit a site, it may create a unique identification number (like BTC081208) that is associated with your browser (your true identity is not known). Such features allow, for example, different ads to be displayed to baseball fans who are visiting spring training sites as opposed to those who are checking out tomorrow night's symphony performance. Not only does this tracking result in tailored ads being displayed as you surf, but it also ensures that the same ads do not keep appearing over and over.

Attachments Although cookies are normally used for good purposes, they, as well as attachments, can be exploited by attackers. **Attachments** are files that are coupled to email messages. Malicious attachments are commonly used to spread viruses, Trojans, and other malware when they are opened. Most users are unaware of the danger of attachments and routinely open any email attachment that they receive, even if it is from an unknown sender. Attackers often include information in the subject line that entices even reluctant users to open the attachment, such as a current event ("Check out this info about yesterday's hurricane") or information about the recipient ("Is this really you in this picture?").

Email-distributed malware frequently takes advantage of personal information contained on the user's computer. For example, some malware can replicate by sending itself as an email attachment to all of the contacts in a user's email address book. The unsuspecting recipients, seeing that an email and attachment arrived from a known person, typically with a provocative subject line, open the attachment and infect their computers.

Session Hijacking It is important that a user who is accessing a secure web application, such as an online bookstore, can be verified so as to prevent an imposter from "jumping in" to the interaction and ordering books that are charged to the victim but are sent to another address. This verification is accomplished through a **session token**, which is a random string assigned to that interaction between the user and the web application currently being accessed (a *session*). When the user logs in to the online bookstore's web server with her account user name and password, the web application server assigns a unique session token, such as *64da9DACOqgoipxqQDdywg*. Each subsequent request from the user's web browser to the web application contains the session token verifying the identity of the user until she logs out.

A session token is usually a string of letters and numbers of variable length. It can be transmitted in different ways: in the URL, in the header of the HTTP requisition, or in the body of the HTTP requisition.

Session hijacking is an attack in which an attacker attempts to impersonate the user by using her session token. A session hijacking attack is shown in Figure 3-7.

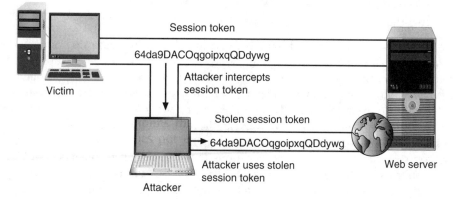

Figure 3-7 Session hijacking attack

An attacker can attempt to obtain the session token in several different ways. One of the most common methods is to use XSS or other attacks to steal the session token cookie from the victim's computer and then use it to impersonate the victim. Other means include eavesdropping on the transmission or guessing the session token. Guessing is successful if the generation of the session tokens is not truly random. In such a case, an attacker can accumulate multiple session tokens and then make a guess at the next session token number.

Although a session hijacking attack may seem to be a network-based attack instead of a client-side application attack, because most session hijacking attacks are performed using techniques like XSS, the CompTIA exam objectives classify this attack as an application attack.

Malicious Add-ons There are two categories of tools that can be added to enhance a user's interaction with a website through his web browser. A **plug-in** is a third-party library that attaches to a web browser and can be embedded inside a webpage. A plug-in adds new functionality to the page being viewed so that users can play music and other multimedia content within the browser or view special graphical images that normally a browser could not play or display. The most widely used plug-ins for web browsers are Java, Adobe Flash player, Apple QuickTime, and Adobe Acrobat Reader. A plug-in, however, affects only the specific page in which it is placed.

Plug-ins can be added to a webpage using the HTML *<embed>* tag or an *<object>* tag.

The second category consists of tools that add functionality to the web browser itself. These are called **add-ons** or **extensions**. Add-ons add a greater degree of functionality to the entire browser. In contrast to plug-ins, add-ons can do the following:

- Create additional web browser toolbars
- Change browser menus
- Be aware of other tabs open in the same browser process
- Process the content of every webpage that is loaded

Security risks exist when using add-ons because attackers can create malicious add-ons to launch attacks against the user's computer. One way in which these malicious add-ons can be written is by using Microsoft's ActiveX. **ActiveX** is not a programming language but a set of rules for how applications under the Microsoft Windows operating system should share information. **ActiveX controls** (add-ons) represent a specific way of implementing ActiveX and are sometimes called ActiveX applications. ActiveX controls can be invoked from webpages through the use of a scripting language or directly by an HTML command. ActiveX controls are like miniature applications that can be run through the web browser: anything a user can do on a computer, an ActiveX control can do, such as deleting files or reformatting a hard drive. Attackers can take advantage of vulnerabilities in ActiveX to perform malicious attacks on a computer.

The risks of using plug-ins are beginning to be reduced. Some web browsers now prohibit plug-ins; other browsers use a "Click to Play" feature that enables a plug-in only after the user gives approval. In addition, the most recent version of HTML known as HTML 5 standardizes sound and video formats so that plug-ins like Flash are no longer needed.

Impartial Overflow Attacks

Some attacks are "impartial" in that they can target either a server or a client. Many of these attacks are designed to "overflow" areas of memory with instructions from the attacker. This type of attack includes buffer overflow attacks, integer overflow attacks, and arbitrary/remote code execution attacks.

Buffer Overflow Attack Consider a teacher working in her office who manually grades a lengthy written examination by marking incorrect answers with a red pen. Because she is frequently interrupted in her grading by students, the teacher places a ruler on the test question she is currently grading to indicate her "return point," or the point at which she should resume the grading. Suppose that two devious students enter her office as she is grading examinations. While one student distracts her attention, the second student silently slides the ruler down from question 4 to question 20. When the teacher returns to her grading, she will resume at the wrong "return point" and not look at the answers for questions 4 through 19.

This scenario is similar to how a buffer overflow attacker attempts to compromise a computer. A storage buffer on a computer typically contains the memory location of the software program that was being executed when another function interrupted the process; that is, the storage buffer contains the "return address" where the computer's processor should resume once the new process has finished. An attacker can substitute his own "return address" in order to point to a different area in the computer's memory that contains his malware code.

A **buffer overflow attack** occurs when a process attempts to store data in RAM beyond the boundaries of a fixed-length storage buffer. This extra data overflows into the adjacent memory locations (a *buffer overflow*). Because the storage buffer typically contains the "return address" memory location, an attacker can overflow the buffer with a new address pointing to the attacker's malware code. A buffer overflow attack is shown in Figure 3-8.

The "return address" is not the only element that can be altered in a buffer overflow attack, but it is one of the most commonly altered elements.

Integer Overflow Attack Consider a digital clock that can display the hours only as *1* to *12*. What happens when the time moves past *12:59*? The clock then "wraps around" to the lowest hour value of *1* again.

On a computer, an *integer overflow* is the condition that occurs when the result of an arithmetic operation—like addition or multiplication—exceeds the maximum size of the integer type used to store it. When this integer overflow occurs, the interpreted value then wraps around from the maximum value to the minimum value.

Normal process

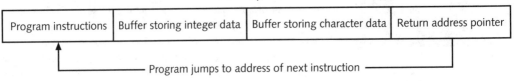

Program jumps to address of next instruction

Buffer overflow

Program instructions	Buffer storing integer data	Buffer storing character data	Return address pointer
		Malware	Fill and overflow buffer	New pointer

Program jumps to attacker malware

Figure 3-8 Buffer overflow attack

For example, an 8-bit signed integer has a maximum value of 127 and a minimum value of −128. If the value 127 is stored in a variable and 1 is added to it, the sum exceeds the maximum value for this integer type and wraps around to become −128.

In an **integer overflow attack,** an attacker changes the value of a variable to something outside the range that the programmer had intended by using an integer overflow. This type of attack could be used in the following situations:

- An attacker could use an integer overflow attack to create a buffer overflow situation. If an integer overflow could be introduced during the calculations for the length of a buffer when a copy is occurring, it could result in a buffer that is too small to hold the data. An attacker could then use this to create her buffer overflow attack.

- A program that calculates the total cost of items purchased would use the number of units sold times the cost per unit. If an integer overflow were introduced when tallying the number of items sold, it could result in a negative value and a resulting negative total cost, indicating that a refund is due the customer.

- A large positive value in a bank transfer could be wrapped around by an integer overflow attack to become a negative value, which could then reverse the flow of money: instead of adding this amount to the victim's account, it could withdraw that amount and later transfer it to the attacker's account.

An extreme example of an integer overflow attack would be withdrawing $1 from an account that has a balance of 0, which could cause a new balance of $4,294,967,295!

Arbitrary/Remote Code Execution Whereas a buffer overflow overwrites data in memory by putting more data in memory than the program can control, a *heap spray* is targeted and inserts data only in certain parts of memory. A heap spray is often used in an **arbitrary/remote code execution** attack.

As its name implies, an arbitrary/remote code execution attack allows an attacker to run programs and execute commands on a different computer. By gaining control of the victim's computer to execute the attacker's commands, the attacker turns it into his own remote computer. Once under the attacker's control, the computer can perform virtually any command from the attacker, from accessing the computer's files to displaying objectionable content on the screen to erasing the entire contents of the hard drive.

Arbitrary/remote code execution attacks often take advantage of malicious attachments. If a user opens a specially crafted file, such as a Microsoft Visio file or a PDF file, the attacker can then gain the same user rights as the current user who is logged on.

Networking-Based Attacks

3.2 Summarize various types of attacks.

In addition to targeting applications, attackers place a high priority on targeting networks in their attacks. This is because exploiting a single vulnerability may expose hundreds or thousands of devices to an attacker. There are several types of attacks that target a network or a process that relies on a network. These include denial of service, interception, poisoning, and attacks on access rights.

Denial of Service (DoS)

Suppose Gabe is having a conversation with Cora in a coffee shop. Suddenly Gabe's friend Mia walks up to the table and starts talking nonstop to Gabe. Gabe would be unable to continue the conversation with Cora because he would be overwhelmed by Mia's voice.

This is essentially what happens in a network **denial of service (DoS)** attack, which is a deliberate attempt to prevent authorized users from accessing a system by overwhelming that system with requests. Most DoS attacks today are actually **distributed denial of service (DDoS)** attacks: instead of using one computer, a DDoS may use hundreds or thousands of zombie computers in a botnet to flood a device with requests.

To expand the previous example, if a "flash mob" of friends suddenly descended upon Gabe and Cora at the coffee shop and all started talking to Gabe at the same time, he would be unable to continue his conversation with Cora because he would be overwhelmed by the number of voices with which he would have to contend. This is similar to what happens in a DDoS attack.

There are different types of DoS attacks. A **ping flood** attack uses the *Internet Control Message Protocol (ICMP)*, which is a network-layer protocol that is part of Transmission Control Protocol/Internet Protocol (TCP/IP), to flood a victim with packets. ICMP is normally used by network diagnostic tasks, such as determining if a host system is active or finding the path used by a packet to reach the host. The **ping** utility sends an ICMP echo request message to a host. The host responds with an ICMP echo response message, indicating that it is still active. In a ping flood attack, multiple computers rapidly send a large number of ICMP echo requests, overwhelming a server (as well as the network) to the extent that it cannot respond quickly enough and will drop legitimate connections to other clients and refuse any new connections.

A real-time map of worldwide DDoS attacks can be seen at www.digitalattackmap.com.

Another DoS attack tricks devices into responding to false requests to an unsuspecting victim. Called a **smurf attack,** an attacker broadcasts a ping request to all computers on the network but changes the address from which the request came to the victim's computer (this impersonation of another computer or device is called **spoofing**). This makes it appear that the victim's computer is asking for a response. Each of the computers then sends a response to the victim's computer so that it is quickly overwhelmed and then crashes or becomes unavailable to legitimate users.

A variety of different attacks use spoofing. For example, because most network systems keep logs of user activity, attackers may spoof their addresses so that their malicious actions will be attributed to valid users, or spoof their network addresses with addresses of known and trusted hosts so that the target computers will accept their packets and act on them.

A **SYN flood attack** takes advantage of the procedures for initiating a session. Under normal network conditions using TCP/IP, a device contacts a network server with a request such as to display a webpage or open a file. This request uses a control message, called a synchronize message or SYN, to initialize the connection. The server responds back with its own SYN along with an acknowledgment (ACK) that it received the initial request, called a SYN +ACK. The server then waits for a reply ACK from the device indicating that it received the server's SYN. To allow for a slow connection, the server might wait for a period of time for the reply. Once the device replies, the data transfer can begin.

It would seem that in order to establish a connection, each device would need to send a SYN and receive an ACK, which would result in four control messages passing back and forth. However, because it is inefficient to send a SYN and ACK in separate messages, one SYN and one ACK are sent together (the SYN+ACK). This results in three messages, which is called a three-way handshake.

In a SYN flood attack against a web server, the attacker sends SYN segments in IP packets to the server. However, the attacker modifies the source address of each packet to computer addresses that do not exist or cannot be reached. The server continues to "hold the line open" and wait for a response (which is not coming) while receiving more false requests and keeping more lines open for responses. After a short period of time, the server runs out of resources and can no longer respond to legitimate requests or function properly. Figure 3-9 shows a server waiting for responses during a SYN flood attack.

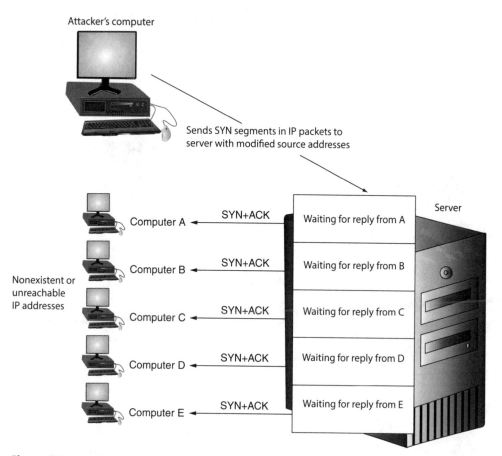

Figure 3-9   SYN flood attack

Interception

Some attacks are designed to intercept network communications. Two of the most common interception attacks are man-in-the-middle and replay attacks.

Man-in-the-Middle   Suppose that Angie, a high school student, is in danger of receiving a poor grade in math. Her teacher, Mr. Ferguson, mails a letter to Angie's parents requesting a conference regarding her performance. However, Angie waits for the mail and removes the letter from the mailbox before her parents come home. She replaces it with a counterfeit letter from Mr. Ferguson that compliments her on her math work, and then forges her parent's signature on the original letter to decline a conference and mails it back to her teacher.

The parents read the fake letter and compliment Angie on her hard work, while Mr. Ferguson wonders why her parents are not concerned about her performance. Angie has conducted a **man-in-the-middle** attack by intercepting legitimate communication and forging a fictitious response to the sender.

Technology-based man-in-the-middle attacks are conducted on networks. This type of attack makes it appear that two computers are communicating with each other, when actually they are sending and receiving data with a computer between them, or the "man-in-the-middle." In Figure 3-10, the victim's computer and the server are communicating without recognizing that an attacker is now intercepting their transmissions.

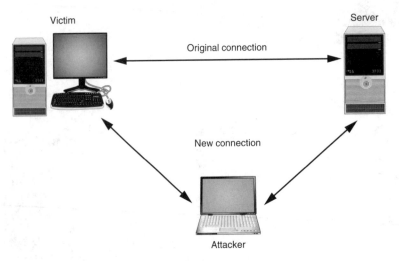

Figure 3-10   Man-in-the-middle attack

As the man-in-the-middle receives data from the devices, it passes it on to the recipient so that neither computer is aware of the man-in-the-middle's existence.

Man-in-the-middle attacks can be active or passive. In a passive attack, the attacker captures the data that is being transmitted, records it, and then sends it on to the original recipient without the attacker's presence being detected. In an active attack, the contents are intercepted and altered before they are sent on to the recipient.

Replay   A **replay** attack is similar to a passive man-in-the-middle attack. Whereas a passive attack sends the transmission immediately, a replay attack makes a copy of the transmission before sending it to the recipient. This copy is then used at a later time (the man-in-the-middle replays it).

A simple replay would involve the man-in-the-middle capturing logon credentials between the computer and the server. Once that session has ended, the man-in-the-middle would attempt to log on and replay the captured credentials.

A more sophisticated attack takes advantage of the communications between a network device and a server. Administrative messages that contain specific network requests are frequently sent between a network device and a server. When the server receives the message, it responds to the sender with another administrative message. Each of these transmissions is encrypted to prevent an attacker from seeing the contents and also contains a code that indicates if it has been tampered with. The server reads the code, and if it recognizes that a message has been tampered with, it does not respond. Using a replay attack, an attacker can capture the message sent from the network device to the server. Later, the attacker can send the original message to the server, and the server may respond, thinking it came from the valid device. Now a trusted relationship has been established between the attacker and the server. Because the attacker knows that he will receive a response from the server each time he sends a valid message, he can use this knowledge as a valuable tool. The attacker can begin to change the content of the captured message and code. If he eventually makes the correct modification, the server will respond, letting the attacker know he has been successful.

Poisoning

Poisoning is the act of introducing a substance that harms or destroys a functional living organism. Two types of attacks inject "poison" into a normal network process to facilitate an attack. These are ARP poisoning and DNS poisoning.

ARP Poisoning TCP/IP requires that logical IP addresses be assigned to each host on a network. However, an Ethernet LAN uses the physical media access control (MAC) address to send packets. In order for a host using TCP/IP on an Ethernet network to find the MAC address of another device based on the IP address, it uses the **Address Resolution Protocol** (**ARP**). If the IP address for a device is known but the MAC address is not, the sending computer sends an ARP packet to all computers on the network that in effect says, "If this is your IP address, send me back your MAC address." The computer with that IP address sends back a packet with the MAC address so the packet can be correctly addressed. This IP address and the corresponding MAC address are stored in an ARP cache for future reference. In addition, all other computers that hear the ARP reply also cache that data.

An attacker can modify the MAC address in the ARP cache so that the corresponding IP address points to a different computer. This is known as **ARP poisoning**. Table 3-4 illustrates the ARP cache before and after a man-in-the-middle attack using ARP poisoning.

Device	IP and MAC address	ARP cache before attack	ARP cache after attack
Attacker	192.146.118.200-AA-BB-CC-DD-02	192.146.118.3=>00-AA-BB-CC-DD-03 192.146.118.4=>00-AA-BB-CC-DD-04	192.146.118.3=>00-AA-BB-CC-DD-03 192.146.118.4=>00-AA-BB-CC-DD-04
Victim 1	192.146.118.300-AA-BB-CC-DD-03	192.146.118.2=>00-AA-BB-CC-DD-02 192.146.118.4=>00-AA-BB-CC-DD-04	192.146.118.2=>00-AA-BB-CC-DD-02 192.146.118.4=>00-AA-BB-CC-DD-(02)
Victim 2	192.146.118.400-AA-BB-CC-DD-04	192.146.118.2=>00-AA-BB-CC-DD-02 192.146.118.3=>00-AA-BB-CC-DD-03	192.146.118.2=>00-AA-BB-CC-DD-02 192.146.118.3=>00-AA-BB-CC-DD-(02)

Table 3-4 ARP poisoning attack

Manually performing a man-in-the-middle attack using ARP poisoning requires sending malicious ARP reply messages and using IP forwarding. However, many automated attack software tools will easily perform ARP poisoning.

Some types of attacks that can be generated using ARP poisoning are listed in Table 3-5.

Attack	Description
Steal data	An attacker can substitute her own MAC address and steal data intended for another device.
Prevent Internet access	An attacker can substitute an invalid MAC address for the network gateway so that no users can access external networks.
Man-in-the-middle	A man-in-the-middle device can be set to receive all communications by substituting that MAC address.
DoS attack	The valid IP address of the DoS target can be substituted with an invalid MAC address, causing all traffic destined for the target to fail.

Table 3-5 Attacks from ARP poisoning

ARP poisoning is successful because there are no authentication procedures to verify ARP requests and replies.

DNS Poisoning The predecessor to today's Internet was a network known as ARPA-net. This network was completed in 1969 and linked together single computers located at each of four different sites (the University of California at Los Angeles, the Stanford Research Institute, the University of California at Santa Barbara, and the University of Utah) with a 50 Kbps connection. Referencing these computers was originally accomplished by assigning an identification number to each computer (IP addresses were not introduced until later). However, as additional computers were added to the network it became more difficult for humans to accurately recall the identification number of each computer.

On Labor Day in 1969, the first test of the ARPAnet was conducted. A switch was turned on, and to almost everyone's surprise, the network worked. Researchers in Los Angeles then attempted to type the word *login* on the computer in Stanford. A user pressed the letter *L* and it appeared on the screen in Stanford. Next, the letter *O* was pressed, and it too appeared. When the letter *G* was typed, however, the network crashed.

What was needed was a *name system* that would allow computers on a network to be assigned both numeric addresses and more friendly human-readable names composed of letters, numbers, and special symbols (called a *symbolic name*). In the early 1970s, each computer site began to assign simple names to network devices and also manage its own **host table** that listed the mappings of names to computer numbers. However, because each site attempted to maintain its own local host table, this resulted in inconsistencies between the sites. A standard master host table was then created that could be downloaded to each site. When TCP/IP was developed, the host table concept was expanded to a hierarchical name system for matching computer names and numbers known as the **Domain Name System (DNS)**, which is the basis for name resolution to IP address today.

Because of the important role it plays, DNS can be the focus of attacks. Like ARP poisoning, **DNS poisoning** substitutes a DNS address so that the computer is automatically redirected to another device. Whereas ARP poisoning substitutes a fraudulent MAC address for an IP address, DNS poisoning substitutes a fraudulent IP address for a symbolic name.

Substituting a fraudulent IP address can be done in two different locations: the local host table, or the external DNS server. TCP/IP still uses host tables stored on the local computer. This is called the TCP/IP *host table name system*. A typical local host table is shown in Figure 3-11. When a user enters a symbolic name, TCP/IP first checks the local host table to determine if there is an entry. If no entry exists, then the external DNS system is used. Attackers can target a local hosts file to create new entries that will redirect users to their fraudulent site, so that, for example, when users enter *www.paypal.com* they are directed to the attacker's look-alike site.

```
# Copyright (c) 1993–1999 Microsoft Corp.
#
# This is a sample HOSTS file used by Microsoft TCP/IP for Windows.
#
# This file contains the mappings of IP addressed to host names. Each
# entry should be kept on an individual line. The IP address should
# be placed in the first column followed by the corresponding host name.
# The IP address and the host name should be separated by at least one
# space.
#
# Additionally, comments (such as these) may be inserted on individual
# lines or following the machine name denoted by a '#' symbol.
#
# for example:
#
#       102.54.94.97        rhino.acme.com        # source server
#       38.25.63.10         x.acme.com            # x client host
#
#

127.0.0.1               localhost
161.6.18.20             www.wku.edu               # Western Kentucky University
74.125.47.99            www.google.com            # My search engine
216.77.188.41           www.att.net               # Internet service provider
204.15.20.80            www.facebook.com
```

Figure 3-11 Sample hosts file
Source: Microsoft Inc.

Host tables are found in the */etc/* directory in UNIX, Linux, and Mac OS X, and are located in the *Windows\System32\drivers\etc* directory in Windows.

A second location that can be attacked is the external DNS server. Instead of attempting to break into a DNS server to change its contents, attackers use a more basic approach. Because DNS servers exchange information among themselves (known as *zone transfers*), attackers will attempt to exploit a protocol flaw and convince the authentic DNS server to accept fraudulent DNS entries sent from the attacker's DNS server. If the DNS server does not correctly validate DNS responses to ensure that they have come from an authoritative source, it will store the fraudulent entries locally and will serve them to users and spread them to other DNS servers.

The Chinese government uses DNS poisoning to prevent Internet content that it considers unfavorable from reaching its citizenry.

The process of a DNS poisoning attack from an attacker who has a domain name of *www .evil.net* with her own DNS server *ns.evil.net* is shown in Figure 3-12.

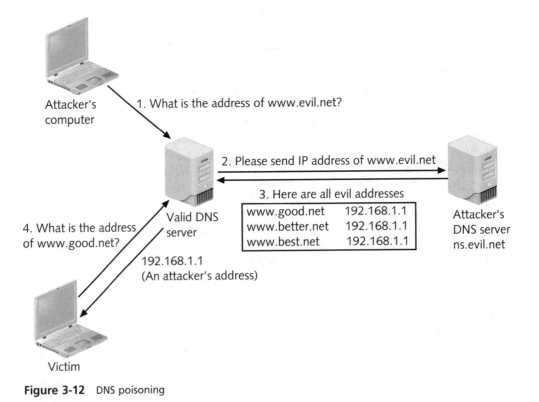

Figure 3-12   DNS poisoning

1. The attacker sends a request to a valid DNS server asking it to resolve the name *www.evil.net*.

2. Because the valid DNS server does not know the address, it asks the responsible name server, which is the attacker's *ns.evil.net*, for the address.

3. The name server *ns.evil.net* sends the address of not only *www.evil.net* but also all of its records (a zone transfer) to the valid DNS server, which then accepts them.

4. Any requests to the valid DNS server will now respond with the fraudulent addresses entered by the attacker.

Attacks on Access Rights

Access rights are privileges to access hardware and software resources that are granted to users. For example, Sophia may be given access rights to only read a file, while Elizabeth has access rights to add content to the file. Two of the attacks that target access rights are privilege escalation and transitive access.

Privilege Escalation Operating systems and many applications have the ability to restrict a user's privileges in accessing its specific functions. **Privilege escalation** is exploiting a vulnerability in software to gain access to resources that the user normally would be restricted from accessing.

Two types of privilege escalation exist. The first is when a user with a lower privilege uses privilege escalation to grant herself access functions reserved for higher-privilege users (sometimes called *vertical privilege escalation*). The second type of privilege escalation is when a user with restricted privileges accesses the different restricted functions of a similar user; that is, Mia does not have privileges to access a payroll program but uses privilege escalation to access Li's account that does have these privileges (*horizontal privilege escalation*).

The difference between privilege escalation and arbitrary/remote code execution is that with privilege escalation the attacker already has an account with low privileges on the targeted system.

Transitive Access *Transitive* is defined as a relation with a property so that if a relation exists between A and B, and there is also a relation between B and C, then there is a relation between A and C. Transitive is often used in mathematics regarding size: if A is smaller than B, and B is smaller than C, then it holds that A is smaller than C, as shown in Figure 3-13. When substituting *trust* for *size*, transitive means that if Alice trusts Bob, and Bob trusts Carol, then Alice trusts Carol (sometimes called *transitive trust*).

In technology this transitive trust can result in **transitive access**, in which System 1 can access System 2, and because System 2 can access System 3, then System 1 can access System 3. However, the intention may not be for System 1 to access System 3, but instead for System 1 to be restricted to accessing only System 2. This sometimes inadvertent and unauthorized access can result in serious security risks. Attackers can take advantage of transitive access that occurs whenever access is built through succeeding systems. By exploiting the sometimes confusing nature of transitive access, attackers can often reach restricted resources.

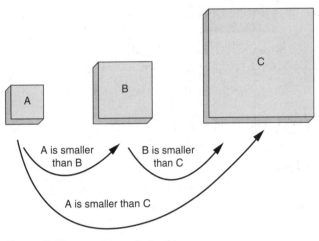

Figure 3-13 Transitive relationship

The classic example of transitive access can be seen in Microsoft's Active Directory. The default is that all domains in a forest trust each other in a two-way transitive trust. When a new child domain is added, it also receives transitive trust. An attacker who joins that child domain can then receive more access rights than was intended.

Chapter Summary

- An important characteristic of server-side web applications is that they create dynamic content based on inputs from the user. However, securing server-side web applications is often considered more difficult than protecting other systems. One reason is because by design these web applications accept user input, which an attacker can potentially use to attack the system.

- A cross-site scripting (XSS) attack is focused not on attacking a web application server to compromise it, but rather on using the server to launch other attacks on computers that access it. An XSS attack uses websites that accept user input without validating it and uses that input in a response without encoding it. An attacker can enter a malicious script into an input field and have that script execute when a victim is tricked into clicking on a malicious link to the page. Another common attack is SQL injection. A website that accepts user input that is not filtered, yet passes it directly to the database, allows that input to manipulate the database processing. Similar to SQL injection, XML injection can inject XML tags and data into a database. A directory traversal/command injection attack allows the attacker to move from the root directory to restricted directories. Once in the restricted directories, the attacker can view confidential files or execute commands.

- A client-side application attack targets vulnerabilities in client applications that interact with a compromised server or that process malicious data. Because HTTP headers can originate from a web browser, an attacker can modify the headers to create an attack. Because HTTP does not have a mechanism for a website to track whether a user has previously visited that site, information that was entered on a previous visit, such as site preferences or the contents of an electronic shopping cart, is stored in a file on the user's local computer. This file is called a cookie. Cookies pose a risk to both security and privacy. Attachments are files that are coupled to email messages and are commonly used to spread viruses, Trojans, and other malware when they are opened.

- Session hijacking is an attack in which an attacker attempts to impersonate the user by using his session token. An attacker can attempt to obtain the session token in several different ways. One of the most common methods is to use XSS or other attacks to steal the session token cookie from the victim's computer and use it to impersonate the victim. Add-ons provide additional functionality to web browsers. There are security risks when using add-ons because attackers can create malicious add-ons to launch attacks against the user's computer. One of the most widely used add-on tools for Windows computers is Microsoft's ActiveX technology, but these ActiveX add-ons present security concerns.

- Some attacks can target either a server or a client by "overflowing" areas of memory with instructions from the attacker. A buffer overflow occurs when a process attempts to store data in RAM beyond the boundaries of a fixed-length storage buffer. This extra data overflows into the adjacent memory locations and, under certain conditions, may cause the computer to stop functioning. An integer overflow attack is the result of an attacker changing the value of a variable to something outside the range that the programmer had intended by using an integer overflow. Whereas a buffer overflow overwrites data in memory by putting more data in memory than the program can control, a heap spray is targeted and only inserts data in certain parts of memory. A heap spray is often used in an arbitrary/ remote code execution attack, in which an attacker runs programs and executes commands on a different computer.

- Networks are a high priority target for attackers. This is because exploiting a single vulnerability may expose hundreds or thousands of devices to an attacker. A denial of service (DoS) attack is a deliberate attempt to prevent a system from performing its normal functions in order to prevent authorized users from access to the system. Different types of DoS attacks exist. Other attacks are designed to intercept network communications. A man-in-the-middle attack attempts to intercept legitimate communication and forge a fictitious response to the sender. A replay attack is similar to a man-in-the-middle attack. Instead of sending the transmission immediately, a replay attack makes a copy of the transmission before sending it to the recipient. This copy is then used at a later time.

- Two types of attacks inject "poison" into a normal network process to facilitate an attack: ARP poisoning and DNS poisoning. In ARP poisoning, an attacker can modify MAC addresses in the ARP cache so that the corresponding IP addresses will point to a different computer. Like ARP poisoning, DNS poisoning substitutes addresses so that the computer is automatically redirected to another device. Whereas ARP poisoning substitutes fraudulent MAC addresses for an IP address, DNS poisoning substitutes fraudulent IP addresses for symbolic names.

■ Access rights are privileges to access hardware and software resources that are granted to users. Privilege escalation involves exploiting a vulnerability in software to gain access to resources that the user normally would be restricted from obtaining. Transitive access involves using a trust relationship between three elements to gain access rights.

Key Terms

ActiveX A set of rules for how applications under the Microsoft Windows operating system should share information.

ActiveX control A specific way of implementing ActiveX that runs through the web browser and functions like a miniature application.

add-on Program that provides additional functionality to web browsers. Also called *extension*.

Address Resolution Protocol (ARP) Part of the TCP/IP protocol for determining the MAC address based on the IP address.

arbitrary/remote code execution An attack that allows an attacker to run programs and execute commands on a different computer.

ARP poisoning An attack that corrupts the ARP cache.

attachment A file that is coupled to an email message and often carries malware.

buffer overflow attack An attack that occurs when a process attempts to store data in RAM beyond the boundaries of a fixed-length storage buffer.

client-side attack An attack that targets vulnerabilities in client applications that interact with a compromised server or process malicious data.

command injection Injecting and executing commands to execute on a server.

cookie A file on a local computer in which a web server stores user-specific information.

cross-site scripting (XSS) An attack that injects scripts into a web application server to direct attacks at clients.

denial of service (DoS) An attack that attempts to prevent a system from performing its normal functions by overwhelming the system with requests.

directory traversal An attack that takes advantage of a vulnerability so that a user can move from the root directory to restricted directories.

distributed denial of service (DDoS) An attack that uses many computers to perform a DoS attack.

DNS poisoning An attack that substitutes DNS addresses so that the computer is automatically redirected to an attacker's device.

Domain Name System (DNS) A hierarchical name system for translating domain names to IP addresses.

extension Another name for *add-on*.

first-party cookie A cookie that is created from the website currently being viewed.

Flash cookie Another name for *locally shared object (LSO)*.

3

host table   A list of the mappings of host names to IP addresses.

HTTP header   Part of HTTP that is comprised of fields that contain the different characteristics of the data that is being transmitted.

HTTP header manipulation   Modifying HTTP headers to create an attack.

integer overflow attack   An attack that is the result of an attacker changing the value of a variable to something outside the range that the programmer had intended.

locally shared object (LSO)   A cookie that is significantly different in size and location from regular cookies, and can store more complex data. Also called *Flash cookie*.

man-in-the-middle   An attack that intercepts legitimate communication and forges a fictitious response to the sender.

persistent cookie   A cookie that is recorded on the hard drive of the computer and does not expire when the browser closes.

ping   A utility that sends an ICMP echo request message to a host.

ping flood   An attack that uses the Internet Control Message Protocol (ICMP) to flood a victim with packets.

plug-in   A third-party library that attaches to a web browser and can be embedded inside a webpage.

privilege escalation   An attack that exploits a vulnerability in software to gain access to resources that the user normally would be restricted from accessing.

replay   An attack that makes a copy of the transmission before sending it to the recipient.

session cookie   A cookie that is stored in Random Access Memory (RAM), instead of on the hard drive, and only lasts only for the duration of a visit to a website.

session hijacking   An attack in which an attacker attempts to impersonate the user by using the user's session token.

session token   A form of verification used when accessing a secure web application.

smurf attack   An attack that broadcasts a ping request to computers yet changes the address so that all responses are sent to the victim.

spoofing   Impersonating another computer or device.

SQL injection   An attack that targets SQL servers by injecting commands to be manipulated by the database.

SYN flood attack   An attack that takes advantage of the procedures for initiating a TCP/IP session.

third-party cookie   A cookie that was created by a third party that is different from the primary website.

transitive access   An attack that exploits the trust relationship between three parties.

XML (Extensible Markup Language)   A markup language that is designed to *carry* data, in contrast to HTML, which indicates how to *display* data.

XML injection   An attack that injects XML tags and data into a database.

zero-day attack   Attack that exploits previously unknown vulnerabilities, so victims have no time (zero days) to prepare for or defend against the attack.

Review Questions

1. Which of these is NOT a reason why securing server-side web applications is difficult?
   a. Although traditional network security devices can block traditional network attacks, they cannot always block web application attacks.
   b. The processors on clients are smaller than on web servers and thus they are easier to defend.
   c. Many web application attacks exploit previously unknown vulnerabilities.
   d. By design dynamic server-side web applications accept user input that can contain malicious code.

2. Which of these is not an HTTP header attack?
   a. Accept-Language
   b. Referer
   c. Response splitting
   d. Content-length

3. What is another name for a locally shared object?
   a. Flash cookie
   b. session cookie
   c. RAM cookie
   d. secure cookie

4. Browser plug-ins _____.
   a. only function on web servers
   b. can be embedded inside a webpage but add-ons cannot
   c. have additional functionality to the entire browser
   d. have been replaced by browser extensions

5. An attacker who manipulates the maximum size of an integer type would be performing what kind of attack?
   a. buffer overflow
   b. real number
   c. heap size
   d. integer overflow

6. What kind of attack is performed by an attacker who takes advantage of the inadvertent and unauthorized access built through three succeeding systems that all trust one another?

   a. privilege rights

   b. heap spray

   c. transitive

   d. vertical escalation

7. Which statement is correct regarding why traditional network security devices cannot be used to block web application attacks?

   a. Traditional network security devices ignore the content of HTTP traffic, which is the vehicle of web application attacks.

   b. Web application attacks use web browsers that cannot be controlled on a local computer.

   c. Network security devices cannot prevent attacks from web resources.

   d. The complex nature of TCP/IP allows for too many ping sweeps to be blocked.

8. What do attackers use buffer overflows to do?

   a. erase buffer overflow signature files

   b. corrupt the kernel so the computer cannot reboot

   c. point to another area in data memory that contains the attacker's malware code

   d. place a virus into the kernel

9. What is unique about a cross-site scripting (XSS) attack compared to other injection attacks?

   a. SQL code is used in an XSS attack.

   b. XSS requires the use of a browser.

   c. XSS does not attack the web application server to steal or corrupt its information.

   d. XSS attacks are rarely used anymore compared to other injection attacks.

10. What is a cookie that was not created by the website being viewed called?

    a. first-party cookie

    b. second-party cookie

    c. third-party cookie

    d. fourth-party cookie

11. What is the basis of an SQL injection attack?

    a. to have the SQL server attack client web browsers

    b. to inject SQL statements through unfiltered user input

    c. to expose SQL code so that it can be examined

    d. to link SQL servers into a botnet

12. Which action cannot be performed through a successful SQL injection attack?

    a. reformat the web application server's hard drive

    b. display a list of customer telephone numbers

    c. discover the names of different fields in a table

    d. erase a database table

13. Which markup language is designed to carry data?

    a. ICMP

    b. HTTP

    c. HTML

    d. XML

14. What type of attack involves an attacker accessing files in directories other than the root directory?

    a. SQL injection

    b. command injection

    c. XML injection

    d. directory traversal

15. Which type of attack modifies the fields that contain the different characteristics of the data that is being transmitted?

    a. XML manipulation

    b. HTML packet

    c. SQL injection

    d. HTTP header

16. What is a session token?

    a. XML code used in an XML injection attack

    b. a random string assigned by a web server

    c. another name for a third-party cookie

    d. a unique identifier that includes the user's email address

17. Which of these is NOT a DoS attack?

    a. SYN flood

    b. ping flood

    c. smurf

    d. push flood

3

18. What type of attack intercepts legitimate communication and forges a fictitious response to the sender?

   a. SIDS

   b. interceptor

   c. man-in-the-middle

   d. SQL intrusion

19. A replay attack _____.

   a. is considered to be a type of DoS attack

   b. makes a copy of the transmission for use at a later time

   c. can be prevented by patching the web browser

   d. replays the attack over and over to flood the server

20. DNS poisoning _____.

   a. floods a DNS server with requests until it can no longer respond

   b. is rarely found today due to the use of host tables

   c. substitutes DNS addresses so that the computer is automatically redirected to another device

   d. is the same as ARP poisoning

Hands-On Projects

If you are concerned about installing any of the software in these projects on your regular computer, you can install the software in the Windows virtual machine created in the Chapter 1 Hands-On Projects 1-3 and 1-4. Software installed within the virtual machine will not impact the host computer.

Project 3-1: Scan Web Browser Plug-ins

Web browser plug-ins and add-ons can be security risks. In this activity you will check the health status of your web browser and any plug-ins using the Qualys BrowserCheck.

1. Use your web browser to go to **https://browsercheck.qualys.com**.

The location of content on the Internet may change without warning. If you are no longer able to access the program through the above URL, use a search engine to search for "Qualys BrowserCheck".

2. Click **Learn more about Qualys BrowserCheck** and read through the features of this program.

3. Return to the home screen.

4. Click **Scan without installing plugin** and then click **Scan Now**.

5. A screen showing any insecure versions of plug-ins or browser updates that are missing will be displayed. If necessary click **Fix It** to address any security issues.

6. Close all windows.

Project 3-2: Configure Microsoft Windows Data Execution Prevention (DEP)

Data Execution Prevention (DEP) is a Microsoft Windows feature that prevents attackers from using buffer overflow to execute malware. Most modern CPUs support an NX (No eXecute) bit to designate a part of memory for containing only data. An attacker who launches a buffer overflow attack to change the "return address" to point to his malware code stored in the data area of memory would be defeated because DEP will not allow code in the memory area to be executed. If an older computer processor does not support NX, then a weaker software-enforced DEP will be enabled by Windows. Software-enforced DEP protects only limited system binaries and is not the same as NX DEP.

DEP provides an additional degree of protection that reduces the risk of buffer overflows. In this project, you will determine if a Microsoft Windows system can run DEP. If it can, you will learn how to configure DEP.

1. The first step is to determine if the computer supports NX. Use your web browser to go to **www.grc.com/securable**. Click **Download now** and follow the default settings to download the application on your computer.

The location of content on the Internet may change without warning. If you are no longer able to access the program through the above URL, use a search engine to search for "GRC securable".

2. Double-click **SecurAble** to launch the program, as shown in Figure 3-14. If it reports that **Hardware D.E.P.** is "No," then that computer's processor does not support NX. Close the SecurAble application.

Figure 3-14 SecurAble results
Source: SecurAble by Gibson Research Corporation

3. The next step is to check the DEP settings in Microsoft Windows. Click **Start** and **Control Panel**.

4. Click **System and Security** and then click **System**.

5. Click **Advanced system settings** in the left pane.

6. Click the **Advanced** tab if necessary.

7. Click **Settings** under **Performance** and then click the **Data Execution Prevention** tab.

8. Windows supports two levels of DEP controls: DEP enabled for only Windows programs and services and DEP enabled for Windows programs and services as well as all other application programs and services. If the configuration is set to *Turn on DEP for essential Windows programs and services only*, click **Turn on DEP for all programs and services except those I select**. This will provide full protection to all programs.

9. If an application does not function properly, it may be necessary to make an exception for that application and not have DEP protect it. If this is necessary, click the **Add** button and then search for the program. Click on the program to add it to the exception list.

10. Close all windows and applications and restart your computer to invoke DEP protection.

Project 3-3: Set Web Browser Security

Web browsers can provide protections against attacks. In this project, you will use the Windows Internet Explorer (IE) Version 11 web browser.

1. Start **Internet Explorer**.

2. Click the **Tools** icon and then click **Internet options** to display the Internet Options dialog box. Click the **General** tab, if necessary.

3. First remove all of the HTML documents and cookies that are in the cache on the computer. Before erasing the files, look at what is stored in the cache. Under **Browsing history** click the **Settings** button and then click the **View files** button to see all of the files. If necessary, maximize the window that displays the files.

4. Click the **Last Checked** column heading to see how long this information has been on the computer (it may be necessary to select the folder view **Details** to see this column heading).

5. Next, select a cookie by locating one in the **Name** column (it will be something like *cookie: windows@microsoft.com*). Double-click the name of the cookie to open it. If you receive a Windows warning message, click **Yes**. What information does this cookie provide? Close the cookie file and open several other cookies. Do some cookies contain more information than others?

6. Close the window listing the cookie files to return to the Website Data Settings dialog box. Click the **Cancel** button.

7. In the Internet Options dialog box under **Browsing history**, click **Delete**.

8. In the Delete Browsing History dialog box, click the items that you want to delete and then click **Delete.**

9. Close the Internet Options dialog box.

10. Click the **Tools** icon and then click **Manage add-ons.**

11. Different categories appear under Add-on Types. Select an add-on that has been added to this browser and view its name, publisher, status, etc., in the details section of the window.

12. Under **Show** select **All add-ons.** Notice in the **Status** column that some add-ons may be enabled and others disabled. Click **Close.**

13. Click the **Tools** icon and then **Internet options.**

14. Click the **Security** tab to display the security options. Click the **Internet** icon if necessary. This is the zone in which all websites are placed that are not in another zone. Under **Security level for this zone** move the slider to look at the various settings.

15. Click **Custom level** and scroll down through the **ActiveX controls and plug-ins.** Would you consider these sufficient? Click **Cancel.**

16. Now place a website in the **Restricted sites** zone. Go to **www .amazon.com** and verify that you can reach this site. Click your **Home** button.

17. Click the **Tools** icon and then click **Internet options** to display the Internet Options dialog box again. Click the **Security** tab and then click **Restricted sites.** Click **Sites,** enter **www.amazon.com,** click **Add,** and then **Close** and **OK.** Now return to that site again. What happens this time? Notice that displays that were previously available no longer appear. Why not? To remove this site, return to the **Restricted sites** to select **www.amazon.com** and click **Remove.**

18. If necessary click the **Tools** icon and then click **Internet Options** to display the Internet Options dialog box again. Click the **Privacy** tab. Drag the slider up and down to view the different privacy settings regarding cookies. Which one should you choose? Choose one and then click **Apply.**

19. Click **OK.**

20. IE also offers tracking protection. Click the **Tools** icon and then click **Safety.**

21. Click **Turn on Tracking Protection.**

22. Click **Your Personalized List** and then click the **Enable** button.

23. You can add sites from which you will be protected in two ways. You can visit the website that has added a script or cookie onto your computer and click the **Settings** button to add or remove the site. Another option is to download a list of sites by going to **www.iegallery.com/en-us/trackingprotectionlists.**

The location of content on the Internet may change without warning. If you are no longer able to access the program through the above URL, use a search engine to search for "Internet Explorer Tracking Protection Lists".

24. Click **Add** next to the name of one of the companies to block tracking from that company. Click **Add List**.

25. Close all windows.

Project 3-4: Hosts File Attack

Substituting a fraudulent IP address can be done by either attacking the Domain Name System (DNS) server or the local host table. Attackers can target a local hosts file to create new entries that will redirect users to their fraudulent site. In this project, you will add a fraudulent entry to the local hosts file.

1. Start your web browser.

2. Go to the Cengage website at **www.cengage.com** and then go to Google at **www.google.com** to verify that the names are correctly resolved.

3. Now search based on IP address. Go to **http://69.32.133.11** for Cengage and **http://173.194.113.146** for Google.

IP addresses are sometimes based on the region in which you live. If you cannot access the above sites by these IP addresses, go to **ipaddress.com/ip_lookup/** and enter the domain name to receive the IP address.

4. Click **Start** and **All Programs** and then **Accessories**.

5. Right-click **Notepad** and then select **Run as administrator**.

6. Click **File** and then **Open**. Click the **File Type** drop-down arrow to change from **Text Documents (*.txt)** to **All Files (*.*)**.

7. Navigate to the file **C:\Windows\System32\drivers\etc\hosts** and open it.

8. At the end of the file enter **173.194.113.146**. This is the IP address of Google.

9. Press **Tab** and enter **www.cengage.com**. In this hosts table, **www .cengage.com** is now resolved to the IP address 69.32.133.11.

10. Click **File** and then **Save**.

11. Open your web browser and then enter the URL **www.cengage.com**. What website appears?

12. Return to the hosts file and remove this entry.

13. Click **File** and then **Save**.

14. Close all windows.

Project 3-5: ARP Poisoning

Attackers frequently modify the Address Resolution Protocol (ARP) table to redirect communications away from a valid device to an attacker's computer. In this project, you will view the ARP table on your computer and make modifications to it. You will need to have another "victim's" computer running on your network (and know the IP address), as well as a default gateway that serves as the switch to the network.

1. Open a Command Prompt window by clicking **Start** and typing **Run** and then pressing **Enter**.

2. Type **cmd** and then press **Enter** to open a command prompt window.

3. To view your current ARP table, type **arp -a** and then press **Enter**. The Internet Address is the IP address of another device on the network while the Physical Address is the MAC address of that device.

4. To determine network addresses, type **ipconfig/all** and then press **Enter**.

5. Record the IP address of the default gateway.

6. Delete the ARP table entry of the default gateway by typing **arp -d** followed by the IP address of the gateway, such as **arp -d 192.168.1.1** and then press **Enter**.

7. Create an automatic entry in the ARP table of the victim's computer by typing **ping** followed by that computer's IP address, such as **ping 192.168.1.100**, and then press **Enter**.

8. Verify that this new entry is now listed in the ARP table by typing **arp -a** and then press **Enter**. Record the physical address of that computer.

9. Add that entry to the ARP table by entering **arp -s** followed by the IP address and then the MAC address.

10. Delete all entries from the ARP table by typing **arp -d**.

11. Close all windows.

Project 3-6: Create an HTTP Header

Because HTTP headers can originate from a web browser, an attacker can modify the headers (called HTTP header manipulation) to create an attack. Although web browsers do not normally allow HTTP header modification, web services are available that allow data from a browser to be modified. One type of HTTP header attack manipulates the Referer field. In this activity, you will modify a Referer field.

1. Use your web browser to go to **www.httpdebugger.com/tools/View HttpHeaders.aspx** to access the MadeForNet HTTP debugger as shown in Figure 3-15.

The location of content on the Internet may change without warning. If you are no longer able to access the program through the above URL, use a search engine to search for "HTTP debugger".

3

HTTP DEBUGGER   Home   Overview   Download   Purchase   Contacts   Free Tools

HTTP Request Viewer, HTTP Response Viewer

Send custom HTTP requests, view the HTTP request/response headers and check your web server settings.

HTTP(S) URL:	For example: http://www.google.com
Content Type:	For example: text/html
Content Data:	Request content data or POST parameters. For example: login=admin&password=pwd
Custom Headers:	For example: Accept-Encoding: gzip,deflate
Referer:	For example: http://www.httpdebugger.com
User Agent:	Internet Explorer ▼
HTTP Version:	● HTTP/1.1 ○ HTTP/1.0
HTTP Method:	● GET ○ POST ○ PUT ○ DELETE ○ HEAD

Submit

Figure 3-15   HTTP debugger
Source: MadeForNet.com

2. Under **HTTP(S) URL:** enter **http://www.cengage.com**.

3. Under **Content Type:** enter **text/html**.

4. Under **Referer:** enter **http://www.google.com**. This will change the referrer from this current site to another site.

5. Under **User Agent** select your web browser.

6. Click **Submit**. Note that the Referer field is changed. How could an attacker use this in an HTTP header attack?

7. Close all windows.

Project 3-7: Manage Flash Cookies

A locally shared object (LSO) is an enhanced cookie used by Adobe Flash and other applications. These cookies cannot be deleted through the browser's normal configuration settings as regular cookies can. Instead, they are managed through the Adobe website. In this project, you will change the settings on LSOs.

1. Use your web browser to go to **www.macromedia.com/support/ documentation/en/flashplayer/help/settings_manager07.html**

> The location of content on the Internet may change without warning. If you are no longer able to access the program through the above URL, use a search engine to search for "Adobe Flash Player Website Storage Settings Panel".
>
> **NOTE**

2. The Global Privacy Settings panel is displayed as shown in Figure 3-16. The first tab is the Global Privacy Settings is for Camera and Microphone. Click **Always ask ...** and then click **Confirm**.

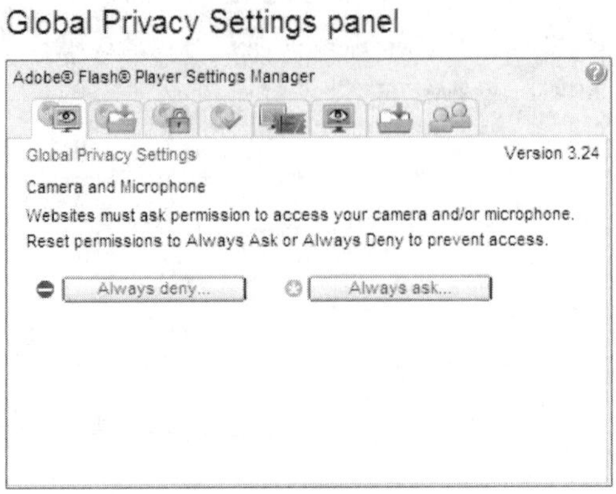

Global Privacy Settings panel

Figure 3-16 Global Privacy Settings panel
Source: Adobe Systems Incorporated

3. Click the next tab, which is the **Global Storage Settings**. Uncheck **Allow third-party Flash content to store data on your computer.**

4. Click the **Global Security Settings** tab. Be sure that either **Always ask** or **Always deny** is selected.

5. Click the **Website Privacy Settings** tab. This regards privacy settings for a camera or microphone. Click **Delete all sites** and then **Confirm.**

6. Close all windows.

Case Projects

Case Project 3-1: DoS Attacks

Denial of service (DoS) attacks can cripple an organization that relies heavily on its web application servers, such as online retailers. What are some of the most widely publicized DoS attacks that have occurred recently? What about attackers who threaten a DoS attack unless a fee is paid? How can DoS attacks be prevented? Write a one-page paper on your research.

Case Project 3-2: Arbitrary/Remote Code Execution Attacks

In recent years the number of arbitrary/remote code execution attacks have skyrocketed. Why is this type of attack so popular with attackers? What are some of the most well-known arbitrary/remote code execution attacks that have occurred? What is the primary means by which attackers infect computers with these attacks? How do these attacks commonly occur? What are the defenses to protect against these attacks? Write a one-page paper on your research.

Case Project 3-3: Injection Attack Defenses

Use the Internet to research defenses against injection attacks. What are the defenses to protect against SQL injection, XML injection, and XSS attacks? How difficult are they to implement? Why are these defenses not used extensively? Write a one-page paper on your research.

Case Project 3-4: Zero-Day Attacks

Attacks that exploit previously unknown vulnerabilities are considered some of the most dangerous attacks. Use the Internet to research these attacks. How are the vulnerabilities discovered? What are some of the most recent zero-day attacks? What defenses are there against them? Write a one-page paper on your research.

Case Project 3-5: Buffer Overflow Attacks

Research the Internet regarding buffer overflow attacks. How do the various types of overflow attacks differ? When did they first start to occur? What can they do and not do? What must a programmer do to prevent a buffer overflow in a program she has written? Write a one-page paper on your research.

Case Project 3-6: Bay Pointe Security Consulting

Bay Pointe Security Consulting (BPSC) provides security consulting services to a wide range of businesses, individuals, schools, and organizations. BPSC has hired you as a technology student to help them with a new project and provide real-world experience to students who are interested in the security field.

Cardinal Car Repair (CCR) is a national repair shop that specializes in repairing minor car door "dings," windshield repair, interior fabric repair, and scratch repair. CCR allows customers to file a claim through its online website. Recently, however, CCR was the victim of an SQL injection attack that resulted in the firing of the security technician. The president of CCR has contacted BPSC to help provide training to the technology staff to prevent further attacks.

1. Create a PowerPoint presentation for CCR about the different types of injection attacks, explaining what they are, how they occur, and what defenses can be set up to prevent them. Your presentation should contain 8 to 10 slides.

2. After the presentation CCR asks BPSC to address other weaknesses in their system. You have been placed on the team to examine potential networking-based attacks. One of your tasks is to create a report for a presentation; you are asked to write a one-page narrative providing an overview of the different types of networking-based attacks of DoS: interception, poisoning, and attacks on access rights.

Case Project 3-7: Community Site Activity

The Information Security Community Site is an online companion to this textbook. It contains a wide variety of tools, information, discussion boards, and other features to assist learners. Go to **community.cengage.com/infosec**. Click JOIN THE COMMUNITY and use the login name and password that you created in Chapter 1. Visit the **Discussions** section and read the following case study.

The crackdown on web browsing privacy is resulting in a tense situation between advertisers and the public. In addition to restricting third-party cookies, several web browsers now provide functionality to limit tracking by online advertisers. The U.S. government has even suggested that a Do Not Track (DNT) list be created that would prohibit websites and advertising networks from monitoring a web surfer's actions. This could allow for greater privacy and perhaps better security. Based on the national Do Not Call list that is designed to prevent telemarketers from making telephone calls to homes, DNT would allow users to sign up for this protection. Because it could not be implemented by users signing up based on their computer's IP address (because it can frequently change on a computer), another proposal is to have a persistent opt-out cookie, meaning that if a specific piece of code similar to a cookie is present on a user's computer, then it would indicate a user's agreement to be tracked or not.

Online advertisers, however, have responded by saying that their ads "pay the bills" for websites and that to restrict tracking would be like requiring television programs to eliminate commercials or magazines to stop accepting print advertisements. The end result would be a dramatic change in browsing. Users who accepted tracking would see all of the website's material, while those who opted out would see only more generalized content. Some websites may begin to charge customers a monthly fee to read their full content.

1. Should tracking be restricted? Would you sacrifice viewing your favorite websites in return for no tracking? Should websites be able to restrict the content that you view based on your choices regarding tracking? If you do not think this solution is a good one, what would you propose? Enter your answers on the InfoSec Community Site discussion board.

part

Application, Data, and Host Security

This part contains just one chapter, but it covers the most important concepts for securing both hardware (the host computer or device) and software (applications). After learning the basics of securing hosts and the applications they run, you will learn about securing data— when it is in transit, residing on a host or storage network, or in use.

Chapter 4   Host, Application, and Data Security

Host, Application, and Data Security

After completing this chapter, you should be able to do the following:

- List the steps for securing a host computer
- Define application security
- Explain how to secure data

Today's Attacks and Defenses

Writing computer software code for an application can be a challenging task when trying to ensure that it contains no flaws, errors, or faults—"bugs." By some estimates commercial off-the-shelf (COTS) software may contain anywhere from one to five bugs per thousand lines of code.[1] Yet even code that is free from operational bugs can have security vulnerabilities, which makes creating secure software even more difficult. Attackers are continually probing to find security weaknesses in software, hoping to exploit small weaknesses and turn them into massive security breaches. The traditional means of verifying the security of software code is very difficult and complex, particularly for large-scale projects. It usually requires highly skilled programmers and engineers with knowledge of both software coding and mathematical theorem-proving techniques to uncover security weaknesses.

Recently the independent research branch of the U.S. Department of Defense known as DARPA (Defense Advanced Research Projects Agency) has entered the software security scene. (The predecessor to DARPA provided funding and oversight for the computer networking project that has grown into today's Internet.) DARPA's mission is to think "outside the box" and, independently of the U.S. military, respond quickly with innovative solutions to address national defense.

DARPA has created a "crowdsourcing" project to uncover software security vulnerabilities (crowdsourcing is obtaining services from a large number of users through the Internet). DARPA Crowd Sourced Formal Verification (CSFV) is designed to determine if large numbers of noncomputer experts can perform formal software verification faster and cheaper than conventional means. CSFV has turned security vulnerability-hunting into game playing: volunteers use online games to help software verification tools root out weaknesses and verify that the code is secure.

The CSFV Verigames web portal offers free online games that can translate players' actions into program annotations to help to verify software code. When users solve puzzles in order to advance to the next level of game play, they are actually generating program annotations and mathematical proofs that can identify flaws in software written in the Java and C programming languages. To date there are five CSFV Verigame online games: CircuitBot (link up a team of robots to carry out a mission), Flow Jam (analyze and adjust a cable network to maximize its flow), Ghost Map (find a path through a brain network), StormBound (unweave the windstorm into patterns of streaming symbols), and Xylem (catalog species of plants using mathematical formulas). Having gamers instead of professionals identify potential problems in software code could help lower the workload of uncovering security flaws significantly. Although the games are not threatening to participants, only users 18 years of age and over are allowed to play, due to government regulations regarding volunteer participants.

Although coding secure software can be a complex process, as shown in the "Today's Attacks and Defenses" vignette, not all defenses against even sophisticated attacks are necessarily complex or difficult to implement. Often attacks—even sophisticated attacks—are successful simply because basic security measures have not been implemented.

Basic security starts with protecting the host, the applications, and the data. The *host*, which can be either a server or a client on a network, runs *applications* that process, save, or transport *data*. Each of these can be an important attack target and demands the necessary protections.

In this chapter, you will first look at security for host systems achieved through both physical means and technology. Next, security devices beyond common general-purpose computers will be studied, followed by an exploration of application security. Finally, you will examine how securing the data itself can provide necessary protections.

4

Securing the Host

2.7 Compare and contrast physical security and environmental controls.

2.9 Given a scenario, select the appropriate control to meet the goals of security.

3.6 Analyze a scenario and select the appropriate type of mitigation and deterrent techniques.

4.3 Given a scenario, select the appropriate solution to establish host security.

Securing the host involves protecting the physical device itself, securing the operating system (OS) software running on the host, and using antimalware software.

Securing Devices

A **security control** is any device or process that is used to reduce risk. That is, it attempts to limit exposure to a danger. There are two levels of security controls. **Administrative controls** are the processes for developing and ensuring that policies and procedures are carried out. In other words, administrative controls are the actions that users *may do*, *must do*, or *cannot do*. The second class of security controls is those that are carried out or managed by devices, called **technical controls**.

Remember from Chapter 1 that the goal of security is not to eliminate all risk, simply because that is not possible. Instead, the goal in designing and implementing controls is to reach a balance between achieving an acceptable level of risk, minimizing losses, and an acceptable level of expense. Some assets, however, must be protected irrespective of the perceived risk. For example, controls based upon regulatory requirements may be required regardless of risk.

The subtypes of controls that can be either technical or administrative (sometimes called **activity phase controls**) may be classified as follows:

- *Deterrent controls.* A **deterrent control** attempts to discourage security violations before they occur.

- *Preventive controls.* **Preventive controls** work to prevent the threat from coming into contact with the vulnerability.

- *Detective controls.* **Detective controls** are designed to identify any threat that has reached the system.
- *Compensating controls.* **Compensating controls** are controls that provide an alternative to normal controls that for some reason cannot be used.
- *Corrective controls.* Controls that are intended to mitigate or lessen the damage caused by the incident are called **corrective controls**.

These controls are summarized in Table 4-1.

Control name	Description	When it occurs	Example
Deterrent control	Discourage attack	Before attack	Signs indicating that the area is under video surveillance
Preventive control	Prevent attack	Before attack	Security awareness training for all users
Detective control	Identify attack	During attack	Installing motion detection sensors
Compensating control	Alternative to normal control	During attack	An infected computer is isolated on a different network
Corrective control	Lessen damage from attack	After attack	A virus is cleaned from an infected server

Table 4-1   Activity phase controls

Security professionals do not universally agree on the nomenclature and classification of activity phase controls. Some researchers divide controls into administrative, logical, and physical. Other security researchers specify up to 18 different activity phase controls.

Many activity phase controls involve the physical security of host devices. Physical security is protecting the devices so that unauthorized users are prohibited from gaining physical access to equipment. Although physically securing devices seems obvious, in practice it can be overlooked because so much attention is focused on preventing attackers from reaching a device electronically. Ensuring that devices—and the applications and data stored on those devices—cannot be physically accessed is important. Securing devices includes external perimeter defenses, internal physical access security, and hardware security.

External Perimeter Defenses External perimeter defenses are designed to restrict access to the areas in which equipment is located. This type of defense includes barriers, guards, and motion detection devices.

Barriers Different types of passive barriers can be used to restrict unwanted individuals or vehicles from entering a secure area. **Fencing** is usually a tall, permanent structure to keep out individuals for maintaining security. Most fencing is accompanied with a **sign** that explains the area is restricted and proper **lighting** so the area can be viewed after dark.

Standard chain link fencing offers limited security because it can easily be circumvented by climbing over it or cutting the links. Most modern perimeter security consists of a fence equipped with other deterrents such as those listed in Table 4-2.

Technology	Description	Comments
Anticlimb paint	A nontoxic petroleum gel-based paint that is thickly applied and does not harden, making any coated surface very difficult to climb.	Typically used on poles, downpipes, wall tops, and railings above head height (8 feet or 2.4 meters).
Anticlimb collar	Spiked collar that extends horizontally for up to 3 feet (1 meter) from the pole to prevent anyone from climbing it; serves as both a practical and visual deterrent.	Used for protecting equipment mounted on poles like cameras or in areas where climbing a pole can be an easy point of access over a security fence.
Roller barrier	Independently rotating large cups (diameter of 5 inches or 115 millimeters) affixed to the top of a fence prevents the hands of intruders from gripping the top of a fence to climb over it.	Often found around public grounds and schools where a nonaggressive barrier is important.
Rotating spikes	Installed at the top of walls, gates, or fences; the tri-wing spike collars rotate around a central spindle.	Designed for high-security areas; can be painted to blend into fencing.

Table 4-2   **Fencing deterrents**

Like fencing, a **barricade** is generally designed to block the passage of traffic. However, barricades are most often used for directing large crowds or restricting vehicular traffic and are generally not designed to keep out individuals. This is because barricades are usually not as tall as fences and can more easily be circumvented by climbing over them. Temporary vehicular traffic barricades are frequently used in construction areas. In order to permanently keep traffic out of a secure area, large modular concrete barricades are often used.

Guards   Whereas barriers act as passive devices to restrict access, human **guards** are considered active security elements. Unlike passive devices, a guard can differentiate between an intruder and someone looking for a lost pet. Guards can also make split-second decisions about when it is necessary to take appropriate action.

Some guards are responsible for monitoring activity that is captured by a video camera. **Video surveillance** uses video cameras to transmit a signal to a specific and limited set of receivers called **closed circuit television (CCTV)**. CCTV is frequently used for surveillance in areas that require security monitoring such as banks, casinos, airports, and military installations. Some CCTV cameras are fixed in a single position pointed at a door or a hallway. Other cameras resemble a small dome and allow guards to move the camera 360 degrees for a full panoramic view. High-end video surveillance cameras are motion-tracking and will automatically follow any movement.

When guards actively monitor a CCTV, it becomes a preventive control: any unauthorized activity seen on video surveillance will result in the guard taking immediate action by either going to the scene or calling for assistance. When a guard does not actively monitor a

CCTV, the video is recorded and, if a security event occurs, the recording is examined later in order to identify the culprit. This would be an example of a detective control.

A video camera monitoring a bank's ATM is an example of a detective control, whereas a camera positioned to watch the entrance of a building is normally considered a preventive control.

Motion Detection **Motion detection** is determining an object's change in position in relation to its surroundings. That is, someone or something has moved in an area in which other objects are still. This movement usually generates an audible **alarm** to warn a guard of an intruder. Motion detection can be performed using the different methods listed in Table 4-3.

Method	Example
Visual	CCTV
Radio frequency	Radar, microwave
Vibration	Seismic sensors
Sound	Microphones
Magnetism	Magnetic sensors
Infrared	Passive and active infrared light sensors

Table 4-3 **Motion detection methods**

Internal Physical Access Security External perimeter defenses are designed to keep an intruder from entering a campus, building, or other area. In the event that unauthorized personnel defeat external perimeter defenses, they will then face internal physical access security, which is focused on the interior of the area. These protections include hardware locks, proximity readers, access lists, mantraps, and protected distribution systems for cabling.

Hardware Locks Hardware locks for doors in residences generally fall into four categories. Most residences have keyed entry locks (use a key to open the lock from the outside), privacy locks (lock the door but have access to unlock it from the outside via a small hole; typically used on bedroom and bathroom doors), patio locks (lock the door from the inside, but it cannot be unlocked from the outside), and passage locks (latch a door closed yet do not lock; typically used on hall and closet doors). The standard keyed entry lock, shown in Figure 4-1, is the most common type of door lock for keeping out intruders, but its security is minimal. Because it does not automatically lock when the door is closed, a user may mistakenly think she is locking a door by closing it when she is not. Also a thin piece of plastic such as a credit card can sometimes be wedged between the lock and the door casing to open it; or the knob itself can be broken off with a sharp blow, such as by a hammer, and then the door can be opened.

4

Figure 4-1   Residential keyed entry lock

Door locks in commercial buildings are typically different from residential door locks. For rooms that require enhanced security, a lever coupled with a **deadbolt lock** is common. This lock extends a solid metal bar into the door frame for extra security as shown in Figure 4-2. Deadbolt locks are much more difficult to defeat than keyed entry locks. The lock cannot be broken from the outside like a preset lock, and the extension of the bar prevents a credit card from being inserted to "jimmy" it open. Deadbolt locks also require that a key be used to both open and lock the door.

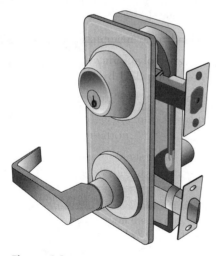

Figure 4-2   Deadbolt lock

NOTE The categories of commercial door locks include storeroom (the outside is always locked, entry is by key only, and the inside lever is always unlocked), classroom (the outside can be locked or unlocked, and the inside lever is always unlocked), store entry double cylinder (includes a keyed cylinder in both the outside and inside knobs so that a key in either knob locks or unlocks both at the same time), and communicating double cylinder lock (includes a keyed cylinder in both outside and inside knobs, and the key unlocks its own knob independently).

However, any residential or commercial door locks that use keys can be compromised if the keys are lost, stolen, or duplicated. To achieve the best security when using keyed door locks, the following lock and key management procedures are recommended:

- Inspect all locks on a regular basis in order to identify physical damage or signs of tampering.
- Receive the approval of a supervisor or other appropriate person before issuing keys.
- Keep track of keys issued, to whom, and the date; and require users to sign their name when receiving keys.
- Master keys should not have any marks identifying them as masters.
- Secure unused keys in a locked safe.
- Establish a procedure to monitor the use of all locks and keys.
- When making duplicates of master keys, mark them "Do Not Duplicate," and wipe out the manufacturer's serial numbers to keep duplicates from being ordered.
- Change locks immediately upon loss or theft of keys.

Because of the difficulties in managing keys for large numbers of users, an alternative to a key lock is a more sophisticated door access system using a *cipher lock* as shown in Figure 4-3. Cipher locks are combination locks that use buttons that must be pushed in the proper sequence to open the door. Although cipher locks may seem similar to a combination padlock, they have more intelligence. A cipher lock can be programmed to allow a certain individual's code to be valid on specific dates and times. For example, an employee's code may be valid to access the computer room from only 8:00 AM to 5:00 PM Monday through Friday. This prevents the employee from entering the room late at night when most other employees are gone. Cipher locks also keep a record of when the door was opened and by which code. A disadvantage of cipher locks is that they can be vulnerable to "shoulder surfing," or an unauthorized user observing the buttons that are pushed on the lock.

Figure 4-3   Cipher lock

Cipher locks are sometimes used in conjunction with a tailgate sensor. Tailgate sensors use multiple infrared beams that are aimed across a doorway and positioned so that as a person walks through the doorway, some beams are activated; the other beams are then activated a fraction of a second later. The beams are monitored and can determine which direction the person is walking. In addition, the number of persons walking through the beam array also can be determined. If only one person is allowed to walk through the beam for a valid set of credentials, an alarm can sound when a second person walks through the beam array immediately behind ("tailgates") the first person without presenting credentials.

Proximity Readers Instead of using a key or entering a code to open a door, a user can use an object (sometimes called a *physical token*) to identify herself in order to gain access to a secure area. One of the most common types of physical tokens is an *ID badge*. ID badges originally contained a photograph of the bearer and were visually screened by security guards. Later ID badges were *magnetic stripe cards* that were "swiped" or contained a *barcode* identifier that was "scanned" to identify the user.

Although the terms *magnetic stripe card* and *magnetic strip card* are often used interchangeably, that is not correct. A *strip* is defined as a long narrow piece of something, usually of uniform width, like a strip of paper. A *stripe*, on the other hand, is a strip of material (like magnetic tape). Technically a *magnetic stripe card* contains a *magnetic strip*.

However, when verifying hundreds or thousands of users at a time, swiping or scanning ID badges can result in a bottleneck. New technologies do not require that an ID badge be visually exposed. Instead, the badge emits a signal identifying the owner; the signal is then detected as the owner moves near a **proximity reader** that receives the signal. Sometimes it is even unnecessary for the bearer to remove the badge from a pocket or purse.

ID badges that can be detected by a proximity reader are often fitted with tiny *radio frequency identification (RFID) tags*. RFID tags, as shown in Figure 4-4, can easily be affixed to the inside of an ID badge and can be read by an RFID proximity reader as the user walks through the turnstile with the badge in a pocket.

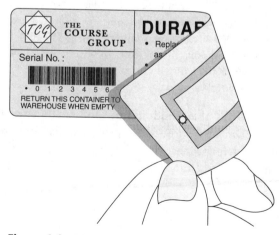

Figure 4-4 RFID tag

RFID tags on ID badges are passive and do not have their own power supply; instead, the tiny electrical current induced in the antenna by the incoming signal from the transceiver provides enough power for the tag to send a response. Because it does not require a power supply, passive RFID tags can be very small (only 0.4 mm × 0.4 mm and thinner than a sheet of paper); yet the amount of data transmitted typically is limited to just an ID number. Passive tags have ranges from about 1/3 inch to 19 feet (10 millimeters to 6 meters). Active RFID tags must have their own power source.

Access List An **access list** is a record or list of individuals who have permission to enter a secure area, along with the time they entered and the time they left the area. Access lists were originally paper documents that users had to sign when entering and leaving a secure area. Today cipher locks and proximity readers can create electronic access lists.

Having a record of individuals who were in the vicinity of a suspicious activity can be valuable. In addition, an access list can also identify whether unauthorized personnel have attempted to access a secure area.

Mantraps A **mantrap** is designed to separate a nonsecured area from a secured area. A mantrap device monitors and controls two interlocking doors to a small room (a vestibule), as shown in Figure 4-5. When in operation, only one door is able to be open at any time. Mantraps are used at high-security areas where only authorized persons are allowed to enter, such as sensitive data processing rooms, cash handling areas, and research laboratories.

Before electronic security was available, vestibules with two locked doors were used to control access into sensitive areas. Individuals attempting to gain access to a secure area would give their credentials to a security officer; the security officer would then open the first door to the vestibule and ask the individuals to enter and wait while their credentials were being checked. If the credentials were approved, the second door would be unlocked; if the credentials were fraudulent, the person would be trapped in the vestibule (a "mantrap").

Protected Distribution Systems (PDS) Cable conduits are hollow tubes that carry copper wire or fiber-optic cables, as shown in Figure 4-6. A **protected distribution system (PDS)** is a system of cable conduits used to protect classified information that is being transmitted between two secure areas. PDS is a standard created by the U.S. Department of Defense (DOD).

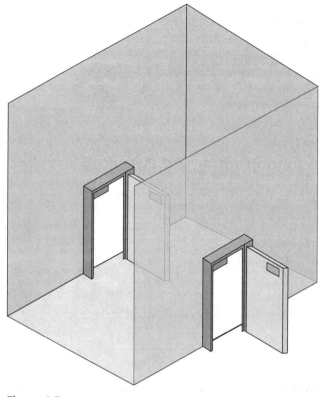

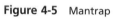

Figure 4-5   Mantrap

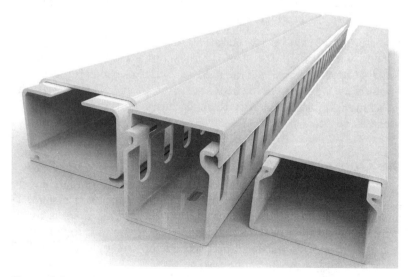

Figure 4-6   Cable conduits
© Peter Sobolev/Shutterstock.com

Two types of PDS are commonly used. In a *hardened carrier PDS*, the data cables are installed in a conduit that is constructed of special electrical metallic tubing or similar material. All of the connections between the different segments are permanently sealed with welds or special sealants. If the hardened carrier PDS is buried underground, such as running between buildings, the carrier containing the cables must be encased in concrete and any manhole covers that give access to the PDS must be locked down. A hardened carrier PDS must be visually inspected on a regular basis.

An alternative to a hardened carrier PDS is an *alarmed carrier PDS*. In this type of PDS, the carrier system is deployed with specialized optical fibers in the conduit that can sense acoustic vibrations that occur when an intruder attempts to gain access to the cables, which triggers an alarm. The advantages of an alarmed carrier PDS are:

- Provides continuous monitoring
- Eliminates the need for periodic visual inspections
- Allows the carrier to be hidden above the ceiling or below the floor
- Eliminates the need for welding or sealing connections

 PDS systems are considered to be so highly secure that they can be used instead of encrypting the transmitted data.

Hardware Security Hardware security is the physical security that specifically involves protecting the hardware of the host system, particularly portable laptops and tablet computers that can easily be stolen. Most portable devices (as well as many expensive computer monitors) have a special steel bracket security slot built into the case. A **cable lock** can be inserted into the security slot of a portable device and rotated so that the cable lock is secured to the device, while a cable connected to the lock can then be secured to a desk or chair. A cable lock is illustrated in Figure 4-7.

When storing a laptop, it can be placed in a **safe** or a **locking cabinet**, which is a ruggedized steel box with a lock. The sizes typically range from small (to accommodate one laptop) to large (for multiple devices). Safes and cabinets also can be prewired for electrical power as well as wired network connections. This allows the laptops stored in the locking cabinet to charge their batteries and receive software updates while not in use.

Securing the Operating System Software

In addition to protecting the hardware, the operating system software that runs on the host must be protected. There are two approaches to securing the operating system. The first is to properly configure the operating system after it has been installed so as to "fortify" it. The second approach is completely different. Instead of attempting to fortify an existing operating system after it is deployed, this approach attempts to tighten the security during the initial design and coding of the operating system.

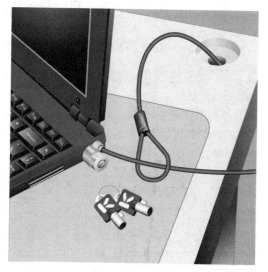

Figure 4-7   Cable lock

Security Through Configuration The security of an OS can be enhanced through the proper configuration of its built-in security features. This can be achieved through a five-step process:

1. Develop the security policy.
2. Perform host software baselining.
3. Configure operating system security settings.
4. Deploy and manage security settings.
5. Implement patch management.

Develop the Security Policy Security starts with an organization determining what actions must be taken to create and maintain a secure environment. That information is recorded in a formal security policy. A **security policy** is a document or series of documents that clearly defines the defense mechanisms an organization will employ in order to keep information secure. A security policy for an operating system may outline which security settings must be turned on and how they are to be configured.

Written security policies are covered in detail in a later chapter.

Perform Host Software Baselining Once the security policy has been created, a security baseline for the host is established. A *baseline* is the standard or checklist against which systems can be evaluated and audited for their level of security (*security posture*). A baseline outlines the major security considerations for a system and becomes the starting point for solid security. A host baseline for the operating system is configuration settings that will be used for each computer in the organization. Whereas the security policy determines *what* must be protected, the baselines are the OS settings that impose *how* the policy will be enforced.

A different security baseline may be needed for each class of computer in the organization because each class performs a different function and thus will need different settings. For example, a security baseline for desktop computers will be different from that for file servers.

Configure Operating System Security Settings After the baseline is established, the security settings on the host operating system can be properly configured. Modern operating systems have hundreds of different security settings that can be manipulated to conform to the baseline. A typical configuration baseline would include changing any default settings that are insecure (such as allowing Guest accounts); eliminating any unnecessary software, services, or protocols (like removing games); and enabling system security features (such as turning on the firewall).

Deploy and Manage Security Settings Instead of recreating the same security configuration on each computer, tools can be used to automate the process. In Microsoft Windows a *security template* is a collection of security configuration settings. These settings typically include the following:

- Account policies
- User rights
- Event log settings
- Restricted groups
- System services
- File permissions
- Registry permissions

Once a single host has been configured properly, a security template from that host can be developed and used for deploying to other systems.

Predefined security templates are also available to be imported to the base host. These settings then can be modified to create a unique security template for all hosts based on the baseline.

A Microsoft Windows security template can be deployed manually, requiring an administrator to access each computer and apply the security template either through using the command line or through using a *snap-in*, which is a software module that provides administrative capabilities for a device. A second method is to use *Group Policy*, which is a feature that provides centralized management and configuration of computers and remote users who are using specific Microsoft directory services known as *Active Directory (AD)*. Group Policy allows a single configuration to be set and then deployed to many or all users.

Implement Patch Management Early operating systems were simply program loaders whose job was to launch applications. As more features and graphical user interfaces (GUIs) were added, they became more complex. Due to the increased length and complexity of operating systems, unintentional vulnerabilities were introduced that could be exploited by attackers. In addition, new attack tools made what were considered secure functions and services on operating systems vulnerable.

Microsoft's first operating system, MS-DOS v1.0, had 4000 lines of code, while Windows 8.1 is estimated to have up to 80 million lines.

4

To address the vulnerabilities in operating systems that are uncovered after the software has been released, software vendors usually deploy a software "fix." A fix can come in a variety of formats. A security **patch** is a publicly released software security update intended to repair a vulnerability; a patch is universal for all customers. A **hotfix** is a software update that addresses a specific customer issue and often may not be distributed outside that customer's organization. A **service pack** is software that is a cumulative package of all patches and hotfixes as well as additional features.

There is no universal agreement on the definition of these terms. For example, whereas most vendors and users refer to a general software security update as a patch, Microsoft calls it a *security update*.

Because patches are produced often, it is important to have a mechanism to ensure that they are installed in a timely fashion. Modern operating systems, such as Red Hat Linux, Apple Mac OS, Ubuntu Linux, and Microsoft Windows, have the ability to perform automatic updates (Microsoft releases its patches regularly on the second Tuesday of each month, called *Patch Tuesday*). The operating system interacts with the vendor's online update service to automatically download and install patches, depending upon the configuration option that is chosen. The automatic update configuration options for most host operating systems allow the user to select the time and the day when the host checks for new important updates (daily or a specific day of the week), what to do when new updates are detected (install updates automatically, download the updates but let the user choose which updates to install, or check for updates but let the user determine those that should be downloaded and installed), and the action to take when recommended updates are available (accept or reject).

A growing trend is to not offer users *any* options regarding patches. Instead, patches are automatically downloaded and installed whenever they become available. This ensures that the software is always up-to-date.

Patches, however, can sometimes create new problems, such as preventing a custom application from running correctly. Organizations that have these types of applications usually test patches when they are released to ensure that they do not adversely affect any customized applications. In these instances, the organization will want to delay the installation of a patch from the vendor's online update service until the patch is thoroughly tested. How can an organization prevent its employees from installing the latest patch until it has passed testing, and yet ensure that all users download and install necessary patches?

The answer is an *automated patch update service*. This service is used to manage patches locally instead of relying upon the vendor's online update service. An automated patch update service typically consists of a component installed on one or more servers inside the corporate network. Because these servers can replicate information among themselves, usually only one of the servers must be connected to the vendor's online update service, as seen in Figure 4-8.

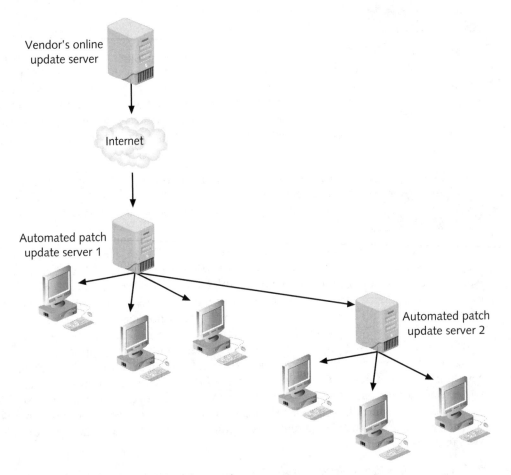

Figure 4-8 Automated patch update service

There are several advantages to an automated patch update service, including:

- Administrators can approve or decline updates for client systems, force updates to install by a specific date, and obtain reports on what updates each computer needs.

- Administrators can approve updates for "detection" only; this allows them to see which computers will require the update without actually installing it.

- Downloading patches from a local server instead of using the vendor's online update service can save bandwidth and time because each computer does not have to connect to an external server.

- Specific types of updates that the organization does not test, such as hotfixes, can be automatically installed whenever they become available.

- Users cannot disable or circumvent updates as they can if their computer is configured to use the vendor's online update service.

Automated patch update services allow administrators in an organizational setting to apply patches in a more controlled and consistent fashion.

Security Through Design Instead of managing the different security options on an operating system that has been deployed, in some cases it is necessary to tighten security during the design and coding of the OS. This is called **OS hardening**. An operating system that has been designed in this way to be secure is a **trusted OS**.

Some of the changes performed through OS hardening to create a trusted OS are listed in Table 4-4.

Hardening technique	Explanation
Least privilege	Remove all *supervisor* or *administrator* accounts that can bypass security settings and instead split privileges into smaller units to provide the least-privileged unit to a user or process.
Reduce capabilities	Significantly restrict what resources can be accessed and by whom.
Read-only file system	Important operating system files cannot be changed.
Kernel pruning	Remove all unnecessary features that may compromise an operating system.

Table 4-4 OS hardening techniques

Securing with Antimalware

Operating system software has continued to add security protections to its core set of features. Third-party antimalware software packages can provide added security. Antimalware software includes antivirus, antispam, popup blockers and antispyware, and host-based firewalls.

Antivirus One of the first antimalware software security applications was **antivirus (AV)** software. This software can examine a computer for any infections as well as monitor computer activity and scan new documents that might contain a virus (this scanning is typically performed when files are opened, created, or closed). If a virus is detected, options generally include cleaning the file of the virus, quarantining the infected file, or deleting the file.

Many AV products scan files by attempting to match known virus patterns against potentially infected files. This is called *static analysis*. The host AV software contains a virus scanning engine and a database of known virus signatures, which are created by extracting a sequence of bytes—a string—found in the virus that then serves as a virus's unique "signature." By comparing the virus signatures against a potentially infected file (called *string scanning*), a match may indicate an infected file. Other variations include *wildcard scanning* (a wildcard is allowed to skip bytes or ranges of bytes instead of looking for an exact match) and *mismatch scanning* (mismatches allow a set number of bytes in the string to be any value regardless of their position in the string). The weakness of static analysis is that the AV vendor must constantly be searching for new viruses, extracting virus signatures, and distributing those updated databases to all users. Any out-of-date signature database could result in an infection.

A newer approach to AV is *dynamic heuristic detection*, which uses a variety of techniques to spot the characteristics of a virus instead of attempting to make matches. One technique used is *code emulation* in which a virtual environment is created that simulates the central processing unit (CPU) and memory of the computer. Any questionable program code is executed in the virtual environment (no actual virus code is executed by the real CPU) to determine if it is a virus.

The difference between static analysis and dynamic heuristic detection is similar to how airport security personnel in some nations screen for terrorists. A known terrorist attempting to go through security can be identified by comparing his face against photographs of known terrorists (static analysis). But what about a new terrorist for whom there is no photograph? Security personnel can look at the person's characteristics—holding a one-way ticket, not checking any luggage, showing extreme nervousness—as possible indicators that the individual may need to be questioned (dynamic heuristic detection).

Antispam Beyond being annoying and disruptive, spam can pose a serious security risk. Spammers often distribute malware as attachments through their spam email messages and can use spam for social engineering attacks.

There are different methods for filtering spam on the host's email client in order to prevent it from reaching the user. One technique is **Bayesian filtering**. The software divides email messages that have been received into two piles, spam and nonspam. The filter then analyzes every word in each email and determines how frequently a word occurs in the spam pile compared to the not-spam pile. A word such as "the" would occur equally in both piles and be given a neutral 50 percent ranking. A word such as "report" may occur frequently in nonspam messages and would receive a 99 percent probability of being a nonspam word, while a word like "sex" may receive a 99 percent probability of being a spam word. Whenever email arrives, the filter looks for the 15 words with the highest probabilities to calculate the message's overall spam probability rating.

Although Bayesian filters are not perfect, they generally trap a much higher percentage of spam than other techniques.

A second method is to create lists of approved or nonapproved senders. A list of senders from whom email messages should be rejected—which can either be created by the user or downloaded from a website—is called a blacklist (the principle of a **blacklist** is to allow everything in unless it appears on the list). A whitelist is just the opposite: it is a list of approved senders; a **whitelist** denies anything from entering unless it is on the list. In addition to blacklists and whitelists, email can be filtered by region or country. Many host email clients also automatically block potentially dangerous types of file attachments, such as *.exe*, *.bat*, *.vbs*, and *.com*.

In addition to email clients, some other applications can take advantage of blacklists and whitelists.

Popup Blockers and Antispyware A *popup* is a small web browser window that appears over a webpage. Most popup windows are created by advertisers and launch as soon as a new website is visited. A **popup blocker** is a separate program or a feature incorporated within a browser that stops popup advertisements from appearing. As a separate program, popup blockers are often part of a package known as **antispyware** that helps prevent computers from becoming infected by different types of spyware. AV and antispyware software share many similarities: they must be regularly updated to defend against the most recent attacks; they can be set to both provide continuous, real-time monitoring as well as perform a complete scan of the entire computer system at one time; and they may trap different types of malware.

A browser popup blocker allows the user to limit or block most popups. Users can select the level of blocking, ranging from blocking all popups to allowing specific popups. When a popup is detected, an alert can be displayed in the browser such as *Popup blocked; to see this popup or additional options click here.*

Host-Based Firewalls A **firewall**, sometimes called a **packet filter**, is designed to prevent malicious network packets from entering or leaving computers or networks. A firewall can be software-based or hardware-based.

Modern operating systems include a **host-based application firewall** that runs as a program on a local system to protect it. These firewalls are application-based. An application running on a host computer may need to send and receive transmissions that normally would be blocked by the firewall. An opening in the firewall can be created by the user simply by approving the application to transmit (called *unblocking*). This is more secure than opening a port on the firewall itself: when a port is opened on the firewall it always remains opened, but when a port is unblocked it is opened only when the application needs it.

Securing Static Environments

4.5 Compare and contrast alternative methods to mitigate security risks in static environments.

Whereas at one time computers were the only technology devices that needed to be protected from an attacker, that is no longer the case. As the number of devices with microprocessors grows exponentially, these are also becoming ripe targets for attackers. These types of devices are sometimes called a **static environment** because unlike traditional computers in which additional hardware can easily be added or attached, these devices generally lack that capability.

Because designing these devices with security in mind has not been a priority, they often can be easily exploited.

Common devices that fall into this category include:

- *Embedded systems.* Whereas a general-purpose personal computer is designed to be flexible and meet a wide range of user needs, an **embedded system** is a computer system with a dedicated function within a larger electrical or mechanical system. Examples of embedded systems include printers, smart TVs, HVAC (heating, ventilation, and air conditioning) controllers, and bank automated teller machines (ATMs). The operating systems of these embedded systems often are stripped-down versions of general-purpose operating systems and may contain many of the same vulnerabilities.

It is estimated that as of early 2014 almost 95 percent of ATMs worldwide were running Microsoft XP Embedded, which was released in 2001.[2]

- *Game consoles.* Like embedded systems, many consumer game consoles contain adaptations of general-purpose operating systems and may contain some of the same vulnerabilities. The increase in network-based *online gaming* has provided an opening for these devices to be exploited. However, it also allows their operating systems to be regularly patched by the vendors.

- *Smartphones.* A *feature phone* is a traditional cellular telephone that includes a limited number of features, such as a camera, an MP3 music player, and ability to send and receive short message service (SMS) text messages. A **smartphone** has all the tools that a feature phone has but also includes an operating system that allows it to run third-party applications (apps). Because it has an operating system, a smartphone offers a broader range of functionality. The two most popular versions of smartphone operating systems are Google's Android and Apple's iOS. Like other operating systems, these smartphone operating systems have vulnerabilities that attackers can exploit.

- *Mainframes.* Very large computing systems that have significant processing capabilities are called **mainframe** systems. These types of systems were first introduced more than 60 years ago. Because of their high cost they are not replaced frequently. The operating systems of older mainframes may lack the ability to be updated in a timely fashion by the vendor.

- *In-vehicle computer systems.* As automobiles become more sophisticated, the number of functions that are controlled by microprocessors continues to increase. Researchers have demonstrated that these in-vehicle computer systems often can be easily manipulated. All cars since 1996 have an On-Board Diagnostics II (OBD-II) connector that is used for troubleshooting. An attacker could plug into the OBD-II connector and change specific vehicle emission settings or erase information captured in an accident that showed the driver was at fault. More treacherous attacks could even control the air bags or antilock braking system (ABS). Other attacks exploit a car's built-in cellular services that provide safety and navigational assistance. An attacker could even use a Trojan in a digital music file played on the car's CD to access the car's systems and turn off the engine, lock the doors, turn off the brakes, and change the odometer readings.

- *SCADA*. Large-scale industrial-control systems are called **SCADA (supervisory control and data acquisition)**. SCADA can be found in military installations, oil pipeline control systems, manufacturing environments, and nuclear power plants. These systems are increasingly becoming the targets of attackers, often because they lack basic security features. One recent attack on a nuclear power plant was introduced to these industrial networks through infected USB flash drives and attempted to take over SCADA computers to give the machinery attached to the SCADA systems new instructions.

Table 4-5 lists some basic defense methods against attacks directed toward devices in static environments.

Method	Description
Network segmentation	Keep devices on their own network separated from the regular network.
Security layers	Build security in layers around the device.
Application firewalls	When feasible, install application firewalls on the device's operating system.
Manual updates	Provide a means for manual software updates when automated updates cannot be used.
Firmware version control	Develop a policy that keeps track of updates to firmware.
Control redundancy and diversity	Keep the operating system code as basic as possible to limit overlapping or unnecessary features.

Table 4-5   **Static environment defense methods**

Application Security

4.1 Explain the importance of application security controls and techniques.

4.5 Compare and contrast alternative methods to mitigate security risks in static environments.

Along with securing the operating system software on hosts and in static environments, there is equally a need to protect the applications that run on the devices. Application security includes application development security and application hardening and patch management.

Application Development Security

Developing, integrating, and updating secure applications has grown increasingly important. As operating systems have become more focused on security and their vendors provide mature patch management systems, attackers are turning their attention to application software that runs on hosts. It is important that security for these applications be considered throughout all phases of the software life cycle, which includes the design, development, testing, deployment, and maintenance of the applications.

Application development security involves application configuration baselines and secure coding concepts.

Application Configuration Baselines As with operating system baselines, standard environment settings in application development can establish a secure baseline. This baseline becomes the foundation on which applications are designed to function in a secure manner within the targeted environment. The standardized environments should include each development system, build system, and test system. Standardization itself must include the system configuration and network configuration.

Secure Coding Concepts Another important step is to implement secure coding concepts and standards. These standards help provide several benefits to the development process:

- Coding standards can help increase the consistency, reliability, and security of applications by ensuring that common programming structures and tasks are handled by similar methods and reducing the occurrence of common logic errors. Coding standards can even cover the use of white-space characters, variable-naming conventions, function-naming conventions, and comment styles.

- Coding standards also allow developers to quickly understand and work with code that has been developed by various members of a development team.

- Coding standards are useful in the code review process as well as in situations where a team member leaves and duties must be assigned to another team member.

Despite their benefits, secure coding concepts still are not being used as they should. One study revealed that 26 percent of the respondents had little or no secure software development processes, and if they did, 59 percent did not follow those processes rigorously.[3]

An example of a coding standard is to use **wrapper functions** to write error-checking routines for preexisting system functions. A wrapper function is a substitute for a regular function that is used in testing. For example, a wrapper function error routine can be written and rigorously tested. Then all calls to the original function itself can be replaced with calls to the wrapper. This allows the programmer to focus on the primary purpose of the code module.

Wrapper functions are often used in securing static environments.

Secure coding concepts include proper error and exception handling and input validation.

Error and Exception Handling One of the important steps in developing secure applications is to account for **errors** (also called **exceptions**), which are faults in a program that occur while the application is running. For example, if a user is asked to provide the name of a file to the application, a number of different conditions can cause an error:

- The user forgets to enter the filename.
- The user enters the name of a file that does not exist.
- The file is locked by another operation and cannot be opened.
- The filename is misspelled.

Each of these actions may cause an error, yet the response to the user should be based on the specific error. It is important that the application be coded in such a way that each error is "caught" and effectively handled. Improper error handling in an application can lead to application failure or, worse, the application entering an insecure state. The following items may indicate potential error-handling issues:

- Failure to check return codes or handle exceptions
- Improper checking of exceptions or return codes
- Handling all return codes or exceptions in the same manner
- Error information that divulges potentially sensitive data

 Improper error handling can be a target of a direct attack if attackers can discover a method of repeatedly causing the application to fail.

One approach to trap errors while testing the application code is to use **fuzz testing** (**fuzzing**). This is a software testing technique that deliberately provides invalid, unexpected, or random data as inputs to a computer program. The program is then monitored to ensure that all errors are trapped. Fuzzing, which is usually done through automated programs, is commonly used to test for security problems in software or computer systems.

Input Validation One specific type of error handling is verifying responses that the user makes to the application. Although these responses could cause the program to abort, they also can be used to inject commands. Improper verification is the cause of several types of attacks, such as cross-site scripting (XSS), SQL injection, and XML injection.

A similar type of attack is a **cross-site request forgery** (**XSRF**); this attack uses the user's web browser settings to impersonate the user. When a web browser receives a request from a web application server, it automatically includes any credentials associated with the site (the IP address, the user's session cookie, any basic authentication credentials, etc.) with the requests. If a user is currently authenticated on a website and is then tricked into loading another webpage, the new page inherits the identity and privileges of the victim to perform an undesired function on the victim's behalf, such as changing the victim's email address and password or making an online purchase.

To prevent cross-site scripting, the program should trap for these user responses. **Input validation** that verified a user's input to an application traditionally has been used for handling untrusted data. However, input validation is not considered the best defense against injection attacks. First, input validation is typically performed after the data is entered by the user but before the destination is known. That means that it is not possible to know which characters could be significantly harmful. Second, some applications must allow potentially harmful characters as input. Although a single apostrophe (') can be used in an XSS attack, it must be permitted when entering a name like *Shawn O'Malley*. A preferred method for trapping user responses is *escaping* (*output encoding*). This technique is used to ensure that characters are treated as data, not as characters that are relevant to the application (such as SQL).

Whereas input validation generally uses the server to perform the validation (**server-side validation**), it is possible to have the client perform the validation (**client-side validation**). In client-side validation all input validations and error recovery procedures are performed by the user's web browser. Although this method does not require server-side scripting, nevertheless it is possible for users to alter or even bypass completely the client-side validation.

Instead of input validation, a more drastic approach to preventing SQL injection attacks is to avoid using SQL relational databases altogether. As an alternative, new nonrelational databases that are better tuned for accessing large data sets, known as **NoSQL**, may be used. The hot debate over which database technology is better is often referred to as the **NoSQL databases vs. SQL database** argument. Due to its less complex nature, NoSQL may have some security advantages over SQL; however, both databases must still be properly implemented and protected against attackers.

Application Hardening and Patch Management

Application hardening is intended to prevent attackers from exploiting vulnerabilities in software applications. In application software these vulnerabilities are often exposed by a failure to properly check the input data entering into the application. Table 4-6 lists different attacks that can be launched using vulnerabilities in applications. It is as important to harden applications as it is to harden the OS.

Attack	Description	Defense
Executable files attack	Trick the vulnerable application into modifying or creating executable files on the system.	Prevent the application from creating or modifying executable files for its proper function.
System tampering	Use the vulnerable application to modify special sensitive areas of the operating system (Microsoft Windows Registry keys, system startup files, etc.) and take advantage of those modifications.	Do not allow applications to modify special areas of the OS.
Process spawning control	Trick the vulnerable application into spawning executable files on the system.	Take away the process spawning ability from the application.

Table 4-6   **Attacks based on application vulnerabilities**

Until recently, application patch management was rare. Because few software companies had implemented patch management systems to deliver updates, users generally were left "in the dark" regarding application software patches or where to acquire them. And it was not always clear that a new version of software addressed a vulnerability or just contained new features. However, more application patch management systems are being developed to patch vulnerabilities.

In 2010, the software vendor Secunia spearheaded an effort to create a common protocol that all application software vendors could use to distribute patches faster. However, no agreement among the vendors could be reached.

Securing Data

2.3 Given a scenario, implement appropriate risk mitigation strategies.

4.4 Implement the appropriate controls to ensure data security.

4

The concept of work has changed dramatically over the last 30 years. Instead of driving to the office for a nine-to-five workday to meet with colleagues and create reports at a desk, work today most likely involves electronic collaboration using mobile technologies—smartphones, tablets, and laptops—over wireless data networks from virtually any location. This means that data, once restricted to papers in the office filing cabinet, now flows freely both in and out of organizations between employees, customers, contractors, and business partners around the world. In addition, the volume of sensitive data has grown exponentially. **Big Data** refers to a collection of data sets so large and complex that it becomes difficult to process using on-hand database management tools or traditional data processing applications. How can all of this data flowing in and out of the organization be protected so that it does not fall into the wrong hands?

One means of securing data is through **data loss prevention (DLP)**. DLP is a system of security tools that is used to recognize and identify data that is critical to the organization and ensure that it is protected. This protection involves monitoring who is using the data and how it is being accessed. DLP's goal is to protect data from any unauthorized users.

DLP is sometimes called Data Leak Prevention.

DLP examines data as it resides in any of three states:

- *Data in-use*. **Data in-use** is data actions being performed by "endpoint devices," such as creating a report from a desktop computer.
- *Data in-transit*. Actions that transmit the data across a network, like an email sent across the Internet, are called **data in-transit**.
- *Data at-rest*. **Data at-rest** is data that is stored on electronic media.

Data that is considered critical to the organization or needs to be confidential can be tagged as such through DLP. A user who then attempts to access the data to disclose it to another unauthorized user will be prevented from doing so.

Most DLP systems use *content inspection*. Content inspection is defined as a security analysis of the transaction within its approved context. Content inspection looks at not only the security level of the data, but also who is requesting it, where the data is stored, when it was requested, and where it is going. DLP systems also can use *index matching*. Documents that have been identified as needing protection, such as the program source code for a new software application, are analyzed by the DLP system and complex computations are conducted based on the analysis. Thereafter, if even a small part of that document is leaked, the DLP system can recognize the snippet as being from a protected document.

Index matching is so sensitive that even if a handful of lines of source code from 10,000 lines of protected code are entered into an email message, the DLP system will identify it.

DLP begins with an administrator creating DLP rules based on the data (what is to be examined) and the policy (what to check for). DLPs can be configured to look for specific data (such as Social Security and credit card numbers), lines of computer software source code, words in a sequence (to prevent a report from leaving the network), maximum file sizes, and file types. Because it can be difficult to distinguish a Social Security number from a mistyped telephone number or a nine-digit online order number, DLP can use *fingerprinting* to more closely identify important data. A fingerprint may consist of a Social Security number along with a name to trigger an alarm. In addition, whitelists and blacklists can be created to prevent specific files from being scanned. These rules are then loaded into a DLP server.

Because the data can be leaked by different means, there are three types of DLP sensors:

- *DLP network sensors.* DLP network sensors are installed on the perimeter of the network to protect data in-transit by monitoring all network traffic. This includes monitoring email, instant messaging, social media interactions, and other web applications. DLP network sensors can even monitor multiple protocols (including HTTP, SMTP, POP, IMAP, FTP, and Telnet).

- *DLP storage sensors.* Sensors on network storage devices are designed to protect data at-rest. These sensors monitor the devices to ensure that the files on the hard drives that store sensitive data are encrypted. They also scan the drives to determine where specific data is stored.

- *DLP agent sensors.* These sensors are installed on each host device (desktop, laptop, tablet, etc.) and protect data in-use. The DLP agent sensors watch for actions such as printing, copying to a USB flash drive, and burning to a CD or DVD. They can also read inside compressed (ZIP) files and binary files (such as older Microsoft Office non-XML files).

One of the drawbacks of DLP agent sensors is that the host device must communicate with the DLP server, which can result in performance issues and may not scale well when more devices are added. To limit the performance impact, DLP agent sensors are "event driven" so that the sensor monitors only for specific user actions, such as copying a file to a USB device or printing a document.

A typical DLP architecture is shown in Figure 4-9.

When a policy violation is detected by the DLP agent, it is reported back to the DLP server. Different actions can then be taken. The information can simply be sent to the server, as shown in Figure 4-10, a screenshot from Google's OpenDLP application. Other actions can include blocking the data, redirecting it to an individual who can examine the request, quarantining the data until later, or alerting a supervisor of the request.

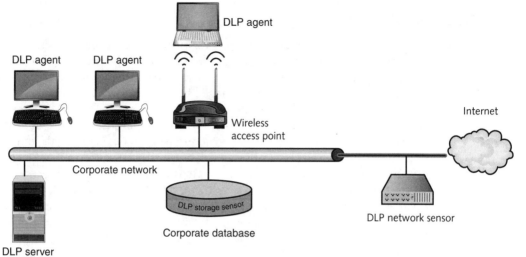

Figure 4-9   DLP architecture

Figure 4-10   DLP report
Source: Google OpenDLP © Andrew Gavin

Chapter Summary

- A security control is any device or process that is used to reduce risk. There are two levels of security controls: administrative controls are the processes for developing and ensuring that policies and procedures are carried out, while technical controls are those that are carried out or managed by devices. Activity phase controls are subtypes of these controls, including deterrent, preventive, detective, compensating, and corrective controls. Many controls involve the physical security of host devices. Fencing is usually a tall, permanent structure to keep out individuals and secure a restricted area. Like fencing, a barricade is generally designed to block the passage of traffic; however, barricades are most often used for directing large crowds or restricting vehicular traffic and generally are not designed to keep out individuals. Whereas barriers act as passive devices to restrict access, human guards are considered active security elements. Some guards are responsible for monitoring activity that is captured by a video camera. Motion detection is determining an object's change in position in relation to its surroundings. This movement usually generates an audible alarm to warn a guard of an intruder.

- Hardware locks for doors are important to protect equipment. The standard keyed entry lock is the most common type of door lock for keeping out intruders, but it provides minimal security. For rooms that require enhanced security, a lever coupled with a deadbolt lock, which extends a solid metal bar into the door frame for extra security, is often used. Because of the difficulties in managing keys for hundreds or thousands of users, an alternative to a key lock is a more sophisticated door access system using a cipher lock. Another option, instead of using a key or entering a code to open a door, is to use a proximity reader that detects an object (sometimes called a physical token) the user carries for identification. A mantrap is designed to separate a nonsecured area from a secured area by controlling two interlocking doors to a small room. A protected distribution system (PDS) is a system of cable conduits that are used to protect classified information that is being transmitted between two highly sensitive areas.

- Hardware security is physical security that involves protecting the hardware of the host system, particularly portable laptops and tablet computers that can easily be stolen. A cable lock can be inserted into a slot in the device and rotated so that cable lock is secured to the device, while a cable connected to the lock can then be secured to a desk or chair. Laptops and other portable devices can be placed in a safe or a locking cabinet, which is a ruggedized steel box with a lock.

- In addition to protecting the hardware, the operating system software that runs on the host also must be protected. The security of an operating system can be enhanced through the proper configuration of its built-in security features. This security starts with an organization first determining what actions must be taken to create and maintain a secure environment. That information is recorded in a formal security policy. Once the security policy has been created, a security baseline for the host is established. A baseline is the standard or checklist against which systems can be evaluated and audited for their security posture. After the baseline is established, the security configuration settings on the host operating system can be properly configured.

4

- Modern operating systems have hundreds of different security settings that can be manipulated to conform to the baseline. Instead of manually creating the same security configuration on each computer, tools can be used to automate the process. To address the vulnerabilities in operating systems that are uncovered after the software has been released, software vendors usually deploy a software "fix," generally known as a security patch. Instead of managing the different security options on an operating system, in some cases it is necessary to instead tighten security during the design and coding of the OS. This is called OS hardening, and an operating system that has been designed in this way to be secure is a trusted OS.

- Operating system and additional third-party antimalware software packages can provide added security. Antivirus (AV) software can examine a computer for any infections as well as monitor computer activity and scan new documents that might contain a virus. Beyond being annoying and disruptive, spam can pose a serious security risk. Several methods for preventing spam from reaching the user exist. A popup blocker can be either a separate program or a feature incorporated within a browser. As a separate program, popup blockers are often part of a package known as antispyware. A firewall is designed to prevent malicious packets from entering or leaving a network. A host-based application software firewall runs as a program on a local system to protect it against attacks.

- As the number of devices with microprocessors grows exponentially, these are also becoming ripe targets for attackers. These types of devices, including embedded systems, game consoles, smartphones, mainframes, in-vehicle computer systems, and supervisory control and data acquisition (SCADA), are sometimes called a static environment. There are basic defense methods against attacks directed toward devices in static environments, such as network segmentation, security layers, application firewalls, manual updates, firmware version control, and controlling redundancy and diversity.

- Protecting the applications that run on the hardware is also an important security step. This involves creating application configuration baselines and implementing secure coding concepts. One of the important steps in developing secure applications is to account for errors while the application is executing. To trap for user responses, input validation has traditionally been used for handling untrusted data. However, input validation is not considered the best defense against injection attacks. A preferred method for validating user responses is escaping (output encoding), which is a technique used to ensure that characters are treated as data, not as characters that are relevant to the application.

- One means of securing data is through data loss prevention (DLP). DLP is a system that can identify critical data, monitor how it is being accessed, and protect it from unauthorized parties. DLP works through content inspection, which is use of centralized management to perform a security analysis of the transaction within its approved context (examining who requested it, what the data is, what medium it is stored on, when it was requested, its destination, etc.). DLP can also use index matching. Documents that have been identified as needing protection, such as the program source code for a new software application, are analyzed by the DLP system, and complex computations are conducted based on the analysis.

Key Terms

access list   A paper or electronic record of individuals who have permission to enter a secure area, the time that they entered, and the time they left the area.

activity phase controls   Subtypes of security controls, classified as deterrent, preventive, detective, compensation, or corrective.

administrative control   Process for developing and ensuring that policies and procedures are carried out, specifying actions that users may do, must do, or cannot do.

alarm   An audible sound to warn a guard of an intruder.

antispyware   Software that helps prevent computers from becoming infected by different types of spyware.

antivirus (AV)   Software that can examine a computer for any infections as well as monitor computer activity and scan new documents that might contain a virus.

barricade   A structure designed to block the passage of traffic.

Bayesian filtering   Spam filtering software that analyzes every word in an email and determines how frequently a word occurs in order to determine if it is spam.

Big Data   A collection of data sets so large and complex that it becomes difficult to process using on-hand database management tools or traditional data processing applications.

blacklist   Permitting everything unless it appears on the list; a list of nonapproved senders.

cable lock   A device that can be inserted into the security slot of a portable device and rotated so that the cable lock is secured to the device to prevent it from being stolen.

client-side validation   Having the client web browser perform all validations and error recovery procedures.

closed circuit television (CCTV)   Video cameras and receivers used for surveillance in areas that require security monitoring.

compensating control   Control that provides an alternative to normal controls that for some reason cannot be used.

corrective control   Control that is intended to mitigate or lessen the damage caused by an incident.

cross-site request forgery (XSRF)   An attack that uses the user's web browser settings to impersonate the user.

data at-rest   Data that is stored on electronic media.

data in-transit   Data that is in transit across a network, such as an email sent across the Internet.

data in-use   A state of data in which actions upon it are being performed by "endpoint devices" such as printers.

data loss prevention (DLP)   A system that can identify critical data, monitor how it is being accessed, and protect it from unauthorized users.

deadbolt lock   A door lock that extends a solid metal bar into the door frame for extra security.

detective control A control that is designed to identify any threat that has reached the system.

deterrent control A control that attempts to discourage security violations before they occur.

embedded system A computer system with a dedicated function within a larger electrical or mechanical system.

errors Faults in a program that occur while the application is running. Also called *exceptions.*

exceptions See *errors.*

fencing Securing a restricted area by erecting a barrier.

firewall Hardware or software that is designed to prevent malicious packets from entering or leaving computers. Also called *packet filter.*

fuzz testing (fuzzing) A software testing technique that deliberately provides invalid, unexpected, or random data as inputs to a computer program.

guard A human who is an active security element.

host-based application firewall A firewall that runs as a program on a local system.

hotfix Software that addresses a specific customer situation and often may not be distributed outside that customer's organization.

input validation Verifying a user's input to an application.

lighting Lights that illuminate an area so that it can be viewed after dark.

locking cabinet A ruggedized steel box with a lock.

mainframe A very large computing system that has significant processing capabilities.

mantrap A device that monitors and controls two interlocking doors to a small room (a vestibule), designed to separate secure and nonsecure areas.

motion detection Determining an object's change in position in relation to its surroundings.

NoSQL A nonrelational database that is better tuned for accessing large data sets.

NoSQL databases vs. SQL databases An argument regarding which database technology is superior. Also called *SQL vs. NoSQL.*

OS hardening Tightening security during the design and coding of the OS.

packet filter Hardware or software that is designed to prevent malicious packets from entering or leaving computers. Also called *firewall.*

patch A general software security update intended to cover vulnerabilities that have been discovered.

popup blocker Either a program or a feature incorporated within a browser that stops popup advertisements from appearing.

preventive controls A control that attempts to prevent the threat from coming in and reaching contact with the vulnerability.

protected distribution system (PDS) A system of cable conduits that is used to protect classified information being transmitted between two secure areas.

proximity reader A device that detects an emitted signal in order to identify the owner.

safe A ruggedized steel box with a lock.

SCADA (supervisory control and data acquisition) Large-scale, industrial-control systems.

security control Any device or process that is used to reduce risk.

security policy A document or series of documents that clearly defines the defense mechanisms an organization will employ to keep information secure.

server-side validation Having the server perform all validations and error recovery procedures.

service pack Software that is a cumulative package of all security updates plus additional features.

sign A written placard that explains a warning, such as notice that an area is restricted.

smartphone A cell phone with an operating system that allows it to run third-party applications (apps).

SQL vs. NoSQL An argument regarding which database technology is better. Also called *NoSQL databases vs. SQL databases*.

static environment Devices in which additional hardware cannot easily be added or attached.

technical controls Security controls that are carried out or managed by devices.

trusted OS An operating system that has been designed through OS hardening.

video surveillance Monitoring activity that is captured by a video camera.

whitelist Permitting nothing unless it appears on the list.

wrapper function A substitute for a regular function that is used in testing.

Review Questions

1. What type of controls are the processes for developing and ensuring that policies and procedures are carried out?

   a. technical controls

   b. active controls

   c. administrative controls

   d. policy controls

2. Which of the following is NOT an activity phase control?

   a. compensating control

   b. detective control

   c. resource control

   d. deterrent control

3. Which of the following is NOT designed to prevent individuals from entering sensitive areas but instead is intended to direct traffic flow?

    a. barricade

    b. fencing

    c. roller barrier

    d. type V controls

4. Which of the following is NOT a motion detection method?

    a. radio frequency

    b. moisture

    c. magnetism

    d. infrared

5. The residential lock most often used for keeping out intruders is the _____.

    a. encrypted key lock

    b. privacy lock

    c. passage lock

    d. keyed entry lock

6. A lock that extends a solid metal bar into the door frame for extra security is the _____.

    a. triple bar lock

    b. deadman's lock

    c. full bar lock

    d. deadbolt lock

7. Which statement about a mantrap is true?

    a. It is illegal in the U.S.

    b. It monitors and controls two interlocking doors to a room.

    c. It is a special keyed lock.

    d. It requires the use of a cipher lock.

8. Which of the following cannot be used along with fencing as a security perimeter?

    a. vapor barrier

    b. rotating spikes

    c. roller barrier

    d. anticlimb paint

4

9. A _____ can be used to secure a mobile device.

    a. mobile connector

    b. cable lock

    c. mobile chain

    d. security tab

10. Which of the following is NOT a characteristic of an alarmed carrier PDS?

    a. periodic visual inspections

    b. continuous monitoring

    c. carrier can be hidden below a floor

    d. eliminates the need to seal connections

11. Which is the first step in securing an operating system?

    a. Develop the security policy.

    b. Implement patch management.

    c. Configure operating system security and settings.

    d. Perform host software baselining.

12. A typical configuration baseline would include each of the following EXCEPT _____.

    a. changing any default settings that are insecure

    b. eliminating any unnecessary software

    c. enabling operating system security features

    d. performing a security risk assessment

13. Which of the following is NOT a Microsoft Windows setting that can be configured through a security template?

    a. Account Policies

    b. User Rights

    c. Keyboard Mapping

    d. System Services

14. _____ allows for a single configuration to be set and then deployed to many or all users.

    a. Active Directory

    b. Group Policy

    c. Snap-In Replication (SIR)

    d. Command Configuration

15. A _____ addresses a specific customer situation and often may not be distributed outside that customer's organization.

  a. rollup

  b. service pack

  c. patch

  d. hotfix

16. Which of the following is NOT an advantage to an automated patch update service?

  a. Administrators can approve or decline updates for client systems, force updates to install by a specific date, and obtain reports on what updates each computer needs.

  b. Downloading patches from a local server instead of using the vendor's online update service can save bandwidth and time because each computer does not have to connect to an external server.

  c. Users can disable or circumvent updates just as they can if their computer is configured to use the vendor's online update service.

  d. Specific types of updates that the organization does not test, such as hotfixes, can be automatically installed whenever they become available.

17. Which of these is NOT a state of data that DLP examines?

  a. data in-use

  b. data in-process

  c. data in-transit

  d. data at-rest

18. How does heuristic detection detect a virus?

  a. A virtualized environment is created and the code is executed in it.

  b. A string of bytes from the virus is compared against the suspected file.

  c. The bytes of a virus are placed in different "piles" and then used to create a profile.

  d. The virus signature file is placed in a suspended chamber before streaming to the CPU.

19. Which of these is a list of approved email senders?

  a. blacklist

  b. whitelist

  c. greylist

  d. greenlist

20. Which statement about data loss prevention (DLP) is NOT true?

    a. It can only protect data while it is on the user's personal computer.

    b. It can scan data on a DVD.

    c. It can read inside compressed files.

    d. A policy violation can generate a report or block the data.

Hands-On Projects

NOTE If you are concerned about installing any of the software in these projects on your regular computer, you can instead install the software in the Windows virtual machine created in the Chapter 1 Hands-On Projects 1-3 and 1-4. Software installed within the virtual machine will not impact the host computer.

Project 4-1: Test Antivirus Software

What happens when antivirus software detects a virus? In this project you will download a virus test file to determine how your AV software reacts. The file downloaded is not a virus but is designed to appear to an antivirus scanner as if it were a virus.

NOTE You need to have antivirus software installed and running on your computer to perform this project.

1. Open your web browser and enter the URL **www.eicar.org/86-0 -Intended-use.html**

NOTE The location of content on the Internet may change without warning. If you are no longer able to access the program through the above URL, use a search engine to search for "EICAR AntiVirus Test File".

2. Read the "INTENDED USE" information.

3. Click **DOWNLOAD**.

4. Click the file **eicar.com,** which contains a fake virus. A dialog box may open that asks if you want to download the file. Wait to see what happens. What does your antivirus software do? Close your antivirus message and if necessary click **Cancel** to stop the download procedure.

5. Now click **eicar_com.zip.** This file contains a fake virus inside a compressed (ZIP) file. What happened? Close your antivirus message and, if necessary, click **Cancel** to stop the download procedure.

If your antivirus software did not prevent you from accessing the eicar_com.zip file, when the File Download dialog box appeared, click **Save** and download the file to your desktop or another location designated by your instructor. When the download is complete, navigate to the folder that contains the file and right-click it. Then, click **Scan for viruses** on the shortcut menu (your menu command might be slightly different). What happened after the scan?

6. Click **eicarcom2.zip**. This file has a double-compressed ZIP file with a fake virus. What happened? Close your antivirus message and, if necessary, click **Cancel** to stop the download procedure.

7. If necessary, erase any files that were saved to your computer.

8. Close all windows.

Project 4-2: Setting Windows Local Security Policy

The Local Group Policy Editor is a Microsoft Management Console (MMC) snap-in that gives a single user interface through which all the Computer Configuration and User Configuration settings of Local Group Policy objects can be managed. The Local Security Policy settings are among the security settings contained in the Local Group Policy Editor. An administrator can use these to set policies that are applied to the computer. In this project, you will view and change local security policy settings.

You will need to be an administrator to open the Local Group Policy Editor.

1. Click **Start**.

2. Type **secpol.msc** into the Search box and then click **secpol**.

You may be prompted at this point for an administrator password or confirmation.

3. First create a policy regarding passwords. Expand **Account Policies** in the left pane and then expand **Password Policy**.

4. Double-click **Enforce password history** in the right pane. This setting defines how many previously used passwords Windows will record. This prevents users from "recycling" old passwords.

5. Change **passwords remembered** to 4.

6. Click **OK**.

7. Double-click **Maximum password age** in the right pane. The default value is 42, meaning that a user must change his password after 42 days.

8. Change **days** to 30.

9. Click **OK**.

10. Double-click **Minimum password length** in the right pane. The default value is a length of 8 characters.

11. Change **characters** to **10**.

12. Click **OK**.

13. Double-click **Password must meet complexity requirements** in the right pane. This setting forces a password to include at least two opposite case letters, a number, and a special character (such as a punctuation mark).

14. Click **Enabled**.

15. Click **OK**.

16. Double-click **Store passwords using reversible encryption** in the right pane. Because passwords should be stored in an encrypted format this setting should not be enabled.

17. If necessary, click **Disabled**.

18. Click **OK**.

19. In the left pane, click **Account lockout policy**.

20. Double-click **Account lockout threshold** in the right pane. This is the number of times that a user can enter an incorrect password before Windows will lock the account from being accessed. (This prevents an attacker from attempting to guess the password with unlimited attempts.)

21. Change **invalid login attempts** to **5**.

22. Click **OK**.

23. Note that the Local Security Policy suggests changes to the **Account lockout duration** and the **Reset account lockout counter after** values to 30 minutes.

24. Click **OK**.

25. Expand **Local Policies** in the left pane and then click **Audit Policy**.

26. Double-click **Audit account logon events**.

27. Check both **Success** and **Failure**.

28. Click **OK**.

29. Right-click **Security Settings** in the left pane.

30. Click **Reload** to have these policies applied.

31. Close all windows.

Project 4-3: Viewing Windows Firewall Settings

In this project, you will view the settings on Windows Firewall.

1. Click **Start** and then click **Control Panel**.

2. Click **System and Security**, then **Windows Firewall**.

3. In the left pane, click **Change notification settings**. Notice that you can either block all incoming connections or be notified when Windows Firewall blocks a program at the firewall. What would be the difference? Which setting is more secure?

4. Now click **Turn off Windows Firewall (not recommended)** (there may be multiple instances of this setting depending on your network).

5. Click **OK**. What warnings appear? Are these sufficient to alert a user?

6. In the left pane, click **Change notification settings**. Click **Turn on Windows Firewall** (there may be multiple instances of this setting depending on your network).

7. Click **OK**.

8. In the left pane, click **Advanced Settings**.

9. Click **Inbound Rules**.

10. Double-click a rule to open the dialog box associated with that rule. Click through the tabs and notice the control that can be configured on firewall rules. Click **Cancel**.

11. Now create a rule that will open a specific port on the computer so that a web server will run and traffic will go through the firewall. Click **New Rule ...** in the right pane to open the New Inbound Rule Wizard dialog box.

12. Click **Port** as the rule type and then click **Next**.

13. If necessary select **TCP** as the protocol.

14. Enter **80** in the **Specific local ports** text box. Click **Next**.

You can open a single port by typing its number, or multiple ports by separating them with a comma, or a port range (such as 80–86).

15. You are asked what to do when the firewall sees inbound traffic on TCP Port 80. Because you want this traffic to reach your web server, click **Allow the connection**.

16. Click **Next**.

17. You are then asked the type of connections to which this rule will apply. To run a web server only for the local computers in your home network, the *Private* option would be selected while deselecting *Public* and *Domain*. For this project, deselect **Private** and **Domain**.

18. Click **Next**.

19. Enter the rule name **Web Server Port 80**.

20. To implement this rule click **Finish**, otherwise click **Cancel**.

21. Close all windows.

Project 4-4: Analyze Files and URLs for Viruses Using VirusTotal

VirusTotal, a subsidiary of Google, is a free online service that analyzes files and URLs in order to identify potential malware. VirusTotal scans and detects any type of binary content, including a Windows executable program, Android, PDFs, and images. VirusTotal is designed to provide a "second opinion" on a file or URL that may have been flagged as suspicious by other AV software. In this project, you will use VirusTotal to scan a file and a URL.

1. Use Microsoft Word to create a document that contains the above paragraph about VirusTotal. Save the document as **VirusTotal.docx**.

2. Now save this document as a PDF. Click **File** and **Save As**.

3. Under **Save as type:** select **PDF (*.pdf)**.

4. Save this file as **YourName-VirusTotal.pdf**.

5. Exit Word.

6. Open your web browser and enter the URL **www.virustotal.com**

The location of content on the Internet may change without warning. If you are no longer able to access the program through the above URL, use a search engine to search for "VirusTotal".

7. If necessary click the **File** tab.

8. Click **Choose File**.

9. Navigate to the location of **YourName-VirusTotal.pdf** and click **Open**.

10. Click **Scan it!**

11. If the **File already analyzed** dialog box opens, click **Reanalyse**.

12. Wait until the analysis is completed.

13. Scroll through the list of AV vendors that have been polled regarding this file. A green checkmark means no malware was detected.

14. Click the **File detail** tab and read through the analysis.

15. Use your browser's back button to return to the VirusTotal home page.

16. Click **URL**.

17. Enter the URL of your school, place of employment, or other site with which you are familiar.

18. Click **Scan it!** If the **URL already analyzed** dialog box opens, click **Reanalyse**.

19. Wait until the analysis is completed.

20. Scroll through the list of vendor analysis. Do any of these sites indicate **Unrate site** or **Malware site**?

21. Click **Additional information**.

22. How could VirusTotal be useful to users? How could it be useful to security researchers? However, could it also be used by attackers to test their own malware before distributing it to ensure that it does not trigger an AV alert? What should be the protections against this?

23. Close all windows.

Case Projects

CASE PROJECTS

Case Project 4-1: Antivirus Comparison

Select four antivirus products, one of which is a free product, and compare their features. Create a table that lists the features. How do they compare with the AV software you currently use? Which would you recommend to others? Why? Create a report on your research.

Case Project 4-2: Analysis of Physical Security

How secure are the host computers at your school or workplace? Perform an analysis of the physical security to protect these devices. Make note of any hardware locks, proximity readers, video surveillance, fencing, etc. Then look at the hardware security around the hosts themselves. What are the strengths? What are the weaknesses? What recommendations would you make for improving host security? Write a one-page paper on your analysis.

Case Project 4-3: Application Patch Management

Select three applications (not operating systems) that you frequently use. How does each of them address patch management? Visit their websites to determine what facilities they have to alert users to new vulnerabilities. Then look at three competing products (for example, if you are examining Microsoft Office, look at OpenOffice) and evaluate their patch management system. What did you discover? Are the patch management systems adequate? Write a one-page paper on your findings.

Case Project 4-4: Open Source Data Loss Prevention

An open source product called opendlp is a free open data loss prevention (DLP) system for monitoring how critical data is accessed. Visit the website **code.google.com/p/opendlp/** and read about opendlp. Then use the Internet to identify three commercial DLP products. Make a list of the features, architecture, strengths, weaknesses, etc. of all of these products. Then determine if each of these products could be used by an attacker to identify vulnerabilities in an organization's data protection. Create a table comparing the products and an analysis of your research.

Case Project 4-5: Game Console Risks

Attacks against game consoles are rapidly increasing. Use the Internet to research attacks on game consoles. How are these attacks carried out? How many attacks have been conducted? What can a "gamer" do to protect herself from these attacks? Write a one-page paper on your findings.

Case Project 4-6: Bay Pointe Security Consulting

Bay Pointe Security Consulting (BPSC) provides security consulting services to a wide range of businesses, individuals, schools, and organizations. BPSC has hired you as a technology student to help them with a new project and provide real-world experience to students who are interested in the security field.

Pack 'n Go (PnG) offers to customers large portable storage units delivered to their home that the customers pack with their personal items. PnG then transports the units locally or over long distance to the end destination. Recently PnG's customer information system, which allows customers to reserve a portable storage unit, was compromised by an attacker. It appears that the attack was the result of a PnG employee's home computer that was successfully attacked and then was used to attack the PnG computers. The result was that storage units were delivered to the driveways of homes where the customers never requested them, which resulted in a large amount of unfavorable media attention. Pack 'n Go has asked BPSC to make a presentation to the staff about securing their staff's home computers, and BPSC has asked you to help the company train its staff on the basics of host security.

1. Create a PowerPoint presentation for the PnG staff about the basic steps in securing a host system, why it is important, what antimalware software should be considered, etc. Because the staff does not have an IT background, the presentation cannot be too technical in nature. Your presentation should contain at least 10 slides.

2. After the presentation, one of PnG's IT staff has contacted you. She has been reading about DLP systems in a trade magazine and wants to know if PnG should look into purchasing a system. Create a memo to PnG's IT department about DLP, explaining what its features are and whether it would be beneficial to the company.

Case Project 4-7: Community Site Activity

The Information Security Community Site is an online companion to this textbook. It contains a wide variety of tools, information, discussion boards, and other features to assist learners. Go to **community.cengage.com/infosec**. Click JOIN THE COMMUNITY and use the login name and password that you created in Chapter 1. Visit the **Discussions** section, and then read the following case study.

Basically there are three types of televisions today. A basic TV uses the Digital Video Broadcasting (DVB) protocol for receiving the cable signal, but the TV itself is relatively "dumb." A media center TV has the basic components of a computer: processor, memory, hard disk, and some type of operating system. These TVs provide wired or wireless home network connections along with USB ports and memory card readers. They also may support other TCP/IP protocols like DHCP, HTTP, and FTP to receive media content or firmware upgrades. At the top end of the TV scale are the newer smart TVs. These Internet-enabled devices are really specialized computers running a version of Linux or Windows with Internet connectivity and a web browser to surf the Web. Users can even download and install apps or widgets and play multiuser games in real time with other users around the world.

Reports by security researchers now show how vulnerable these TVs can be. A set of fuzz testing tools was used to test different TVs from different vendors. What they found was that each of these TVs failed multiple tests and was vulnerable to a variety of attacks, such as a denial of service (DoS) attack against a media center or smart TV to cause it to crash. In addition, malware can be installed that turns the TV into a zombie that attacks other computers and TVs or turns on the cameras and microphones of the attached game players to spy on users. Other malware can steal the credit card numbers or the passwords used to pay and access on-demand streaming services that are stored on the TVs. And this malware can easily be transported to other computers through the home network or by tricking the user through social engineering to insert a USB flash drive into the TV, which is then carried to other devices.

What do you think? Who should be responsible for protecting smart TVs? The customer or the vendor? Should the vendor send out regular patch updates for security purposes? What if vendors were to charge for this feature? Should users be given the option to pay? Or should all vendors be required to keep these TVs protected? Enter your answers on the Community Site discussion board.

References

1. "Information Innovation Office," *DARPA*, accessed Jan. 24, 2014, www.darpa.mil/Our_Work/I2O/Programs/Crowd_Sourced_Formal_Verification_(CSFV).aspx.

2. Summers, Nick, "ATMs lurch into a new century," *Bloomberg Businessweek*, Jan 20–26, 2014, pp. 37–38.

3. Rotibi, Bola, "Failure to invest in secure software delivery puts businesses at risk," *Creative Intellect Consulting*, Feb. 21, 2011, retrieved Mar. 25, 2011, www.creativeintellectuk.com/?p=212.

## part III

Cryptography

This part introduces you to an essential element of modern network security: cryptography (encrypting and decrypting data). Chapter 5 defines cryptography, illustrates its basic concepts, and shows how it is implemented through both software and hardware. Chapter 6 continues with more advanced cryptography topics such as digital certificates, public key infrastructure (PKI), and transport encryption protocols.

## chapter 5

Basic Cryptography

After completing this chapter, you should be able to do the following:

- Define cryptography
- Describe hash, symmetric, and asymmetric cryptographic algorithms
- List the various ways in which cryptography is used

Today's Attacks and Defenses

With today's super-fast computers and the advancements in cryptography it would seem that an encrypted message dating back 70 years could easily be broken. However, that proved not to be the case in this fascinating incident.

In 1982 David and Anne Martin were renovating a fireplace that had been sealed off for many years in their 17th-century house in the village of Bletchingley, England. In the chimney, the Martins discovered the remains of a carrier pigeon with a small scarlet capsule attached to its leg. The red color of the capsule marked the bird as a military carrier pigeon for the Allied Forces in World War II. Inside the capsule was a message written in code. There were 27 groups of five letters or numbers, on thin paper the size of a cigarette paper. The message read:

AOAKN HVPKD FNFJW YIDDC RQXSR DJHFP GOVFN MIAPX PABUZ WYYNP
CMPNW HJRZH NLXKG MEMKK ONOIB AKEEQ WAOTA RBQRH DJOFM
TPZEH LKXGH RGGHT JRZCQ FNKTQ KLDTS FQIRW AOAKN 27 1525/6

At the bottom of the coded message were two items that were not in code: "Number of Copies Sent: Two" and "Sender: Serjeant [sic] W. Stot." Additional sets of numbers (NURP 40 TW194 and NURP 37 DK 76) probably indicated the military number of the two birds who carried the message.

The Martins contacted several British government authorities about their find, but at the time there was no interest in the bird's message. However, in 2012, Bletchley Park, which served as the headquarters of British Intelligence code breakers during World War II and is now a museum, took an interest in the message. It turns out this message may have been ultra-secret. First, although Bletchley Park (only five miles from the Martin's house) used carrier pigeons during World War II, none of its official messages were sent in code; they were all written in longhand. Second, messages were never carried by more than one bird. Evidently this bird's message may have been part of a top-secret program.

In late 2012 the British government's Government Communications Headquarters, which is responsible for code breaking, examined the encrypted message. After top government code breakers spent months using super-fast computers to attempt to break the code, they finally announced that the code could not be cracked (a few amateur sleuths have claimed to have deciphered the message, but these claims have proved to be false).

Why is it so tough to break this code? The reason is that the code was written using a one-time pad, or OTP. An OTP uses as a key a random set of letters that only the sender and recipient know. If an OTP is truly random, is used only one time, and

(continued)

is kept secret by the sender and receiver, it can be virtually impossible to crack. That seems to be the case in this incident.

We may never know what message that pigeon 40TW194 was carrying. Yet, as a Government Communications Headquarters spokesperson said, "It is a tribute to the skills of the wartime code makers that, despite working under severe pressure, they devised a code that was undecipherable both then and now."[1]

Consider an attorney who wants to protect important documents stored at his office. The attorney may erect a fence surrounding his property, install strong door locks, and place cameras over the doors in order to deter thieves. Yet, as important as these defenses are, they nevertheless could be breached, and in some cases rather easily. For the attorney to securely safeguard those documents, he would need to store them in a safe that is protected by a combination lock as a second line of defense. Even if thieves were able to climb over the fence, break the door locks, and circumvent the cameras to enter the office, the intruders then would have to break the code to the combination lock before reaching the documents. This would require a much higher level of both time and expertise, and generally would defeat all but the most sophisticated and determined thieves.

In information security this same approach is used to protect data. Physical and technical security, such as motion detection devices and firewalls, are important in keeping out data thieves. Yet, for high-value data that must be fully protected, a second level of protection also should be used: encryption. This means that even if attackers penetrate the host and reach the data, they still must uncover the key to unlock the encrypted contents, a virtually impossible task if the encryptions are properly applied. And as more data today is taken off-premises by employees to be used in the field or at home, it becomes increasingly important to protect this mobile data with encryption.

In this chapter, you will learn how encryption can be used to protect data. You will first learn what cryptography is and how it can be used for protection. Then you will examine how to protect data using three common types of encryption algorithms: hashing, symmetric encryption, and asymmetric encryption. Finally, you see how to use cryptography on files and disks to keep data secure.

Defining Cryptography

6.1 Given a scenario, utilize general cryptography concepts.

Defining cryptography involves understanding what it is and what it can do. It also involves understanding how cryptography can be used as a security tool to protect data.

What Is Cryptography?

"Scrambling" data so that it cannot be read is a process known as **cryptography** (from Greek words meaning *hidden writing*). Cryptography is the science of transforming information into a secure form so that unauthorized persons cannot access it.

Whereas cryptography scrambles a message so that it cannot be understood, **steganography** hides the existence of the data. What appears to be a harmless image can contain hidden data, usually some type of message, embedded within the image. Steganography takes the data, divides it into smaller sections, and hides it in unused portions of the file, as shown in Figure 5-1. Steganography may hide data in the file header fields that describe the file, between sections of the *metadata* (data that is used to describe the content or structure of the actual data), or in the areas of a file that contain the content itself. Steganography can use a wide variety of file types— image files, audio files, video files, etc.—to hide messages and data.

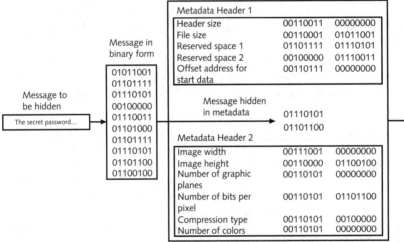

Figure 5-1 Data hidden by steganography

Photo: Chris Parypa Photography/Shutterstock.com

NOTE Government officials suspect that terrorist groups routinely use steganography to exchange information. A picture of a sunrise posted on a website may actually contain secret information, although it appears harmless.

Cryptography's origins date back centuries. One of the most famous ancient cryptographers was Julius Caesar. In messages to his commanders, Caesar shifted each letter of his messages three places down in the alphabet, so that an *A* was replaced by a *D*, a *B* was replaced by an *E*, and so forth. Changing the original text into a secret message using cryptography is known as **encryption**. When Caesar's commanders received his messages, they reversed the process (such as substituting a *D* for an *A*) to change the secret message back to its original form. This is called **decryption**.

Data in an unencrypted form is called **cleartext** data. Cleartext data is "in the clear" and thus can be displayed as is without any decryption being necessary. **Plaintext** data is cleartext data that is to be encrypted and is the result of decryption as well. Plaintext may be considered as a special instance of cleartext.

Plaintext should not be confused with "plain text." Plain text is text that has no formatting (such as bolding or underlining) applied.

Plaintext data is input into a cryptographic **algorithm,** which consists of procedures based on a mathematical formula used to encrypt and decrypt the data. A **key** is a mathematical value entered into the algorithm to produce **ciphertext**, or encrypted data. Just as a key is inserted into a door lock to lock the door, in cryptography a unique mathematical key is input into the encryption algorithm to "lock down" the data by creating the ciphertext. Once the ciphertext needs to be returned to plaintext, the reverse process occurs with a decryption algorithm and key. The cryptographic process is illustrated in Figure 5-2.

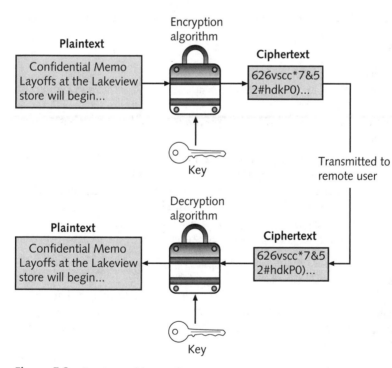

Figure 5-2 Cryptographic process

Cryptography and Security

Cryptography can provide basic security protection for information because access to the keys can be limited. Cryptography can provide five basic protections:

- *Confidentiality.* Cryptography can protect the confidentiality of information by ensuring that only authorized parties can view it. When private information, such as a list of employees to be laid off, is transmitted across the network or stored on a file server, its contents can be encrypted, which allows only authorized individuals who have the key to see it.

- *Integrity.* Cryptography can protect the integrity of information. Integrity ensures that the information is correct and no unauthorized person or malicious software has altered that data. Because ciphertext requires that a key must be used in order to open the data before it can be changed, cryptography can ensure its integrity. The list of employees to be laid off, for example, can be protected so that no names can be added or deleted by unauthorized personnel.

- *Availability.* Cryptography can help ensure the availability of the data so that authorized users who possess the key can access it. Instead of storing an important file on a hard drive that is locked in a safe to prevent unauthorized access, an encrypted file can be immediately available from a central file server to authorized individuals who have been given the key. The list of employees to be laid off could be stored on a network server and available to the director of Human Resources for review because she has the algorithm key.

The confidentiality, integrity, and availability of information are covered in Chapter 1.

- *Authentication.* The authentication of the sender can be verified through cryptography. Specific types of cryptography, for example, can prevent a situation such as circulation of a list of employees to be laid off that appears to come from a manager, but in reality was sent by an imposter.

- *Non-repudiation.* Cryptography can enforce nonrepudiation. *Repudiation* is defined as denial; nonrepudiation is the inability to deny. In information technology, **non-repudiation** is the process of proving that a user performed an action, such as sending an email message. Non-repudiation prevents an individual from fraudulently "reneging" on an action. The non-repudiation features of cryptography can prevent a manager from claiming he never sent the list of employees to be laid off to an unauthorized third party.

A practical example of non-repudiation is Alice taking her car into a repair shop for service and signing an estimate form of the cost of repairs and authorizing the work. If Alice later returns and claims she never approved a specific repair, the signed form can be used as non-repudiation.

The security protections afforded by cryptography are summarized in Table 5-1. Not all types of cryptography provide all five protections.

It is generally recognized that cryptography is too important to allow the use of untested algorithms and that using proven technologies is important. This does not mean, however, that older algorithms are necessarily more secure than newer ones. Each must be evaluated for its own strengths.

Characteristic	Description	Protection
Confidentiality	Ensures that only authorized parties can view the information	Encrypted information can only be viewed by those who have been provided the key.
Integrity	Ensures that the information is correct and no unauthorized person or malicious software has altered that data	Encrypted information cannot be changed except by authorized users who have the key.
Availability	Ensures that data is accessible to authorized users	Authorized users are provided the decryption key to access the information.
Authentication	Provides proof of the genuineness of the user	Proof that the sender was legitimate and not an imposter can be obtained.
Non-repudiation	Proves that a user performed an action	Individuals are prevented from fraudulently denying that they were involved in a transaction.

Table 5-1   **Information protections by cryptography**

Cryptographic Algorithms

6.1 Given a scenario, utilize general cryptography concepts.

6.2 Given a scenario, use appropriate cryptographic methods.

One of the fundamental differences in cryptographic algorithms is the amount of data that is processed at a time. Some algorithms use a **stream cipher**. A stream cipher takes one character and replaces it with one character, as shown in Figure 5-3.

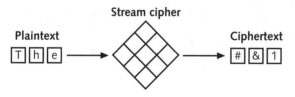

Figure 5-3   Stream cipher

The simplest type of stream cipher is a *substitution cipher*. Substitution ciphers simply substitute one letter or character for another (a *monoalphabetic substitution cipher*), as shown in Figure 5-4. A more complex stream cipher that can be more difficult to break is a *homoalphabetic substitution cipher* that maps a single plaintext character to multiple ciphertext characters. For example, an *F* may map to *ILS*.

Although a homoalphabetic substitution cipher creates several ciphertext characters for each plaintext character, it is still considered a stream cipher because it processes one plaintext character at a time.

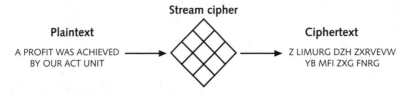

A B C D E F G H I J K L M N O P Q R S T U V W X Y Z — **Plaintext letters**
Z Y X W V U T S R Q P O N M L K J I H G F E D C B A — **Substitution letters**

Stream cipher

Plaintext   **Ciphertext**

A PROFIT WAS ACHIEVED ⟶   ⟶ Z LIMURG DZH ZXRVEVW
BY OUR ACT UNIT   YB MFI ZXG FNRG

Figure 5-4 Substitution cipher

Other algorithms make use of a **block cipher**. Whereas a stream cipher works on one character at a time, a block cipher manipulates an entire block of plaintext at one time. The plaintext message is divided into separate blocks of 8 to 16 bytes, and then each block is encrypted independently. For additional security, the blocks can be randomized.

Stream and block ciphers each have advantages and disadvantages. A stream cipher is fast when the plaintext is short, but can consume much more processing power if the plaintext is long. In addition, stream ciphers are more prone to attack because the engine that generates the stream does not vary; the only change is the plaintext itself. Because of this consistency, an attacker can examine streams and may be able to determine the key. Block ciphers are considered more secure because the output is more random. When using a block cipher, the cipher is reset to its original state after each block is processed. This results in the ciphertext being more difficult to break.

Recently a third type has been introduced called a **sponge function**. A sponge function takes as input a string of any length, and returns a string of any requested variable length. This function repeatedly applies a process on the input that has been *padded* with additional characters until all characters are used (*absorbed* in the *sponge*).

There are three broad categories of cryptographic algorithms. These are known as hash algorithms, symmetric cryptographic algorithms, and asymmetric cryptographic algorithms.

Along with discussing these cryptographic algorithms, the following sections review their comparative strengths and performance where appropriate.

Hash Algorithms

The most basic type of cryptographic algorithm is a one-way hash algorithm. A **hash** algorithm creates a unique "digital fingerprint" of a set of data and is commonly called *hashing*. This fingerprint, called a **digest** (sometimes called a *message digest* or *hash*), represents the contents. Although hashing is considered a cryptographic algorithm, its purpose is not to create ciphertext that can later be decrypted. Instead, hashing is "one-way" in that its contents cannot be used to reveal the original set of data. Hashing is used primarily for comparison purposes.

A secure hash that is created from a set of data cannot be reversed. For example, if 12 is multiplied by 34 the result is 408. If a user was asked to determine the two numbers used to create the number 408, it would not be possible to "work backward" and derive the original numbers with absolute certainty because there are too many mathematical possibilities (204 +204, 407+1, 999–591, 361+47, etc.). Hashing is similar in that it is used to create a value, but it is not possible to determine the original set of data.

Although hashing and checksums are similar in that they both create a value based on the contents of a file, hashing is not the same as creating a checksum. A checksum is intended to verify (*check*) the integrity of data and identify data-transmission errors, while a hash is designed to create a unique digital fingerprint of the data.

A hashing algorithm is considered secure if it has these characteristics:

- *Fixed size*. A digest of a short set of data should produce the same size as a digest of a long set of data. For example, a digest of the single letter *a* is 86be7afa339d0fc7cfc 785e72f578d33, while a digest of 1 million occurrences of the letter *a* is 4a7f5723f95 4eba1216c9d8f6320431f, the same length.

- *Unique*. Two different sets of data cannot produce the same digest, which is known as a *collision*. Changing a single letter in one data set should produce an entirely different digest. For example, a digest of *Sunday* is 0d716e73a2a7910bd4ae63407056d79b while a digest of *sunday* (lowercase *s*) is 3464eb71bd7a4377967a30da798a1b54.

- *Original*. It should be impossible to produce a data set that has a desired or predefined hash.

- *Secure*. The resulting hash cannot be reversed in order to determine the original plaintext.

Hashing is used primarily to determine the integrity of a message or contents of a file. In this case, the digest serves as a check to verify that the original contents have not changed. For example, digest values are often posted on websites in order to verify the integrity of files that can be downloaded. A user can create a digest on a file after it has been downloaded and then compare that value with the original digest value posted on the website. A match indicates that the integrity of the file has been preserved. This is shown in Figure 5-5.

A variation that provides improved security is the **Hashed Message Authentication Code (HMAC)**. A *message authentication code (MAC)* combines a "shared secret key" that only the sender and receiver know along with the message. When the receiver gets the message, she knows that it came from the sender because only he has the secret key. This serves to authenticate the sender of the message. However, a MAC does not encrypt the message itself. An HMAC is a hash-based message authentication code in which a hash function is applied to both the key and the message. HMAC is widely used by Internet security protocols to verify the integrity of transmitted data during secure communications.

Hashing can be used to verify the integrity of data. The protections provided by hashing are seen in Table 5-2.

At one time in some countries a customer's automated teller machine (ATM) card stored the digest of the customer's personal identification number (PIN) on the back of the card. When the PIN was entered on the ATM, it was hashed and then compared with the digest stored on the back of the card. If the numbers matched, the customer's identity was verified. This prevented a thief from easily using a stolen card. These types of cards, however, are no longer used.

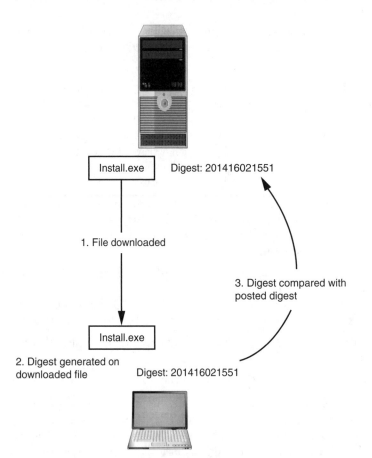

Install.exe   Digest: 201416021551

1. File downloaded

3. Digest compared with posted digest

Install.exe

2. Digest generated on downloaded file   Digest: 201416021551

Figure 5-5   Verifying file integrity with digests

Characteristic	Protection?
Confidentiality	No
Integrity	Yes
Availability	No
Authenticity	No
Nonrepudiation	No

Table 5-2   Information protections by hashing cryptography

The most common hash algorithms are Message Digest, Secure Hash Algorithm, Whirlpool, and RIPEMD.

Message Digest (MD) One of the most common one-way hash algorithms is the **Message Digest** (MD), which has three different versions. *Message Digest 2 (MD2)* was one of the early hash algorithms. It takes plaintext of any length and creates a digest 128 bits in length. MD2 divides the plaintext into multiple 128-bit sections. If the message is less than 128 bits, however, extra padding is added. MD2 was developed in 1989 and was optimized to run on Intel-based microcomputers that processed 8 bits at a time. MD2 is no longer considered secure.

Message Digest 4 (MD4) was developed in 1990 for computers that processed 32 bits at a time. Like MD2, MD4 creates a digest of 128 bits. The plaintext message itself is padded to a length of 512 bits instead of 128 bits as with MD2. Flaws in the MD4 hash algorithm have prevented this MD from being widely accepted.

Despite the fact that it contained flaws, MD4 was responsible for influencing several of the secure one-way hash algorithms that are used today.

Message Digest 5 (MD5), the current MD version and a revision of MD4, was created the following year and designed to address MD4's weaknesses. Like MD4, the length of a message is padded to 512 bits in length. The hash algorithm then uses four variables of 32 bits each in a round-robin fashion to create a value that is compressed to generate the digest. Weaknesses have been revealed in the compression function that could lead to collisions, so some security experts recommend that a more secure hash algorithm be used instead.

Secure Hash Algorithm (SHA)

A more secure hash than MD is the **Secure Hash Algorithm (SHA)**. Like MD, the SHA is a family of hashes. The first version was *SHA-0*, which due to a flaw was withdrawn shortly after it was first released. Its successor, *SHA-1*, was developed in 1993 by the U.S. National Security Agency (NSA) and the National Institute of Standards and Technology (NIST). It is patterned after MD4 and MD5, but creates a digest that is 160 bits instead of 128 bits in length. SHA pads messages of less than 512 bits with zeros and an integer that describes the original length of the message. The padded message is then run through the SHA algorithm to produce the digest.

Recent calculations have indicated that if the number of integrated circuits doubles every 18–24 months (as predicted by "Moore's Law"), by 2018 servers could have enough power to crack SHA-1. One researcher says that by 2021 hardware will be so cheap that cracking SHA-1 will be a university student's research project![2]

Another family of SHA hashes are known as *SHA-2*. SHA-2 actually is comprised of six variations: SHA-224, SHA-256, SHA-384, SHA-512, SHA-512/224, and SHA-512/256 (the last number indicates the length in bits of the digest that is generated). SHA-2 is currently considered to be a secure hash.

In 2007, an open competition for a new *SHA-3* hash algorithm was announced. Of the 51 entries that were accepted to Round 1 of the competition, only 14 were selected for Round 2 (one of the entries rejected was a new MD6). In late 2010, five finalists moved to Round 3. In late 2012 the final winner of the competition was announced. The winning algorithm, Keccak (pronounced *catch-ack*), was created by four security researchers from Italy and Belgium. Keccak will become NIST's SHA-3 hash algorithm.

The NIST considers SHA-2 to be secure and suitable for general use, so SHA-3 may initially serve as a fallback option in the event that SHA-2 becomes broken.

One of the design goals of SHA-3 was for it to be dissimilar to previous hash algorithms like MD5 and SHA-0, SHA-1, and SHA-2. Because successful attacks have been launched against MD5 and SHA-0 as well as theoretical attacks on SHA-1, making SHA-3 different would prevent attackers from building upon any previous work to compromise hashing algorithms. SHA-3 uses a sponge function instead of stream or block ciphers.

Because SHA-3 is relatively compact, it may soon find its way into smart devices such as sensors in a building's security system or remotely controlled home appliances.

Whirlpool *Whirlpool* is a relatively recent cryptographic hash function that has received international recognition and adoption by standards organizations, including the International Organization for Standardization (ISO). Named after the first galaxy recognized to have a spiral structure, it creates a digest of 512 bits. Whirlpool is being implemented in several new commercial cryptography applications.

According to its creators, Whirlpool will not be patented and can be freely used for any purpose.

RACE Integrity Primitives Evaluation Message Digest (RIPEMD) Another hash was developed by the Research and Development in Advanced Communications Technologies (RACE), an organization that is affiliated with the European Union (EU). **RIPEMD** stands for **RACE Integrity Primitives Evaluation Message Digest**, which was designed after MD4.

The primary design feature of RIPEMD is two different and independent parallel chains of computation, the results of which are then combined at the end of the process. There are several versions of RIPEMD, all based on the length of the digest created. RIPEMD-128 is a replacement for the original RIPEMD and is faster than RIPEMD-160. RIPEMD-256 and RIPEMD-320 reduce the risk of collisions but do not provide any higher levels of security.

Table 5-3 illustrates the digests generated from several different one-way hash algorithms using the original phrase *CengageLearning*.

Symmetric Cryptographic Algorithms

The original cryptographic algorithms for encrypting and decrypting data are symmetric cryptographic algorithms. **Symmetric cryptographic algorithms** use the same single key to encrypt and decrypt a document. Unlike hashing in which the hash is not intended to be decrypted, symmetric algorithms are designed to encrypt and decrypt the ciphertext. Data encrypted with a symmetric cryptographic algorithm by Alice will be decrypted when

Hash	Digest
MD2	c4b4c4568a42895c68e5d507d7f0a6ca
MD4	9a5b5cec21dd77d611e04e10f902e283
MD5	0e41799d87f1179c1b8c38c318132236
RipeMD160	d4ec909f7b0f7dfb6fa45c4c91a92962649001ef
SHA-1	299b20adfec43b1e8fade03c0e0c61fc51b55420
SHA-256	133380e0ebfc19e91589c2feaa346d3e679a7529fa8d03617fcd661c997d7287
Whirlpool	1db4f64211028432d31ec9f0201244d59c11ff04dcf5c3dc97cc4cef700ad0c20d1943853202 20038ae9680da453f64d0062b09eabd8a157ebe147cd9233dd1d
SHA-3	c298d1ec129b04495f399cbc5c44b8023e213ebe27b78f689046a72e436e0e0 1d47302bbc8a857695594106d63571b95933a6 7b389802ceb2ef9b078297cfcc3

Table 5-3 **Digests generated from one-time hash algorithms**

received by Bob. It is therefore essential that the key be kept private (confidential), because if an attacker obtained the key he could read all the encrypted documents. For this reason, symmetric encryption is also called **private key cryptography**. Symmetric encryption is illustrated in Figure 5-6 where identical keys are used to encrypt and decrypt a document.

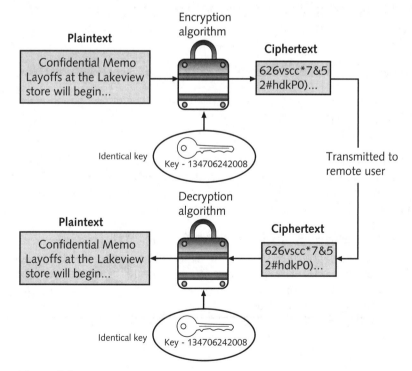

Figure 5-6 Symmetric (private key) cryptography

Symmetric cryptography can provide strong protections against attacks as long as the key is kept secure. The protections provided by symmetric cryptography are summarized in Table 5-4.

Characteristic	Protection?
Confidentiality	Yes
Integrity	Yes
Availability	Yes
Authenticity	No
Non-repudiation	No

Table 5-4   **Information protections by symmetric cryptography**

Common symmetric cryptographic algorithms include the Data Encryption Standard, Triple Data Encryption Standard, Advanced Encryption Standard, and several other algorithms.

Data Encryption Standard (DES)
One of the first widely popular symmetric cryptography algorithms was the **Data Encryption Standard** (DES). The predecessor of DES was a product originally designed in the early 1970s by IBM called Lucifer that had a key length of 128 bits. The key was later shortened to 56 bits and renamed DES. The U.S. government officially adopted DES as the standard for encrypting nonclassified information.

DES effectively catapulted the study of cryptography into the public arena. Until the deployment of DES, cryptography was studied almost exclusively by military personnel. The popularity of DES helped move cryptography implementation and research to academic and commercial organizations.

DES is a block cipher. It divides plaintext into 64-bit blocks and then executes the algorithm 16 times. Four modes of DES encryption exist. Although DES was once widely implemented, its 56-bit key is no longer considered secure and has been broken several times. It is not recommended for use.

Triple Data Encryption Standard (3DES)
Triple Data Encryption Standard (3DES) is designed to replace DES. As its name implies, 3DES uses three rounds of encryption instead of just one. The ciphertext of one round becomes the entire input for the second iteration. 3DES employs a total of 48 iterations in its encryption (3 iterations times 16 rounds). The most secure versions of 3DES use different keys for each round, as shown in Figure 5-7. By design 3DES performs better in hardware than as software.

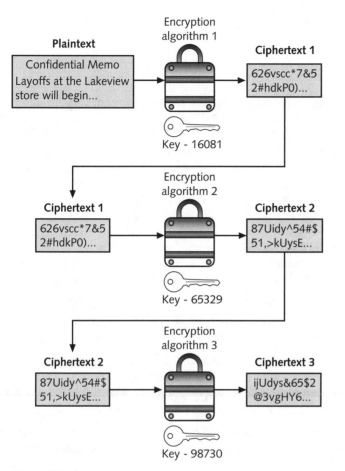

Figure 5-7   3DES

In some versions of 3DES, only two keys are used, but the first key is repeated for the third round of encryption. The version of 3DES that uses three keys is estimated to be 2 to the power of 56 times stronger than DES.

Although 3DES addresses several of the key weaknesses of DES, it is no longer considered the most secure symmetric cryptographic algorithm.

Advanced Encryption Standard (AES) The **Advanced Encryption Standard (AES)** is a symmetric cipher that was approved by the NIST in late 2000 as a replacement for DES. The process began with the NIST publishing requirements for a new symmetric algorithm and requesting proposals. After a lengthy process that required the cooperation of the U.S. government, industry, and higher education, five finalists were chosen, with the ultimate winner being an algorithm known as Rijndael, but more often referred to as AES, that is now the official standard for encryption by the U.S. government.

Vincent Rijmen, one of the co-creators of AES, is also one of the designers of Whirlpool.

AES performs three steps on every block (128 bits) of plaintext. Within step 2, multiple rounds are performed depending upon the key size: a 128-bit key performs 9 rounds, a 192-bit key performs 11 rounds, and a 256-bit key, known as AES-256, uses 13 rounds. Within each round, bytes are substituted and rearranged, and then special multiplication is performed based on the new arrangement. To date, no attacks have been successful against AES.

Other Algorithms Several other symmetric cryptographic algorithms also exist. *Rivest Cipher (RC)* is a family of cipher algorithms designed by Ron Rivest. He developed six ciphers, ranging from RC1 to RC6 (but did not release RC1 and RC3). *RC2* is a block cipher that processes blocks of 64 bits. **RC4** is a stream cipher that accepts keys up to 128 bits in length. *RC5* is a block cipher that can accept blocks and keys of different lengths. *RC6* has three key sizes (128, 192, and 256 bits) and performs 20 rounds on each block.

The algorithm referred to as *International Data Encryption Algorithm (IDEA)* dates back to the early 1990s and is used in European nations. It is a block cipher that processes 64 bits with a 128-bit key with 8 rounds. It is generally considered to be secure.

Blowfish is a block cipher algorithm that operates on 64-bit blocks and can have a key length from 32 to 448 bits. Blowfish was designed to run efficiently on 32-bit computers. To date, no significant weaknesses have been identified. A later derivation of Blowfish known as **Twofish** is also considered to be a strong algorithm, although it has not been used as widely as Blowfish.

A **one-time pad (OTP)** combines plaintext with a random key. It is the only known method to perform encryption that cannot be broken mathematically. It also does not require the use of a computer.

OTPs were used by special operations teams and resistance groups during World War II as well as by intelligence agencies and spies during the Cold War.

A *pad* is a long sequence of random letters. These letters are combined with the plaintext message to produce the ciphertext. To decipher the message, the recipient must have a copy of the pad to reverse the process. As its name implies, the pad should be used only one time and then destroyed.

To encipher a message, the position in the alphabet of the first letter in the plaintext message is added to the position in the alphabet of the first random letter from the pad. For example, if *SECRET* is to be encrypted using the pad *CBYFEA*, the first letter *S* (#19 of the alphabet) is added to the first letter of the pad *C* (#3 of the alphabet) and then 1 is subtracted (19+3−1=21). This results in *U* (#21 of the alphabet). Each letter is similarly encrypted (any number larger than 26 is "wrapped" around to the start of the alphabet). To decipher a message, the recipient takes the first letter of the ciphertext and subtracts the first random letter from the pad (any negative numbers are wrapped around to the end of the alphabet). An OTP is illustrated in Table 5-5.

Plaintext	Position in alphabet	Pad	Position in alphabet	Calculation	Result
S	19	C	3	19+3−1=21	U
E	5	B	2	5+2−1=6	F
C	3	Y	25	3+25−1=1	A
R	18	F	6	18+6−1=23	W
E	5	E	5	5+5−1=9	I
T	20	A	1	20+1−1=20	T

Table 5-5 OTP

As long as the pad is a random string of characters, is kept secret, and is not reused, ciphertext like *GRTUSVIFAIHAIUJ* generated by an OTP is considered to be unbreakable.

Asymmetric Cryptographic Algorithms

If Bob wants to send an encrypted message to Alice using symmetric encryption, he must be sure that she has the key to decrypt the message. Yet how should Bob get the key to Alice? He cannot send it electronically through the Internet, because that would make it vulnerable to interception by attackers. Nor can he encrypt the key and send it, because Alice would not have a way to decrypt the encrypted key. This example illustrates the primary weakness of symmetric encryption algorithms: distributing and maintaining a secure single key among multiple users, who are often scattered geographically, poses significant challenges.

A completely different approach from symmetric cryptography is **asymmetric cryptographic algorithms,** also known as **public key cryptography.** Asymmetric encryption uses two keys instead of only one. These keys are mathematically related and are known as the public key and the private key. The **public key** is known to everyone and can be freely distributed, while the **private key** is known only to the individual to whom it belongs. When Bob wants to send a secure message to Alice, he uses Alice's public key to encrypt the message. Alice then uses her private key to decrypt it. Asymmetric cryptography is illustrated in Figure 5-8.

Asymmetric encryption was developed by Whitfield Diffie and Martin Hellman of the Massachusetts Institute of Technology (MIT) in 1975.

Several important principles regarding asymmetric cryptography are:

- *Key pairs*. Unlike symmetric cryptography that uses only one key, asymmetric cryptography requires a pair of keys.
- *Public key*. Public keys by their nature are designed to be "public" and do not need to be protected. They can be freely given to anyone or even posted on the Internet.
- *Private key*. The private key should be kept confidential and never shared.

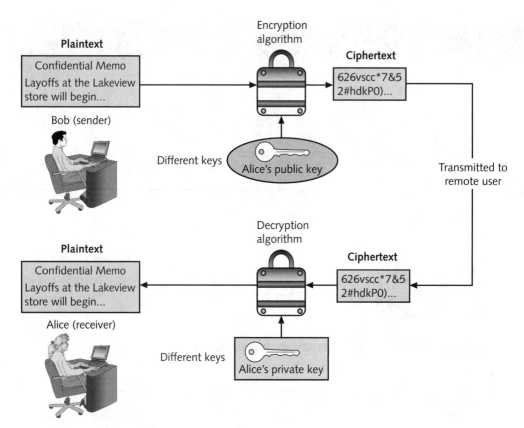

Figure 5-8 Asymmetric (public key) cryptography

- *Both directions.* Asymmetric cryptography keys can work in both directions. A document encrypted with a public key can be decrypted with the corresponding private key. In the same way, a document encrypted with a private key can be decrypted with its public key.

Asymmetric cryptography also can be used to provide proofs. Suppose that Alice receives an encrypted document that says it came from Bob. Although Alice can be sure that the encrypted message was not viewed or altered by someone else while being transmitted, how can she know for certain that Bob was actually the sender? Because Alice's public key is widely available, anyone could use it to encrypt the document. Another individual could have created a fictitious document, encrypted it with Alice's public key, and then sent it to Alice while pretending to be Bob. Alice's key can verify that no one read or changed the document in transport, but it cannot verify the sender.

Proof can be provided with asymmetric cryptography, however, by creating a **digital signature,** which is an electronic verification of the sender. A handwritten signature on a paper document serves as proof that the signer has read and agreed to the document. A digital signature is much the same, but can provide additional benefits. A digital signature can:

- *Verify the sender.* A digital signature serves to confirm the identity of the person from whom the electronic message originated.

- *Prevent the sender from disowning the message.* The signer cannot later attempt to disown it by claiming the signature was forged (nonrepudiation).

- *Prove the integrity of the message.* A digital signature can prove that the message has not been altered since it was signed.

The basis for a digital signature rests on the ability of asymmetric keys to work in both directions (a public key can encrypt a document that can be decrypted with a private key, and the private key can encrypt a document that can be decrypted by the public key). The steps for Bob to send a digitally signed message to Alice are:

1. After creating a memo, Bob generates a digest on it.

2. Bob then encrypts the digest with his private key. This encrypted digest is the digital signature for the memo.

3. Bob sends both the memo and the digital signature to Alice.

4. When Alice receives them, she decrypts the digital signature using Bob's public key, revealing the digest. If she cannot decrypt the digital signature, then she knows that it did not come from Bob (because only Bob's public key is able to decrypt the digest generated with his private key).

5. Alice then hashes the memo with the same hash algorithm Bob used and compares the result to the digest she received from Bob. If they are equal, Alice can be confident that the message has not changed since he signed it. If the digests are not equal, Alice will know the message has changed since it was signed.

These steps are illustrated in Figure 5-9.

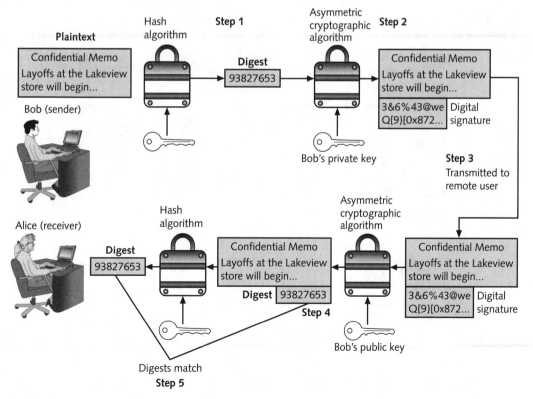

Figure 5-9 Digital signature

Using a digital signature does not encrypt the message itself. In the example, if Bob wanted to ensure the privacy of the message, he also would have to encrypt it using Alice's public key.

Public and private keys may result in confusion regarding whose key to use and which key should be used. Table 5-6 lists the practices to be followed when using asymmetric cryptography.

Action	Whose key to use	Which key to use	Explanation
Bob wants to send Alice an encrypted message	Alice's key	Public key	When an encrypted message is to be sent, the recipient's, and not the sender's, key is used.
Alice wants to read an encrypted message sent by Bob	Alice's key	Private key	An encrypted message can be read only by using the recipient's private key.
Bob wants to send a copy to himself of the encrypted message that he sent to Alice	Bob's key	Public key to encrypt Private key to decrypt	An encrypted message can be read only by the recipient's private key. Bob would need to encrypt it with his public key and then use his private key to decrypt it.
Bob receives an encrypted reply message from Alice	Bob's key	Private key	The recipient's private key is used to decrypt received messages.
Bob wants Susan to read Alice's reply message that he received	Susan's key	Public key	The message should be encrypted with Susan's key for her to decrypt and read with her private key.
Bob wants to send Alice a message with a digital signature	Bob's key	Private key	Bob's private key is used to encrypt the hash.
Alice wants to see Bob's digital signature	Bob's key	Public key	Because Bob's public and private keys work in both directions, Alice can use his public key to decrypt the hash.

Table 5-6   **Asymmetric cryptography practices**

No user other than the owner should have the private key.

Asymmetric cryptography can provide strong protections. These protections are summarized in Table 5-7.

RSA   The asymmetric algorithm **RSA** was published in 1977 and patented by MIT in 1983. RSA is the most common asymmetric cryptography algorithm and is the basis for several products.

Characteristic	Protection?
Confidentiality	Yes
Integrity	Yes
Availability	Yes
Authenticity	Yes
Non-repudiation	Yes

Table 5-7 Information protections by asymmetric cryptography

RSA stands for the last names of its three developers, Ron Rivest, Adi Shamir, and Leonard Adleman.

The RSA algorithm multiplies two large prime numbers (a prime number is a number divisible only by itself and 1), p and q, to compute their product ($n = pq$). Next, a number e is chosen that is less than n and a prime factor to $(p-1)(q-1)$. Another number d is determined, so that $(ed-1)$ is divisible by $(p-1)(q-1)$. The values of e and d are the public and private exponents. The public key is the pair (n,e) while the private key is (n,d). The numbers p and q can be discarded.

An illustration of the RSA algorithm using very small numbers is as follows:

1. Select two prime numbers, p and q (in this example $p = 7$ and $q = 19$)
2. Multiply p and q together to create $n(7 * 19 = 133)$
3. Calculate m as $p-1 * q-1$ ($[7-1] * [19-1]$ or $6 * 18 = 108$)
4. Find a number e so that it and m have no common positive divisor other than $1(e = 5)$
5. Find a number d so that $d = (1 + n * m)/e$ or ($[1 + 133 * 108]/5$ or $14{,}364/5 = 2875$)

For this example, the public key n is 133 and e is 5, while for the private key n is 133 and d is 2873.

RSA is slower than other algorithms. DES is approximately 100 times faster than RSA in software and between 1000 and 10,000 times as fast in hardware.

Elliptic Curve Cryptography (ECC) Elliptic curve cryptography (ECC) was first proposed in the mid-1980s. Instead of using large prime numbers as with RSA, elliptic curve cryptography uses sloping curves. An elliptic curve is a function drawn on an X-Y axis as a gently curved line. By adding the values of two points on the curve, a third point on the curve can be derived, of which the inverse is used as illustrated in Figure 5-10. With ECC, users share one elliptic curve and one point on the curve. One user chooses a secret random number and computes a public key based on a point on the curve; the other user does the same. They can now exchange messages because the shared public keys can generate a private key on an elliptic curve.

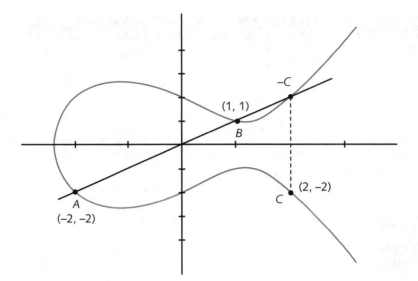

Figure 5-10 Elliptic curve cryptography (ECC)

ECC is considered as an alternative for prime-number-based asymmetric cryptography for mobile and wireless devices. Because mobile devices are limited in terms of computing power due to their smaller size, ECC offers security that is comparable to other asymmetric cryptography but with smaller key sizes. This can result in faster computations and lower power consumption.

NTRUEncrypt A relatively new asymmetric cryptographic algorithm is *NTRUEncrypt*. NTRUEncrypt uses a different foundation than prime numbers (RSA) or points on a curve (ECC). Instead, it uses *lattice-based cryptography* that relies on a set of points in space, as illustrated in Figure 5-11. In addition to being faster than RSA and ECC, it is believed the NTRUEncrypt will be more resistant to quantum computing attacks.

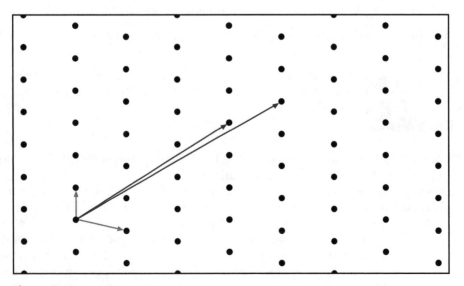

Figure 5-11 Lattice-based cryptography

NTRUEncrypt is used to encrypt customer credit card information at gasoline service stations that is then transmitted through satellites, and has been approved for use in the financial services industry.

Quantum Cryptography Quantum cryptography attempts to use the unusual and unique behavior of microscopic objects to enable users to securely develop and share keys as well as to detect eavesdropping. Research in quantum cryptography started in the late 1960s with the first proposed techniques appearing in 1984.

Quantum cryptography is not the same as quantum computing, yet both may impact the future of cryptography. A quantum computer is fundamentally different from a classical computer and can factor numbers very quickly, which could be used to crack the keys in symmetric and asymmetric cryptography. However, because quantum cryptography does not depend on difficult mathematical problems for its security, it is not threatened by the development of quantum computers.

Quantum cryptography exploits the properties of microscopic objects such as photons. A possible scenario for quantum cryptography is as follows:

1. Using a special device, Alice observes photons randomly that have specific circular, diagonal, or other types of polarizations. She records the polarization of each photon and sends them to Bob.

2. When Bob receives the photons, he randomly measures the polarization of each and records it.

3. Bob then tells Alice publicly what his measurements types were, but not the results of the measurements.

4. Alice responds by telling Bob which measurement types were correct. Alice and Bob then convert the correct types to a string of bits that forms their secret key.

If quantum cryptography is found to be commercially feasible, it may hold the potential for introducing an entirely new type of cryptography.

Key Exchange Despite the fact that asymmetric cryptography allows two users to send encrypted messages using separate public and private keys, it does not completely solve the problem of sending and receiving keys (**key exchange**), such as exchanging a symmetric private key. One solution is to make the exchange outside of the normal communication channels, called **out-of-band**. For example, Alice could hire Charlie to carry a USB flash drive containing the key directly to Bob.

How could an employee of an embassy located in a foreign country send and receive secret messages with her home nation? Using a telephone or other electronic communications would be risky, since these lines could be tapped. The solution is to use a separate means of communications, such as diplomatic bags containing paper memos and documents carried by trusted couriers. This is an example of an out-of-band exchange of secret information.

There are different solutions for a key exchange that occurs within the normal communications channel (**in-band**) of cryptography, including:

- *Diffie-Hellman (DH)*. The **Diffie-Hellman (DH)** key exchange requires Alice and Bob to each agree upon a large prime number and related integer. Those two numbers can be made public, yet Alice and Bob, through mathematical computations and exchanges of intermediate values, can separately create the same key.

- *Diffie-Hellman Ephemeral (DHE)*. Whereas DH uses the same keys each time, **Diffie-Hellman Ephemeral (DHE)** uses different keys. **Ephemeral keys** are temporary keys that are used only once and then discarded.

- *Elliptic Curve Diffie–Hellman (ECDH)*. **Elliptic Curve Diffie–Hellman (ECDH)** uses elliptic curve cryptography instead of prime numbers in its computation.

- *Perfect forward secrecy*. Public key systems that generate random public keys that are different for each session are called **perfect forward secrecy**. The value of perfect forward secrecy is that if the secret key is compromised, it cannot reveal the contents of more than one message.

Using Cryptography

4.4 Implement the appropriate controls to ensure data security.

6.2 Given a scenario, use appropriate cryptographic methods.

Cryptography should be used to secure any and all data that needs to be protected. This includes individual files, databases, removable media, or data on mobile devices. Cryptography can be applied through either software or hardware.

Encryption Through Software

Encryption can be implemented through cryptographic software running on a system. This can be applied to individual files by using the software to encrypt and decrypt each file. The encryption also can be performed on a larger scale through the file system or by encrypting the entire disk drive.

File and File System Cryptography Encryption software can be used to encrypt or decrypt files one-by-one. However, this can be a cumbersome process. Instead, protecting groups of files, such as all files in a specific folder, can take advantage of the operating system's file system. A *file system* is a method used by operating systems to store, retrieve, and organize files.

Protecting individual files or multiple files through file system cryptography can be performed using software such as Pretty Good Privacy and Microsoft Windows Encrypting File System.

Pretty Good Privacy (PGP/GPG) One of the most widely used asymmetric cryptography systems for files and email messages on Windows systems is a commercial product called **Pretty Good Privacy (PGP)**. A similar program known as **GNU Privacy Guard (GPG)** is an open-source product. GPG versions run on Windows, UNIX, and Linux operating systems. Messages encrypted by PGP can generally be decrypted by GPG and vice versa.

PGP and GPG use both asymmetric and symmetric cryptography. PGP/GPG generates a random symmetric key and uses it to encrypt the message. The symmetric key is then encrypted using the receiver's public key and sent along with the message. When the recipient receives a message, PGP/GPG first decrypts the symmetric key with the recipient's private key. The decrypted symmetric key is then used to decrypt the rest of the message.

PGP uses symmetric cryptography because it is faster than asymmetric cryptography.

PGP uses RSA for protecting digital signatures and 3DES or IDEA for symmetric encryption. GPG is unable to use IDEA because IDEA is patented. Instead, GPG uses one of several open-source algorithms.

Microsoft Windows Encrypting File System (EFS)

Microsoft's *Encrypting File System (EFS)* is a cryptography system for Windows operating systems that use the Windows NTFS file system. Because EFS is tightly integrated with the file system, file encryption and decryption are transparent to the user. Any file created in an encrypted folder or added to an encrypted folder is automatically encrypted. When an authorized user opens a file, it is decrypted by EFS as data is read from a disk; when a file is saved, EFS encrypts the data as it is written to a disk.

EFS files are encrypted with a single symmetric key, and then the symmetric key is encrypted twice: once with the user's EFS public key (to allow transparent decryption), and once with the recovery agent's key to allow data recovery. When a user encrypts a file, EFS generates a *file encryption key* (FEK) to encrypt the data. The FEK is encrypted with the user's public key, and the encrypted FEK is then stored with the file. When decrypting, EFS decrypts the FEK by using the user's private key, and then decrypts the data by using the FEK.

Files can be marked for encryption in several ways:

- A user can set the encryption attribute for a file in the Advanced Attributes dialog box.
- Storing the file in a file folder set for encryption will automatically encrypt the file.
- The *Cipher.exe* command-line utility can be used to encrypt files.

When using EFS, you should first encrypt the folder and then move the files to be protected into that folder. Also, do not encrypt the entire drive that contains the system folder; this could significantly decrease performance and even cause the system to not boot.

Whole Disk Encryption

Cryptography can be applied to entire disks. This is known as **whole disk encryption** and protects all data on a hard drive. One example of whole disk encryption software is that included in Microsoft Windows known as *BitLocker* drive encryption software. BitLocker encrypts the entire system volume, including the Windows Registry and any temporary files that might hold confidential information. BitLocker prevents attackers from accessing data by booting from another operating system or placing the hard drive in another computer.

When using BitLocker, the user must provide authentication before the system boots by entering a PIN or inserting a USB flash drive that contains a startup key.

Hardware Encryption

Software encryption suffers from the same fate as any application program: it can be subject to attacks to exploit its vulnerabilities. As another option, cryptography can be embedded in hardware to provide an even higher degree of security. Hardware encryption cannot be exploited like software encryption. Hardware encryption can be applied to USB devices and standard hard drives. More sophisticated hardware encryption options include the trusted platform module and the hardware security model.

USB Device Encryption Many instances of data leakage are the result of USB flash drives being lost or stolen. Although this data can be secured with software-based cryptographic application programs, vulnerabilities in these programs can open the door for attackers to access the data.

As an alternative, encrypted hardware-based USB devices like flash drives can be used to prevent these types of attacks. These drives resemble standard USB flash drives, with several significant differences:

- Encrypted hardware-based USB drives will not connect to a computer until the correct password has been provided.
- All data copied to the USB flash drive is automatically encrypted.
- The external cases are designed to be tamper-resistant so attackers cannot disassemble the drives.
- Administrators can remotely control and track activity on the devices.
- Compromised or stolen drives can be remotely disabled.

One hardware-based USB encrypted drive allows administrators to remotely prohibit accessing the data on a device until it can verify its status, to lock out the user completely the next time the device connects, or even to instruct the drive to initiate a self-destruct sequence to destroy all data.

Hard Disk Drive Encryption Just as an encrypted hardware-based USB flash drive will automatically encrypt any data stored on it, self-encrypting hard disk drives (HDDs) can protect all files stored on them. When the computer or other device with a self-encrypting HDD is initially powered up, the drive and the host device perform an authentication process. If the authentication process fails, the drive can be configured to simply deny any access to the drive or even perform a "cryptographic erase" on specified blocks of data (a cryptographic erase deletes the decryption keys so that all data is permanently encrypted and unreadable). This also makes it impossible to install the drive on another computer to read its contents.

Self-encrypting HDDs are commonly found in copiers and multifunction printers as well as point-of-sale systems used in government, financial, and medical environments.

Trusted Platform Module (TPM) The **Trusted Platform Module** (TPM) is essentially a chip on the motherboard of the computer that provides cryptographic services. For example, TPM includes a true random number generator instead of a pseudorandom number generator (PRNG) as well as full support for asymmetric encryption (TPM can also generate public and private keys). Because all of this is done in hardware and not through the software of the operating system, malicious software cannot attack it. Also, TPM can measure and test key components as the computer is starting up. It will prevent the computer from booting if system files or data have been altered. With TPM, if the hard drive is moved to a different computer, the user must enter a recovery password before gaining access to the system volume.

Cryptographic software can take advantage of services provided by TPM.

Hardware Security Module (HSM) A **Hardware Security Module** (HSM) is a secure cryptographic processor. An HSM includes an onboard key generator and key storage facility, as well as accelerated symmetric and asymmetric encryption, and can even back up sensitive material in encrypted form. Most HSMs are LAN-based appliances that can provide services to multiple devices.

In 2005, the U.S. National Security Agency (NSA) identified a set of cryptographic algorithms that, when used together, are the "preferred method" for ensuring the security and integrity of information passed over public networks such as the Internet. These are called *Suite B* and are comprised of encryption using AES 128- or 256-bit keys, digital signatures with the ECC with 256- and 384-bit numbers, key exchange using ECDHE, and hashing based on SHA-2. The NSA's *Suite A* contains classified algorithms for highly sensitive communication and is not released to the public.

Chapter Summary

- Cryptography is the science of transforming information into a secure form so that unauthorized persons cannot access it. Unlike steganography, which hides the existence of data, cryptography masks the content of documents or messages so that they cannot be read or altered. The original data, called plaintext, is input into a cryptographic encryption algorithm that has a mathematical value (a key) used to create ciphertext. Because access to the key can be restricted, cryptography can provide confidentiality, integrity, availability, authenticity, and nonrepudiation. One of the fundamental differences in cryptographic algorithms is the amount of data that is processed at a time. A stream cipher takes one character and replaces it with one character while a block cipher manipulates an entire block of plaintext at one time. A sponge function takes as input a string of any length, and returns a string of any requested variable length.

■ Hashing creates a unique digital fingerprint called a digest that represents the contents of the original material. Hashing is not designed for encrypting material that will be later decrypted; it is used only for comparison. If a hash algorithm produces a fixed-size hash that is unique, and the original contents of the material cannot be determined from the hash, the hash is considered secure. Common hashing algorithms are Message Digest, Secure Hash Algorithm, Whirlpool, and RIPEMD.

■ Symmetric cryptography, also called private key cryptography, uses a single key to encrypt and decrypt a message. Symmetric cryptographic algorithms are designed to decrypt the ciphertext. Symmetric cryptography can provide strong protections against attacks as long as the key is kept secure. Common symmetric cryptographic algorithms include Data Encryption Standard, Triple Data Encryption Standard, Advanced Encryption Standard, and several other algorithms.

■ Asymmetric cryptography, also known as public key cryptography, uses two keys instead of one. These keys are mathematically related and are known as the public key and the private key. The public key is widely available and can be freely distributed, while the private key is known only to the recipient of the message and must be kept secure. Asymmetric cryptography keys can work in both directions. A document encrypted with a public key can be decrypted with the corresponding private key, and a document encrypted with a private key can be decrypted with its public key. Asymmetric cryptography also can be used to create a digital signature, which verifies the sender, proves the integrity of the message, and prevents the sender from disowning the message. Common asymmetric cryptographic algorithms include RSA, elliptic curve, quantum cryptography, and NTRUEncrypt. There are different solutions for a key exchange that occurs within the normal communications channel (called in-band) of cryptography.

■ Cryptography can be applied through either software or hardware. Software-based cryptography can protect large numbers of files on a system or an entire disk. One of the most widely used asymmetric cryptography systems for files and email messages on Windows systems is a commercial product called Pretty Good Privacy (PGP); a similar open-source program is known as GNU Privacy Guard (GPG). Microsoft's Encrypting File System (EFS) is a cryptography system for Windows operating systems. Cryptography also can be applied to entire disks, known as whole disk encryption.

■ Hardware encryption cannot be exploited like software cryptography. Hardware encryption devices can protect USB devices and standard hard drives. More sophisticated hardware encryption options include the Trusted Platform Module and the Hardware Security Model.

Key Terms

Advanced Encryption Standard (AES) A symmetric cipher that was approved by the NIST in late 2000 as a replacement for DES.

algorithm Procedures based on a mathematical formula used to encrypt and decrypt the data.

asymmetric cryptographic algorithm Cryptography that uses two mathematically related keys.

block cipher A cipher that manipulates an entire block of plaintext at one time.

Blowfish A block cipher that operates on 64-bit blocks and can have a key length from 32 to 448 bits.

ciphertext Data that has been encrypted.

cleartext Unencrypted data.

cryptography The science of transforming information into a secure form so that unauthorized persons cannot access it.

Data Encryption Standard (DES) A symmetric block cipher that uses a 56-bit key and encrypts data in 64-bit blocks.

decryption The process of changing ciphertext into plaintext.

Diffie-Hellman (DH) A key exchange that requires all parties to agree upon a large prime number and related integer so that the same key can be separately created.

Diffie-Hellman Ephemeral (DHE) A Diffie-Hellman key exchange that uses different keys.

digest The unique digital fingerprint created by a one-way hash algorithm.

digital signature An electronic verification of the sender.

elliptic curve cryptography (ECC) An algorithm that uses elliptic curves instead of prime numbers to compute keys.

Elliptic Curve Diffie–Hellman (ECDH) A Diffie-Hellman key exchange that uses elliptic curve cryptography instead of prime numbers in its computation.

encryption The process of changing plaintext into ciphertext.

ephemeral key A temporary key that is used only once before it is discarded.

GNU Privacy Guard (GPG) Free and open-source software that is commonly used to encrypt and decrypt data.

Hardware Security Module (HSM) A secure cryptographic processor.

hash An algorithm that creates a unique digital fingerprint.

Hashed Message Authentication Code (HMAC) A hash function that is applied to both the key and the message.

in-band Exchanging secure information within normal communication channels.

key A mathematical value entered into a cryptographic algorithm to produce encrypted data.

key exchange The process of sending and receiving secure cryptographic keys.

Message Digest (MD)   A common hash algorithm with several different versions.

Message Digest 5 (MD5)   The current version of MD.

non-repudiation   The process of proving that a user performed an action.

one-time pad (OTP)   Combining plaintext with a random key to create ciphertext that cannot be broken mathematically.

out-of-band   Exchanging secure information outside the normal communication channels.

perfect forward secrecy   Public key systems that generate random public keys that are different for each session.

plaintext   Cleartext data that is to be encrypted and decrypted by a cryptographic algorithm.

Pretty Good Privacy (PGP)   A commercial product that is commonly used to encrypt files and messages.

private key   An asymmetric encryption key that does have to be protected.

private key cryptography   Cryptographic algorithms that use a single key to encrypt and decrypt a message.

public key   An asymmetric encryption key that does not have to be protected.

public key cryptography   Cryptography that uses two mathematically related keys.

quantum cryptography   A type of asymmetric cryptography that attempts to use the unusual and unique behavior of microscopic objects to enable users to securely develop and share keys.

RACE Integrity Primitives Evaluation Message Digest (RIPEMD)   A hash algorithm that uses two different and independent parallel chains of computation and then combines the result at the end of the process.

RC4   An RC stream cipher that will accept keys up to 128 bits in length.

RSA   The most common asymmetric cryptography algorithm.

Secure Hash Algorithm (SHA)   A secure hash algorithm that creates more secure hash values than Message Digest (MD) algorithms.

sponge function   A cryptographic function that applies a process on the input that has been padded with additional characters until all characters are used.

steganography   Hiding the existence of data within another type of file.

stream cipher   An algorithm that takes one character and replaces it with one character.

symmetric cryptographic algorithm   Encryption that uses a single key to encrypt and decrypt a message.

Triple Data Encryption Standard (3DES)   A symmetric cipher that was designed to replace DES.

Trusted Platform Module (TPM)   A chip on the motherboard of the computer that provides cryptographic services.

Twofish   A derivation of the Blowfish algorithm that is considered to be strong.

whole disk encryption   Cryptography that can be applied to entire disks.

Review Questions

1. The Hashed Message Authentication Code (HMAC) _____.
   a. encrypts only the key
   b. encrypts the key and the message
   c. encrypts only the message
   d. encrypts the DHE key only

2. What is the latest version of the Secure Hash Algorithm?
   a. SHA-2
   b. SHA-3
   c. SHA-4
   d. SHA-5

3. All of the following can be broken mathematically EXCEPT _____.
   a. AES
   b. 3DES
   c. SHA
   d. OTP

4. Elliptic Curve Diffie–Hellman (ECDH) is an example of _____.
   a. in-band key exchange
   b. out-of-band key exchange
   c. SHA-1 key management
   d. AES key certification

5. Which of the following key exchanges uses the same keys each time?
   a. Diffie-Hellman Ephemeral (DHE)
   b. Diffie-Hellman (DH)
   c. Diffie-Hellman-RSA (DHRSA)
   d. Elliptic Curve Diffie-Hellman (ECDH)

6. Public key systems that generate random public keys that are different for each session are called _____.
   a. Public Key Exchange (PKE)
   b. Elliptic Curve Diffie-Hellman (ECDH)
   c. Diffie-Hellman (DH)
   d. perfect forward secrecy

5

7. What is data called that is to be encrypted by inputting it into an cryptographic algorithm?

   a. plaintext

   b. cleartext

   c. opentext

   d. ciphertext

8. Which of these is NOT a basic security protection for information that cryptography can provide?

   a. risk loss

   b. integrity

   c. confidentiality

   d. authenticity

9. The areas of a file in which steganography can hide data include all of the following EXCEPT _____.

   a. in data that is used to describe the content or structure of the actual data

   b. in the directory structure of the file system

   c. in the file header fields that describe the file

   d. in areas that contain the content data itself

10. Proving that a user sent an email message is known as _____.

    a. repudiation

    b. integrity

    c. non-repudiation

    d. availability

11. A(n) _____ is not decrypted but is only used for comparison purposes.

    a. stream

    b. digest

    c. algorithm

    d. key

12. Which of these is NOT a characteristic of a secure hash algorithm?

    a. Collisions should be rare.

    b. The results of a hash function should not be reversed.

    c. The hash should always be the same fixed size.

    d. A message cannot be produced from a predefined hash.

13. Which protection is provided by hashing?
    a. authenticity
    b. confidentiality
    c. integrity
    d. availability

14. Which of these is the strongest symmetric cryptographic algorithm?
    a. Advanced Encryption Standard
    b. Data Encryption Standard
    c. Triple Data Encryption Standard
    d. Rivest Cipher (RC) 1

15. If Bob wants to send a secure message to Alice using an asymmetric cryptographic algorithm, which key does he use to encrypt the message?
    a. Alice's private key
    b. Alice's public key
    c. Bob's public key
    d. Bob's private key

16. A digital signature can provide each of the following benefits EXCEPT _____.
    a. prove the integrity of the message
    b. verify the receiver
    c. verify the sender
    d. enforce nonrepudiation

17. Which asymmetric cryptographic algorithm is the most secure?
    a. SHA-2
    b. BTC-2
    c. RSA
    d. ME-14

18. Which asymmetric encryption algorithm uses prime numbers?
    a. EFS
    b. quantum computing
    c. ECC
    d. RSA

19. The Trusted Platform Module (TPM) _____.
    a. allows the user to boot a corrupted disk and repair it
    b. is available only on Windows computers running BitLocker
    c. includes a pseudorandom number generator (PRNG)
    d. provides cryptographic services in hardware instead of software

20. Which of these has an onboard key generator and key storage facility, as well as accelerated symmetric and asymmetric encryption, and can back up sensitive material in encrypted form?

    a. Trusted Platform Module (TPM)

    b. self-encrypting hard disk drives (HDDs)

    c. encrypted hardware-based USB devices

    d. Hardware Security Module (HSM)

Hands-On Projects

If you are concerned about installing any of the software in these projects on your regular computer, you can instead install the software in the Windows virtual machine created in the Chapter 1 Hands-On Projects 1-3 and 1-4. Software installed within the virtual machine will not impact the host computer.

Project 5-1: Using OpenPuff Steganography

Unlike cryptography that scrambles a message so that it cannot be viewed, steganography hides the existence of the data. In this project, you will use OpenPuff to create a hidden message.

1. Use your web browser to go to **embeddedsw.net/OpenPuff_Steganography_Home.html**.

It is not unusual for websites to change the location of files. If the URL above no longer functions, open a search engine and search for "OpenPuff".

2. Click **Source Page** and then click **Manual** to open the OpenPuff manual. Save this file to your computer. Read through the manual to see the different features available.

3. Click your browser's back button to return to the home page.

4. Click **OpenPuff** to download the program.

5. Navigate to the location of the download and uncompress the Zip file on your computer.

6. Now create a carrier file that will contain the hidden message. Open a Windows search box and enter **Snipping Tool**.

For added security OpenPuff allows a message to be spread across several carrier files.

7. Launch **Snipping Tool**.

8. Under **New** click **Window Snip**.

9. Capture the image of one of the pages of the OpenPuff manual. Click **File** and **Save As**. Enter **Carrier1.png** and save to a location such as the desktop.

10. Now create the secret message to be hidden. Create a new Word file and enter **This is a secret message**.

11. Save this file as **Message.docx**.

12. Exit Word.

13. Create a Zip file from **Message**. Navigate to the location of this file through Windows Explorer and click the right mouse button.

14. Click **Send to** and select **Compressed (zipped) folder** to create the Zip file.

15. Navigate to the OpenPuff directory and double-click **OpenPuff.exe**.

16. Click **Hide**.

 Under Bit selection options, note the wide variety of file types that can be used to hide a message

17. Under (**1**) create three unrelated passwords and enter them into **Cryptography (A)**, **(B)**, and **(C)**.

18. Under (**2**) locate the message to be hidden. Click **Browse** and navigate to the file **Message.zip**. Click **Open**.

19. Under (**3**) select the carrier file. Click **Add** and navigate to **Carrier1.pdf** and click **Open** as shown in Figure 5-12.

20. Click **Hide Data!**

21. Navigate to a different location than that of the carrier files and click **OK**.

22. After the processing has completed, navigate to the location of the carrier file that contains the message and open the file. Can you detect anything different with the file now that it contains the message?

23. Now uncover the message. Close the OpenPuff Data Hiding screen to return to the main menu.

24. Click **Unhide**.

25. Enter the three passwords.

26. Click **Add Carriers** and navigate to the location of **Carrier1** that contains the hidden message.

27. Click **Unhide!** and navigate to a location to deposit the hidden message. When it has finished processing click **OK**.

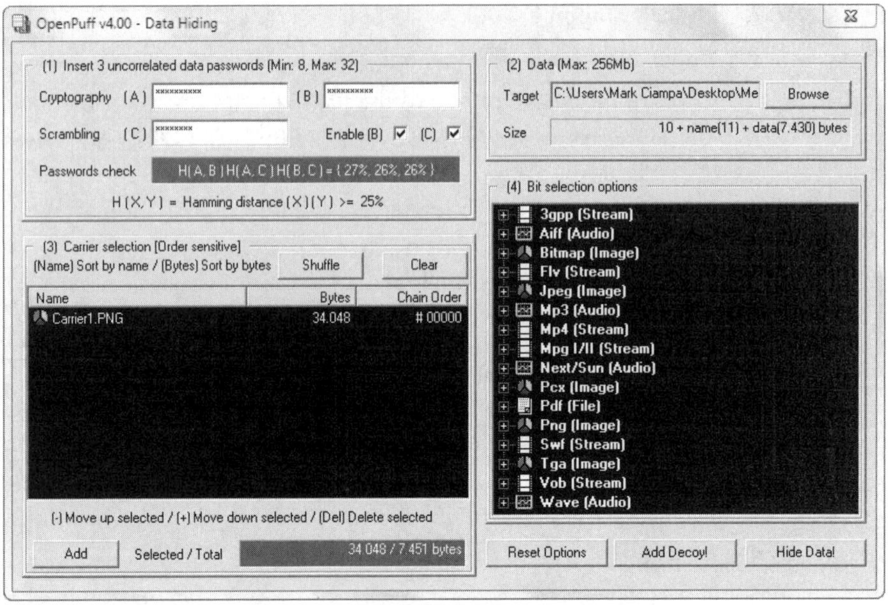

Figure 5-12 OpenPuff
Source: EmbeddedSW.net

28. Click **Done** after reading the report.

29. Go to that location and you will see **Message.zip**.

30. Close OpenPuff and close all windows.

Project 5-2: Running an RSA Cipher Demonstration

The steps for encryption using RSA can be illustrated in a Java applet on a website. In this project, you will observe how RSA encrypts and decrypts.

It is recommended that you review the section earlier in this chapter regarding the steps in the RSA function.

1. Use your web browser to go to **people.cs.pitt.edu/~kirk/cs1501/notes/rsademo/**.

It is not unusual for websites to change the location of files. If the URL above no longer functions, open a search engine and search for "RSA Cipher Demonstration".

2. Read the information about the demonstration.

3. Click **key generation page**.

4. Change the first prime number (P) to 7.

5. Change the second prime number (Q) to 5.

6. Click **Proceed.**

7. Read the information in the popup screen and record the necessary numbers. Close the screen when finished.

8. Click **Encryption Page.**

9. Next to **Enter Alice' Exponent key, E:** enter 5 as the key value from the previous screen.

10. Under **Enter Alice' N Value:** enter 35.

11. Click **Encrypt.** Read the message and record the values. Close the screen when finished.

12. Click **Decryption Page.**

13. Next to **Enter the encrypted message** enter **1.**

14. Next to **Enter your N value:** enter 35.

15. Next to **Enter your private key, D:** enter 5.

16. Click **Proceed.** Note that **1** has been decrypted to **A.**

17. Close all windows.

Project 5-3: Installing Command-Line Hash Generators and Comparing Hashes

In this project, you will download different command-line hash generators to compare hash digest values.

1. Use your web browser to go to **md5deep.sourceforge.net.**

It is not unusual for websites to change the location of files. If the URL above no longer functions, open a search engine and search for "MD5DEEP".

2. Click **Download md5deep and hashdeep.**

3. Click **Windows binary** and download the latest version of the program.

These programs are run from a command prompt instead of by double-clicking an icon. It is recommended that the programs be stored on a USB flash drive or on the root directory (C:\) to make navigating to them easier.

4. Using Windows Explorer, navigate to the location of the downloaded file. Right-click the file and then click **Extract All** to extract the files.

5. Create a Microsoft Word document with the contents **Now is the time for all good men to come to the aid of their country.**

6. Save the document as **Country1.docx** in the directory that contains the hash digest generator files and then close the document.

7. Start a command prompt by clicking **Start,** entering **cmd,** and then pressing **Enter.**

8. Navigate to the location of the downloaded files.

9. Enter **MD5DEEP Country1.docx** to start the application that creates an MD5 digest of **Country1.docx** and then press **Enter**. What is the length of this digest?

10. Now enter **MD5DEEP MD5DEEP.TXT** to start the application that creates an MD5 digest of the accompanying documentation file **MD5DEEP.TXT** and then press **Enter**. What is the length of this digest? Compare it to the digest of **Country1.docx**. What does this tell you about the strength of the MD5 digest?

11. Launch Microsoft Word and then open **Country1.docx**.

12. Remove the period at the end of the sentence so it says **Now is the time for all good men to come to the aid of their country** and then save the document as **Country2.docx** in the directory that contains the hash digest generator files. Close the document.

13. At the command prompt, enter **MD5DEEP Country2.docx** to start the application that creates an MD5 hash of **Country2.docx** and then press **Enter**. What difference does removing the period make to the digest?

14. Return to the command prompt and perform the same comparisons of **Country1.docx** and **Country2.docx** using **sha1deep.exe** (SHA-1), **sha256deep.exe** (SHA-256), and **whirlpooldeep.exe** (Whirlpool). What observations can you make regarding the length of the digests between **Country1.docx** and **Country2.docx** for each hash algorithm? What do you observe regarding the differences between hash algorithms as you compare MD5 with SHA-1, SHA-256 with Whirlpool, etc.?

15. Enter **Exit** at the command prompt.

Project 5-4: Installing GUI Hash Generators and Comparing Digests

In this project, you will download a GUI hash generator and compare the results of various hash algorithms.

1. Use your web browser to go to **implbits.com/Products/HashTab.aspx**.

It is not unusual for websites to change the location of files. If the URL above no longer functions, open a search engine and search for "Hash Tab".

2. Click **Windows Download**.

3. Click **Download Now!**

4. Enter an email address to receive a direct link to download the file.

5. Follow the default instructions to install Hash Tab.

6. Click the right mouse button on the Windows **Start** icon.

7. Click **Open Windows Explorer**.

8. Navigate to the document **Country1.docx**.

9. Click once on **Country1.docx** and then right-click.

10. Click **Properties**.

11. Notice that there is a new tab, **File Hashes**. Click this tab to display the digests for this file, as illustrated in Figure 5-13.

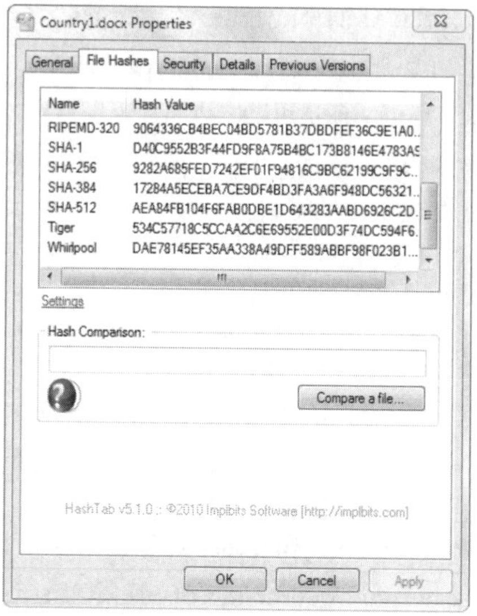

Figure 5-13   File Hashes tab
Source: Implbits Software LLC

12. Click **Settings**.

13. Click the **Select All** button.

14. Click **OK**.

15. Scroll through the different digests generated. How do the new SHA-3 digests compare with other digests?

16. Click **Compare a file**.

17. Navigate to the file **Country2.docx** and then click **Open**.

18. A digest is generated on this file. What tells you that the digests are not the same?

19. Which program would you prefer to use, a GUI or command-line one-way hash? Why?

20. Close all windows.

Project 5-5: Using Microsoft's Encrypting File System (EFS)

Microsoft's Encrypting File System (EFS) is a cryptography system for Windows operating systems that uses the Windows NTFS file system. Because EFS is tightly integrated with the file system, file encryption and decryption are transparent to the user. In this project, you will turn on and use EFS.

1. Create a Word document with the contents of the first two paragraphs under **Today's Attacks and Defenses** on the first page of this chapter.

2. Save the document as **Encrypted.docx**.

3. Save the document again as **Not Encrypted.docx**.

4. Right-click the **Start** button and then click **Open Windows Explorer**.

5. Navigate to the location of **Encrypted.docx**.

6. Right-click **Encrypted.docx**.

7. Click **Properties**.

8. Click the **Advanced** button.

9. Check the box **Encrypt contents to secure data**. This document is now protected with EFS. All actions regarding encrypting and decrypting the file are transparent to the user and should not noticeably affect any computer operations. Click **OK**.

10. Click **OK** to close the Encrypted Properties dialog box.

11. Launch Microsoft Word and then open **Encrypted.docx**. Was there any delay in the operation?

12. Now open **Not Encrypted.docx**. Was it any faster or slower?

13. Retain these two documents for use in the next project. Close Word.

Project 5-6: Using TrueCrypt

As an alternative to EFS, third-party applications can be downloaded to protect files with cryptography. In this project, you will download and install TrueCrypt.

1. Use your web browser to go to **www.truecrypt.org**.

It is not unusual for websites to change the location of files. If the URL above no longer functions, open a search engine and search for "TrueCrypt".

2. Click **Downloads**.

3. Under **Latest Stable Version** click **Download**.

4. Follow the default installation procedures to install TrueCrypt. Click **No** if you are asked to view the tutorial.

5. Launch TrueCrypt by clicking **Start** and then entering **TrueCrypt**.

6. When the main TrueCrypt window displays, click the **Create Volume** button.

7. A TrueCrypt volume can be in a file (called a container), in a partition or drive. A TrueCrypt container is like a normal file in that it can be moved, copied, and deleted. Be sure that **Create an encrypted file container** is selected. Click **Next**.

8. Under **Volume Type**, be sure that **Standard TrueCrypt volume** is selected. Click **Next**.

9. Under **Volume Location**, click **Select File**.

10. Enter **TrueCrypt Encrypted Volume** next to **File name** and select the location for this file. Click **Save**.

11. Click **Next**.

12. Under **Encryption Algorithm**, be sure that **AES** is selected. Click **Next**.

13. Under **Volume Size**, enter **1** and be sure that **MB** is selected. Click **Next**.

14. Under **Volume Password**, read the requirements for a password and then enter a strong password to protect the files. Enter it again under **Confirm** and then click **Next**.

15. When the **Volume Format** dialog box displays, move your mouse as randomly as possible within the window for at least 30 seconds. The mouse movements are used to strengthen the encryption keys.

16. Click **Format**. It is now creating the TrueCrypt Encrypted Volume container. When it is finished, click **OK**.

17. Click **Exit**.

18. Now you must mount this container as a volume. Select a drive letter that is not being used by clicking on it.

19. Click **Select File**.

20. Navigate to the location where you saved the TrueCrypt Encrypted Volume container and then click **Open**.

21. Click **Mount**.

22. When prompted, enter your TrueCrypt container password and then click **OK**.

23. The volume will now display as mounted. This container is entirely encrypted, including file names and free space, and functions like a real disk. You can copy, save, or move files to this container disk and they will be encrypted as they are being written. Minimize this window.

24. Open the file **Encrypted.docx**.

25. Save this file as **TrueCrypt Encrypted.docx** and save it in your TrueCrypt container (use the drive letter that you selected above).

26. Close this document.

27. Open the document from your TrueCrypt container. Did it take any longer to open now that it is encrypted? Close the document again.

28. Maximize the TrueCrypt window and then click **Dismount** to stop your container. A container will also be unmounted when you log off.

29. Based on your experiences with TrueCrypt and EFS, which do you prefer? Why? What advantages and disadvantages do you see for both applications?

30. Close all windows.

Case Projects

CASE PROJECTS

Case Project 5-1: Hash Algorithm Comparison

Research the different hash algorithms (Message Digest, Secure Hash Algorithm, Whirlpool, and RIPEMD) and then create a table that compares them. Include the size of the digest, the number of rounds needed to create the hash, block size, who created it, what previous hash it was derived from, its strengths, and its weaknesses.

Case Project 5-2: One-Time Pad (OTP) Research

Use the Internet to research OTPs: who was behind the initial idea, when they were first used, in what applications they were found, how they are used today, etc. Then visit an online OTP creation site such as *www.braingle.com/ brainteasers/codes/onetimepad.php* and practice creating your own ciphertext with OTP. If possible exchange your OTPs with other students to see how you might try to break them. Would it be practical to use OTPs? Why or why not? Write a one-page paper on your findings.

Case Project 5-3: Blowfish

Several security researchers claim that Blowfish has better performance than other symmetric encryption algorithms and does not have any known security vulnerabilities. Research Blowfish and create a one-page paper that outlines its strengths, weaknesses, how it is currently being used, etc. Based on your research, do you agree that Blowfish may be a top choice?

Case Project 5-4: Diffie-Hellman Research

How does Diffie-Hellman work? Use the Internet to research this key-sharing function. Then visit the website *dkerr.home.mindspring.com/diffie_hellman_ calc.html* to see how values are created. Write a one-page paper on Diffie-Hellman.

Case Project 5-5: USB Device Encryption

Use the Internet to select four USB flash drives that support hardware encryption. Create a table that compares all four and their features. Be sure to include any unique features that the drives may have along with their costs. Which would you recommend? Why? Write a one-page paper on your research.

Case Project 5-6: SHA-3 Research

Use the Internet to research SHA-3 (Keccak). How is it similar to other hash algorithms? How is it different? What are its strengths and weaknesses? Write a one-page paper on your research.

Case Project 5-7: Bay Pointe Security Consulting

Bay Pointe Security Consulting (BPSC) provides security consulting services to a wide range of businesses, individuals, schools, and organizations. BPSC has hired you as a technology student to help them with a new project and provide real-world experience to students who are interested in the security field.

National Meteorological Services (NMS) offers in-depth weather forecasting services to airlines, trucking firms, event planners, and other organizations that need the latest and most accurate weather forecasting services. NMS has discovered that their forecast information, which was being sent out as email attachments to its customers, was being freely distributed without NMS's permission, and in some instances was being resold by their competitors. NMS wants to look into encrypting these weather forecast documents, but is concerned that its customers may find decrypting the documents cumbersome. The company also wants to provide to their customers a level of assurance that these documents originate from NMS and have not been tampered with. NMS has asked BPSC to make a presentation about different solutions, and BPSC has asked you to help them prepare it.

1. Create a PowerPoint presentation about encryption and the different types of encryption. Include the advantages and disadvantages of each. Your presentation should contain at least 10 slides.

2. After the presentation, an NMS officer asks for your recommendation regarding meeting their needs for encryption. Create a memo communicating the actions you believe would be best for the company to take.

Case Project 5-8: Community Site Activity

The Information Security Community Site is an online companion to this textbook. It contains a wide variety of tools, information, discussion boards, and other features to assist learners. Go to **community.cengage.com/infosec**. Click JOIN THE COMMUNITY and use the login name and password that you created in Chapter 1. Visit the **Discussions** section, and then read the following case study.

This is a true story (with minor details changed). Microsoft had uncovered several licensing discrepancies in its software that clients were using while claiming they had purchased it from an authorized software retailer. The sale of one software package to a company in Tampa was traced back to a retailer in Pennsylvania, and yet the retailer had no record of any sales to the Tampa company. A private security consulting agency was called in, and they discovered that the network system administrator "Ed" in Pennsylvania was downloading pirated software from the Internet and selling it to customers as legitimate software behind the company's back. Ed had sold almost a half-million dollars in illegal software. The security firm also noticed a high network bandwidth usage. Upon further investigation they found that Ed was using one of the company's servers as a pornographic website with more than 50,000 images and 2500 videos. In addition, a search of Ed's desktop computer uncovered a spreadsheet with hundreds of credit card numbers from the company's e-commerce site. The security firm speculated that Ed was either selling these card numbers to attackers or using them himself.

The situation was complicated by the fact that Ed was the only person who knew certain administrative passwords for the core network router and firewall, network switches, the corporate virtual private network (VPN), the entire Human Resources system, the email server, and the Windows Active Directory. In addition, the company had recently installed a Hardware Security Module (HSM) to which only Ed had the password. The security consultant and the Pennsylvania company were worried about what Ed might do if he was confronted with the evidence, since essentially he could hold the entire organization hostage or destroy virtually every piece of useful information.

A plan was devised. The company invented a fictitious emergency situation at one of their offices in California that required Ed to fly there overnight. The long flight gave the security team a window of about five and a half hours during which Ed could not access the system (the flight that was booked for Ed did not have wireless access). Working as fast as they could, the team mapped out the network and reset all the passwords. When Ed landed in California, the chief operating officer was there to meet him and Ed was fired on the spot.

Now it's your turn to think outside of the box. What would you have done to keep Ed away so you could reconfigure the network? Or how could you have tricked Ed into giving up the passwords without revealing to him that he was under suspicion? Record your answers on the Community Site discussion board.

References

1. Cowell, Alan, "Code found on pigeon baffles British cryptographers," *New York Times*, Nov. 24, 2012, accessed Feb. 5, 2014, www.nytimes.com/2012/11/24/world/europe/code-found-on-pigeon-baffles-british-cryptographers.html?_r=0.

2. Schneier, Bruce, "When will we see collisions for SHA-1?," *Schneier on Security*, Oct. 5, 2012, accessed Feb. 5, 2014, https://www.schneier.com/blog/archives/2012/10/when_will_we_se.html.

## chapter 6

Advanced Cryptography

After completing this chapter, you should be able to do the following:

- Define digital certificates
- List the various types of digital certificates and how they are used
- Describe the components of Public Key Infrastructure (PKI)
- List the tasks associated with key management
- Describe the different transport encryption protocols

Today's Attacks and Defenses

Did the U.S. government try to insert a secret weakness into a cryptographic algorithm so they could read encrypted documents?

The Computer Security Law of 1987 was passed by the U.S. Congress to improve the security and privacy of sensitive data on federal computer systems. One part of this law tasked the U.S. National Institute of Standards and Technology (NIST) to create standards by working with the National Security Agency (NSA). The NSA advertises itself as the "home to America's codemakers and codebreakers,"[1] and has provided information to U.S. decision makers and military leaders for more than 50 years.

In the 1990s the NSA was instrumental in working with IBM on the development of the Data Encryption Standard (DES). However, a controversy arose about the NSA's influence. The agency was accused of tampering with the standard by requiring that changes be made from the original algorithm's design. These changes were made without any explanation. Several years later it was revealed that IBM's researchers had discovered a potential weakness in DES and informed the NSA, which then mandated the changes so the algorithm would be resistant to attacks. So instead of weakening DES, the NSA actually helped strengthen it. In addition to DES, the NIST-NSA partnership was later responsible for the Advanced Encryption Standard (AES).

However, in 2013 documents were leaked that suggested the NSA's influence on another standard may have been intentionally harmful and introduced weaknesses to the algorithm. In 2006 a standard was released that outlined four algorithms for securely generating random numbers that were used as part of a cryptographic algorithm. Whereas three of the algorithms were considered sound, a fourth algorithm raised controversy. Called Dual_EC_DRBG and based on elliptic curve technology, this algorithm not only was slow but also had a bias in that some numbers appeared more often than other numbers (and thus were not truly random). Although some argued that the Dual_EC_DRBG standard should be dropped, it was kept at the NSA's insistence. The agency said that it was worth including because of its theoretical basis and that it should be difficult to predict the numbers the algorithm would generate as long as the elliptic curve discrete logarithm problem remained difficult to solve.

Soon after the standard was published, a more serious problem with Dual_EC_DRBG was uncovered. As with DES, the Dual_EC_DRBG algorithm includes certain parameters that have to be chosen by the algorithm designer, namely, the elliptic curve and a chosen point on that curve. In 2007 two Microsoft researchers discovered that the point and the curve were related to one another by another number X. If X was

(continued)

known, then someone could examine the random numbers generated by the algorithm and subsequently predict the numbers that would be generated in the future, thus breaking the encryption. In short, any algorithm that used the random numbers generated by Dual_EC_DRBG could be compromised. The leaked 2013 documents suggested that the NSA intentionally sabotaged Dual_EC_DRBG.

What does it all mean? Like DES, was the NSA making Dual_EC_DRBG stronger by requiring these changes? Or were they attempting to incorporate a "backdoor" weakness that could allow them to read encrypted data? For now there is no way to know for certain. All that is certain is that Dual_EC_DRBG will never be widely used.

Cryptography has clear benefits for safeguarding sensitive data for end users. Hashing can ensure the integrity of a file (to guarantee that no one has tampered with it), symmetric encryption can protect the confidentiality of an email message (to ensure that no one has read it), and asymmetric encryption can verify the authenticity of the sender and enforce nonrepudiation (to prove that the sender is who he claims to be and cannot deny sending it). These cryptographic benefits can be implemented by individual users on their desktop computers or mobile devices.

Hashing, symmetric encryption, asymmetric encryption, and nonrepudiation are covered in Chapter 5.

Yet when cryptography is utilized in the enterprise, a level of complexity is added. What happens if an employee has encrypted an important proposal yet suddenly falls ill and cannot return to work? Where is her key stored? Who can have access to it? And how can the keys of hundreds or even thousands of employees be managed?

These and other issues relating to cryptography move the discussion from the basic mechanics of how end users can take advantage of cryptography to a higher level of the advanced cryptographic procedures that often are found in the enterprise. In this chapter you will learn about advanced cryptography. First you will learn about digital certificates and how they can be used. Next, you will explore public key infrastructure and key management. Finally, you will look at different transport cryptographic algorithms to see how cryptography is used on data that is being transported.

Digital Certificates

6.1 Given a scenario, utilize general cryptography concepts.

6.3 Given a scenario, use appropriate PKI, certificate management and associated components.

One of the common applications of cryptography is digital certificates. Using digital certificates involves understanding their purpose, knowing how they are managed, and determining which type of digital certificate is appropriate for different situations.

Defining Digital Certificates

Suppose that Alice receives an encrypted document that says it came from Bob. Although Alice can be sure that the encrypted message was not viewed or altered by someone else while being transmitted, how can she know for certain that Bob was actually the sender? Because Alice's public key is widely available, an attacker could have created a fictitious document, encrypted it with Alice's public key, and then sent it to Alice while pretending to be Bob. Although Alice's key can verify that no one read or changed the document in transport, it cannot verify the sender.

Proof can be provided with asymmetric cryptography by creating a *digital signature*. After creating a memo, Bob generates a digest on it and then encrypts the digest with his private key before sending both the memo and the digital signature to Alice. When she receives them, she decrypts the digital signature using Bob's public key, revealing the digest (if she cannot decrypt the digital signature then she knows that it did not come from Bob). Alice then hashes the memo with the same hash algorithm Bob used and compares the result to the digest she received from Bob. If they are equal, Alice can be confident that the message has not changed since he signed it.

The digital signature process is illustrated in Figure 5-9.

However, there is a weakness with digital signatures: they do not confirm the true identity of the sender. Digital signatures only show that the private key of the sender was used to encrypt the digital signature, but they do not definitively prove *who* the sender was. If Alice receives a message with a digital signature claiming to be from Bob, she cannot know for certain that it is the "real" Bob whose public key she is retrieving.

For example, suppose Bob created a message along with a digital signature and sent it to Alice. However, Mallory intercepted the message. He then created his own set of public and private keys using Bob's identity. Mallory could then create a new message and digital signature (with the imposter private key) and send them to Alice. Upon receiving the message and digital signature, Alice would unknowingly retrieve the imposter public key (thinking it belonged to Bob) and decrypt it. Alice would be tricked into thinking Bob had sent it when in reality it came from Mallory. This interception and imposter public key are illustrated in Figure 6-1.

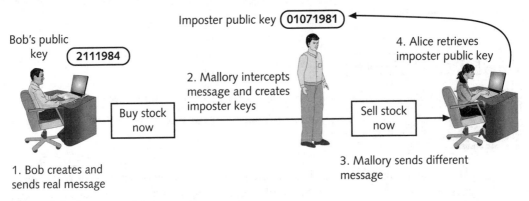

Figure 6-1 Imposter public key

Suppose that Bob wanted to ensure that Alice receives his real public key and not the imposter public key. He could travel to Alice's city, knock on her front door, and say, "I'm Bob and here's my key."

Yet how would Alice even know *this* was the real Bob and not Mallory in disguise? For verification she could ask to see Bob's passport. This is a document that is provided by a *trusted third party*. Although Alice may not initially trust Bob because she does not know him, she will trust the government agency that required Bob to provide proof of his identity when he applied for the passport. Using a trusted third party who has verified Bob, and who Alice also trusts, would help to solve the problem.

This is the concept behind a digital certificate. A **digital certificate** is a technology used to associate a user's identity to a public key and that has been "digitally signed" by a trusted third party. This third party verifies the owner and that the public key belongs to that owner. When Bob sends a message to Alice, he does not ask her to retrieve his public key from a central site; instead, Bob attaches the digital certificate to the message. When Alice receives the message with the digital certificate, she can check the signature of the trusted third party on the certificate. If the signature was signed by a party that she trusts, then Alice can safely assume that the public key contained in the digital certificate is actually from Bob. Digital certificates make it possible for Alice to verify Bob's claim that the key belongs to him and prevent a man-in-the-middle attack that impersonates the owner of the public key.

A digital certificate typically contains the following information:

- Owner's name or alias
- Owner's public key
- Name of the issuer
- Digital signature of the issuer
- Serial number of the digital certificate
- Expiration date of the public key

NOTE A digital certificate is basically a container for a public key. However, certificates also can contain other user-supplied information, such as an email address, postal address, and basic registration information, such as the country or region, postal code, age, and gender of the user. And digital certificates can be used to identify objects other than users, such as servers and applications.

Managing Digital Certificates

Several entities and technologies are used for the management of digital certificates. These include the Certificate Authority (CA) and Registration Authority (RA), along with a Certificate Repository (CR). Also, there must be a means to revoke certificates.

Certificate Authority (CA) When a new car is purchased, it is necessary to register that car with the state in which the owner lives. The new owner may visit the local county courthouse or similar venue to fill out the appropriate paperwork and pay the required fee. This information is usually then forwarded to the state capital, where the state's department of motor vehicles issues an official car title that is sent to the new owner.

The department of motor vehicles in the state capital in this example is similar to the **Certificate Authority (CA)**. A CA serves as the trusted third-party agency that is responsible for issuing the digital certificates. A CA can be external to the organization, such as a commercial CA that charges for the service, or it can be a CA internal to the organization that provides this service to employees.

 Technically a CA is a *Certification* Authority because its function is to certify; it is not an *authority* on certificates. However, today it often is called a *Certificate* Authority.

The general duties of a CA include:

- Generate, issue, and distribute public key certificates
- Distribute CA certificates
- Generate and publish certificate status information
- Provide a means for subscribers to request revocation
- Revoke public key certificates
- Maintain the security, availability, and continuity of the certificate issuance signing functions

A subscriber requesting a digital certificate first generates the public and private keys. Next she generates a **Certificate Signing Request (CSR)**, which is a specially formatted encrypted message that validates the information the CA requires to issue a digital certificate. Table 6-1 lists the information found in a CSR. Once the CA receives and verifies the CSR, it inserts the public key into the certificate. Finally, these certificates are digitally signed with the private key of the issuing CA.

Name	Description	Example
Common name	Fully qualified domain name (FQDN) of the server	www.acompany.net
Business name	Legal name of organization	A Company, Inc.
Department	Division of the organization	Information Technology
City	City of the organization	Tampa
State	State of the organization	FL
Country	Two-letter code of country	US
Email address	Address of contact person	cio@acompany.net

Table 6-1   **Certificate Signing Request content**

Because digital certificates are used extensively on the Internet, web browsers are preconfigured with a default list of CAs. A list of CAs in the Google Chrome web browser is illustrated in Figure 6-2.

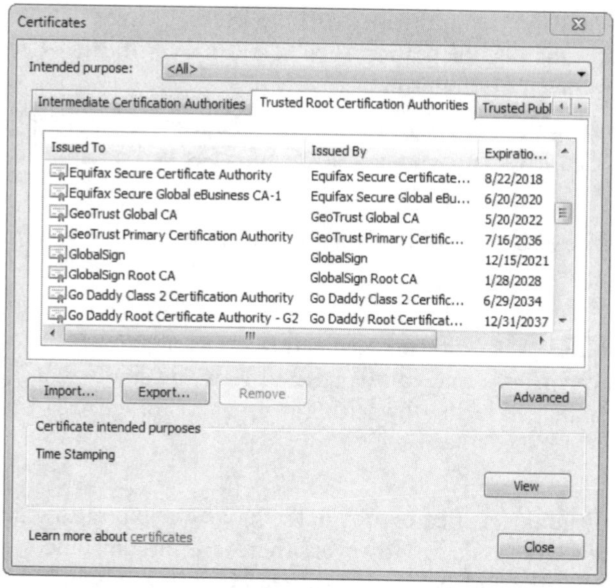

Figure 6-2   Web browser default CAs
Source: Google Chrome web browser

Registration Authority (RA) In the previous example, the local county courthouse where the new car owner filled out the appropriate paperwork and paid the required fee is similar to the **Registration Authority (RA)** function, which is a subordinate entity designed to handle specific CA tasks such as processing certificate requests and authenticating users. Although the registration function could be implemented directly with the CA, there are advantages to using separate RAs. If there are many entities that require a digital certificate, or if these are spread out across geographical areas, using a single centralized CA may create bottlenecks or inconveniences. Using one or more RAs, sometimes called *Local Registration Authorities (LRAs)*, who can "off-load" these registration functions, can create an improved workflow.

The general duties of an RA include:

- Receive, authenticate, and process certificate revocation requests
- Identify and authenticate subscribers
- Obtain a public key from the subscriber
- Verify that the subscriber possesses the asymmetric private key corresponding to the public key submitted for certification

The primary function of an RA is to verify the identity of the individual. The person requesting a digital certificate can be identified to the RA in several ways:

- *Email.* In the simplest form, the owner may be identified only by an email address. Although this type of digital certificate might be sufficient for basic email communication, it is insufficient for other activities, such as transferring money online.

- *Documents.* An RA can confirm the authenticity of the person requesting the digital certificate by requiring specific documentation such as a birth certificate or copy of an employee badge that contains a photograph.
- *In person.* In some instances, the RA might require the applicant to apply in person to prove his existence and identity by providing a government-issued passport or driver's license.

After the identity is verified, the RA can initiate the certification process with a CA on behalf of that person.

Certificate Repository (CR) A **Certificate Repository (CR)** is a publicly accessible centralized directory of digital certificates that can be used to view the status of a digital certificate. This directory can be managed locally by setting it up as a storage area that is connected to the CA server.

Certificate Revocation Digital certificates normally have an expiration date, such as one year from the date they were issued. However, there are circumstances that may be cause for the certificate to be revoked before it expires. Some reasons may be benign, such as when the certificate is no longer used or the details of the certificate, such as the user's address, have changed. Other circumstances may be more dangerous. For example, if someone were to steal a user's private key, she could impersonate the victim through using digital certificates without the other users being aware of it. In addition, what would happen if digital certificates were stolen from a CA? The thieves could then issue certificates to themselves that would be trusted by unsuspecting users. It is important that the CA publishes approved certificates as well as revoked certificates in a timely fashion; otherwise, it could lead to a situation in which security may be compromised.

There have been several incidences of digital certificates stolen from CAs. One Dutch CA firm had its servers compromised because they used outdated and unpatched software, and did not even have anti-virus software installed that could have alerted them when the attackers planted the malware on the servers. Attackers stole 531 certificates and distributed them, resulting in more than 300,000 IP addresses accessing sites in just one month that were displaying a fake certificate for Google.com. And almost 99 percent of those IP addresses originated in Iran. It is surmised that the fake Google.com certificate was used primarily to spy on Iranians' Gmail accounts and that the culprit was the Iranian government looking to locate and crack down on dissidents.

The current status of a certificate can be checked to determine if it has been revoked by two means. The first is to use a **Certificate Revocation List (CRL)**, which serves as a list of certificate serial numbers that have been revoked. Many CAs maintain an online CRL that can be queried by entering the certificate's serial number. In addition, a local computer receives updates on the status of certificates and maintains a local CRL, as illustrated in Figure 6-3.

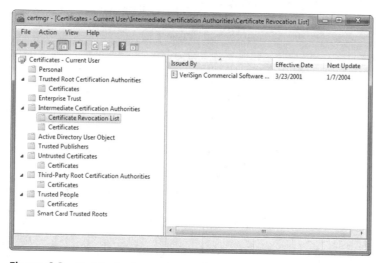

Figure 6-3   Certificate Revocation List (CRL)
Source: Microsoft Windows

The second method is an **Online Certificate Status Protocol (OCSP)**, which performs a real-time lookup of a certificate's status. OCSP is called a request-response protocol. The browser sends the certificate's information to a trusted entity like the CA, known as an *OCSP Responder*. The OCSP Responder then provides immediate revocation information on that one specific certificate.

Until recently all modern web browsers (Internet Explorer, Firefox, Safari on Mac OS X, some versions of Opera, and Google Chrome) used OCSP. However, if the web browser cannot reach the OCSP Responder server, such as when the server is down, then the browser receives back the message that there is a network error (called a *soft-fail*) and the revocation check is simply ignored. Because of this weakness, Google Chrome decided that it would no longer support OCSP but instead would rely entirely on CRLs that are downloaded to Chrome.

A variation of OCSP is called *OCSP stapling*. OCSP requires the OCSP Responder to provide responses to every web client of a certificate in real time, which may create a high volume of traffic. With OCSP stapling, web servers send queries to the OCSP Responder server at regular intervals to receive a signed time-stamped OCSP response. When a client's web browser attempts to connect to the web server, the server can include (*staple*) in the handshake with the web browser the previously received OCSP response. The browser then can evaluate the OCSP response to determine if it is trustworthy. OCSP stapling is illustrated in Figure 6-4.

Types of Digital Certificates

There are different categories of digital certificates. The most common categories are personal digital certificates, server digital certificates, and software publisher digital certificates. There are also standards for digital certificates.

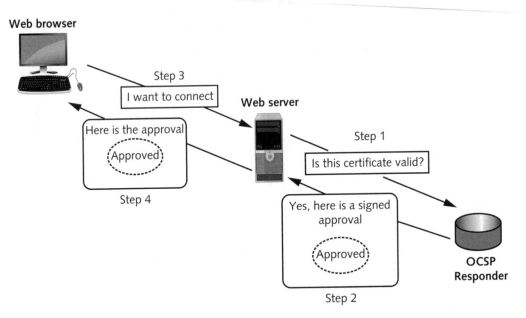

Figure 6-4 OCSP stapling

Any object that has a digital certificate associated with it is technically called an *end-entity*.

Class 1: Personal Digital Certificates

Personal digital certificates (Class 1) are issued by an RA directly to individuals. Personal digital certificates are frequently used to secure email transmissions. Typically these require only the user's name and email address in order to receive this certificate.

In addition to email messages, digital certificates also can be used to authenticate the authors of documents. For example, a user can create a Microsoft Word or Adobe Portable Document Format (PDF) document and then use a digital certificate to create a digital signature.

Class 2: Server Digital Certificates

Server digital certificates are often issued from a web server to a client, although they can be distributed by any type of server, such as an email server. Server digital certificates perform two functions. First, they can ensure the authenticity of the web server. Server digital certificates enable clients connecting to the web server to examine the identity of the server's owner. A user who connects to a website that has a server digital certificate issued by a trusted CA can be confident that the data transmitted to the server is used only by the person or organization identified by the certificate.

Some CAs issue only entry-level certificates that provide domain-only validation; that is, they only authenticate that an organization has the right to use a particular domain name. These certificates indicate nothing regarding the individuals behind the site.

Second, server digital certificates can ensure the authenticity of the cryptographic connection to the web server. Sensitive connections to web servers, such as when a user needs to enter a credit card number to pay for an online purchase, need to be protected. Web servers can set up secure cryptographic connections so that all transmitted data is encrypted by providing the server's public key with a digital certificate to the client. This handshake between web browser and web server is illustrated in Figure 6-5.

1.   The web browser sends a message ("ClientHello") to the server that contains information including the list of cryptographic algorithms that the client supports.

2.   The web server responds ("ServerHello") by indicating which cryptographic algorithm will be used. It then sends the server digital certificate to the browser.

3.   The web browser verifies the server certificate (such as making sure it has not expired) and extracts the server's public key. The browser generates a random value (called the *pre-master secret*), encrypts it with the server's public key, and sends it back to the server ("ClientKeyExchange").

4.   The server decrypts the message and obtains the browser's pre-master secret. Because both the browser and server now have the same pre-master secret, they can each create the same *master secret*. The master secret is used to create **session keys**, which are symmetric keys to encrypt and decrypt information exchanged during the session and to verify its integrity.

 One of the goals of the handshake is to generate keys for symmetric encryption using 3DES or AES. No public keys or certificates are involved once the handshake is completed.

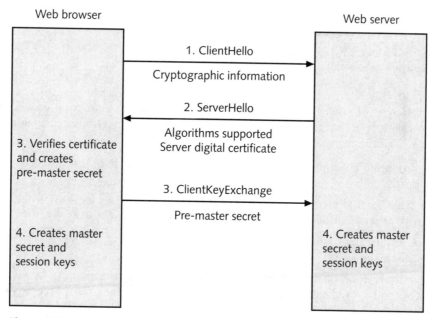

Figure 6-5   Server digital certificate handshake

Most server digital certificates combine both server authentication and secure communication between clients and servers on the web, although these functions can be separate. A server digital certificate that both verifies the existence and identity of the organization and securely encrypts communications displays a padlock icon in the web browser. Clicking the padlock icon displays information about the digital certificate along with the name of the site, as shown in Figure 6-6 (Google Chrome browser).

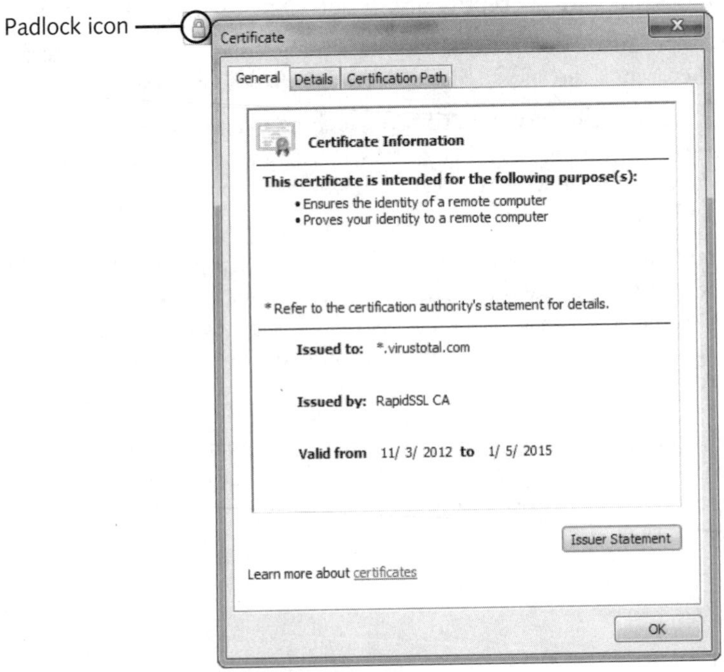

Padlock icon

Certificate

General | Details | Certification Path

Certificate Information

This certificate is intended for the following purpose(s):
- Ensures the identity of a remote computer
- Proves your identity to a remote computer

* Refer to the certification authority's statement for details.

Issued to: *.virustotal.com

Issued by: RapidSSL CA

Valid from 11/ 3/ 2012 **to** 1/ 5/ 2015

Issuer Statement

Learn more about certificates

OK

Figure 6-6 Padlock icon and certificate information
Source: Google Chrome web browser

An enhanced type of server digital certificate is the *Extended Validation SSL Certificate (EV SSL)*. This type of certificate requires more extensive verification of the legitimacy of the business. Requirements include:

- The CA must pass an independent audit verifying that it follows the EV standards.
- The existence and identity of the website owner, including its legal existence, physical address, and operational presence, must be verified by the CA.
- The CA must verify that the website is the registered holder and has exclusive control of the domain name.
- The authorization of the individual(s) applying for the certificate must be verified by the CA, and a valid signature from an officer of the company must accompany the application.

In addition, web browsers can visually indicate to users that they are connected to a website that uses the higher-level EV SSL by using colors on the address bar. A web browser that accesses a site that uses EV SSL displays the address bar shaded in green along with the site's name. The address bar displays in red if the site is known to be dangerous.

Class 3: Software Publisher Digital Certificates *Software publisher digital certificates* are provided by software publishers. The purpose of these certificates is to verify that their programs are secure and have not been tampered with.

The remaining two classes of digital certificates are specialized. Class 4 is for online business transactions between companies, while Class 5 is for private organizations or governmental security.

X.509 Digital Certificates The most widely accepted format for digital certificates is defined by the International Telecommunication Union (ITU) *X.509* international standard. Digital certificates following this standard can be read or written by any application that follows X.509. The current version is X.509 v3. Table 6-2 shows the structure of an X.509 certificate.

X.509 systems also include a method for creating a Certificate Revocation List (CRL).

Field name	Explanation
Certificate version number	0 = Version 1, 1 = Version 2, 2 = Version 3
Serial number	Unique serial number of certificate
Issuer signature algorithm ID	"Issuer" is Certificate Authority
Issuer X.500 name	Certificate Authority name
Validity period	Start date/time and expiration date/time
Subject X.500 name	Private key owner
Subject public key information	Algorithm ID and public key value
Issuer unique ID	Optional; added with Version 2
Subject unique ID	Optional; added with Version 2
Extensions	Optional; added with Version 3
Signature	Issuer's digital signature

Table 6-2   X.509 structure

Public Key Infrastructure (PKI)

6.3 Given a scenario, use appropriate PKI, certificate management and associated components.

One of the important management tools for the use of digital certificates and asymmetric cryptography is public key infrastructure. Public key infrastructure involves public key cryptography standards, trust models, and managing PKI.

What Is Public Key Infrastructure (PKI)?

One single digital certificate between Alice and Bob involves multiple entities and technologies. Asymmetric cryptography must be used to create the public and private keys, an RA must verify Bob's identity, the CA must issue the certificate, the digital certificate must be placed in a CR and moved to a CRL when it expires, and so on. In an organization where multiple users have multiple digital certificates, it can quickly become overwhelming to individually manage all of these entities. In short, there needs to be a consistent means to manage digital certificates.

Public key infrastructure (PKI) is what you might expect from its name: it is the underlying infrastructure for the management of public keys used in digital certificates. PKI is a framework for all of the entities involved in digital certificates for digital certificate management—including hardware, software, people, policies, and procedures—to create, store, distribute, and revoke digital certificates. In short, PKI is digital certificate management.

PKI is sometimes erroneously applied to a broader range of cryptography topics beyond managing digital certificates. It is sometimes defined as that which supports other public key-enabled security services or certifies users of a security application. PKI should be understood as the framework for digital certificate management.

Public Key Cryptography Standards (PKCS)

Public key cryptography standards (PKCS) are a numbered set of PKI standards that have been defined by the RSA Corporation. Although they are informal standards, today they are widely accepted in the industry. These standards are based on the RSA public key algorithm. Currently, PKCS is composed of the 15 standards detailed in Table 6-3.

Applications and products that are developed by vendors may choose to support the PKCS standards. For example, as shown in Figure 6-7, Microsoft Windows provides native support for exporting digital certificates based on PKCS #7 and #12.

Trust Models

Trust may be defined as confidence in or reliance on another person or entity. One of the principal foundations of PKI is that of trust: Alice must trust that the public key in Bob's digital certificate actually belongs to him.

A **trust model** refers to the type of trust relationship that can exist between individuals or entities. In one type of trust model, **direct trust**, a relationship exists between two individuals

PKCS standard number	Current version	PKCS standard name	Description
PKCS #1	2.1	RSA Cryptography Standard	Defines the encryption and digital signature format using RSA public key algorithm
PKCS #2	N/A	N/A	Originally defined the RSA encryption of the message digest; now incorporated into PKCS #1
PKCS #3	1.4	Diffie-Hellman Key Agreement Standard	Defines the secret key exchange protocol using the Diffie-Hellman algorithm
PKCS #4	N/A	N/A	Originally defined specifications for the RSA key syntax; now incorporated into PKCS #1
PKCS #5	2.0	Password-Based Cryptography Standard	Describes a method for generating a secret key based on a password; known as the Password-Based Encryption (PBE) Standard
PKCS #6	1.5	Extended-Certificate Syntax Standard	Describes an extended-certificate syntax; currently being phased out
PKCS #7	1.5	Cryptographic Message Syntax Standard	Defines a generic syntax for defining digital signature and encryption
PKCS #8	1.2	Private Key Information Syntax Standard	Defines the syntax and attributes of private keys; also defines a method for storing keys
PKCS #9	2.0	Selected Attribute Types	Defines the attribute types used in data formats defined in PKCS #6, PKCS #7, PKCS #8, and PKCS #10
PKCS #10	1.7	Certification Request Syntax Standard	Outlines the syntax of a request format sent to a CA for a digital certificate
PKCS #11	2.20	Cryptographic Token Interface Standard	Defines a technology-independent device interface, called Cryptoki, that is used for security tokens, such as smart cards
PKCS #12	1.0	Personal Information Exchange Syntax Standard	Defines the file format for storing and transporting a user's private keys with a public key certificate
PKCS #13	Under development	Elliptic Curve Cryptography Standard	Defines the elliptic curve cryptography algorithm for use in PKI; describes mechanisms for encrypting and signing data using elliptic curve cryptography
PKCS #14	Under development	Pseudorandom Number Generation Standard	Covers pseudorandom number generation (PRNG)
PKCS #15	1.1	Cryptographic Token Information Format Standard	Defines a standard for storing information on security tokens

Table 6-3 PKCS standards

6

Certificate Export Wizard

Export File Format
Certificates can be exported in a variety of file formats.

Select the format you want to use:

○ DER encoded binary X.509 (.CER)

○ Base-64 encoded X.509 (.CER)

● Cryptographic Message Syntax Standard - PKCS #7 Certificates (.P7B)
   ☑ Include all certificates in the certification path if possible

○ Personal Information Exchange - PKCS #12 (.PFX)
   ☐ Include all certificates in the certification path if possible
   ☐ Delete the private key if the export is successful
   ☐ Export all extended properties

○ Microsoft Serialized Certificate Store (.SST)

Learn more about certificate file formats

[< Back] [Next >] [Cancel]

Figure 6-7 Microsoft Windows PKCS support
Source: Microsoft Windows

because one person knows the other person. Because Alice knows Bob—she has seen him, she can recognize him in a crowd, she has spoken with him—she can trust that the digital certificate that Bob personally gives to her contains his public key.

A **third-party trust** refers to a situation in which two individuals trust each other because each trusts a third party. If Alice does not know Bob, this does not mean that she can never trust his digital certificate. Instead, if she trusts a third-party entity who knows Bob, then she can trust that his digital certificate with the public key is Bob's.

An example of a third-party trust is a courtroom. Although the defendant and prosecutor may not trust one another, they both can trust the judge (a third party) to be fair and impartial. In that case, they implicitly trust each other because they share a common relationship with the judge.

Essentially three PKI trust models use a CA. These are the hierarchical trust model, the distributed trust model, and the bridge trust model.

A less secure trust model that uses no CA is called the "web of trust" model and is based on direct trust. Each user signs his digital certificate and then exchanges certificates with all other users. Because all users trust each other, each user can sign the certificate of all other users. Pretty Good Privacy (PGP) uses the web of trust model.

Hierarchical Trust Model The **hierarchical trust model** assigns a single hierarchy with one master CA called the *root*. This root signs all digital certificate authorities with a single key. A hierarchical trust model is illustrated in Figure 6-8.

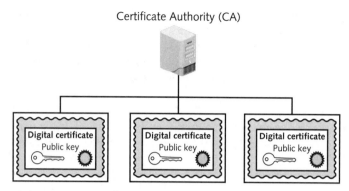

Figure 6-8   Hierarchical trust model

A hierarchical trust model can be used in an organization where one CA is responsible for only the digital certificates for that organization. However, on a larger scale, a hierarchical trust model has several limitations. First, if the CA's single private key were to be compromised, then all digital certificates would be worthless. Also, having a single CA who must verify and sign all digital certificates may create a significant backlog.

Distributed Trust Model   Instead of having a single CA, as in the hierarchical trust model, the **distributed trust model** has multiple CAs that sign digital certificates. This essentially eliminates the limitations of a hierarchical trust model. The loss of a CA's private key would compromise only those digital certificates for which it had signed, and the workload of verifying and signing digital certificates can be distributed. In addition, these CAs can delegate authority to other intermediate CAs to sign digital certificates. A distributed trust model is illustrated in Figure 6-9.

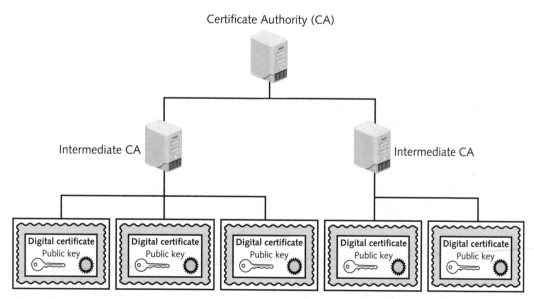

Figure 6-9   Distributed trust model

The distributed trust model is the basis for most end-user digital certificates used on the Internet. There are *trusted root certification authorities* as well as subordinate *intermediate certification authorities* (these can be seen in the tabs in Figure 6-2 and in the left pane in Figure 6-3). This allows a "chain" to be established: a web browser trusts the intermediate CA because the certificate was issued through a higher-level trusted root CA that it trusts.

To simplify the relationships in the chain, all certificates contain *Issued To* and *Issued By* fields so that the web browser can determine the trusted root CA. However, certificates issued by a trusted root CA do not use these fields because the trusted root CA issues the certificates itself.

Bridge Trust Model The **bridge trust model** is similar to the distributed trust model in that there is no single CA that signs digital certificates. However, with the bridge trust model there is one CA that acts as a "facilitator" to interconnect all other CAs. This facilitator CA does not issue digital certificates; instead, it acts as the hub between hierarchical trust models and distributed trust models. This allows the different models to be linked together. The bridge trust model is shown in Figure 6-10.

Managing PKI

An organization that uses multiple digital certificates on a regular basis needs to properly manage those digital certificates. This includes establishing policies and practices and determining the life cycle of a digital certificate.

Certificate Policy A *certificate policy (CP)* is a published set of rules that govern the operation of a PKI. The CP provides recommended baseline security requirements for the use and operation of CA, RA, and other PKI components. A CP should cover such topics as CA or RA obligations, user obligations, confidentiality, operational requirements, and training.

Many organizations create a single CP to support not only digital certificates but also digital signatures and all encryption applications.

Certificate Practice Statement (CPS) A *certificate practice statement (CPS)* is a more technical document than a CP. A CPS describes in detail how the CA uses and manages certificates. Additional topics for a CPS include how end users register for a digital certificate, how to issue digital certificates, when to revoke digital certificates, procedural controls, key pair generation and installation, and private key protection.

Certificate Life Cycle Digital certificates should not last forever. Employees leave, new hardware is installed, applications are updated, and cryptographic standards evolve. Each of

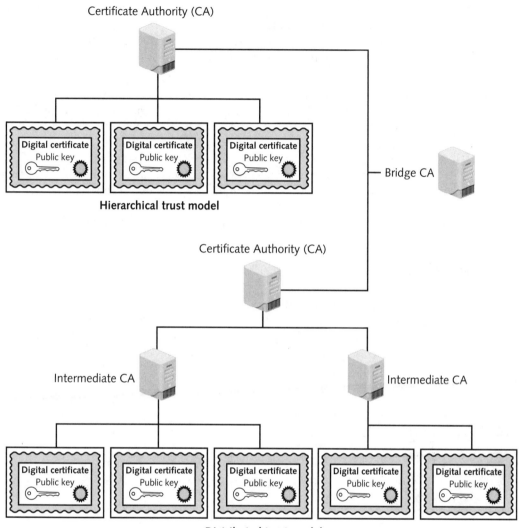

Certificate Authority (CA)

Digital certificate
Public key

Digital certificate
Public key

Digital certificate
Public key

Bridge CA

Hierarchical trust model

Certificate Authority (CA)

Intermediate CA

Intermediate CA

Digital certificate
Public key

Digital certificate
Public key

Digital certificate
Public key

Digital certificate
Public key

Digital certificate
Public key

Distributed trust model

Figure 6-10 Bridge trust model

these changes affects the usefulness of a digital certificate. The life cycle of a certificate is typically divided into four parts:

1. *Creation.* At this stage the certificate is created and issued to the user. Before the digital certificate is generated, the user must be positively identified. The extent to which the user's identification must be confirmed can vary, depending upon the type of certificate and any existing security policies. Once the user's identification has been verified, the request is sent to the CA for a digital certificate. The CA can then apply its appropriate signing key to the certificate, effectively signing the public key. The relevant fields can be updated by the CA, and the certificate is then forwarded to the RA (if one is being used). The CA also can keep a local copy of the certificate it generated. A certificate, once issued, can be published to a public directory if necessary.

2. *Suspension.* This stage could occur once or multiple times throughout the life of a digital certificate if the certificate's validity must be temporarily suspended. This may occur, for example, when an employee is on a leave of absence. During this time it may be important that the user's digital certificate not be used for any reason until she returns. Upon the user's return, the suspension can be withdrawn or the certificate can be revoked.

3. *Revocation.* At this stage the certificate is no longer valid. Under certain situations a certificate may be revoked before its normal expiration date, such as when a user's private key is lost or compromised. When a digital certificate is revoked, the CA updates its internal records and any CRL with the required certificate information and timestamp (a revoked certificate is identified in a CRL by its certificate serial number). The CA signs the CRL and places it in a public repository so that other applications using certificates can access this repository in order to determine the status of a certificate.

Either the user or the CA can initiate a revocation process.

4. *Expiration.* At the expiration stage the certificate can no longer be used. Every certificate issued by a CA must have an expiration date. Once it has expired, the certificate may not be used any longer for any type of authentication and the user will be required to follow a process to be issued a new certificate with a new expiration date.

Key Management

6.1 Given a scenario, utilize general cryptography concepts.

6.3 Given a scenario, use appropriate PKI, certificate management and associated components.

Because keys form the foundation of PKI systems, it is important that they be carefully managed. Proper key management includes key storage, key usage, and key handling procedures.

Key Storage

The means of storing keys in a PKI system is important. Public keys can be stored by embedding them within digital certificates, while private keys can be stored on the user's local system. The drawback to software-based storage is that it may leave keys open to attacks: vulnerabilities in the client operating system, for example, can expose keys to attackers.

Storing keys in hardware is an alternative to software-based storage. For storing public keys, special CA root and intermediate CA hardware devices can be used. Private keys can be stored on smart cards or in tokens.

TIP Whether private keys are stored in hardware or software, it is important that they be adequately protected. To ensure basic protection, never share the key in plaintext, always store keys in files or folders that are themselves password protected or encrypted, do not make copies of keys, and destroy expired keys.

Key Usage

If more security is needed than a single set of public and private keys, multiple pairs of dual keys can be created. One pair of keys may be used to encrypt information, and the public key can be backed up to another location. The second pair would be used only for digital signatures, and the public key in that pair would never be backed up.

Key Handling Procedures

Certain procedures can help ensure that keys are properly handled. These procedures include:

- *Escrow.* **Key escrow** refers to a process in which keys are managed by a third party, such as a trusted CA. In key escrow, the private key is split and each half is encrypted. The two halves are registered and sent to the third party, which stores each half in a separate location. A user can then retrieve the two halves, combine them, and use this new copy of the private key for decryption. Key escrow relieves the end user from the worry of losing her private key. The drawback to this system is that after the user has retrieved the two halves of the key and combined them to create a copy of the key, that copy of the key can be vulnerable to attacks.

- *Expiration.* Keys have expiration dates. This prevents an attacker who may have stolen a private key from being able to decrypt messages for an indefinite period of time. Some systems set keys to expire after a set period of time by default.

- *Renewal.* Instead of letting a key expire and then creating a new key, an existing key can be renewed. With renewal, the original public and private keys can continue to be used and new keys do not have to be generated. However, continually renewing keys makes them more vulnerable to theft or misuse.

- *Revocation.* Whereas all keys should expire after a set period of time, a key may need to be revoked prior to its expiration date. For example, the need for revoking a key may be the result of an employee being terminated from his position. Revoked keys cannot be reinstated. The CA should be immediately notified when a key is revoked and then the status of that key should be entered on the CRL.

- *Recovery.* What happens if an employee is hospitalized for an extended period, yet the organization for which she works needs to transact business using her keys? Different techniques may be used. Some CA systems have an embedded key recovery system in which a **key recovery agent (KRA)** is designated, who is a highly trusted person responsible for recovering lost or damaged digital certificates. Digital certificates can then be archived along with the user's private key. If the user is unavailable or if the certificate is lost, the certificate with the private key can be recovered. Another technique is known as *M-of-N control*. A user's private key is encrypted and divided into a specific number of parts, such as three. The parts are distributed to other individuals, with an overlap so that multiple individuals have the same part. For example, the three parts could be distributed to six people, with two people each having the same part. This is known as the N group. If it is necessary to recover the key, a smaller subset of the N group, known as the M group, must meet and agree that the key should be recovered. If a majority of the M group can agree, they can then piece the key together. M-of-N control is illustrated in Figure 6-11.

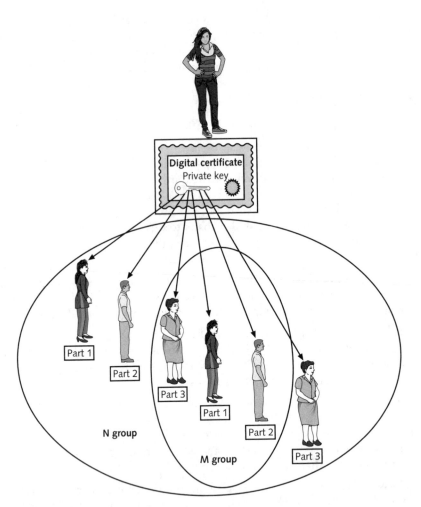

Figure 6-11 M-of-N control

The reason for distributing parts of the key to multiple users is that the absence of one member would not prevent the key from being recovered.

- *Suspension.* The revocation of a key is permanent; key suspension is for a set period of time. For example, if an employee is on an extended medical leave it may be necessary to suspend the use of her key for security reasons. A suspended key can be later reinstated. As with revocation, the CA should be immediately notified when a key is suspended, and the status of that key should be checked on the CRL to verify that it is no longer valid.

- *Destruction.* Key destruction removes all private and public keys along with the user's identification information in the CA. When a key is revoked or expires, the user's information remains on the CA for audit purposes.

Cryptographic Transport Protocols

6

1.4 Given a scenario, implement common protocols and services.

6.2 Given a scenario, use appropriate cryptographic methods.

In addition to protecting data in-use and data at-rest, cryptography is most often used to protect data in-transit across a network. The most common cryptographic transport protocols include Secure Sockets Layer (SSL), Transport Layer Security (TLS), Secure Shell (SSH), Hypertext Transport Protocol Secure (HTTPS), and IP security (IPsec).

Secure Sockets Layer (SSL)

One of the most common cryptographic transport algorithms is **Secure Sockets Layer (SSL)**. This protocol was developed by Netscape in 1994 in response to the growing concern over Internet security. The design goal of SSL was to create an encrypted data path between a client and a server that could be used on any platform or operating system. SSL took advantage of the relatively new cryptographic algorithm Advanced Encryption Standard (AES) instead of the weaker Data Encryption Standard (DES).

Over time updates to SSL were released. Today SSL version 3.0 is the version most web servers support.

Transport Layer Security (TLS)

Transport Layer Security (TLS) is another cryptographic transport algorithm. Although SSL and TLS are often used interchangeably or in conjunction with each other (*TLS/SSL*), this is not correct. SSL v3.0 served as the basis for TLS v1.0 (and is sometimes erroneously called *SSL 3.1*). Although TLS v1.0 was considered marginally more secure than SSL v3.0, subsequent versions of TLS (v1.1 and v1.2) are significantly more secure and address several vulnerabilities present in SSL v3.0 and TLS v1.0.

Despite the fact that TLS v1.1 and v1.2 are significantly more secure than SSL v3.0, many websites still support weaker versions of SSL and TLS in order to provide the broadest range of compatibility for older web browsers. Table 6-4 lists a survey of web servers that use SSL and TLS (servers may support multiple protocols).[2]

Protocol supported	Percentage of websites	Protocol security strength
SSL v2.0	23.0	Should not be used
SSL v3.0	99.3	Considered obsolete
TLS v1.0	97.7	Must be carefully configured
TLS v1.1	29.6	No known vulnerabilities
TLS v1.2	32.3	No known vulnerabilities

Table 6-4   **Website support of SSL and TLS**

In early 2014 a vulnerability in OpenSSL, an open-source software implementation of SSL and TLS, was discovered. This vulnerability was part of OpenSSL's relatively new "Heartbeat Extension" that is used to ensure that the other party in a client-server communication is still active. The vulnerability, called "Heartbleed," allowed attackers to access data in the web server's memory and steal the cryptographic keys used to encrypt and decrypt communications. Owners of web servers were forced to quickly patch the vulnerability on their servers.

As noted in steps 1 and 2 in Figure 6-5, the web browser provides a list of all the cryptographic algorithms that it supports, but the web server makes the ultimate decision of which will be used.

A **cipher suite** is a named combination of the encryption, authentication, and message authentication code (MAC) algorithms that are used with SSL and TLS. These are negotiated between the web browser and web server during the initial connection handshake. Depending on the different algorithms that are selected, the overall security of the transmission may be either strong or weak. For example, using RC4 instead of AES would significantly weaken the cipher suite. Another factor is the length of the keys. Keys of less than 2048 bits are considered weak, keys of 2048 bits are considered good, while keys of 4096 bits are strong.

Cipher suites typically use descriptive names to indicate their components. For example, CipherSuite *SSL_RSA_WITH_RC4_128_MD5* specifies that RSA will be used for key exchange and authentication algorithm, RC4 encryption algorithm using a 128–bit key will be used, and MD5 will be the MAC algorithm.

Secure Shell (SSH)

Secure Shell (SSH) is an encrypted alternative to the Telnet protocol that is used to access remote computers. SSH is a Linux/UNIX-based command interface and protocol for securely accessing a remote computer. SSH is actually a suite of three utilities—slogin, ssh, and scp—that are secure versions of the unsecure UNIX counterpart utilities. These commands are summarized in Table 6-5. Both the client and server ends of the connection are authenticated using a digital certificate, and passwords are protected by being encrypted. SSH can even be used as a tool for secure network backups.

UNIX command name	Description	Syntax	Secure command replacement
rlogin	Log on to remote computer	rlogin *remotecomputer*	slogin
rcp	Copy files between remote computers	rcp *[options] localfile remotecomputer:filename*	scp
rsh	Executing commands on a remote host without logging on	rsh *remotecomputer command*	ssh

Table 6-5 SSH commands

The first version of SSH was released in 1995 by a researcher at the Helsinki University of Technology after his university was the victim of a password-sniffing attack.

Hypertext Transport Protocol Secure (HTTPS)

One common use of TLS and SSL is to secure Hypertext Transport Protocol (HTTP) communications between a browser and a web server. This secure version is actually "plain" HTTP sent over SSL or TLS and is called **Hypertext Transport Protocol Secure (HTTPS)**. HTTPS uses port 443 instead of HTTP's port 80. Users must enter URLs with *https://* instead of *http://*.

Another cryptographic transport protocol for HTTP was Secure Hypertext Transport Protocol (SHTTP). However, it was not as secure as HTTPS and is now considered obsolete.

IP Security (IPsec)

Internet Protocol Security (IPsec) is a protocol suite for securing Internet Protocol (IP) communications. IPSec encrypts and authenticates each IP packet of a session between hosts or networks. IPSec can provide protection to a much wider range of applications than SSL or TLS.

IPsec is considered to be a *transparent* security protocol. It is transparent to the following entities:

- *Applications*. Programs do not have to be modified to run under IPsec.
- *Users*. Unlike some security tools, users do not need to be trained on specific security procedures (such as encrypting with PGP).
- *Software*. Because IPsec is implemented in a device such as a firewall or router, no software changes must be made on the local client.

Unlike SSL, which is implemented as a part of the user application, IPsec is located in the operating system or the communication hardware. IPsec is more likely to operate at a faster speed because it can cooperate closely with other system programs and the hardware.

IPsec provides three areas of protection that correspond to three IPsec protocols:

- *Authentication.* IPsec authenticates that packets received were sent from the source. This is identified in the header of the packet to ensure that no man-in-the-middle attacks or replay attacks took place to alter the contents of the packet. This is accomplished by the *Authentication Header (AH)* protocol.

- *Confidentiality.* By encrypting the packets, IPsec ensures that no other parties were able to view the contents. Confidentiality is achieved through the *Encapsulating Security Payload (ESP)* protocol. ESP supports authentication of the sender and encryption of data.

- *Key management.* IPsec manages the keys to ensure that they are not intercepted or used by unauthorized parties. For IPsec to work, the sending and receiving devices must share a key. This is accomplished through a protocol known as *Internet Security Association and Key Management Protocol/Oakley (ISAKMP/Oakley)*, which generates the key and authenticates the user using techniques such as digital certificates.

IPsec supports two encryption modes: transport and tunnel. *Transport mode* encrypts only the data portion (payload) of each packet yet leaves the header unencrypted. The more secure *tunnel mode* encrypts both the header and the data portion. IPsec accomplishes transport and tunnel modes by adding new headers to the IP packet. The entire original packet (header and payload) is then treated as the data portion of the new packet. This is illustrated in Figure 6-12. Because tunnel mode protects the entire packet, it is generally used in a network-to-network communication. Transport mode is used when a device must see the source and destination addresses to route the packet. For example, a packet sent from a client computer to the local IPsec-enabled firewall would be sent in transport mode so the packet can be transported through the local network. Once it reached the firewall, it would be changed to tunnel mode before being sent on to the Internet. The receiving firewall would then extract, decrypt, and authenticate the original packet before it is routed to the final destination computer.

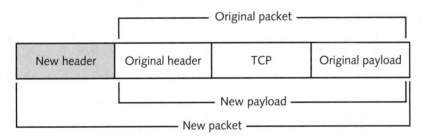

Figure 6-12   New IPsec packet using tunnel mode

In IPv4, IPsec is an optional protocol. In IPv6, IPsec is integrated into the IP protocol and is native on all packets. Although all IPv6 nodes must have IPsec available, the actual use of IPsec in IPv6 is optional.

Chapter Summary

- Digital signatures can be used to show the identity of the sender, but because the public key is available for anyone to obtain, an imposter could post a public key under another person's name. To avoid this impersonation, a third party can be used to verify the owner's identity. A digital certificate is the user's public key that has been digitally signed by a trusted third party who verifies the owner and that the public key belongs to that owner. It also binds the public key to the certificate.

- An entity that issues digital certificates for others is known as a Certificate Authority (CA). Users provide information to a CA that verifies their identity. A subordinate entity, called a Registration Authority (RA), is used to handle some CA tasks such as processing certificate requests and authenticating users. A Certificate Repository (CR) is a list of approved digital certificates. Revoked digital certificates are listed in a Certificate Revocation List (CRL), which can be accessed to check the certificate status of other users. The status also can be checked through the Online Certificate Status Protocol (OCSP). Because digital certificates are used extensively on the Internet, all modern web browsers are preconfigured with a default list of CAs and the ability to automatically update certificate information.

- Personal digital certificates are issued by an RA to individuals, primarily for protecting email correspondence and individual documents. Server digital certificates typically perform two functions. First, they can ensure the authenticity of the web server. Second, server certificates can ensure the authenticity of the cryptographic connection to the web server. Software publisher certificates are provided by software publishers and are used to verify that their programs are secure and have not been tampered with. The most widely accepted format for digital certificates is the X.509 international standard.

- A public key infrastructure (PKI) is a framework for all of the entities involved in digital certificates—including hardware, software, people, policies, and procedures—to create, store, distribute, and revoke digital certificates. PKI is essentially digital certificate management. Public Key Cryptography Standards (PKCS) is a numbered set of PKI standards. Although they are informal standards, they are widely accepted today.

- One of the principal foundations of PKI is that of trust. Three basic PKI trust models use a CA. The hierarchical trust model assigns a single hierarchy with one master CA called the root, who signs all digital certificate authorities with a single key. The bridge trust model is similar to the distributed trust model. No single CA signs digital certificates, and yet the CA acts as a facilitator to interconnect all other CAs. The distributed trust model has multiple CAs that sign digital certificates.

- An organization that uses multiple digital certificates on a regular basis needs to properly manage those digital certificates. Such management includes establishing policies and practices and determining the life cycle of a digital certificate. Because keys form the very foundation of PKI systems, it is important that they be carefully managed.

- Cryptography is commonly used to protect data in-transit. Secure Sockets Layer (SSL) is one of the most widely used cryptographic transport protocols. Modern versions of the Transport Layer Security (TLS) are a more secure alternative to SSL.

A cipher suite is a named combination of the encryption, authentication, and message authentication code (MAC) algorithms that are used with SSL and TLS. Secure Shell (SSH) is a Linux/UNIX-based command interface and protocol for securely accessing a remote computer communicating over the Internet. Hypertext Transport Protocol Secure (HTTPS), a secure version for web communications, is HTTP sent over SSL or TLS. IP security (IPsec) is a set of protocols developed to support the secure exchange of packets.

Key Terms

bridge trust model   A trust model with one CA that acts as a facilitator to interconnect all other CAs.

Certificate Authority (CA)   A trusted third-party agency that is responsible for issuing digital certificates.

Certificate Repository (CR)   A publicly accessible centralized directory of digital certificates that can be used to view the status of a digital certificate.

Certificate Revocation List (CRL)   A repository that lists revoked digital certificates.

Certificate Signing Request (CSR)   A specially formatted encrypted message that validates the information the CA requires to issue a digital certificate

cipher suite   A named combination of the encryption, authentication, and message authentication code (MAC) algorithms that are used with SSL and TLS.

digital certificate   A technology used to associate a user's identity to a public key, in which the user's public key is digitally signed by a trusted third party.

direct trust   A type of trust model in which a relationship exists between two individuals because one person knows the other person.

distributed trust model   A trust model that has multiple CAs that sign digital certificates.

hierarchical trust model   A trust model that has a single hierarchy with one master CA.

Hypertext Transport Protocol Secure (HTTPS)   A secure version of HTTP sent over SSL or TLS.

Internet Protocol Security (IPsec)   A set of protocols developed to support the secure exchange of packets between hosts or networks.

key escrow   A process in which keys are managed by a third party, such as a trusted CA.

key recovery agent (KRA)   A highly trusted person responsible for recovering lost or damaged digital certificates.

Online Certificate Status Protocol (OCSP)   A protocol that performs a real-time lookup of a certificate's status.

public key infrastructure (PKI)   A framework for managing all of the entities involved in creating, storing, distributing, and revoking digital certificates.

Registration Authority (RA)   A subordinate entity designed to handle specific CA tasks such as processing certificate requests and authenticating users.

Secure Shell (SSH)   A Linux/UNIX-based command interface and protocol for securely accessing a remote computer.

Secure Sockets Layer (SSL)   A protocol originally developed by Netscape for securely transmitting data.

session keys   Symmetric keys to encrypt and decrypt information exchanged during a handshake session between a web browser and web server.

third-party trust   A trust model in which two individuals trust each other because each individually trusts a third party.

Transport Layer Security (TLS)   A protocol that is more secure than SSL and guarantees privacy and data integrity between applications.

trust model   The type of trust relationship that can exist between individuals or entities.

Review Questions

1. A _____ is a specially formatted encrypted message that validates the information the CA requires to issue a digital certificate.

   a. Certificate Signing Request (CSR)

   b. digital digest

   c. FQDN form

   d. digital certificate

2. _____ performs a real-time lookup of a digital certificate's status.

   a. Certificate Revocation List (CRL)

   b. Online Certificate Status Protocol (OCSP)

   c. CA Registry Database (CARD)

   d. Real-Time CA Verification (RTCAV)

3. _____ are symmetric keys to encrypt and decrypt information exchanged during the session and to verify its integrity.

   a. Session keys

   b. Encrypted signatures

   c. Digital digests

   d. Digital certificates

4. Which of these is considered the weakest cryptographic transport protocol?

   a. SSL v2.0

   b. TLS v1.0

   c. TLS v1.1

   d. TLS v1.3

5. The strongest technology that would assure Alice that Bob is the sender of a message is a(n) _____.

   a. digital signature

   b. encrypted signature

   c. digital certificate

   d. digest

6. A digital certificate associates _____.

   a. a user's private key with the public key

   b. a private key with a digital signature

   c. a user's public key with his private key

   d. the user's identity with his public key

7. Digital certificates can be used for each of these EXCEPT _____.

   a. to encrypt channels to provide secure communication between clients and servers

   b. to verify the identity of clients and servers on the Web

   c. to verify the authenticity of the Registration Authorizer

   d. to encrypt messages for secure email communications

8. An entity that issues digital certificates is a _____.

   a. Certificate Authority (CA)

   b. Signature Authority (SA)

   c. Certificate Signatory (CS)

   d. Digital Signer (DS)

9. A centralized directory of digital certificates is called a(n) _____.

   a. Digital Signature Approval List (DSAP)

   b. Certificate Repository (CR)

   c. Authorized Digital Signature (ADS)

   d. Digital Signature Permitted Authorization (DSPA)

10. In order to ensure a secure cryptographic connection between a web browser and a web server, a(n) _____ would be used.

    a. web digital certificate

    b. email web certificate

    c. server digital certificate

    d. personal digital certificate

11. A digital certificate that turns the address bar green is a(n) _____.

    a. Personal Web-Client Certificate

    b. Advanced Web Server Certificate (AWSC)

    c. X.509 Certificate

    d. Extended Validation SSL Certificate

12. The _____-party trust model supports CA.

    a. first

    b. second

    c. third

    d. fourth

13. Public Key Cryptography Standards (PKCS) _____.

    a. are widely accepted in the industry

    b. are used to create public keys only

    c. define how hashing algorithms are created

    d. have been replaced by PKI

14. Which statement is NOT true regarding hierarchical trust models?

    a. The root signs all digital certificate authorities with a single key.

    b. It assigns a single hierarchy with one master CA.

    c. It is designed for use on a large scale.

    d. The master CA is called the root.

15. Which of these is NOT where keys can be stored?

    a. in tokens

    b. in digests

    c. on the user's local system

    d. embedded in digital certificates

16. Public key infrastructure (PKI) _____.

    a. creates private key cryptography

    b. is the management of digital certificates

    c. requires the use of an RA instead of a CA

    d. generates public/private keys automatically

17. A(n) _____ is a published set of rules that govern the operation of a PKI.

    a. enforcement certificate (EF)

    b. certificate practice statement (CPS)

    c. certificate policy (CP)

    d. signature resource guide (SRG)

18.   Which of these is NOT part of the certificate life cycle?

    a.   revocation

    b.   authorization

    c.   creation

    d.   expiration

19.   _____ refers to a situation in which keys are managed by a third party, such as a trusted CA.

    a.   Key escrow

    b.   Remote key administration

    c.   Trusted key authority

    d.   Key authorization

20.   _____ is a protocol for securely accessing a remote computer.

    a.   Secure Shell (SSH)

    b.   Secure Sockets Layer (SSL)

    c.   Secure Hypertext Transport Protocol (SHTTP)

    d.   Transport Layer Security (TLS)

Hands-On Projects

If you are concerned about installing any of the software in these projects on your regular computer, you can instead install the software in the Windows virtual machine created in the Chapter 1 Hands-On Projects 1-3 and 1-4. Software installed within the virtual machine will not impact the host computer.

Project 6-1: SSL Server and Client Tests

In this project, you will use online tests to determine the security of web servers and your local web browser.

    1.   Go to **www.ssllabs.com/ssltest/index.html**.

It is not unusual for websites to change the location of files. If the URL above no longer functions, open a search engine and search for "Qualys SSL Server Test".

    2.   Click the first website listed under **Recent Best-Rate**.

3. Note the grade given for this site. Click the IP address under **Server** (if multiple IP addresses are listed, select one of the addresses) to display the results similar to that seen in Figure 6-13.

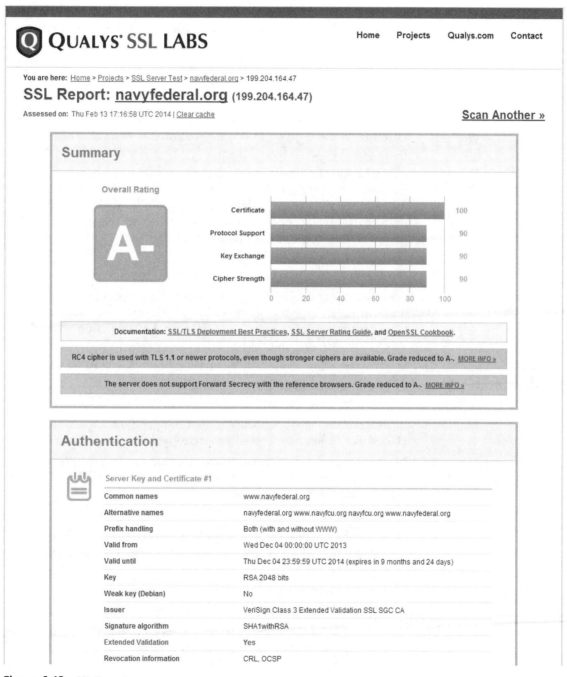

Figure 6-13 SSL Report
Source: Qualys SSL Labs

4. Under **Summary** note the **Overall Rating** along with the scores for **Certificate, Protocol Support, Key Exchange,** and **Cipher Strength**, which make up the cipher suite.

5. If this site did not receive an Overall Rating of *A* under **Summary**, you will see the reasons listed. Read through these. Would you agree? Why?

6. Scroll down through the document and read through the **Authentication** information. Note the information supplied regarding the digital certificates.

7. Scroll down to **Configuration**. Note the list of protocols supported and not supported. If this site was to increase its security, which protocols should it no longer support? Why?

8. Under **Cipher Suites** interpret the suites listed. Notice that they are given in server-preferred order. In order to increase its security, which cipher suite should be listed first? Why?

9. Under **Handshake Simulation** select the web browser and operating system that you are using or is similar to what you are using (*IE 11/Win 8.1* is using Microsoft Internet Explorer 11 running under Windows 8.1). Read through the capabilities of this client interacting with this web server. Note particularly the order of preference of the cipher suites. Click the browser's back button when finished.

10. Scroll to the top of the page, then click **Scan Another >>**.

11. This time select one of the **Recent Worst-Rated** sites. As with the previous excellent example, now review the **Summary, Authentication, Configuration, Cipher Suites,** and **Handshake Simulation**. Would you agree with this site's score?

12. If necessary return to the **SSL Report** page and click **Scan Another >>**.

13. Enter the name of your school or work URL and generate a report. What score did it receive?

14. Review the **Summary, Authentication, Configuration, Cipher Suites,** and **Handshake Simulation**. Would you agree with this site's score?

15. Make a list of the top five vulnerabilities that you believe should be addressed in order of priority. If possible, share this with any IT personnel who may be able to take action.

16. Click **Projects**.

17. Now test the capabilities of your web browser. Click **SSL Client Test**. Review the capabilities of your web browser. Print or take a screen capture of this page.

18. Close this web browser.

19. Now open a different web browser on this computer or on another computer.

20. Go to **www.ssllabs.com/projects/index.html** and click **SSL Client Test** to compare the two scores. From a security perspective, which browser is better? Why?

21. Close all windows.

Project 6-2: Viewing Digital Certificates

In this project, you will view digital certificate information using Microsoft Internet Explorer.

1. Use your web browser to go to **www.google.com**.

2. Note that although you did not enter *https://*, nevertheless Google created a secure HTTPS connection. Why would it do that?

3. Click the padlock icon in the browser address bar.

4. Click **View certificates**.

5. Note the general information displayed under the **General** tab.

6. Now click the **Details** tab. The fields are displayed for this X.509 digital certificate.

7. Click **Valid to** to view the expiration date of this certificate.

8. Click **Public key** to view the public key associated with this digital certificate. Why is this site not concerned with distributing this key? How does embedding the public key in a digital certificate protect it from impersonators?

9. Click the **Certification Path** tab. Because web certificates are based on the distributed trust model, there is a "path" to the root certificate. Click the root certificate and click the **View Certificate** button. Click the **Details tab** and then click **Valid to**. Why is the expiration date of this root certificate longer than that of the website certificate? Click **OK** and then click **OK** again to close the Certificate window.

10. Now view all the certificates in this web browser. Click the **Tools** icon and then **Internet options**.

11. Click the **Content** tab.

12. Click the **Certificates** button.

13. Click **Trusted Root Certification Authorities** to view the root certificates in this web browser. Why are there so many?

14. Click the **Advanced** button.

15. Under **Export format**, what is the default format? Click the **down arrow**. Which PKCS format can this information be downloaded to? Why this format only?

16. Close all windows.

Project 6-3: Viewing Digital Certificate Revocation Lists (CRL) and Untrusted Certificates

Revoked digital certificates are listed in a Certificate Revocation List (CRL), which can be accessed to check the certificate status of other users. In this project, you will view the CRL and any untrusted certificates on your computer.

1. Click **Start** and then type **cmd** and press **Enter**.

2. Type **certmgr.msc** and then press **Enter**.

3. In the left pane, expand **Trusted Root Certification Authorities**.

4. In the left pane, click **Certificates**. These are the CAs approved for this computer.

5. In the left pane, expand **Intermediate Certification Authorities**.

6. Click **Certificates** to view the intermediate CAs.

7. Click **Certificate Revocation List**.

8. In the right pane, all revoked certificates will display. Select a revoked certificate and double-click it, as illustrated in Figure 6-14.

Figure 6-14 Certificate Revocation List information
Source: Microsoft Windows

9. Read the information about it and click fields for more detail if necessary. Why do you think this certificate has been revoked? Close the Certificate Revocation List by clicking the **OK** button.

10. In the left pane, expand **Untrusted Certificates**.

11. Click **Certificates**. The certificates that are no longer trusted are listed in the right pane.

12. Double-click one of the untrusted certificates. Read the information about it and click fields for more detail if necessary. Why do you think this certificate is no longer trusted?

13. Click **OK** to close the Certificate dialog box.

14. Close all windows.

Project 6-4: Downloading and Installing a Digital Certificate

In this project, you will download and install a free email digital certificate.

1. Go to **www.comodo.com/home/email-security/free-email-certificate.php**.

It is not unusual for websites to change the location of files. If the URL above no longer functions, open a search engine and search for "Comodo Free Secure Email Certificate".

2. Click **Free Email Certificate**.

3. You will be taken to the **Application for Secure Email Certificate**. If a **Web Access Confirmation** dialog box displays, click **Yes**.

4. Enter the requested information. Based on the information requested, how secure would you rate this certificate? Under which circumstances would you trust it? Why? Click **I ACCEPT** and then click **Next**.

5. If a **Web Access Confirmation** dialog box displays, click **Yes**.

6. Open your email account that you entered in the application and open the email from Comodo.

7. Click **Click & Install Comodo Email Certificate**.

8. Verify that the certificate is installed. Click **Start** and then type **cmd** and press **Enter**.

9. Type **certmgr.msc** and then press **Enter**.

10. In the left pane, expand **Personal**.

11. In the left pane, click **Certificates**. Your personal certificate should display.

12. Close all windows.

Project 6-5: Using a Digital Certificate for Signing Documents

In this project, you will use the digital certificate in Microsoft Outlook 2013.

1. Start Microsoft Outlook 2013.

2. Create an email message to send to yourself.

3. Click the **OPTIONS** tab.

4. Click the arrow next to **More Options**.

5. Click the **Security Settings** button.

6. Click **Add digital signature to this message**.

7. Click **OK** and then click **Close** in the dialog box.

8. Click **Send**.

9. Note that when the message displays, the icon contains a seal indicating that it was signed.

10. Open the message and note that it states who the signer was.

11. Close all windows.

Case Projects

CASE PROJECTS

Case Project 6-1: HTTPS Web Browser–Web Server Interaction

Search the Internet for information regarding the interaction between web browser and web server using HTTPS from initial handshake to close of the session. Create a detailed drawing of the steps and also annotate each step with additional detail.

Case Project 6-2: Key Management Life Cycle

Draw a diagram that illustrates what a key management life cycle would look like. How long should a key be valid? What steps should be taken when a key is about to expire? Who should be responsible for keys, the user or the organization? Annotate your diagram with steps that should be taken at each step along the cycle.

Case Project 6-3: Certificate Authorities (CAs)

Microsoft Windows comes configured with many digital certificates from trusted publishers. These certificates allow software to be downloaded and installed automatically. Use the Microsoft Management Console (MMC) to go through this list of approved publishers. How many have you heard of? How many are unknown? Select three of the publishers and research their organizations on the Internet. Write a one-paragraph summary of each CA.

Case Project 6-4: HTTPS

Hypertext Transport Protocol Secure (HTTPS) is becoming increasingly more popular as a security protocol for web traffic. Some sites automatically use HTTPS for all transactions (like Google), while others require that users must configure it in their settings. Some argue that HTTPS should be used on all web traffic. What are the advantages of HTTPS? What are its disadvantages? How is it different from HTTP? How must the server be set up for HTTPS transactions? How would it protect you using a public Wi-Fi connection at a local coffee shop? Should all Web traffic be required to use HTTPS? Why or why not? Write a one-page paper of your research.

Case Project 6-5: TLS

TLS is becoming the most popular cryptographic transport protocol used on web servers. Use the Internet to research TLS. What are its strengths? What are its weaknesses? How can they be addressed? Write a one-page paper of your research.

Case Project 6-6: Bay Pointe Security Consulting

Bay Pointe Security Consulting (BPSC) provides security consulting services to a wide range of businesses, individuals, schools, and organizations. BPSC has hired you as a technology student to help them with a new project and provide real-world experience to students who are interested in the security field.

Marathon Gardening is a statewide landscaping business with offices and facilities in more than 20 locations. Marathon has just hired its first security manager who proposes using digital certificates for all enhanced security. Marathon would like a training session from BPSC to its employees about digital certificates.

1. Create a PowerPoint presentation that provides an overview of cryptography with specific emphasis on digital signatures, digital certificates, and PKI. The presentation should be at least eight slides in length.

2. The security manager has now proposed that all email correspondence, both internal between Marathon employees and external to all Marathon business partners and customers, should use digital certificates. Several IT staff employees are concerned about this proposal. They have asked you for your opinion on using digital certificates for all email messages. Write a one-page memo to Marathon about the pros and cons of this approach.

Case Project 6-7: Community Site Activity

The Information Security Community Site is an online companion to this textbook. It contains a wide variety of tools, information, discussion boards, and other features to assist learners. Go to **community.cengage.com/infosec**. Sign in with the login name and password that you created in Chapter 1.

Read again *Today's Attacks and Defenses* at the beginning of the chapter. Should the government require backdoors in cryptographic algorithms so that they can read communications between enemies of the country? Or is that a violation of its citizens' privacy? Take both the "pro" and "con" sides to this argument and present three to five reasons for each side. Then, give your opinion. Record your answer on the Community Site discussion board.

References

1. "About NSA," *National Security Agency*, Nov. 29, 2011, retrieved Feb. 11, 2014, www.nsa.gov/about/index.shtml.

2. "SSL Pulse," *Trustworthy Internet Movement*, Feb. 2, 2014, retrieved Apr. 22, 2014, https://www.trustworthyinternet.org/ssl-pulse/.

Network Security

The chapters in Part IV deal with securing an enterprise computer network. In Chapter 7, you will learn the fundamental concepts of network security through standard network devices, network security hardware, and network technology and design. In Chapter 8, you will learn how to implement network security as a network administrator.

Network Security Fundamentals

After completing this chapter, you should be able to do the following:

- List the different types of network security devices and how they can be used
- Explain how network technologies can enhance security
- Describe secure network design elements

Today's Attacks and Defenses

One of the largest security breaches in history exposed the payment card data and personal information of 110 million customers of one of the U.S.'s largest retailers. Although the exact details are shrouded in secrecy, it appears that the lack of basic network security surrounding the retailer's own network played a significant role in the attack.

Attackers often start by "island hopping." Instead of attempting to break into a major retailer's secure data network, attackers search for weaker third-party contractors who have been given access to the retailer's network, such as heating, ventilation, and air-conditioning (HVAC) subcontractors. For example, these HVAC subcontractors generally are responsible for installing and managing new refrigeration systems at the retailers. The refrigeration systems are connected to the retailer's data network so that they can be monitored remotely. Subcontractors are given a username and password to access the retailer's network in order to manage these HVAC systems.

This attack probably started with attackers sending out spear phishing emails to the retailer's many different subcontractors. One HVAC subcontractor in Pennsylvania fell victim to the attack. An employee opened the phishing email and the employee's computer was infected with the attacker's malware. The malware was able to go undetected because the HVAC subcontractor was protecting its computers with a free version of antivirus (AV) software. This AV software is an "on-demand" scanner: it looks for malware only when it is initiated by the user and does not scan continuously as most AV software does. Once the attackers had infected the employee's computer, they penetrated the HVAC subcontractor's network and stole the login credentials to access the retailer's network.

The retailer's network is a vast structure of servers, subnetworks, and computers. How did the attackers know how to navigate this network to find what they were looking for? The answer is that information about the retailer's network was freely available to them. This retailer posted information about its network on the Web. Using a simple Google search, the attackers may have found the retailer's web "Supplier Portal" that contains information for subcontractors, vendors, and suppliers regarding how to submit invoices online through the retailer's payment system, instructions on submitting work orders, and other valuable information about their network. This portal even contained Microsoft Excel files for the subcontractors. The attackers may have downloaded these files and then searched through their metadata. One Excel file revealed that it was created on a specific date by a company employee who printed it on a printer on the retailer's network in the Windows domain "\\TCMPSPRINT04P\". This helped the attackers begin to construct the layout of the retailer's internal network so they could then focus their attack.

(continued)

The retailer made another critical error by not segmenting its network. The part of the network for the vendors and suppliers like HVAC subcontractors was not separated from the customer payment information network. Once the attackers had penetrated the payment system for vendors, they could easily jump to the customer information system. The attackers then loaded malware onto the retailer's network servers, which in turn downloaded the malware to the point-of-sale (POS) devices that are used to scan customer payment cards in each of the retailer's stores. Whenever a customer scanned his or her card, the malware grabbed that information from the POS device.

One more network mistake made by the retailer was not monitoring its own network. The attackers brazenly took over one of the retailer's own servers on the internal network to create a control server. After collecting six days' worth of data, the control server started downloading the stolen information to an FTP server that was part of a hijacked website the attackers had also compromised. These transmissions occurred several times each day over a two-week period. If the retailer had been monitoring data leaving its network, perhaps 11 GB of data on 110 million customers would not have been stolen, or the breach would have been discovered much earlier.

At one time the terms *information security* and *network security* were virtually synonymous. That was because the network was viewed as the protecting wall around which client computers could be kept safe. A secure network would keep attackers away from the devices on the inside.

This approach, however, was later seen to be untenable. There are simply too many entry points that circumvent the network and allow malware to enter. For example, users could bring an infected USB flash drive and insert it into their computer, thus introducing malware while bypassing the secure network. Also, malware started taking advantage of common network protocols, such as Hypertext Transfer Protocol (HTTP), and could not always be detected or blocked by network security devices.

This is not to say that network security is unimportant. Having a secure network is essential to a comprehensive information security posture. Not all applications are designed and written with security and reliability in mind, so it falls on the network to provide protection. Also, network-delivered services can scale better for larger environments and can complement server and application functionality. And because an attacker who can successfully penetrate a computer network may have access to hundreds or even thousands of desktop systems, servers, and storage devices, a secure network defense still remains a critical element in any organization's security plan. Organizations should make network defenses one of the first priorities in protecting information.

This chapter explores network security. You will investigate how to build a secure network through network devices, network technologies, and by the design of the network itself.

Security Through Network Devices

1.1 Implement security configuration parameters on network devices and other technologies.

1.2 Given a scenario, use secure network administration principles.

1.3 Explain network design elements and components.

1.4 Given a scenario, implement common protocols and services.

3.6 Analyze a scenario and select the appropriate type of mitigation and deterrent techniques.

4.3 Given a scenario, select the appropriate solution to establish host security.

A basic level of security can be achieved through using the security features found in standard network hardware. And because networks typically contain multiple types of network hardware, this allows for **layered security**, also called **defense in depth**. If only one defense mechanism is in place, an attacker only has to circumvent that single defense. Instead, a network with layered security will make it more difficult for an attacker because he must have all the tools, knowledge, and skills to break through the various layers. A layered approach also can be useful in resisting a variety of attacks. Layered network security, which provides the most comprehensive protection, can be achieved by using both standard networking devices as well as hardware designed primarily for security or that provides a significant security function.

Standard Network Devices

The security functions of standard network devices can be used to provide a degree of network security. These network devices can be classified based on their function in the OSI model. In 1978, the *International Organization for Standardization (ISO)* released a set of specifications that was intended to describe how dissimilar computers could be connected together on a network. The ISO demonstrated that what happens on a network device when sending or receiving traffic can be best understood by portraying this transfer as a series of related steps that take place. Looking at what happens during each step and how it relates to the previous or next steps can help compartmentalize computer networking and make it easier to understand. The ISO called its work the *Open Systems Interconnection (OSI)* reference model. After a revision in 1983, the OSI reference model is still used today. The OSI reference model illustrates how a network device prepares data for delivery over the network to another device, and how data is to be handled when it is received.

Started in 1947, the goal of the ISO is to promote international cooperation and standards in the areas of science, technology, and economics. Today groups from more than 160 countries belong to this organization that is headquartered in Geneva, Switzerland.

The key to the OSI reference model is *layers*. The model breaks networking steps down into a series of seven layers. Within each layer, different networking tasks are performed. In addition, each layer cooperates with the layers immediately above and below it. The OSI model gives a visual representation of how a computer prepares data for transmission and how it receives data from the network, and illustrates how each layer provides specific services and shares with the layers above and below it. Table 7-1 describes the OSI layers.

Layer number	Layer name	Description	Function
Layer 7	Application Layer	The top layer, Application, provides the user interface to allow network services.	Provides services for user applications
Layer 6	Presentation Layer	The Presentation Layer is concerned with how the data is represented and formatted for the user.	Is used for translation, compression, and encryption
Layer 5	Session Layer	This layer has the responsibility of permitting the two parties on the network to hold ongoing communications across the network.	Allows devices to establish and manage sessions
Layer 4	Transport Layer	The Transport Layer is responsible for ensuring that error-free data is given to the user.	Provides connection establishment, management, and termination as well as acknowledgments and retransmissions
Layer 3	Network Layer	The Network Layer picks the route the packet is to take, and handles the addressing of the packets for delivery.	Makes logical addressing, routing, fragmentation, and reassembly available
Layer 2	Data Link Layer	The Data Link Layer is responsible for dividing the data into frames. Some additional duties of the Data Link Layer include error detection and correction (for example, if the data is not received properly, the Data Link Layer would request that it be retransmitted).	Performs physical addressing, data framing, and error detection and handling
Layer 1	Physical Layer	The job of this layer is to send the signal to the network or receive the signal from the network.	Involved with encoding and signaling, and data transmission and reception

Table 7-1   OSI reference model

NOTE Several different mnemonics can be used to memorize the layers of the OSI model. These include *All People Seem To Need Data Processing* (for Layers 7–1) and *Please Do Not Throw Sausage Pizza Away* (for Layers 1–7).

Standard network devices can be classified by the OSI layer at which they function. These devices include switches, routers, load balancers, and proxies.

NOTE Several different data units are represented at the various layers of the OSI model. These data units include bit (Physical), bit/frame (Data Link), packet/datagram (Network), segment (Transport), and data (Session, Presentation, and Application).

Switches Early local area networks (LANs) used a *hub*, which is a standard network device for connecting multiple network devices together so that they function as a single network segment. Hubs worked at the Physical Layer (Layer 1) of the OSI model. This means that they did not read any of the data passing through them and thus were ignorant of the source and destination of the frames. A hub would receive only incoming frames, regenerate the electrical signal, and then send all the frames received out to all other devices connected to the hub. Each device would then decide if the frame was intended for it (and retain it) or if it was intended for another device (and then ignore it). In essence, a hub was a multiport repeater: whatever it received, it then passed on.

Because a hub repeated all frames to all the attached network devices, it significantly—and unnecessarily—increased network traffic. But hubs were also a security risk because an attacker could install software or a hardware device that captured and decoded packets on one client connected to a hub and then view all traffic traveling through the hub by using a **protocol analyzer,** which captures packets to decode and analyze their contents. Because most protocol analyzers can filter out unwanted packets and reconstruct packet streams, an attacker could capture a copy of a file that was being transmitted, read email messages, view the contents of webpages, and see unprotected passwords.

 Because of their impact on network traffic and inherent security vulnerability, hubs are rarely used today. Some organizations even prohibit the use of hubs.

Like a hub, a network **switch** is a device that connects network devices together. However, unlike a hub, a switch has a degree of "intelligence." Operating at the Data Link Layer (Layer 2), a switch can learn which device is connected to each of its ports, and then forward only frames intended for a specific device (*unicast*) or frames sent to all devices (*broadcast*). A switch learns by examining the media access control (MAC) address of frames that it receives and then associates its port with the MAC address of the device connected to that port. This improves network performance and provides better security. An attacker who installs software to capture packets on a computer attached to a switch will see only frames that are directed to that device and not those directed to other network devices.

Although a switch limits the frames that are sent to devices, it is still important for a network administrator to be able to monitor network traffic. This helps to identify and troubleshoot network problems, such as a network interface card (NIC) that is defective and sending out malformed packets. Monitoring traffic on switches generally can be done in two ways. First, a managed switch on an Ethernet network that supports *port mirroring* allows the administrator to configure the switch to copy traffic that occurs on some or all ports to a designated monitoring port on the switch. Port mirroring is illustrated in Figure 7-1, where the monitoring computer is connected to the mirror port and can view all network traffic (the monitoring computer can be a standalone device or a computer that runs protocol analyzer software).

A second method for monitoring traffic is to install a *network tap (test access point)*. A network tap is a separate device that can be installed on the network. A network tap is illustrated in Figure 7-2.

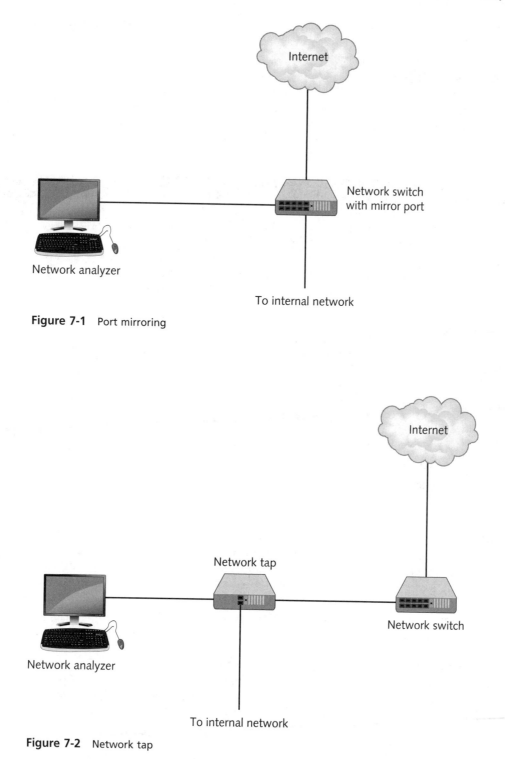

Figure 7-1   Port mirroring

Figure 7-2   Network tap

A network tap is generally best for high-speed networks that have a large volume of traffic, while port mirroring is better for networks with light traffic.

Because a switch can still be used for capturing traffic, it is important that the necessary defenses be implemented to prevent unauthorized users from gathering this data. These attacks and defenses are summarized in Table 7-2.

Type of attack	Description	Security defense
MAC flooding	An attacker can overflow the switch's address table with fake MAC addresses, forcing it to act like a hub, sending packets to all devices.	Use a switch that can close ports with too many MAC addresses.
MAC address impersonation	If two devices have the same MAC address, a switch may send frames to each device. An attacker can change the MAC address on her device to match the target device's MAC address.	Configure the switch so that only one port can be assigned per MAC address.
ARP poisoning	The attacker sends a forged ARP packet to the source device, substituting the attacker's computer MAC address.	Use an ARP detection appliance.
Port mirroring	An attacker connects his device to the switch's mirror port.	Secure the switch in a locked room.
Network tap	A network tap is connected to the network to intercept frames.	Keep network connections secure by restricting physical access.

Table 7-2   Protecting the switch

Routers Operating at the Network Layer (Layer 3), a **router** is a network device that can forward packets across different computer networks. When a router receives an incoming packet, it reads the destination address and then, using information in its routing table, sends the packet to the next network toward its destination. Routers also can perform a security function. The router can be configured to filter out specific types of network traffic. For example, a router can be set to disallow IP-directed broadcasts or incoming packets that have invalid addresses.

Load Balancers *Load balancing* is a technology that can help to evenly distribute work across a network. Requests that are received can be allocated across multiple devices such as servers. To the user, this distribution is transparent and appears as if a single server is providing the resources. Load-balancing technology provides these advantages:

- The probability of overloading a single server is reduced.
- Each networked computer can benefit from having optimized bandwidth.
- Network downtime can be reduced.

Load balancing can be performed either through software running on a computer or as a dedicated hardware device known as a **load balancer**. Load balancers are often grouped into two categories known as *Layer 4 load balancers* and *Layer 7 load balancers*. Layer 4 load balancers act upon data found in Network and Transport layer protocols such as Internet Protocol (IP), Transmission Control Protocol (TCP), File Transfer Protocol (FTP), and User Datagram Protocol (UDP). Layer 7 load balancers distribute requests based on data found in Application layer protocols such as HTTP. Although both Layer 4 and Layer 7 load balancers can distribute work based on a "round-robin" rotation to all devices equally or to those devices that have the least number of connections, Layer 7 load balancers also can use HTTP headers, cookies, or data within the application message itself to make a decision on distribution.

Load balancing that is used for distributing HTTP requests received is sometimes called *IP spraying*.

The use of a load balancer has security advantages. Because load balancers generally are located between routers and servers, they can detect and stop attacks directed at a server or application. A load balancer can be used to detect and prevent denial-of-service (DoS) and protocol attacks that could cripple a single server. Some load balancers can hide HTTP error pages or remove server identification headers from HTTP responses, denying attackers additional information about the internal network.

Proxies In the human world, a *proxy* is a person who is authorized to act as the substitute or agent on behalf of another person. For example, an individual who has been granted the power of attorney for a sick relative can make decisions and take actions on behalf of that person as her proxy.

Several different types of proxies are used in computer networking. These devices act as substitutes on behalf of the primary device. A **proxy server** is a computer or an application program that intercepts user requests from the internal secure network and then processes that request on behalf of the user. A proxy server is illustrated in Figure 7-3.

When an internal client requests a service such as a file or a webpage from an external web server, it normally would connect directly with that remote server. In a network using a proxy server, the client first connects to the proxy server, which checks its memory to see if a previous request already has been fulfilled and whether a copy of that file or page is residing on the proxy server in its temporary storage area (*cache*). If it is not, the proxy server connects to the external web server using its own IP address (instead of the internal client's address) and requests the service. When the proxy server receives the requested item from the web server, the item is then forwarded to the client. Access to proxy servers is configured in a user's web browser, as shown in Figure 7-4. An **application-aware proxy** is a special proxy server that "knows" the application protocols that it supports. For example, an *FTP proxy server* implements the protocol FTP.

Although proxy servers have some disadvantages, such as the added expense and the fact that caches may not always be current, they have several advantages:

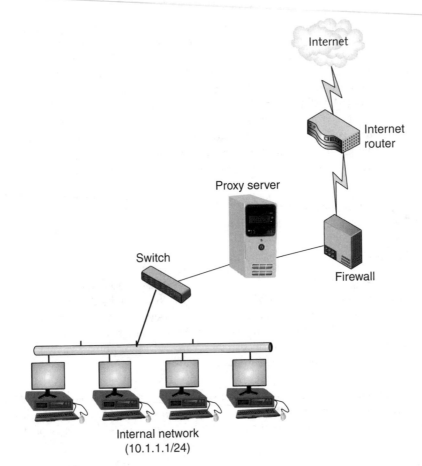

Figure 7-3   Proxy server

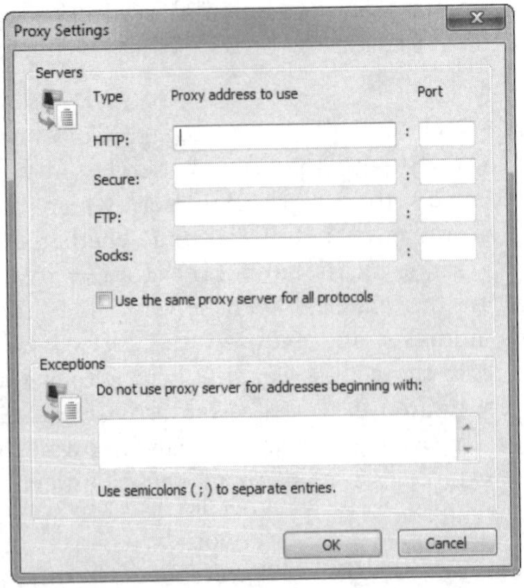

Figure 7-4   Configuring access to proxy servers (Internet Explorer)
Source: Microsoft Windows

- *Increased speed.* Because proxy servers can cache material, a request can be served from the cache instead of retrieving the webpage through the Internet.

- *Reduced costs.* A proxy server can reduce the amount of bandwidth usage because of the cache.

- *Improved management.* A proxy server can block specific webpages and/or entire websites. Some proxy servers can block entire categories of websites such as entertainment, pornography, or gaming sites.

- *Stronger security.* Acting as the intermediary, a proxy server can protect clients from malware by intercepting it before it reaches the client. In addition, a proxy server can hide the IP address of client systems inside the secure network. Only the proxy server's IP address is used on the open Internet.

A **reverse proxy** does not serve clients but instead routes incoming requests to the correct server. Requests for services are sent to the reverse proxy that then forwards them to the server. To the outside user, the IP address of the reverse proxy is the final IP address for requesting services, yet only the reverse proxy can access the internal servers. Proxy and reverse proxy servers are illustrated in Figure 7-5.

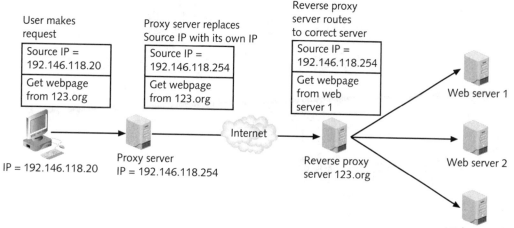

Figure 7-5   Reverse proxy

Encrypted traffic entering the network must first be decrypted in order for a load balancer to direct requests to different servers. A reverse proxy can be the point at which this traffic is decrypted.

Network Security Hardware

Although standard networking devices can provide a degree of security, hardware devices that are specifically designed for security can give a much higher level of protection. These devices include network firewalls, spam filters, virtual private network concentrators, Internet content filters, web security gateways, intrusion detection and prevention systems, and Unified Threat Management appliances.

Network Firewalls Although a host-based application software firewall that runs as a program on one client is different from a hardware-based network firewall designed to protected an entire network, their functions are essentially the same: to inspect packets and either accept or deny entry. Hardware firewalls are usually located outside the network security perimeter as the first line of defense, as shown in Figure 7-6.

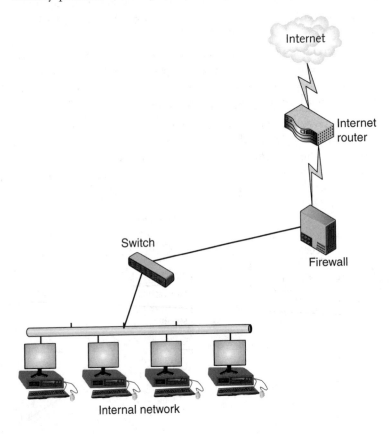

Figure 7-6   Firewall location

 Host-based application firewalls are covered in more detail in Chapter 4.

Packets can be filtered by a firewall in one of two ways. *Stateless packet filtering* looks at the incoming packet and permits or denies it based on the conditions that have been set by the administrator. *Stateful packet filtering* keeps a record of the state of a connection between an internal computer and an external device and then makes decisions based on the connection as well as the conditions. For example, a stateless packet filter firewall might allow a packet to pass through because it is intended for a specific computer on the network. However, a stateful packet filter would not let the packet pass if that internal network computer did not first request the information from the external server.

A firewall can take different actions when it receives a packet: *allow* (let the packet pass through and continue on its journey), *drop* (prevent the packet from passing into the network and send no response to the sender), *reject* (prevent the packet from passing into the network but send a message to the sender that the destination cannot be reached), or *ask* (inquire what action to take). These firewall actions can be determined by two methods. Traditional firewalls are rule-based while more modern firewalls are application-based.

Rule-Based Firewalls A *rule-based firewall* uses a set of individual instructions to control actions, called **firewall rules**. These rules are a single line of textual information containing such information as:

- *Source address.* The source address is the location of the origination of the packet (where the packet is *from*). Addresses generally can be indicated by a specific IP address or range of addresses, an IP mask, the MAC address, or host name.

- *Destination address.* This is the address the connection is attempting to reach (where the packet is going *to*). These addresses can be indicated in the same way as the source address.

- *Source port.* The source port is the TCP/IP port number being used to send packets of data through. Options for setting the source port often include a specific port number, a range of numbers, or *Any* (port).

- *Destination port.* This setting gives the port on the remote computer or device that the packets will use. Options include the same as for the source port.

- *Protocol:* The protocol defines the protocol (such as *TCP, UDP, TCP or UDP, ICMP, IP*) that is being used when sending or receiving packets of data.

- *Direction.* The direction shows the direction of traffic for the data packet (*In*, *Out*, or *Both*).

- *Action.* The action setting indicates what the firewall should do when the conditions of the rule are met. These options may be *Allow, Drop, Reject,* or *Ask*.

Each firewall rule is a separate instruction processed in sequence that tells the firewall precisely what action to take with each packet that comes through it. The rules are stored together in one or more text files that are read when the firewall starts. Rule-based systems are static in nature and cannot do anything other than what they have been expressly configured to do. Although this makes them more straightforward to configure, they are less flexible and cannot adapt to changing circumstances.

Firewall rules are essentially an *IF-THEN* construction. *IF* these rule conditions are met, *THEN* the action occurs.

Application-Aware Firewalls A more "intelligent" firewall is an **application-aware firewall**, sometimes called a *next-generation firewall (NGFW)*. Application-aware firewalls operate at a higher level by identifying the applications that send packets through the firewall and then make decisions about the application instead of filtering packets based on granular rule settings like the destination port or protocol. A special type of application-aware firewall is a **web application firewall**. A web application firewall is a special type of firewall that looks at the applications using HTTP.

7

Applications can be identified by application-aware firewalls through predefined application signatures, header inspection, or payload analysis. In addition, application-aware firewalls can learn new applications by watching how they behave and even create a baseline of normal behaviors so that an alert can be raised if the application deviates from the baseline.

An example of how an application-aware firewall and a rule-based firewall compare can be seen in how they filter specific web applications. An organization may frown upon employees using the network during normal business hours to stream online movies, but still need to provide employees with access to an online sales application. Setting a rule in a rule-based firewall to prevent streaming video (HTTP on Port 80) would also stop access to the online sales application. An application-aware firewall, in contrast, can distinguish between these two applications and allow access to the sales application while blocking streaming video, social networking, and gaming. Or it could allow these applications but limit bandwidth consumption to give priority to business applications.

A web application firewall, which can be a separate hardware appliance or a software plug-in, can run on a server or client device, can block specific websites or attacks that attempt to exploit known vulnerabilities in specific client software, and can even block cross-site scripting (XSS) and SQL injection attacks.

Spam Filters Beyond being annoying and disruptive, spam can pose a serious security risk. "Spammers" can distribute malware through their email messages as attachments and use spam for social engineering attacks. Due to the high volume of spam, most organizations use enterprise-wide spam filters to block spam before it ever reaches the client.

Email systems use two TCP/IP protocols to send and receive messages: the *Simple Mail Transfer Protocol (SMTP)* handles outgoing mail, while the *Post Office Protocol (POP)*, more commonly known as *POP3* for the current version, is responsible for incoming mail. The SMTP server listens on port 25 while POP3 listens on port 110.

Another inbound email protocol is Internet Message Access Protocol (IMAP). While POP3 is a "store-and-forward" service, IMAP is "remote" email storage. With IMAP, the email resides on the server and can be accessed from virtually any device.

One method for filtering spam is for the organization to install its own corporate spam filter. This filter works with the receiving email server, which is typically based on the SMTP for sending email and the POP3 for retrieving email. There are two options for installing a corporate spam filter:

- *Install the spam filter with the SMTP server.* This is the simplest and most effective approach to installing a spam filter. The spam filter and SMTP server can run together on the same computer or on separate computers. The filter (instead of the SMTP server) is configured to listen on port 25 for all incoming email messages and then pass the non-spam email to the SMTP server that is listening on another port (such as port 26). This configuration prevents the SMTP server from notifying the spammer that it was unable to deliver the message. Installation of the spam filter with the SMTP server is shown in Figure 7-7.

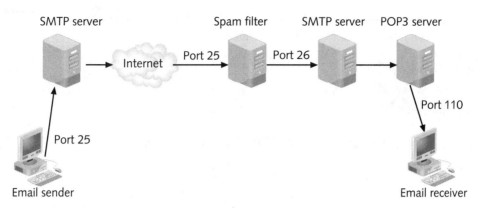

Figure 7-7   Spam filter with SMTP server

- *Install the spam filter on the POP3 server.* Although the spam filter can be installed on the POP3 server, this would mean that all spam must first pass through the SMTP server and be delivered to the user's mailbox. This can result in increased costs for storage, transmission, backup, and deletion. This configuration is shown in Figure 7-8.

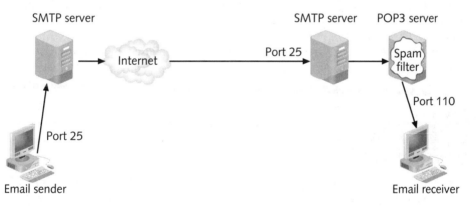

Figure 7-8   Spam filter on POP3 server

SMTP servers can forward email sent from an email client to a remote domain, known as SMTP relay. However, if SMTP relay is not controlled, an attacker can use it to forward spam and disguise his identity to make himself untraceable. An uncontrolled SMTP relay is known as an SMTP open relay. The defenses against SMTP open relay are to turn off mail relay altogether so that all users send and receive email from the local SMTP server only or to limit relays to only local users.

Another method to filter spam is for the organization to contract with a third-party entity that filters out spam. All email is directed to the third party's remote spam filter where it is cleansed before it is redirected to the organization. This redirection can be accomplished by changing the *MX (mail exchange) record.* The MX record is an entry in the Domain Name System (DNS) that identifies the mail server responsible for handling that domain name. To redirect mail to the third party's remote server, the MX record is changed to show the new recipient.

Multiple MX records can be configured in DNS to enable the use of primary and backup mail servers. Each MX record can be prioritized with a preference number that indicates the order in which the mail servers should be used.

Virtual Private Network (VPN) Concentrators An unsecured public network should never be used for sensitive data transmissions. One solution could be to encrypt documents before transmitting them. However, there are drawbacks. First, the user must consciously perform a separate action (such as encrypt a document) or use specific software (such as PGP) in order to transmit a secure document. The time and effort required to do so, albeit small, may discourage users from protecting their documents. A second drawback is that these actions protect only documents that are transmitted; all other communications, such as accessing corporate databases, are not secure.

A more secure solution is to use a virtual private network (VPN). A **virtual private network (VPN)** is a technology that enables authorized users to use an unsecured public network, such as the Internet, as if it were a secure private network. It does this by encrypting *all* data that is transmitted between the remote device and the network and not just specific documents or files. This ensures that any transmissions that are intercepted will be indecipherable. There are two common types of VPNs. A *remote-access VPN* or *virtual private dial-up network (VPDN)* is a user-to-LAN connection used by remote users. The second type is a *site-to-site VPN*, in which multiple sites can connect to other sites over the Internet.

The "dial-up" in the name VPDN reflects the fact that these once required a dial-up connection using an analog telephone system. A dial-up connection is no longer necessary.

VPN transmissions are achieved through communicating with endpoints. An *endpoint* is the end of the tunnel between VPN devices. An endpoint can be software on a local computer, a dedicated hardware device such as a **VPN concentrator** (which aggregates hundreds or thousands of VPN connections), or integrated into another networking device such as a firewall. Depending upon the type of endpoint that is being used, client software may be required on the devices that are connecting to the VPN. Hardware devices that have a *built-in VPN* endpoint handle all VPN setup, encapsulation, and encryption in the endpoint. Client devices are not required to run any special software and the entire VPN process is transparent to them.

Different "tunneling" protocols—enclosing a packet within another packet—can be used for VPN transmissions. A site-to-site VPN may use either *generic routing encapsulation (GRE)*, which is a framework for how to package the guest protocol for transport over the Internet protocol (IP), or Internet protocol security (IPsec). IPsec has two "subprotocols" that are used in VPN:

- *Encapsulated Security Payload (ESP)*. ESP encrypts the data that is being transmitted using a symmetric key.

- *Authentication Header (AH).* AH creates a digest of the packet header. This helps to hide certain information such as the sender's source address until it reaches its destination.

A remote-access VPN generally uses either IPsec or the *Layer 2 Tunneling Protocol (L2TP)*. VPNs can be software-based or hardware-based. Software-based VPNs, often used on mobile devices like laptops in which the VPN endpoint is actually software running on the device itself, offer the most flexibility in how network traffic is managed. However, software-based VPNs generally do not have as good performance or security as a hardware-based VPN. Hardware-based VPNs, typically used for site-to-site connections, are more secure, have better performance, and can offer more flexibility than software-based VPNs. This is because only the network devices manage the VPN functions and relieve the device from performing any VPN activities. Hardware-based VPNs generally are used for connecting two local area networks through a VPN tunnel.

Internet Content Filters *Internet content filters* monitor Internet traffic and block access to preselected websites and files. A requested webpage is displayed only if it complies with the specified filters. Unapproved websites can be restricted based on the Uniform Resource Locator or URL (**URL filtering**) or by searching for and matching keywords such as *sex* or *hate* (**content inspection**) as well as looking for malware (**malware inspection**). Table 7-3 lists several features of Internet content filters.

Feature	Description
URL filtering and content inspection	Network administrators can block access to specific websites or allow only specific websites to be accessed while all others are blocked. Blocking can be based on keywords, URL patterns, or lists of prohibited sites.
Malware inspection and filtering	Filters can assess if a webpage contains any malicious elements or exhibits any malicious behavior, and then flag questionable pages with a warning message.
Prohibiting file downloads	Executable programs (.exe), audio or video files (.mp3, .avi, .mpg), and archive files (.zip, .rar) can be blocked.
Profiles	Content-specific websites, such as adult, hacking, and virus-infected websites, can be blocked.
Detailed reporting	Administrators can monitor Internet traffic and identify users who attempt to foil the filters.

Table 7-3   **Internet content filter features**

Web Security Gateways Internet content filters monitor Internet traffic and block access to preselected websites and files. This makes them *reactive* security measures that only defend against known threats from known malicious sites. In contrast, a **web security gateway** can block malicious content in real time as it appears (without first knowing the URL of a dangerous site). Web security gateways enable a higher level of defense by examining the content through application-level filtering. For example, a web security gateway can block the following web-based traffic:

- Adware and spyware
- Cookies
- Instant messengers
- P2P (peer-to-peer) file sharing
- Script exploits
- TCP/IP malicious code attacks

Intrusion Detection and Prevention An intrusion detection system (IDS) is a device that can detect an attack as it occurs. IDS systems can use different methodologies for monitoring for attacks. In addition, IDS can be installed on either local hosts or networks. An extension of IDS is an intrusion prevention system (IPS).

Monitoring Methodologies Monitoring involves examining network traffic, activity, transactions, or behavior in order to detect security-related anomalies. There are four monitoring methodologies: anomaly-based monitoring, signature-based monitoring, behavior-based monitoring, and heuristic monitoring.

Anomaly-based monitoring is designed for detecting statistical anomalies. First, a baseline of normal activities is compiled over time. (A *baseline* is a reference set of data against which operational data is compared.) Whenever there is a significant deviation from this baseline, an alarm is raised. An advantage of this approach is that it can detect the anomalies quickly without trying to first understand the underlying cause. However, normal behavior can change easily and even quickly, so anomaly-based monitoring is subject to *false positives*, or alarms that are raised when there is no actual abnormal behavior. In addition, anomaly-based monitoring can impose heavy processing loads on the systems where they are being used. Finally, because anomaly-based monitoring takes time to create statistical baselines, it can fail to detect events before the baseline is completed.

A second method for auditing usage is to examine network traffic, activity, transactions, or behavior and look for well-known patterns, much like antivirus scanning. This is known as **signature-based monitoring** because it compares activities against a predefined signature. Signature-based monitoring requires access to an updated database of signatures along with a means to actively compare and match current behavior against a collection of signatures. One of the weaknesses of signature-based monitoring is that the signature databases must be constantly updated, and as the number of signatures grows, the behaviors must be compared against an increasingly large number of signatures. Also, if the signature definitions are too specific, signature-based monitoring can miss variations.

Behavior-based monitoring attempts to overcome the limitations of both anomaly-based monitoring and signature-based monitoring by being adaptive and proactive instead of reactive. Rather than using statistics or signatures as the standard by which comparisons are made, behavior-based monitoring uses the "normal" processes and actions as the standard. Behavior-based monitoring continuously analyzes the behavior of processes and programs on a system and alerts the user if it detects any abnormal actions, at which point the user can decide whether to allow or block the activity. One of the advantages of behavior-based monitoring is that it is not necessary to update signature files or compile a baseline of statistical behavior before monitoring can take place. In addition, behavior-based monitoring can more quickly stop new attacks.

The final method takes a completely different approach and does not try to compare actions against previously determined standards (like anomaly-based monitoring and signature-based monitoring) or behavior (like behavior-based monitoring). Instead, it is founded on *experience-based techniques*. Known as **heuristic monitoring**, it attempts to answer the question, *Will this do something harmful if it is allowed to execute?* Heuristic (from the Greek word for *find* or *discover*) monitoring is similar to antivirus heuristic detection. However, instead of creating a virtual environment in which to test a threat, IDS heuristic monitoring uses an algorithm to determine if a threat exists. Table 7-4 illustrates how heuristic monitoring could trap an application that attempts to scan ports that the other methods may not catch.

Antivirus heuristic detection is covered in Chapter 4.

Monitoring methodology	Trap application scanning ports?	Comments
Anomaly-based monitoring	Depends	Only if this application has tried to scan previously and a baseline has been established
Signature-based monitoring	Depends	Only if a signature of scanning by this application has been previously created
Behavior-based monitoring	Depends	Only if this action by the application is different from other applications
Heuristic monitoring	Yes	IDS is triggered if any application tries to scan multiple ports

Table 7-4 **Methodology comparisons to trap port scanning application**

Types of IDS Two basic types of IDS exist. A **host-based intrusion detection system (HIDS)** is a software-based application that runs on a local host computer that can detect an attack as it occurs. A HIDS is installed on each system, such as a server or desktop, that needs to be protected. A HIDS relies on agents installed directly on the system being protected. These agents work closely with the operating system, monitoring and intercepting requests in order to prevent attacks. HIDSs typically monitor the following desktop functions:

- *System calls.* Each operation in a computing environment starts with a *system call*. A system call is an instruction that interrupts the program being executed and requests a service from the operating system. HIDS can monitor system calls based on the process, mode, and action being requested.

- *File system access.* System calls usually require specific files to be opened in order to access data. A HIDS works to ensure that all file openings are based on legitimate needs and are not the result of malicious activity.

- *System Registry settings.* The Windows *Registry* maintains configuration information about programs and the computer. HIDS can recognize unauthorized modification of the Registry.

- *Host input/output.* HIDS monitors all input and output communications to watch for malicious activity. For example, if the system never uses instant messaging and suddenly a threat attempts to open an IM connection from the system, the HIDS would detect this as anomalous activity.

 HIDSs are designed to integrate with existing antivirus, antispyware, and firewalls that are installed on the local host computer.

However, there are disadvantages to HIDS, including:

- It cannot monitor any network traffic that does not reach the local system.
- All log data is stored locally.
- It tends to be resource-intensive and can slow down the system.

Just as a software-based HIDS monitors attacks on a local system, a **network intrusion detection system (NIDS)** watches for attacks on the network. As network traffic moves through the network, NIDS sensors—usually installed on network devices such as firewalls and routers—gather information and report back to a central device. A NIDS may use one or more of the evaluation techniques listed in Table 7-5.

Technique	Description
Protocol stack verification	Some attacks use invalid IP, TCP, UDP, or ICMP protocols. A protocol stack verification can identify and flag invalid packets, such as several fragmented IP packets.
Application protocol verification	Some attacks attempt to use invalid protocol behavior or have a telltale signature (such as DNS poisoning). The NIDS will reimplement different application protocols to find a pattern.
Creating extended logs	A NIDS can log unusual events and then make these available to other network logging monitoring systems.

Table 7-5 NIDS evaluation techniques

 A NIDS is not limited to inspecting incoming network traffic. Often valuable information about an ongoing attack can be gained from observing outgoing traffic as well. A system that has been turned into a zombie will produce large amounts of outgoing traffic, and a NIDS that examines both incoming and outgoing traffic can detect it.

Once an attack is detected, a NIDS can perform different actions to sound an alarm and log the event. These alarms may include sending email, page, or a cell phone message to the network administrator or even playing an audio file that says "Attack is taking place."

An **application-aware IDS** is a specialized IDS. Instead of applying all IDS rules to all traffic flows, an application-aware IDS is capable of using "contextual knowledge" in real time. It can know the version of the operating system or which application is running as well as what vulnerabilities are present in the systems being protected. This "context" improves the speed and accuracy of IDS decisions and reduces the risk of false positives.

Intrusion Prevention Systems (IPSs) As its name implies an *intrusion prevention system (IPS)* not only monitors to detect malicious activities like an IDS but also attempts to prevent them by stopping the attack. A **network intrusion prevention system (NIPS)** is similar to a NIDS in that it monitors network traffic to immediately react to block a malicious attack. One of the major differences between a NIDS and a NIPS is its location. A NIDS has sensors that monitor the traffic entering and leaving a firewall, and reports back to the central device for analysis. A NIPS, on the other hand, would be located "in line" on the firewall itself. This can allow the NIPS to more quickly take action to block an attack.

Similar to an application-aware IDS, an **application-aware IPS** knows such information as the applications that are running as well as the underlying operating systems so that it can provide a higher degree of accuracy regarding potential attacks.

Unified Threat Management (UTM) Security Appliances Because different types of network security hardware—firewalls, Internet content filters, web security gateways, etc.—each provide a different defense, a network may require multiple devices for comprehensive protection. This can make it cumbersome to manage all of these devices. An alternative is an integrated device that combines several security functions, called a **Unified Threat Management (UTM)** security product. Such multipurpose security appliances provide an array of security functions, such as:

- Antispam and antiphishing
- Antivirus and antispyware
- Bandwidth optimization
- Content filtering
- Encryption
- Firewall
- Instant messaging control
- Intrusion protection
- Web filtering

UTMs once were called *all-in-one network security appliances.*

Security Through Network Technologies

1.3 Explain network design elements and components.

Network technologies can also help to secure a network. Two such technologies are network address translation and network access control.

Network Address Translation (NAT)

Network address translation (NAT) is a technique that allows private IP addresses to be used on the public Internet. *Private IP addresses*, which are listed in Table 7-6, are IP addresses that are not assigned to any specific user or organization; instead, they can be used by anyone on the private internal network. Private addresses function as regular IP addresses on an internal network; however, if a packet with a private address makes its way to the Internet, the routers drop that packet.

 Strictly speaking, NAT is not a specific device, technology, or protocol. It is a technique for substituting IP addresses.

Class	Beginning address	Ending address
Class A	10.0.0.0	10.255.255.255
Class B	172.16.0.0	172.31.255.255
Class C	192.168.0.0	192.168.255.255

Table 7-6 Private IP addresses

NAT replaces a private IP address with a public IP address. As a packet leaves a network, NAT removes the private IP address from the sender's packet and replaces it with an alias IP public address, as shown in Figure 7-9. The NAT software maintains a table of the private IP addresses and alias public IP addresses. When a packet is returned to NAT, the process is reversed. A variation of NAT is *port address translation (PAT)*. Instead of giving each outgoing packet a different IP address, each packet is given the same IP address but a different TCP port number. This allows a single public IP address to be used by several users.

 PAT is typically used on home routers that allow multiple users to share one IP address received from an Internet service provider (ISP).

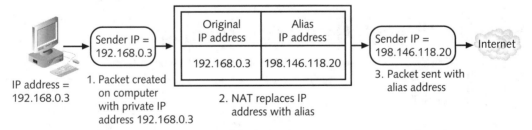

Figure 7-9 Network address translation (NAT)

A device using NAT, such as a NAT router, also can provide a degree of security. Because all outgoing traffic flows through the NAT router, it knows which packets were sent out and what it expects to receive. What happens if a packet arrives at the NAT router for an internal network device but the request for that packet was not first sent out through the router? If the initial request did not come through the NAT router, the router will discard all unsolicited packets so that they never enter the internal network. In this way the NAT router acts like a firewall by discarding unwanted packets. Another element of security that NAT provides is masking the IP addresses of internal devices. An attacker who captures the packet on the Internet cannot determine the actual IP address of the sender. Without that address, it is more difficult to identify and attack a computer.

Network Access Control (NAC)

The waiting room at a doctor's office is an ideal location for the spread of germs. The patients waiting in this confined space are obviously ill and many have weakened immune systems. During the cold and flu season, doctors routinely post notices that anyone who has flulike symptoms should not come to the waiting room so that other patients will not be infected. Suppose that a physician decided to post a nurse at the door of the waiting room to screen patients. Anyone who came to the waiting room and exhibited flulike symptoms would be directed to a separate quarantine room away from the normal patients. Here the person could receive specialized care without impacting others.

This is the logic behind **network access control (NAC)**. NAC examines the current state of a system or network device before it is allowed to connect to the network. Any device that does not meet a specified set of criteria, such as having the most current antivirus signature or the software firewall properly enabled, is allowed to connect only to a "quarantine" network where the security deficiencies are corrected. After the problems are solved, the device is connected to the normal network. The goal of NAC is to prevent computers with suboptimal security from potentially infecting other computers through the network.

 NAC also can be used to ensure that systems not owned by the organization, such as those owned by customers, visitors, and contractors, can be granted access without compromising security.

An example of the NAC process is illustrated in Figure 7-10 using the Microsoft Network Access Protection (NAP) terminology:

1. The client performs a self-assessment using a System Health Agent (SHA) to determine its current security posture.

2. The assessment, known as a Statement of Health (SoH), is sent to a server called the Health Registration Authority (HRA). This server enforces the security policies of the network. It also integrates with other external authorities such as antivirus and patch management servers in order to retrieve current configuration information.

3. If the client is approved by the HRA, it is issued a Health Certificate.

4. The Health Certificate is then presented to the network servers to verify that the client's security condition has been approved.

5. If the client is not approved, it is connected to a quarantine network where the deficiencies are corrected, and then the computer is allowed to connect to the network.

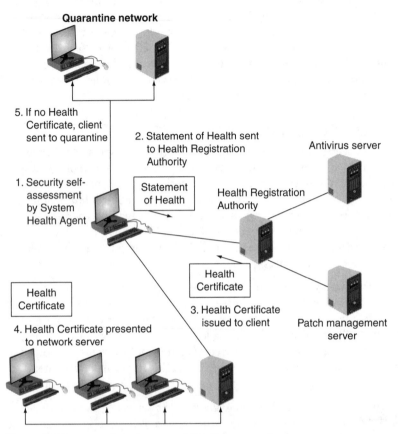

Figure 7-10 Network access control (NAC) framework

NAC typically uses one of two methods for directing the client to a quarantine network and then later to the production network. The first method is the use of a Dynamic Host Configuration Protocol (DHCP) server. The unapproved client is first leased an IP address to the quarantine network and then later leased an IP address to the production network. The second method actually uses a technique often used by attackers known as Address Resolution Protocol (ARP) poisoning. With this method the ARP table is manipulated on the client so that it connects to the quarantine network.

ARP poisoning is covered in Chapter 3.

NAC can be an effective tool for identifying and correcting systems that do not have adequate security installed and preventing these devices from infecting others.

Security Through Network Design Elements

1.3 Explain network design elements and components.

The design of a network can provide a secure foundation for resisting attackers. Elements of a secure network design include creating demilitarized zones, subnetting, using virtual LANs, and remote access.

Demilitarized Zone (DMZ)

Imagine a bank that located its automated teller machine (ATM) in the middle of their vault. This would be an open invitation for disaster by inviting every outside user to enter the secure vault to access the ATM. Instead, the ATM and the vault should be separated so that the ATM is located in a public area that anyone can access, while the vault is restricted to trusted individuals. In a similar fashion, locating public-facing servers such as web and email servers inside the secure network is also unwise. An attacker only has to break out of the security of the server to find herself inside the secure network.

In order to allow untrusted outside users access to resources such as web servers, most networks employ a **demilitarized zone (DMZ)**. The DMZ functions as a separate network that rests outside the secure network perimeter: untrusted outside users can access the DMZ but cannot enter the secure network.

Figure 7-11 illustrates a DMZ that contains a web server and an email server that are accessed by outside users. In this configuration, a single firewall with three network interfaces is used: the link to the Internet is on the first network interface, the DMZ is formed from the second network interface, and the secure internal LAN is based on the third network interface. However, this makes the firewall device a single point of failure for the network, and it also must take care of all the traffic to both the DMZ and internal network. A more secure approach is to have two firewalls, as seen in Figure 7-12. In this configuration, an attacker would have to breach two separate firewalls to reach the secure internal LAN.

Some consumer routers claim to support a DMZ, and yet do not allow a true DMZ. Rather, they allow only one local device to be exposed to the Internet for Internet gaming or videoconferencing by forwarding all the ports at the same time to that one device.

Subnetting

The TCP/IP protocol uses IP addresses, which are 32-bit (4-byte) addresses such as *192.146.118.20*. IP addresses are actually two addresses: one part is a network address (such as *192.146.118*) and one part is a host address (such as *20*). This split between the network and host portions of the IP address originally was set on the boundaries between the bytes (called *classful addressing*). Improved addressing techniques introduced in 1985 allowed an IP address to be split anywhere within its 32 bits. This is known as **subnetting** or **subnet addressing**. Instead of just having networks and hosts, with subnetting, networks essentially can be divided into three parts: network, subnet, and host. Each network can

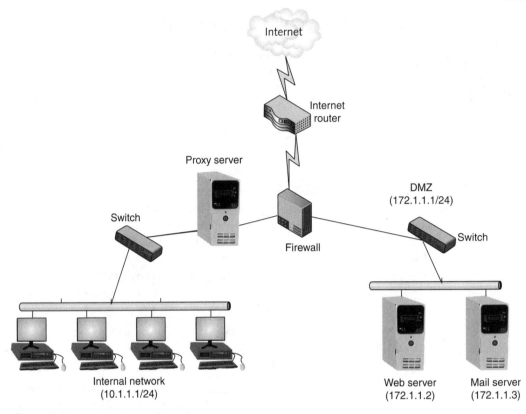

Figure 7-11   DMZ with one firewall

contain several subnets, and each subnet connected through different routers can contain multiple hosts. Subnets are illustrated in Figure 7-13, and the advantages of subnetting are listed in Table 7-7.

Subnets also can improve network security. Security is enhanced by subnetting a single network into multiple smaller subnets in order to isolate groups of hosts. Networks can be subnetted so that each department, remote office, campus building, floor in a building, or group of users can have its own subnetwork. Network administrators can utilize network security tools to make it easier to regulate who has access in and out of a particular subnetwork. Also, because wireless subnetworks, research and development subnetworks, finance subnetworks, human resource subnetworks, and subnetworks that face the Internet can all be separate, subnet addresses are instantly recognizable so that the source of potential security issues can be quickly addressed. For example, any IP address beginning with 192.168.50 can indicate mobile users, 192.168.125 may designate executive users, and 192.168.200 can indicate wireless network users.

Subnetting does not necessarily have to be tied to the design of the physical network.

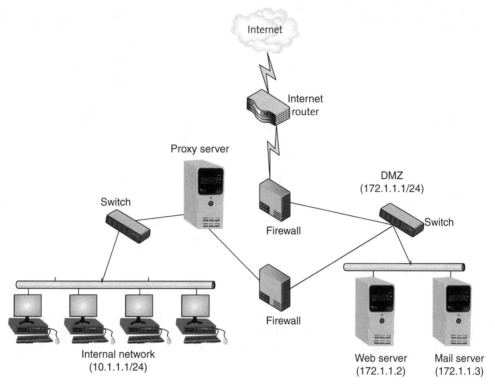

Figure 7-12 DMZ with two firewalls

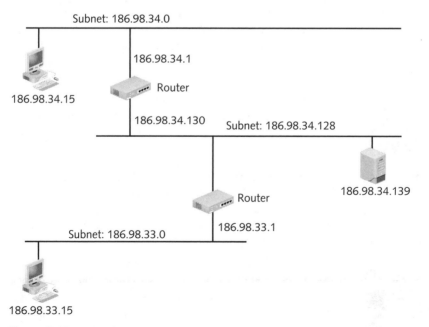

Figure 7-13 Subnets

Advantage	Explanation
Decreased network traffic	Broadcasts to network hosts are generally limited to individual subnets.
Flexibility	The number of subnets and hosts on each subnet can be customized for each organization and easily changed as necessary.
Improved troubleshooting	Tracing a problem on a subnet is faster and easier than on a single large network.
Improved utilization of addresses	Because networks can be subdivided, the number of wasted IP addresses generally is reduced.
Minimal impact on external routers	Because only routers within the organization are concerned with routing between subnets, routers outside the organization do not have to be updated to reflect changes.
Reflection of physical network	Hosts can be grouped together into subnets that more accurately reflect the way they are organized in the physical network.

Table 7-7   Advantages of subnetting

Another security advantage of using subnets is that it allows network administrators to hide the internal network layout. Because subnets are visible only within the organization, outsiders cannot see the internal network's structure. This can make it more difficult for attackers to target their attacks.

Virtual LANs (VLANs)

Networks are usually segmented by using switches to divide the network into a hierarchy. *Core switches* reside at the top of the hierarchy and carry traffic between switches, while *workgroup switches* are connected directly to the devices on the network. It is often beneficial to group similar users together, such as all the members of the Accounting department. However, grouping by user sometimes can be difficult because all users may not be in the same location and served by the same switch.

Core switches must work faster than workgroup switches because core switches must handle the traffic of several workgroup switches.

It is possible to segment a network by separating devices into logical groups. This is known as creating a **virtual LAN (VLAN)**. A VLAN allows scattered users to be logically grouped together even though they may be physically attached to different switches. This can reduce network traffic and provide a degree of security similar to subnetting; VLANs can be isolated so that sensitive data is transported only to members of the VLAN.

There are differences between subnetting and VLANs. Subnets are subdivisions of IP address classes (Class A, B, or C) and allow a single Class A, B, or C network to be used instead of multiple networks. VLANs are devices that are connected logically rather than physically, either through the port they are connected to or by their media access control (MAC) address.

VLAN communication can take place in two ways. If multiple devices in the same VLAN are connected to the same switch, the switch itself can handle the transfer of packets to the members of the VLAN group. However, if VLAN members on one switch need to communicate with members connected to another switch, a special "tagging" protocol must be used, either a proprietary protocol or the vendor-neutral IEEE 802.1Q. These special protocols add a field to the packet that "tags" it as belonging to the VLAN.

NOTE Another security advantage of VLANs is that they can be used to prevent direct communication between servers, which can bypass firewall or IDS inspection. Servers that are placed in separate VLANs will require that any traffic headed toward the default gateway for inter-VLAN routing be inspected.

Remote Access

Users who work away from the office have become commonplace today. These include telecommuters (who work occasionally or regularly from a home office), sales representatives who travel to meet distant customers, and workers who may be in another city at a conference or training. Organizations typically provide avenues for these remote users to access corporate resources as if they were sitting at a desk in the office. It is important to maintain strong security for these remote communications because the transmissions are routed through networks or devices that the organization does not manage and secure.

Remote access refers to any combination of hardware and software that enables remote users to access a local internal network. Remote access provides remote users with the same access and functionality as local users through a VPN or dial-up connection. This service includes support for remote connection and logon and then displays the same network interface as the normal network.

Chapter Summary

- Standard network security devices can be used to provide a degree of network security. Hubs should not be used in a network because they repeat all frames to all attached network devices, allowing an attacker to easily capture traffic and analyze its contents. A more secure network device is a switch. A switch forwards frames only to specific devices instead of all devices, thus limiting what a protocol analyzer can detect. A router can forward packets across computer networks. Because packets move through the router, the router can be configured to filter out specific types of network traffic. A load balancer can direct requests to different servers based on a variety of factors. Because load balancers are generally located between routers and servers they can detect and stop attacks directed at a server or application. A proxy server is a computer or an application program that intercepts user requests from the internal secure network and then processes that request on behalf of the user. Acting as the intermediary, a proxy server can protect clients from malware by intercepting it before it reaches the client. In addition, a proxy server can hide the IP address of client systems inside the secure network. A reverse proxy does not serve clients but instead routes incoming requests to the correct server.

- Hardware devices that are specifically designed for security can give a much higher level of protection. A hardware-based network firewall is designed to inspect packets and either accept or deny entry. These are located outside the network security perimeter as the first line of defense. Firewalls can either be rule-based or application-aware, and can use stateless packet filtering or stateful packet filtering. One method for filtering spam is for the organization to install its own corporate spam filter. This filter works with the receiving email server, which is typically based on the SMTP for sending email and the POP3 for retrieving email. Another method to filter spam is for the organization to contract with a third-party entity that filters out spam.

- A virtual private network (VPN) uses an unsecured public network, such as the Internet, as if it were a secure private network. It does this by encrypting all data that is transmitted between the remote device and the network. A VPN concentrator aggregates hundreds or thousands of connections. Internet content filters monitor Internet traffic and block access to preselected websites and files. A web security gateway can block malicious content in "real time" as it appears without first knowing the URL of a dangerous site.

- An intrusion detection system (IDS) is designed to detect an attack as it occurs. Monitoring involves examining network traffic, activity, transactions, or behavior in order to detect security-related anomalies. There are four monitoring methodologies: anomaly-based monitoring, signature-based monitoring, behavior-based monitoring, and heuristic monitoring. A host intrusion detection system (HIDS) is a software-based application that runs on a local host computer. A network intrusion detection system (NIDS) watches for attacks on the network. As network traffic moves through the network, NIDS sensors (usually installed on network devices such as firewalls and routers) gather information and report back to a central device. A network intrusion prevention system (NIPS) is similar to a NIDS in that it monitors network traffic to immediately react to block the malicious attack, but it can react more quickly than a NIDS. Integrated devices, called Unified Threat Management (UTM) products, are multipurpose security appliances that provide an array of security functions.

- Network technologies also can help secure a network. Network address translation (NAT) discards packets that were not requested by an internal network device and also hides the IP addresses of internal network devices from attackers by substituting a private address with a public address. Network access control (NAC) looks at the current security posture of a system and, if it is deficient, prohibits it from connecting to the network, sending it instead to a remediation network for the deficiency to be corrected.

- Several methods can be used to design a secure network. A demilitarized zone (DMZ) functions as a separate network that rests outside the secure network perimeter so untrusted outside users can access the DMZ but cannot enter the secure network. Subnetting involves dividing a network into subnets that are connected through a series of routers. This can improve security by regulating the users who can access a specific subnet. Similar to subnetting, a virtual LAN (VLAN) allows users who may be scattered across different campuses or floors of a building to be logically grouped. Like subnetting, VLANs can isolate sensitive traffic. Remote access refers to any combination of hardware and software that enables remote users to access a local internal network.

Key Terms

anomaly-based monitoring A monitoring technique used by an intrusion detection system (IDS) that creates a baseline of normal activities and compares actions against the baseline. Whenever there is a significant deviation from this baseline, an alarm is raised.

application-aware firewall A firewall that can identify the applications that send packets through the firewall and then make decisions about the applications.

application-aware IDS A specialized intrusion detection system (IDS) that is capable of using "contextual knowledge" in real time.

application-aware IPS An intrusion prevention system (IPS) that knows information such as the applications that are running as well as the underlying operating systems.

application-aware proxy A special proxy server that knows the application protocols that it supports.

behavior-based monitoring A monitoring technique used by an IDS that uses the normal processes and actions as the standard and compares actions against it.

content inspection Searching incoming web content to match keywords.

defense in depth A defense that uses multiple types of security devices to protect a network. Also called *layered security*.

demilitarized zone (DMZ) A separate network that rests outside the secure network perimeter: untrusted outside users can access the DMZ but cannot enter the secure network.

firewall rules A set of individual instructions to control the actions of a firewall.

heuristic monitoring A monitoring technique used by an intrusion detection system (IDS) that uses an algorithm to determine if a threat exists.

host-based intrusion detection system (HIDS) A software-based application that runs on a local host computer that can detect an attack as it occurs.

intrusion detection system (IDS) A device that detects an attack as it occurs.

layered security A defense that uses multiple types of security devices to protect a network. Also called *defense in depth*.

load balancer A dedicated network device that can direct requests to different servers based on a variety of factors.

malware inspection Searching for malware in incoming web content.

network access control (NAC) A technique that examines the current state of a system or network device before it is allowed to connect to the network.

network address translation (NAT) A technique that allows private IP addresses to be used on the public Internet.

network intrusion detection system (NIDS) A technology that watches for attacks on the network and reports back to a central device.

network intrusion prevention system (NIPS) A technology that monitors network traffic to immediately react to block a malicious attack.

protocol analyzer Hardware or software that captures packets to decode and analyze their contents.

7

proxy server   A computer or an application program that intercepts user requests from the internal secure network and then processes those requests on behalf of the users.

remote access   Any combination of hardware and software that enables remote users to access a local internal network.

reverse proxy   A computer or an application program that routes incoming requests to the correct server.

router   A device that can forward packets across computer networks.

signature-based monitoring   A monitoring technique used by an intrusion detection system (IDS) that examines network traffic to look for well-known patterns and compares the activities against a predefined signature.

subnetting (subnet addressing)   A technique that uses IP addresses to divide a network into network, subnet, and host.

switch   A device that connects network segments and forwards only frames intended for that specific device or frames sent to all devices.

Unified Threat Management (UTM)   Network hardware that provides multiple security functions.

URL filtering   Restricting access to unapproved websites.

virtual LAN (VLAN)   A technology that allows scattered users to be logically grouped together even though they may be attached to different switches.

virtual private network (VPN)   A technology that enables use of an unsecured public network as if it were a secure private network.

VPN concentrator   A device that aggregates VPN connections.

web application firewall   A special type of application-aware firewall that looks at the applications using HTTP.

web security gateway   A device that can block malicious content in real time as it appears (without first knowing the URL of a dangerous site).

Review Questions

1. Which secure feature does a load balancer NOT provide?

    a. hide HTTP error pages

    b. remove server identification headers from HTTP responses

    c. filter packets based on protocol settings

    d. block denial-of-service (DoS) attacks

2. Which of these would NOT be a filtering mechanism found in a firewall rule?

    a. source address

    b. date

    c. protocol

    d. direction

3. A(n) _____ can identify the application that send packets and then make decisions about filtering based on it.

   a. application-aware firewall

   b. reverse proxy

   c. Internet content filter

   d. web security gateway

4. Which function does an Internet content filter NOT perform?

   a. URL filtering

   b. malware inspection

   c. content inspection

   d. intrusion detection

5. How does network address translation (NAT) improve security?

   a. It discards unsolicited packets.

   b. It filters based on protocol.

   c. It masks the IP address of the NAT device.

   d. NATs do not improve security.

6. How does a virtual LAN (VLAN) allow devices to be grouped?

   a. based on subnets

   b. logically

   c. directly to hubs

   d. only around core switches

7. Which device is easiest for an attacker to take advantage of in order to capture and analyze packets?

   a. hub

   b. switch

   c. router

   d. load balancer

8. Which of these is NOT an attack against a switch?

   a. MAC address impersonation

   b. ARP poisoning

   c. MAC flooding

   d. ARP address impersonation

9. Which statement regarding a demilitarized zone (DMZ) is NOT true?

   a. It can be configured to have one or two firewalls.

   b. It provides an extra degree of security.

   c. It typically includes an email or web server.

   d. It contains servers that are used only by internal network users.

10. Which statement about network address translation (NAT) is true?

    a. It can be stateful or stateless.

    b. It substitutes MAC addresses for IP addresses.

    c. It removes private addresses when the packet leaves the network.

    d. It can be found only on core routers.

11. Which of these is NOT an advantage of a load balancer?

    a. The risk of overloading a desktop client is reduced.

    b. Network hosts can benefit from having optimized bandwidth.

    c. Network downtime can be reduced.

    d. DoS attacks can be detected and stopped.

12. A(n) _____ intercepts internal user requests and then processes those requests on behalf of the users.

    a. content filter

    b. host detection server

    c. proxy server

    d. intrusion prevention device

13. A reverse proxy _____.

    a. only handles outgoing requests

    b. is the same as a proxy server

    c. must be used together with a firewall

    d. routes incoming requests to the correct server

14. Which is the preferred location for installation of a spam filter?

    a. on the POP3 server

    b. with the SMTP server

    c. on the local host client

    d. on the proxy server

15. A _____ watches for attacks and sounds an alert only when one occurs.

    a. firewall

    b. network intrusion prevention system (NIPS)

    c. proxy intrusion device

    d. network intrusion detection system (NIDS)

16. A multipurpose security device is known as _____.

    a. Cohesive Attack Management System (Co-AMS)

    b. Proxy Security System (PSS)

    c. Intrusion Detection/Prevention (ID/P)

    d. Unified Threat Management (UTM)

17. Each of these can be used to hide information about the internal network EXCEPT _____.

    a. a protocol analyzer

    b. subnetting

    c. a proxy server

    d. network address translation (NAT)

18. What is the difference between a network intrusion detection system (NIDS) and a network intrusion prevention system (NIPS)?

    a. There is no difference; a NIDS and a NIPS are equal.

    b. A NIPS can take actions more quickly to combat an attack.

    c. A NIDS provides more valuable information about attacks.

    d. A NIPS is much slower because it uses protocol analysis.

19. If a device is determined to have an out-of-date virus signature file, then Network Access Control (NAC) can redirect that device to a network by _____.

    a. a Trojan horse

    b. TCP/IP hijacking

    c. Address Resolution Protocol (ARP) poisoning

    d. DHCP man-in-the-middle

20. A firewall using _____ is the most secure type of firewall.

    a. stateful packet filtering

    b. network intrusion detection system replay

    c. stateless packet filtering

    d. reverse proxy analysis

7

Hands-On Projects

If you are concerned about installing any of the software in these projects on your regular computer, you can instead install the software in the Windows virtual machine created in the Chapter 1 Hands-On Projects 1-3 and 1-4. Software installed within the virtual machine will not impact the host computer.

Project 7-1: Configuring the Windows Firewall

In this project you will edit configuration settings on the Windows Firewall.

The Windows Firewall uses three different profiles: domain (when the computer is connected to a Windows domain), private (when connected to a private network, such as a work or home network), and public (used when connected to a public network, such as a public Wi-Fi). A computer may use multiple profiles, so that a business laptop computer may use the domain profile at work, the private profile when connected to the home network, and the public profile when connected to a public Wi-Fi network. Windows asks whether a network is public or private when you first connect to it.

1. Click **Start**, then **Control Panel**, then **System and Security**, and finally **Windows Firewall**.

2. Click **Turn Windows Firewall on or off**. Be sure that the Windows Firewall is turned on for both private and public networks.

3. Under **Public network settings** check **Block all incoming connections, including those in the list of allowed apps**. This provides an extra level of security when using a public network such as a free Wi-Fi network by preventing a malicious incoming connection from another computer on the network. Click **OK**.

4. To allow an inbound connection from an installed application, in the left pane click **Allow an app or feature through Windows Firewall**.

5. Each program or feature of Windows can be chosen to allow an incoming connection on public or private networks. Click **Allow another app**.

6. From here you can select an app that will permit an incoming connection. Because this is a security risk, click **Cancel**.

7. Now check the configuration properties of the Windows Firewall. Click **Advanced settings**.

8. Click **Windows Firewall Properties**.

9. Note the settings on each of the profiles by clicking the **Domain Profile, Private Profile,** and **Public Profile** tabs. Is there any difference in the settings between these profiles? Why?

10. On each tab under Settings, click **Customize.** Be sure that **Display a notification** is set to **Yes.** Why would this be important?

11. Click **OK** to return to the Windows Firewall with Advanced Security page.

12. In addition to being application-aware, the Windows Firewall also can be configured for firewall rules. Click **Outbound Rules** in the left pane to block a program from reaching the Internet.

13. In the right pane, click **New Rule ...**

14. Click **Port** and then **Next.**

In addition to ports, Windows Firewall also can block by program (*Program*) or even by program, port, and IP address (*Custom*).

TIP

7

15. If necessary, click **TCP.**

16. Next to **Specific remote ports:** enter 80. Click **Next.**

17. If necessary, click **Block the connection.** Click **Next.**

18. Be sure that this new rule applies to all three domains. Click **Next.**

19. Under **Name:** enter **Blocking Port 80.** Click **Finish.**

20. Now open a web browser and try to connect to the Internet. What happens?

21. Click the **Back** button to return to the Windows Firewall screen and click **Action** and **Restore Default Policy** to disable this rule. Click **OK.**

22. Select **Outbound Rules** in the left pane. In the right pane, click **New Rule ...**

23. Click **Custom** and **Next.**

24. If necessary click **All programs** and **Next.**

25. Note that you can configure a firewall rule based on protocol, protocol number, local port, and remote port.

26. Click **Cancel.**

27. Close all windows.

Project 7-2: Using Behavior-Based Monitoring Tools

Instead of using statistics or signatures as the standard by which comparisons are made, behavior-based monitoring uses the "normal" processes and actions as the standard. Behavior-based monitoring continuously analyzes the behavior of processes and programs on a system and signals alerts if it detects any abnormal actions so the user can then decide whether to allow or block the activity. In this project, you will download and install ThreatFire, a behavior-based monitoring tool.

1. Use your web browser to go to **www.threatfire.com/download.**

The location of content on the Internet may change without warning. If you are no longer able to access the program through the above URL, use a search engine to search for "ThreatFire".

2. Click **Get Free.**

3. Click **Save** and then save the file to a location on your computer such as the desktop or other location.

4. When the file has finished downloading, click **Run** and follow the default settings to install ThreatFire. During the installation, you may see the PC Security Check Required window. If so, click **Start Scan** and once the scan is completed click **Continue.**

5. After installation, a tutorial will appear regarding how the software works. Read through the tutorial by clicking the **Next** button.

6. You may be prompted to reboot your computer. Restart your system.

7. After your computer has restarted, launch ThreatFire.

8. Click **Advanced Tools.**

9. Click **Custom Rule Settings.**

10. Click the **Process Lists** tab.

11. Click the **Uncheck All** button under **Email and Browsers:** to turn off all of those listed as trusted. Then go back and select only those that are installed on this system.

12. Click **Apply** and then **OK.**

13. Click **Settings.**

14. Click **Sensitivity Level.**

15. Move the slider to **5,** the highest level.

16. Use your system as you normally would. What actions does ThreatFire take? Would you recommend this as a supplement to antivirus software that relies on signature updates?

17. Close all windows.

Project 7-3: Using an Internet Content Filter

Internet content filters are used to block inappropriate content. In this project, you will download and install the filter K9 Web Protection.

1. Use your web browser to go to **www1.k9webprotection.com.**

The location of content on the Internet may change without warning. If you are no longer able to access the program through the above URL, use a search engine to search for "K9 Web Protection".

2. Click **Free Download.**

3. Be sure the radio button **Get K9 Free for your home** is selected. Enter the requested information and then click **Request License**.

4. Go to the email account that you entered and click **Download K9 Web Protection**.

5. Click the operating system that you are using.

6. Click **Save** and save the file to your computer.

7. Click **Run** and follow the instructions to install it to your computer.

8. When the installation is complete, reboot the computer.

9. Launch **Blue Coat K9 Web Protection Admin**.

10. Click **SETUP**.

11. Enter your password.

12. Under **Web Categories to Block**, note the different levels of options available.

13. Click **Custom**.

14. Under **Other Categories**, click **Block All**.

15. Click on the other options under **Setup** and note the different configuration settings.

16. Under **Web Categories to Block**, click **Monitor**.

17. Click **Save**.

18. Click **Logout**.

19. Open your web browser. Enter the URL **www.google.com**. What happens now that the filter is installed?

20. Close all windows.

Project 7-4: Configure a Windows Client for Network Access Protection

Network access control (NAC) examines the current state of a system or network device before it is allowed to connect to the network to prevent computers with suboptimal security from potentially infecting other computers through the network. Any device that does not meet a specified set of criteria, such as having the most current antivirus signature or the software firewall properly enabled, is only allowed to connect to a "quarantine" network where the security deficiencies are corrected. The Microsoft NAC solution is called Microsoft Network Access Protection. In this project you will explore the configuration options for configuring a Windows client for Network Access Protection.

In order to fully implement Network Access Protection, it would be necessary to install the Network Policy Server and create a System Health Validator on a Microsoft Windows 2012 Server. Those steps will not be performed in this project.

1. In Microsoft Windows 8, enter **services.msc** at the Start screen.

2. In the **Services** dialog box, scroll down to **Network Access Protection Agent** and double-click it. This will open the Network Access Protection Agent Properties dialog box.

3. Change Startup type from **Manual** to **Automatic**. This will cause the Windows service that supports Network Access Protection to start automatically when it is needed.

4. Click **Start** under Service status to launch the service. Click **OK**.

5. Close the Services dialog box.

6. At the Start screen, enter **napclcfg.msc**, which will open the NAP Client Configuration dialog box.

7. In the left pane, click **Enforcement Clients**. Because you want to enforce health policies when a client computer attempts to obtain an IP address from the DHCP server, double-click **DHCP Quarantine Enforcement Client**.

8. The DHCP Quarantine Enforcement Client Properties dialog box appears. Click the check box **Enable this enforcement client** and then click **OK**.

9. In the left pane, click **User Interface Settings**. The NAP status user interface provides information about the NAP agents that are enabled on the computer, network enforcement status, and remediation status. This can be used to inform users regarding what is happening to their computer if it is sent to a quarantine VLAN. It also can provide contact information so that users can receive assistance if necessary.

10. In the center pane, double-click **User Interface** to open the User Interface Properties dialog box.

11. The Title appears as a banner at the top of the NAP Status dialog box with a maximum character length of 40. Enter **IT Department-Organization X**.

12. The Description appears below the title. Enter **Call the IT Helpdesk at x3659 for assistance**.

13. The Image can be a logo of the organization of file type .jpg, .bmp, or .gif. Click **Cancel**.

14. Expand **Health Registration Settings** in the left pane.

15. Click **Request Policy**. This allows you to configure the security mechanisms that the client computer uses to communicate with a Health Registration Authority (HRA) server.

16. In the left pane under Health Registration Settings, click **Trusted Server Groups**. This is the point at which you can specify which HRA servers you want the computer to communicate with.

If there is more than one HRA server in a trusted server group, you can specify the order in which client computers attempt to contact the servers. This is useful if you have several HRA servers in different network segments or domains and you want to prioritize which servers a client attempts to access first. You must configure at least one trusted server group; otherwise, a client computer will not know how to contact an HRA server to obtain a certificate of health.

17. Close the NAP Client Configuration dialog box.

18. Close all windows.

Case Projects

CASE PROJECTS

Case Project 7-1: Subnetting and VLANs for Security

Select a network at your school or place of work and acquire information regarding its design (you may want to speak with the network administrator, or your instructor may provide the information for you). Draw a map of the network layout, and then redesign the network using subnets and/or VLANs with the goal of making the network more secure. Draw a map of your new secure network layout. What changes did you make? Why did you make them? Include a paragraph describing your changes.

Case Project 7-2: UTM Comparison

Create a table of three to five popular UTM devices available today. Include the vendor name, pricing, a list of features, the type of protections it provides, etc. Based on your research, assign a value of 1–5 (lowest to highest) that you would give that UTM. Include a short explanation of why you gave it that ranking.

Case Project 7-3: Load-Balancing Algorithms

Different algorithms are used to make decisions on load balancing. These include random allocation, round-robin, weighted round-robin, round-robin DNS load balancing, and others. Use the Internet to research load-balancing algorithms. Create a table that lists at least five algorithms and their advantages and disadvantages. Do any of these algorithms compromise security? Write a one-page paper on your research.

Case Project 7-4: Network Firewall Comparison

Use the Internet to identify three network firewalls, and create a chart that compares their features. Note if they are rule-based or application-aware, perform stateless or stateful packet filtering, what additional features they include (IDS, content filtering, etc.), their costs, etc. Which would you recommend? Why?

Case Project 7-5: Bay Pointe Security Consulting

Bay Pointe Security Consulting (BPSC) provides security consulting services to a wide range of businesses, individuals, schools, and organizations. BPSC has hired you as a technology student to help them with a new project and provide real-world experience to students who are interested in the security field.

Eagle Trail Real Estate is a statewide residential and commercial real estate company. Because the company was the victim of several recent attacks, Eagle

7

Trail wants to completely change its network infrastructure. Currently the company has a small IT staff, so they have contracted with BPSC to make recommendations and install the new equipment. First, however, they have asked BPSC to give a presentation to their executive staff about network security.

1. Create a PowerPoint presentation for the executive staff about network security. Include what it is, why it is important, and how it can be achieved using network devices, technologies, and design elements. Because the staff does not have an IT background, the presentation cannot be too technical in nature. Your presentation should contain at least 10 slides.

2. Eagle Trail has been working with BPSC and is debating if they should use UTM network security appliances or separate devices (firewall, Internet content filters, NIDS, etc.). Because they appreciated your first presentation, they want your opinion on this subject. Create a memo that outlines the advantages and disadvantages of each approach, and gives your recommendation.

Case Project 7-6: Community Site Activity

The Information Security Community Site is an online companion to this textbook. It contains a wide variety of tools, information, discussion boards, and other features to assist learners. Go to **community.cengage.com/infosec**. Sign in with the login name and password that you created in Chapter 1.

Some schools and libraries use Internet content filters to prohibit users from accessing undesirable websites. These filters are designed to protect individuals, but some claim it is a violation of their freedom. What are your opinions about Internet content filters? Do they provide protection for users or are they a hindrance? Who should be responsible for determining which sites are appropriate and which are inappropriate? And what punishments should be enacted against individuals who circumvent these filters? Visit the Community Site discussion board and post how you feel about Internet content filters.

## chapter 8

Administering a Secure Network

After completing this chapter, you should be able to do the following:

- List and describe the functions of common network protocols
- Explain how network administration principles can be applied
- Define different network applications and how they can be secured

Today's Attacks and Defenses

Administering a secure network involves much more than installing security updates and monitoring for intrusions. It also requires making rational decisions regarding security. But sometimes security decisions are anything but rational.

The Economic Development Administration (EDA) is part of the U.S. Department of Commerce. Recently another government agency, the Department of Homeland Security (DHS), warned the Commerce Department that a potential malware infection could be occurring within its networks. After investigating, the security administrators at the Commerce Department identified the potentially infected computers as belonging to the EDA, and the EDA was contacted about this problem. The email sent by Commerce Department security administrators to the EDA said that they found 146 EDA systems that might be infected.

The next day the Commerce Department sent a follow-up email with a correction. Instead of 146 potential EDA computers, there actually were only two computers that were infected. The Commerce Department asked the EDA to reimage the two computers to clean them of any malware. According to the U.S. Inspector General's report on the incident, however, the second email was vague and did not point out that the first email was inaccurate. The EDA interpreted the second email as a confirmation of the first warning. After performing an analysis on the two computers listed in the second email and finding evidence of malware infections, the EDA believed they were being instructed to clean at least 146 systems. When the EDA said that there were too many computers to reimage (although across a network, 50 computers can easily be reimaged in one day), the Commerce Department assumed—incorrectly—that the EDA had found more computers that were infected.

The next month the chief information officer (CIO) of the EDA ordered that their computers should be isolated from the network. Soon after this, the CIO decided that *all* EDA computers should be physically destroyed. The instruction sent out was not to just clean or replace the infected hard drives, but to crush all the computer systems—along with mice and keyboards. The order would destroy more than $3 million worth of EDA computer systems. Over the next six months the EDA spent all of the money allocated for destruction—more than $170,000—crushing computers. When the money ran out, the EDA had to stop its misguided efforts. The EDA then requested from the Commerce Department's IT Review Board more than $26 million over the next three years to fund its remaining destruction and recovery efforts. The request was denied and an investigation was launched. The end result was that the EDA spent 50 percent of its entire IT budget, or about $2.7 million, in personnel and related costs to fix just two infected computers.

(continued)

The Department of Commerce later launched a "comprehensive incident response improvement project." This project paid a third party to review how the department had responded and hired three experienced incident handlers, along with installing a new security incident tracking system. It is unknown how much this new project will ultimately cost taxpayers.

As you learned in the previous chapter, building a secure network through network devices, network technologies, and appropriate network design are important steps for keeping information secure. Yet the job does not end there. Properly administering the network is also critical for security. A network that is not properly maintained through proven administrative procedures is at a high risk to be compromised by attackers.

This chapter looks at administering a secure network. First you will explore common network protocols, which are important to use in maintaining a secure network. Next you will investigate basic network administration principles. Finally, you will look at securing three popular types of network applications: IP telephony, virtualization, and cloud computing.

8

Common Network Protocols

1.4 Given a scenario, implement common protocols and services.

4.4 Implement the appropriate controls to ensure data security.

In the world of international politics, *protocols* are the forms of ceremony and etiquette. These rules of conduct and communication are to be observed by foreign diplomats and heads of state while working in a different country. If they were to ignore these protocols, they would risk offending the citizens of the host country, which might lead to a diplomatic incident or, even worse, a war.

Computer networks also have protocols, or rules for communication. These protocols are essential for proper communication to take place between network devices. The most common protocol used today for both local area networks (LANs) and the Internet is **Transmission Control Protocol/Internet Protocol (TCP/IP)**. TCP/IP is not one single protocol; instead, it comprises several protocols that all function together (called a *protocol suite*). The two major protocols that make up its name, *TCP* and *IP*, are considered the most important protocols. IP is the protocol that functions primarily at the Open Systems Interconnection (OSI) Network Layer (Layer 3) to provide addressing and routing. TCP is the main Transport Layer (Layer 4) protocol that is responsible for establishing connections and the reliable data transport between devices.

IP is responsible for addressing packets and sending them on the correct route to the destination, while TCP is responsible for reliable packet transmission.

TCP/IP uses its own four-layer architecture that includes Network Interface, Internet, Transport, and Application layers. This corresponds generally to the OSI reference model, as illustrated in Figure 8-1. The TCP/IP architecture gives a framework for the dozens of various protocols and several high-level applications that comprise the suite.

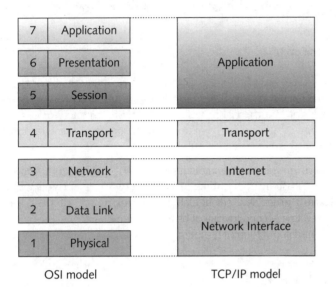

7	Application		
6	Presentation		Application
5	Session		
4	Transport		Transport
3	Network		Internet
2	Data Link		Network Interface
1	Physical		

OSI model   TCP/IP model

Figure 8-1 OSI model vs. TCP/IP model

The Physical Layer is omitted in the TCP/IP model. This is because TCP/IP views the Network Interface Layer as the point where the connection between the TCP/IP protocol and the networking hardware occurs.

Several of the basic TCP/IP protocols that relate to security are Internet Control Message Protocol (ICMP), Simple Network Management Protocol (SNMP), Domain Name System (DNS), file transfer and storage protocols, NetBIOS, and Telnet. In addition, a new and more secure version of IP is designed to replace the current version.

There are other TCP/IP security-related protocols such as Secure Sockets Layer (SSL), Transport Layer Security (TLS), Secure Shell (SSH), Hypertext Transfer Protocol Secure (HTTPS), and Internet Protocol Security (IPSec). These are covered in Chapter 6.

Internet Control Message Protocol (ICMP)

Different IP devices on a network often need to share between them specific information. However, IP does not have the capability for devices to exchange these low-level control messages. The communications between devices is handled by one of the core protocols of TCP/IP, namely, **Internet Control Message Protocol (ICMP)**. ICMP messages are divided into two classes:

- *Informational and query messages.* These messages are used for devices to exchange information and perform testing. They are generated either by an application or simply on a regular basis by devices to provide information to other devices.

- *Error messages.* ICMP error messages provide feedback to another device about an error that has occurred. These messages can be sent as the result of basic errors (such as a requested service is not available or that a device cannot be reached) or more advanced situations (such as a web security gateway does not have sufficient buffering capacity to forward a packet).

Although it is technically a protocol, ICMP is more a structure for the exchange of information and error messages.

Each ICMP message contains four fields:

1. *Type.* The Type field identifies the general category of the ICMP message. Types 0–40 are commonly used while types 42–255 are reserved.

2. *Code.* The Code field gives specific additional information regarding the Type field. Table 8-1 lists some of the most common codes of the 16 different code values for Type 3, *Destination Unreachable.*

3. *Checksum.* This field is used to verify the integrity of the message.

4. *Message Body.* The Message Body field contains information about the specific ICMP message.

ICMP messages that report errors also will include the header and the first 64 data bits of the packet that caused the problem. This helps to diagnose the problem.

Type 3 code value	Description
0	Destination network unreachable
1	Destination host unreachable
2	Destination protocol unreachable
3	Destination port unreachable
5	Source route failed
6	Destination network unknown
7	Destination host unknown
9	Communication with destination network administratively prohibited
12	Host unreachable for Type of Service

Table 8-1 **Common ICMP code values for Type 3, Destination Unreachable**

Several attacks take advantage of ICMP:

- *Network discovery*. An attacker can use ICMP messages as one of the first steps in reconnaissance to discover information about the hosts that are part of the network. This can include sending individual ICMP echo requests to the broadcast addresses of a network and sending an ICMP address mask request to a host on the network to determine the subnet mask.

- *Smurf attack*. Attackers can broadcast a *ping* request (which uses ICMP) to all computers on the network but change the address from which the request came to that of the target. This makes it appear that the target computer is asking for a response from all computers. Each of the computers then responds to the target server, overwhelming it and causing it to crash or be unavailable to legitimate users.

- *ICMP redirect attack*. In this attack, an ICMP redirect packet is sent to the victim that asks the host to send its packets to another "router," which is actually a malicious device.

- *Ping of death*. A malformed ICMP *ping* that exceeds the size of an IP packet is sent to the victim's computer. This can cause the host to crash.

Simple Network Management Protocol (SNMP)

The **Simple Network Management Protocol (SNMP)** is a popular protocol used to manage network equipment and is supported by most network equipment manufacturers. It allows network administrators to remotely monitor, manage, and configure devices on the network. SNMP functions by exchanging management information between networked devices.

SNMP can be found not only on core network devices such as switches, routers, and wireless access points, but also on some printers, copiers, fax machines, and even uninterruptible power supplies (UPSs).

Each SNMP-managed device must have an agent or a service that listens for commands and then executes them. These agents are protected with a password, called a *community string*, in order to prevent unauthorized users from taking control of a device. There are two types of community strings: a *read-only* string will allow information from the agent to be viewed, and a *read-write* string allows settings on the device to be changed.

There were several security vulnerabilities with the use of community strings in the first two versions of SNMP, known as SNMPv1 and SNMPv2. First, the default SNMP community strings for read-only and read-write were *public* and *private*, respectively. Administrators who did not change these default strings left open the possibility of an attacker taking control of the network device. Also, community strings were transmitted as cleartext with no attempt to encrypt the contents. Because of the security vulnerabilities of SNMPv1 and SNMPv2, SNMPv3 uses usernames and passwords along with encryption to foil an attacker's attempt to view the contents.

It is recommended that SNMPv3 be used in place of SNMPv1 and SNMPv2.

Domain Name System (DNS)

The *Domain Name System (DNS)* is a TCP/IP protocol that resolves (maps) a symbolic name (*www.cengage.com*) with its corresponding IP address (*69.32.133.11*). The DNS database is organized as a hierarchy (tree). Yet to store the entire database of names and IP addresses in one location would present several problems. First, it would cause a bottleneck and slow down the Internet with all users trying to access a single copy of the database. Second, if something happened to this one database, the entire Internet would be affected.

Instead of being on only one server, the DNS database is divided and distributed to many different servers on the Internet, each of which is responsible for different areas of the Internet. The steps of a DNS lookup (which uses TCP/IP port 53) are as follows, illustrated in Figure 8-2.

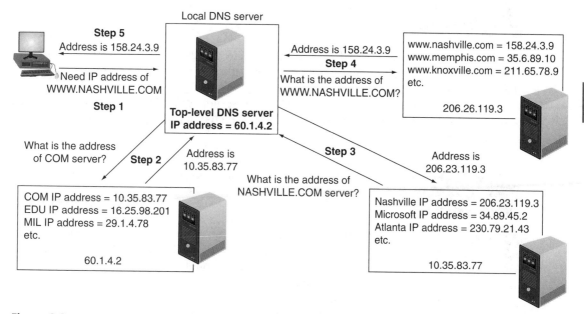

Figure 8-2   DNS lookup

Step 1. The request for the IP address of the site *www.nashville.com* is first compared against the local host table to determine if there is an entry. If no entry exists, the request travels from the user's computer to the local DNS server that is part of the LAN to which it is connected.

Step 2. The local DNS server does not know the IP address of *www.nashville.com*, yet it does know the IP address of a DNS server that contains the top-level domains and their IP numbers. A request is sent to this top-level domain DNS server.

Step 3. This top-level DNS server sends back the IP address of the DNS server that contains information about addresses that end in *.COM*. The local DNS server then sends a request to this second DNS server, which contains the IP address of the DNS server that contains the information about *nashville.com*.

Step 4. After receiving back that information, the local DNS server contacts the third DNS server responsible for *nashville*, which looks up the IP address of *www.nashville.com*.

Step 5. This information is finally returned to the local DNS server, which sends it back to the user's computer.

Because of the important role it plays, DNS is often the focus of attacks. *DNS poisoning* substitutes addresses so that the computer is redirected to another device. That is, an attacker replaces a valid IP address with a fraudulent IP address for a symbolic name. Substituting a fraudulent IP address can be done in two different locations: the local host table, or the external DNS server.

DNS poisoning is covered in Chapter 3.

DNS poisoning can be prevented by using the latest editions of the DNS software known as *BIND*, or *Berkeley Internet Name Domain*. These editions make DNS servers less trusting of the information passed to them by other DNS servers and ignore any DNS records received that are not directly relevant to the query. A newer secure version of DNS known as *Domain Name System Security Extensions (DNSSEC)* allows DNS information to be digitally signed so that an attacker cannot forge DNS information.

A variation on DNS poisoning involves substituting a false MX (mail exchange) record. This results in all email being sent to the attacker.

A second attack using DNS is almost the reverse of DNS poisoning; instead of sending a zone transfer to a valid DNS server, an attacker asks the valid DNS server for a zone transfer, known as a *DNS transfer*. With this information it would be possible for the attacker to map the entire internal network of the organization supporting the DNS server. Often a zone transfer may contain hardware and operating system information for each network device, providing the attacker with even more valuable information.

File Transfer Protocols

In its early days, prior to the development of the World Wide Web and Hypertext Transfer Protocol (HTTP), the Internet was primarily a medium for transferring files from one device to another. Today transferring files is still considered an important task. Two TCP/IP protocols are used for transferring files. These are File Transfer Protocol (FTP) and Secure Copy Protocol (SCP).

File Transfer Protocol (FTP) Transferring files can be performed using the **File Transfer Protocol (FTP)**, which is an unsecure TCP/IP protocol. FTP is used to connect to an FTP server, much in the same way that HTTP links to a web server. A "light" version of FTP known as **Trivial File Transfer Protocol (TFTP)** uses a small amount of memory but has limited functionality. It is often used for the automated transfer of configuration files between devices.

There are several different methods for using FTP on a local computer:

- *From a command prompt.* Commands can by typed at an operating system prompt, such as *ls* (list files), *get* (retrieve a file from the server), and *put* (transfer a file to the server).

- *Using a web browser.* Instead of prefacing a URL with the protocol *http://*, the FTP protocol is entered with a preface of *ftp://*.

- *Using an FTP client.* A separate FTP client application can be installed that displays files on the local host as well as the remote server. These files can be dragged and dropped between devices. The FTP client FileZilla is shown in Figure 8-3.

File Edit View Transfer Server Bookmarks Help					

| Host: | | Username: | | Password: | | Port: | | Quickconnect | ▼ |

Response:	MFF modify;UNIX.group;UNIX.mode;
Response:	MLST modify*;perm*;size*;type*;unique*;UNIX.group*;UNIX.mode*;UNIX.owner*;
Response:	REST STREAM
Response:	SIZE
Response:	211 End
Status:	Server does not support non-ASCII characters.
Status:	Connected
Status:	Retrieving directory listing

Local site:	C:\Users\Mark Ciampa\Documents\	▼		Remote site:	/	▼

Documents		revels
CyberLink		roger
HRBlock		Romero
Listen or Transcribe		ses

Filename	▲	Filename	▲
Listen or Transcribe		Haselhoff	
My Music		hill	
My Pictures		HMM	
My Videos		Honaker	

11 files and 11 directories. Total size: 2,616,890 bytes	1 file and 55 directories. Total size: 302 bytes

Server/Local file	Direction	Remote file	Size	Priority	Status
mciampa@ftp.thom...					
C:\Users\Mark Cia...	-->	/MichelleCan...	6,065,718	Normal	
C:\Users\Mark Cia...	-->	/MichelleCan...	6,065,718	Normal	
C:\Users\Mark Cia...	-->	/MichelleCan...	29,223	Normal	
C:\Users\Mark Cia...	-->	/MichelleCan...	29,365	Normal	
C:\Users\Mark Cia...	-->	/MichelleCan...	26,899	Normal	
C:\Users\Mark Cia...	-->	/MichelleCan...	10,068	Normal	
C:\Users\Mark Cia...	-->	/MichelleCan...	22,525	Normal	
C:\Users\Mark Cia...	-->	/MichelleCan...	26,227	Normal	
C:\Users\Mark Cia...	-->	/MichelleCan...	1,861,286	Normal	

Queued files (34)   Failed transfers   Successful transfers

Figure 8-3 FTP client
Source: FileZilla

FTP servers can be configured to allow unauthenticated users to transfer files, known as *anonymous FTP* or *blind FTP*.

Using FTP behind a firewall can present a set of challenges. FTP typically uses two ports: TCP port 21 is the FTP control port used for passing FTP commands, and TCP port 20 is the FTP data port through which data is sent and received. Using *FTP active mode*, an FTP client initiates a session to a server by opening a *command channel* connection to the server's TCP port number 21. A file transfer is requested by the client by sending a *PORT* command to the server, which then attempts to initiate a *data channel* connection back to the client on TCP port 20. The client's firewall, however, may see this data channel connection request from the server as unsolicited and drop the packets. This can be avoided by using *FTP passive mode*. In passive mode, the client initiates the data channel connection, yet instead of using the *PORT* command, the client sends a *PASV* command on the command channel. The server responds with the TCP port number to which the client should connect to establish the data channel (typically port 1025 to 5000).

Increased security can be established by restricting the port range used by the FTP service and then creating a firewall rule that allows FTP traffic only on those allowed port numbers.

Several security vulnerabilities are associated with using FTP. First, FTP does not use encryption, so any usernames, passwords, and files being transferred are in cleartext and could be accessed by using a protocol analyzer. Also, files being transferred by FTP are vulnerable to man-in-the-middle attacks where data is intercepted and then altered before being sent to the destination.

There are two options for secure transmissions over FTP. **FTP Secure (FTPS)** uses Secure Sockets Layer (SSL) or Transport Layer Security (TLS) to encrypt commands sent over the control port (port 21) in an FTP session. FTPS is actually a file transport layer resting on top of SSL or TLS, meaning that it uses the FTP protocol to transfer files to and from SSL or TLS-enabled FTP servers. However, a weakness of FTPS is that although the control port commands are encrypted, the data port (port 20) may or may not be encrypted. This is because a file that has already been encrypted by the user would not need to be encrypted again by FTPS and incur the additional overhead.

The second option is to use **Secure FTP (SFTP)**. There are several differences between SFTP and FTPS. First, FTPS is a combination of two technologies (FTP and SSL or TLS), whereas SFTP is an entire protocol itself and is not pieced together with multiple parts. Second, SFTP uses only a single TCP port instead of two ports like FTPS. Finally, SFTP encrypts and compresses all data and commands (FTPS may not encrypt data).

The abbreviation *SFTP* is the same as that for the *Simple File Transfer Protocol.* However, Simple File Transfer Protocol was never widely used, so today SFTP refers to Secure FTP.

Secure Copy Protocol (SCP) Another protocol used for file transfers is **Secure Copy Protocol (SCP)**. SCP is an enhanced version of *Remote Copy Protocol (RCP)*. SCP encrypts files and commands, yet has limitations. For example, a file transfer cannot be interrupted and then resumed in the same session; the session must be completely terminated and then restarted. SCP is found mainly on UNIX and Linux platforms.

Storage Protocols

The amount of data that is being stored has grown almost beyond imagination. Whereas at one time a single terabyte of storage was considered massive, today that is no longer the case (Table 8-2 lists different storage capacities). Between 2006 and 2011, the amount of available digital data worldwide increased from 200 EB to almost 2 ZB, and it is estimated that there will be 8 ZB of digital data stored by 2015. Organizations must cope with storing massive amounts of their data. Almost 70 percent of companies with more than 500 employees manage more than 100 TB of data storage, and nearly 40 percent manage more than 1 PB.[1]

Name	Size	Description
Gigabyte (GB)	1000 megabytes	1 GB can hold the contents of a shelf of books 30 feet long
Terabyte (TB)	1000 gigabytes	10 TB can hold the entire printed collection of the Library of Congress
Petabyte (PB)	1000 terabytes	The contents of 20 million four-drawer filing cabinets could be stored in 1 PB
Exabyte (EB)	1000 petabytes	All of the words ever spoken by the whole of mankind throughout history would consume 5 EB
Zettabyte (ZB)	1000 exabytes	Virtually nothing with which to compare it

Table 8-2 Storage capacities

8

As storage capacities have grown, so also has network traffic to transmit these massive amounts of data. On the Internet it is estimated that global traffic will increase by 32 percent annually, when traffic itself will easily reach 1 ZB. By 2015, the data equivalent of every movie ever filmed will cross through the Internet every 5 minutes.[2]

In the enterprise the standard data storage facilities and networking protocols cannot always cope with the need to store and transmit large volumes of data. Most organizations have turned to using a **storage area network (SAN)**, which is a dedicated network storage facility that provides access to data storage over a high-speed network. SANs consolidate different storage facilities—disk arrays, tape libraries, and even "optical jukeboxes" that can load thousands of discs by robotic arms—so they are accessible to servers. The different storage facilities actually appear as a single pool of locally attached devices.

Unlike a SAN, which is essentially a network that provides access to multiple storage devices, network attached storage (NAS) is a technology in which a single storage device is attached to a local area network.

Several different high-speed storage network protocols are used by SANs. **iSCSI (Internet Small Computer System Interface)** is an IP-based storage networking standard for linking data storage facilities. Because it works over a standard IP network, iSCSI can transmit data over LANs, wide area networks (WANs), and the Internet. **Fibre Channel (FC)** is a high-speed storage network protocol that can transmit up to 16 gigabits per second. A variation of FC is **Fibre Channel over Ethernet (FCoE)** that encapsulates Fibre Channel frames over Ethernet networks. This allows Fibre Channel to use fast Ethernet networks while preserving the Fibre Channel protocol.

It is important that not only SAN data storage but also the storage network protocols be secured. An iSCSI network should be designed so that the SAN cannot be directly accessed by clients. Instead, a SAN should have its own dedicated switch that is inaccessible from clients. This is seen in Figure 8-4.

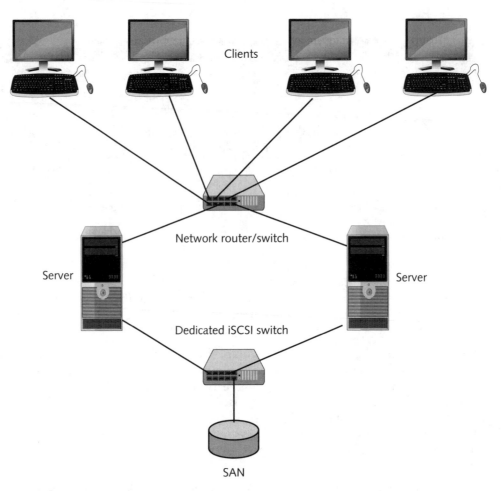

Figure 8-4 iSCSI dedicated switch

Fibre Channel has several security mechanisms built-in, one of which is *FC zones*. There are two types of FC zones. In an *FC hard zone*, all zone members are identified by a physical port number on the switch. This helps to ensure that data transfer cannot occur between unauthorized zone members because it is restricted by the FC hardware switch. Instead of being controlled by the FC hardware switch, an *FC soft zone* is software-based. When a device logs in, it queries the server for available devices and only the devices in the same zone are made available while other devices are hidden. In an FC soft zone, however, the switch does not restrict data transfer as in an FC hard zone, so unauthorized zone members can see restricted data.

NetBIOS

NetBIOS (Network Basic Input/Output System) is a transport protocol used by Microsoft Windows systems to allow applications on separate computers to communicate over a LAN. In modern networks NetBIOS normally runs over TCP/IP through the *NetBIOS over TCP/IP (NBT)* protocol. This results in each computer in the network having both an IP address plus a NetBIOS name.

The default setting for Windows computers is to use NetBIOS settings from the DHCP server. However, if a static IP address is being used on the local host or if the DHCP server cannot provide the NetBIOS setting, then NetBIOS over TCP/IP will be enabled.

An attacker who determines that NetBIOS is running on a LAN can use an application to gather information regarding the network in order to design an attack. Specifically he can determine:

- Computer names
- Contents of the remote name cache including IP addresses
- List of local NetBIOS names
- List of resolved names

Due to the security risks with NetBIOS, it is recommended that it be disabled or used only if necessary on the specific devices that require it.

Because of security concerns, many corporate networks prohibit the use of NetBIOS.

Telnet

Telnet is an older TCP/IP protocol for text-based communication. In addition, Telnet is also an application. This application is a terminal emulation program that runs on a local computer that connects to a server on the network. Commands can be entered using the Telnet application to the remote server as if the user was at the server itself.

Because it dates back to 1969, Telnet contains several security vulnerabilities. Telnet does not encrypt data so any passwords sent over Telnet to log into the server can easily be discovered. In addition, security weaknesses have been uncovered within this protocol. It is recommended that Secure Shell (SSH) be used instead of Telnet.

SSH is covered in Chapter 6.

IPv6

The current version of the IP protocol is version 4 and is called *IPv4*. Developed in 1981, long before the Internet was universally popular, IPv4 has several weaknesses. One of the

8

weaknesses is the number of available IP addresses. An IP address is 32 bits in length, providing about 4.3 billion possible IP address combinations. This no longer is sufficient for the number of devices that are being connected to the Internet. Another weakness is that of security. Due to its structure, IPv4 can be subject to several types of attacks.

Prior to the release of IPv4 in 1981, the total number of IP addresses available was only 255.

The solution to these weaknesses is the next generation of the IP protocol called **Internet Protocol version 6 (IPv6)**. IPv6 addresses the weaknesses of IPv4 and also provides several other significant improvements. One of the ways to understand the differences between IPv4 and IPv6 is to compare the structure of their headers. This is illustrated in Figure 8-5, and several of the differences are summarized in Table 8-3.

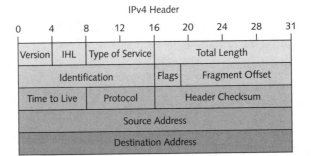

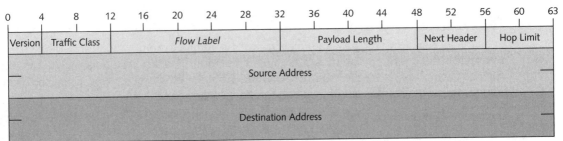

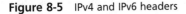

Figure 8-5 IPv4 and IPv6 headers

The number of IPv6 addresses is 340,282,366,920,463,463,374,607, 431,768,211,456 or 340 trillion, trillion, trillion addresses. This translates to 665 million billion IP addresses per square meter on earth.

IPv6 has several enhanced security features. Cryptographic protocols are part of the core protocol that provides secure data communication. In addition, new authentication headers prevent IP packets from being tampered or altered.

IPv4 field name	IPv6 field name	Explanation
Internet Header Length (IHL)	Not used	IPv6 uses a fixed packet header size of 40 bytes, so information always appears in the same place. This is a much smaller header size than IPv4 because packets contain only the header information that they need. The smaller size speeds up finding information in the packet and processing the packet.
Type of Service	Traffic Class	Currently there are no standard requirements for the content of this field.
Not Used	Flow Label	Packets belonging to the same stream, session, or flow share a common flow value, making it more easily recognizable without looking deeper into the packet.
Total Length	Payroll Length	Payroll Length, which includes any additional headers, no longer includes the length of the header (as in IPv4), so the host or router does not need to check if the packet is large enough to hold the IP header.
Time to Live (TTL)	Hop Limit	TTL was a misnomer because it never contained an actual time value.
Protocol	Next Header	This indicates the type of header that follows.
Source Address and Destination Address	Source Address and Destination Address	These serve the same function in IPv6 except they are expanded from 32 bits to 128 bits.

Table 8-3   Comparison of IPv4 and IPv6 headers

Network Administration Principles

1.2 Given a scenario, use secure network administration principles.

3.6 Analyze a scenario and select the appropriate type of mitigation and deterrent techniques.

Administering a network can be a difficult task; administering a *secure* network can be even more challenging. It is important that network security administration follow a **rule-based management** approach, which is the process of administration that relies on following procedural and technical rules, instead of creating security elements "on the fly." There are different types of rules. *Procedural rules* may be defined as the authoritative and prescribed direction for conduct. For information security, procedural rules can be external to the organization (such as the Health Insurance Portability and Accountability Act of 1996, the Sarbanes-Oxley Act of 2002, or the Gramm-Leach-Bliley Act) or internal (such as corporate policies and procedures). The procedural rules in turn, dictate *technical rules*. Technical rules may involve configuring a firewall or proxy server to conform to the procedural rules.

Technical rules should never dictate procedural rules.

It is the role of the network administrator to follow a rule-based management approach. This typically involves following rules that address device security, monitoring and analyzing logs, network design management, and port security.

Device Security

Because new devices are continually added to the network, securing devices is a never-ending task yet is key in maintaining a network's security. Device security includes establishing a secure router configuration and implementing flood guards.

Secure Router Configuration One of the most important network appliances on a network today is the router. Operating at the Network Layer (Layer 3), a router forwards packets across computer networks. Routers also can perform a security function; because packets move through the router, it can be configured to filter out specific types of network traffic. It is vital that the router's configuration provides a secure network environment and also that the configuration be performed in a secure manner.

Basic secure router configuration includes those tasks listed in Table 8-4.

Task	Explanation
Create a network design	Prior to any configuration, a network diagram that illustrates the router interfaces should be created. This diagram should reflect both the LAN and wide area network (WAN) interfaces.
Use a meaningful router name	Because the name of the router appears in the command line during router configuration, it helps ensure that commands are given to the correct router. For example, if the name *Internet_Router* is assigned to the device, the displayed command prompt would be *Internet_Router (config)#*.
Secure all ports	All ports to the router should be secured. This includes both physical ports (sometimes called the *console port* and *auxiliary port*) and inbound ports from remote locations (sometimes known as *VTY* for *virtual teletype*).
Set a strong administrator password	Most routers allow a user to access the command line in *user mode*, yet an administrator password is required to move to *privileged mode* for issuing configuration commands.
Make changes from the console	The configuration of the router should be performed from the console and not a remote location. This configuration can then be stored on a secure network drive as a backup and not on a laptop or USB flash drive.

Table 8-4 Secure router configuration tasks

Flood Guard One of the most dreaded attacks is *denial of service (DoS)* or *distributed denial of service (DDoS)*, which attempts to prevent a system from performing its normal functions through a deliberate attempt to prevent authorized users from access to the system. One type of DoS attack is a SYN flood attack that takes advantage of the procedures for initiating a session. In a SYN flood attack against a web server, the attacker sends SYN segments in IP packets to the server but modifies the source address of each packet to addresses that do not exist or cannot be reached. The server continues to wait for a response while receiving more false requests and can run out of resources so that it can no longer respond to legitimate requests or function properly.

 DoS attacks are covered in Chapter 3.

One defense against DoS and DDoS SYN flood attacks is to use a **flood guard**. A flood guard is a feature that controls a device's tolerance for unanswered service requests and helps to prevent a DoS attack. A network administrator can set the maximum number of "developing" connections that the device will tolerate. Once that limit is reached, each inbound SYN directed to the affected server is intercepted and dropped, and an empty SYN +ACK packet is returned. Flood guards are commonly found on firewalls, intrusion detection systems (IDS), and intrusion prevention systems (IPS).

Monitoring and Analyzing Logs

A **log** is a record of events that occur. **Security logs** are particularly important because they can reveal the types of attacks that are being directed at the network and if any of the attacks were successful. A security **access log** can provide details regarding requests for specific files on a system while an **audit log** is used to record which user performed an action and what that action was. System **event logs** document any unsuccessful events and the most significant successful events (some system event logs can be tailored to specify the types of events that are recorded). The types of information that can be recorded might include the date and time of the event, a description of the event, its status, error codes, service name, and user or system that was responsible for launching the event.

Monitoring system logs is an important step that can benefit an organization in different ways. These include:

- A routine review and analysis of logs helps to identify security incidents, policy violations, fraudulent activity, and operational problems shortly after they have occurred.

- Logs can be useful for performing auditing analysis, supporting the organization's internal investigations, and identifying operational trends and long-term problems.

- Logs can provide documentation that the organization is complying with laws and regulatory requirements.

Many logs are generated by network devices. Virtually every network device, both standard network devices (switches, routers, load balancers, proxies, etc.) and network security devices (firewalls, Internet content filters, web security gateways, IPS and IDS, Unified Threat Management appliances, etc.), can create logs. Network device logs can be very valuable in maintaining a secure defense system. For example, the types of items that would be examined in a firewall log include:

- *IP addresses that are being rejected and dropped.* It is not uncommon for the owner of a firewall to track down the owner of the site from which the packets are originating and ask why someone at his site is probing these ports. The owner may be able to pinpoint the perpetrator of the probe, even if the owner is an Internet Service Provider (ISP).

- *Probes to ports that have no application services running on them.* Attackers often try to determine if specific ports are already in use in order to target them for attack. If several probes appear directed at an obscure port number, it may be necessary to investigate if malware is associated with it.

- *Source-routed packets.* Packets with a source address internal to the network but that originates from outside the network could indicate that an attacker is attempting to spoof an internal address in order to gain access to the internal network.

- *Suspicious outbound connections.* Outbound connections from a public web server could be an indication that an attacker is launching attacks against others from the web server.

- *Unsuccessful logins.* If several unsuccessful logins come from the same domain, it may be necessary to create a new rule to drop all connections from that domain or IP address.

Network device logs that provide the most beneficial security data, in order of importance, are listed in Table 8-5.

Device	Explanation
Firewalls	Firewall logs can be used to determine whether new IP addresses are attempting to probe the network and if stronger firewall rules are necessary to block them. Outgoing connections, incoming connections, denied traffic, and permitted traffic should all be recorded.
Network intrusion detection systems (NIDS) and network intrusion prevention systems (NIPS)	Intrusion detection and intrusion prevention systems record detailed security log information on suspicious behavior as well as any attacks that are detected. In addition, these logs also record any actions NIPS used to stop the attacks.
Web servers	Web servers are usually the primary target of attackers. These logs can provide valuable information about the type of attack that can help in configuring good security on the server.
DHCP servers	DHCP server logs can identify new systems that mysteriously appear and then disappear as part of the network. They can also show what hardware device had which IP address at a specific time.
VPN concentrators	VPN logs can be monitored for attempted unauthorized access to the network.
Proxies	As intermediate hosts through which websites are accessed, these devices keep a log of all URLs that are accessed through them. This information can be useful when determining if a zombie is "calling home."
Domain Name System (DNS)	A DNS log can create entries in a log for all queries that are received. Some DNS servers also can create logs for error and alert messages.
Email servers	Email servers can show the latest malware attacks that are being launched through the use of attachments.
Routers and switches	Router and switch logs provide general information about network traffic.

Table 8-5 Device logs with beneficial security data

Some NIDS run periodically instead of continuously so they generate log entries in batches instead of on an ongoing basis.

However, there are several problems with *log management*, or generating, transmitting, storing, analyzing, and disposing of computer security log data. This is due to:

- *Multiple devices generating logs.* As noted, virtually every network device, both standard network devices and network security devices, can create logs. And each device may interpret an event in a different context, so that a router looks at a single event differently than a firewall does. This can create a confusing mix of log data.

- *Very large volume of data.* Because each device generates its own data, a very large amount of data can accumulate in a very short period of time. In addition, many devices record all events, even those that are not security-related, which increases even more the amount of data that is generated. Filtering through this large volume of data can be overwhelming.

- *Different log formats.* Perhaps the biggest obstacle to log management is that different devices record log information in different formats and even with different data captured. Combining multiple logs, each with a different format, can be a major challenge.

One solution to log management is to use a centralized device log analyzer. These systems are designed to collect and consolidate logs from multiple sources for easy analysis. An example of a centralized device log manager is illustrated in Figure 8-6.

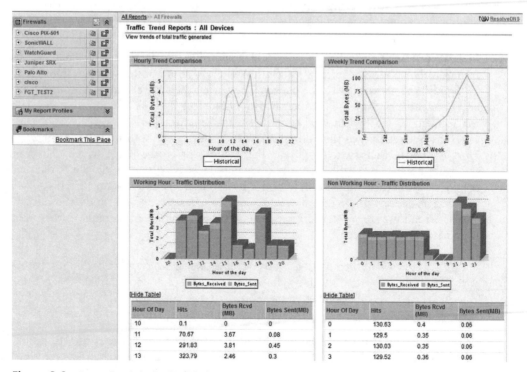

Figure 8-6 Centralized device log analyzer

Source: ManageEngine.com

Network Design Management

In addition to device security and monitoring and analyzing logs, several network design management principles should be followed to ensure that security and the viability of the network are maintained. Network separation to prevent bridging, loop protection, and VLAN management are three principles that should be considered.

Network Separation One of the important rules of network design is to separate secure parts of the network from unsecure parts. That is, the part of the network that contains customer credit card information should not be accessible from the part of the network that manages heating and cooling systems. One way to provide network separation is to physically separate users by connecting them to different switches and routers. This prevents bridging and even prevents a reconfigured device from allowing that connection to occur.

In the early 2000s, a technology known as *air gap* was introduced as a means of network separation. Two servers, one facing the external Internet and the other facing the internal secure network, were connected by a single air gap switch that was connected to only one server at a time. When a packet arrived from the Internet, the server passed it to the switch, which stripped the TCP header, stored the packet in memory, and then disconnected from the Internet server. It then connected to the internal server and forwarded the packet, where the header was recreated before the packet was sent to the internal LAN. The process was reversed for outgoing packets. The physical separation of the networks (the air gap) and the stripping of headers were designed to remove potential vulnerabilities. The technology was not widely adopted.

Loop Protection In Figure 8-7, Host Z, which is connected to Switch A, wants to send frames to Host X on Segment 2. Because Switch A does not know where Host X is located, it "floods" the network with the packet. The packet then travels down Segment 1 to Switch B and Segment 2 to Switch C. Switch B then adds Host Z to its lookup table that it maintains for Segment 1, and Switch C also adds it to its lookup table for Segment 3. Yet if Switch B or C has not yet learned the address for Host Z, they will both flood Segment 2 looking for Host X; that is, each switch will take the packet sent by the other switch and flood it back out again because they still do not know where Host X is located. Switch A then will receive the packet from each segment and flood it back out on the other segment. This *switching loop* causes a *broadcast storm* as the frames are broadcast, received, and rebroadcast by each switch. Broadcast storms can cripple a network in a matter of seconds to the point that no legitimate traffic can occur.

Because the headers that a Layer 2 switch examines do not have a time to live (TTL) value, a packet could loop through the network indefinitely.

Broadcast storms can be prevented with **loop protection**, which uses the IEEE 802.1d standard *spanning-tree algorithm (STA)*. STA can determine that a switch has multiple ways to communicate with a host and then determine the best path while blocking out other paths.

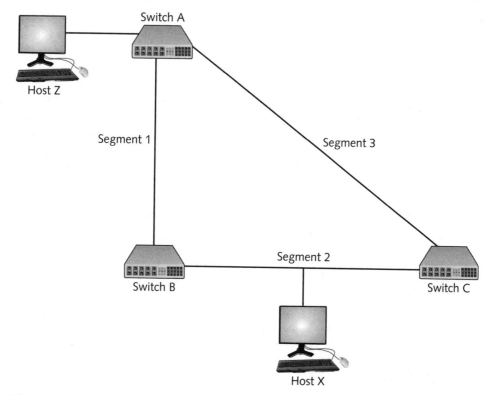

Figure 8-7 Broadcast storm

Although STA determines the best path, it also registers the other paths in the event that the primary path is unavailable.

VLAN Management It is possible to segment a network by physical devices grouped into logical units through a *virtual LAN (VLAN)*. This allows scattered users to be logically grouped together even though they may be attached to different switches, thus reducing network traffic and providing a degree of security.

VLANs are covered in Chapter 7.

Some general principles for managing VLANs are:

- Configure empty switch ports to connect to an unused VLAN.
- Change any default VLAN names.
- Configure the ports on the switch that pass tagged VLAN packets to explicitly forward specific tags.
- Configure VLANs so that public devices, such as a web application server, are not on a private VLAN, forcing users to have access to that VLAN.

Port Security

Securing physical ports is an important step in network management. Ports can be secured through disabling unused interfaces, using MAC limiting and filtering, and through IEEE 802.1x.

Disabling Unused Interfaces Disabling unused interfaces is a security technique to turn off ports on a network device that are not required, such as a switch. This is an important security step that is often overlooked. A switch or router without port security allows attackers to connect to unused ports to access the network. It is important that all interfaces be secured before a router or switch is deployed. The network administrator should navigate to each unused interface and issue the appropriate shutdown command.

MAC Limiting and Filtering In addition to disabling unused interfaces, another step in port security is **MAC limiting and filtering**. This will filter and limit the number of media access control (MAC) addresses allowed on a single port. A port can be set to a limit of only 1 and a specific MAC address can be assigned to that port. This enables only a single authorized host to connect through that port; attempts to access the interface by a host not listed will result in a security violation.

Usually the maximum number of secure MAC addresses for an interface can be set between 1 and 132, with the default at 1.

Often different configuration options for setting MAC limiting and filtering exist. Table 8-6 lists the options for one brand of switch.

Configuration setting	Explanation
Static	The MAC addresses are manually entered and then stored on the device.
Dynamic	The MAC addresses are automatically learned and stored; when the switch restarts, the settings are erased.
Sticky	The MAC addresses are automatically learned and stored along with any addresses that were learned prior to using the Sticky configuration. If this configuration is disabled, the addresses are kept in memory but are removed from the table.

Table 8-6 MAC limiting and filtering configuration options

Because of the variations in configuration options, it is important to know the functions of each option and then to select the best setting.

IEEE 802.1x The IEEE 802.1x standard provides the highest degree of port security by implementing port-based authentication. This protocol authenticates users on a per-switch port basis by permitting access to valid users but effectively disabling the port if authentication fails. This prevents an unauthenticated device from receiving any network traffic until its identity can be verified. It also strictly limits access to the device that provides the authentication to prevent attackers from reaching it. Figure 8-8 illustrates the steps in an 802.1x authentication procedure.

Figure 8-8   IEEE 802.1x process

1. The device (called a *supplicant*) requests from the *authenticator* permission to join the network.

2. The authenticator asks the supplicant to verify its identity.

3. The supplicant sends identity information to the authenticator.

4. The authenticator passes the identity credentials on to an *authentication server*, whose only job is to verify the authentication of devices. The identity information is sent in an encrypted form.

5. The authentication server verifies or rejects the supplicant's identity and returns the information to the authenticator.

6. If approved, the supplicant can now join the network and transmit data.

 **NOTE** Although IEEE 802.1x is commonly used on wireless networks, it can be used for wired networks as well. For example, in a public conference room, an RJ-45 network connection may be accessible to both trusted employees and untrusted public users. IEEE 802.1x permits the trusted employees to access both the secure internal corporate network and the Internet, while restricting public users to Internet access only from the same network connection.

Securing Network Applications and Platforms

 **SECURITY+**
1.3 Explain network design elements and components.

2.1 Explain the importance of risk related concepts.

4.3 Given a scenario, select the appropriate solution to establish host security.

4.4 Implement the appropriate controls to ensure data security.

Several relatively new network applications and platforms require special security considerations. These applications include IP telephony, virtualization, and cloud computing.

IP Telephony

A wave of change is sweeping all forms of digital communications. This change is an effort to unify divergent forms of communication into a single mode of transmission by shifting to an all-digital technology infrastructure. One of the most visible of these unification efforts is the convergence of voice and data traffic over a single Internet Protocol (IP) network. Using IP, various services such as voice, video, and data can be combined (*multiplexed*) and transported under a universal format. **IP telephony** is using a data-based IP network to add digital voice clients and new voice applications onto the IP network.

 Although IP telephony and Voice over IP (VoIP) are sometimes viewed as being identical, in reality they are not. VoIP is the underlying technology used to digitize and transmit voice traffic over an IP telephony system.

IP telephony offers significant enhancements over traditional telephone systems. An IP telephony application can be easily developed that personalizes the treatment of incoming calls. For example, a college instructor's application-enabled IP phone can display a list of students and direct the phone system how to handle incoming calls from a particular student. As a result, this can allow an important call to ring through to the wireless IP telephone the faculty member carries to the classroom, when under normal circumstances calls are blocked. If the incoming caller ID is blocked or does not match any of the student phone numbers, the traditional time-of-day routing schematic remains in effect and the call forwards to voicemail. Or, as an option, the call may be instructed to roll to a voice mailbox where a specific prerecorded message established just for this student will play.

IP telephony offers many benefits to an organization, including:

- *Cost savings.* The cost of convergence technologies is low in comparison to startup costs for new traditional telephone equipment.

- *Simplified management.* Instead of managing separate voice and data networks, convergence provides the functionality of managing and supporting a single network for all applications.

- *Application development.* New applications can be developed more quickly with fewer resources and at a lower cost on a converged network. Instead of developing applications based on a vendor's proprietary operating environment, IP-based systems allow organizations to write data and voice applications using industry-standard data language and protocols.

- *Reduced infrastructure requirements.* The requirements of the wired infrastructure are reduced, as multiple cable drops to the desktop are no longer required because one connection supports both data and telephony.

- *Reduced regulatory requirements.* Local telephone exchanges are heavily regulated. The Internet, as an information service, is essentially unregulated or is regulated differently, which can provide competitive advantages.

- *Increased user productivity.* Users are no longer forced to learn different interfaces to access information and to communicate because artificial boundaries no longer exist between applications. For example, separate email and voicemail boxes are no longer required.

Designing a unified network of voice, video, and data traffic may enhance security because only one network must be managed and defended. However, IP telephony networks are not immune to attack. Because they use IP networks, they may be vulnerable to attackers. Table 8-7 lists several IP telephony vulnerabilities that may be exploited.

Vulnerability	Description
Operating systems	"Softphones" that operate on standard PCs are vulnerable to operating system attacks.
VoIP protocols	Many of the common VoIP protocols do not provide adequate call-party authentication, end-to-end integrity protection, and confidentiality measures.
Lack of encryption	Voice protocols do not encrypt call-signaling and voice streams, so identities, credentials, and phone numbers of callers can be captured using protocol analyzers.
Network acknowledgment	Attackers can flood VoIP targets with DoS-type attacks that can degrade service, force calls to be dropped prematurely, and render certain VoIP equipment incapable of processing calls.
Spam	Spam over Internet telephony can carry unsolicited sales calls and other nuisance messages, and programs can download hidden malware to softphones.

Table 8-7   IP telephony vulnerabilities

NOTE An attacker can use captured account information to impersonate a user to a customer representative or self-service portal, where she can change the calling plan to permit calls to 900 numbers or to blocked international numbers. She also can access voicemail or change a call forwarding number.

Virtualization

Virtualization is a means of managing and presenting computer resources by function without regard to their physical layout or location. For example, computer storage devices on a SAN can be virtualized so that multiple physical storage devices can be viewed as a single logical unit.

One type of virtualization in which an entire operating system environment is simulated is known as **host virtualization**. Instead of using a physical computer, a *virtual machine*, which is a simulated software-based emulation of a computer, is created instead. The *host system* (the operating system installed on the computer's hardware) runs a *hypervisor* that manages the virtual machine operating systems and supports one or more *guest systems* (a foreign virtual operating system). For example, a computer that boots to Windows (host) would run Microsoft Hyper-V (hypervisor) to support a virtual machine of Linux (guest). Host virtualization is illustrated in Figure 8-9.

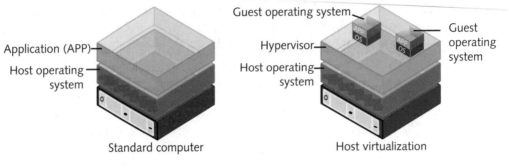

Figure 8-9 Host virtualization

NOTE Virtualization is used extensively to consolidate network and web servers so that multiple virtual servers can run on a single physical computer. Because a typical server utilizes only about 10 percent of its capacity, there is excess capacity for running virtual machines on a physical server.

Virtualization has several advantages. First, new virtual server machines can be quickly made available (**host availability**), and resources such as the amount of Random Access Memory (RAM) or hard drive space can easily be expanded or contracted as needed (**host elasticity**). Also, virtualization can reduce costs. Instead of purchasing one physical server to run one network operating system and its applications, a single physical server can run multiple virtual machines. This results in a significant cost savings in that fewer physical computers must be purchased and maintained. In addition, the cost of electricity to run these servers as well as keep data center server rooms cool is also reduced.

Another advantage of server virtualization is that it can be beneficial in providing uninterrupted server access to users. Data centers need to have the ability to schedule planned "downtime" for servers to perform maintenance on the hardware or software. Often it is difficult, however, to find a time when users will not be inconvenienced by the downtime. This can be addressed by virtualization that supports *live migration*; this technology enables a virtual machine to be moved to a different physical computer with no impact to the users. The virtual machine stores its current state onto a shared storage device immediately before the migration occurs. The virtual machine is then reinstalled on another physical computer and accesses its storage with no noticeable interruption to users. Live migration also can be used for *load balancing*; if the demand for a service or application increases, network managers can quickly move this high-demand virtual machine to another physical server with more RAM or CPU resources.

Host virtualization also has several security-related advantages:

- The latest patches can be downloaded and run in a virtual machine to determine **patch compatibility**, or the impact on other software or even hardware. This is used instead of installing the patch on a production computer and then being forced to "roll back" to the previous configuration if it does not work properly.

- A **snapshot** of a particular state of a virtual machine can be saved for later use. A user can make a snapshot before performing extensive modifications or alterations to the virtual machine, and then the snapshot can be reloaded so that the virtual machine is at the beginning state before the changes were made. Multiple snapshots can be made, all at different states, and loaded as needed.

- Testing the existing security configuration, known as **security control testing**, can be performed using a simulated network environment on a computer using multiple virtual machines. For example, one virtual machine can virtually attack another virtual machine on the same host system to determine vulnerabilities and security settings. This is possible because all of the virtual machines can be connected through a virtual network.

- A virtual machine can be used to test for potential malware. A suspicious program can be loaded into an isolated virtual machine and executed (**sandboxing**). If the program is malware, it will impact only the virtual machine, and it can easily be erased and a snapshot reinstalled. This is how antivirus software using dynamic heuristic detection can spot the characteristics of a virus.

 Dynamic heuristic detection is covered in Chapter 4.

Yet, security for virtualized environments can be a concern:

- A guest operating system that has remained dormant for a period of time may not contain the latest patches and other security updates, even though the same underlying host operating system has been updated. When the guest is launched, it will be vulnerable until properly updated.

- Not all hypervisors have the necessary security controls to keep out determined attackers. If a single hypervisor is compromised, multiple virtual servers will be at risk.

- Existing security tools, such as antivirus, antispam, and IDS, were designed for single physical servers and do not always adapt well to multiple virtual machines.

- Virtual machines must be protected from both outside networks and other virtual machines on the same physical computer. In a network without virtual machines, external devices such as firewalls and IDS that reside between physical servers can help prevent one physical server from infecting another physical server, but no such physical devices exist between virtual machines.

Cloud Computing

Cloud computing, which is a pay-per-use computing model in which customers pay only for the online computing resources they need, has emerged as a revolutionary concept that can dramatically impact all areas of IT, including network design, applications, procedures, and even personnel. Cloud computing is changing the face of IT to such an extent that the history of computing may one day be distinguished as "pre-cloud" and "post-cloud."

Although various definitions of cloud computing have been proposed, the definition from the National Institute of Standards and Technology (NIST) may be the most comprehensive: *Cloud computing is a model for enabling convenient, on-demand network access to a shared pool of configurable computing resources (e.g., networks, servers, storage, applications, and services) that can be rapidly provisioned and released with minimal management effort or service provider interaction.*[3] Cloud computing can be understood when it is compared to a similar model known as *hosted services*. In a hosted services environment, servers, storage, and the supporting networking infrastructure are shared by multiple "tenants" (users and organizations) over a remote network connection that has been contracted for a specific period of time. As more resources are needed (such as additional storage space or computing power), the tenant must contact the hosted service and negotiate an additional fee as well as sign a new contract for those new services as opposed to the pay-per-use model that cloud computing employs. As computing needs increase or decrease, cloud computing resources can be quickly (and automatically) scaled up or down. Table 8-8 lists the characteristics of cloud computing.

Characteristic	Explanation
On-demand self-service	The consumer can automatically increase or decrease computing resources without requiring any human interaction from the service provider.
Universal client support	Virtually any networked device (desktop, laptop, smartphone, tablet, etc.) can access the cloud computing resources.
Invisible resource pooling	The physical and virtual computing resources are pooled together to serve multiple, simultaneous consumers that are dynamically assigned or reassigned according to the consumers' needs; the customer has little or no control or knowledge of the physical location of the resources.
Immediate elasticity	Computing resources can be increased or decreased quickly to meet demands.
Metered services	Fees are based on the computing resources used.

Table 8-8   Cloud computing characteristics

There are different types of clouds. A **public cloud** is one in which the services and infrastructure are offered to all users with access provided remotely through the Internet. Unlike a public cloud that is open to anyone, a **community cloud** is a cloud that is open only to specific organizations that have common concerns. For example, because of the strict data requirements of the Health Insurance Portability and Accountability Act of 1996 (HIPAA), a community cloud open only to hospitals may be used. A **private cloud** is created and maintained on a private network. Although this type offers the highest level of security and control (because the company must purchase and maintain all the software and hardware), it also reduces any cost savings. A **hybrid cloud** is a combination of public and private clouds. **Cloud storage** has no computational capabilities but only provides remote file storage.

There are three services models in cloud computing:

- **Software as a Service (SaaS).** In this model the cloud computing vendor provides access to the vendor's software applications running on a cloud infrastructure. These applications, which can be accessed through a web browser, do not require any installation, configuration, upgrading, or management from the user.

- **Platform as a Service (PaaS).** Unlike SaaS in which the application software belonging to the cloud computing vendor is used, in PaaS consumers can install and run their own specialized applications on the cloud computing network. Although customers have control over the deployed applications, they do not manage or configure any of the underlying cloud infrastructure (network, servers, operating systems, storage, etc.).

- **Infrastructure as a Service (IaaS).** In this model, the customer has the highest level of control. The cloud computing vendor allows customers to deploy and run their own software, including operating systems and applications. Consumers have some control over the operating systems, storage, and their installed applications, but do not manage or control the underlying cloud infrastructure.

As cloud computing increases in popularity, enhanced features are being added. For example, Amazon Web Services (AWS) has an enhancement to their Virtual Private Cloud infrastructure. Organizations can now create a network topology in the AWS cloud that closely resembles their own physical data center including public, private, and demilitarized zones (DMZs). They also can create Internet gateways, use network address translation (NAT), and create security groups that can filter traffic.

Despite its impact on IT, cloud computing raises significant security concerns. It is important that the cloud provider guarantee that the means are in place by which authorized users are given access while imposters are denied. Also, all transmissions to and from "the cloud" must be adequately protected. Finally, the customer's data must be properly isolated from that of other customers, and the highest level of application availability and security must be maintained.

Some cloud providers offer their customers the option of running their applications in the cloud on hardware that is exclusively dedicated to them in order to provide enhanced security.

Chapter Summary

- The most common protocol used today for local area networks (LANs) and the Internet is Transmission Control Protocol/Internet Protocol (TCP/IP). TCP/IP is not a single protocol; instead, it is a suite of protocols that all function together. One of the core protocols of TCP/IP is the Internet Control Message Protocol (ICMP). ICMP is used by devices to communicate updates or error information to other devices. Several different attacks use ICMP messages. The Simple Network Management Protocol (SNMP) allows network administrators to remotely monitor, manage, and configure devices on the network. SNMP functions by exchanging management information between networked devices. There were several security vulnerabilities with the use of community strings in early versions of SNMP that have been addressed in the most recent version. The Domain Name System (DNS) is a TCP/IP protocol that resolves an IP address with its equivalent symbolic name. The DNS is a database, organized as a hierarchy or tree, of the name of each site on the Internet and its corresponding IP number. Because of the important role it plays, DNS can be the focus of attacks.

- Transferring files is most commonly performed using the File Transfer Protocol (FTP), which is part of the TCP/IP suite. FTP is used to connect to an FTP server, much in the same way that HTTP links to a web server. Several vulnerabilities are associated with using FTP. There are two options for secure transmissions over FTP. FTPS (FTP using Secure Sockets Layer) is a file transport layer resting "on top" of SSL/TLS. SFTP (Secure FTP) is an entire secure file transfer protocol and not separate elements added together. Another protocol used for file transfers is the Secure Copy Protocol (SCP), although it is found mainly on UNIX and Linux platforms.

- In the enterprise the standard data storage facilities and networking protocols cannot always cope with the need to store and transmit large volumes of data. Most organizations have turned to using a storage area network (SAN), which is a dedicated network storage facility that provides access to data storage over a high-speed network. There are several different high-speed storage network protocols that are used by SANs, including iSCSI (Internet Small Computer System Interface), Fibre Channel (FC), and Fibre Channel over Ethernet (FCoE). NetBIOS (Network Basic Input/Output System) is a transport protocol used by Microsoft Windows systems for allowing applications on separate computers to communicate over a LAN. Due to the security risks with NetBIOS, it is recommended that it be disabled. Telnet is a TCP/IP protocol and application for text communication. Telnet contains several security vulnerabilities and is not recommended for use. Because of the weaknesses of the current version of IP, known as IPv4, the next generation of the IP protocol called IPv6 addresses these weaknesses and also provides several other significant security improvements.

- One of the most important network appliances on a network today is the router. It is vital that the router's configuration provide a secure network environment and that the configuration be performed in a secure manner. A defense against DoS and DDoS SYN flood attacks is to use a flood guard. A flood guard is a feature that controls a device's tolerance for unanswered service requests and helps to prevent a DoS attack. A log is a record of events that occur. Security logs are particularly important because they can reveal the types of attacks that are being directed at the network and if any of the attacks were successful.

- One important rule of network design is to separate secure parts of the network from unsecure parts. That is, the part of the network that contains customer credit card information should not be accessible from the part of the network that manages heating and cooling systems. One way to provide network separation is to physically separate users by connecting them to different switches and routers. A switching loop in a network causes broadcast storms as the frames are broadcast, received, and rebroadcast by each switch. Broadcast storms can be eliminated by the loop protection of the IEEE 802.1d standard spanning-tree algorithm (STA). It is possible to segment a network by physical devices grouped into logical units through a virtual LAN (VLAN). This allows scattered users to be logically grouped together even though they may be attached to different switches, thus reducing network traffic and providing a degree of security.

- Securing ports is an important step in network management. Disabling unused ports on a network device, such as a switch, is an important security step that is often overlooked. Another step in port security is MAC limiting and filtering, which filters and limits the number of media access control (MAC) addresses allowed on a single port. A standard known as IEEE 802.1x provides the highest degree of port security. IEEE 802.1x blocks all traffic on a port-by-port basis until the client is authenticated using credentials stored on an authentication server.

■ Several relatively new network applications require special security considerations. IP telephony is adding digital voice clients and new voice applications onto the IP network. IP telephony networks are not immune to attack; because they use IP networks, they may be vulnerable to attackers. Virtualization is a means of managing and presenting computer resources by function without regard to their physical layout or location. One type of virtualization in which an entire operating system environment is simulated is known as host virtualization. Security for virtualized environments can be a concern. A growing number of virtualization security tools are available. Cloud computing is a revolutionary concept. Cloud computing is a "pay-per-use" model in which customers pay only for the online computing resources that they need at the present time. Despite its promise to dramatically impact IT, cloud computing also has security concerns.

Key Terms

access log   A log that can provide details regarding requests for specific files on a system.

audit log   A log that is used to record which user performed an action and what that action was.

cloud computing   A pay-per-use computing model in which customers pay only for the online computing resources that they need, and the resources can be easily scaled.

cloud storage   A cloud system that has no computational capabilities but provides remote file storage.

community cloud   A cloud that is open only to specific organizations that have common concerns.

disabling unused interfaces   A security technique to turn off ports on a network device that are not required.

event log   Log that documents any unsuccessful events and the most significant successful events.

Fibre Channel (FC)   A high-speed storage network protocol that can transmit up to 16 gigabits per second.

Fibre Channel over Ethernet (FCoE)   A high-speed storage network protocol that encapsulates Fibre Channel frames over Ethernet networks.

File Transfer Protocol (FTP)   An unsecure TCP/IP protocol that is commonly used for transferring files.

flood guard   A feature that controls a device's tolerance for unanswered service requests and helps to prevent a DoS or DDoS attack.

FTP Secure (FTPS)   A TCP/IP protocol that uses Secure Sockets Layer or Transport Layer Security to encrypt commands sent over the control port (port 21) in an FTP session.

host availability   The ability to quickly make new virtual server machines available.

8

host elasticity   The ability to easily expand or contract resources in a virtualized environment.

host virtualization   A type of virtualization in which an entire operating system environment is simulated.

hybrid cloud   A combination of public and private clouds.

IEEE 802.1x   A standard that authenticates users on a per-switch port basis by permitting access to valid users but effectively disabling the port if authentication fails.

Infrastructure as a Service (IaaS)   A cloud computing model in which customers have the highest level of control and can deploy and run their own software.

Internet Control Message Protocol (ICMP)   A TCP/IP protocol that is used by devices to communicate updates or error information to other devices.

Internet Protocol version 6 (IPv6)   The next generation of the IP protocol that addresses weaknesses of IPv4 and provides several significant improvements.

IP telephony   Using a data-based IP network to add digital voice clients and new voice applications onto the IP network.

iSCSI (Internet Small Computer System Interface)   An IP-based storage networking standard for linking data storage facilities.

log   A record of events that occur.

loop protection   Technique to prevent broadcast storms by using the IEEE 802.1d standard spanning-tree algorithm (STA).

MAC limiting and filtering   A security technique to limit the number of media access control (MAC) addresses allowed on a single port.

NetBIOS (Network Basic Input/Output System)   An older transport protocol used by Microsoft Windows systems for allowing applications on separate computers to communicate over a LAN.

patch compatibility   The impact of a patch on other software or even hardware.

Platform as a Service (PaaS)   A cloud service in which consumers can install and run their own specialized applications on the cloud computing network.

private cloud   A cloud that is created and maintained on a private network.

public cloud   A cloud in which the services and infrastructure are offered to all users with access provided remotely through the Internet.

rule-based management   The process of administration that relies on following procedural and technical rules.

sandboxing   Using a virtual machine to run a suspicious program to determine if it is malware.

Secure Copy Protocol (SCP)   A TCP/IP protocol used mainly on UNIX and Linux devices that securely transports files by encrypting files and commands.

Secure FTP (SFTP)   A secure TCP/IP protocol that is used for transporting files by encrypting and compressing all data and commands.

security control testing   Testing the existing security configuration.

security log   Log that can reveal the types of attacks that are being directed at the network and if any of the attacks were successful.

Simple Network Management Protocol (SNMP)   A TCP/IP protocol that exchanges management information between networked devices. It allows network administrators to remotely monitor, manage, and configure devices on the network.

snapshot   An instance of a particular state of a virtual machine that can be saved for later use.

Software as a Service (SaaS)   A model of cloud computing in which the vendor provides access to the vendor's software applications running on a cloud infrastructure.

storage area network (SAN)   A dedicated network storage facility that provides access to data storage over a high-speed network.

Telnet   An older TCP/IP protocol and an application used for text-based communication.

Transmission Control Protocol/Internet Protocol (TCP/IP)   The most common protocol suite used today for local area networks (LANs) and the Internet.

Trivial File Transfer Protocol (TFTP)   A light version of FTP that uses a small amount of memory and has limited functionality.

virtualization   A means of managing and presenting computer resources by function without regard to their physical layout or location.

8

Review Questions

1. Which high-speed storage network protocols used by a SAN is IP-based?
   a. iSCSI
   b. FC
   c. FCoE
   d. XSAN

2. Which Fibre Channel zone is the most restrictive?
   a. FC hard zone
   b. FC soft zone
   c. FC port zone
   d. FC interface zone

3. An attacker can use NetBIOS to determine each of the following EXCEPT _____.
   a. computer names
   b. contents of the remote name cache
   c. list of remote NetBIOS names
   d. list of resolved names

4. Which type of log can provide details regarding requests for specific files on a system?

    a. event log

    b. access log

    c. audit log

    d. SysFile log

5. Which type of device log contains the most beneficial security data?

    a. email log

    b. switch log

    c. firewall log

    d. router log

6. Which type of cloud is offered to all users?

    a. hybrid cloud

    b. private cloud

    c. public cloud

    d. community cloud

7. Which of these would NOT be a valid Internet Control Message Protocol (ICMP) error message?

    a. Host Unreachable

    b. Network Unreachable

    c. Destination Network Unknown

    d. Router Delay

8. Internet Control Message Protocol (ICMP) is used by each of these attacks EXCEPT _____.

    a. ICMP poisoning

    b. smurf DoS attack

    c. ICMP redirect attack

    d. ping of death

9. Which version of Simple Network Management Protocol (SNMP) is considered the most secure?

    a. SNMPv2

    b. SNMPv3

    c. SNMPv4

    d. SNMPv5

10. Which Domain Name System (DNS) attack replaces a fraudulent IP address for a symbolic name?

    a. DNS replay

    b. DNS masking

    c. DNS poisoning

    d. DNS forwarding

11. Which of these is the most secure protocol for transferring files?

    a. SCP

    b. SFTP

    c. FTPS

    d. FTP

12. Each of these is a technique for securing a router EXCEPT _____.

    a. making all configuration changes remotely

    b. securing all ports

    c. setting a strong administrator password

    d. using a meaningful router name

13. Which statement about a flood guard is true?

    a. It is a separate hardware appliance that is located inside the DMZ.

    b. It prevents DoS or DDoS attacks.

    c. It can be used on either local host systems or network devices.

    d. It protects a router from password intrusions.

14. Each of these is an entry in a firewall log that should be investigated EXCEPT _____.

    a. IP addresses that are being rejected and dropped

    b. successful logins

    c. suspicious outbound connections

    d. IP addresses that are being rejected and dropped

15. If a group of users must be separated from other users, which is the most secure network design?

    a. Use a VLAN.

    b. Connect them to different switches and routers.

    c. Use a subnet mask.

    d. It is impossible to separate users on a network.

16. Why is loop protection necessary?

    a. It makes a DMZ more secure.

    b. It denies attackers from launching DDoS attacks.

    c. It prevents a broadcast storm that can cripple a network.

    d. It must be installed before IEEE 802.1d can be implemented.

17. What does MAC limiting and filtering do?
    a. It limits devices that can connect to a switch.
    b. It allows only approved wireless devices to connect to a network.
    c. It prevents Address Resolution Protocol spoofing.
    d. It provides security for a router.

18. In a network using IEEE 802.1x, a supplicant _____.
    a. must use IEEE 802.11d to connect to the network
    b. makes a request to the authenticator
    c. contacts the authentication server directly
    d. can only be a wireless device

19. Which statement is true regarding security for a computer that boots to Apple Mac OS X and then runs a Windows virtual machine?
    a. The security of the Apple Mac OS X completely protects the Windows virtual machine.
    b. The hypervisor protects both the Apple Mac OS X and Windows operating systems.
    c. The security of the Windows virtual machine completely protects the Apple Mac OS X.
    d. The Windows virtual machine needs its own security.

20. Which of the following is NOT a security concern of virtualized environments?
    a. Virtual machines must be protected from both the outside world and also from other virtual machines on the same physical computer.
    b. Physical security appliances are not always designed to protect virtual systems.
    c. Virtual servers are less expensive than their physical counterparts.
    d. Live migration can immediately move one virtualized server to another hypervisor.

Hands-On Projects

HANDS-ON PROJECTS

NOTE If you are concerned about installing any of the software in these projects on your regular computer, you can instead install the software in the Windows virtual machine created in the Chapter 1 Hands-On Projects 1-3 and 1-4. Software installed within the virtual machine will not impact the host computer.

Project 8-1: Using an Application Sandbox

A sandbox isolates a program in order to prevent malware from permanently infecting a computer. In this project, you will download and use an application sandbox.

1. Use your web browser to go to **www.sandboxie.com**.

The location of content on the Internet may change without warning. If you are no longer able to access the program through the above URL, use a search engine to search for "Sandboxie".

2. Click **Download Now**.
3. Click the **Sandboxie** icon to download the Sandboxie.
4. Install the application **SandboxieInstall.exe** by accepting the default settings. Click **OK** in the Software Compatibility dialog box.
5. Read the **Getting Started Tutorial – Sandbox** by clicking **Next** on each screen and click **Finish**.
6. Right-click **Sandbox DefaultBox** in Sandboxie.
7. Click **Run Sandboxed**.
8. Click **Run Web Browser**.
9. Your default web browser will launch in a sandboxed environment.
10. If necessary, maximize your web browser.
11. Move your mouse pointer to the top edge of the web browser window. Notice that a yellow border appears around the window indicating it is sandboxed.
12. Use your web browser to navigate to several websites that you commonly use. Does the sandbox slow down the web browser?
13. Close your web browser.
14. Now configure Sandboxie to sandbox a different application. Return to the Sandbox DefaultBox.
15. Right-click **Sandbox DefaultBox** in Sandboxie.
16. Click **Run Sandboxed**.
17. Click **Run Any Program**.
18. When the [#] **Run Sandboxed – DefaultBox** [#] appears, enter **Notepad** and click **OK**.
19. Notepad will now launch in the sandbox. Move your mouse cursor over the window and note that it displays a yellow border.
20. Close Notepad.
21. Close all windows.

Project 8-2: Create a Virtual Machine from a Physical Computer

The VMware vCenter Converter will create a virtual machine from an existing physical computer. In this project, you will download and install vCenter.

1. Use your web browser to go to **www.vmware.com/products/converter/**.

The location of content on the Internet may change without warning. If you are no longer able to access the program through the above URL, use a search engine to search for "VMware vCenter".

2. Click **Download Now**.

3. Click **Create an account**, enter the requested information, and click **Continue**. Then enter your username and password, and click **Log in**. Enter the required details and click **I Agree**.

4. Click **Register**. Click **I agree** and then click **Continue**.

5. Click **Start Download Manager**.

6. When the download completes, click **Launch**.

7. Follow the instructions to install vCenter.

8. Launch vCenter to display the VMware vCenter Converter Standalone menu.

9. Click **Convert machine**.

10. Under **Specify the powered-on machine**, click **This local machine**. Click **Next**.

11. Next to **Select destination type:**, click **VMware Workstation or other VMware virtual machine**.

12. Under **Select a location for the virtual machine:**, click **Browse**.

13. Navigate to a location to store the new virtual machine. Click **Next** and then click **Next** again.

14. Click **Finish** to create the virtual machine from the physical machine.

15. When the vCenter has finished, note the location of the image. It will be used in the next project.

16. Close all windows.

Project 8-3: Load the Virtual Machine

In this project, you will download a program to load the virtual machine created in Project 8-2.

1. Use your web browser to go to **my.vmware.com/web/vmware/downloads**.

The location of content on the Internet may change without warning. If you are no longer able to access the program through the above URL, use a search engine to search for "VMware Player".

2. Click the **All Products** tab, then scroll down to VMware Player and click **View Download Components**.

If in Project 8-2 you chose to create the virtual machine as a VMware Workstation, you should download and install the evaluation version of VMware Workstation instead.

3. Click **Download** next to **VMware Player and VMware Player Plus for Windows**.

4. When the download completes, follow the instructions to install VMware Player.

5. Start VMware Player after the installation completes. Click **Open a Virtual Machine**.

6. Navigate to the location of the virtual machine created in Project 8-2 and follow the instructions to open it.

7. Use VMware Player to navigate through this virtual machine. How easy was it to create a virtual machine from a physical machine?

8. Close all windows.

Project 8-4: View SNMP Management Information Base (MIB) Elements

SNMP information is stored in a management information base (MIB), which is a database for different objects. In this project, you will view MIBs.

1. Use your web browser to go to **www.mibdepot.com**.

The location of content on the Internet may change without warning. If you are no longer able to access the program through the above URL, use a search engine to search for "MIB Depot".

2. In the left pane, click **Single MIB View**.

3. Scroll down and click **Linksys** in the right pane. This will display the Linksys MIBs summary information.

4. In the left pane, click **v1 & 2 MIBs** to select the SNMP Version 1 and Version 2 MIBs.

5. In the right pane, click **LINKSYS-MIB** under **MIB Name (File Name)**. This will display a list of the Linksys MIBs.

6. Click **Tree** under **Viewing Mode** in the left pane. The MIBs are now categorized by Object Identifier (OID). Each object in a MIB file has an OID associated with it, which is a series of numbers separated by dots that represent where on the MIB "tree" the object is located.

7. Click **Text** in the left pane to display textual information about the Linksys MIBs. Scroll through the Linksys MIBs and read several of the descriptions. How could this information be useful in troubleshooting?

8. Now look at the Cisco MIBs. Click **Vendors** in the left pane to return to a vendor list.

9. Scroll down and click **Cisco Systems** in the right pane. How many total Cisco MIB objects are listed? Why is there a difference?

10. In the right pane, click the link **Traps**.

11. Scroll down to **Trap 74**, which begins the list of Cisco wireless traps. Notice the descriptive names assigned to the wireless traps.

12. Now scroll down to **Traps 142-143** and click the name **bsnAPIfDown**. Read the description for this SNMP trap. When would it be invoked? Click the browser's **Back** arrow to return to the listing.

13. Close all windows.

Project 8-5: Viewing Logs Using the Microsoft Windows Event Viewer

In this project, you will view logs on a Microsoft Windows computer.

1. Launch Event Viewer by clicking **Start** and then type **Administrative Tools** in the Search programs and files box.

2. Click the **Administrative Tools** folder and then double-click **Event Viewer**.

3. The Event Viewer opens to the Overview and Summary page that displays all events from all Windows logs on the system. The total number of events for each type that have occurred is displayed along with the number of events of each type that have occurred over the last seven days, the last 24 hours, or the last hour. Click the **+ (plus)** sign under each type of event in the Summary of Administrative Events to view events that have occurred on this system.

4. Select a specific event and then double-click it to display detailed information on the event. Is this information in a format that a custodian could use when examining a system? Is it in a format that an end-user would find helpful?

5. When finished, click the **Back** arrow to return to the Overview and Summary page.

6. In the left pane under **Event Viewer** (**Local**), double-click **Windows Logs** to display the default generated logs, if necessary.

7. Double-click **Security**.

8. Select a specific event and then double-click it to display detailed information on the event. When finished, click **Close** and the **Back** arrow to return to the Overview and Summary page.

9. In the left pane under **Event Viewer** (**Local**), double-click **Applications and Services Logs** to display the default generated logs, if necessary.

10. Select a specific event and double-click it to display detailed information on the event. When finished, click **Close** and then double-click **Event Viewer** (**Local**) in the left pane. Leave this window open for the next project.

Project 8-6: Creating a Custom View in Microsoft Windows Event Viewer

Microsoft Windows Event Viewer also can be used to create custom logs and collect copies of events from different systems. In this project, you will use the Event Viewer to create a custom log.

1. If necessary, launch Event Viewer by clicking **Start** and then typing **Administrative Tools** in the Search programs and files box. Click the **Administrative Tools** folder and then double-click **Event Viewer**.

2. In the right pane entitled Actions, click **Create Custom View**.

3. Under **Logged** click the **drop-down arrow** next to **Any time**. Several options appear of times to log the events. Click **Custom range** and note that you can create a specific time period to log these events. Click **Cancel** and be sure the **Logged** setting is **Any time** in order to capture all events.

4. Under **Event level**, check each box (**Critical, Error, Warning, Information, Verbose**) in order to capture all levels of events.

5. Under **By source**, click the radio button if necessary and then click the **drop-down arrow** next to **Event sources**. Scroll through the list of sources that can be used to create a log entry.

6. For this custom view, instead of selecting specific sources, you will use log entries collected from default logs. Under **By log**, click the radio button if necessary and then click the **drop-down arrow** next to **Event logs**.

7. Click the **+ (plus)** sign by **Windows Logs** and also **Applications and Services Logs**. Any of these logs can be used as input into your custom logs. Click the box next to **Windows Logs** to select all of the available Windows logs.

8. You also can include or exclude specific events. Be sure that is selected.

9. Next to **Keywords** select **Classic**.

10. Next to **User** be sure that is selected so that any user who logs in to this system will have log entries created.

11. Your completed dialog box will look like that shown in Figure 8-10. Click **OK**. If an Event Viewer dialog box appears, click **Yes**.

12. In the **Save Filter to Custom View** dialog box, next to **Name**, enter **All Events**.

13. Next to **Description**, enter **All Events**. Click **OK**.

14. In the left pane under **Event Viewer (Local)**, double-click **Custom Views** if necessary to display the custom view. Display your view by clicking on it.

15. Close Event Viewer and all windows.

16. Reboot the system.

17. If necessary, launch Event Viewer by clicking **Start** and then typing **Administrative Tools** in the Search programs and files box. Click the **Administrative Tools** folder and then double-click **Event Viewer**.

8

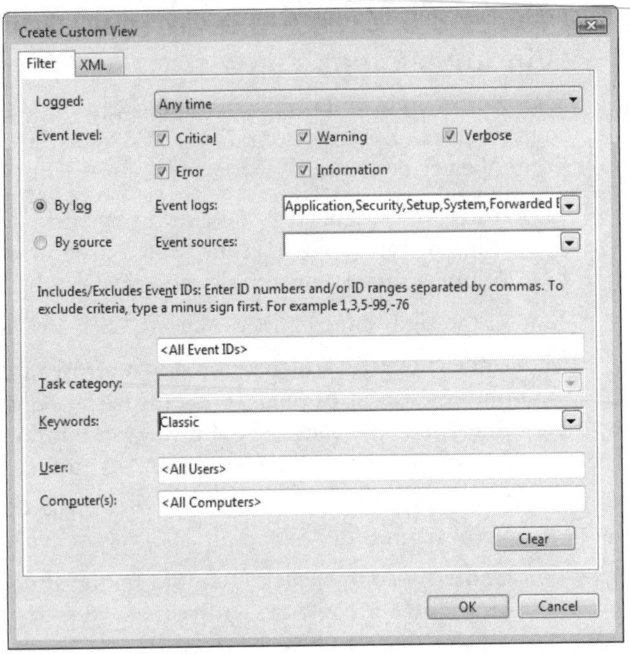

Figure 8-10 Create Custom View dialog box
Source: Microsoft Windows

18. In the left pane under **Event Viewer (Local)**, double-click **Custom Views** if necessary to display the custom views. Display your view by clicking it. What new events have occurred?

19. Close all windows.

Project 8-7: Creating a Subscription in Microsoft Windows Event Viewer

Although log entries can be exported into event files (*.evtx), it can be cumbersome to view multiple files from different systems. Microsoft Windows can collect copies of events from multiple systems and store them locally. This is known as a subscription. In this project, you will perform the steps for creating a subscription.

Creating a subscription from multiple computers requires that a Windows firewall exception be added to each computer along with adding an account with administrator privileges to the Event Log Readers group on each source computer. Because these actions may impact the security policy of systems, in this activity you will not actually create a working subscription but instead will explore the steps necessary to create a subscription.

1. Launch Event Viewer as shown in Project 8-6.

2. In the left pane, click **Subscriptions**. In the right pane entitled **Actions**, click **Create Subscription**.

You may be asked to start the Windows Event Collector Service if it is not already running. Click Yes.

3. Under **Subscription name:**, enter your name followed by **Subscription**.

4. Under **Description:**, enter **Events compiled from systems**.

5. Under **Destination log:**, click the **drop-down arrow**. Note that events from other computers can be combined with the event logs on this local system or collected in the Forwarded Events log. For this activity be sure that **Forwarded Events** is selected.

6. Be sure that **Collector initiated** is chosen under **Subscription type and source computers**. This means that the local system will contact the other systems for their log entries.

7. Under **Events to collect:**, click the **drop-down arrow** next to **Select Events**.

8. Select **Copy from existing Custom View**.

9. In the Open Custom View dialog box, select the custom view created in Project 8-6. Click **Open**.

10. The custom view appears. Click **OK**. If necessary, click **Yes** in the dialog box.

11. Click the **Advanced** button. You will see three event delivery optimization method options:

    - *Normal*. This ensures the reliable delivery of events and does not attempt to conserve bandwidth but instead is for events to be delivered quickly. This method pulls content from remote computers five items at a time.

    - *Minimize Bandwidth*. The Minimize Bandwidth option ensures that the least amount of bandwidth is used for this service. This is chosen to limit the frequency of network connections that are made to gather log events.

    - *Minimize Latency*. This method is used when events must be collected as quickly as possible. This is an appropriate choice for collecting alerts or critical events.

12. Be sure that **Normal** is selected and then click **OK**.

13. If this subscription were to be created, you would click OK and then configure each system appropriately. Because this subscription is not actually to be created, click **Cancel**.

14. Close all windows.

Case Projects

Case Project 8-1: SAN Comparisons

Use the Internet to research iSCSI, FC, and FCoE SANs. How do they function? What are their features? What are the advantages of each type? What are the disadvantages? Create a table comparing the SANs. If you were to recommend a SAN for your school or business, which would you choose? Why?

Case Project 8-2: IPv6 ICMP

In IPv4, ICMP provides error reporting and flow control features. Although this functionality is still part of IPv6, there are additional roles that ICMP plays in this latest version of IP. These include fragmentation, neighbor discovery, and State-Less Address AutoConfiguration (SLAAC). In addition, many ICMP messages are sent as multicast instead of only unicast. Yet IPv6 ICMP raises a new set of security concerns. Use the Internet to research the ICMP under IPv6 and what the security concerns are. Write a one-page paper on your findings.

Case Project 8-3: Comparing Cloud Computing Features

As cloud computing increases in popularity, enhanced features are continually being added. For example, Amazon Web Services (AWS) supports a Virtual Private Cloud infrastructure through which organizations can create a network topology in the AWS cloud that closely resembles their own physical data center. Research AWS's Virtual Private Cloud or another cloud vendor's similar offering. What are your impressions? Would this be something that an organization should consider? What are its technical limitations? Write a one-page summary of your research.

Case Project 8-4: Centralized Device Log Analyzers

Use the Internet to research four different centralized device log analyzers. Create a table comparing their benefits, the platforms they support, their advantages and disadvantages, and costs. Which would you recommend? Why?

Case Project 8-5: Cloud Computing Benefits

Would your school or place of work benefit from cloud computing? Identify at least two cloud computing vendors and research their features and costs. Then look at one element of your school or work's network infrastructure and apply it to cloud computing. Would it be feasible? Why or why not? Write a one-page paper on your research and opinions.

Case Project 8-6: Bay Pointe Security Consulting

Bay Pointe Security Consulting (BPSC) provides security consulting services to a wide range of businesses, individuals, schools, and organizations. BPSC has hired you as a technology student to help them with a new project and provide real-world experience to students who are interested in the security field.

Performance Engineered Lubricants (PEL) is a regional petroleum manufacturing and distribution company. PEL is interested in moving to cloud computing, and they have contracted with BPSC to make recommendations.

1. Create a PowerPoint presentation for PEL regarding cloud computing. Include a definition of cloud computing, how it can be used, and why it is important. Your presentation should contain at least 10 slides.

2. PEL is enthusiastic about cloud computing, but is unsure about whether SaaS, PaaS, or IaaS would be best for them. They have multiple customized software applications for the blending of different petroleum products. Create a memo that outlines the advantages and disadvantages of each approach, and give your recommendation.

Case Project 8-7: Community Site Activity

The Information Security Community Site is an online companion to this textbook. It contains a wide variety of tools, information, discussion boards, and other features to assist learners. Go to **community.cengage.com/infosec**. Sign in with the login name and password that you created in Chapter 1. Visit the **Discussions** section, and then read the following case study.

A hospital decided to use cloud computing for processing and storage in order to save costs. After several months it was discovered that the cloud provider's storage facilities were compromised and patient information was stolen. The hospital maintained that the cloud provider should be punished and fined for the breach, while the provider responded that it was still the hospital's responsibility under HIPAA to secure patient information and the hospital was ultimately responsible.

Who do you think should be responsible? The cloud provider or the hospital? If the cloud provider is responsible, then should software companies like Microsoft be held liable for a vulnerability in their software that results in a data breach on a Microsoft server in a LAN? Where does the responsibility for the user end and the vendor begin?

References

1. Shainer, Gilad, "Storage disaggregation in the data center," *Data Center Knowledge*, Oct. 18, 2013, accessed Feb. 22, 2014, http://www.datacenterknowledge.com/archives/2013/10/18/storage-disaggregation-in-the-data-center/.

2. Goldman, David, "Video and mobile are breaking the Internet," *CNN Money*, Jun. 1, 2011, accessed Mar. 6, 2014, http://money.cnn.com/2011/06/01/technology/cisco_visual_networking_index/.

3. Mell, Peter, and Grance, Tim, "The NIST definition of cloud computing," NIST Computer Security Division Computer Security Resource Center. Oct. 7, 2009, accessed Apr. 2, 2011, http://csrc.nist.gov/groups/SNS/cloud-computing/.

part V

Mobile Security

In our increasingly wireless and mobile world, mobile security has come to the forefront of security issues. In this part, you will learn how to secure wireless networks (Chapter 9) and mobile devices (Chapter 10).

Chapter 9   Wireless Network Security
Chapter 10   Mobile Device Security

Wireless Network Security

After completing this chapter, you should be able to do the following:

- Describe the different types of wireless network attacks
- List the vulnerabilities in IEEE 802.11 security
- Explain the solutions for securing a wireless network

Today's Attacks and Defenses

The most significant feature of a Wi-Fi network is the fact that the wireless signal is not confined to a cable as in a traditional network but instead is broadcast through the air. Because Wi-Fi signals are not restricted by walls or doors, the user has unprecedented mobility and can freely roam while still connected to the network. However, this feature is also a security liability. Because a wireless signal is not confined within the walls of a building, an unauthorized user can pick up the signal outside a building's security perimeter. An intruder lurking in the parking lot with a wireless laptop, for example, could intercept wireless signals. This would allow an attacker to access the secure internal network, infect it with malware, or eavesdrop on the wireless transmissions to read everything that is being sent and received.

Now a new product is available that can confine a Wi-Fi signal and prevent it from leaving a room. This unlikely solution is a special type of wallpaper. A French researcher who is the scientific director of the French pulp and paper research institute *Centre Technique du Papier* has created wallpaper with a snowflake pattern that blocks Wi-Fi signals. Called MetaPaper, it is printed in conductive metallic ink on nonconductive paper and is 99 percent effective in blocking Wi-Fi signals. Unlike a special paint introduced by Japanese scientists in 2009 that blocks transmissions of all wireless frequencies, MetaPaper blocks only Wi-Fi signals. This allows wireless transmissions using emergency frequencies to pass through the wallpaper.

But MetaPaper can do more than protect a Wi-Fi network by restricting its signal within the walls of a room. Just as MetaPaper can be used to keep the signal from leaking out, it also can be used to stop a signal from entering a room. Although Wi-Fi never has been proven to be harmful to human health, some organizations like hospitals have indicated they want to stop these signals from entering for either privacy or health reasons. In addition, MetaPaper can be used in areas in which a "quiet space" is necessary, such as in a cinema or a theatre. And it also can help make a Wi-Fi signal more efficient by blocking competing signals.

It is estimated that MetaPaper will sell for approximately $12 per square meter (10.7 square feet) and may generate sales of up to $38 million in France alone within a year. The goal is to reduce the price of MetaPaper so that it costs no more than conventional wallpaper.

It is difficult to think of a technology over the last decade with a greater impact on our lives than wireless data communications. Because it is no longer necessary to remain connected by cable to a network, users are free to surf the Web, check email, download electronic books, or watch videos from virtually anywhere. Free wireless Internet connections are available in coffee shops and restaurants worldwide. Students use wireless data services on their school's campus in order to access instructional material as well as remain connected to friends. Travelers can have wireless access while waiting in airports, traveling on airplanes and trains, and working in their hotel rooms. At work, employees can access remote data during meetings and in conference rooms, thus significantly increasing their productivity. Wireless also has spurred the growth of many other new technologies, such as portable tablet devices. Although wireless voice communication started the revolution in the 1990s, wireless data communications are the driving force in the 21st century. It has truly become a wireless world.

Statistics confirm how widespread wireless technology has become. Each year, hundreds of millions of wireless data devices are sold. Virtually all laptop, notebook, and tablet computers as well as smartphones have wireless data capabilities. Since 2007, the number of locations where wireless data services are available has increased 40 percent annually. According to some estimates, by 2014 there will be 1.4 billion devices shipped annually that support wireless data standards, and these devices will transmit the amount of wireless data traffic equal to almost one billion DVDs.[1] By the end of 2011, one quarter of all households around the world, or 439 million households, were using wireless data technology, with South Korea leading the way with over 80 percent of its households using wireless (the U.S. was eighth with 61 percent). It is estimated that by 2016, more than 800 million households will have wireless data technology installed.[2] Considering that wireless local area networks were not even available until 2000, their widespread installation is that much more amazing.

Yet, because of the nature of wireless transmissions and the vulnerabilities of early wireless networking standards, wireless networks have been prime targets for attackers. There have been significant changes in wireless network security, however, to the point that today wireless security technology and standards provide users with security comparable to that their wired counterparts enjoy.

This chapter explores wireless network security. You will first investigate the attacks on wireless devices that are common today. Next, you will explore different wireless security mechanisms that have proven to be vulnerable. Finally, you will examine several secure wireless protections.

Wireless Attacks

3.4 Explain types of wireless attacks.

There are several attacks that can be directed against wireless data systems. These attacks can be directed against Bluetooth systems, near field communication devices, and wireless local area networks.

Bluetooth Attacks

Bluetooth is the name given to a wireless technology that uses short-range radio frequency (RF) transmissions and provides rapid ad hoc or "on-the-fly" device pairings. Named after the 10th-century Danish King Harald "Bluetooth" Gormsson, who was responsible for unifying Scandinavia, it was originally designed in 1994 by the cellular telephone company Ericsson as a way to replace wires with radio-based technology. Bluetooth has moved well beyond its original design. Bluetooth technology enables users to connect wirelessly to a wide range of computing and telecommunications devices. It provides for virtually instantaneous connections between a Bluetooth-enabled device and receiver, such as a cellular smartphone connecting with a car's communication system or a laptop computer with a Bluetooth mouse. Several of these Bluetooth-enabled product pairings are listed in Table 9-1.

Category	Bluetooth pairing	Usage
Automobile	Hands-free car system with cell phone	Drivers can speak commands to browse the cell phone's contact list, make hands-free phone calls, or use its navigation system.
Home entertainment	Stereo headphones with portable music player	Users can create a playlist on a portable music player and listen through a set of wireless headphones or speakers.
Photographs	Digital camera with printer	Digital photos can be sent directly to a photo printer or from pictures taken on one cell phone to another phone.
Computer accessories	Computer with keyboard and mouse	Small travel mouse can be linked to a laptop or a full-size mouse and keyboard that can be connected to a desktop computer.
Gaming	Video game system with controller	Gaming devices and video game systems can support multiple controllers, while Bluetooth headsets allow gamers to chat as they play.
Sports and fitness	Heart-rate monitor with wristwatch	Athletes can track heart rates while exercising by glancing at their watch.
Medical and health	Blood pressure monitors with smartphones	Patient information can be sent to a smartphone, which can then send an emergency phone message if necessary.

Table 9-1 Bluetooth products

Bluetooth is finding its way into unlikely devices. A Victorinox Swiss Army pocketknife model has Bluetooth technology that can be used to remotely control a computer when projecting a PowerPoint presentation. The pocketknife also serves as a 32 GB USB flash drive that has a biometric fingerprint scanner. And since pocketknives cannot be carried onto an airplane, one version of the pocketknife lacks a sharp blade.

Bluetooth is a *Personal Area Network (PAN)* technology designed for data communication over short distances. The current version is Bluetooth v4.0 (a subset is known as Bluetooth Low Energy), yet all Bluetooth devices are backward compatible with previous versions. Most Bluetooth devices have a range of 33 feet (10 meters) and can transmit 1 million bits per second (Mbps).

 The IEEE 802.15.1-2005 Wireless Personal Area Network standard was based on the Bluetooth v1.2 specifications. The IEEE, however, has discontinued its relationship with Bluetooth so that any future Bluetooth versions will not become IEEE standards.

There are two types of Bluetooth network topologies. The first is a *piconet*. When two Bluetooth devices come within range of each other, they automatically connect with one another. One device is the *master*, and controls all of the wireless traffic. The other device is known as a *slave*, which takes commands from the master. Slave devices that are connected to the piconet and are sending transmissions are known as *active slaves*; devices that are connected but are not actively participating are called *parked slaves*. An example of a piconet is illustrated in Figure 9-1.

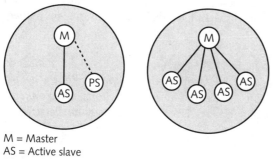

M = Master
AS = Active slave
PS = Parked slave

Figure 9-1   Bluetooth piconet

If multiple piconets cover the same area, a Bluetooth device can be a member in two or more overlaying piconets. A group of piconets in which connections exist between different piconets is called a *scatternet*. A scatternet is illustrated in Figure 9-2.

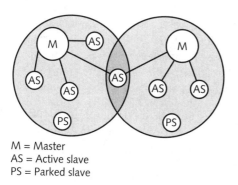

M = Master
AS = Active slave
PS = Parked slave

Figure 9-2   Bluetooth scatternet

Due to the ad hoc nature of Bluetooth piconets and scatternets, attacks on wireless Bluetooth technology are not uncommon. Two Bluetooth attacks are bluejacking and bluesnarfing.

Bluejacking Bluejacking is an attack that sends unsolic____ssages to Bluetooth-enabled devices. Usually bluejacking involves sending text mes____t images and sounds also can be transmitted. Bluejacking is usually considered more annoying than harmful because no data is stolen; however, many Bluetooth users resent receiving unsolicited messages.

Bluejacking has been used for advertising purposes by vendors.

Bluesnarfing Bluesnarfing is an attack that accesses unauthorized information from a wireless device through a Bluetooth connection, often between cell phones and laptop computers. In a bluesnarfing attack, the attacker copies emails, calendars, contact lists, cell phone pictures, or videos by connecting to the Bluetooth device without the owner's knowledge or permission.

To prevent bluesnarfing, Bluetooth devices should be turned off when not being used or when in a room with unknown people. Another option is to set Bluetooth on the device as *undiscoverable*, which keeps Bluetooth turned on, yet it cannot be detected by another device.

Near Field Communication (NFC) Attacks

Although it might appear that the trend for wireless devices would be to transmit *faster* and *farther*, that is not always the case. In many settings, low speed and low power are more desirable. A device using low power can be much smaller in size, even down to the size of a penny. Applications using low rate technologies include motion sensors that control lights or alarms, light wall switches, meter reader devices, game controllers for interactive toys, tire pressure monitors in cars, passive infrared sensors for building automation systems, and inventory tracking devices.

Recognizing the need for these smaller, low-power devices, the IEEE 802.15.4 standard was approved in 2003. This standard addresses requirements for RF transmissions that require low power consumption as well as low cost. The 802.15.4 devices operate up to 164 feet (50 meters) at different frequencies, depending on the data rate.

One of these low speed and power technologies is **near field communication (NFC)**. NFC is a set of standards primarily for smartphones and smart cards that can be used to establish communication between devices in close proximity. Once the devices are either tapped together or brought within several centimeters of each other, two-way communication is established. NFC's ease of use has opened the door for a wide range of practical short-range communications. Programmable tags—small NFC-enabled pieces of paper or plastic that sell for only a few dollars—can communicate with smartphones to trigger an action. Some tags are preprogrammed to perform a specific task, while others require users to download an application to customize each tag with one of several dozen possible actions. Here are some examples of how NFC programmable tags might be used:

- NFC programmable tags can be placed on spice containers in a kitchen. The chef can tap her smartphone against a bottle of spice and the device automatically performs a web search for recipes featuring that spice.

- A smartphone can tap an NFC tag affixed to a business card to automatically download the contact information to the phone.

- Attendees of a social event can be given NFC-enabled bracelets linked to their email addresses. As they sample hundreds of different foods and drinks, attendees can tap their bracelets against NFC readers to vote for their favorite foods or have the recipes of that dish emailed to them.

NFC devices are increasingly used in *contactless payment systems* in which a consumer can pay for a purchase by simply tapping a store's payment terminal with their smartphone. Users store credit card and store loyalty card information in a "virtual wallet" on the smartphone to pay for purchases at an NFC-enabled point-of-sale (PoS) checkout device. Figure 9-3 shows one such contactless payment system.

Figure 9-3 Contactless payment system
© scyther5/Shutterstock.com

NOTE NFC-enabled mobile phone shipments reached 416 million units in 2014, and by 2018 the market is predicted to reach 1.2 billion devices.[3] With the exception of Apple, every major cell phone manufacturer has announced plans to incorporate NFC into its smartphone devices.

The use of NFC contactless payment systems has risks because of the nature of this technology. The risks and defenses of using NFC are listed in Table 9-2.

Vulnerability	Explanation	Defense
Eavesdropping	The NFC communication between device and terminal can be intercepted and viewed.	Because an attacker must be extremely close to pick up the signal, users should be aware of this. Also, some NFC applications can perform encryption.
Data manipulation	Attackers can jam an NFC signal so transmission cannot occur.	Some NFC devices can monitor for data manipulation attacks.
Man-in-the-middle attack	An attacker can intercept the NFC communications between devices and forge a fictitious response.	Devices can be configured in *active-passive* pairing so one device only sends while the other can only receive.
Device theft	The theft or loss of a smartphone could allow an attacker to use that phone for purchases.	Smartphones should be protected with passwords or PINs.

Table 9-2   **NFC risks and defenses**

Wireless Local Area Network (WLAN) Attacks

A **wireless local area network (WLAN)** is designed to replace or supplement a wired local area network (LAN). Devices such as tablets, laptop computers, smartphones, and printers that are within 460 feet (140 meters) of a centrally located connection device can send and receive information at transmission speeds that typically range from 54 Mbps to as high as 7 billion bits per second (Gbps).

It is important to know about the history and specifications of IEEE WLANs, the hardware necessary for a wireless network, and the different types of WLAN attacks directed at both the enterprise and home users.

IEEE WLANs For computer networking and wireless communications, the most widely known and influential organization is the *Institute of Electrical and Electronics Engineers (IEEE)*, which dates back to 1884. In the early 1980s, the IEEE began work on developing computer network architecture standards. This work was called Project 802, and quickly expanded into several different categories of network technology.

One of the most well-known IEEE standards is 802.3, which set specifications for Ethernet local area network technology.

In 1990, the IEEE started work to develop a standard for wireless local area networks (WLANs) operating at 1 and 2 Mbps. Several proposals were recommended before a draft was developed. This draft, which went through seven different revisions, took seven years to complete. In 1997, the IEEE approved the final draft known as *IEEE 802.11*.

Although bandwidth of 2 Mbps was seen as acceptable in 1990 for wireless networks, by 1997 it was no longer sufficient for more recent network applications. The IEEE body revisited the 802.11 standard shortly after it was released to determine what changes could be made to increase the speed. In 1999, a new *IEEE 802.11b* amendment was created, which added two higher speeds (5.5 Mbps and 11 Mbps) to the original 802.11 standard. At the same time the IEEE also issued another standard with even higher speeds, the *IEEE 802.11a* standard with a speed of 54 Mbps.

The success of the IEEE 802.11b standard prompted the IEEE to reexamine the 802.11b and 802.11a standards to determine if a third intermediate standard could be developed. This "best of both worlds" approach would preserve the stable and widely accepted features of 802.11b but increase the data transfer rates to those similar to 802.11a. The *IEEE 802.11g* standard was formally ratified in 2003 and can support devices transmitting at 54 Mbps.

In 2004, the IEEE began work on a dramatically new WLAN standard that would significantly increase the speed, range, and reliability of wireless local area networks. Known as *IEEE 802.11n*, it was ratified in 2009. The 802.11n standard has four significant improvements over previous standards: speed (600 Mbps), coverage area (doubles the indoor range and triples the outdoor range of coverage), increased resistance to interference, and strong security.

Work on an updated standard to support the demand for wireless video delivery was started in 2011 called *IEEE 802.11ac*. Building upon many of the enhancements introduced in 802.11n, this new standard, ratified in early 2014, has data rates over 7 Gbps. Table 9-3 compares the different IEEE WLAN standards.

	802.11	802.11b	802.11a	802.11g	802.11n	802.11ac
Frequency	2.4 GHz	2.4 GHz	5 GHz	2.4 GHz	2.4 & 5 GHz	5 GHz
Nonoverlapping channels	3	3	23	3	21	21
Maximum data rate	2 Mbps	11 Mbps	54 Mbps	54 Mbps	600 Mbps	7.2 Gbps
Indoor range (feet/meters)	65/20	125/38	115/35	115/35	230/70	115/35
Outdoor range (feet/meters)	328/100	460/140	393/120	460/140	820/250	460/140
Ratification date	1997	1999	1999	2003	2009	2014

Table 9-3   IEEE WLAN standards

IEEE 802.11ac will be backwards compatible with 802.11n devices operating in the 5 GHz spectrum only.

WLAN Hardware   Different types of hardware are used in WLANs. A *wireless client network interface card adapter* performs the same functions as a wired adapter with one major exception: there is no external cable RJ-45 connection. In its place is an antenna (sometimes embedded into the adapter) to send and receive signals through the airwaves.

An *access point (AP)* consists of three major parts:

- An antenna and a radio transmitter/receiver to send and receive wireless signals
- Special bridging software to interface wireless devices to other devices
- A wired network interface that allows it to connect by cable to a standard wired network

An AP has two basic functions. First, it acts as the "base station" for the wireless network. All wireless devices with a wireless NIC transmit to the AP, which in turn, redirects the signal if necessary to other wireless devices. The second function of an AP is to act as a bridge between the wireless and wired networks. The AP can be connected to the wired network by a cable, allowing all the wireless devices to access through the AP the wired network (and vice versa), as shown in Figure 9-4.

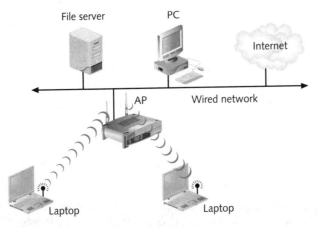

Figure 9-4 Access point (AP) in WLAN

For a small office or home, instead of using an enterprise-grade AP, another device is commonly used. This device combines multiple features into a single hardware device. These features often include those of an AP, firewall, router, dynamic host configuration protocol (DHCP) server, along with other features. Strictly speaking these devices are *residential WLAN gateways* as they are the entry point from the Internet into the wireless network. However, most vendors instead choose to label their products as *wireless broadband routers* or simply *wireless routers*.

WLAN Enterprise Attacks In a traditional wired network, a well-defined boundary or "hard edge" protects data and resources. There are two types of hard edges. The first is a network hard edge. A wired network typically has one point (or a limited number of points) through which data must pass from an external network to the secure internal network. This single data entry point makes it easier to defend against attacks because any attack must likewise pass through this one point. A device like a firewall can be used to block attacks from entering the network. The combination of a single entry point plus security devices that can defend it make up a network's hard edge, which protects important data and resources. This is illustrated in Figure 9-5.

The second hard edge is made up of the walls of the building that houses the enterprise. Because these walls keep out unauthorized personnel, attackers cannot physically access computing devices or network equipment to steal data or infect computers. In other words, the walls serve to physically separate computing resources from attackers.

The introduction of WLANs in enterprises, however, has changed these hard edges to "blurred edges." Instead of a network hard edge with a single data entry point, a WLAN

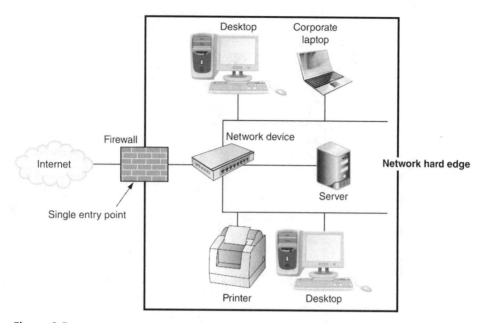

Figure 9-5 Network hard edge

9

can contain multiple entry points. As shown in Figure 9-6, the RF signals from APs create several data entry points into the network through which attackers can inject attacks or steal data. This makes it difficult to create a hard network edge. In addition, because RF signals extend beyond the boundaries of the building, the walls cannot be considered as a physical hard edge to keep away attackers. An attacker sitting in a car well outside of the building's security perimeter can still easily pick up a wireless RF signal to eavesdrop on data transmissions or inject malware behind the firewall. An AP whose security settings have not been set (*open AP*) or have been improperly configured can allow attackers access to the network.

In addition to creating multiple entry points, several different wireless attacks can be directed at the enterprise. These include rogue access points, evil twins, intercepting wireless data, wireless replay attacks, and wireless denial of service attacks.

Rogue Access Point Hannah wants to have wireless access in the employee break room and conference room next to her office. However, her employer's IT staff turns down her request for a wireless network. Hannah decides to take the matter into her own hands: she purchases an inexpensive consumer wireless router and secretly brings it into her office and connects it to the wired network, thus providing wireless access to the employees in her area. Unfortunately, Hannah also has provided open access to an attacker sitting in his car in the parking lot who picks up the wireless signal. This attacker can then circumvent the security protections of the company's network.

Hannah has installed a **rogue access point** (*rogue* means someone or something that is deceitful or unreliable). A rogue AP is an unauthorized AP that allows an attacker to bypass many

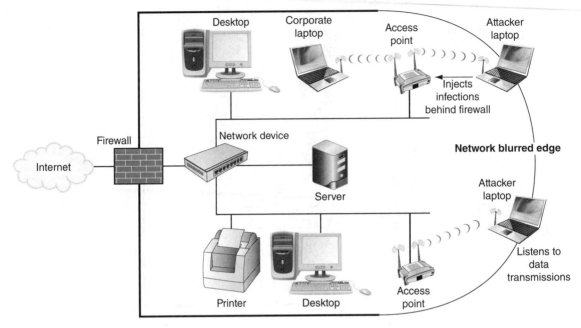

Figure 9-6 Network blurred edge

of the network security configurations and opens the network and its users to attacks. For example, although firewalls are typically used to restrict specific attacks from entering a network, an attacker who can access the network through a rogue access point is behind the firewall.

 Rogue APs do not even have to be separate network devices. The wireless Hosted Network function in Microsoft Windows makes it possible to virtualize the physical wireless network interface card into multiple virtual wireless NICs (Virtual WiFi) that can be accessed by a software-based wireless AP (SoftAP). This means that any computer can easily be turned into a rogue AP. And some smartphone apps allow these devices to function as APs.

Evil Twin Whereas a rogue AP is set up by an internal user, an **evil twin** is an AP that is set up by an attacker. This AP is designed to mimic an authorized AP, so a user's mobile device like a laptop or tablet will unknowingly connect to this evil twin instead. Attackers can then capture the transmissions from users to the evil twin AP.

Figure 9-7 illustrates rogue AP and evil twin attacks on an enterprise network, which further create a "blurred edge" to a corporate network.

Intercepting Wireless Data One of the most common wireless attacks is intercepting and reading data (*packet sniffing*) that is being transmitted. An attacker can pick up the RF signal from an open or misconfigured AP and read any confidential wireless transmissions. To make matters worse, if the attacker manages to connect to the enterprise wired network

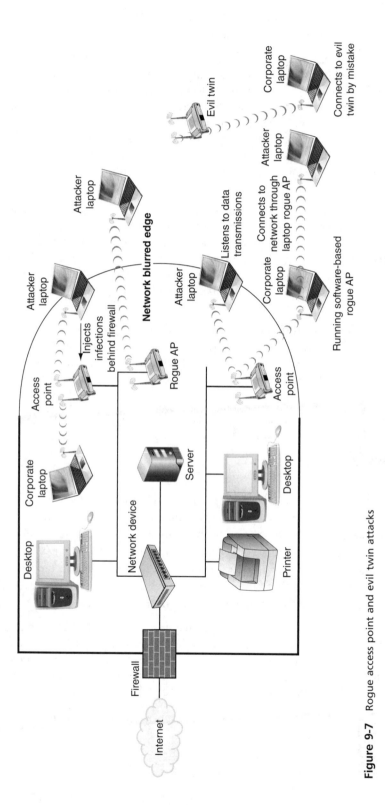

Figure 9-7 Rogue access point and evil twin attacks

through a rogue AP, she also could read broadcast and multicast wired network traffic that leaks from the wired network to the wireless network.

Just as wired network traffic can be viewed by a stand-alone protocol analyzer device or a computer that runs protocol analyzer software, wireless traffic also can be captured to decode and analyze the contents of packets. However, capturing wireless data using network protocol analyzer software requires that the wireless NIC be in the correct mode. Wireless network interface card adapters can operate in one of six modes: master (when the card acts as an AP), managed (when the station acts as a normal client), repeater, mesh, ad hoc, or monitor mode (also called Radio Frequency Monitor or RFMON). It is necessary for the wireless NIC to operate in monitor mode so that it can capture frames without first being associated with an AP.

In earlier versions of Microsoft Windows, the Microsoft Windows Network Driver Interface Specification (NDIS) did not support monitor mode, and only data frames could be displayed. Later versions of Windows added some support for monitor mode, yet this is dependent upon specific types of cards. Unlike Windows, Linux does support monitor mode so that most cards and their drivers can easily display wireless traffic.

The type of wired network traffic that could be read through the wireless network includes Internet Group Management Protocol (IGMP), Interior Gateway Routing Protocol (IGRP), Open Shortest Path First (OSPF), Spanning Tree Protocol (STP), Cisco's Hot Standby Router Protocol (HSRP), Virtual Router Redundancy Protocol (VRRP), and NetBIOS traffic.

Although a discussion of these protocols and traffic types are beyond the scope of this textbook, using a WLAN to read this data could yield significant information to an attacker regarding the wired enterprise network.

Wireless Replay Attack Another wireless attack is "hijacking" the wireless connection. Using an evil twin, an attacker can trick a corporate mobile device to connect to the imposter device instead. The attacker could then perform a wireless man-in-the-middle attack. This type of attack makes it appear that the wireless device and the network computers are communicating with each other, when actually they are sending and receiving data through an evil twin AP (the "man-in-the-middle"). As the man-in-the-middle receives data from the devices, it passes it on to the recipient so that neither computer is aware of the man-in-the-middle's existence.

Man-in-the-middle attacks can be active or passive. In an active attack, the contents are intercepted and altered before they are forwarded to the recipient. In a passive attack, the attacker captures the data that is being transmitted (such as usernames and passwords), records it, and then sends it on to the original recipient without the attacker's presence being detected. This is called a **wireless replay** attack.

Wired man-in-the-middle and replay attacks are covered in Chapter 3.

as an active man-in-the-middle attack will modify or inject content into a message, ther type of wireless attack can actually inject wireless packets into the enterprise network. For example, an attacker's application could examine incoming wireless packets, and, if the packet data matches a pattern specified in a configuration file, inject custom content onto the network to redirect traffic to an attacker's server. In yet another type of attack, a routing protocol attack, the attacker injects specific packets into the network to redirect a traffic stream through another router that is controlled by the attacker.

Wireless Denial of Service Attack Because wireless devices operate using RF signals, there is the potential for two types of signal interference. The wireless device itself may be the source of interference for other devices, and signals from other devices can disrupt wireless transmissions. Several types of devices transmit a radio signal that can cause incidental interference with a WLAN. These devices include microwave ovens, elevator motors, photocopying machines, certain types of outdoor lighting systems, theft protection devices, cordless telephones, microwave ovens, and Bluetooth devices. These may cause errors or completely prevent transmission between a wireless device and an AP.

Interference is nothing new for a computer data network. Even when using cables to connect network devices, interference from fluorescent light fixtures and electric motors can disrupt data transmission. The solution for wireless devices is the same as that for standard cabled network devices: locate the source of the interference and eliminate the interference. This can be done by moving an access point away from a photocopying machine or microwave oven, for example.

Attackers can likewise use intentional RF interference to flood the RF spectrum with enough interference to prevent a device from effectively communicating with the AP. This wireless DoS attack prevents the transmission of data to or from network devices. In one type of wireless DoS attack, an attacker can intentionally flood the RF spectrum with extraneous RF signal "noise" that creates interference and prevents communications from occurring. This is called **RF jamming**.

RF jamming attacks generally are rare because sophisticated and expensive equipment is necessary to flood the RF spectrum with enough interference to impact the network. In addition, because a very powerful transmitter must be used at a relatively close range to execute the attack, it is possible to identify the location of the transmitter and therefore identify the source of the attack.

Another wireless DoS attack takes advantage of an IEEE 802.11 design weakness. This weakness is the implicit trust of management frames that are transmitted across the wireless network, which includes information such as the sender's source address. Because IEEE 802.11 requires no verification of the source device's identity (and so all management frames are sent in an unencrypted format), an attacker can easily craft a fictitious frame that pretends to come from a trusted client when in reality it is from a malicious attacker. Different types of frames can be "spoofed" by an attacker to prevent a client from being able to remain connected to the WLAN. A client must be both authenticated and associated with an AP before being accepted into the wireless network, and when the client leaves the network this is accomplished through the exchange of deauthentication and disassociation management frames. An attacker can create false deauthentication or disassociation frames that are sent to an AP that appear to come from another client device, causing the client to disconnect from the AP. Although the client device can send another authentication request to an AP, an attacker can continue to send spoofed frames to sever any reconnections.

The amendment IEEE 802.11w was designed to protect against wireless DoS attacks. However, it only protects specific management frames instead of all management frames, it requires updates to both the AP and the wireless clients, and it may interfere with other security devices. For these reasons, it has not been widely implemented.

Manipulating duration field values is another wireless DoS attack. The 802.11 standard provides an option using the Request to Send/Clear to Send (RTS/CTS) protocol. A Request to Send (RTS) frame is transmitted by a mobile device to an AP that contains a duration field indicating the length of time needed for both the transmission and the returning acknowledgment frame. The AP, as well as all stations that receive the RTS frame, are alerted that the medium will be reserved for a specific period of time. Each receiving station stores that information in its net allocation vector (NAV) field, and no station can transmit if the NAV contains a value other than zero. An attacker can send a frame with the duration field set to an arbitrarily high value (the maximum is 32767), thus preventing other devices from transmitting for lengthy periods of time.

Wireless Home Attacks Attacks against home WLANs are considered easy due to the fact that most home users fail to configure any security on their home networks. Although many home users consider it to be an inconvenience to properly set the security on their wireless router, home users face several risks from attacks on their insecure wireless networks. Among other things, attackers can:

- *Steal data.* On a computer in the home WLAN, an attacker could access any folder with file sharing enabled. This essentially provides an attacker full access to steal sensitive data from the computer.

- *Read wireless transmissions.* Usernames, passwords, credit card numbers, and other information sent over the WLAN could be captured by an attacker.

- *Inject malware.* Because attackers could access the network behind a firewall, they could inject viruses and other malware onto the computer.

- *Download harmful content.* In several instances, attackers have accessed a home computer through an unprotected WLAN and downloaded child pornography to the computer, and then turned that computer into a file server to distribute the content. When authorities have traced the files back to that computer, the unsuspecting owner has been arrested and his equipment confiscated.

Attackers can easily identify unprotected home wireless networks through **war driving**. War driving is searching for wireless signals from an automobile or on foot using a portable computing device. After the wireless signal has been detected, the next step is to document and then advertise the location of the wireless LANs for others to use. Early WLAN users copied a system that hobos used during the Great Depression to indicate friendly locations. Wireless networks were identified by drawing on sidewalks or walls around the area of the network, known as **war chalking**. War chalking symbols are shown in Figure 9-8. Today the location of WLANs discovered through war driving are posted on websites.

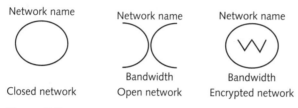

Closed network   Open network   Encrypted network

Figure 9-8   War chalking symbols

 War driving is derived from the term *war dialing*. When telephone modems were popular in the 1980s and 1990s, an attacker could program the device to randomly dial telephone numbers until a computer answered the call. This random process of searching for a connection was known as war dialing, so the word for randomly searching for a wireless signal became known as war driving.

In order to properly conduct war driving, several tools are necessary. These tools are listed in Table 9-4.

Tool	Purpose
Mobile computing device	A mobile computing device with a wireless NIC can be used for war driving. This includes a standard portable computer, a pad computer, or a smartphone.
Wireless NIC adapter	Many war drivers prefer an external wireless NIC adapter that connects into a USB or other port and has an external antenna jack.
Antenna(s)	Although all wireless NIC adapters have embedded antennas, attaching an external antenna will significantly increase the ability to detect a wireless signal.
Software	Client utilities and integrated operating system tools provide limited information about a discovered WLAN. Serious war drivers use more specialized software.
Global positioning system (GPS) receiver	Although this is not required, it does help to pinpoint the location more precisely if this information will be recorded or shared with others.

Table 9-4   War driving tools

Vulnerabilities of IEEE Wireless Security

1.5 Given a scenario, troubleshoot security issues related to wireless networking.

3.4 Explain types of wireless attacks.

The original IEEE 802.11 committee recognized that wireless transmissions could be vulnerable. Because of this, they implemented several wireless security protections in the 802.11 standard, while leaving other protections to be applied at the WLAN vendor's discretion. Several of these protections, though well intended, were vulnerable and led to multiple attacks. These vulnerabilities can be divided into four categories: Wired Equivalent Privacy (WEP), Wi-Fi Protected Setup (WPS), MAC address filtering, and SSID broadcasting.

Wired Equivalent Privacy (WEP)

Wired Equivalent Privacy (WEP) is an IEEE 802.11 security protocol designed to ensure that only authorized parties can view transmitted wireless information. WEP accomplishes this confidentiality by encrypting the transmissions. WEP relies on a shared secret key that is known only by the wireless client and the AP. The same secret key must be entered on the AP and on all devices before any transmissions can occur, because it is used to encrypt any packets to be transmitted as well as decrypt packets that are received. IEEE 802.11 WEP shared secret keys must be a minimum of 64 bits in length. Most vendors add an option to use a longer 128-bit shared secret key for higher security.

The shared secret key is combined with an **initialization vector (IV)**, which is a 24-bit value that changes each time a packet is encrypted. The IV and the key are combined and used as a seed for generating a random number necessary in the encryption process. The IV and encrypted ciphertext are both transmitted to the receiving device. Upon arrival, the receiving device first separates the IV from the encrypted text and then combines the IV with its own shared secret key to decrypt the data.

WEP has several security vulnerabilities. First, to encrypt packets, WEP can use only a 64-bit or 128-bit number, which is made up of a 24-bit IV and either a 40-bit or 104-bit default key. Even if a longer 128-bit number is used, the length of the IV still remains at 24 bits. The relatively short length of the IV limits its strength, since shorter keys are easier to break than longer keys.

Second, WEP implementation violates the cardinal rule of cryptography: anything that creates a detectable pattern must be avoided at all costs. This is because patterns provide an attacker with valuable information to break the encryption. The implementation of WEP creates a detectable pattern for attackers. Because IVs are 24-bit numbers, there are only 16,777,216 possible values. An AP transmitting at only 11 Mbps can send and receive 700 packets each second. If a different IV were used for each packet, then the IVs would start repeating in fewer than seven hours (a "busy" AP can produce duplicates in fewer than five hours). An attacker who captures packets for this length of time can see the duplication and use it to crack the code.

Recent techniques have reduced the amount of time to crack WEP down to minutes.

Wi-Fi Protected Setup (WPS)

Wi-Fi Protected Setup (WPS) is an optional means of configuring security on wireless local area networks. Introduced by the Wi-Fi Alliance in early 2007, it is designed to help users who have little or no knowledge of security to quickly and easily implement security on their WLANs.

There are two common WPS methods. The PIN method utilizes a Personal Identification Number (PIN) printed on a sticker of the wireless router or displayed through a software setup wizard. The user types the PIN into the wireless device (like a wireless tablet, laptop computer, or smartphone) and the security configuration automatically occurs. This is the mandatory model, and all devices certified for WPS must support it. The second method is the push-button method: the user pushes buttons (usually an actual button on the wireless router and a virtual one displayed through a software setup wizard on the wireless device) and the security configuration takes place. Support for this model is mandatory for wireless routers and optional for connecting devices.

More than 5800 different wireless devices have been certified by the Wi-Fi Alliance to run WPS.

However, there are significant design and implementation flaws in WPS using the PIN method:

- There is no lockout limit for entering PINs, so an attacker can make an unlimited number of PIN attempts.

- The last PIN character is only a checksum.

- The wireless router reports the validity of the first and second halves of the PIN separately, so essentially an attacker has to break only two short PIN values (a four-character PIN and a three-character PIN).

Due to the PIN being broken down into two shorter values, only 11,000 different PINs must be attempted before determining the correct value. If the attacker's computer can generate 1.3 PIN attempts per second (or 46 attempts per minute), the attacker can crack the PIN in less than four hours and become connected to the WLAN. This effectively defeats security restrictions regarding allowing only authorized users to connect to the wireless network.

Some wireless vendors are implementing additional security measures for WPS, such as limiting the amount and frequency of PIN guesses. Unless it can be verified that WPS supports these higher levels of security, it is recommended that WPS be disabled through the wireless router's configuration settings.

MAC Address Filtering

One means of protecting a WLAN is to control which devices are permitted to join the network. Wireless access control is intended to limit a user's admission to the AP: only those who are authorized are able to connect to the AP and thus become part of the wireless LAN.

The most common type of wireless access control is **Media Access Control (MAC) address filtering**. The MAC address is a hardware address that uniquely identifies each node of a network. The MAC address is a unique 48-bit number that is "burned" into the network interface card adapter when it is manufactured. This number consists of two parts: a 24-bit organizationally unique identifier (OUI), sometimes called a "company ID," which references the company that produced the adapter, and a 24-bit individual address block (IAB), which uniquely identifies the card itself. A typical MAC address is illustrated in Figure 9-9.

Organizationally unique   Individual address
identifier (OUI)   block (IAB)

00-50-F2-7C-62-E1

Figure 9-9 MAC address

Other names for the MAC address are vendor address, vendor ID, NIC address, Ethernet address, hardware address, and physical address.

The IEEE 802.11 standard permits controlling but does not specify how it is to be implemented. Since a wireless device can be identified by its MAC address, however, virtually all wireless AP vendors implement MAC address filtering as the means of access control. A wireless client device's MAC address is entered into software running on the AP, which then is used to permit or deny a device from connecting to the network. As shown in Figure 9-10, restrictions can be implemented in one of two ways: a specific device can be permitted access into the network or the device can be blocked.

Wireless MAC Filter :	⦿ Enable ◯ Disable	
Prevent :	◯ Prevent PCs listed from accessing the wireless ———	— Keep out only these devices
Permit only :	⦿ Permit only PCs listed to access the wireless network ——	— Allow in only these devices
	Save Setting Cancel Changes	

Figure 9-10 MAC address filtering

MAC address filtering is usually implemented by permitting instead of preventing, because it is not possible to know the MAC addresses of all of the devices that are to be excluded.

Filtering by MAC address has several vulnerabilities. First, MAC addresses are initially exchanged between wireless devices and the AP in an unencrypted format. An attacker using a protocol analyzer can easily see the MAC address of an approved device and then substitute it on her own device.

 MAC address substitution is possible on Microsoft Windows computers because the MAC address of the wireless NIC is read and then that value is stored in the Windows Registry database, which can easily be changed.

Another weakness of MAC address filtering is that managing a large number of MAC addresses can pose significant challenges. The sheer number of users often makes it difficult to manage all of the MAC addresses. As new users are added to the network and old users leave, keeping track of MAC address filtering demands almost constant attention. For this reason, MAC address filtering is not always practical in a large and dynamic wireless network.

Disabling SSID Broadcasts

Another means of controlling access to the WLAN uses the **Service Set Identifier (SSID)** of the wireless network. The SSID serves as the user-supplied network name of a wireless network and generally can be any alphanumeric string up to 32 characters. Although normally the SSID is broadcast so that any device can see it, the broadcast can be restricted. Then only those users that know the "secret" SSID in advance would be allowed to access the network.

Some wireless security sources encourage users to configure their APs to prevent the broadcast (beaconing) of the SSID, and instead require the user to enter the SSID manually on the wireless device. Although this may seem to provide protection by not advertising the SSID, it provides only a weak degree of security and has several limitations:

- The SSID can be easily discovered even when it is not contained in beacon frames because it is transmitted in other management frames sent by the AP. Attackers with protocol analyzers can still detect the SSID.

- Turning off the SSID broadcast may prevent users from being able to freely roam from one AP coverage area to another.

- It is not always possible or convenient to turn off SSID beaconing. SSID beaconing is the default mode in virtually every AP, and not all APs allow beaconing to be turned off.

 Older versions of Microsoft Windows, when receiving signals from both a wireless network that is broadcasting an SSID and one that is not broadcasting the SSID, will always connect to the AP that is broadcasting its SSID. If a device using this older version is connected to an AP that is not broadcasting its SSID, and another AP is turned on that is broadcasting its SSID, the device will automatically disconnect from the first AP and connect to the AP that is broadcasting.

Wireless Security Solutions

 1.5 Given a scenario, troubleshoot security issues related to wireless networking.

3.4 Explain types of wireless attacks.

5.2 Given a scenario, select the appropriate authentication, authorization or access control.

6.2 Given a scenario, use appropriate cryptographic methods.

As a result of the wireless security vulnerabilities in IEEE and Wi-Fi Alliance technologies, both organizations worked to create comprehensive security solutions. The results from the IEEE, known as *802.11i*, served as the foundation for the Wi-Fi Alliance's Wi-Fi Protected Access (WPA) and Wi-Fi Protected Access 2 (WPA2). WPA and WPA2 are the primary wireless security solutions today. In addition, there are other security steps that can be taken.

Wi-Fi Protected Access (WPA)

As the IEEE worked on the 802.11i standard, the Wi-Fi Alliance grew impatient and decided that wireless security could no longer wait. In October 2003 it introduced its own **Wi-Fi Protected Access (WPA)**. One of the design goals of WPA was to fit into the existing WEP engine without requiring extensive hardware upgrades or replacements. There were two modes of WPA. *WPA Personal* was designed for individuals or small office/home office (SOHO) settings, which typically have 10 or fewer employees. A more robust *WPA Enterprise* was intended for larger enterprises, schools, and government agencies. WPA addresses both encryption and authentication.

Temporal Key Integrity Protocol (TKIP) Encryption The heart and soul of WPA is a newer encryption technology called **Temporal Key Integrity Protocol (TKIP)**. TKIP functions as a "wrapper" around WEP by adding an additional layer of security but still preserving WEP's basic functionality. TKIP's enhancements are in three basic areas: the required key length is increased from 64 bits to 128 bits (making it harder to break), the IV is increased from 24 bits to 48 bits (effectively eliminating collisions), and a unique "base key" is created for each wireless device using a master key derived in the authentication process along with the sender's unique MAC address (this key is used with the IV to create unique keys for each packet).

With WEP, a small 40-bit encryption key must be manually entered on APs and devices. This key does not change and is the basis for encryption for all transmissions. By contrast, TKIP uses a longer 128-bit *per-packet key*. The per-packet functionality of TKIP means that it dynamically generates a new key for each packet, thus preventing collisions. The result is that TKIP dynamically generates unique keys to encrypt every data packet that is wirelessly communicated during a session.

 When using TKIP there are 280 trillion possible keys that can be generated for a given data packet. If a wireless device was transmitting 10,000 packets per second with WEP, collisions could occur in 90 minutes; TKIP **NOTE** ensures that collisions would not occur for more than 900 years.

WPA also includes a *Message Integrity Check (MIC)*, designed to prevent an attacker from conducting active or passive man-in-the-middle attacks by capturing, altering, and resending data packets. MIC provides a strong mathematical function in which the receiver and the transmitter each compute and then compare the MIC. If it does not match, the data is assumed to have been tampered with and the packet is dropped. There is also an optional MIC countermeasure in which all clients are deauthenticated and new associations are prevented for one minute if a MIC error occurs.

Preshared Key (PSK) Authentication Authentication for WPA Personal is accomplished by using a **preshared key (PSK)**. In cryptography, a PSK is a value that has been previously shared using a secure communication channel between two parties. In a WLAN, a PSK is slightly different. It is a secret value that is manually entered on both the AP and each wireless device, making it essentially identical to the "shared secret" used in WEP. Because this secret key is not widely known, it may be assumed that only approved devices have the key value. Devices that have the secret key are then automatically authenticated by the AP.

Although using PSK has several weaknesses—the key must be kept secret, it can be difficult to manage multiple devices, the key itself may be weak, keys must be entered manually—the alternative requires a significant investment in hardware and software. Authentication for enterprises should use the higher-level authentication process, but for home users, PSK is the option of choice.

WPA Vulnerabilities Although an improvement over WEP, WPA nevertheless has weaknesses. One of the design goals of WPA was to fit into the existing WEP engine without requiring extensive hardware upgrades or replacements. Because most existing WEP devices at the time WPA was released had very limited central processing unit (CPU) capabilities—with many APs operating at less than 40 MHz—a series of compromises had to be made. This allowed WEP to be modified to run WPA through software-based firmware upgrades on the AP and software upgrades on wireless devices, but these constraints limited the security of WPA, which was designed only as an interim short-term solution to address the critical WEP vulnerabilities and was not seen as a long-term solution. The vulnerabilities in WPA center around two areas, namely, key management and passphrases.

Improper management of the PSK keys can expose a WLAN to attackers. PSK key management weaknesses include the following:

- Like WEP, the distribution and sharing of PSK keys is performed manually without any technology security protections. The keys can be distributed by telephone, email, or a text message (none of which are secure). Any user who obtains a key is assumed to be authentic and approved.

- Standard security practices call for keys to be changed on a regular basis. Changing the PSK key requires reconfiguring the key on every wireless device and on all APs.

- To allow a guest user to have access to a PSK WLAN, the key must be given to that guest. Once the guest departs, this shared secret must be changed on all devices to ensure adequate security for the PSK WLAN.

A second area of PSK vulnerability is the use of passphrases. A PSK is a passphrase (consisting of letters, digits, punctuation, etc.) that is between 8 and 63 characters in length. PSK passphrases of fewer than 20 characters can be subject to attacks to crack the passphrase. If a user created a PSK passphrase of fewer than 20 characters that was a dictionary word, then a match may be found and the passphrase broken.

NOTE   The problem with short passphrases was noted even in the IEEE standard, which says: "Keys derived from the passphrase provide relatively low levels of security, especially with keys generated from short passwords, since they are subject to dictionary attack. Use of the key hash is recommended only where it is impractical to make use of a stronger form of user authentication. A key generated from a passphrase of less than about 20 characters is unlikely to deter attacks."

Wi-Fi Protected Access 2 (WPA2)

In March 2001 the IEEE started work on addressing wireless security. This work was based on new wireless security mechanisms as opposed to transitional solutions such as WPA. After three years of effort, in June 2004 the *IEEE 802.11i* wireless security standard was ratified. Also known as the *robust security network (RSN)*, 802.11i provides a solid wireless security model.

In September 2004, the Wi-Fi Alliance introduced **Wi-Fi Protected Access 2 (WPA2)**, which was the second generation of WPA security. WPA2 is based on the final IEEE 802.11i standard and is almost identical to it. The difference between WPA2 and IEEE 802.11i is that WPA2 allows wireless clients using TKIP to operate in the same WLAN, whereas IEEE 802.11i does not permit them to do so. As with WPA, there are two modes of WPA2, *WPA2 Personal* for individuals or small office/home offices (SOHOs) and *WPA2 Enterprise* for larger enterprises, schools, and government agencies. WPA2 addresses the two major security areas of WLANs, namely, encryption and authentication.

AES-CCMP Encryption The WPA2 standard addresses encryption by using the Advanced Encryption Standard (AES) block cipher. AES performs three steps on every block (128 bits) of plaintext. Within the second step, multiple iterations (called rounds) are performed depending upon the key size: a 128-bit key performs 9 rounds, a 192-bit key performs 11 rounds, and a 256-bit key, known as AES-256, performs 13 rounds. Within each round, bytes are substituted and rearranged, and then special multiplication is performed based on the new arrangement. For the WPA2 implementation of AES, a 128-bit key length is used in four stages that make up one round, and each round is then performed 10 times.

The encryption protocol used for WPA2 is the **Counter Mode with Cipher Block Chaining Message Authentication Code Protocol (CCMP)** and specifies the use of CCM (a general-purpose cipher mode algorithm providing data privacy) with AES. The Cipher Block Chaining Message Authentication Code (CBC-MAC) component of CCMP provides data integrity and authentication. CCM itself does not require that a specific block cipher be used, but the most secure cipher AES is mandated by the WPA2 standard. For this reason, CCMP for WLANs is sometimes designated as *AES-CCMP*.

Although CCMP uses a completely different encryption algorithm than TKIP, there are similarities to the process. Both CCMP and TKIP use a 128-bit key for encryption. Also, CCMP includes a 48-bit value that is sent in cleartext, as does TKIP. Although TKIP calls this value a TKIP sequence counter (TSC), CCMP more properly calls it a packet number (PN). Finally, both methods use a 64-bit MIC value. However, CCMP's MIC protects everything in the 802.11 Media Access Control (MAC) header (except for the duration field), while the TKIP MIC protects only the source and destination addresses.

 Despite the fact that AES is an efficient block cipher, CCMP still requires a separate encryption processor.

IEEE 802.1x Authentication Authentication for the WPA2 Enterprise model uses the *IEEE 802.1x* standard. This standard, originally developed for wired networks,

provides a greater degree of security by implementing port-based authentication. IEEE 802.1x blocks all traffic on a port-by-port basis until the client is authenticated using credentials stored on an authentication server. This prevents an unauthenticated device from receiving any network traffic until its identity can be verified. It also strictly limits access to the device that provides the authentication to prevent attackers from reaching it.

 IEEE 802.1x is covered in Chapter 8.

It is important that the communication between the supplicant, authenticator, and authentication server in an IEEE 802.1x configuration be secure. A framework for transporting the authentication protocols is known as the **Extensible Authentication Protocol (EAP)**. EAP was created as a more secure alternative than the weak **Challenge-Handshake Authentication Protocol (CHAP)** and **Password Authentication Protocol (PAP)**. Despite its name, EAP is a *framework* for transporting authentication protocols instead of the authentication protocol itself. EAP essentially defines the format of the messages and uses four types of packets: *request, response, success*, and *failure*. Request packets are issued by the authenticator and ask for a response packet from the supplicant. Any number of request–response exchanges may be used to complete the authentication. If the authentication is successful, a success packet is sent to the supplicant; if not, a failure packet is sent.

 An EAP packet contains a field that indicates the function of the packet (such as response or request) and an identifier field used to match requests and responses. Response and request packets also have a field that indicates the type of data being transported (such as an authentication protocol) along with the data itself.

The two common EAP protocols are:

- **Lightweight EAP (LEAP)**. LEAP is a proprietary EAP method developed by Cisco Systems and is based on the Microsoft implementation of CHAP. It requires mutual authentication used for WLAN encryption using Cisco client software (there is no native support for LEAP in Microsoft Windows operating systems). However, CHAP user credentials are not strongly protected and can be compromised, making LEAP vulnerable to specific types of attacks. Cisco now recommends that users migrate to a more secure EAP than LEAP.

- **Protected EAP (PEAP)**. PEAP is designed to simplify the deployment of 802.1x by using Microsoft Windows logins and passwords. PEAP is considered a more flexible EAP scheme because it creates an encrypted channel between the client and the authentication server, and the channel then protects the subsequent user authentication exchange. To create this channel, the PEAP client first authenticates the PEAP authentication server using enhanced authentication.

The seven different EAP protocols supported in WPA2 Enterprise are listed in Table 9-5. WPA2 can even support new EAP types as they become available.

EAP name	Description
EAP-TLS	This Internet Engineering Task Force (IETF) global standard protocol uses digital certificates for authentication.
EAP-TTLS/MSCHAPv2	This EAP protocol securely tunnels client password authentication within Transport Layer Security (TLS) records.
PEAPv0/EAP-MSCHAPv2	This version of EAP uses password-based authentication.
PEAPv1/EAP-GTC	PEAPv1 uses a changing token value for authentication.
EAP-FAST	This EAP protocol securely tunnels any credential form for authentication (such as a password or a token) using TLS.
EAP-SIM	EAP-SIM is based on the subscriber identity module (SIM) card installed in mobile phones and other devices that use Global System for Mobile Communications (GSM) networks.
EAP-AKA	This EAP uses the Universal Mobile Telecommunications System (UMTS) Subscriber Identity Module (USIM) for authentication.

Table 9-5 EAP protocols supported by WPA2 Enterprise

Despite the fact that WPA2 provides the optimum level of wireless security and has been mandatory for all wireless devices certified by the Wi-Fi Alliance since March 2006, there are still a surprising number of WLAN networks that do not implement it. In a recent analysis by this author, 23 different WLANs were discovered in one residential neighborhood. Thirteen of those networks, or 56 percent, used the weak WEP encryption and open key authentication. The other WLANs used WPA (four) or had no security (three), and only three networks used the secure WPA2. In another test, 26 WLANs were found, with six running WPA2, three using WPA, and 17 open (unsecured).

Additional Wireless Security Protections

Other security steps can be taken to protect a wireless network. These include captive portal APs, rogue AP discovery tools, power level controls, antennas, and site surveys.

Captive Portal APs A home user who installs a WLAN can simply launch a web browser to give immediate and unlimited access to the Internet. In a public area that is served by a WLAN, however, opening a web browser will rarely give immediate Internet access because the owner of the WLAN usually wants to advertise itself as providing this service, or wants the user to read and accept an Acceptable Use Policy (AUP) before using the WLAN. And sometimes a "general" authentication, such as a password given to all current hotel guests, must be entered before being given access to the network. This type of information, approval, or authentication can be supported through a **captive portal AP**. A captive portal AP uses a standard web browser to provide information, and gives the wireless user the opportunity to agree to a policy or present valid login credentials, providing a higher degree of security.

When accessing a public WLAN, users should consider using a virtual private network (VPN) to encrypt all transmissions.

Rogue AP Discovery Tools The problem of rogue APs is of increasing concern to organizations. Several methods can be used to detect a rogue AP by continuously monitoring the RF airspace. This requires a special sensor called a *wireless probe*, a device that can monitor the airwaves for traffic. There are four types of wireless probes:

- *Wireless device probe.* A standard wireless device, such as a portable laptop computer, can be configured to act as a wireless probe. At regular intervals during the normal course of operation, the device can scan and record wireless signals within its range and report this information to a centralized database. This scanning is performed when the device is idle and not receiving any transmissions. When a large number of mobile devices are used as wireless device probes, it can provide a high degree of accuracy in identifying rogue access points.

- *Desktop probe.* Instead of using a mobile wireless device as a probe, a desktop probe utilizes a standard desktop PC. A universal serial bus (USB) wireless network interface card adapter is plugged into the desktop computer to monitor the RF frequency in the area for transmissions.

- *Access point probe.* Some AP vendors have included in their APs the functionality of detecting neighboring APs, friendly APs as well as rogue APs. However, this approach is not widely used. The range for a single AP to recognize other APs is limited because APs are typically located so that their signals overlap only in such a way as to provide roaming to wireless users.

- *Dedicated probe.* A dedicated probe is designed to exclusively monitor the RF frequency for transmissions. Unlike access point probes that serve as both an AP and a probe, dedicated probes monitor only the airwaves. Dedicated probes look very similar to standard access points.

Once a suspicious wireless signal is detected by a wireless probe, the information is sent to a centralized database where WLAN management system software compares it to a list of approved APs. Any device not on the list is considered a rogue AP. The WLAN management system can instruct the switch to disable the port to which the rogue AP is connected, thus severing its connection to the wired network.

Power Level Controls Another security feature on some APs is the ability to adjust the level of power at which the WLAN transmits. On devices with that feature, the power can be adjusted so that less of the signal leaves the premises and reaches outsiders.

For IEEE WLANs, the maximum transmit power is 200 milliwatts (mW). APs that can adjust the power level usually permit the level to be adjusted in predefined increments, such as 1, 5, 20, 30, 40, 100, or 200 mW.

Antennas APs use antennas that radiate out a signal in all directions. Because these devices are generally positioned to provide the broadest area of coverage, APs should be located near the middle of the coverage area. Generally the AP can be secured to the ceiling or high on a wall. It is recommended that APs be mounted as high as possible for two reasons: there may be fewer obstructions for the RF signal, and to prevent thieves from stealing the device. For security purposes, the AP and its antenna should be positioned so that, when possible, a minimal amount of signal reaches beyond the security perimeter of the building or campus. Another option is to use an antenna that will focus its signal in a more concentrated direction toward authorized users instead of broadcasting it over a wide area.

Site Surveys Ensuring that a wireless LAN can provide its intended functionality and meet its required design goals can best be achieved through a **site survey**. A site survey is an in-depth examination and analysis of a wireless LAN site. There are several reasons for conducting a site survey, such as achieving the best possible performance from the WLAN, determining the best location for APs, ensuring that the coverage will fulfill the organization's requirements, and mapping any nearby wireless networks to determine existing radio interference. A site survey also can be used to enhance the security of a WLAN. The survey can provide the optimum location of the APs so that a minimum amount of signal extends past the boundaries of the organization to be accessible to attackers.

Chapter Summary

- Bluetooth is a wireless technology that uses short-range RF transmissions. It enables users to connect wirelessly to a wide range of computing and telecommunications devices by providing for rapid "on-the-fly" connections between Bluetooth-enabled devices. There are two types of Bluetooth network topologies: a piconet and a scatternet. Two of the common attacks on wireless Bluetooth technology are bluejacking, which is sending unsolicited messages, and bluesnarfing, or accessing unauthorized information from a wireless device through a Bluetooth connection.

- Near field communication (NFC) is a set of standards primarily for smartphones and smart cards that can be used to establish communication between devices in close proximity. Once the devices are either tapped together or brought very close to each other, a two-way communication is established. NFC devices are increasingly used in contactless payment systems so that a consumer can pay for a purchase by simply tapping a store's payment terminal with their smartphone. There are risks with using NFC contactless payment systems because of the nature of this technology.

- A wireless local area network (WLAN) is designed to replace or supplement a wired LAN. The IEEE has developed six standards for WLANs. An enterprise WLAN requires a wireless client network interface card adapter and an AP for communications, whereas a home network uses a wireless router instead of an AP. Due to the nature of wireless transmissions, wireless networks are targets for attackers. In a traditional wired network, the security of the network itself along with the walls and doors of the secured building protects the data and resources. Because an RF signal can easily extend past the protective perimeter of a building and because an AP can provide unauthorized entry points into the network, WLANs are frequently the target of attackers.

- A rogue AP is an unauthorized AP that allows an attacker to bypass network security and opens the network and its users to attacks. An evil twin is an AP that is set up by an attacker to mimic an authorized AP and capture the transmissions from users. One of the most common wireless attacks is intercepting and reading data that is being transmitted. In addition, if the attacker manages to connect to the enterprise wired network through a rogue AP, she could also read broadcast and multicast wired network traffic. In wireless replay attacks, attackers capture the data that is being transmitted, record it, and then send it on to the original recipient without their presence being detected. Attackers likewise can use intentional RF interference to flood the RF spectrum with enough interference to prevent a device from effectively communicating with the AP, performing a wireless DoS attack that prevents the transmission of data to or from network devices. Home wireless networks that are not protected are subject to attackers stealing data, reading transmissions, or injecting malware behind the firewall. Attackers can easily identify unprotected home wireless networks through war driving.

- The original IEEE 802.11 committee recognized that wireless transmissions could be vulnerable and implemented several wireless security protections in the 802.11 standard, while leaving other protections to be applied at the WLAN vendor's discretion. Despite their intended design, several of these protections were vulnerable and led to attacks. Wired Equivalent Privacy (WEP) was designed to ensure that only authorized parties can view transmitted wireless information by encrypting transmissions. WEP relies on a secret key that is shared between the wireless client device and the AP that is combined with an initialization vector (IV). However, WEP has several security vulnerabilities. Wi-Fi Protected Setup (WPS) is an optional means of configuring security on wireless local area networks and is designed to help users who have little or no knowledge of security to quickly and easily implement security on their WLANs. However, there are significant design and implementation flaws in WPS.

- One method of controlling access to the WLAN so that only approved users can be accepted is to limit a device's access to AP. Virtually all wireless AP vendors choose to use Media Access Control (MAC) address filtering. Filtering by MAC address, however, has several vulnerabilities. One weakness is that MAC addresses are initially exchanged between wireless devices and the AP in an unencrypted format. For a degree of protection, some wireless security sources encourage users to configure their APs to prevent the beacon frame from including the Service Set Identifier (SSID) and instead require the user to enter the SSID manually on the wireless device. Although this may seem to provide protection by not advertising the SSID, it provides only a weak degree of security.

- Wi-Fi Protected Access (WPA) was designed to fit into the existing WEP engine without requiring extensive hardware upgrades or replacements. WPA replaces WEP with the Temporal Key Integrity Protocol (TKIP), which uses a longer key and dynamically generates a new key for each packet that is created. WPA authentication for WPA Personal is accomplished by using preshared key (PSK) technology. A key must be created and entered into both the access point and all wireless devices ("shared") prior to ("pre") the devices communicating with the AP. Vulnerabilities still exist in WPA in two areas: key management and passphrases.

- Wi-Fi Protected Access 2 (WPA2) is the second generation of WPA security. Encryption under WPA2 is accomplished by using AES-CCMP. WPA2

9

authentication is accomplished by the IEEE 802.1x standard. Because it is important that the communication between the supplicant, authenticator, and authentication server in an IEEE 802.1x configuration be secure, a framework for transporting the authentication protocols is known as the Extensible Authentication Protocol (EAP). EAP is a framework for transporting authentication protocols by defining the format of the messages.

- Other steps can be taken to protect a wireless network. A captive portal AP uses a standard web browser to provide information and give the wireless user the opportunity to agree to a policy or present valid login credentials, providing a higher degree of security. The problem of rogue APs is of increasing concern to organizations. Several methods can be used to detect a rogue AP by continuously monitoring the RF airspace. This requires a special sensor called a wireless probe, a device that can monitor the airwaves for traffic. Another security feature on some APs is the ability to adjust the level of power at which the WLAN transmits. On devices with that feature, the power can be adjusted so that less of the signal leaves the premises and reaches outsiders. For security purposes, the AP and its antenna should be positioned so that, when possible, a minimal amount of signal reaches beyond the security perimeter of the building or campus. A site survey is an in-depth examination and analysis of a WLAN site. A survey can provide the optimum location of the APs so that a minimum amount of signal extends past the boundaries of the organization to be accessible to attackers.

Key Terms

bluejacking   An attack that sends unsolicited messages to Bluetooth-enabled devices.

bluesnarfing   An attack that accesses unauthorized information from a wireless device through a Bluetooth connection.

Bluetooth   A wireless technology that uses short-range radio frequency (RF) transmissions and provides rapid ad hoc device pairings.

captive portal AP   An infrastructure that is used on public access WLANs to provide a higher degree of security.

Challenge-Handshake Authentication Protocol (CHAP)   A weak authentication protocol that has been replaced by the Extensible Authentication Protocol (EAP).

Counter Mode with Cipher Block Chaining Message Authentication Code Protocol (CCMP)   The encryption protocol used for WPA2 that specifies the use of a general-purpose cipher mode algorithm providing data privacy with AES.

evil twin   An AP set up by an attacker to mimic an authorized AP and capture transmissions, so a user's device will unknowingly connect to this evil twin instead of the authorized AP.

Extensible Authentication Protocol (EAP)   A framework for transporting authentication protocols that defines the format of the messages.

initialization vector (IV)   A 24-bit value used in WEP that changes each time a packet is encrypted.

Lightweight EAP (LEAP)   A proprietary EAP method developed by Cisco Systems requiring mutual authentication used for WLAN encryption using Cisco client software.

Media Access Control (MAC) address filtering   A method for controlling access to a WLAN based on the device's MAC address.

near field communication (NFC)   A set of standards primarily for smartphones and smart cards that can be used to establish communication between devices in close proximity.

Password Authentication Protocol (PAP)   A weak authentication protocol that has been replaced by the Extensible Authentication Protocol (EAP).

preshared key (PSK)   The authentication model used in WPA that requires a secret key value to be entered into the AP and all wireless devices prior to communicating.

Protected EAP (PEAP)   An EAP method designed to simplify the deployment of 802.1x by using Microsoft Windows logins and passwords.

RF jamming   Intentionally flooding the radio frequency (RF) spectrum with extraneous RF signal "noise" that creates interference and prevents communications from occurring.

rogue access point   An unauthorized AP that allows an attacker to bypass many of the network security configurations and opens the network and its users to attacks.

Service Set Identifier (SSID)   The alphanumeric user-supplied network name of a WLAN.

site survey   An in-depth examination and analysis of a wireless LAN site.

Temporal Key Integrity Protocol (TKIP)   The WPA and WPA2 encryption technology.

war chalking   The process of documenting and then advertising the location of wireless LANs for others to use.

war driving   Searching for wireless signals from an automobile or on foot using a portable computing device.

Wi-Fi Protected Access (WPA)   The original set of protections from the Wi-Fi Alliance designed to address both encryption and authentication.

Wi-Fi Protected Access 2 (WPA2)   The second generation of WPA security from the Wi-Fi Alliance that addresses authentication and encryption on WLANs and is currently the most secure model for Wi-Fi security.

Wi-Fi Protected Setup (WPS)   An optional means of configuring security on wireless local area networks primarily intended to help users who have little or no knowledge of security to quickly and easily implement security on their WLANs. Due to design and implementation flaws, WPS is not considered secure.

Wired Equivalent Privacy (WEP)   An IEEE 802.11 security protocol designed to ensure that only authorized parties can view transmitted wireless information. WEP has significant vulnerabilities and is not considered secure.

wireless local area network (WLAN)   A wireless network designed to replace or supplement a wired local area network (LAN).

wireless replay   A passive attack in which the attacker captures transmitted wireless data, records it, and then sends it on to the original recipient without the attacker's presence being detected.

Review Questions

1. Which technology is predominately used for contactless payment systems?

    a. wireless local area network (WLAN)

    b. Bluetooth

    c. near field communication (NFC)

    d. Temporal Key Integrity Protocol (TKIP)

2. Bluetooth falls under the category of _____.

    a. local area network (LAN)

    b. short area network (SAN)

    c. paired-device network (PDN)

    d. personal area network (PAN)

3. Which of these IEEE WLANs has the highest data rate?

    a. 802.11b

    b. 802.11n

    c. 802.11g

    d. 802.11ac

4. Which of these technologies is NOT found in a wireless broadband router?

    a. wireless probe

    b. firewall

    c. router

    d. access point

5. Why is a rogue AP a security vulnerability?

    a. It uses the weaker IEEE 802.15.ax protocol.

    b. It allows an attacker to bypass many of the network security configurations.

    c. It requires the use of vulnerable wireless probes on all mobile devices.

    d. It conflicts with other network firewalls and can cause them to become disabled.

6. Which of these is NOT a risk when a home wireless router is not securely configured?

    a. An attacker can steal data from any folder with file sharing enabled.

    b. Usernames, passwords, credit card numbers, and other information sent over the WLAN could be captured by an attacker.

    c. Only 50 percent of the packets will be encrypted.

    d. Malware can be injected into a computer connected to the WLAN.

7. Which of these Wi-Fi Protected Setup (WPS) methods is vulnerable?

   a. PIN method

   b. push-button method

   c. piconet method

   d. NFC method

8. If Cora tries to access a free public Wi-Fi at a local coffee shop that requires her to first agree to an Acceptable Use Policy (AUP) before continuing, what type of AP has she encountered?

   a. web-based

   b. captive portal

   c. rogue

   d. Internet content filter

9. What is the unauthorized access of information from a wireless device through a Bluetooth connection called?

   a. bluejacking

   b. bluesnarfing

   c. Bluetooth snatching

   d. Bluetooth spoofing

10. The primary design of a(n) _____ is to capture the transmissions from legitimate users.

    a. rogue access point

    b. WEP

    c. evil twin

    d. Bluetooth grabber

11. Which of these is a vulnerability of MAC address filtering?

    a. The user must enter the MAC.

    b. MAC addresses are initially exchanged between wireless devices and the AP in an unencrypted format.

    c. APs use IP addresses instead of MACs.

    d. Not all operating systems support MACs.

12. Which of these is NOT a limitation of turning off the SSID broadcast from an AP?

    a. Users can more easily roam from one WLAN to another.

    b. The SSID can easily be discovered, even when it is not contained in beacon frames, because it still is transmitted in other management frames sent by the AP.

    c. Turning off the SSID broadcast may prevent users from being able to freely roam from one AP coverage area to another.

    d. Some versions of operating systems favor a network that broadcasts an SSID over one that does not.

13. What is the primary weakness of wired equivalent privacy (WEP)?

    a. It functions only on specific brands of APs.

    b. Its usage creates a detectable pattern.

    c. It slows down a WLAN from 104 Mbps to 16 Mbps.

    d. Initialization vectors (IVs) are difficult for users to manage.

14. WPA replaces WEP with _____.

    a. WPA2

    b. Temporal Key Integrity Protocol (TKIP)

    c. Cyclic Redundancy Check (CRC)

    d. Message Integrity Check (MIC)

15. A preshared key (PSK) of fewer than _____ characters may be subject to an attack if that key is a common dictionary word.

    a. 20

    b. 32

    c. 48

    d. 64

16. A WEP key that is 128 bits in length _____.

    a. has an initialization vector (IV) that is the same length as a WEP key of 64 bits

    b. cannot be cracked because it is too long

    c. cannot be used on access points that use passphrases

    d. is less secure than a WEP key of 64 bits because shorter keys are stronger

17. AES-CCMP is the encryption protocol standard used in _____.

    a. Bluetooth

    b. WPA2

    c. IEEE 802.11

    d. WPA

18. What is the Extensible Authentication Protocol (EAP)?

    a. a framework for transporting authentication protocols

    b. a subset of WPA2

    c. the protocol used in TCP/IP for authentication

    d. a technology used by IEEE 802.11 for encryption

19. Which technology should be used instead of LEAP?

    a. STREAK

    b. PEAP

    c. LEAP-2

    d. REAP

20. Which of these is NOT a type of wireless AP probe?

   a. wireless device probe

   b. WNIC probe

   c. dedicated probe

   d. AP probe

Hands-On Projects

If you are concerned about installing any of the software in these projects on your regular computer, you can instead install the software in the Windows virtual machine created in the Chapter 1 Hands-On Projects 1-3 and 1-4. Software installed within the virtual machine will not impact the host computer.

You do not need a mobile laptop or notebook computer to complete these projects. An inexpensive USB wireless network interface card adapter can be inserted in the USB port of a desktop computer in order to turn it into a wireless device.

9

Project 9-1: Viewing WLAN Security Information with Vistumbler

Vistumbler can be used to display the security information that is beaconed out from WLANs. Note that Vistumbler does not allow you to "crack" any WLANs but instead only displays information. In this project, you will use Vistumbler to view this information. This project works best when you are in an area in which you can pick up multiple WLAN signals.

1. Use your web browser to go to **www.vistumbler.net**.

The location of content on the Internet may change without warning. If you are no longer able to access the program through the above URL, use a search engine and search for "Vistumbler".

2. Click **EXE Installer (Mirror)**.

3. Follow the prompts to download and install Vistumbler.

4. If the program does not start after the installation is complete, launch Vistumbler.

5. If necessary, expand the window to full screen.

6. Click **Scan APs**. If no networks appear, click **Interface** and then select the appropriate wireless NIC interface.

7. Note the columns **Signal** and **High Signal**. How could this be used in a site survey?

8. Click **Graph 1**.

9. Click one of the APs displayed at the bottom of the screen. Allow Vistumbler to accumulate data over several minutes. What information is displayed on this graph?

10. Click **Graph 2**.

11. Click another one of the APs displayed at the bottom of the screen. Allow Vistumbler to accumulate data over several minutes. What information is displayed on this graph? How is this different from the previous graph?

12. Click **No Graph** to return to the previous screen.

13. Use the horizontal scroll bar to move to the right. Note the columns **Authentication, Encryption, Manufacturer,** and **Radio Type**. How would this information be useful to an attacker?

14. Use the horizontal scroll bar to move back to the far left.

15. In the left page, expand the information under **Authentication**. What types are listed?

16. Expand the information under these types and note the information given for the wireless LAN signals. What device does **Mac Address** point to? How could this be useful to an attacker?

17. In the left page, expand the information under **Encryption**. What types are listed? Which types are most secure? Which types are least secure?

18. Expand the information under these types and note the information given for each WLAN.

19. Record the total number of different WLANs that you are able to detect, along with the number of encryption types. Which type is most common?

20. Compile all the information from other students regarding the total number of different WLANs and the number of encryption types. Does it surprise you? Why or why not?

21. One of the features of Vistumbler is its ability to use audio and text-to-speech information so that the location and strength of WLANs can be detected without the need to constantly monitor the screen. Be sure that the speakers on the laptop computer are turned on.

22. Click **Options**.

23. Click **Speak Signals**. Now Vistumbler will "speak" the percentage of signal strength.

24. Now carry the laptop away from the AP and note the changes. How would this be helpful to an attacker?

25. Close Vistumbler.

26. Close all windows.

Project 9-2: Substitute a MAC Address Using SMAC

Although MAC address filters are often relied upon to prevent unauthorized users from accessing a wireless LAN, MAC addresses can easily be spoofed. In this project, you will substitute a MAC address.

1. Open your web browser and enter the URL **www.klcconsulting.net/ smac.**

The location of content on the Internet may change without warning. If you are no longer able to access the program through the above URL, use a search engine and search for "KLC Consulting SMAC".

2. Scroll down to **FREE Download – SMAC 2.0.**

3. Click **Download Site 3**.

4. When the file finishes downloading, run the program and follow the default installation procedures.

5. Click **Finish** to launch SMAC and accept the license agreement.

6. When prompted for a Registration ID, click **Proceed**. SMAC displays the network interface card adapters that it discovers, as seen in Figure 9-11.

9

ID	Active	Spoofed	Network Adapter	IP Address	Active MAC
0009	Yes	No	Dell Wireless 1390 WLAN Mini-Card	192.168.1.62	00-19-7E-6A-C8-8B
0029	Yes	No	VMware Virtual Ethernet Adapter for VMnet1	192.168.76.1	00-50-56-C0-00-01
0031	Yes	No	VMware Virtual Ethernet Adapter for VMnet8	192.168.209.1	00-50-56-C0-00-08
0036	Yes	No	VirtualBox Host-Only Ethernet Adapter	169.254.242.20	08-00-27-00-40-DB

Figure 9-11 SMAC main window
Source: KLC Consulting, Inc.

If the message **SMAC has determined that you have insufficient registry access** appears, close the SMAC application if necessary. Single click on the SMAC icon and then click the right mouse button. Click **Run as administrator**.

7. If there are multiple network interface card adapters listed, click on each adapter. Does the **Active MAC Address** change? Why?

8. Click on a network adapter and then click the **Random** button to change the MAC address. It is displayed in the **New Spoofed MAC Address**.

9. Click the **Random** button to create a new MAC address.

10. Click the down arrow under the **New Spoofed MAC Address** to view the manufacturer associated with this OUI.

11. Does the OUI change?

12. Click the down arrow under the **New Spoofed MAC Address** to view the manufacturers again. Select a different manufacturer. What happens to the OUI?

13. Click the **Random** button several more times to create new MAC addresses based on this manufacturer.

Because this is an Evaluation mode copy of SMAC, you are not able to actually change the MAC address. In the Full Feature mode, you would click on **Update MAC** as the next step.

14. Close all windows.

15. To reenable your original MAC, launch SMAC and then click **Remove MAC**.

16. Reboot the computer.

Project 9-3: Use Microsoft Windows Netsh Commands

The Windows Netsh commands for a wireless local area network (WLAN) provide the means to configure wireless connectivity and security settings using a command line instead of a graphical user interface (GUI). Benefits of the wireless Netsh interface include easier wireless deployment as an alternative to Group Policy, ability to configure clients to support multiple security options, and even the ability to block undesirable networks. In this project, you will explore some of the Netsh commands.

For this project you will need a computer running Microsoft Windows that has a wireless NIC and can access a wireless LAN.

1. In Microsoft Windows, access **All Programs**, and then click **Accessories**.

2. Right-click **Command Prompt** and then select **Run as administrator** from the context menu. This will open the Windows command window in elevated privilege mode.

3. Type **netsh** and then press **Enter**. The command prompt will change to *netsh>*.

4. Type **wlan** and then press **Enter**. The command prompt will change to *netsh wlan>*.

5. Type **show drivers** and then press **Enter** to display the wireless NIC driver information. It may be necessary to scroll back toward the top to see all the information.

6. Next view the WLAN interfaces for this computer. Type **show interfaces** and then press **Enter**. Record the SSID value, and the name of the Profile.

7. Now look at the global wireless settings for this computer. Type **show settings** and then press **Enter**.

8. Display all of the available networks to this computer. Type **show networks** and then press **Enter**.

9. Windows creates a profile for each network that you connect to. To display those profiles, type **show profiles** and then press **Enter**. If there is a profile of a network that you no longer use, type **delete profile name=** *profile-name*.

10. Now disconnect from your current WLAN by typing **disconnect** and then press **Enter**. Note the message you receive, and observe the status in your system tray.

11. Reconnect to your network by typing **connect name=***profile-name* **ssid=** *ssid-name* as recorded above and then press **Enter**.

12. Netsh allows you to block specific networks. Select another network name that you currently are not connected to. Type **show networks,** press **Enter**, and then record the SSID of that network you want to block. Type **add filter permission = block ssid=***ssid-name* **networktype =** **infrastructure** and then press **Enter**.

13. Type **show networks** and then press **Enter**. Does the network that you blocked above appear in the list?

14. Now display the blocked network (but do not allow access to it). Type **set blockednetworks display=show** and then press **Enter**.

15. Type **show networks** and then press **Enter**. Does the network that you blocked above appear in the list?

16. Click the wireless icon in your system tray. Does the network appear in this list?

17. Click the wireless icon in your system tray. What appears next to the name of this blocked network? Click the name of the network. What does it say?

18. Now reenable access to the blocked network by typing **delete filter permission = block ssid=***ssid-name* **networktype = infrastructure** and then press **Enter**.

19. Type **Exit** and then press **Enter**.

20. Type **Exit** again and then press **Enter** to close the command window.

Project 9-4: Configuring Access Points—WPA2 and WPS

The ability to properly configure an AP is an important skill for any wireless network professional as well as, to a lesser degree, for end-users. In this project you will use an online emulator from D-Link to configure an AP's legacy security settings.

1. Use your web browser to go to **support.dlink.com/emulators/ dap1522/**.

The location of content on the Internet may change without warning. If you are no longer able to access the program through the above URL, use a search engine and search for "D-Link emulator 1522".

2. Click **DAP-1522 AP Mode**.

3. The emulated login screen will appear. Click **Login** without entering a password.

4. An emulated Setup screen displaying what a user would see when configuring an actual DAP-1522 is displayed.

5. Under **MANUAL WIRELESS NETWORK SETUP**, click the button **Manual Wireless Network Setup**.

6. Under **WIRELESS SECURITY MODE**, click the down arrow in the **Security Mode:** options. What are the choices listed? Click **WPA-Personal**.

7. Under **WPA**, click the down arrow next to **WPA Mode:**. What choices are listed? When would you use **Auto (WPA or WPA2)**?

8. Press the Escape key to close the dropdown menu, and then click the down arrow next to **Cipher Type:**. What options are listed? When would you use **TKIP and AES**?

9. The **Passphrase** box under **PRE-SHARED KEY** is where you would enter the PSK. Because it is important that this value be strong, it is recommended that you use a password generation program. Leave this D-Link site link up and open another tab on your web browser.

10. Go to **www.grc.com/passwords.htm**.

11. Under **63 random printable ASCII characters**, select that value and copy it into your clipboard by right-clicking and selecting **Copy**.

12. Return to the D-Link page.

13. Click in the **Passphrase** box and paste this value from the clipboard by right-clicking and selecting **Paste**.

Because the passphrase only has to be entered once on the AP and once on each wireless device, it does not have to be a passphrase that must be committed to memory. Instead, it can be a long and complicated passphrase to enhance security. Under normal circumstances the passphrase now would be entered on each wireless device and saved in a password management application so it can be retrieved when needed.

14. Under **WIRELESS SECURITY MODE**, click the down arrow next to **Security Mode:**. Change it to **WPA-Enterprise**. What new information is requested? Why?

15. Under **WI-FI PROTECTED SETUP (ALSO CALLED WNC 2.0 IN WINDOWS VISTA)**, note that it is enabled by default. Is this good or bad? Why?

16. Uncheck the box next to **Enable:**.

17. Close all windows.

Case Projects

CASE PROJECTS

Case Project 9-1: Wireless Security Websites

It is important to keep abreast of the latest wireless security vulnerabilities and attacks so that your wireless network can be made secure. Using Internet search engines, research websites that contain information about wireless security. Find the top three sites that you would recommend. Which sites have the most up-to-date information? Who sponsors these sites? What other types of valuable information are on the sites? Write a one-page paper on what you find and comparing the sites.

Case Project 9-2: Is War Driving Legal?

Use the Internet to research the legality of war driving. Is it considered illegal? Why or why not? If it is not illegal, do you think it should be? What should be the penalties? Create a report on your research.

Case Project 9-3: EAP

Use the Internet to research information on four different EAP protocols that are supported in WPA2 Enterprise (see Table 9-5). Write a brief description of each and indicate the relative strength of its security. Write a one-page paper on your research.

Case Project 9-4: Your Wireless Security

Is the wireless network you own as secure as it should be? Examine your wireless network or that of a friend or neighbor and determine which security model it uses. Next, outline the steps it would take to move it to the next highest level. Estimate how much it would cost and how much time it would take to increase the level. Finally, estimate how long it would take you to replace all the data on your computer if it was corrupted by an attacker, and what you might lose. Would this be motivation to increase your current wireless security model? Write a one-page paper on your work.

Case Project 9-5: Open Source Wireless Protocol Analyzers

Whereas at one time protocol analyzers were proprietary and expensive, today there are several excellent protocol analyzers that are open source or free products, such as Wireshark, Colasoft's Capsa, Packetyzer, and others. Research three open source or free protocol analyzers. Which product would you recommend for capturing and analyzing wireless traffic? Why? Write a paper on the information that you find.

Case Project 9-6: Bay Pointe Security Consulting

Bay Pointe Security Consulting (BPSC) provides security consulting services to a wide range of businesses, individuals, schools, and organizations. BPSC has hired you as a technology student to help them with a new project and provide real-world experience to students who are interested in the security field.

Pomodoro Fresco is a regional Italian pizza chain that provides free open wireless access to its customers and secure wireless access for its staff. However, Pomodoro Fresco was using WPA for securing its staff network but was using a short and weak password, and an attacker accessed the WLAN. The company now wants to install a much more secure wireless network, and they have asked BPSC to make a presentation about their options. BPSC has asked you to help them in the presentation.

1. Create a PowerPoint presentation for the staff about the threats against WLANs and the weaknesses of the IEEE 802.11 security protocols. Also include information about the more secure WPA2. Your presentation should contain at least 10 slides.

2. After the presentation, Atrium Inns is trying to decide if they should install a captive portal for their customer WLAN. Create a memo to Atrium outlining the advantages and disadvantages, along with your recommendation.

Case Project 9-7: Community Site Activity

The Information Security Community Site is an online companion to this textbook. It contains a wide variety of tools, information, discussion boards, and other features to assist learners. Go to **community.cengage.com/infosec**. Sign in with the login name and password that you created in Chapter 1.

Unencrypted wireless data is a treasure trove for attackers, who can capture virtually anything you transmit. Even if you visit a website that says it is protected, often only the username and password are protected. Once you get past the authentication, it reverts to unprotected transmissions. The website then sends a cookie to your computer that your web browser uses for all subsequent requests. If an attacker can get that cookie, called session hijacking or "sidejacking," then she can impersonate you and access your account. Grabbing this cookie is fairly easy if you are on an unencrypted wireless network.

To illustrate just how vulnerable one can be to session hijacking using a WLAN, two researchers created Firesheep, a free open-source Firefox browser extension. Anyone can install this add-on and then connect to an unencrypted wireless network. If the person clicks "Start Capturing," then when anyone on the WLAN visits a site that is known by Firesheep, like Facebook, Twitter,

Amazon, Dropbox, Wordpress, or Flickr, you will see his name and probably his photo displayed. Double-click the name and you will be logged in as that person to that account. Although the antidote is to use only WPA2 encrypted WLAN sites, this is generally not possible in a public Wi-Fi hotspot.

Is this type of application illegal? Would the ability to hijack accounts violate federal wiretapping laws? Would the creators of Firesheep be liable for prosecution? Are the researchers making software that enables unauthorized access to other users' accounts with the intention of facilitating that crime? Or because they are not actively engaged in committing a crime, should they not be prosecuted? Post your thoughts about free speech, censorship, and privacy over Firesheep on the discussion board.

References

1. John Cox, "Wi-Fi client surge forces new look at WLAN designs," *Network World*, Jun. 20, 2011.

2. Jia Wu, "A quarter of households worldwide now have wireless home networks," *Strategy Analytics*, www.strategyanalytics.com/default.aspx?mod=pressreleaseviewer&a0=5193.

3. Patterson, Sean, "NFC finally coming to most smartphones," *WebProNews*, Feb. 27, 2014, accessed Mar. 1, 2014, www.webpronews.com/nfc-finally-coming-to-most -smartphones-2014-02.

9

## chapter 10

Mobile Device Security

After completing this chapter, you should be able to do the following:

- List and compare the different types of mobile devices
- Explain the risks associated with mobile devices
- List ways to secure a mobile device
- Explain how to apply mobile device app security
- Describe how to implement BYOD security

Today's Attacks and Defenses

One of the greatest risks to mobile phones is not that determined attackers will circumvent the secure technology defenses on the phone to steal important data. Instead, it's the risk of the owner laying the phone down in a public place and then walking off without it. A recent study looked at what actually happens to lost phones in order to determine how vulnerable the information stored on them may be.[1]

In this study, called the *Honey Stick Project*, security researchers loaded 50 smartphones with a collection of simulated corporate and personal data. No security features such as login passwords or PINs were enabled on any of the devices. The phones also had installed a hidden program that could remotely monitor how they were being used and from what location. Phones were then intentionally left in several different environments with heavy pedestrian traffic, such as malls, food courts, elevators, transit stops, and student unions in New York City, Washington D.C., Los Angeles, San Francisco Bay, and Ottawa, Canada. As "finders" picked up the "lost" phones, the details of which apps and data were being accessed were then secretly transmitted back to a central database.

The results of the Honey Stick Project were revealing. Finders attempted to access business-related apps or data on 83 percent of the phones, and on 45 percent of the devices attempts were made to access the corporate email client. The file *HR Salaries* was accessed on 53 percent of the phones while *HR Cases* was accessed on 40 percent of the devices. The app *Remote Admin* was used on almost half of the lost devices. The researchers concluded that when a business-connected mobile device is lost, there is more than an 80 percent chance that the finder will attempt to access corporate data or networks.

Sensitive personal information also was accessed by the finders. On 96 percent of the lost phones an attempt was made to access at least one of the apps or files. About 9 out of every 10 devices showed attempts to access personal apps or data, and access to social networking accounts and personal email were each attempted on 60 percent of the devices. Although it could be argued that this occurred simply because the finder was trying to identify the phone's owner, attempts to access other apps might illustrate a more sinister motive. A personal online banking app was accessed on 43 percent of the devices, attempts to access a private photos app occurred on 72 percent of the phones, and a *Saved Passwords* file was accessed on 57 percent of the phones. In addition, on two-thirds of the phones the finder attempted to click through the login or password reset screens.

The use of one of the lost phones was fairly typical. This phone was first accessed just 5 minutes after it was lost. The finder first went through the salary, banking, and Facebook information on the phone, and later connected to a computer while the

(continued)

finder attempted to access the corporate network. The phone then traveled 150 miles while the finder accessed Facebook 21 times over a 45-minute period and looked at the folder containing passwords nine times. The next day the phone shut down completely and disappeared.

In short, 89 percent of the finders accessed personal information and 83 percent accessed business information on the lost phones. And despite the fact that the owner's phone number and email address were clearly marked in a contacts app, of the 50 devices lost, only 25 offers to help were received.

If a time traveler living just 10 years ago could be transported to today's world, it is likely that he would be shocked at how mobile devices have dramatically changed the way we live. Watching cars pass on the road he would observe that a high percentage of drivers are talking or sending text messages on their mobile phones, often in violation of laws that prohibit it. Sitting in a classroom he would see that most students are using their mobile tablet devices to read e-textbooks, access online files, and take notes. Strolling through the mall he would be amazed to see shoppers scan bar codes on their smartphones to determine if the same item is offered at another store in the mall at a lower price or if it would be cheaper to just immediately order it online. All of these dramatic changes might even discourage our time traveler from jumping ahead another 10 years to see what a world filled with even more mobile devices would be like.

The statistics confirm that mobile devices have changed—and are continuing to change—our everyday lives. It is estimated that between 2013 and 2016 more than 5 billion smartphones will be sold.[2] The wireless penetration (or the number of active wireless mobile devices divided by the total population) in the U.S. is now 102 percent. Almost 40 percent of all U.S. households no longer use wired phones but instead rely entirely on mobile cell phones. The number of annual text messages sent between mobile devices has gone from almost zero just a few years ago to more than 2.1 trillion annually.[3] In 2013, for the first time in the history of the personal computer (PC), the sales of PCs declined from the previous year, falling 10 percent.[4] This was due almost entirely to mobile tablet computers replacing PCs and laptops. Clearly the mobile device revolution is upon us.

Just as users have flocked to mobile devices, so too have attackers. Because mobile devices have become the primary, if not exclusive, computing device for a growing number of users, there has been a dramatic increase in malware and attacks directed at these devices. And unlike desktop computers that can be protected by walls and locked doors, the mobile devices themselves—which can be used virtually anywhere in the world—also must be constantly protected from loss or theft.

In this chapter, you will explore mobile device security. You will begin by looking at the different types of mobile devices. Next, you will look at the risks associated with these devices. Then, you will explore how to secure these devices and the applications running on them. Finally, you will study how enterprises wrestle with how users can bring their own personal mobile devices and connect them to the secure corporate network without compromising that network.

10

Types of Mobile Devices

Defining the characteristics of a mobile device can be like trying to hit a "moving target" because the features found on mobile devices are constantly evolving as mobile device vendors add the "latest and greatest" features to their devices to differentiate their products from those of competitors and entice users to upgrade or purchase new devices. Despite their ever-changing feature sets, however, there are some basic characteristics of mobile devices that differentiate them from other computing devices. These characteristics include:

- Small form factor
- Wireless data network interface for accessing the Internet, such as Wi-Fi or cellular data connection
- Mobile operating system
- Applications (*apps*) that can be acquired through different means, such as downloaded from the Web, included with the operating system, or provided by the wireless data carrier
- Data synchronization capabilities with a separate computer or remote servers
- Local nonremovable data storage

In addition, other features that may be optional can be found on most mobile devices. These features include:

- Digital camera(s)
- Global Positioning System (GPS)
- Microphone
- Removable storage media
- Support for using the device itself as removable storage for another computing device
- Wireless cellular connection for voice communications
- Wireless personal area network interfaces like Bluetooth or near field communications

There are several different types of mobile devices. These include portable computers, tablets, smartphones, wearable technology, and legacy devices. In addition, most of these devices have removable storage capabilities.

Portable Computers

As a class *portable computers* are devices that closely resemble standard desktop computers. These portable computers have similar hardware (keyboard, hard disk drive, RAM, etc.) and run the same operating systems (Windows, Apple Mac OS, or Linux) and application software (Microsoft Office, web browsers, etc.) that are found on a general-purpose desktop computer. The primary difference is that portable computers are smaller self-contained devices that can easily be transported from one location to another while operating on battery power.

A *laptop* computer is regarded as the earliest portable computer. A laptop is designed to replicate the abilities of a desktop computer with only slightly less processing power yet is small enough to be used on a lap or small table. These devices generally weigh over six pounds (2.7 kilograms or kg), depending on their size, construction materials, and integrated hardware, and are considered cumbersome to transport in a carrying case for an extended period of time. Laptops have multiple hardware ports, such as Universal Serial Bus (USB), Extended Serial Advanced Technology Attachment (eSATA), and wired network ports (RJ-45). They also have optical drives (DVD or Blu-ray) and may accommodate limited hardware upgrades.

Although often considered to be the same, a laptop computer and a notebook computer are different. A *notebook* computer is a smaller version of a laptop computer and is considered a lightweight personal computer. Notebook computers typically weigh less than laptops and are small enough to fit easily inside a briefcase. These portable computers are designed to include only the most basic frequently used features of a standard computer in a smaller size that is easy to carry. Unlike laptop computers, notebooks have a limited number of hardware ports, do not include optical drives, and often cannot be upgraded. Table 10-1 compares the features of laptop and notebook computers.

Feature	Laptop	Notebook
Size	Larger devices with display screens ranging from 10 to 19 inches (25.4 to 48.3 cm)	Smaller devices designed to fit easily into a small bag or briefcase
Optical drives	Integrated into the device	Not included but can be attached externally
Processor	Slightly less powerful than desktops	Generally not as powerful as laptops
Cooling capacities	Includes fan similar to desktop	Does not require fan due to less powerful processor
Intended use	Replicates functionality of desktop system	Portable personal device for essential computing functions

Table 10-1   Laptop vs. notebook computers

NOTE   The first commercially successful portable computer was the Osborne 1, released in 1981. Its screen was only 5 inches (13 centimeters), and it had a single floppy disk drive. Weighing in at a hefty 23.5 pounds (10.7 kg), it was said to be more "luggable" than portable.

A relatively new class of portable computers is the *subnotebook* computer, sometimes called an *ultrabook* (Intel/Windows) or *air* (Apple). These devices are even smaller than standard notebooks and use low-power processors and solid state drives (SSDs). They generally have a high-definition multimedia interface (HDMI) port along with a limited number of USB hardware ports. Figure 10-1 shows a subnotebook computer.

NOTE   Because laptops, notebooks, and subnotebooks use the same hardware and run the same software as standard desktop computers, they face the same risks of attack. An additional risk is that these portable computers also are subject to theft or loss.

Figure 10-1 Subnotebook computer
© Creativa/Shutterstock.com

A new type of computing device that resembles a laptop computer is a *web-based* computer. It contains a limited version of the Linux operating system and a web browser with an integrated media player. Web-based computers are designed to be used primarily while connected to the Internet. No traditional software applications can be installed, and no user files are stored locally on the device. Instead, the device accesses online web apps and saves user files on the Internet.

Tablets

Tablets are portable computing devices that are generally larger than smartphones and smaller than notebooks, and are focused on ease of use. Tablets generally lack a built-in keyboard and instead rely on a touch screen. Tablets are often classified by their screen size. The two most common categories of tablet screen sizes are 5–8.5 inches (12.7–21.5 cm) and 8.5–10 inches (12.7–25.4 cm). The weight of tablets is generally less than 1.5 pounds (0.68 kg), and they are less than 1/2 inch (1.2 cm) thick. Figure 10-2 shows a typical tablet computer.

Designed for user convenience, tablets are thinner, lighter, easier to carry, and more intuitive to use than portable computers. Whereas portable computers are designed for performance, tablets are primary display devices that can accommodate limited user input. Tablet computers have an operating system that allows them to run third-party apps. The most popular operating systems for tablets are Apple iOS, Google Android, and Microsoft Windows. It is estimated that by 2016 the number of tablets shipped will exceed portable computer shipments.[5]

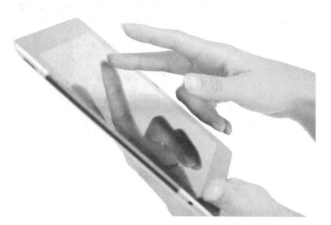

Figure 10-2   Tablet computer
© maximino/Shutterstock.com

 **NOTE** Tablets are purchased more often in mature markets like the U.S., while laptops sell better in emerging markets. This is because laptops are often the only computing devices in a household in emerging markets, whereas in mature markets tablets supplement existing computer resources.

Smartphones

A *feature phone* is a traditional cellular telephone that includes a limited number of features, such as a camera, an MP3 music player, and ability to send and receive *short message service (SMS)* text messages. Many feature phones are designed to highlight a single feature, such as the ability to take high-quality photos or provide a large amount of memory for music storage.

A **smartphone** has all the tools that a feature phone has but also includes an operating system that allows it to run apps and access the Internet. Because it has an operating system, a smartphone offers a broader range of functionality. Users can install apps that perform a wide variety of functions for productivity, social networking, music, and so forth, much like a standard computer. In fact, because of this ability to run apps, smartphones are essentially handheld personal computers. As the popularity of smartphones has increased, the sales of feature phones have decreased. Table 10-2 lists the worldwide market share of smartphones and feature phones.

Wearable Technology

A new class of mobile technology consists of devices that can be worn by the user instead of carried. Known as *wearable technology*, these devices can provide even greater flexibility and mobility.

One wearable technology device is an optical head-mounted display. The most common display is a "wearable computer" known as Google Glass. Google Glass can be activated in response to the user's voice commands by saying "*OK Glass*" or tilting the head 30 degrees upward. Then a specific voice command (called a "voice action") can be given, such as requesting directions

10

Year	Smartphone market share (%)	Feature phone market share (%)
2011	35	46
2012	46	41
2013	54	38
2014	58	35
2015	62	33
2016	67	28

Table 10-2 Smartphone vs. feature phone worldwide market share[6]

(*Give me directions to Tampa, Florida*), issuing a command to make a web search (*Google Cengage Learning*), or an action to use one of the device's features (*Take a picture* or *Record a video*). Google Glass also can be manipulated by a touchpad on the side of the device. When a user slides her finger backward on the touchpad it displays current events, such as the weather, while sliding the finger forward shows past events, such as phone calls or photos. Google Glass is shown in Figure 10-3.

Figure 10-3 Google Glass
© Joe Seer/Shutterstock.com

Another wearable technology is a *smart watch*. This device can serve as an accessory to a smartphone so that users can easily glance at the watch to view messages without the need to remove the smartphone from a bag or pocket. The device also may have its own set of sensors and software features to function independently. For example, it could serve as a control device for home automation systems.

Although optical head-mounted displays and smart watches currently are not widely available, it is predicted that this wearable technology will become very popular and could ultimately replace other mobile devices.

Legacy Devices

Several different mobile devices are no longer widely in use and are considered legacy devices. One of the first mobile devices was a *personal digital assistant (PDA)*. A PDA was a handheld mobile device that was intended to replace paper systems. These devices often included an appointment calendar, an address book, a "to-do" list, a calculator, and the ability to record limited notes. PDAs that included a wireless data connection also included an email client and a limited-edition web browser. Most PDAs had a touchscreen for entering data while others had a rudimentary keyboard that contained only a numeric keypad or thumb keyboard. Popular in the 1990s and early 2000s, PDAs fell out of favor as smartphones gained in popularity.

A *netbook* computer was a small, inexpensive, and lightweight portable computer. In order to be affordable, netbooks used low-powered processors, featured small screens and keyboards, omitted optical storage, and could not be upgraded. The screen sizes ranged from 5 to 12 inches (12.7 to 30.4 cm) and weighed only 2.2 pounds (1 kg). The popularity of netbooks declined once tablet computers were introduced.

Mobile Device Removable Storage

Mobile devices use *flash memory* for storage, which is a nonvolatile solid state electronic storage that can be electrically erased and reused. Whereas all mobile devices have local nonremovable storage capabilities, most devices also support removable data storage. This removable storage includes large form factor and small form factor storage.

Large Form Factor Storage A credit card–sized peripheral that slides into a slot on a laptop computer can add additional functionality, much like a card device can be inserted into the bus expansion slot on a desktop computer. Originally these cards were known as PCMCIA (Personal Computer Memory Card International Association) cards, and later the name was changed to *PC Card*.

The PC Card standard defines three form factors for three types of PC Cards. All three card types are the same length and width and use the same 68-pin connector. The cards differ only in their thickness. Table 10-3 lists the dimensions and typical uses of different PC Cards.

Laptops in the 1990s usually were configured with two PC Card Type II slots with no barrier in between them. This allowed for the installation of either two Type II cards or one Type III card. Today laptops often have a single Type II slot, while notebooks and tablets have no PC Card slots.

PC Card type	Length (mm)	Width (mm)	Thickness (mm)	Typical uses
Type I	85.6	54	3.3	Memory
Type II	85.6	54	5.0	Input/output devices
Type III	85.6	54	10.5	Rotating mass storage devices

Table 10-3 PC Card form factors

An enhanced type of PC Card is the *CardBus*. CardBus is a 32-bit bus in the PC Card form factor. CardBus also includes a bus mastering feature, which allows a controller on the bus to talk to other devices or memory without going through the CPU.

 A notch on the left front of a CardBus device prevents it from being inserted into a slot that can accept only PC Cards. Most new slots are compatible with both CardBus and PC Card devices.

Today PC Card and CardBus devices are being replaced by *ExpressCard* technology. ExpressCard is designed to deliver higher-performance modular expansion in a smaller size. There are two standard ExpressCard form factors: the ExpressCard/34 module (34 mm × 75 mm) and the ExpressCard/54 module (54 mm × 75 mm). Both formats are 5 mm thick (the same as the Type II PC Card) yet 10.6 mm shorter than a PC Card.

Small Form Factor Storage *CompactFlash (CF)* is small form factor (43 × 36 × 3.3 mm for Type I, and 43 × 36 × 5 mm for Type II) that is generally used as a mass storage device format for portable electronic devices. Similar to CF, a **Secure Digital (SD)** card is another small form factor storage media. SD has evolved from its inception in 1999 from a single card type and size to a variety of different types and sizes. The SD format includes four card "families" available in three different form factors with different speed ratings. The four families are:

- Standard-Capacity (SDSC)
- High-Capacity (SDHC)
- eXtended-Capacity (SDXC)
- Secure Digital Input Output (SDIO)

 A variation of the SDIO is an SD card that is a combination of a wireless NIC and storage. Once inserted into a digital camera, this type of SD card can wirelessly transmit pictures across the network to a desktop or laptop's hard disk drive or to a wireless printer.

Currently there are three sizes of SD cards: *full SD, miniSD*, and *microSD*. Full SD memory cards are typically used in personal computers, video cameras, digital cameras, and other large consumer electronics devices. The microSD and miniSD cards are commonly used in smaller electronic devices like smartphones and tablets. A microSD card is illustrated in Figure 10-4.

Figure 10-4   microSD card
© ExaMedia Photography/Shutterstock.com

 Adapters are available for microSD cards to fit a full SD card slot. This gives the ability to move the card from a laptop computer to a tablet.

SD speed classes were designed to support video recording. There are two types of speed classes, the standard speed class and the ultra high speed (UHS) speed class. These are listed in Table 10-4.

Class	Class ranking	Minimum speed (MB per second)	Application
Standard speed class	2	2	SD video recording
Standard speed class	4	4	High-definition (HD) video recording
Standard speed class	6	6	HD video recording
Standard speed class	10	10	Full HD video recording and still HD recording
UHS speed class	U1	10	Real-time broadcasts
UHS speed class	U3	30	4K resolution video files

Table 10-4   SD speed classes

Mobile Device Risks

 4.2 Summarize mobile security concepts and technologies.

There are several security risks associated with using mobile devices. These include limited physical security, connecting to public networks, location tracking, installing unsecured applications, accessing untrusted content, and bring your own device (BYOD) risks.

Limited Physical Security

The greatest asset of a mobile device—its portability—is also considered its greatest vulnerability. Mobile devices are used in a wide variety of locations (coffee shops, hotels, conferences, employee homes) that are outside of the organization's normal physical perimeter. Devices can easily be lost or stolen, and any unprotected data on the device could be retrieved by the thief. These examples illustrate the problem:

- A mobile device like a laptop is stolen on average once every 50 seconds. The location where the most laptops are stolen in North America is Chicago, followed by Houston, Detroit, and Los Angeles.[7]

- One-third of all laptops stolen in the U.S. go missing from public schools. Residential property is the second most common location.[8]

- Consumer-owned laptops are most often stolen in August and September (as students return to school) and November and December (during holiday shopping).[9]

Laptop theft is especially prevalent at airports. The airport with the highest number of thefts is Atlanta, followed by Miami, Orlando, Chicago, Los Angeles, and San Francisco. Table 10-5 lists the top five areas where airport laptop theft occurs.[10]

Area of airport	Percentage of laptops stolen
Luggage/storage area	29
Terminal/boarding area	22
Other	19
Airplane	18
Check-in/security	12

Table 10-5 **Top five areas for airport laptop theft**

Almost one-third of all laptops stolen or left behind at airport security are never recovered.[11]

In addition to loss or theft, merely using a mobile device in a public area can be considered a risk. Users must constantly guard against shoulder surfing by strangers who want to view sensitive information being displayed on the phone or view a user's password as it is being entered.

Shoulder surfing is covered in Chapter 2.

Connecting to Public Networks

Mobile devices must use public external networks for their Internet access. Because these networks are beyond the control of the organization, attackers can eavesdrop on the data transmissions and view sensitive information. In addition, these open networks may be susceptible to man-in-the-middle or replay attacks.

Location Tracking

Mobile devices with *global positioning system (GPS)* capabilities typically run **location services**. These services can identify the location of a person carrying a mobile device or a specific store or restaurant. This enables the location of a friend to be identified or the address of the nearest coffee shop to be displayed. Location services are used extensively by social media, navigation systems, weather systems, and other mobile-aware applications. One increasing use of location services is to enable a smartphone to immediately display a coupon whenever a user comes in close proximity to a store or restaurant.

Mobile devices using location services are at increased risk of targeted physical attacks. An attacker can easily determine where the user and the mobile device are currently located, and use that information to follow the user in order to steal the mobile device or inflict harm upon the person. In addition, attackers can compile over time a list of people with whom the user associates and the types of activities they perform in particular locations in order to craft attacks.

Installing Unsecured Applications

Software for traditional desktop computers is generally purchased from large and reputable vendors or is developed in-house. In contrast, mobile devices are designed to easily locate, acquire, and install apps from a variety of sources. These sources range from large reputable vendors to single-person developers and even hobbyists. Many apps are free while others can be purchased at a nominal cost. In many cases, however, these apps do not include security features.

Currently there are two dominant operating systems for mobile devices, Apple iOS and Google Android, on which the apps function. These two operating systems are very different and have different levels of security.

Two other operating systems for mobile devices are Microsoft Windows Phone and Blackberry. The market share for these products, however, is currently very small.

Apple iOS The Apple iOS operating system, developed by Apple for their mobile devices, is a closed and proprietary architecture. This makes it much more difficult for attackers to create an app that could compromise it and become a security risk. In addition, iOS uses its App Store, which is part of Apple iTunes, as the sole source for distributing apps. iTunes is Apple's "mobile ecosystem" infrastructure that is used to download apps, organize them, and even play digital audio and video on personal computers and other Apple products (iPod Touch, iPhone, iPad, etc.). All iOS apps must first be reviewed and approved by Apple before they can be made available on the iTunes Store. This allows Apple to screen for malicious apps and prevent them from being posted.

With more than one million apps in the Apple App Store, however, mobile app developers face stiff competition to have their app recognized and generate revenue. As a result, many app developers generate supplementary revenue by selling user data generated through the app to advertising networks and analytics companies. In addition, this user data collected by the app and sent back to the developer for distribution is transmitted without encryption so that an attacker could access it.

One recent study compared the top 200 iOS and Android apps (both paid and free) and found that iOS apps exhibited a greater percentage of risky behaviors than Android apps. Approximately 91 percent of iOS apps exhibit at least one risky behavior (compared to 83 percent of Android apps). Table 10-6 lists the percentage of Apple iOS free and paid apps that exhibit risky behavior.[12]

Risky behavior	Free apps (%)	Paid apps (%)
Location tracking	62	49
Access address book	35	31
Access calendar	2	3
Identify user or device	24	27
Share data with ad networks	48	27

Table 10-6　Apple iOS apps risky behavior

CAUTION Some Apple apps are designed to *circumvent* security. One app allows users to bypass entering a password on their desktop or notebook Mac. First the user installs the app on both their iPhone and Mac. Then when the user wants to log into her Mac she simply knocks twice (or taps hard) on the iPhone screen and the iPhone app then creates a connection with the Mac using Bluetooth and transmits the Mac password to the computer. If the user has a weak iPhone password, uses a short personal identification number (PIN), or has no login security on the iPhone (approximately half of iPhone users do not set their phones up with a screen lock), then an attacker who accesses the iPhone could have complete access to it as well as the entire contents of the Mac.

Google Android Unlike Apple iOS, the Google **Android** operating system for mobile devices is not proprietary but is entirely open for anyone to use or even modify. Apps for Android devices can be downloaded from the Google Play store (which does not screen apps like Apple does) or can be downloaded from an unofficial third-party website (called *sideloading*).

Generally this makes Android apps highly risky. One report says that the number of malicious Android apps worldwide increased by an additional 350,000 in one six-month period. Most of these malicious apps are imitations of legitimate popular apps or are Trojans. About 44 percent of these malicious apps are designed to trick users into downloading costly services, such as sending expensive text messages (with the malware developer receiving a portion of the charges). Other malicious Android apps steal user data (24 percent) or load adware (17 percent).[13]

Accessing Untrusted Content

Mobile devices have the ability to access untrusted content that other types of computing devices generally do not have. One example is *Quick Response (QR)* codes. These codes are a matrix or two-dimensional barcode first designed for the automotive industry in Japan. QR codes consist of black modules (square dots) arranged in a square grid on a white background, which can be read by an imaging device such as a mobile device's camera. A QR code for the Cengage Learning website is illustrated in Figure 10-5.

Figure 10-5　QR code

QR codes have become popular outside the automotive industry because of their fast readability and greater storage capacity compared to standard barcodes. Applications for these codes include product tracking, item identification, time tracking, document management, and general marketing. QR codes can store website URLs, plain text, phone numbers, email addresses, or virtually any alphanumeric data up to 4296 characters.

QR codes are internationally standardized.

An attacker can create an advertisement listing a reputable website, such as a bank, but include a QR code that contains a malicious URL. Once the user snaps a picture of the QR code using his mobile device's camera, the code directs the web browser on his mobile device to the attacker's imposter website or to a site that immediately downloads malware.

Bring Your Own Device (BYOD) Risks

Due to the widespread use of mobile devices, it is not always feasible to require an employee to carry a company-owned smartphone along with his own personal cell phone. Many organizations have adopted a *bring your own device (BYOD)* policy, which allows users to use their own personal mobile devices for business or organizational purposes.

Several risks are associated with BYOD:

- Users may erase the installed built-in limitations on their smartphone (called *jailbreaking* on Apple iOS devices or *rooting* on Android devices) to provide additional functionality. However, this also disables the built-in operating system security features on the phone.

- Personal mobile devices are often shared among family members and friends, subjecting sensitive corporate data installed on a user's device to outsiders.

- Different mobile devices have different hardware and different versions of operating systems, all of which contain different levels and types of security features. Technical support staff may be called upon to support hundreds of different mobile devices, creating a nightmare for establishing a security baseline.

- Mobile devices may be connected to a user's personal desktop computer that is infected, thus infecting the mobile device and increasing the risk of the organization's network becoming infected when the mobile device connects to it.

- There may be difficulties in securing the personal smartphone from an employee who was fired so that any corporate data on it can be erased.

Securing Mobile Devices

4.2 Summarize mobile security concepts and technologies.

Securing mobile devices requires several steps. These include the initial setup of the device, its ongoing management, and how to deal with the theft or loss of the device.

Device Setup

Several configurations should be considered when initially setting up a mobile device for use. These include disabling unused features, enabling screen locks, using encryption, and controlling access to devices.

Disable Unused Features Mobile devices include a wide variety of features for the user's convenience. However, each of these can also serve as a threat vector. It is important to disable unused features and turn off those that do not support the business use of the phone or that are rarely used. One of the features that should be disabled if it is not being regularly used is Bluetooth wireless data communication in order to prevent bluejacking and bluesnarfing.

Bluetooth is covered in Chapter 9.

Enable Lock Screen A **lock screen** prevents the mobile device from being used until the user enters the correct passcode such as a PIN or password. Lock screens should be configured so that whenever the device is turned on or is left idle for a period of time, the user must enter the passcode. Most mobile devices can be set to have the screen automatically lock after anywhere from 30 seconds to 30 minutes of inactivity.

A lock screen is a different setting from the *sleep time* setting that regulates when the device goes into a hibernation mode.

Some mobile devices can be configured so that after a specific number of failed attempts to enter the correct passcode, such as when a thief is trying to guess the code, additional security protections will occur, including:

- *Extend lockout period*. If an incorrect passcode is entered a specific number of times, the lockout period will be extended. For example, if the incorrect passcode is enter five consecutive times, the mobile device will remain completely locked for one minute. If the incorrect code is entered again after one minute, the device will stay locked for double that time, or two minutes. For each successive incorrect entry, the lockout period will double.

- *Reset to factory settings*. If an incorrect passcode is entered a set number of times, the user will be prompted to enter a special phrase to continue. If the phrase is correctly entered, then the user will have only one more opportunity to enter the correct passcode. If an incorrect passcode is entered again, the device will automatically reset to its factory settings and erase any data stored on it.

Most mobile devices have different options for the type of passcode that can be entered. Although they are the most secure option, strong passwords are seldom used on mobile devices. Instead, a popular but less secure option is to draw or swipe a specific pattern connecting dots, as illustrated in Figure 10-6.

10

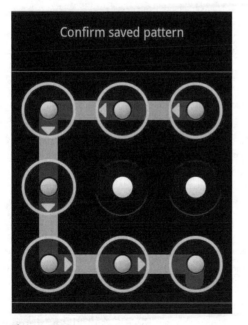

Figure 10-6 Swipe pattern
Source: OnlineAndroidTips.com

The least effective code is a short PIN. Many users opt to set a short four-digit PIN, similar to those used with a bank's automated teller machine (ATM). However, short PIN codes provide only a limited amount of security. An analysis of 3.4 million users' four-digit (0000–9999) PINs that were compromised revealed that users create predictable PIN patterns. The PIN *1234* was used in more than one out of every 10 PINs. Table 10-7 lists the five most common PINs and their frequency of use. Of the 10,000 potential PIN combinations, 26.83 percent of all PINs could be guessed by attempting just the top 20 most frequent PINs.[14]

PIN	Frequency of use (%)
1234	10.71
1111	6.01
0000	1.88
1212	1.19
7777	0.74

Table 10-7   **Most common PINs**

The research also revealed that the least common PIN was *8068*, which appeared in only 25 of the 3.4 million PINs.

Use Encryption Mobile devices that contain sensitive data should have that data encrypted to protect it. However, currently neither Apple iOS nor Google Android provide native cryptography, so third-party apps must be installed to provide encryption.

There are two encryption options. Full device encryption can be enabled to apply protection to all data stored on the device. Another option on mobile devices that contain both personal and corporate data is separating data storage into "containers" and encrypting only the sensitive data. This "containerization" also helps companies avoid data ownership privacy issues and legal concerns regarding a user's personal data stored in a BYOD setting. In addition, it allows companies to delete only business data when necessary without touching personal data. Third-party software is available to create containers on a mobile device's internal memory or the data can be separately stored on the device's removable storage microSD card.

Control Access A key to securing mobile devices is to control access to the device and its data by limiting who is authorized to use the information. Whereas lock screens can help restrict users from accessing the device itself through authentication, at a higher corporate level decisions must be made on who can access the data well before it is downloaded onto a mobile device.

Some organizations focus their efforts on securing the mobile device itself. With the proliferation of devices in a BYOD environment, however, this can be very difficult. Thus organizations are now beginning to focus their efforts on the *data* instead of just the *device* by extending data loss prevention to mobile devices.

Data loss prevention is covered in Chapter 4.

Device and App Management

Once the device is initially configured, both the device and its apps must be managed. There are two tools for facilitating this management, mobile device management and mobile application management.

Mobile Device Management (MDM)

Mobile device management (MDM) tools allow a device to be managed remotely by an organization. Typically MDM involves a server component, which sends out management commands to the mobile devices, and a client component, which runs on the mobile device to receive and implement the management commands. An administrator can then perform *over the air (OTA)* updates or configuration changes to one device, groups of devices, or all devices.

Some of the features that MDM tools provide include the ability to:

- Rapidly enroll new mobile devices (**on-boarding**) and quickly remove devices (**off-boarding**) from the organization's network
- Apply or modify default device settings
- Enforce encryption settings, antivirus updates, and patch management
- Display an acceptable use policy that requires consent before allowing access
- Configure email, calendar, contacts, Wi-Fi, and virtual private network (VPN) profiles OTA
- Discover devices accessing enterprise systems
- Approve or quarantine new mobile devices
- Distribute and manage public and corporate apps
- Securely share and update documents and corporate policies
- Detect and restrict jailbroken and rooted devices
- Selectively erase corporate data while leaving personal data intact

MDM also can facilitate **asset tracking,** or maintaining an accurate record of company-owned mobile devices, as well as **inventory control**, which is the operation of stockrooms where mobile devices are stored prior to their dispersal to employees.

Mobile Application Management (MAM)

Whereas MDM focuses on the device, **mobile application management (MAM)**, also called **application control**, comprises the tools and services responsible for distributing and controlling access to apps. These apps can be internally developed or commercially available apps.

MDM provides a high degree of control over the device but a lower level of control on the apps, whereas MAM gives a higher level of control over apps but less control over the device.

10

MAM initially controlled apps through *app wrapping*, which sets up a "dynamic" library of software routines and adds to an existing program (binary) to restrict parts of an app. For example, an app could be wrapped so that when it was launched a passcode had to be entered before it could be used. Another example is that a wrapped app could require a VPN for specific communications. Using an MAM originally required the use of an MDM as well, although newer versions of some mobile device operating systems have MAM incorporated into the software itself.

Device Loss or Theft

One of the greatest risks of a mobile device is the loss or theft of the device. Unprotected devices can be used to access corporate networks or view sensitive data stored on them. In order to reduce the risk of theft or loss:

- Keep the mobile device out of sight when traveling in a high-risk area.
- Avoid becoming distracted by what is on the device. Always maintain an awareness of your surroundings.
- When holding a device, use both hands to make it more difficult for a thief to snatch.
- Do not use the device on escalators or near transit train doors.
- White or red headphone cords may indicate they are connected to an expensive device. Consider changing the cord to a less conspicuous color.
- If a theft does occur, do not resist or chase the thief. Instead, take note of the suspect's description, including any identifying characteristics and clothing, and then call the authorities. Also contact the organization or wireless carrier and change all passwords for accounts accessed on the device.

If a mobile device is lost or stolen, several different security features can be used to locate the device or limit the damage. Many of these can be used through either MDM, a feature in the operating system, or an installed third-party app. These features are listed in Table 10-8.

Security feature	Explanation
Alarm	The device can generate an alarm even if it is on mute.
Last known location	If the battery is charged to less than a specific percentage, the device's last known location can be indicated on an online map.
Locate	The current location of the device can be pinpointed on a map through the device's GPS.
Remote lockout	The mobile device can be remotely locked and a custom message sent that is displayed on the login screen.
Thief picture	A thief who enters an incorrect passcode three times will have her picture taken through the device's on-board camera and emailed to the owner.

Table 10-8 Security features for locating lost or stolen mobile devices

If a lost or stolen device cannot be located, it may be necessary to perform **remote wiping**, which will erase sensitive data stored on the mobile device. This ensures that even if a thief is able to access the device, no sensitive data will be compromised.

Mobile Device App Security

4.2 Summarize mobile security concepts and technologies.

In addition to securing the mobile device, the apps on the device also should be secured. Just as the data can be encrypted, so too can the app itself if it is an application created in-house that could provide insight to an attacker about the corporate network or is an app that a competitor might want to steal. Also, apps can require that the user provide authentication such as a passcode before access is granted. In addition, MDMs can support *application whitelisting*, which ensures that only preapproved apps can run on the device.

MDMs also can enforce **geo-fencing**. Geo-fencing uses the device's GPS to define geographical boundaries where the app can be used. For example, a tablet containing patient information that leaves the hospital grounds or an employee who attempts to enter a restricted area with a device can result in an alert sent to an administrator. Geo-fencing requires the app to support **geo-tagging**, which is adding geographical identification data.

Geo-fencing is commonly used in law enforcement. An individual under house arrest is fitted with an ankle bracelet that will alert authorities if the individual leaves the house.

Many MDMs allow users to store usernames and passwords within the device itself. Known as **credential management** it serves as a "vault" for storing valuable authentication information. In addition, cryptographic keys can be stored and managed on the device.

10

BYOD Security

4.2 Summarize mobile security concepts and technologies.

There are several benefits of BYOD for companies:

- *Management flexibility*. BYOD eases the management burden by eliminating the need to select a wireless data carrier and manage plans for employees.

- *Less oversight*. Organizations do not need to monitor employee telecommunications usage for overages or extra charges.

- *Cost savings*. Because employees are responsible for their own mobile device purchases and wireless data plans (or receive a small monthly stipend), the company can save money.

- *Increased employee performance*. Employees are more likely to be productive while traveling or working away from the office if they are comfortable with their device.

- *Simplified IT infrastructure.* By using BYOD, companies do not have to support a remote data network for employees.

- *Reduced internal service.* BYOD reduces the strain on IT help desks because users will be primarily contacting their wireless data carrier for support.

In addition, users are eager to accept this flexibility. The user BYOD benefits include:

- *Choice of device.* Users want the freedom of choosing the type of mobile device they like instead of being forced to accept a corporate device that may not meet their individual needs.

- *Choice of carrier.* Most users have identified a specific wireless data carrier they want to use and often resist being forced to use a carrier with whom they have experienced a poor past relationship.

- *Convenience.* Many users already have their own device and want the convenience of using only a single device.

- *Attraction.* BYOD can be an appealing recruitment incentive for prospective employees.

Yet there are significant risks associated with BYOD, as spelled out in the section earlier in this chapter, "Bring Your Own Device (BYOD) Risks." BYOD security must be carefully thought out before implementing BYOD. MDMs and MAMs are important in managing BYOD devices.

Chapter Summary

- There are several different types of mobile devices. Portable computers are devices that closely resemble standard desktop computers. A laptop is designed to replicate the abilities of a desktop computer with only slightly less processing power yet is small enough to be used on a lap or small table. A notebook computer is a smaller version of a laptop computer that is designed to include only the most basic frequently used features of a standard computer in a smaller size that is easy to carry. A relatively new class of portable computers is the subnotebook computer that is even smaller than the standard notebook. Web-based computers are designed to be used primarily while connected to the Internet.

- Tablet computers are portable computing devices smaller than portable computers, larger than smartphones, and focused on ease of use. Tablets generally lack a built-in keyboard and rely on a touch screen. A smartphone includes an operating system that allows it to run apps and access the Internet, and it offers a broader range of functionality. A new class of mobile technology is wearable technology, devices that can be worn by the user instead of being carried. Mobile devices use flash memory for storage. All mobile devices have local nonremovable storage capabilities, and most devices also support removable data storage. A credit-card–sized peripheral that slides into a slot on a laptop computer can add additional functionality much like a card device that can be inserted into the bus expansion slot on a desktop computer. A Secure Digital (SD) card is a small form factor storage media and includes four card "families" available in three different form factors with different speed ratings.

- Several risks are associated with using mobile devices. Mobile devices are used in a wide variety of locations that are outside of the organization's normal physical perimeter. Devices can easily be lost or stolen, and any unprotected data on the device can be retrieved by a thief. Mobile devices must use public external networks for their Internet access. Because these networks are beyond the control of the organization, attackers can eavesdrop on data transmissions and view sensitive information. Mobile devices with GPS capabilities can run location services to identify the location of a person carrying a mobile device. This places the user at an increased risk of targeted physical attacks. Mobile devices are designed to easily locate, acquire, and install apps from a variety of sources. In many cases, security features may not be included in these apps. Currently there are two dominant operating systems for mobile devices, Apple iOS and Google Android, and these two operating systems are very different and have different levels of security. Mobile devices have the ability to access untrusted content that other types of computing devices generally do not have. Many organizations have adopted a bring your own device (BYOD) policy, which allows users to use their own personal mobile devices for business purposes. There are several risks associated with BYOD.

- Several configurations should be considered when initially setting up a mobile device. It is important to disable unused features and turn off those that do not support the business use of the device or that are rarely used. A lock screen prevents the mobile device from being used until the user enters the correct passcode. Some mobile devices can be configured so that after a specific number of failed attempts to enter the correct passcode, such as when a thief is trying to guess the code, additional security protections will occur. Mobile devices that contain sensitive data should have that data encrypted to protect it. A key to securing mobile devices is to control access to the device and its data by limiting who is authorized to use the information. At a corporate level, decisions must be made about who can access the data well before it is downloaded onto a mobile device.

- Mobile device management (MDM) tools allow a device to be managed remotely. Typically MDM involves a server component, which sends out management commands to the mobile devices, and a client component, which runs on the mobile device to receive and implement the management commands. MDM can facilitate asset tracking as well as inventory control. Mobile application management (MAM) consists of the tools and services responsible for distributing and controlling access to apps. If a mobile device is lost or stolen, several different security features can be used to locate the device or limit the damage. Many of these can be used through either MDM, a feature in the operating systems, or an installed third-party app. If the device cannot be located, it may be necessary to perform remote wiping, which will erase sensitive data stored on the mobile device.

- The apps on a mobile device also should be secured. MDMs can support application whitelisting, which ensures that only preapproved apps can be run on the device. In addition, MDMs can enforce geo-fencing. Geo-fencing uses the device's GPS to define geographical boundaries where the app can be used. There are several benefits of BYOD for companies and employees. Due to the risks of BYOD, however, BYOD security must be carefully thought out before implementation.

Key Terms

Android   The Google operating system for mobile devices that is not proprietary.

application control   See *mobile application management (MAM)*.

asset tracking   Maintaining an accurate record of company-owned mobile devices.

credential management   A secure repository for storing valuable authentication information on a mobile device.

geo-fencing   Using a mobile device's GPS to define geographical boundaries where an app can be used.

geo-tagging   Adding or allowing geographical identification data in a mobile app.

inventory control   The operation of stockrooms where mobile devices are stored prior to their dispersal.

iOS   The operating system for Apple mobile devices that is a closed and proprietary architecture.

location services   Services that can identify the location of a person carrying a mobile device or a specific store or restaurant.

lock screen   A technology that prevents a mobile device from being used until the user enters the correct passcode.

mobile application management (MAM)   The tools and services responsible for distributing and controlling access to apps. Also called *application control*.

mobile device management (MDM)   Tools that allow a device to be managed remotely.

off-boarding   The ability to quickly remove devices from the organization's network.

on-boarding   The ability to rapidly enroll new mobile devices.

remote wiping   The ability to remotely erase sensitive data stored on a mobile device.

Secure Digital (SD)   A small form factor storage media of a variety of different types and sizes.

smartphone   A mobile cell phone that has an operating system for running apps and accessing the Internet.

tablet   Portable computing device that is generally larger than smartphones and smaller than notebooks, and is focused on ease of use.

Review Questions

1. Which technology is NOT a characteristic of a mobile device?

   a.   physical keyboard

   b.   small form factor

   c.   local nonremovable data storage

   d.   data synchronization capabilities

2. Each optional feature is found on most mobile devices EXCEPT _____.
   a. digital camera
   b. microphone
   c. operating system
   d. removable storage media

3. Which type of computer most closely resembles a desktop computer?
   a. notebook
   b. subnotebook
   c. laptop
   d. netbook

4. Tablet computers are designed for _____.
   a. processing capabilities
   b. ease of use
   c. wireless connection speed
   d. hardware upgrades

5. One of the first mobile devices was a _____.
   a. personal digital assistant (PDA)
   b. tablet
   c. smartphone
   d. notebook

6. Which of these is NOT a size of SD cards?
   a. smallSD
   b. miniSD
   c. microSD
   d. full SD

7. Which of these is NOT a risk of connecting a mobile device to a public network?
   a. Public networks are beyond the control of the employee's organization.
   b. Public networks may be susceptible to man-in-the-middle attacks.
   c. Public networks are faster than local networks and can spread malware more quickly to mobile devices.
   d. Replay attacks can occur on public networks.

8. Mobile devices using _____ are at increased risk of targeted physical attacks.
   a. GPS
   b. captive portals
   c. location services
   d. Internet filters

10

9. What is one reason Android devices are considered to be at a higher security risk than iOS devices?

    a. iOS has been available longer and has more of its vulnerabilities worked out.

    b. Android apps can be sideloaded.

    c. All Android apps are free.

    d. Apple apps are written in a more secure binary language.

10. Which of these can a QR code NOT contain?

    a. image

    b. URL

    c. email address

    d. phone number

11. What prevents a mobile device from being used until the user enters the correct passcode?

    a. swipe identifier (SW-ID)

    b. keyboard

    c. touch pad

    d. lock screen

12. Bob has attempted to enter the passcode for his mobile device but keeps entering the wrong code. Now he is asked to enter a special phrase to continue. This means that Bob's mobile device is configured to _____.

    a. reset to factory settings

    b. extend the lockout period

    c. use PIN codes as passcodes

    d. double the amount of time he is prevented from accessing his device

13. What does containerization do?

    a. It splits operating system functions only on specific brands of mobile devices.

    b. It places all keys in a special vault.

    c. It slows down a mobile device to half speed.

    d. It separates personal data from corporate data.

14. What allows a device to be managed remotely?

    a. mobile device management (MDM)

    b. mobile application management (MAM)

    c. mobile resource management (MRM)

    d. mobile wrapper management (MWM)

15. Which of these is NOT a security feature for locating a lost or stolen mobile device?

    a. remote lockout

    b. last known good configuration

    c. alarm

    d. thief picture

16. What enforces the location in which an app can function by tracking the location of the mobile device?

    a. location resource management

    b. geo-fencing

    c. geo-tagging

    d. Graphical Management Tracking (GMT)

17. Which of these is NOT an advantage of BYOD for an organization?

    a. flexibility

    b. cost increases

    c. increased employee performance

    d. reduced internal service

18. Which mobile device is the smallest?

    a. subnotebook

    b. laptop

    c. notebook

    d. desktop

19. Where does a web-based computer store user files?

    a. on its hard disk drive

    b. on the Internet

    c. on a microSD card

    d. on a Type II PC card

20. Which of these is NOT a type of SD card?

    a. Standard-Capacity

    b. High-Capacity

    c. Low-Capacity

    d. eXtended-Capacity

10

Hands-On Projects

If you are concerned about installing any of the software in these projects on your regular computer, you can instead install the software in the Windows virtual machine created in the Chapter 1 Hands-On Projects 1-3 and 1-4. Software installed within the virtual machine will not impact the host computer.

Project 10-1: Creating and Using QR Codes

Quick Response (QR) codes can be read by an imaging device such as a mobile device's camera or online. In this project you will create and use QR codes.

1. Use your web browser to go to **www.qrstuff.com**.

The location of content on the Internet may change without warning. If you are no longer able to access the program through the above URL, use a search engine and search for "QR Stuff".

2. First create a QR code. Under **DATA TYPE** be sure that **Website URL** is selected.

3. Under **CONTENT** enter the URL **http://www.cengagebrain.com** as illustrated in Figure 10-7. Note how the **QR CODE PREVIEW** changes.

4. Under **OUTPUT TYPE**, click **DOWNLOAD** to download an image of the QR code.

5. Navigate to the location of the download and open the image. Is there anything you can tell by looking at this code?

6. Now use an online reader to interpret the QR code. Use your web browser to go to **qr4.cloudapp.net/Free-Online-QR-Code-Reader.aspx**.

The location of content on the Internet may change without warning. If you are no longer able to access the program through the above URL, use a search engine and search for "Free Online QR Code Reader".

7. Under **QR Code Services**, click **Choose File**.

8. Navigate to the location of the QR code that you downloaded on your computer and click **Open**.

9. Click **Upload QR Code Image**.

10. Under **QR Code Contents**, what does it display? How could an attacker use a QR code to direct a victim to a malicious website?

11. Return to **www.qrstuff.com**.

Figure 10-7   QR code
Source: qrstuff.com

10

12. Click **Google Maps Location** under **DATA TYPE**.

13. Under **Or use the field below to geo-locate an address** to enter an address with which you are familiar. Click **go**.

14. The latitude and longitude will be automatically entered under **CONTENT**.

15. Under **OUTPUT TYPE**, click **DOWNLOAD** to download an image of this QR code.

16. Navigate to the location of the download and open the image. How does it look different from the previous QR code? Is there anything you can tell by looking at this code?

17. Use your web browser to return to **qr4.cloudapp.net/Free-Online-QR -Code-Reader.aspx**.

18. Under **QR Code Services**, click **Choose File**.

19. Navigate to the location of the Google Maps Location QR code that you downloaded on your computer and click **Open**.

20. Click **Upload QR Code Image**.

21. Under **QR Code Contents** a URL will be displayed. Paste this URL into a web browser.

22. What does the browser display? How could an attacker use this for a malicious attack?

23. Return to **www.qrstuff.com**.

24. Click each option under **DATA TYPE** to view the different items that can be created by a QR code. Select three and indicate how they could be used by an attacker.

25. Close all windows.

Project 10-2: Software to Locate a Missing Laptop

If a mobile device is lost or stolen, there are several different security features that can be used to locate the device or limit the damage. Many of these can be used through an installed third-party app. In this project you will download and install software that can locate a missing laptop computer. Note that for this project a portable computer or desktop computer can be used.

1. Open your web browser and enter the URL **preyproject.com**.

The location of content on the Internet may change without warning. If you are no longer able to access the program through the above URL, use a search engine and search for "Prey Project".

2. Click **FAQ**.

3. Read through the questions so you will understand what Prey does.

4. Click **Download**.

5. Select the latest version for your computer.

6. When the file finishes downloading, run the program and follow the default installation procedures.

7. Click **Finish** to configure the Prey settings.

8. Be sure that **New user** is selected. Click **Next**.

9. Enter your information to create an account and click **Create**.

10. Go to **panel.preyproject.com**.

11. Enter your login information, and on the **All your devices** page, click the name of your recently added device.

12. You will then receive in your email a link to go to the Prey control panel. Save this link for future reference.

13. Click the question mark next to **Get active connections** to change the setting from **NO** to **YES**.

14. Do the same with each of the other settings that by default are set to **NO** and change them to **YES**.

15. Click **Save changes**.

16. Click the **Hardware** tab to review the hardware settings from this device.

17. Click **Main**.

18. Under **Actions to perform**, click the question mark next to **Alarm** to change from **Off** to **On**. What does this function perform?

19. Click the question mark next to **Alert** to change from **Off** to **On**. What does this function perform?

20. Click **Save changes**.

21. Move the slider from **OK** to **MISSING** to begin the tracking process.

22. It may take up to 10 minutes for the alarm to sound depending on how frequently the device checks into Prey.

23. When a report is generated, click **Reports** and read the information about the location of the device. Would this be sufficient information to find the missing device?

24. Click **Main**.

25. Move the slider from **Missing** to **OK**.

26. Click **Save changes**.

27. Close all windows.

Project 10-3: Installing Bluestacks Android Emulator

In this project you will install an Android emulator on a personal computer to test different antimalware tools.

Depending on your computer's configuration, it may be necessary to disable any virtualization software that is running prior to installing the Bluestacks emulator.

1. Use your web browser to go to **www.bluestacks.com**

The location of content on the Internet may change without warning. If you are no longer able to access the program through the above URL, use a search engine and search for "Bluestacks".

2. Click **DOWNLOAD XP, VISTA, WIN7/8**.

3. When the download is complete, launch the installation file and accept the defaults to install Bluestacks. Note that this installation may take several minutes to complete.

4. Once the application starts, press F11 if necessary to go from full screen mode to a smaller window.

5. If the **One time setup** screen appears, click **Continue**. You will need a Google account in order to access apps from the Google Play Store. In the **Add a Google Account** screen, answer the question **Do you want to add an existing account or create a new one?** by clicking either **Existing** if you already have an account or **New** to create an account. Follow the prompts in order to sign in or create your new account.

6. If you are asked **Join Google+**, click **Not now**.

7. Uncheck **Keep this phone backed up with my Google Account**. Click **Next**.

8. When the **One time setup** screen appears again, click **Continue**.

10

9. Under **Enable App Sync,** enter your Google account password.

10. When asked **Do you want the browser to remember this password?** click **Not now.**

11. When the **One time setup** screen appears again, click **Let's go!**

12. Remain in Bluestacks for the next project.

Project 10-4: Installing Security Apps Using Bluestacks Android Emulator

In this project you will download and install Android apps to test different antimalware tools. You must complete Project 10-3 before proceeding with this project.

1. Click **Accept.**

2. In the Google Play Store, click **APPS.**

3. Click the magnifying glass to open the online search tool.

If you were not asked to complete the "One Time Setup" in the previous project, you may be asked to perform that function now.

4. Enter **Lookout Security & Antivirus,** as illustrated in Figure 10-8.

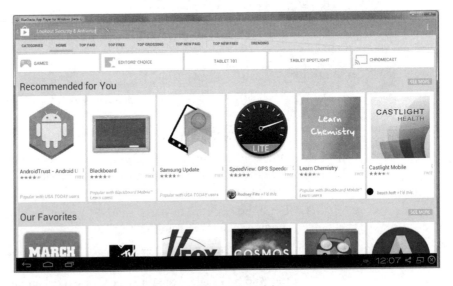

Figure 10-8 Searching for Lookout Security & Antivirus
Source: Lookout.com

5. If necessary, click on the Lookout Security & Antivirus icon.

6. Click **INSTALL.**

7. Click **ACCEPT.**

8. After Lookout has installed, click **OPEN.**

9. The **Welcome to Lookout!** screen appears. Click **Next**.

10. After reading the explanations about Lookout, click **Next** on each successive screen. Click **Done** on the final screen.

11. Create a password and enter it under **Password** and **Confirm password**.

12. Click **Start Protecting**.

13. If you are asked to upgrade, click **No Thanks**.

14. Click **Continue to Lookout Free**.

15. Click **Done**.

16. Click **Change Settings**.

17. Read through these configuration settings. Would you consider them adequate for a mobile device? Why or why not?

18. Click the **Home** button.

19. Under **RECENTLY PLAYED**, click **Lookout**.

20. Click **Scan Now** to scan the apps contained in Bluestacks. Would this be easy to use on a mobile device?

21. Explore the different options of Lookout.

22. Click the **Home** button.

23. Under **RECENTLY PLAYED**, click **Search**.

24. Enter **Security** and press **Enter**.

25. Scroll down through the different apps available.

26. Select a different mobile antivirus app and install it. Compare its features to Lookout. Which do you prefer? Why?

27. Click the **Home** button.

28. Under **RECENTLY PLAYED**, click **Search**.

29. Enter **Security** and press **Enter**.

30. Select a different security app and install it. How easy were these apps to install and configure? How do they compare with comparable desktop antimalware apps?

31. Close all windows.

Case Projects

CASE PROJECTS

Case Project 10-1: Mobile Device Management Tools

Use the Internet to identify and compare three different mobile device management (MDM) tools. Create a table that lists their various features for on-boarding, off-boarding, configuration, quarantine, modification of device settings, etc. Which of the tools would you recommend? Why?

Case Project 10-2: Mobile Application Management Tools

Although not as widely used as MDMs, mobile application management (MAM) tools can provide a higher degree of security by securing apps on a mobile device. Use the Internet to identify and compare three different MAM tools and create a table that compares their features. Which would you recommend? Why? Write a one-page paper on your research.

Case Project 10-3: App Wrapping Alternatives

MAM initially controlled apps through app wrapping, which sets up a "dynamic" library of software routines and adds to an existing program (binary) that restricts parts of an app. However, due to both technical and legal issues, app wrapping was not widely implemented. Recent versions of the Apple iOS include app wrapping alternatives, as does the Samsung KNOX technology. Use the Internet to research alternatives to app wrapping. How did app wrapping work? What were the problems encountered with it? What are the current alternatives? Would you consider them useable? Why? Write a one-page paper on your research.

Case Project 10-4: Security for Missing Mobile Devices

If a mobile device is lost or stolen, several different security features can be used to locate the device or limit the damage. Many of these can be used through an installed third-party app. Use the Internet to identify four apps, two each for iOS and Android, and create a table that compares their features. Use the information in Table 10-8 as a starting point. Create your own table comparing their different features. Include a paragraph that outlines which app you would prefer for iOS and Android.

Case Project 10-5: BYOD Policy

Use the Internet to locate BYOD policies from two different organizations. After reading that information, create your own BYOD policy for your school or place of employment. What restrictions should be enforced? What control should the organization have over personal devices? Write a one-page paper on the information that you find.

Case Project 10-6: Bay Pointe Security Consulting

Bay Pointe Security Consulting (BPSC) provides security consulting services to a wide range of businesses, individuals, schools, and organizations. BPSC has hired you as a technology student to help them with a new project and provide real-world experience to students who are interested in the security field.

The president of Mount Juliet College is considering implementing a BYOD policy for all employees. Although there is strong support from the faculty and staff, there is resistance from the IT department. Mount Juliet College has asked BPSC to make a presentation about BYOD, and BPSC has asked you to help them in the presentation.

1. Create a PowerPoint presentation for the staff about the advantages and risks of BYOD. Be sure to cover these from the perspective of the organization, the IT department, and the end-user. Your presentation should contain at least eight slides.

2. After the presentation, the IT director at Mount Juliet College sent to the president and you an email with a link to a blog that says BYODs are a "disaster waiting to happen" and would result in chaos for any organization. The president has asked you to provide additional information on tools that can be used to support BYODs. Write a one-page memo listing the features of MDMs and MAMs.

Case Project 10-7: Community Site Activity

The Information Security Community Site is an online companion to this textbook. It contains a wide variety of tools, information, discussion boards, and other features to assist learners. Go to **community.cengage.com/infosec**. Sign in with the login name and password that you created in Chapter 1.

Many developers of apps generate supplementary revenue by selling user data generated through the apps to advertising networks and analytics companies. Some app developers do not disclose that they do this, while others "bury" this information in the license agreement. However, users are not allowed to use the app unless they agree to sharing their data; that is, there is no facility to use the app without sharing your personal data.

Should this be allowed? What should be the penalty for an app developer that captures and shares your data with a third party if that possibility has not been disclosed to you? Should there be a provision that you would still be able to use the app if you disabled its data sharing feature? Post your thoughts about app data sharing on the discussion board.

10

References

1. "The Honey Stick project home page," *Streetwise Security Zone*, www.streetwise -security-zone.com/members/streetwise/adminpages/honeystickproject.

2. Charlie Rose, "Charlie Rose talks to Qualcomm's Paul Jacobs," *Bloomberg Businessweek*, Jan. 14–20, 2013, p. 37.

3. "Your wireless life," *The Wireless Association*, Nov. 2013, accessed Mar. 4, 2014, www.ctia.org/your-wireless-life/how-wireless-works/wireless-quick-facts.

4. Steven Vaughan-Nichols, "What a surprise! 2013 was a lousy year for PC sales," *ZD Net*, Jan. 10, 2014, accessed Mar. 4, 2014, www.zdnet.com/what-a-surprise-2013-was -a-lousy-year-for-pc-sales-7000025002/.

5. "Tablet computer sales will overtake notebooks by 2016," *VB/Mobile*, Aug. 15, 2012, accessed Sep. 3, 2012, http://venturebeat.com/2012/08/15/tablet-computer-sales-will -overtake-notebooks-by-2016/.

6. "Smartphones see accelerated rise to dominance," *HIS iSuppli Market Research*, Aug. 28, 2012, accessed Sep. 3, 2012, www.isuppli.com/Mobile-and-Wireless-Communications/News/Pages/Smartphones-See-Accelerated-Rise-to-Dominance.aspx.

7. "Absolute Software 2011 computer theft report," *Absolute Software*, May 23, 2012, accessed Sep. 2, 2012, http://blog.absolute.com/absolute-software-2011-computer-theft-report/.

8. *Ibid.*

9. *Ibid.*

10. "Computer theft report infographic," *Absolute Software*, Aug. 29, 2012, accessed Sep. 2, 2012, http://blog.absolute.com/computer-theft-report-infographic/.

11. "Op-Ed: A reporter's worst nightmare," *News Is My Business*, Aug. 20, 2012, accessed Sep. 2, 2012, http://newsismybusiness.com/op-ed-a-reporters-worst-nightmare/.

12. "Winter 2014 app reputation report," *Appthority*, accessed Mar. 9, 2014, https://www.appthority.com/resources.

13. "TrendLabs 2012 mobile threat and security roundup: Repeating history," accessed Mar. 9, 2014, www.trendmicro.com/cloud-content/us/pdfs/security-intelligence/reports/rpt-repeating-history.pdf.

14. "Pin analysis," *DataGenetics*, accessed Mar. 10, 2014, http://datagenetics.com/blog/september32012/index.html.

## part VI

Access Control and Identity Management

A foundation principle of security is that only approved users be allowed to access resources. In this part, you will learn how to control access (Chapter 11) and authenticate users (Chapter 12).

Chapter 11   Access Control Fundamentals

Chapter 12   Authentication and Account Management

Access Control Fundamentals

After completing this chapter, you should be able to do the following:

- Define access control and list the four access control models
- Describe how to implement access control
- Explain the different types of authentication services

Today's Attacks and Defenses

"She looks after every tax dollar as if it were her own," was the glowing praise heaped upon Rita Crundwell by a city commissioner for her exemplary work as city comptroller of Dixon, Illinois. However, the commissioner was more accurate than he may have imagined. The very next year Crundwell pleaded guilty to embezzling an astonishing $53 million from her city over 20 years, the largest known embezzlement to have ever occurred in the public sector. Her scheme unfolded only when she took an extended vacation away from work.[1]

Best known as Ronald Reagan's boyhood home, Dixon is a northern Illinois community of 16,000 about 100 miles west of Chicago. Crundwell began working for the city when she was only 17, still in high school. In 1983, she became city treasurer and comptroller, overseeing all of Dixon's finances. Crundwell was well-known and well-liked in the community.

In late 1990 Crundwell opened an account at a local bank. Designated as the "Reserve Sewer Capital Development Account—Reserve Fund (RSCDA)," no other city employee knew of its existence. The next year she quietly transferred more than $181,000 of the city's money to her account. Each year thereafter she became bolder in stealing from Dixon, so that in 2008 alone she transferred $5.8 million into her RSCDA account.

Crundwell began to live a lavish lifestyle on the city's money. She poured millions of dollars into her RC Quarter Horses business. She built a large ranch in Dixon, traveled in expensive motor homes (one cost in excess of $2.1 million) to various quarter horse competitions, and invested heavily in quarter horses. Once she spent $335,000 to purchase two horses and an additional $260,000 for a new horse trailer to transport them. Because her salary was only $80,000, Dixon residents raised questions about Crundwell's lavish lifestyle. The concerns were quickly brushed aside by rumors that a wealthy investor was providing funds for her quarter horse business. Another rumor claimed that her family owned all the cell phone towers in Illinois.

In sharp contrast, the city of Dixon suffered dramatically due to Crundwell's thefts. Dixon started reporting significant annual deficits, often more than $1 million each year. The police department could not purchase needed equipment; aging vehicles could not be replaced; grass at the city cemetery was not cut; and during the last 10 years of Crundwell's embezzlement, the city resurfaced an average of 6.5 blocks out of more than 100 miles of paved roads. When city department heads asked Crundwell about funding for their departments, she simply replied that the city did not have the money.

Crundwell's scheme unraveled in late 2011 when she took an extended vacation. During her absence a city employee opened her mail, discovered the RSCDA account

(continued)

and her checks, and turned the information over to the mayor, who immediately called the Federal Bureau of Investigation (FBI). Crundwell was later arrested and pled guilty. She was sentenced to 20 years in prison, the maximum allowable sentence. She also was ordered to pay back the entire $53.7 million. Her assets—including 400 horses, three houses, jewelry, and property in Florida—were seized and sold, recovering about $10 million. In addition, Dixon sued its auditors for not detecting the fraud and reached a settlement of $40 million.

It is speculated that despite the massive amounts of money stolen, the embezzlement scheme by Crundwell might have continued had she not taken an extended vacation.

Consider an employee named Braden who returns to the office one evening to finish a report. When he enters the building, he must first pass the night security guard. Braden shows his ID badge, but because the guard only works nights, he does not know Braden. The guard takes time to examine the photo on Braden's ID badge and compare it to his face, as well as to ask questions that only the "real" Braden would know. Once Braden's identity is confirmed, the guard allows him to enter the building. However, Braden cannot go into just any office in the building; he has been given a key that opens only his office door, thus restricting his admission to only that room.

The actions of the security guard and the restrictions placed on Braden's key are similar to those used in information security. A user first must be identified as an authorized user, such as by logging in with a user name and password to a laptop computer. Because that laptop connects to the corporate network that contains critical data, it is important also to restrict user access to only the software, hardware, and other resources for which the user has been approved. These two acts—authenticating only approved users and controlling their access to resources—are important foundations in information security.

This chapter introduces you to the principles and practices of controlling access. You will first examine access control terminology, the four standard control models, and their best practices. Then you will investigate implementing access control. Finally, you will explore authentication services, which are used to verify approved users. Additional authentication techniques will be explored in the next chapter.

What Is Access Control?

2.1 Explain the importance of risk-related concepts.

5.2 Given a scenario, select the appropriate authentication, authorization or access control.

As its name implies, **access control** is granting or denying approval to use specific resources; it is controlling access. *Physical access control* consists of fencing, hardware door locks, and mantraps to limit contact with *devices*. In a similar way, *technical access control* consists of technology restrictions that limit users on computers from accessing *data*. Access control has a set of associated terminology used to describe its actions. There are four standard access control models as well as specific practices used to enforce access control.

 Most home users have full privileges on their personal computers so they can install programs, access files, or delete folders at will and give no thought to access control. In the enterprise, however, where multiple individuals access information, access control is essential.

Access Control Terminology

Consider the following scenario: Gabe is babysitting Mia one afternoon. Before leaving the house, his mother tells Gabe that a package delivery service is coming to pick up a box, which is inside the front door. Soon there is a knock at the door, and as Gabe looks out he sees the delivery person standing on the porch. Gabe asks her to display her employee credentials, which the delivery person is pleased to do. Gabe then opens the door and allows her inside, but only to the area by the front door, to pick up the box.

This scenario illustrates the basic steps in limiting access. The package delivery person first presents her *identification* to Gabe to be reviewed. A user accessing a computer system would likewise present credentials or identification, such as a user name, when logging on to the system. Checking the delivery person's credentials to be sure that they are authentic and not fabricated is *authentication*. Computer users, likewise, must have their credentials authenticated to ensure that they are who they claim to be, often by entering a password, fingerprint scan, or other means of authentication. *Authorization*, granting permission to take the action, is the next step. Gabe allowed the package delivery person to enter the house because she had been preapproved by Gabe's mother and her credentials were authentic. Likewise, once users have presented their identification and been authenticated, they can be authorized to log in to the system. Gabe, however, allowed the package delivery person access only to the area by the front door in order to retrieve the box; he did not allow her to go upstairs or into the kitchen. Likewise, computer users are granted *access* only to the specific services, devices, applications, and files needed in order to perform their job duties. The basic steps in this access control process are summarized in Table 11-1.

Action	Description	Scenario example	Computer process
Identification	Review of credentials	Delivery person shows employee badge	User enters user name
Authentication	Validate credentials as genuine	Gabe reads badge to determine it is real	User provides password
Authorization	Permission granted for admittance	Gabe opens door to allow delivery person in	User authorized to log in
Access	Right given to access specific resources	Delivery person can only retrieve box by door	User allowed to access only specific data

Table 11-1 Basic steps in access control

Although *authorization* and *access* are often used as synonymous, in technical access control, they are different steps. A computer user may receive *authorization* (be granted permission) to log in to a system by presenting valid identification and authentication, and yet that authorization does not always provide *access* to specific resources.

Other terminology is used to describe how computer systems impose technical access control:

- *Object*. An object is a specific resource, such as a file or a hardware device.
- *Subject*. A subject is a user or a process functioning on behalf of the user that attempts to access an object.
- *Operation*. The action that is taken by the subject over the object is called an operation. For example, a user (subject) may attempt to delete (operation) a file (object).

Individuals are given different roles in relationship to access control objects or resources. These roles are summarized in Table 11-2.

Role	Description	Duties	Example
Owner	Person responsible for the information	Determines the level of security needed for the data and delegates security duties as required	Determines that the file SALARY.XLSX can be read only by department managers
Custodian	Individual to whom day-to-day actions have been assigned by the owner	Periodically reviews security settings and maintains records of access by end-users	Sets and reviews security settings on SALARY.XLSX
End-user	User who accesses information in the course of routine job responsibilities	Follows organization's security guidelines and does not attempt to circumvent security	Opens SALARY.XLSX

Table 11-2   **Roles in access control**

11

Instead of the formal term *custodian*, the more generic term *administrator* is most commonly used to describe this role.

Figure 11-1 illustrates the technical access control process and terminology.

A common attack that exploits vulnerabilities in access control to gain access to restricted resources is called privilege escalation. Privilege escalation was covered in Chapter 3.

Access Control Models

Consider a network system administrator who needs to act as an access control custodian. One afternoon she must give a new employee access to specific servers and files. With tens

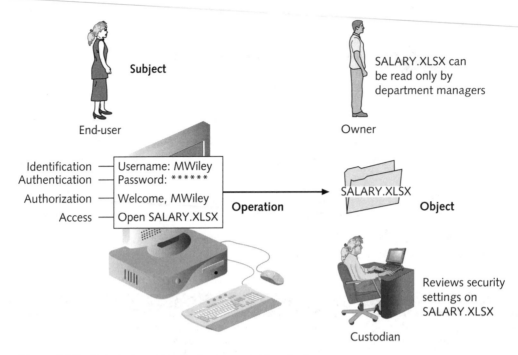

Figure 11-1 Technical access control process and terminology

of thousands of files scattered across a multitude of different servers, and with the new employee being given different access privileges to each file (for example, he can view one file but not edit it, and in a different file he can edit but not delete), controlling access could prove to be a daunting task. However, this job is made easy by the fact that the hardware and software have a predefined *framework* that the custodian can use for controlling access. This framework is called an **access control model** and is embedded in the software and hardware. The custodian can use the appropriate model to configure the necessary level of control.

 Access control models that are used by custodians for access control are neither created nor installed by custodians or users. Instead, these models are already part of the software and hardware.

There are four major access control models: Discretionary Access Control (DAC), Mandatory Access Control (MAC), Role Based Access Control (RBAC), and Rule Based Access Control (RBAC).

 These are variously referred to as access control models, methods, modes, techniques, or types. Note that Rule Based Access Control uses the same four-letter abbreviation (RBAC) as Role Based Access Control.

Discretionary Access Control (DAC) The Discretionary Access Control (DAC) model is the least restrictive. With the DAC model, every object has an owner, who has total control over that object. Owners can create and access their objects freely. In addition, the owner can give permissions to other subjects over these objects. For example, with DAC, Amanda could access the files EMPLOYEES.XLSX and SALARIES.XLSX as well as paste the contents of EMPLOYEES.XLSX into a newly created document MY_DATA.XLSX. She also could give Abby access to all of these files but allow Brian to only read EMPLOYEES. XLSX.

DAC is used on operating systems such as most types of UNIX and Microsoft Windows. Figure 11-2 illustrates the types of control that a Windows owner has over an object. These controls can be configured so that another user can have full or limited access over a file, printer, or other object.

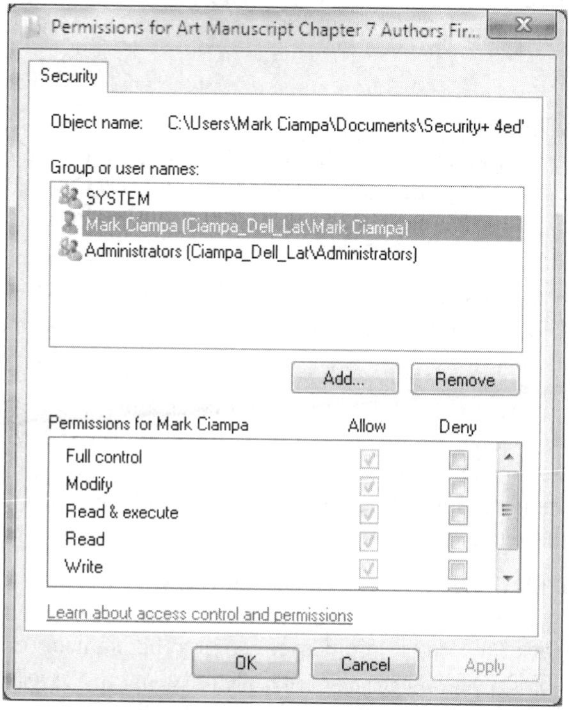

Figure 11-2 Windows Discretionary Access Control (DAC)
Source: Microsoft Windows

DAC has two significant weaknesses. First, although it gives a degree of freedom to the subject, DAC poses risks in that it relies on decisions by the end-user to set the proper level of security. As a result, incorrect permissions might be granted to a subject or permissions might be given to an unauthorized subject. A second weakness is that a subject's permissions will be "inherited" by any programs that the subject executes. Attackers often take advantage of this inheritance because end-users frequently have a high level of privileges. Malware that is downloaded onto a user's computer that uses the DAC model would then run at the same high level as the user's privileges.

One method of controlling DAC inheritance is to automatically reduce the user's privilege level. For example, Microsoft Windows uses Internet Explorer Enhanced Protected Mode, which prevents malware from executing code through the use of elevated privileges. A user with administrative privileges who accesses the Internet using Internet Explorer will automatically have reduced privileges during that web session. This helps prevent user and system files or settings from being changed without the user's explicit permission.

Mandatory Access Control (MAC) The opposite of DAC is the most restrictive access control model known as **Mandatory Access Control** (**MAC**). MAC assigns users' access controls strictly according to the custodian's desires. This is considered the most restrictive access control model because the user has no freedom to set any controls. This model is typically found in military settings in which security is of supreme importance.

There are two key elements to MAC:

- *Labels*. In a system using MAC, every entity is an object (laptops, files, projects, and so on) and is assigned a classification label. These labels represent the relative importance of the object, such as *confidential, secret*, and *top secret*. Subjects (users, processes, and so on) are assigned a privilege label (sometimes called a *clearance*).

- *Levels*. A hierarchy based on the labels is also used, both for objects and subjects. *Top secret* has a higher level than *secret*, which has a higher level than *confidential*.

MAC grants permissions by matching object labels with subject labels based on their respective levels. To determine if a file can be opened by a user, the object and subject labels are compared. The subject must have an equal or greater level than the object in order to be granted access. For example, if the object label is *top secret*, yet the subject has only a lower *secret* clearance, access is denied. Subjects cannot change the labels of objects or other subjects in order to modify the security settings.

In the original MAC model, all objects and subjects were assigned a numeric access level and the access level of the subject had to be higher than that of the object in order for access to be granted. For example, if EMPLOYEES.XLSX was assigned Level 500 while SALARIES.XLSX was assigned Level 700, then a user with an assigned level of 600 could access EMPLOYEES.XLSX (Level 500) but not SALARIES.XLSX (Level 700). This model was later modified to use labels instead of numbers.

There are two major implementations of MAC. The first is called the *lattice model*. A *lattice* is a type of screen or fencing that is used as a support for climbing garden plants. Different "rungs" on the MAC lattice model have different security levels, and subjects are assigned a "rung" on the lattice just as objects are. There can even be multiple lattices placed beside each other to allow for different groups of labels. For example, one subject label lattice could use the clearances *confidential, secret*, and *top secret* while a corresponding subject label lattice could use *public, restricted*, and *top clearance*. The rungs of each subject lattice would still align with the rungs on the object security lattice.

Another implementation of MAC is the *Bell-LaPadula (BLP) model*. Although this model is very similar to the lattice model, it contains an additional restriction not found in the original lattice model. This protection prevents subjects from creating a new object or performing specific functions on objects that are at a lower level than their own. For example, a user with clearance *secret* should not have the ability to open a document at the *secret* level and then paste its contents to a newly created document at the *confidential* level. A variation of the BLP model is the *Biba Integrity model*, which goes beyond the BLP model and adds protecting data integrity in addition to confidentiality.

Microsoft Windows uses a MAC implementation called *Mandatory Integrity Control (MIC)*. Based on the Biba model, MIC ensures data integrity by controlling access to securable objects. A *security identifier (SID)* is a unique number issued to the user, group, or session. Each time a user logs in, the system retrieves the SID for that user from the database, and then uses that SID to identify the user in all subsequent interactions with Windows security. Windows links the SID to an *integrity level*. Objects such as files, processes, services, and devices are assigned integrity levels—low, medium, high, and system—that determine their levels of protection or access. In order to write to or delete an object, the integrity level of the subject must be equal to or greater than the object's level. This ensures that processes running with a low integrity level cannot write to an object with a medium integrity level.

MIC works in addition to Windows DAC. Windows first checks any requests against MIC, and if they pass, then it checks DAC.

This can be seen in practice through a Window's feature known as *User Account Control (UAC)*. The standard user (lower level) who attempts to install software (higher level) is first required by UAC to enter the higher-level administrative password before being allowed to proceed (which elevates the action to the higher level). As an additional check, an administrative user also must confirm the action (yet he does not need to enter the administrative password, as shown in Figure 11-3). In this way, UAC attempts to match the subject's privilege level with that of the object.

11

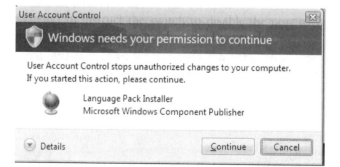

Figure 11-3 Windows User Account Control (UAC) prompt
Source: Microsoft Windows

The Windows UAC interface also provides extended information. A shield icon warns users if they attempt to access any feature that requires UAC permission. In addition, the UAC prompt includes a description of the requested action to inform the user of the requested action. The UAC prompts are color-coded to indicate the level of risk, from red (highest risk) to gray (lowest risk).

Role Based Access Control (RBAC) The third access control model is **Role Based Access Control (RBAC)**, sometimes called *Non-Discretionary Access Control*. RBAC is considered a more "real-world" access control than the other models because the access under RBAC is based on a user's job function within an organization. Instead of setting permissions for each user or group, the RBAC model assigns permissions to particular roles in the organization, and then assigns users to those roles. Objects are set to be a certain type, to which subjects with that particular role have access. For example, instead of creating a user account for Ahmed and assigning specific privileges to that account, the role *Business_Manager* can be created based on the privileges an individual in that job function should have. Then Ahmed and all other business managers in the organization can be assigned to that role. The users and objects inherit all of the permissions for the role.

Roles are different from groups. Although users may belong to multiple groups, a user under RBAC can be assigned only one role. In addition, under RBAC, users cannot be given permissions beyond those available for their role.

Rule Based Access Control (RBAC) The **Rule Based Access Control (RBAC)** model, also called the *Rule-Based Role-Based Access Control (RB-RBAC)* model or *automated provisioning*, can dynamically assign roles to subjects based on a set of rules defined by a custodian. Each resource object contains a set of access properties based on the rules. When a user attempts to access that resource, the system checks the rules contained in that object to determine if the access is permissible.

Rule Based Access Control is often used for managing user access to one or more systems, where business changes may trigger the application of the rules that specify access changes. For example, a subject on Network A wants to access objects on Network B, which is located on the other side of a router. This router contains the set of access control rules and can assign a certain role to the user, based on her network address or protocol, which will then determine whether she will be granted access. Similar to MAC, Rule Based Access Control cannot be changed by users. All access permissions are controlled based on rules established by the custodian or system administrator.

Table 11-3 summarizes the features of the four access control models.

Best Practices for Access Control

Enforcing technical access control using the access control models is only one means of providing security. In addition, establishing a set of "best practices" for limiting access also can help secure systems and their data. These practices include separation of duties, job rotations, least privilege, implicit deny, and mandatory vacations.

Name	Restrictions	Description
Mandatory Access Control (MAC)	End-user cannot set controls	Most restrictive model
Discretionary Access Control (DAC)	Subject has total control over objects	Least restrictive model
Role Based Access Control (RBAC)	Assigns permissions to particular roles in the organization and then users are assigned to roles	Considered a more "real-world" approach
Rule Based Access Control (RBAC)	Dynamically assigns roles to subjects based on a set of rules defined by a custodian	Used for managing user access to one or more systems

Table 11-3   Access control models

Separation of Duties News headlines such as "County Official Charged with Embezzlement" appear all too frequently. Often this fraud results from a single user being trusted with a set of responsibilities that place the person in complete control of the process. For example, one person may be given total control over the collection, distribution, and reconciliation of money. If no other person is involved, it may be too tempting for that person to steal, knowing that nobody else is watching and that there is a good chance the fraud will go undetected. To counteract this possibility, most organizations require that more than one person be involved with functions that relate to handling money, because it would require a conspiracy of all the individuals in order for fraud to occur.

Likewise, a foundational principle of computer access control is not to give one person total control. Known as **separation of duties**, this practice requires that if the fraudulent application of a process could potentially result in a breach of security, the process should be divided between two or more individuals. For example, if the duties of the owner and the custodian are performed by a single individual, it could provide that person with total control over all security configurations. It is recommended that these responsibilities be divided so that the system is not vulnerable to the actions performed by a single person.

Job Rotation Another way to prevent one individual from having too much control is to use **job rotation**. Instead of one person having sole responsibility for a function, individuals are periodically moved from one job responsibility to another. Employees can rotate either within their home department or across positions in other departments. The best rotation procedure involves multiple employees rotating across many positions for different lengths of time to gain exposure to different roles and functions.

Job rotation has several advantages:

- It limits the amount of time that individuals are in a position to manipulate security configurations.

- It helps to expose any potential avenues for fraud by having multiple individuals with different perspectives learn about the job and uncover vulnerabilities that someone else may have overlooked.

- Besides enhancing security, job rotation also can reduce "burnout," increase employee satisfaction, provide a higher level of employee motivation, enhance and improve skills and competencies leading to promotional advancement, and provide an increased appreciation for peers and decreased animosity between departments.

Job rotation, however, also has disadvantages. In some cases employees may not be in a specific job long enough to develop proficiency, and productivity may be lost in the time it takes to train employees in new tasks. Also, job rotation is often limited to less specialized positions. For these reasons, job rotation may not always be practical.

Least Privilege Consider the rooms in a large office building, each of which has a door with a lock. Different classifications of employees can be provided different keys to open doors based on their jobs. For example, a typical office worker would not be given a key that opens every door in the building. There simply is no need for this classification of worker to have access to the contents of every room. If that key were lost or stolen, the thief could easily enter any office at any time to remove its contents. Instead, a typical office worker would be provided only a key that opens the door to his office because that is all that is needed for the worker to do his job. A member of the building's security staff, on the other hand, would have a key that could open any office because her job function would require it.

Limiting access to rooms in a building is a model of the information technology security principle of **least privilege**. Least privilege in access control means that only the minimum amount of privileges necessary to perform a job or function should be allocated. This helps reduce the attack surface by eliminating unnecessary privileges that could provide an avenue for an attacker.

Least privilege should apply both to users and to processes running on the system. For processes, it is important that they be designed so that they run at the minimum security level needed in order to correctly function. Users also should be given only those privileges for which they need to perform their required tasks. Different options for securely providing privileges exist. For example, in Apple Mac OS X and Linux/UNIX systems, the system administrator can give specific users or groups access to higher-level commands without revealing the main root password to those users or groups. A user must simply enter the *sudo* (superuser do) command, which prompts the user for his personal password and confirms the request to execute a command (previously approved by the system administrator). The *sudo* command also logs all actions as an audit trail.

One of the reasons why home computers are so frequently and easily compromised is that they use an account with administrative rights. A more secure option is to use an account with lower privileges and then invoke administrative privileges only when necessary. For Apple Mac OS X users, one option is to use the *sudo* command. Windows users can right-click a program from the Start menu and select *Run as administrator*.

Although least privilege is recognized as an important element in security, the temptation to assign higher levels of privileges is great due to the challenges of assigning users lower security levels. Several of those challenges are listed in Table 11-4.

Earlier versions of Windows placed severe restrictions on a standard user to the extent that modifying power management settings and installing new fonts were prohibited. Later versions of Windows allowed more freedom by giving standard users the ability to modify settings that posed no security risks.

Challenge	Explanation
Legacy applications	Many older software applications were designed to run only with a high level of privilege. Many of these applications were internally developed and are no longer maintained or are third-party applications that are no longer supported. Redeveloping the application may be seen as too costly. An alternative is to run the application in a virtualized environment.
Common administrative tasks	In some organizations, basic system administration tasks are performed by the user, such as connecting printers or defragmenting a disk. Without a higher level of privilege, users must contact the help desk so that a technician can help with the tasks.
Software installation/upgrade	A software update that is not centrally deployed can require a higher privilege level, which can mean support from the local help desk. This usually results in decreased productivity and increased support costs.

Table 11-4   Challenges of least privilege

Implicit Deny Implicit deny in access control means that if a condition is not explicitly met, the request for access is rejected. (*Implicit* means that something is implied or indicated but not actually expressed.) For example, a network router may have a rule-based access control restriction. If no conditions match the restrictions, the router rejects access because of an implicit *deny all* clause: any action that is not explicitly permitted is denied. When creating access control restrictions, it is recommended that unless the condition is specifically met, access should be denied.

The DAC models that use *explicit deny* have stronger security because access control to all users is denied by default and permissions must be explicitly granted to approved users.

11

Mandatory Vacations In many fraud schemes, the perpetrator must be present every day in order to continue the fraud or keep it from being exposed. Many organizations require **mandatory vacations** for all employees to counteract this. For sensitive positions within an organization, an audit of the employees' activities is usually scheduled while they are away on vacation.

Implementing Access Control

1.2 Given a scenario, use secure network administration principles.

4.4 Implement the appropriate controls to ensure data security.

5.2 Given a scenario, select the appropriate authentication, authorization or access control.

5.3 Install and configure security controls when performing account management, based on best practices.

Several technologies can be used to implement access control. These include access control lists, Group Policy, and account restrictions.

Access Control Lists (ACLs)

An **access control list (ACL)** is a set of permissions that is attached to an object. This list specifies which subjects are allowed to access the object and what operations they can perform on it. When a subject requests to perform an operation on an object, the system checks the ACL for an approved entry in order to decide if the operation is allowed.

 ACLs are the oldest and most basic form of access control. These became popular in the 1970s with the growth of multiuser systems, particularly UNIX systems, when it became necessary to limit access to files and data on shared systems. Later, as multiuser operating systems for personal use became popular, the concept of ACLs was added to them. Today all major operating systems—UNIX/Linux, Apple Mac, and Windows—make use of ACLs at some level.

Although ACLs can be associated with any type of object, these lists are most often viewed in relation to files maintained by the operating system. For example, a user setting permissions in a UNIX DAC operating system would use the commands *setfacl* and *getacl l* (to set and display ACL settings, respectively), as shown in Figure 11-4. Operating systems with graphical user interfaces, such as Microsoft Windows, display a table of permissions like that shown previously in Figure 11-2.

```
$ setfacl -m user:tdk:rw- samplefile
$ getacl samplefile
# file: samplefile
# owner: reo
# group: sysadmin
user::rw-user:
tdk:rw-             #effective:r--
group::r--          #effective:r--
mask:r--
other:r--
```

Figure 11-4 UNIX file permissions

The structure behind ACL tables can be complex. In the Microsoft Windows, Linux, and Mac OS X operating systems, each entry in the ACL table is known as an *access control entry (ACE)*. In Windows, the ACE includes four items of information:

- *An SID for the user account, group account, or logon session.* An SID is a unique number issued to the user, group, or session that is used to identify the user in all subsequent interactions with Windows security.

- *An access mask that specifies the access rights controlled by the ACE.* An *access mask* is a value that specifies the rights that are allowed or denied, and is also used to request access rights when an object is opened.

- *A flag that indicates the type of ACE.* This flag corresponds to a particular set of operations that can be performed on an object.

- *A set of flags that determines whether objects can inherit permissions.*

When an SID has been used as the unique identifier for a user or group, it cannot ever be used again to identify another user or group.

Although widely used, ACLs have limitations. First, using ACLs is not efficient. The ACL for each file, process, or resource must be checked every time the resource is accessed. ACLs control not only user access to system resources but also application and system access as well. This means that in a typical computing session ACLs are checked whenever a user accesses files, when applications are opened (along with the files and applications those applications open and modify), when the operating system applications perform functions, and so on. A second limitation to ACLs is that they can be difficult to manage in an enterprise setting where many users need to have different levels of access to many different resources. Selectively adding, deleting, and changing ACLs on individual files, or even groups of files, can be time-consuming and open to errors, particularly if changes must be made frequently.

Group Policies

In an organization with hundreds of computers, how can access control be implemented? One solution for organizations using Microsoft Windows is to use **Group Policy**. This is a Microsoft Windows feature that provides centralized management and configuration of computers and remote users using the Microsoft directory services Active Directory (AD). Group Policy is usually used in enterprise environments to enforce access control by restricting user actions that may pose a security risk, such as changing access to certain folders or downloading executable files. Group Policy can control an object's script for logging on and off the system, folder redirection, Internet Explorer settings, and Windows Registry settings (the *registry* is a database that stores settings and options for the operating system).

Group Policy settings are stored in *Group Policy Objects (GPOs)*. These objects may, in turn, be linked to multiple domains or websites, which allows for multiple systems and users to be updated by a change to a single GPO. Group Policies are analyzed and applied for computers when they start up and for users when they log in. Every 1 to 2 hours, the system looks for changes in the GPO and reapplies them as necessary.

11

The time period to look for changes in the GPO can be adjusted.

A *Local Group Policy (LGP)* has fewer options than a Group Policy. Generally a LGP is used to configure settings for systems that are not part of Active Directory. Although older versions of Windows using LGP could not be used to apply policies to individual users or groups of users, recent Windows versions support multiple Local Group Policy objects, which allows setting Local Group Policy for individual users.

Although Group Policies can assist custodians in managing multiple systems, some security settings configured by Group Policy can be circumvented by a determined user. For this reason, Group Policy is often viewed as a way to establish a security configuration baseline for users, but not as an "ironclad" security solution.

Account Restrictions

Another means of enforcing access control is to place restrictions on user accounts. Two common account restrictions are time-of-day restrictions and account expiration.

Time-of-Day Restrictions Time-of-day restrictions can be used to limit when a user can log in to a system or access resources. In addition to time-of-day restrictions, some programs can also even restrict what websites are viewed and which programs are used by specific users. When setting these restrictions, a custodian would typically indicate the times a user is restricted from accessing the system or resources. Figure 11-5 illustrates time-of-day restrictions implemented by indicating the specific days and times, while Figure 11-6 shows setting the restrictions with a graphical interface.

Days to Block:	Time of day to block:
☑ Sunday	Start Blocking 18 Hour 30 Minute
☐ Monday	End Blocking 24 Hour 0 Minute ☐ All Day
☑ Tuesday	
☑ Wednesday	**Time Zone**
☐ Thursday	(GMT-06:00) Central America, Central Time (US & Canada) ▼
☑ Friday	☐ Automatically adjust for daylight savings time
☑ Saturday	

Figure 11-5 Time-of-day restrictions setting specific times and days

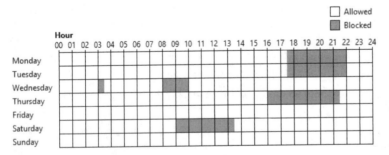

Figure 11-6 Time-of-day restrictions using a GUI

Source: Microsoft Windows

Time-of-day restrictions in a Windows environment can be set through a Group Policy.

Account Expiration *Orphaned accounts* are user accounts that remain active after an employee has left an organization, while a *dormant account* is one that has not been accessed for a lengthy period of time. These types of accounts can be a security risk. For example, an employee who left under unfavorable circumstances may be tempted to "get even" with the organization by stealing or erasing sensitive information through her account. Dormant accounts that are left unchecked can provide an avenue for an attacker to exploit without the fear of the actual user or a system administrator noticing.

Several recommendations for dealing with orphaned or dormant accounts include:

- *Establish a formal process.* It is important that a formal procedure be in place for disabling accounts for employees who are dismissed or resign from the organization.
- *Terminate access immediately.* It is critical that access be ended as soon as the employee is no longer part of the organization.
- *Monitor logs.* Current employees are sometimes tempted to use an older dormant account instead of their own account. Monitoring logs can help prevent use of other accounts.

Locating and terminating orphaned and dormant accounts, however, still remains a problem for many organizations. To assist with controlling orphaned and dormant accounts, **account expiration** can be used. Account expiration is the process of setting a user's account to expire. Account expiration is not the same as password expiration. Account expiration indicates when an account is no longer active; password expiration sets the time when a user must create a new password in order to access his account. Account expiration can be explicit, in that the account expires on a set date, or it can be based on a specific number of days of inactivity. For example, in a Linux or UNIX system, when an account is created, an option allows for a set number of days after a password has expired before the account itself will be disabled.

 The Last Logon attribute in Microsoft Active Directory (AD) does not store the date and time of when an account was last accessed but instead records a value such as *128271382542862359*, which is the number of 100-nanosecond intervals that have elapsed since January 1, 1601. Fortunately, there is a simple way to convert this to a more common date and time format.

11

Authentication Services

3.5 Explain types of application attacks.

5.1 Compare and contrast the function and purpose of authentication services.

A user accessing a computer system must present credentials or identification when logging in to the system. Verifying the person's credentials to be sure that they are genuine and the user actually is who she claims to be is the process of *authentication*. Authentication services can be provided on a network by a dedicated authentication, authorization, and accounting (AAA) server or by an authentication server, which is a server that performs only authentication. The most common type of authentication and AAA servers are RADIUS, Kerberos, Terminal Access

Control Access Control Systems (TACACS), generic servers built on the Lightweight Directory Access Protocol (LDAP), and Security Assertion Markup Language (SAML).

RADIUS

RADIUS, or **Remote Authentication Dial In User Service**, was developed in 1992 and quickly became the industry standard with widespread support across nearly all vendors of networking equipment. RADIUS was originally designed for remote dial-in access to a corporate network. However, the word *Remote* in the name RADIUS is now almost a misnomer because RADIUS authentication is used for more than connecting to remote networks. With the development of IEEE 802.1x port security for both wired and wireless LANs, RADIUS has seen even greater usage.

 IEEE 802.1x is covered in Chapter 8 for wired networks and in Chapter 9 for wireless networks.

A RADIUS client is not the device requesting authentication, such as a desktop system or wireless notebook computer. Instead, a RADIUS client is typically a device such as a wireless access point (AP) or dial-up server that is responsible for sending user credentials and connection parameters in the form of a RADIUS message to a RADIUS server. The RADIUS server authenticates and authorizes the RADIUS client request, and sends back a RADIUS message response. RADIUS clients also send RADIUS accounting messages to RADIUS servers. The strength of RADIUS is that messages are never sent directly between the wireless device and the RADIUS server. This prevents an attacker from penetrating the RADIUS server and compromising security.

 RADIUS standards also support the use of what are called RADIUS proxies. A RADIUS proxy is a computer that forwards RADIUS messages between RADIUS clients, RADIUS servers, and other RADIUS proxies.

The detailed steps for RADIUS authentication with a wireless device in an IEEE 802.1x network, which are illustrated in Figure 11-7, are:

1. A wireless device, called the *supplicant* (it makes an "appeal" for access), sends a request to an AP requesting permission to join the WLAN. The AP prompts the user for the user ID and password.

2. The AP, serving as the *authenticator* that will accept or reject the wireless device, creates a data packet from this information called the *authentication request*. This packet includes information such as identification of the specific AP that is sending the authentication request and the user name and password. For protection from eavesdropping, the AP (acting as a RADIUS client) encrypts the password before it is sent to the RADIUS server. The authentication request is sent over the network from the AP to the RADIUS server. This communication can be done over either a local area network or a wide area network. This allows the RADIUS clients to be remotely located from the RADIUS server. If the RADIUS server cannot be reached, the AP can usually route the request to an alternate server.

3. When an authentication request is received, the RADIUS server validates that the request is from an approved AP and then decrypts the data packet to access the user name and password information. This information is passed on to the appropriate security user database. This could be a text file, UNIX password file, a commercially available security system, or a custom database.

4. If the user name and password are correct, the RADIUS server sends an authentication acknowledgment that includes information on the user's network system and service requirements. For example, the RADIUS server may tell the AP that the user needs TCP/IP. The acknowledgment can even contain filtering information to limit a user's access to specific resources on the network. If the user name and password are not correct, the RADIUS server sends an authentication reject message to the AP and the user is denied access to the network. To ensure that requests are not responded to by unauthorized persons or devices on the network, the RADIUS server sends an authentication key, or signature, identifying itself to the RADIUS client.

5. If accounting is also supported by the RADIUS server, an entry is started in the accounting database.

6. Once the server information is received and verified by the AP, it enables the necessary configuration to deliver the wireless services to the user.

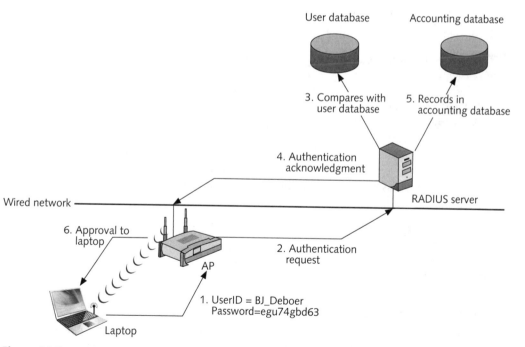

Figure 11-7   RADIUS authentication

RADIUS allows an organization to maintain user profiles in a central database that all remote servers can share. Doing so increases security, allowing a company to set up a policy that can be applied at a single administered network point. Having a central service also means that it is easier to track usage for billing and for keeping network statistics.

Kerberos

Kerberos is an authentication system developed by the Massachusetts Institute of Technology (MIT) in the 1980s and used to verify the identity of networked users. Named after a three-headed dog in Greek mythology that guarded the gates of Hades, Kerberos uses encryption and authentication for security. Kerberos will function under Windows, Apple Mac OS X, and Linux.

Kerberos is used most often by universities and government agencies.

Kerberos has often been compared to using a driver's license to cash a check. A state agency, such as the Department of Motor Vehicles (DMV), issues a driver's license that has these characteristics:

- It is difficult to copy.
- It contains specific information (name, address, weight, height, etc.).
- It lists restrictions (must wear corrective lenses, etc.).
- It will expire at some future date.

Kerberos, which works in a similar fashion, is typically used when a user attempts to access a network service and that service requires authentication. The user is provided a ticket that is issued by the Kerberos authentication server, much as a driver's license is issued by the DMV. This ticket contains information linking it to the user. The user presents this ticket to the network for a service. The service then examines the ticket to verify the identity of the user. If the user is verified, he is then accepted. Kerberos tickets share some of the same characteristics as a driver's license: tickets are difficult to copy (because they are encrypted), they contain specific user information, they restrict what a user can do, and they expire after a few hours or a day. Issuing and submitting tickets in a Kerberos system is handled internally and is transparent to the user.

Kerberos is available as a free download.

Terminal Access Control Access Control System (TACACS)

Similar to RADIUS, **Terminal Access Control Access Control System (TACACS)** is an authentication service commonly used on UNIX devices that communicates by forwarding user authentication information to a centralized server. The centralized server can be either a TACACS database or a database such as a Linux or UNIX password file with TACACS protocol support. The first version was simply called TACACS, while a later version introduced in 1990 was known as **Extended TACACS (XTACACS)**. The current version is **TACACS+**.

TACACS is a proprietary system developed by Cisco Systems.

There are several differences between TACACS+ and RADIUS. These are summarized in Table 11-5.

Feature	RADIUS	TACACS+
Transport protocol	User Datagram Protocol (UDP)	Transmission Control Protocol (TCP)
Authentication and authorization	Combined	Separated
Communication	Unencrypted	Encrypted
Interacts with Kerberos	No	Yes
Can authenticate network devices	No	Yes

Table 11-5   **Comparison of RADIUS and TACACS+**

Lightweight Directory Access Protocol (LDAP)

A *directory service* is a database stored on the network itself that contains information about users and network devices. It contains information such as the user's name, telephone extension, email address, login name, and other facts. The directory service also keeps track of all the resources on the network and a user's privileges to those resources, and grants or denies access based on the directory service information. Directory services make it much easier to grant privileges or permissions to network users.

The International Organization for Standardization (ISO) created a standard for directory services known as *X.500*. The purpose of the X.500 standard was to standardize how the data was stored so that any computer system could access these directories. It provides the capability to look up information by name (a *white-pages service*) and to browse and search for information by category (a *yellow-pages service*). The information is held in a *directory information base (DIB)*. Entries in the DIB are arranged in a tree structure called the *directory information tree (DIT)*. Each entry is a named object and consists of a set of attributes. Each attribute has a defined attribute type and one or more values. The directory defines the mandatory and optional attributes for each class of object. Each named object may have one or more object classes associated with it.

The X.500 standard itself does not define any representation for the data stored like user names. What is defined is the structural form of names. Systems that are based on the X.500, such as Microsoft Active Directory, define their own representation.

The X.500 standard defines a protocol for a client application to access an X.500 directory called the *Directory Access Protocol (DAP)*. However, the DAP is too large to run on a personal computer. The **Lightweight Directory Access Protocol (LDAP)**, sometimes called X.500 Lite, is a simpler subset of DAP. The primary differences between DAP and LDAP are:

- Unlike X.500 DAP, LDAP was designed to run over TCP/IP, making it ideal for Internet and intranet applications. X.500 DAP requires special software to access the network.

- LDAP has simpler functions, making it easier and less expensive to implement.

- LDAP encodes its protocol elements in a less complex way than X.500 that enables it to streamline requests.

 LDAP was originally developed by Netscape Communications and the University of Michigan in 1996.

If the information requested is not contained in the directory, DAP only returns an error to the client requesting the information, which must then issue a new search request. By contrast, LDAP servers return only results, making the distributed X.500 servers appear as a single logical directory.

By default LDAP traffic is transmitted in cleartext. LDAP traffic can be made secure by using Secure Sockets Layer (SSL) or Transport Layer Security (TLS). This is known as **Secure LDAP** or *LDAP over SSL (LDAPS)*.

LDAP makes it possible for almost any application running on virtually any computer platform to obtain directory information. Because LDAP is an open protocol, applications need not worry about the type of server hosting the directory. Today many LDAP servers are implemented using standard relational database management systems as the engine, and communicate via the Extensible Markup Language (XML) documents served over the hypertext transport protocol (HTTP).

However, a weakness of LDAP is that it can be subject to **LDAP injection attacks**. These attacks, similar to SQL injection attacks, can occur when user input is not properly filtered. This may allow an attacker to construct LDAP statements based on user input statements. The attacker could then retrieve information from the LDAP database or modify its content. The defense against LDAP injection attacks is to examine all user input before processing.

 SQL injection attacks are covered in Chapter 3.

Security Assertion Markup Language (SAML)

Security Assertion Markup Language (SAML) is an Extensible Markup Language (XML) standard that allows secure web domains to exchange user authentication and authorization data. This allows a user's login credentials to be stored with a single identity provider instead of being stored on each web service provider's server. SAML is used extensively for online e-commerce business-to-business (B2B) and business-to-consumer (B2C) transactions.

XML is covered in Chapter 3.

The steps of a SAML transaction, which are illustrated in Figure 11-8, are:

1. The user attempts to reach a website of a service provider that requires a username and password.

2. The service provider generates a SAML authentication request that is then encoded and embedded into a URL.

3. The service provider sends a redirect URL to the user's browser that includes the encoded SAML authentication request, which is then sent to the identity provider.

4. The identity provider decodes the SAML request and extracts the embedded URL. The identity provider then attempts to authenticate the user either by asking for login credentials or by checking for valid session cookies.

5. The identity provider generates a SAML response that contains the authenticated user's username, which is then digitally signed using asymmetric cryptography.

6. The identity partner encodes the SAML response and returns that information to the user's browser.

7. Within the SAML response, there is a mechanism so that the user's browser can forward that information back to the service provider, either by displaying a form that requires the user to click on a *Submit* button or by automatically sending to the service provider.

8. The service provider verifies the SAML response by using the identity provider's public key. If the response is successfully verified, the user is logged in.

11

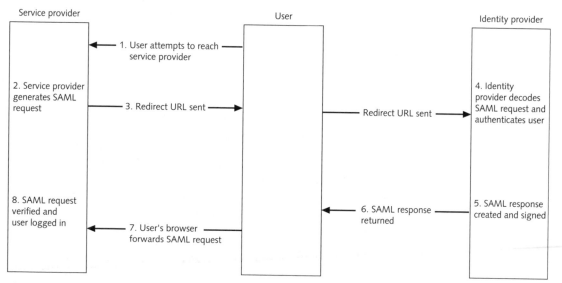

Figure 11-8 SAML transaction

 SAML works with multiple protocols including Hypertext Transfer Protocol (HTTP), Simple Mail Transfer Protocol (SMTP), and File Transfer Protocol (FTP).

Chapter Summary

- Access control is the process by which resources or services are denied or granted. Physical access control consists of protections to limit contact with devices, while technical access control is the technology restrictions that limit users on computers from accessing data. Access control has its own set of terminology. Hardware and software have a predefined *framework* that the custodian can use for controlling access; this is called an access control model. There are four major access control models. The Discretionary Access Control model gives the user full control over any objects that he owns. In the Mandatory Access Control model, the end-user cannot change any security settings. Role Based Access Control maps the user's job function with security settings. Rule Based Access Control dynamically assigns roles based on a set of rules.

- Best practices for implementing access control include separation of duties (dividing a process between two or more individuals), job rotation (periodically moving workers from one job responsibility to another), using the principle of least privilege (giving users only the minimal amount of privileges necessary in order to perform their job functions), using implicit deny (rejecting access unless it is specifically granted), and mandatory vacations (requiring that employees take periodic vacations).

- Implementing access control methods include using access control lists (ACLs), which are provisions attached to an object. ACLs define which subjects are allowed to access which objects and specify which operations they can perform. Group Policy is a Microsoft Windows feature that provides centralized management and the configuration of computers that use Active Directory. Time of day restrictions limit when a user can log into a system or access resources. Account expiration specifies when a user's account expires.

- Authentication services can be provided on a network by a dedicated AAA or authentication server. RADIUS, or Remote Authentication Dial In User Service, has become the industry standard with widespread support across nearly all vendors of networking equipment. The strength of RADIUS is that messages are never directly sent between the wireless device and the RADIUS server. This prevents an attacker from penetrating the RADIUS server and compromising security. Kerberos is an authentication system used to verify the identity of networked users. Similar to RADIUS, Terminal Access Control Access Control System (TACACS), XTACACS, and TACACS+ are protocol specifications that forward user name and password information to a centralized server. A directory service is a database stored on the network itself that contains information about users and network devices, including all the resources on the network and a user's privileges to those resources, and can grant or deny access based on the directory service information. One implementation of a directory service as an authentication is the Lightweight Directory Access

Protocol (LDAP). Security Assertion Markup Language (SAML) is an XML standard that allows secure web domains to exchange user authentication and authorization data with one another.

Key Terms

access control   The mechanism used in an information system for granting or denying approval to use specific resources.

access control list (ACL)   A set of permissions that is attached to an object.

access control model   A predefined framework found in hardware and software that a custodian can use for controlling access.

account expiration   The process of setting a user's account to expire.

Discretionary Access Control (DAC)   The least restrictive access control model in which the owner of the object has total control over it.

Extended TACACS (XTACACS)   The second version of the Terminal Access Control Access Control System (TACACS) authentication service.

Group Policy   A Microsoft Windows feature that provides centralized management and configuration of computers and remote users.

implicit deny   Rejecting access unless a condition is explicitly met.

job rotation   The act of moving individuals from one job responsibility to another.

Kerberos   An authentication system developed by the Massachusetts Institute of Technology (MIT) and used to verify the identity of networked users.

LDAP injection attack   An attack that constructs LDAP statements based on user input statements, allowing the attacker to retrieve information from the LDAP database or modify its content.

least privilege   Providing only the minimum amount of privileges necessary to perform a job or function.

Lightweight Directory Access Protocol (LDAP)   A protocol for a client application to access an X.500 directory.

Mandatory Access Control (MAC)   The most restrictive access control model, typically found in military settings in which security is of supreme importance.

mandatory vacations   Requiring that all employees take vacations.

Remote Authentication Dial In User Service (RADIUS)   An industry standard authentication service with widespread support across nearly all vendors of networking equipment.

Role Based Access Control (RBAC)   A "real-world" access control model in which access is based on a user's job function within the organization.

Rule Based Access Control (RBAC)   An access control model that can dynamically assign roles to subjects based on a set of rules defined by a custodian.

Secure LDAP   Transporting LDAP traffic over Secure Sockets Layer (SSL) or Transport Layer Security (TLS).

11

Security Assertion Markup Language (SAML) An Extensible Markup Language (XML) standard that allows secure web domains to exchange user authentication and authorization data.

separation of duties The practice of requiring that processes should be divided between two or more individuals.

TACACS+ The current version of the Terminal Access Control Access Control System (TACACS) authentication service.

Terminal Access Control Access Control System (TACACS) An authentication service commonly used on UNIX devices that communicates by forwarding user authentication information to a centralized server. The current version is TACACS+.

time-of-day restriction Limitation imposed as to when a user can log in to a system or access resources.

Review Questions

1. What is the current version of TACACS?

    a. XTACACS

    b. TACACS+

    c. TACACS v5

    d. TRACACS

2. How is the Security Assertion Markup Language (SAML) used?

    a. It is a backup to a RADIUS server.

    b. It allows secure web domains to exchange user authentication and authorization data.

    c. It is an authenticator in IEEE 802.1x.

    d. It is no longer used because it has been replaced by LDAP.

3. A RADIUS authentication server requires that the _____ be authenticated first.

    a. user

    b. authentication server

    c. supplicant

    d. authenticator

4. Which of these is NOT part of the makeup of the AAA elements in network security?

    a. auditing usage (accounting)

    b. controlling access to network resources (authentication)

    c. enforcing security policies (authorization)

    d. determining user need (analyzing)

5. With the development of IEEE 802.1x port security, the _____ authentication server has seen even greater usage.

   a. RADIUS

   b. RDAP

   c. DAP

   d. AAA

6. Which authentication protocol is available as a free download that runs on Microsoft Windows, Apple Mac OS X, and Linux?

   a. LDAP

   b. IEEE 802.1x

   c. RADIUS

   d. Kerberos

7. What is the version of the X.500 standard that runs on a personal computer over TCP/IP?

   a. Lite RDAP

   b. DAP

   c. LDAP

   d. IEEE X.501

8. A user entering her user name would correspond to the _____ action in access control.

   a. authentication

   b. identification

   c. authorization

   d. access

9. A process functioning on behalf of the user who attempts to access a file is known as a(n) _____.

   a. object

   b. operation check

   c. subject

   d. resource

10. What is the name given to the individual who periodically reviews security settings and maintains records of access by users?

    a. supervisor

    b. custodian

    c. owner

    d. manager

11

11. In the _____ model, the end-user cannot change any security settings.

    a. Discretionary Access Control

    b. Restricted Access Control

    c. Security Access Control

    d. Mandatory Access Control

12. Which statement about Rule Based Access Control is true?

    a. It requires that a custodian set all rules.

    b. It is considered obsolete today.

    c. It dynamically assigns roles to subjects based on rules.

    d. It is considered a real-world approach by linking a user's job function with security.

13. _____ in access control means that if a condition is not explicitly met, then access is to be rejected.

    a. Prevention control

    b. Denial of duties

    c. Implicit deny

    d. Explicit rejection

14. Which of these is a set of permissions that is attached to an object?

    a. access control list (ACL)

    b. Subject Access Entity (SAE)

    c. object modifier

    d. security entry designator

15. Which Microsoft Windows feature provides centralized management and configuration of computers and remote users who are using Active Directory?

    a. Windows Register Settings

    b. AD Management Services (ADMS)

    c. Group Policy

    d. Resource Allocation Entities

16. A(n) _____ constructs LDAP statements based on user inputs in order to retrieve information from the database or modify its contents.

    a. RBASE plug-in attack

    b. SQL/LDAP insert attack

    c. modified Trojan attack

    d. LDAP injection attack

17. What is the least restrictive access control model?
    a. Discretionary Access Control (DAC)
    b. Role Based Access Control (RBAC)
    c. Mandatory Access Control (MAC)
    d. Rule Based Access Control (RBAC)

18. The principle known as _____ in access control means that each user should be given only the minimal amount of privileges necessary for that person to perform his job function.
    a. mandatory limitations
    b. enterprise security
    c. least privilege
    d. deny all

19. A(n) _____ is the person who is responsible for the information, determines the level of security needed for the data, and delegates security duties as required.
    a. owner
    b. administrator
    c. custodian
    d. end-user

20. In the Mandatory Access Control (MAC) model, every subject and object _____.
    a. must be given a number from 200–900
    b. is restricted and cannot be accessed
    c. is assigned a label
    d. can be changed by the owner

11

Hands-On Projects

If you are concerned about installing any of the software in these projects on your regular computer, you can instead install the software in the Windows virtual machine created in the Chapter 1 Hands-On Projects 1-3 and 1-4. Software installed within the virtual machine will not impact the host computer.

Project 11-1: Using Windows Local Group Policy Editor

The Windows Local Group Policy (LGP) has fewer options than a Group Policy, and generally an LGP is used to configure settings for systems that are not part of

Active Directory. In this project you will explore different options of using the Windows LGP.

1. Click **Start** and type **mmc**.

2. Click **File** and **Add/Remove Snap-in**.

3. In **Add or Remove Snap-ins** dialog box, click **Group Policy Object Editor** and click **Add**.

4. In the **Select Group Policy Object** dialog box, click **Browse**.

5. Click **This computer** and then **OK**.

6. Click **Finish**.

7. Click **OK** to display the Console Root screen as shown in Figure 11-9.

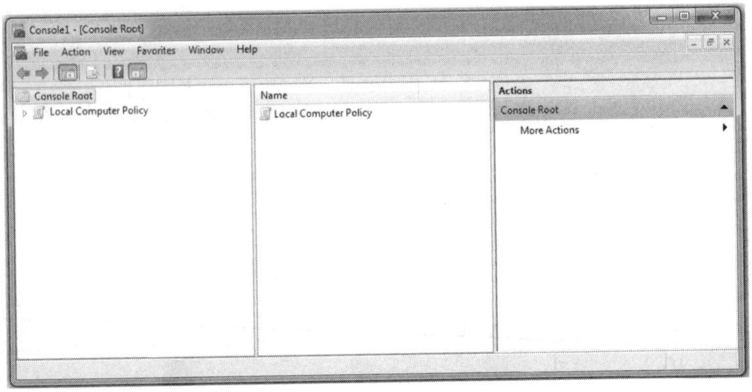

Figure 11-9   Console Root screen
Source: Microsoft Windows

8. Administrative Templates are registry-based policy settings that appear in the Local Group Policy Editor. In the left pane under **Console Root,** click **Local Computer Policy.**

9. Double-click **Computer Configuration**.

10. Double-click **Administrative Templates.**

11. Click **All Settings.** In the middle pane scroll down through the different LPGs that can be set on the local computer. Which settings can you identify that directly relate to security?

12. Now change the LGP so that only strong TLS cryptography will be used. In the left pane, double-click **Network**.

13. Click **SSL Configuration Settings**.

14. In the center pane, double-click **SSL Cipher Suite Order**. This identifies which SSL suites will be supported.

15. Click **Enabled** if necessary.

16. Open a blank Notepad document.

17. Now copy and paste all suites listed in the left pane under **SSL Cipher Suites** into the Notepad document. Note that this is one continuous line with no line breaks and no additional space.

18. Locate **SSL_CK_RC4_128_WITH_MD5,** which is one of the weakest SSL cipher suites.

19. Erase this listing. Make sure that there are no additional space or commas.

20. Copy this line onto the clipboard and paste it under **SSL Cipher Suites.**

21. Click **Apply.**

22. Click **OK.**

23. Close all windows.

Project 11-2: Using Discretionary Access Control to Share Files in Windows

Discretionary Access Control can be applied in Microsoft Windows. In this project, you will set up file sharing with other users.

You should have a standard user named "Abby Lomax" created in Windows and a Notepad document Sample.txt created by an administrative user in order to complete this assignment.

1. Right-click the file **Sample.txt.**

2. To see the current permissions on this file, click **Properties,** and then click the **Security** tab.

3. Click your user name and then click **Edit.**

4. Under **Permissions for [user],** click **Deny** for the **Read** attribute.

5. Click **Apply** and **Yes** at the warning dialog box.

6. Click **OK** in the Properties dialog box and then click **OK** in the Sample.txt dialog box.

7. Double-click the file **Sample.txt** to open it. What happens?

8. Now give permissions to Abby Lomax to open the file. Right-click the file **Sample.txt.**

9. Click **Share with** and then click **Specific people.**

10. Click the drop-down arrow and select **Abby Lomax.** Click **Add.**

11. Click **Share.**

12. Click **Done** when the sharing process is completed.

13. Now log in as Abby Lomax. Click **Start** and the **right arrow** and then **Switch User.**

14. Log in as Abby Lomax.

15. Right-click **Start** and then click **Explore.**

16. Navigate to your account name and locate the file Sample.txt.

17. Double-click **Sample.txt** to open the file. Using DAC, permissions have been granted to another user.

18. Close all windows.

Project 11-3: Enabling IEEE 802.1x

In this project, you will enable support for 802.1x on a Microsoft Windows computer with a wired connection (there are a different steps for wireless devices).

 You must be logged in as an Administrator for this project.

1. First you must enable the Wired AutoConfig service, which by default is turned off. Click the **Start** button and in the **Search** box, type **services.msc** and then press **Enter.**

2. If you are prompted by UAC, enter the password or click **Yes.**

3. In the **Services** dialog box, click the **Standard** tab at the bottom of the screen.

4. Scroll down to **Wired AutoConfig** and then right-click it and click **Start.** The service is now enabled.

5. Open the Network Connections by clicking the **Start** button and then clicking **Control Panel.**

6. Click **Network and Internet.**

7. Click **Network and Sharing Center.**

8. In the left pane, click **Change adapter settings.**

9. Double-click the network interface card being used.

10. Click **Properties.**

11. If you are prompted by UAC, enter the password or click **Yes.**

12. Click **Authentication.**

13. Click **Enable IEEE 802.1X authentication** if necessary.

14. If necessary, under Choose a network authentication method, select **Microsoft Protected EAP (PEAP).**

15. Click **Additional Settings** and view the different IEEE 802.1X options.

16. Click **Cancel.**

17. Click **OK.**

18. Close all windows.

Project 11-4: Explore User Account Control (UAC)

Microsoft Windows provides several options with user account control (UAC). In this project, you will configure and test UAC.

1. First ensure that UAC is set at its highest level. Click the **Start** button and then click **Control Panel**.

2. Click **System and Security**.

3. Under Action Center, click **Change User Account Control settings**.

4. The User Account Control Settings dialog box displays. If necessary, move the slider up to the higher level of **Always notify**.

5. Click **OK**.

6. In the Control Panel menu, under System, click **Allow remote access**.

7. The UAC confirmation box displays. Click **No**.

8. In the Control Panel menu, under Action Center, click **Change User Account Control settings**.

9. The User Account Control settings dialog box displays. Move the slider down to the lowest level of **Never notify**.

10. Click **OK**.

11. In the Control Panel menu, under System, click **Allow remote access**. What happens?

12. Return to the Control Panel menu, and under Action Center, click **Change User Account Control settings**.

13. Change the account settings to **Notify me only when apps try to make changes to my computer**.

14. Now try to click **Allow remote access**. What happens?

15. Return to the Control Panel menu, and under Action Center, click **Change User Account Control settings**.

16. Change the account settings to **Notify me only when apps try to make changes to my computer (do not dim my desktop)**.

17. Now try to click **Allow remote access**. What happens?

18. Return to the Control Panel menu, and under Action Center, click **Change User Account Control settings**.

19. The User Account Control Settings dialog box displays. Move the slider up to the higher level of **Always notify**.

20. Click **OK**.

21. Close all windows.

Case Projects

CASE PROJECTS

Case Project 11-1: Security Assertion Markup Language (SAML)

Use the Internet to research SAML. What are its features? How is it being used? What are its advantages and disadvantages? Write a one-page paper on your research.

Case Project 11-2: User Account Control (UAC)

Microsoft Windows User Account Control (UAC) provides a higher level of security for users. Research UAC using the Internet. What were its design goals? Were they achieved? How secure is UAC? What are its strengths? What are its weaknesses? Write a one-page paper on your findings.

Case Project 11-3: Best Practices for Access Control

Search the Internet for one instance of a security breach that occurred for each of the four best practices of access control (separation of duties, job rotation, least privilege, and implicit deny). Write a short summary of that breach. Then rank these four best practices from most effective to least effective. Give an explanation of your rankings.

Case Project 11-4: Group Policies

Write a one-page paper on Microsoft's Group Policies. Explain what they are, how they can be used, and what their strengths and weaknesses are.

Case Project 11-5: TACACS+

How does TACACS+ work? In what settings is it most likely to be found? How widespread is its usage? What are its advantages? What are its disadvantages? When would you recommend using it over RADIUS or Kerberos? Use the Internet to answer these questions about TACACS+ and write a one-page paper on your findings.

Case Project 11-6: LDAP

Use the Internet to research LDAP. Describe the settings in which it would be used and what its different database options are. Write a one-page paper on your research.

Case Project 11-7: Bay Pointe Security Consulting

Bay Pointe Security Consulting (BPSC) provides security consulting services to a wide range of businesses, individuals, schools, and organizations. BPSC has hired you as a technology student to help them with a new project and provide real-world experience to students who are interested in the security field.

Built-Right Construction is a successful developer of commercial real estate projects. Built-Right has caught the attention of Premiere Construction, a national builder, who wants to purchase Built-Right to make them a subsidiary. Premiere Construction has contracted with BPSC to help them provide training to the Built-Right office staff regarding best practices of access control. BPSC has asked you for assistance on this project.

1. Create a PowerPoint presentation for the staff about the best practices of access control (separation of duties, job rotation, least privilege, and implicit deny). Explain what each is and how it can be used to create a secure environment. Because the staff does not have an IT background,

the presentation cannot be too technical in nature. Your presentation should contain at least 10 slides.

2. After the presentation, Premiere Construction has asked you how best to handle the staff's objections regarding these practices, because some of the staff members see them as restrictive. Create a memo to Premiere Construction on how you would address those objections in the next round of training.

Case Project 11-8: Community Site Activity

The Information Security Community Site is an online companion to this textbook. It contains a wide variety of tools, information, discussion boards, and other features to assist learners. Go to **community.cengage.com/infosec**. Sign in with the login name and password that you created in Chapter 1.

It is your first week in technical support at a local college. An instructor has called the help desk saying that she cannot install a new software application on her desktop computer, and you have been asked to visit her office to make the installation. (The policy at the college is that all systems have least privilege and, for security reasons, users cannot install applications.) When you arrive at her office, you are immediately confronted with an angry instructor who complains that she cannot do her job because of all the restrictions. She demands that you provide her with the ability to install her own applications. Two other instructors hear the commotion and come to her office with the same complaints.

What is the best way to handle the situation? Should you try to explain the reasoning behind the restrictions? Or should you simply say, "That's the way it is" and walk away? Or is there a better approach? Enter your answers on the Community Site discussion board.

11

Reference

1. Babwin, Don, "Rita Cundwell sentencing: Nearly 20 years for ex-comptroller who stole $53 million from town," *Huffington Post*, Feb. 14, 2013, retrieved Mar. 31, 2014, www.huffingtonpost.com/2013/02/14/rita-crundwell-sentencing_0_n_2685121.html.

## chapter 12

Authentication and Account Management

After completing this chapter, you should be able to do the following:

- Describe the different types of authentication credentials
- Explain what single sign-on can do
- List the account management procedures for securing passwords

Today's Attacks and Defenses

Imagine you just discovered that your entire digital life has been "trashed." Every email stored in your Gmail account is deleted. All of the data on your Mac-Book notebook has been erased. Everything on your iPhone smartphone and your iPad tablet has been wiped clean. Your credit numbers stored on Amazon are exposed. And someone has been using your Twitter account to broadcast racist and homophobic messages. What a nightmare! But that's exactly what happened recently to reporter Mat Honan.[1] Despite the fact that Mat had good passwords on his accounts and devices, one attacker was able to trash Mat's digital life in the space of one hour. And the attacker did not try to break Mat's passwords but circumvented them by exploiting customer service representatives by telephone.

One Friday afternoon Mat was playing with his daughter when his iPhone suddenly powered off. Since he was expecting a phone call, he plugged the phone in to recharge the battery. However, it rebooted to the setup screen. Because Mat's phone automatically backed up online to Apple's iCloud service, he attempted to connect to iCloud to restore his data, but when he entered his iCloud password it was rejected. He then connected his iPhone to his MacBook notebook computer to restore it from a backup he had performed just a few days before. When he opened his MacBook, however, a message popped up that said his Google Gmail login account information was wrong. Then the screen on his MacBook went gray and asked for a four-digit PIN.

What Mat did not know was that he had been a victim of multiple attacks that afternoon. Why? "I just liked your username," is what the attacker later told Mat. That attacker started with Mat's Twitter account, which the attacker then found was linked to Mat's personal website. On his website Mat had listed his Google Gmail account. The attacker then went to Google's account recovery page and entered Mat's Gmail address to view an obscured version of the alternative email address Mat had on file to which a password reset link could be sent. When Gmail displayed *m****n@me.com* the attacker knew that Mat had an Apple account (*me.com* is an Apple email domain). But the attacker also needed Mat's billing address and last four digits of his credit card number. The attacker found Mat's billing address by conducting a *whois* search on his personal web domain. But what about the last four digits of his credit card? How could the attacker find that information?

The attacker called Amazon, pretending to be Mat, and said he wanted to add a new credit card number to his account. Amazon asked for verification of Mat's name, address, and the email address on file. The attacker provided this newly uncovered

(continued)

information and then gave a new credit card number. Next the attacker called back to Amazon and said he had lost access to his account. When asked, the attacker again provided Mat's name, address, and new credit card number from the just-completed phone call. The attacker was then able to add a new email address (his own) to Mat's account and have a password reset sent to that new email address, which he then used to reset Mat's Amazon password. After logging in to Amazon, the attacker could see all of Mat's credit cards on file, so he now had the last four digits of all of Mat's credit card numbers.

The attacker then called AppleCare, provided Mat's information, and was able to reset Mat's Apple password to his own. From there the attacker launched the "Find My Mac" feature and pretended Mat's MacBook had been stolen. He performed a remote data wipe on Mat's MacBook, iPhone, and iPad devices. Although the "Find My Mac" app does create a four-digit PIN in order to reverse the data wipe if necessary, only the attacker, of course, knew the new PIN. By exploiting the customer service procedures employed by Apple and Amazon, the attacker was able to get into Mat's iCloud service and destroy his digital life.

Mat says that in many ways this attack was his fault. His different accounts were all "daisy-chained" together, so that by accessing his linked Gmail and Amazon account, the attacker was able to get into his Apple ID and Twitter accounts. Even though Mat had good passwords on his accounts and devices, the attacker circumvented them. According to Matt, the greatest loss was photos of his young daughter, which were all stored on his Apple devices and iCloud services. He had no other backups, so those photos were lost forever.

Recall the scenario in Chapter 11 regarding the employee Braden who returned to the office one evening to finish a report. When he entered the building, Braden first had to pass the night security guard, display his photo ID badge, and answer questions from the guard. The guard took time to determine that the person holding the badge was the "genuine" Braden, and not an imposter who might have stolen Braden's badge. Once his identity was confirmed, Braden was allowed to enter the building. However, he could go only into his own office, because he had previously been assigned a key for only his own office door.

Whereas restricting Braden to just his office is similar to the concept of access control, the actions of the night security guard to verify Braden's identity parallel the act of *authentication* in information security. Authentication is the process of ensuring that the person desiring access to resources is *authentic*, and not an imposter.

In this chapter we will study authentication and the secure management of user accounts that enforces authentication. First you will look at the different types of authentication credentials that can be used to verify a user's identity. Next you will see how a single sign-on might be used. Finally, you will look into the techniques and technology used to manage user accounts in a secure fashion.

Authentication Credentials

2.7 Compare and contrast physical security and environmental controls.

3.2 Summarize various types of attacks.

5.2 Given a scenario, select the appropriate authentication, authorization or access control.

6.2 Given a scenario, use appropriate cryptographic methods.

Consider this scenario: Ermanno works on a local military base. Each afternoon he stops at the gym on the base to exercise. After Ermanno locks his car, he walks into the club and is recognized by Li, the clerk at the desk. Li congratulates Ermanno for winning the recent competition for doing the most pushups in one minute. She then allows him to pass on to the locker room. Once inside the locker room, Ermanno opens his locker's combination lock with a series of numbers that he has memorized. While he is exercising, Kristen walks over to Ermanno and says, "I knew it was you doing those pushups even though I could not see your face. Nobody comes close to doing as many as you can. Congratulations on winning the trophy."

In this scenario, Ermanno has been demonstrated to be *genuine* or *authentic*, and not an imposter, by five separate elements. These are illustrated in Figure 12-1 and explained below:

Key fob (what he has)

Military base (where he is)

© Sasha Fenix/Shutterstock.com

Facial characteristics (what he is)

Pushups (what he does)

Combination lock (what he knows)

Figure 12-1 Ermanno's authenticity

- *Somewhere he is.* Because the military base is surrounded by fencing and guards, an imposter Ermanno would not be approved to enter the base. This means that the *location* of Ermanno can help prove his authenticity.

- *Something he has.* By locking the doors of his car with his car's wireless key fob, an item that only the real Ermanno would possess, what he *has* helps to prove his genuineness.

- *Something he is.* Access to the locker room is protected by what Ermanno *is*. Li has to recognize his unique characteristics (his hair color, face, body type, voice, etc.) before he will be allowed to enter the locker room, so these characteristics serve to confirm his authenticity.

- *Something he knows.* The contents of Ermanno's locker are protected by what only the real Ermanno *knows*, namely, the lock combination. The lock will not open for an imposter, but only for the real Ermanno who knows the combination.

- *Something he does.* Because only Ermanno is able to do the record number of pushups, what he *does* helps to uniquely prove his authenticity.

Because only the real or "authentic" Ermanno possesses these elements—where he is, what he has, what he is, what he knows, and what he does—they can be considered as types of **authentication** or proof of his genuineness. This authentication confirms his identity and can be used to protect his belongings by preventing access by an imposter.

In information technology (IT), these five elements are known as **authentication factors** (sometimes called *authentication credentials*). Although there are many different authentication credentials that can be presented to an IT system in order to verify the genuineness of the user, all credentials can be classified into one of these five categories.

What You Know: Passwords

In most systems, a user logging in would be asked to *identify* himself. This is done by entering an identifier known as the **username**, such as *F_McGee*. Yet because anyone could enter this username, the next step is for the user to *authenticate* himself by proving that he actually is *F_McGee*. This is often done by providing information that only he would know, namely, a password. A **password** is a secret combination of letters, numbers, and/or characters that only the user should have knowledge of. Passwords are the most common type of authentication today.

Despite their widespread use, passwords provide only weak protection. Although there are several different attacks that can be launched against passwords, actions can be taken to strengthen passwords.

Password security has been exploited since the early days of computers. In 1961 MIT developed the Compatible Time-Sharing System (CTSS) in which passwords were first used in to authenticate computer users. In the spring of 1962, a Ph.D. researcher, who had been allotted only four hours per week of computing resources, submitted a request to the CTSS computer to print the list of all password files. Because there were no safeguards, the computer produced the list, which the researcher then used to log in with other users' passwords and gain more computing time.

Password Weaknesses The weakness of passwords centers on human memory. Human beings can memorize only a limited number of items. Passwords place heavy loads on human memory in multiple ways:

- The most effective passwords are long and complex. However, these are difficult for users to memorize and then accurately recall when needed.

- Users must remember passwords for many different accounts. Most users have accounts for different computers and mobile devices at work, school, and home; multiple email accounts; online banking; Internet site accounts; and so on. In one study, 28 percent of a group of users had more than 13 passwords each,[2] while in another study a group of 144 users had an average of 16 passwords per user.[3]

- For the highest level of security, each account password should be unique, which further strains human memory.

- Many security policies mandate that passwords expire after a set period of time, such as every 45–60 days, when a new one must be created. Some security policies even prevent a previously used password from being recycled and used again, forcing users to repeatedly memorize new passwords.

 Tennessee was the first state to pass a law in 2013 that makes it a crime to share certain types of passwords, even with family members or friends. It is illegal to share online subscriptions to entertainment services, even if permission has been given by the owner of the password. Violators who steal more than $500 of content can be charged with a felony.

Because of the burdens that passwords place on human memory, users take shortcuts to help them memorize and recall their passwords. The first shortcut is to use a *weak password*. Weak passwords use a common word as a password (*princess*), a short password (*desk*), a predictable sequence of characters (*abc123*), or personal information (*Hannah*) in a password. Even when users attempt to create stronger passwords, they generally follow predictable patterns of *appending* and *replacing*:

- *Appending*. When users combine letters, numbers, and punctuation (*character sets*), they do it in a pattern. Users typically append one character set with another set or sets. Most often they only add a number after letters (*caitlin1* or *cheer99*). If they add all three character sets, it is in the sequence *letters+punctuation+number* (*amanda.7* or *chris#6*).

- *Replacing*. Users also use replacements in predictable patterns. Generally a zero is used instead of the letter *o* (*passw0rd*), the digit *1* for the letter *i* (*denn1s*), or a dollar sign for an *s* (*be$tfriend*).

Attackers are aware of these patterns in passwords and can search for them, dramatically weakening passwords and make it easier for attackers to crack them.

Another common shortcut is to reuse the same password for multiple accounts. Although this makes it easier for the user, it also makes it easier for an attacker who compromises one account to access other accounts.

The alarming use of weak passwords can be easily illustrated. Several recent attacks have stolen tens of millions of passwords, which later were posted on the Internet. An analysis of one theft of 32 million user passwords showed that 30 percent of users had created passwords of only five or six characters, while just 12 percent of the user passwords were a stronger nine characters in length. Almost one in every five users created a password that was one of the 5000 most common passwords, including names, slang words, dictionary words, or trivial passwords (consecutive digits, adjacent keyboard keys, etc.). The 10 most common passwords found and their number of occurrences are listed in Table 12-1.

Rank	Password	Number of users with password
1	123456	290,731
2	12345	79,078
3	123456789	76,790
4	Password	61,958
5	iloveyou	51,622
6	princess	35,231
7	rockyou	22,588
8	1234567	21,726
9	12345678	20,553
10	abc123	17,542

Table 12-1   Ten most common passwords

Some applications now test for the most common passwords and warn users if they try to use a common password. One program checks a password against the 10,000 most common passwords used today.

A noted security expert summarized the password problem well by stating:

> *The problem is that the average user can't and won't even try to remember complex enough passwords to prevent attacks. As bad as passwords are, users will go out of the way to make it worse. If you ask them to choose a password, they'll choose a lousy one. If you force them to choose a good one, they'll write it [down] and change it back to the password they changed it from the last month. And they'll choose the same password for multiple applications.*[4]

Attacks on Passwords   Most average users think that passwords are compromised by an attacker guessing a password by typing different variations. Although it may be possible for an attacker to enter different passwords at the login prompt to attempt to guess a password, in reality this is not practical. Even at two or three tries per second, it could take thousands of years to guess the right password. In addition, most accounts can be set to disable all logins after a limited number of incorrect attempts (such as five), thus locking out the attacker. Instead of randomly guessing a password, attackers use far more sophisticated methods. Attacks that can be used to discover a password include:

- *Social engineering.* Passwords can be revealed through social engineering attacks, including phishing, shoulder surfing, and dumpster diving.

- *Capturing.* There are several methods that can be used to capture passwords. A keylogger on a computer can capture the passwords that are entered on the keyboard. While passwords are in transit, man-in-the-middle and replay attacks can be used. A protocol analyzer also can capture transmissions that contain passwords.

- *Resetting.* If an attacker can gain physical access to a user's computer, she can erase the existing password and reset it to a new password. Password reset programs require that the computer be rebooted from an optical drive or USB flash drive that usually contains a version of a different operating system along with the password reset program. For example, to reset a password on a Microsoft Windows computer, a USB flash drive with Linux and the password reset program would be used.

These attacks, however, have their limitations, such as the need to physically access a user's computer or watch the user enter a password. Most password attacks today instead use *offline cracking.* When a password is created, a one-way hash algorithm creates a unique digital fingerprint digest (sometimes called a *message digest* or *hash*) of the password. This digest is then stored instead of the original cleartext password. When a user attempts to log in, she enters her password and a digest is then created from it. The two digests are compared, and if they match, the user is authenticated.

Hash algorithms are covered in Chapter 5.

With offline cracking, attackers steal the file of password digests and load that file onto their own computers. They can then attempt to discover the passwords by comparing the stolen digests with their own digests that they have created, called *candidates.* Several offline cracking techniques attempt to match a known password digest with stolen digests. These are brute force, dictionary, hybrid, rainbow tables, and password collections.

When cracking passwords, attackers use computers with multiple graphics processing units (GPUs). Whereas the central processing unit (CPU) of a computer can do a wide variety of tasks, a GPU, which is separate from the CPU, is used to render screen displays on computers. GPUs are very good at performing video processing, which involves the very repetitive work of performing the same function over and over to large groups of pixels on the screen. This makes GPUs superior to CPUs at repetitive tasks like breaking passwords. Recently a security researcher created a computer cluster of five servers and 25 GPUs and was able to generate 350 billion password candidates per second.[5]

Brute Force In an automated **brute force attack**, every possible combination of letters, numbers, and characters is used to create candidate digests that are then matched against those in the stolen digest file. This is the slowest yet most thorough method. Using an auto-mated brute force attack program, an attacker enters into the attack program the following types of parameters:

- *Password length.* The minimum and maximum lengths of the passwords to be generated (such as a range from *1–15*) can be entered.

- *Character set.* This is the set of letters, symbols, and characters that make up the password. Because not all systems accept the same character set for passwords, if characters can be eliminated from the character set, this will dramatically increase the speed of the attack.

- *Language.* Many programs allow different languages to be chosen, such as Arabic, Dutch, English, French, German, Italian, Portuguese, Russian, or Spanish.

- *Pattern.* If any part of the password is known, a pattern can be entered to reduce the number of passwords generated. A question mark (?) can replace one symbol and an asterisk (*) can replace multiple symbols. For example, if the first two letters of a six-character password were known to be *sk*, the pattern could be *sk????*.

- *Skips.* Because most passwords are wordlike combinations of letters, some brute force attack programs can be set to skip nonsensical combinations of characters (*wqrghea*) so that only passwords such as *elmosworld* and *carkeys* are created.

Dictionary Attack   Another common password attack is a **dictionary attack**. A dictionary attack begins with the attacker creating digests of common dictionary words as candidates and then comparing them against those in a stolen digest file. A dictionary attack is shown in Figure 12-2. Dictionary attacks can be successful because users often create passwords that are simple dictionary words.

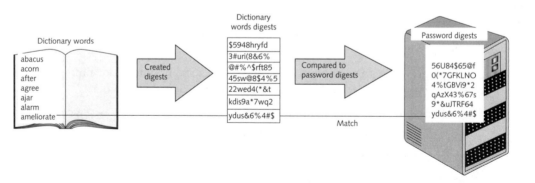

Figure 12-2   Dictionary attack

A dictionary attack that uses a set of dictionary words and compares it with the stolen digests is known as a **pre-image attack**, in that one known digest (dictionary word) is compared to an unknown digest (stolen digest). A **birthday attack** is slightly different, in that the search is for *any* two digests that are the same.

A birthday attack is named after a mathematical phenomenon known as the birthday paradox. If you are trying to find another person who has the same birthday as you, then you must ask 253 people to have a 50 percent chance that at least one of them shares your birthday. But if you want to find only two people who share same birthday, regardless of the day, fewer people must be queried. Within a group of only 23 people, there is a 50 percent chance that two will share the same birthday.

Hybrid Attack A variation of the dictionary attack is the **hybrid attack**. This attack combines a dictionary attack with a brute force attack and will slightly alter dictionary words by adding numbers to the end of the password, spelling words backward, slightly misspelling words, or including special characters such as @, $, !, or %.

Rainbow Tables Although brute force and dictionary attacks were once the primary tools used by attackers to crack stolen digest passwords, more recently attackers have used **rainbow tables**. Rainbow tables make password attacks easier by creating a large pregenerated data set of candidate digests.

There are two steps in using a rainbow table. First is creating the table itself. Next, that table is used to crack a password. A rainbow table is a compressed representation of cleartext passwords that are related and organized in a sequence (called a *chain*). To create a rainbow table, each chain begins with an initial password that is hashed and then fed into a function that produces a different cleartext password. This process is repeated for a set number of rounds. The initial password and the last digest value of the chain comprise a rainbow table entry.

Using a rainbow table to crack a password also requires two steps. First, the password to be broken is hashed and run through the same procedure used to create the initial table. This results in the initial password of the chain. Then the process is repeated, starting with this initial password until the original digest is found. The password used at the last iteration is the cracked password.

Although generating a rainbow table requires a significant amount of time, once it is created it has three significant advantages over other password attack methods:

- A rainbow table can be used repeatedly for attacks on other passwords.
- Rainbow tables are much faster than dictionary attacks.
- The amount of memory needed on the attacking machine is greatly reduced.

Rainbow tables are freely available for download on the Internet.

Password Collections A watershed moment in password attacks occurred in late 2009. An attacker using an SQL injection attack broke into a server belonging to a developer of several popular social media applications. This server contained more than 32 million user passwords, all in cleartext. These passwords were later posted on the Internet.

Attackers seized this opportunity to examine actual user passwords. These passwords provided two key elements for password attacks. First, this "treasure-trove" collection of passwords gave attackers, for the first time, a large corpus of real-world passwords. Because users repeat their passwords on multiple accounts, attackers could now use these passwords as candidate passwords in their attacks. It is estimated that in excess of 100 million passwords were stolen and published online in one year alone. Websites now host lists of these leaked passwords along with statistical analysis that attackers can utilize.

In addition, these password collections have provided attackers insight into the strategic thinking of how users create passwords. For example, on those occasions when users mix uppercase and lowercase in passwords, users tend to capitalize at the beginning of the password, much like writing a sentence. Likewise, punctuation and numbers are more likely to appear at the end of the password, again mimicking standard sentence writing. And a high percentage of passwords were comprised of a name and date, such as *Braden2008*. Such insights can be valuable to attackers in designing a "mask" (such as *?dabcdef -2 ?l?u ?1?1? 2?2?2?2?2*) to crack passwords. Password mask attacks can significantly reduce the amount of time needed to break a password when compared to a raw brute force attack.

Password Defenses There are four primary defenses against password attacks. These include password complexity, credential management, password hashing algorithms, and salts.

Password Complexity One insight into creating complex and strong passwords is to examine how a password attack program attempts to break a password.[6] Most passwords consist of a *root* (not necessarily a dictionary word but generally "pronounceable") along with an *attachment*, either an ending suffix (about 90 percent of the time) or a prefix (10 percent). An attack program will first test the password against 1000 common passwords (such as *123456*, *password1*, and *letmein*). If it is not successful, it then combines these common passwords with 100 common suffixes (such as *1, 4u,* and *abc*). This results in almost 100,000 different combinations that can crack 25 percent of all passwords. Next the program (in order) uses 5000 common dictionary words, 10,000 names, 100,000 comprehensive dictionary words, and combinations from a phonetic pattern dictionary, varying the dictionary words between lowercase (the most common), initial uppercase (the second most common), all uppercase, and then final character as uppercase. The program also makes common substitutions with letters in the dictionary words, such as $ for *s*, @ for *a*, 3 for *E*, etc. Finally, it uses a variation of attachments, such as:

- Two-digit combinations
- Dates from 1900 to the present
- Three-digit combinations
- Single symbols (#, $, %)
- Single digit plus single symbol
- Two-symbol combinations

Understanding how a password attack program attempts to break a password can lead to the following general observations regarding creating passwords:

- Do not use passwords that consist of dictionary words or phonetic words.
- Do not repeat characters (*xxx*) or use sequences (*abc, 123, qwerty*).

- Do not use birthdays, family member names, pet names, addresses, or any personal information.

- Do not use short passwords. A strong password should be a minimum of 15 characters in length.

A longer password is always more secure than a shorter password because the longer a password is, the more attempts an attacker must make in order to determine it. The formula for determining the number of possible passwords given the number of characters that can be used in the password and the password length is

Number-of-Keyboard-Keys ^ Password-Length = Total-Number-of-Possible-Passwords.

Table 12-2 illustrates the number of possible passwords for different password lengths using a standard 95-key keyboard. Longer passwords force attackers to spend significantly more time attempting to break them.

Keyboard keys	Password length	Number of possible passwords
95	2	9025
95	3	857,375
95	4	81,450,625
95	5	7,737,809,375
95	6	735,091,890,625

Table 12-2 Number of possible passwords

One way to make passwords stronger is to use nonkeyboard characters, or special characters that do not appear on the keyboard, thus extending the number of possible keys beyond 95. These characters are created by holding down the *ALT* key while simultaneously typing a number on the numeric keypad (but not the numbers across the top of the keyboard). For example, *ALT + 0163* produces the £ symbol. A list of all the available nonkeyboard characters can be seen by clicking *Start* and entering *charmap.exe*, and then clicking on a character. The code ALT + 0*xxx* will appear in the lower-left corner of the screen (if that character can be reproduced in Windows). Figure 12-3 shows a Windows character map.

TIP

Apple has a built-in password generator feature that is often overlooked. When creating a new password, you can click the key icon that is next to the "New Password" field in order to bring up the Apple Password Assistant. The assistant can generate a password based on several choices: Memorable, Letters and Numbers, Numbers Only, Random, or FIPS-181 compliant (FIPS stands for the Federal Information Processing Standards, issued by the National Institute of Standards and Technology). A "Length" slider can set the password length, while a "Quality" indicator gives the strength of your password.

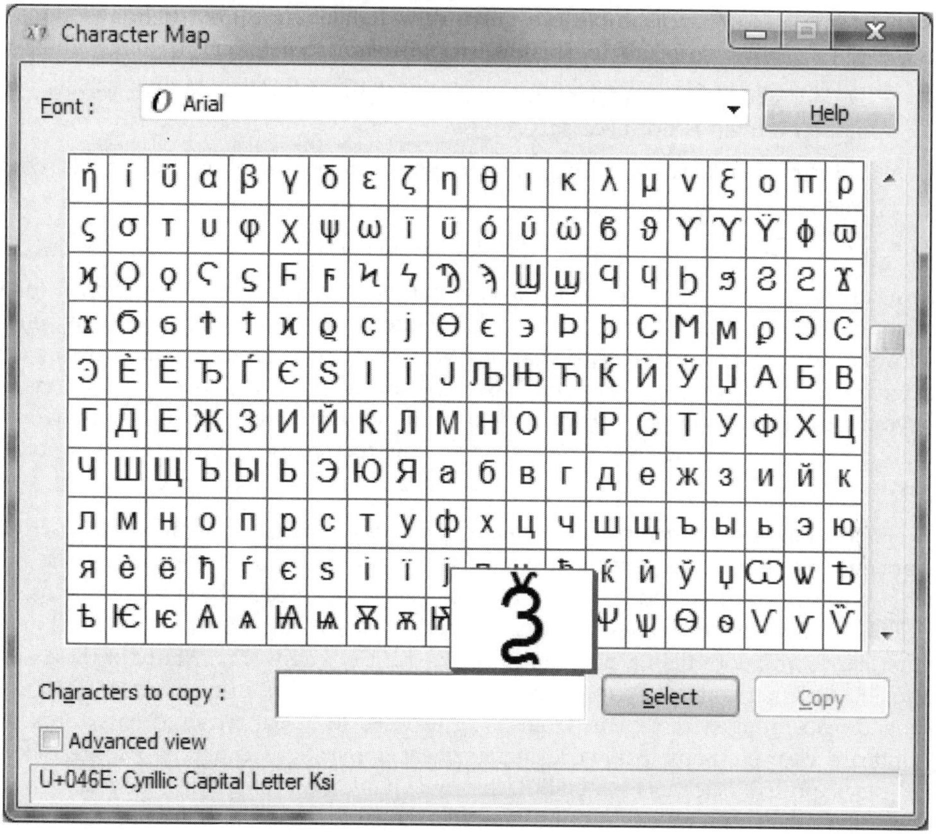

Figure 12-3 Windows character map
Source: Microsoft Windows

Credential Management Equally important to creating good passwords is to properly manage password credentials. For an organization, one important defense against password cracking is to prevent attackers from capturing the password digest files. There are several defenses against the theft of these files:

- Do not leave a computer running unattended, even if it is in a locked office. All screensavers should be set to resume only when a password is entered.

- Do not set a computer to boot from an optical drive or USB flash drive.

- Password-protect the ROM BIOS.

- Physically lock the computer case so that it cannot be opened.

Good credential management also includes the following:

- Change passwords frequently.

- Do not reuse old passwords.

- Never write a password down.

- Have a unique password for each account.

- If it is necessary for a user to access another user's account, a temporary password should be set up and then immediately changed.

- Do not allow a computer to automatically sign into an account or record a password so that a login is not necessary.

- Do not enter passwords on public access computers or other individuals' computers that could be infected.

- Do not enter a password while using an unencrypted wireless network.

A secure solution to credential management is to rely on technology rather than human memory to store and manage passwords. Modern web browsers contain a function that allows a user to save a password that has been entered while using the browser or through a separate dialog box that "pops up" over the browser. Browser-based solutions, however, have disadvantages. Users are restricted to using the computer that has that password information previously stored, they must avoid clearing the passwords from the computer, and the passwords may be vulnerable if another user is allowed access to the computer.

A better solution is *password management applications*. These programs let a user create and store multiple strong passwords in a single user "vault" file that is protected by one strong master password. Users can retrieve individual passwords as needed by opening the user file, thus freeing the user from the need to memorize multiple passwords. Yet most password management applications are more than a password-protected list of passwords. Many of these applications also include drag-and-drop capabilities, enhanced encryption, in-memory protection that prevents the operating system cache from being exposed to reveal retrieved passwords, and timed Clipboard clearing. Some password management applications can even require that a specific key file be present (such as on a USB flash drive) in addition to entering the master password to open the vault. This means that if the vault file was stolen, it could not be opened.

Password Hashing Algorithms Although passwords are hashed before being stored, not all hash algorithms for passwords are considered equal.

Microsoft Windows operating systems hash passwords in two ways. The first is known as the **LM (LAN Manager) hash**. The LM hash is not actually a hash, because a hash is a mathematical function used to fingerprint the data. The LM hash instead uses a *cryptographic one-way function (OWF)*: instead of encrypting the password with another key, the password itself is the key. The LM hash is considered to be a very weak function for storing passwords. First, the LM hash is not case sensitive, meaning that there is no difference between uppercase (*A*) and lowercase (*a*). This significantly reduces the character set that an attacker must use. Second, the LM hash splits all passwords into two 7-character parts. If the original password is fewer than 14 characters, it simply pads the parts; if it is longer, the extra characters are dropped. This means that an attacker attempting to break an LM hash must break only two 7-character passwords from a limited character set.

To address the security issues in the LM hash, Microsoft later introduced the **NTLM (New Technology LAN Manager) hash**. Unlike the LM hash, the NTLM hash does not limit stored passwords to two 7-character parts. In addition, it is case sensitive and has a larger character set of 65,535 characters. The original version of NTLM uses a weak cryptographic function and does not support more recent cryptographic methods; Microsoft recommends that it should not be used. The current version is **NTLMv2** and uses the Hashed Message Authentication Code (HMAC) with MD5.

Most Linux systems by default use MD5 for hashing passwords. On several systems, stronger versions of SHA-256 or SHA-512 can be substituted. Apple Mac OS X uses SHA-1 hashes.

Using general-purpose hash algorithms like MD5 and SHA, however, is not considered secure for creating digests because these hashing algorithms are designed to create a digest as quickly as possible. The fast speed of general-purpose hash algorithms works in an attacker's favor. When an attacker is creating candidate digests, a general-purpose hashing algorithm can rapidly create a very large number of passwords for matching purposes.

A more secure approach for creating password digests is to use a specialized password hash algorithm that is intentionally designed to be slower. This would then limit the ability of an attacker to crack passwords because it requires significantly more time to create each candidate digest, thus slowing down the entire cracking process. This is called **key stretching**.

Two popular key stretching password hash algorithms are **bcrypt** and **PBKDF2**. These can be configured to require more time to create a digest. A network administrator can specify the number of iterations (*rounds*), which sets how "expensive" (in terms of computer time and/or resources) the password hash function will be. Whereas the increased time is a minor inconvenience when one user logs in and waits for the password digest to be generated, it can significantly reduce attackers' speed of generating candidates.

Using a general password algorithm, an attacker could generate about 95^8 candidate passwords in 5.5 hours. However, using bcrypt, in that same time only 71,000 candidate passwords could be generated.

Salts In order to increase the strength of hashed passwords, a salt also can be used. A **salt** consists of a random string that is used in hash algorithms. Passwords can be protected by adding a random string to the user's cleartext password before it is hashed. Table 12-3 compares simplistic unsalted and salted passwords.

12

Username	Password	Unsalted password hash	Random salt	Salted password	Salted password hash
Alice	apple	4r9g8	&hgu$	&hgu$apple	r$wdc
Bob	banana	3ca53	#x!@3	#x!@3banana	ei832
Carol	carrot	8dusi	5!%vX	5!%vXcarrot	5t9ri
Devin	banana	3ca53	9*^cs	9*^csbanana	xde4z
Elisa	eggplant	4v37d	={4*f	={4*feggplant	i8s74

Table 12-3   Unsalted and salted passwords

Salts make dictionary attacks and brute force attacks for cracking large number of passwords much slower (although they do not benefit cracking just one password), and also limit the impact of rainbow tables. Another benefit of a salt is that if two users choose the same password, this will not help the attacker. In Table 12-3, both Bob and Devin selected the same password (*banana*) that resulted in the same unsalted hashed password (*3ca53*). Without salts, an attacker who is able to crack Bob's password would also immediately know Devin's password without performing any computations. By adding salts, however, each password digest will be different.

Although it is possible to use the same salt, for the highest level of security, salts should be random for each user password. This requires that both the salt, which is added to the user's cleartext password when it is entered upon login, and the stored password digest be protected.

What You Have: Tokens, Cards, and Cell Phones

Another type of authentication credential is based on the approved user having a specific item in his possession. Such items are often used in conjunction with passwords. Because the user is using more than one type of authentication credential—both what a user knows (the password) and what the user has—this type of authentication credential is called **multifactor authentication**. (Using just one type of authentication is called **single-factor authentication**.)

The most common items that are used for authentication are tokens, cards, and cell phones.

Tokens A **token** is typically a small device (usually one that can be affixed to a keychain) with a window display, as shown in Figure 12-4. Instead of the user presenting a password (what she knows), a token introduces a different form of authentication based on what the person has (a token). Tokens can be used to create a **one-time password (OTP)**, an authentication code that can be used only once or for a limited period of time.

Figure 12-4   Token

There are two types of OTPs. A **time-based one-time password (TOTP)** changes after a set time period. As illustrated in Figure 12-5, the token and a corresponding authentication server share an algorithm (each user's token has a different algorithm), and the token generates a code from the algorithm once every 30 to 60 seconds. This code is valid for only the brief period of time that it is displayed on the token. When the user logs in, she enters her username along with the code currently being displayed on the token. When the authentication server receives it, the server looks up the algorithm associated with that specific user, generates its own code, and then compares it with what the user entered. If they are identical, the user is authenticated. An attacker who steals the code would have to use it within the token's time limit.

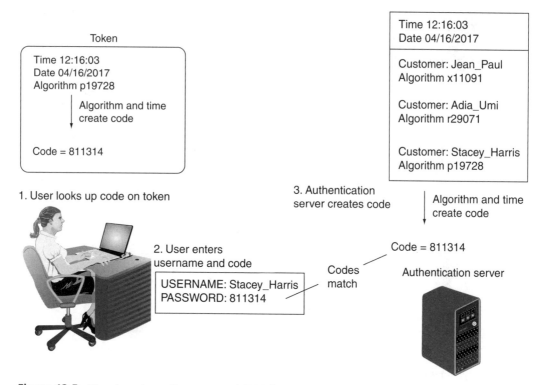

Figure 12-5 Time-based one-time password (TOTP)

The code is not transmitted to the token; instead, both the token and authentication server have the same algorithm and time setting.

12

Instead of changing after a set number of seconds, an **HMAC-based one-time password (HOTP)** is "event-driven" and changes when a specific event occurs, such as when a user enters a personal identification number (PIN) on the token's keypad, which triggers the token to create a random code. For example, after entering the PIN *1694*, the code *190411* is displayed.

Tokens have several advantages over passwords. First, standard passwords are static: they do not change unless the user is forced to create a new password. Because passwords do not change frequently, this can give an attacker a lengthy period of time in which to crack and then use the password. In contrast, tokens produce dynamic passwords that change frequently. Second, a user might not know if an attacker has stolen her password, and confidential information could be accessed without the user knowing it was taking place. If a token is stolen, it would become obvious and steps could be taken immediately to disable that account.

Intel recently introduced Intel Identity Protection Technology (IPT) that functions on Intel ultrabook mobile devices. Using what Intel calls "embedded, restricted-access components forged in silicon," IPT generates from the CPU a unique TOTP code every 30 seconds and displays it on the laptop's screen. Users can then enter their password and the code on a website for multifactor authentication.

Cards Several types of cards can be used as authentication credentials. A **smart card**, as illustrated in Figure 12-6, contains an *integrated circuit chip* that can hold information, which then can be used as part of the authentication process. Smart cards can be either contact cards, which contain a tell-tale "pad" allowing electronic access to the contents of the chip, or contactless cards that do not require physical contact with the card itself.

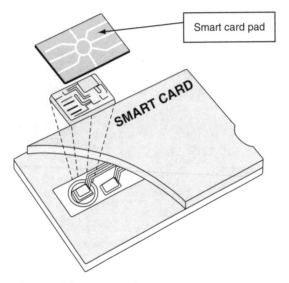

Figure 12-6   Smart card

One type of smart card is currently being distributed by the U.S. government. A **common access card (CAC)** is a U.S. Department of Defense (DoD) smart card that is used for identification of active-duty and reserve military personnel along with civilian employees and special contractors. A CAC resembles a credit card. In addition to an integrated circuit chip, it has a bar code and magnetic stripe along with the bearer's picture and printed information. This card can be used to authenticate the owner as well as for encryption. The smart card standard covering all U.S. government employees is the **Personal Identity Verification (PIV)** standard.

Cell Phones Tokens and cards are increasingly being replaced today with cell phones. A code can be sent to a user's cell phone through an app on the device or as a text message when using TOTP. Cell phones also allow a user to send a request via the phone to receive an HOTP authorization code.

What You Are: Biometrics

In addition to authentication based on what a person knows or has, another category rests on the features and characteristics of the individual. This type of "what you are" authentication involves standard biometrics and cognitive biometrics.

Standard Biometrics
Standard **biometrics** uses a person's unique physical characteristics for authentication (what he *is*). Standard biometrics can use fingerprints or other unique characteristics of a person's face, hands, or eyes (irises and retinas) to authenticate a user. Fingerprint scanners have become the most common type of standard biometric device. Every user's fingerprint consists of a number of ridges and valleys, with ridges being the upper skin layer segments of the finger and valleys the lower segments. In one method of fingerprint scanning, the scanner locates the point where these ridges end and split, converts them into a unique series of numbers, and then stores the information as a template. A second method creates a template from selected locations on the finger.

Biometrics is commonly used in physical security. Access to a secure area may be restricted to only those who fingerprint or retina is scanned.

There are two basic types of fingerprint scanners. A *static fingerprint scanner* requires the user to place the entire thumb or finger on a small oval window on the scanner. The scanner takes an optical "picture" of the fingerprint and compares it with the fingerprint image on file. The other type of scanner is known as a *dynamic fingerprint scanner*. A dynamic fingerprint scanner has a small slit or opening, as shown in Figure 12-7.

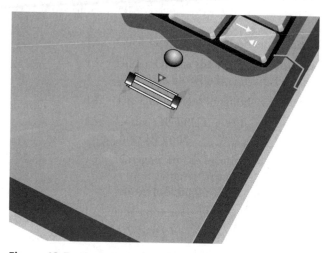

Figure 12-7 Dynamic fingerprint scanner

Dynamic fingerprint scanners work on the same principle as stud finders that carpenters use to locate wood studs behind drywall. This is known as capacitive technology.

Standard biometrics has two disadvantages. The first is the cost. Biometric readers (hardware scanning devices) must be installed at each location where authentication is required. The second disadvantage is that biometric readers are not always foolproof and can reject authorized users while accepting unauthorized users. These errors are mainly due to the many facial or hand characteristics that must be scanned and then compared.

Although biometrics is sometimes advertised as the solution to passwords, there still are issues with biometrics. Users cannot hide their biometrics, so it is possible to "steal" someone's characteristics by lifting a fingerprint from a glass, photographing an iris, or recording a voice and then using the copy to trick the biometric reader. And unlike passwords that can easily be reset if compromised, it may not be possible to "reset" biometric data.

Cognitive Biometrics   Whereas standard biometrics considers a person's physical characteristics, the field of **cognitive biometrics** is related to the perception, thought process, and understanding of the user. Cognitive biometrics is considered to be much easier for the user to remember because it is based on the user's life experiences. This also makes it more difficult for an attacker to imitate.

One type of cognitive biometrics is picture gesture authentication (PGA) for touch-enabled devices. Users select a picture to use for which there should be at least 10 "points of interest" on the photograph that could serve as "landmarks" or places to touch, connect with a line, or draw a circle around. Specific gestures—tap, line, or circle—are then used to highlight any parts of the picture and these gestures are recorded. When logging in, a user reproduces those same gestures on the photograph, as illustrated in Figure 12-8. In order for an attacker to replicate these actions, she would need to know the parts of the image that were highlighted, the order of the gestures, as well as the direction, and the starting and ending points, of the circles and lines.

Picture passwords can still be vulnerable to attacks. An attacker who is shoulder surfing may be able to see a user's gestures, or finger smudges left on the screen may provide enough clues for an attacker to replicate the actions. In addition, security researchers have found that one of the most common methods used in this authentication process was using a photo of a person and triple tapping on the face. The most common face tap is the eyes, followed by nose and jaw.[7]

A similar example of cognitive biometrics requires the user to identify specific faces. Users are provided a random set of photographs of different faces, typically three to seven, to serve as their password. They are taken through a "familiarization process" that is intended to imprint the faces in the user's mind. When the user logs in, he must select his assigned faces from three to five different groups, with each group containing nine faces. These groups are presented one at a time until all the faces have been correctly identified.

Figure 12-8   Picture gesture authentication

Photo © Pressmaster/Shutterstock.com (numbers and lines added)

Another example of cognitive biometrics based on a life experience that the user remembers begins with the user selecting one of several "memorable events" in her lifetime, such as taking a special vacation, celebrating a personal achievement, or attending a specific family dinner. Then the user is asked specific questions about that memorable event, such as what type of food was served, how old the person was when the event occurred, where the event was located, who was in attendance, and the reason for the event. The user authenticates by answering the same series of questions when logging in.

Cognitive biometrics is considered much easier for the end-user and may provide a higher degree of protection. It is predicted that cognitive biometrics could become a key element in authentication in the future.

What You Do: Behavioral Biometrics

Another type of authentication is based on actions that the user is uniquely qualified to perform. This is sometimes called **behavioral biometrics**. Two examples are keystroke dynamics and voice recognition.

12

Keystroke Dynamics One type of behavioral biometrics is *keystroke dynamics*, which attempts to recognize a user's unique typing rhythm. All users type at a different pace. During World War II, the U.S. military could distinguish enemy coders who tapped out Morse code from Allied coders by their unique rhythms. A study funded by the U.S. National Bureau of Standards concluded that the keystroke dynamics of entering a user-name and password could provide up to 98 percent accuracy.[8]

Keystroke dynamics uses two unique typing variables. The first is known as *dwell time*, which is the time it takes for a key to be pressed and then released. The second characteristic is *flight time*, or the time between keystrokes (both "down" when the key is pressed and "up" when the key is released are measured). Multiple samples are collected to form a user typing template, as shown in Figure 12-9. When the user enters his username and password, they are sent, along with the user's individual typing sample obtained by entering the username and password, to the authentication server. If both the password and the typing sample match, those stored on the authentication server, and the user is approved; if the typing template does not match even though the password does, the user is not authenticated. This is shown in Figure 12-10.

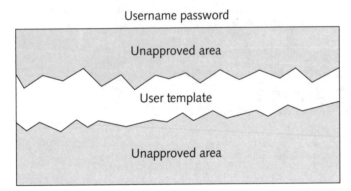

Figure 12-9   Typing template

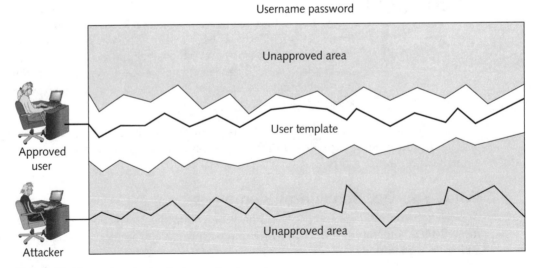

Figure 12-10   Authentication by keystroke dynamics

Keystroke dynamics holds a great deal of potential. Because it requires no specialized hardware and because the user does not have to take any additional steps beyond entering a username and password, some security experts predict that keystroke dynamics will become widespread in the near future.

Voice Recognition
Because all users' voices are different, voice recognition can be used to authenticate users based on the unique characteristics of a person's voice. Several characteristics make each person's voice unique, from the size of the head to age. These differences can be quantified and a user voice template can be created, much like the template used in keystroke dynamics.

Voice recognition is not to be confused with speech recognition, which accepts spoken words for input as if they had been typed on the keyboard.

One of the concerns regarding voice recognition is that an attacker could record the user's voice and then create a recording to use for authentication. However, this would be extremely difficult to do. Humans speak in phrases and sentences instead of isolated words. The *phonetic cadence*, or speaking two words together in a way that one word "bleeds" into the next word, becomes part of each user's speech pattern. It would be extremely difficult to capture several hours of someone's voice, parse it into separate words, and then combine the words in real time to defeat voice recognition security.

To protect against voice biometric attacks, identification phrases can be selected that would rarely (if ever) come up in normal speech, or random phrases can be displayed for the user to repeat.

Where You Are: Geolocation

A final type of authentication can be based where the user is located. Known as **geolocation**, it is the identification of the location of a person or object using technology. Although geolocation may not uniquely identify the user, it can indicate if an attacker is trying to perform a malicious action from a location different from the normal location of the user.

For example, where does Alice normally access her bank's website? If it is typically from her home computer on nights and weekends, then this information can be used to establish a geolocation pattern based on the Internet Protocol (IP) address of Alice's computer. If a computer located in China attempts to access her bank's website, this may be an indication that an attacker instead of Alice is at work. Geolocation is done to some degree by most banks, so that generally a bank will turn down requests for wire transfers from overseas locations unless the user has specifically approved such a transfer in advance with the bank.

In addition to geolocation, the time of day, Internet service provider, and basic PC configuration also can be used to determine if the user is authentic.

Geolocation is not restricted to banking. Many websites will not allow a user to access an account if the computer is located in North Carolina when normally the access is from Tennessee. The website may require a second type of authentication, such as a code sent as a text message to a cell phone number on file, before the user can be authenticated.

Single Sign-On

5.2 Given a scenario, select the appropriate authentication, authorization or access control.

One of the problems facing users today is the fact that they have multiple accounts across multiple platforms that all ideally use a unique username and password. The difficulty in managing all of these different authentication credentials frequently causes users to compromise and select the least burdensome password and then use it for all accounts. A solution to this problem is to have one username and password to gain access to all accounts so that the user has only one username and password to remember.

This is the idea behind *identity management*, which is using a single authentication credential that is shared across multiple networks. When those networks are owned by different organizations, it is called **federated identity management (FIM)**, or just **federation**. One application of FIM is called **single sign-on (SSO)**, or using one authentication credential to access multiple accounts or applications. SSO holds the promise of reducing the number of usernames and passwords that users must memorize (potentially, to just one).

Several large Internet providers support SSO, but only for their own suite of services and applications. For example, a Google user can access all of the features of the site, such as Gmail, Google Docs and Spreadsheets, Calendar, and Picasa photo albums, by entering a single username and password. However, the SSO is restricted to Google applications (not "federated" with other organizations) and is centrally located at Google.

There are several implementations of web-based FID systems. Examples of some popular SSOs include Microsoft Account, OpenID, and OAuth.

Microsoft Account

Microsoft has promoted SSO technology for several years. In 1999 Microsoft introduced *.NET Passport* before changing the name to *Microsoft Passport Network*. The name was changed again to *Windows Live ID* in 2006 as an SSO for web commerce. Today the technology is simply known as *Microsoft Account*. Although Windows Live ID was originally designed as a federated identity management system that would be used by a wide variety of web servers, because of security issues and privacy concerns, Windows Live ID received limited support. Microsoft Account is similar to Windows Live ID and serves as the authentication system for different Microsoft products.

Microsoft Account, like Windows Live ID, requires a user to create a standard username and password. When the user wants to log in to a website that supports Microsoft Account, the user is redirected to the nearest authentication server, which asks for the username and password over a secure connection. Once authenticated, the user is given an encrypted time-limited "global" cookie that is stored on her computer along with an encrypted ID tag. This ID tag is then sent to the website that the user wants to log into. The website uses this ID tag for authentication and stores its own encrypted and time-limited "local" cookie on the user's computer. The use of "global" and "local" cookies is the basis of Microsoft Account. When the user logs out of her Microsoft account, these cookies are erased.

OpenID

Unlike Microsoft Account, which is proprietary and has centralized authentication, *OpenID* is a decentralized open-source FIM that does not require specific software to be installed on the desktop. OpenID is a Uniform Resource Locator (URL)–based identity system. An OpenID identity is only a URL backed up by a username and password. OpenID provides a means to prove that the user owns that specific URL.

OpenID is completely decentralized. Users can choose the server with which they are most comfortable or can run their own server if they choose.

The steps for creating and using OpenID are as follows:

1. The user goes to a free website that provides OpenID accounts, such as MyOpenID.com, and creates an account with a username (*Me*) and password. The user is then given the OpenID account of *Me.myopenid.com*.

2. When the user visits a website like BuyThis.com that requires him to sign in, he can instead choose to use OpenID. He simply enters his OpenID URL, *Me.myopenid.com*.

3. BuyThis.com redirects him to MyOpenID.com where he is required to enter his password to authenticate himself and indicate he trusts BuyThis.com with his identity.

4. MyOpenID.com sends him back to BuyThis.com, where he is now authenticated.

What is actually created is a webpage that is used for authentication. The user can even go to Me@myopenid.com, although very little information exists there.

OpenID does have some security weaknesses. One weakness is that OpenID depends on the URL identifier routing to the correct server, which depends on a domain name server (DNS) that may have its own security weaknesses. In its current format, OpenID is generally not considered strong enough for most banking and e-commerce websites. However, OpenID is considered suitable for other less secure sites.

Open Authorization (OAuth)

Consider Abby who wants to post photos online of her latest vacation for her friends. Abby starts by first logging into her account on an online storage site (*Box.net*) to upload her photos from her cell phone. Then she accesses her favorite photo sharing site (*Flickr.com*) to post her photos along with her comments. Abby must log in to this site with another user-name and password. After the photos are posted, she then accesses her online contact list (*Gmail.google.com*) to create a list of her friends to whom she wants to show her photos; again, Abby uses another username and password for her Gmail account. She then goes to her social media site (*Facebook.com*) to spread the word, and once again must enter a username and password.

A technology to avoid using multiple passwords is an open-source service similar to OpenID called *Open Authorization (OAuth)*. OAuth permits users to share resources stored on one site with a second site without forwarding their authentication credentials to the other site. It also allows for different applications to seamlessly share data across sites. This would enable Abby to send her photos to *Box*, which would then automatically communicate with *Flickr*, *Gmail*, and *Facebook*.

OAuth relies upon token credentials. A user sends her authentication credentials to a server (such as a web application server) and also authorizes the server to issue token credentials to a third-party server. These token credentials are used in place of transferring the user's user-name and password. The tokens are not generic, but are for specific resources on a site for a limited period of time.

TIP Token credentials include a token identifier, which is a unique random string of characters that is encrypted to protect the token from being used by unauthorized parties. Token credentials can be revoked at any time by the user without affecting other token credentials issued to other sites.

Account Management

4.2 Summarize mobile security concepts and technologies.

5.2 Given a scenario, select the appropriate authentication, authorization or access control.

5.3 Install and configure security controls when performing account management, based on best practices.

Managing credentials such as passwords in user accounts can be accomplished by setting restrictions regarding the creation and use of passwords. Although these restrictions can be performed on a user-by-user basis, this quickly becomes cumbersome and is a security risk: it is too easy to overlook one setting in one user account and create a security vulnerability.

A preferred approach is to assign privileges by group. In a Microsoft Windows environment, there are two categories of group password settings. The first category is called *Password Policy Settings* and is configured by using Group Policy at the domain level. There are six common domain password policy settings called password setting objects. These objects are detailed in Table 12-4.

Microsoft Group Policy is covered in Chapter 11.

Attribute	Description	Recommended setting
Enforce password history	Determines the number of unique new passwords a user must use before an old password can be reused (from 0 to 24).	24 new passwords
Maximum password age	Determines how many days a password can be used before the user is required to change it. The value of this setting can be between 0 and 999.	90 days
Minimum password age	Determines how many days a new password must be kept before the user can change it (from 0 to 999). This setting is designed to work with the Enforce password history setting so that users cannot quickly reset their passwords the required number of times, and then change back to their old passwords.	1 day
Minimum password length	Determines the minimum number of characters a password can have (0–28).	12 characters
Passwords must meet complexity requirements	Determines whether the following are used in creating a password: Passwords cannot contain the user's account name or parts of the user's full name that exceed two consecutive characters; must contain characters from three of the following four categories—English uppercase characters (A through Z), English lowercase characters (a through z), digits (0 through 9), and nonalphabetic characters (!, $, #, %).	Enabled
Store passwords using reversible encryption	Provides support for applications that use protocols which require knowledge of the user's password for authentication purposes. An attacker who can circumvent the encryption will be able to log on to the network with these passwords.	Disabled

Table 12-4   Password policy settings (Windows Group Policy)

Although older versions of Microsoft Windows Server Active Directory domains allow only one password policy that is applied to all users in the domain, versions beginning with Windows Server 2008 provide organizations with a way to define different password policies for different sets of users in a domain. This helps to mitigate problems associated with users who have different accounts or roles.

12

The second category is the *Account Lockout Policy*, which is an Active Directory Domain Services (AD DS) security feature. The lockout prevents a login after a set number of failed login attempts within a specified period and also can specify the length of time that the lockout is in force. This helps prevent attackers from online guessing of user passwords. These settings are listed in Table 12-5.

Attribute	Description	Recommended setting	Comments
Account lockout duration	Determines the length of time a locked account remains unavailable before a user can try to log in again (a value of *0* sets account to remain locked out until an administrator manually unlocks it).	15 minutes	Setting this attribute too high may increase help desk calls from users who unintentionally lock themselves out.
Account lockout threshold	Determines the number of failed login attempts before a lockout occurs.	30 invalid attempts	Setting this attribute too low may result in attackers using the lockout state as a denial of service (DoS) attack by triggering a lockout on a large number of accounts.
Reset account lockout counter after	Determines the length of time before the account lockout threshold setting resets to zero.	15 minutes	This reset time must be less than or equal to the value for the account lockout duration setting.

Table 12-5   Account lockout policy settings (Windows Active Directory)

In addition to account policy enforcement, other steps should be taken as well. For example, generic accounts should be prohibited, and user access should be subject to continuous monitoring and review. Also, care must be taken with **transitive trust**. Transitive trust is a two-way relationship that is automatically created between parent and child domains in a Microsoft Active Directory Forest. When a new domain is created, it shares resources with its parent domain by default, which can enable an authenticated user to access resources in both the child and the parent.

Chapter Summary

- Different authentication credentials can be presented to an information technology system to verify the genuineness of the user. These can be classified into five categories: what you know, what you have, what you are, what you do, and where you are.

- The most common "what you know" type of authentication is a password. A password is a secret combination of letters, numbers, and/or characters that only the user should have knowledge of and is the most common type of authentication in use today. Passwords provide a weak degree of protection because they rely on human memory. Human beings have a finite limit to the number of items that they can memorize. Because of the burdens that passwords place on human memory, users often take shortcuts to help them recall their passwords.

- Although there are several different types of password attacks, the most common password attacks today use offline cracking. Attackers steal the file of password digests and then load that file onto their own computers so they can attempt to discover the passwords by comparing the stolen digest passwords with candidate digests that they have created. An automated brute force attack uses every possible combination of letters, numbers, and characters to create candidates that are matched with those in the stolen file. A dictionary attack begins with the attacker creating digests of common dictionary words, which are then compared with those in a stolen password file. The hybrid attack slightly alters dictionary words. Attackers often use rainbow tables, which make password attacks easier by creating a large pregenerated data set of encrypted passwords. Large collections of stolen password files have allowed attackers to create a larger number of accurate candidates and to understand how users create passwords.

- There are several defenses against password attacks. The most basic is password complexity, or creating long and complex passwords. Credential management involves properly managing passwords, often by using technology instead of human memory. Another defense is to use a password hashing algorithm instead of a general-purpose hash algorithm. Salts, or random strings added to passwords, also can make passwords more difficult for attackers to break.

- Another type of authentication credential is based on the approved user having a specific item in her possession ("what you have"). A token is typically a small device (usually one that can be affixed to a keychain) with a window display that generates a code from the algorithm once every 30 to 60 seconds. Several different types of cards can be used as authentication credentials. A smart card contains an integrated circuit chip that can hold information, which can then be used as part of the authentication process. Tokens and cards are being replaced with cell phones.

- The features and characteristics of the individual ("what you are") can serve as authentication. Standard biometrics uses a person's unique physical characteristics for authentication. Cognitive biometrics is related to the perception, thought process, and understanding of the user. Cognitive biometrics is considered to be much easier for the user because it is based on the user's life experiences, which also makes it very difficult for an attacker to imitate.

- Behavioral biometrics, or "what you do," authenticates by normal actions that the user performs. Behavioral biometric technologies include keystroke dynamics and voice recognition. A final type of authentication, geolocation, is the identification of the location ("where you are") of a person or object using technology. Although geolocation may not uniquely identify the user, it can indicate if an attacker is trying to perform a malicious action from a location different from the normal location of the user.

- One of the problems facing users today is that they have multiple accounts across multiple platforms that all ideally use a unique username and password. The difficulty in managing all these different authentication credentials frequently causes users to compromise and select the least burdensome password and then use it for all accounts. A solution to this problem is to have one username and password to gain access to all accounts so that the user has only one username and password to remember. This is called single sign-on (SSO). Examples of some of the popular SSOs include Microsoft Account, OpenID, and OAuth.

12

- Managing the passwords in user accounts can be accomplished by setting restrictions regarding the creation and use of passwords. Although these restrictions can be performed on a user-by-user basis, this quickly becomes cumbersome and is a security risk: it is too easy to overlook one setting in one user account and create a security vulnerability. It may be more secure for an administrator to set these restrictions in a Group Policy.

Key Terms

authentication   Proving that a user is genuine, and not an imposter.

authentication factors   Five elements that can prove the genuineness of a user: what you know, what you have, what you are, what you do, and where you are.

bcrypt   A popular key stretching password hash algorithm.

behavioral biometrics   Authenticating a user by the unique actions that the user performs.

birthday attack   An attack that searches for any two digests that are the same.

brute force attack   A password attack in which every possible combination of letters, numbers, and characters is used to create encrypted passwords that are matched against those in a stolen password file.

cognitive biometrics   Authenticating a user through the perception, thought process, and understanding of the user.

common access card (CAC)   A U.S. Department of Defense (DoD) smart card used for identification of active-duty and reserve military personnel along with civilian employees and special contractors.

dictionary attack   A password attack that creates encrypted versions of common dictionary words and compares them against those in a stolen password file.

federated identity management (FIM) (or federation**)**   Single sign-on for networks owned by different organizations.

geolocation   The identification of the location of a person or object using technology.

HMAC-based one-time password (HOTP)   A one-time password that changes when a specific event occurs.

hybrid attack   A password attack that slightly alters dictionary words by adding numbers to the end of the password, spelling words backward, slightly misspelling words, or including special characters.

key stretching   A password hashing algorithm that requires significantly more time than standard hashing algorithms to create the digest.

LM (LAN Manager) hash   A cryptographic function found in older Microsoft Windows operating systems used to fingerprint data.

multifactor authentication   Using more than one type of authentication credential.

NTLM (New Technology LAN Manager) hash   A hash used by modern Microsoft Windows operating systems for creating password digests.

NTLMv2   The current version of the New Technology LAN Manager hash.

one-time password (OTP)   An authentication code that can be used only once or for a limited period of time.

password   A secret combination of letters, numbers, and/or characters that only the user should have knowledge of.

PBKDF2   A popular key stretching password hash algorithm.

Personal Identity Verification (PIV)   A U.S. government standard for smart cards that covers all government employees.

pre-image attack   An attack in which one known digest is compared to an unknown digest.

rainbow tables   Large pregenerated data sets of encrypted passwords used in password attacks.

salt   A random string that is used in hash algorithms.

single-factor authentication   Using one type of authentication credential.

single sign-on (SSO)   Using one authentication credential to access multiple accounts or applications.

smart card   A card that contains an integrated circuit chip that can hold information used as part of the authentication process.

standard biometrics   Using fingerprints or other unique physical characteristics of a person's face, hands, or eyes for authentication.

time-based one-time password (TOTP)   A one-time password that changes after a set period of time.

token   A small device that can be affixed to a keychain with a window display that shows a code to be used for authentication.

transitive trust   A two-way relationship that is automatically created between parent and child domains in a Microsoft Active Directory Forest.

12

username   An identifier of a user logging into a system.

Review Questions

1. Which authentication factor is based on a unique talent that a user possesses?

    a. what you have

    b. what you are

    c. what you do

    d. what you know

2. Which of these is NOT a characteristic of a weak password?

    a. a common dictionary word

    b. a long password

    c. using personal information

    d. using a predictable sequence of characters

3. Which attack is an attempt to compare a known digest to an unknown digest?
   a. pre-image attack
   b. birthday attack
   c. configuration attack
   d. SNIP attack

4. Which of these algorithms is the weakest for creating password digests?
   a. SHA-1
   b. MD-5
   c. LM (LAN Manager) hash
   d. NTLM (New Technology LAN Manager) hash

5. How is key stretching effective in resisting password attacks?
   a. It takes more time to generate candidate password digests.
   b. It requires the use of GPUs.
   c. It does not require the use of salts.
   d. The license fees are very expensive to purchase and use it.

6. Which of these is NOT a reason why users create weak passwords?
   a. A lengthy and complex password can be difficult to memorize.
   b. A security policy requires a password to be changed regularly.
   c. Having multiple passwords makes it hard to remember all of them.
   d. Most sites force users to create weak passwords even though they do not want to.

7. What is a hybrid attack?
   a. an attack that uses both automated and user input
   b. an attack that combines a dictionary attack with an online guessing attack
   c. a brute force attack that uses special tables
   d. an attack that slightly alters dictionary words

8. A TOTP token code is valid _____.
   a. for as long as it appears on the device
   b. for up to 24 hours
   c. only while the user presses SEND
   d. until an event occurs

9. What is a token system that requires the user to enter the code along with a PIN called?

   a. single-factor authentication system

   b. token-passing authentication system

   c. dual-prong verification system

   d. multifactor authentication system

10. Which of these is a U.S. Department of Defense (DoD) smart card that is used for identification of active-duty and reserve military personnel?

    a. Personal Identity Verification (PIV) card

    b. Common Access Card (CAC)

    c. Government Smart Card (GSC)

    d. Secure ID Card (SIDC)

11. Keystroke dynamics is an example of which type of biometrics?

    a. behavioral

    b. resource

    c. cognitive

    d. adaptive

12. Creating a pattern of where a user accesses a remote web account is an example of _____.

    a. geolocation

    b. Time-Location Resource Monitoring (TLRM)

    c. keystroke dynamics

    d. cognitive biometrics

13. Which of these is a decentralized open-source FIM that does not require specific software to be installed on the desktop?

    a. Windows Live ID

    b. SSO Login Resource (SSO-LR)

    c. Windows CardSpace

    d. OpenID

14. Which human characteristic is NOT used for biometric identification?

    a. retina

    b. face

    c. weight

    d. fingerprint

12

15. _____ biometrics is related to the perception, thought processes, and understanding of the user.

    a. Cognitive

    b. Standard

    c. Intelligent

    d. Behavioral

16. Using one authentication credential to access multiple accounts or applications is known as _____.

    a. credentialization

    b. identification authentication

    c. single sign-on

    d. federal login

17. What is a disadvantage of biometric readers?

    a. cost

    b. speed

    c. size

    d. standards

18. Which single sign-on (SSO) technology depends on tokens?

    a. OAuth

    b. CardSpace

    c. OpenID

    d. All SSO technologies use tokens.

19. Why should the account lockout threshold not be set too low?

    a. It could decrease calls to the help desk.

    b. The network administrator would have to reset the account manually.

    c. The user would not have to wait too long to have her password reset.

    d. It could result in denial of service (DoS) attacks.

20. Which one-time password is event-driven?

    a. HOTP

    b. TOTP

    c. ROTP

    d. POTP

Hands-On Projects

If you are concerned about installing any of the software in these projects on your regular computer, you can instead install the software in the Windows virtual machine created in the Chapter 1 Hands-On Projects 1-3 and 1-4. Software installed within the virtual machine will not impact the host computer.

Project 12-1: Use an Online Rainbow Table Cracker

Although brute force and dictionary attacks were once the primary tools used by attackers to crack stolen digest passwords, more recently attackers have used rainbow tables. Rainbow tables make password attacks easier by creating a large pregenerated data set of candidate digests. In this project, you will create a hash on a password and then crack it with an online rainbow table cracker to demonstrate the speed of using rainbow tables.

1. The first step is to use a general-purpose hash algorithm to create a password hash. Use your web browser to go to **www.fileformat.info/ tool/hash.htm**.

The location of content on the Internet may change without warn- ing. If you are no longer able to access the program through the above URL, use a search engine and search for "Fileformat.info".

2. Under **String hash**, enter the simple password **apple123** in the **Text:** line.
3. Click **Hash**.
4. Scroll down the page and copy the MD4 hash of this password to your Clipboard by selecting the text, right-clicking, and choosing **Copy**.
5. Open a new tab on your web browser.
6. Go to **https://crackstation.net/**.
7. Paste the MD4 hash of *apple123* into the text box beneath **Enter up to 10 non-salted hashes:**.
8. In the RECAPTCHA box, enter the current value being displayed in the box that says **Type the text**.
9. Click **Crack Hashes**.
10. How long did it take this online rainbow table to crack this hash?
11. Click the browser tab to return to FileFormat.Info.
12. Under **String hash**, enter the longer password **12applesauce** in the **Text:** line.
13. Click **Hash**.

14. Scroll down the page and copy the MD4 hash of this password to your Clipboard.

15. Click to browser tab to return to the CrackStation site.

16. Paste the MD4 hash of *12applesauce* into the text box beneath **Enter up to 10 non-salted hashes:**.

17. In the RECAPTCHA box, enter the current value being displayed in the box that says **Type the text**.

18. Click **Crack Hashes**.

19. How long did it take this online rainbow table to crack this stronger password hash?

20. Click the browser tab to return to FileFormat.Info and experiment by entering new passwords, computing their hash, and testing them in the CrackStation site. If you are bold, enter a string hash that is similar to a real password that you use.

21. What does this tell you about the speed of rainbow tables? What does it tell you about how easy it is for attackers to crack weak passwords?

22. Close all windows.

Project 12-2: Keystroke Dynamics

One type of behavioral biometrics is keystroke dynamics, which attempts to recognize a user's unique typing rhythm. In this project, you will download an application that illustrates keystroke dynamics.

1. Use your web browser to go to **www.epaymentbiometrics.ensicaen.fr/ index.php/app/resources/65**.

 The location of content on the Internet may change without warning. If you are no longer able to access the program through the above URL, use a search engine and search for "GreyC-Keystroke Software".

2. Under **Download the application**, select the appropriate version for your computer.

3. After the file downloads, uncompress the files.

4. Navigate to the directory of the files and double-click **GreycKeystroke.exe**.

5. Click **OK** to launch the application.

6. Click **Parameters**.

7. Point to **Password**.

8. This is the text that will be entered to determine your keystroke dynamics. Replace the current text with **Cengage Learning** and press **Enter**.

9. Now register yourself. Click **Execution Mode**.

10. Point to **Enroll User**.

11. In **User name**, enter your name and press **Enter**.

12. Now you will determine your keystroke dynamics.

13. Under **Password:** type **Cengage Learning** and press **Enter**.

14. Notice that the graphs illustrate your keystroke dynamics for the time between two keys pressure, time between two keys release, time between one release and one pressure, and time between one pressure and one release.

15. Now change the color of the next attempt and run the test again. Click **View**.

16. Click **Graph color**.

17. Click **green**.

18. Under **Password:** type **Cengage Learning** and press **Enter**.

19. Your graph should look similar to the first attempt.

20. Now run the test with a partner. Click **Execution Mode**.

21. Click **Enroll User**.

22. Ask your partner to enter his or her name, and press **Enter**.

23. Click **View**, then click **Graph color**.

24. Click **blue**.

25. Ask your partner under **Password:** to type **Cengage Learning** and press **Enter**.

26. Click **View**, then click **Graph color**.

27. Click **black**.

28. Ask your partner under **Password:** to type **Cengage Learning** and press **Enter**.

29. The results may look similar to Figure 12-11. How different are the dynamics between you and your partner?

30. Now determine the mean (average) of the keystroke dynamics for your partner. Click **View**.

31. Point to **Show mean vector**.

32. Select your partner's name.

33. Notice that another line appears with the average of your partner.

34. Now show your average. Click **View**, then click **Show mean vector**.

35. Select your name.

36. Can you determine that your keyboard dynamics are different from your partner's through these graphs?

37. To run the test again, click **View** and **Clear graph**.

38. Close GreyC Keystroke when finished and close all windows.

12

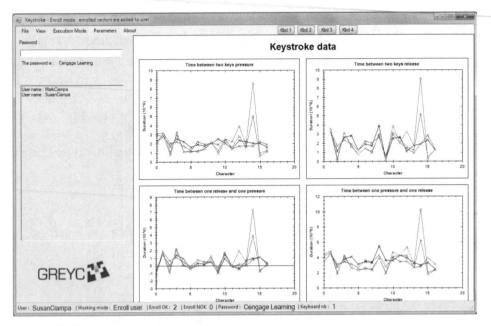

Figure 12-11 GreyC Keystroke Dynamics
Source: www.epaymentbiometrics.ensicaen.fr/index.php/app/resources/65

Project 12-3: Download and Install a Password Management Program

The drawback to using strong passwords is that they can be very difficult to remember, particularly when a unique password is used for each account that a user has. As another option, password management programs allow users to store account information such as a username and password. These programs are themselves protected by a single strong password. One example of a password storage program is KeePass Password Safe, which is an open-source product. In this project, you will download and install KeePass.

1. Use your web browser to go to **keepass.info** and then click **Downloads**.

The location of content on the Internet may change without warning. If you are no longer able to access the program through the above URL, use a search engine and search for "KeePass".

2. Under **Professional Edition,** locate the most recent portable version of KeePass and click it to download the application. Save this file in a location such as your desktop, a folder designated by your instructor, or your portable USB flash drive. When the file finishes downloading, install the program. Accept the installation defaults.

Because this is the portable version of KeePass it does not install under Windows. In order to use it, you must double-click the filename KeePass.exe.

3. Launch KeePass to display the opening screen.

4. Click **File** and **New** to start a password database. Enter a strong master password for the database to protect all of the passwords in it. When prompted, enter the password again to confirm it.

5. Click **Edit** and **Add Entry**. You will enter information about an online account that has a password that you already use.

6. Create a group by clicking **Edit** and then **Add Group** and then enter **Web Sites**.

7. Select the **Web Sites** group and click **Edit** and then **Add Entry**.

8. Enter a title for your website (such as *Google Gmail*) under **Title**.

9. Under **User name,** enter the username that you use to log in to this account.

10. Erase the entries under **Password** and **Repeat** and enter the password that you use for this account and confirm it.

11. Enter the URL for this account under **URL**.

12. Click **OK**.

13. Click **File** and **Save**. Enter your last name as the filename and then click **Save**.

14. Exit KeePass.

15. If necessary, navigate to the location of KeePass and double-click the file **KeePass.exe** to launch the application.

16. Enter your master password to open your password file.

17. If necessary, click the group to locate the account you just entered; it will be displayed in the right pane.

18. Click under **URL** to go to that website.

19. Click KeePass in the taskbar so that the window is now on top of your browser window.

20. Drag and drop your username from KeePass into the login username box for this account in your web browser.

21. Drag and drop your password from KeePass for this account.

22. Click the button on your browser to log in to this account.

23. Because you can drag and drop your account information from KeePass, you do not have to memorize any account passwords and can instead create strong passwords for each account. Is this an application that would help users create and use strong passwords? What are the strengths of such password programs? What are the weaknesses? Would you use KeePass?

24. Close all windows.

12

Project 12-4: Use Cognitive Biometrics

Cognitive biometrics holds great promise for adding two-factor authentication without placing a tremendous burden on the user. In this project, you will participate in a demonstration of Passfaces.

1. Use your web browser to go to **www.passfaces.com/demo**.

The location of content on the Internet may change without warning. If you are no longer able to access the program through the above URL, use a search engine and search for "Passfaces demo".

2. Under **First Time Users,** enter the requested information and then click **START THE DEMO.**

3. Click **Start the Demo.**

4. Accept **demo** as the name and then click **OK.**

5. When asked, click **NEXT** to enroll now.

6. When the **Enroll in Passfaces** dialog box displays, click **NEXT.**

7. Look closely at the three faces you are presented with. After you feel familiar with the faces, click **NEXT.**

8. You will then be asked to think of associations with the first face (who it looks like or who it reminds you of). Follow each step with the faces and then click **NEXT** after each face.

9. When the **STEP 2 Practice Using Passfaces** dialog box displays, click **NEXT.**

10. You will then select your faces from three separate screens, each of which has nine total faces. Click on the face (which is also moving as a hint).

11. You can practice one more time. Click **NEXT.**

12. When the **STEP 3 Try Logging On with Passfaces** dialog box displays, click **NEXT.** Identify your faces, and click **NEXT.**

13. Click **DONE** and click **OK.**

14. Click **Try Passfaces** and then click **Logon.**

15. Click **OK** under the username and identify your faces.

16. Is this type of cognitive biometrics effective? If you came back to this site tomorrow, would you remember the three faces?

17. Close all windows.

Project 12-5: Create an OpenID Account

OpenID is a decentralized open-source FIM that does not require specific software to be installed on the desktop. OpenID is a Uniform Resource Locator (URL)–based identity system. In this project you create an OpenID account.

1. Use your web browser to go to **pip.verisignlabs.com/**, which is the Personal Identity Provider OpenID site of VeriSign Labs.

The location of content on the Internet may change without warning. If you are no longer able to access the program through the above URL, use a search engine and search for "PIP OpenID sites".

2. Click **Get Started Now.**

3. Enter the requested information and then click **Create Account.**

4. Click **My Account** and then click **Browse** next to the Personal Icon. Locate an image on your computer. Click **Open.** Click **Save Settings.**

5. Go to your email account and read the information about your account.

6. Record your identity URL and then click **Sign Out.**

7. Use your web browser to return to **pip.verisignlabs.com/**.

8. Click **Sign In.**

9. Enter your **user name** and **password** and click **Sign In** to test the password.

Your username is not your identity URL but instead is the username you entered when you created the account.

Remember that there is no restriction on how websites can use the information you enter. It is best not to enter any more information than you consider absolutely necessary.

10. Click **Sign Out.**

11. Close all windows.

Project 12-6: Use an OpenID Account

In this project, you will use the OpenID account that you created in the previous project.

1. Use your web browser to go to **www.livejournal.com/openid/**.

The location of content on the Internet may change without warning. If you are no longer able to access the program through the above URL, use a search engine and search for "LiveJournal OpenID".

2. Enter your identity URL in the Your OpenID URL text box.

3. Click **Login.**

12

4. You will be returned to the Personal Identity Portal OpenID site of VeriSign Labs. Enter your username and password and click **Sign In**.

5. Click **Allow**. You are returned to the LiveJournal website.

6. Log out of LiveJournal.

7. Do you consider OpenID easy to use? Would you recommend it to other users? How secure does it seem to you? Would you use it for accessing your bank information? Why or why not?

8. Close all windows.

Case Projects

CASE PROJECTS

Case Project 12-1: Testing Password Strength

How strong are your passwords? Various online tools can provide information on password strength, but not all feedback is the same. First, assign the numbers 1 through 3 to three of the passwords you are currently using, and write down the number (not the password) on a piece of paper. Then, enter those passwords into these three online password testing services:

- How Secure Is My Password (*howsecureismypassword.net/*)
- Check Your Password (*www.microsoft.com/security/pc-security/ password-checker.aspx*)
- The Password Meter (*www.passwordmeter.com/*)

Record next to each number the strength of that password as indicated by these three online tools. Then use each online password tester to modify the password by adding more random numbers or letters to increase its strength. How secure are your passwords? Would any of these tools encourage someone to create a stronger password? Which provided the best information? Create a one-paragraph summary of your findings.

Case Project 12-2: Password Management Applications

Research at least four password management applications, one of which is a stand-alone application and another of which is a browser-based application. Create a table that lists and compares their features. Which would you recommend? Why? Create a report on your findings.

Case Project 12-3: Create Your Own Cognitive Biometric Memorable Event

What type of cognitive biometric "memorable event" do you think would be effective? Design your own example that is different from those given in the chapter. There should be five steps, and each step should have at least seven options. The final step should be a fill-in-the-blank user response. Compare your steps with those of other learners. Which do you think would be the easiest for users?

Case Project 12-4: Standard Biometric Analysis

Use the Internet and other sources to research the two disadvantages of standard biometrics, cost, and error rates. Select one standard biometric technique (fingerprint, palm print, iris, facial features, etc.) and research the costs for having biometric readers for that technique located at two separate entrances into a building. Next, research ways in which attackers attempt to defeat this particular standard biometric technique. Finally, how often will this technique reject authorized users while accepting unauthorized users compared to other standard biometric techniques? Based on your research, would you recommend this technique? Why or why not? Write a one-page paper on your findings.

Case Project 12-5: Open Authentication (OAuth)

Use the Internet to research OAuth. What is the technology behind it? What are its strengths? What are its weaknesses? Will it replace OpenID? Would you recommend it for secure applications like online banking? Write a one-page paper on your analysis.

Case Project 12-6: Bay Pointe Security Consulting

Bay Pointe Security Consulting (BPSC) provides security consulting services to a wide range of businesses, individuals, schools, and organizations. BPSC has hired you as a technology student to help them with a new project and provide real-world experience to students who are interested in the security field.

"It's Late" is a regional coffee shop that serves "quick, casual food" such as sandwiches, soups, and salads. Each location also provides free wireless LAN access to its customers. Recently one of the location's networks was successfully attacked and personal customer information was stolen, such as names, email addresses, birthdates, and similar information. The attack was traced to a manager's account that used the name of his spouse as the password. The new director of IT has asked BPSC to assist them by conducting a workshop regarding the risks of weak passwords and how to create and manage strong passwords.

1. Create a PowerPoint presentation for the executive management about the weaknesses and risks of using passwords, and how employees should create strong passwords. Your presentation should contain at least 10 slides.

2. After the presentation, the It's Late director of IT has contacted you. She recently read an article in a trade magazine about SSO and believes that this could be a solution to their problem. Create a memo to this director about SSO and how it could or could not address the password issue.

Case Project 12-7: Community Site Activity

The Information Security Community Site is an online companion to this textbook. It contains a wide variety of tools, information, discussion boards, and other features to assist learners. Go to **community.cengage.com/infosec**. Sign in with the login name and password that you created in Chapter 1.

Take the challenge to convince three of your friends that they must strengthen their passwords. Create a script of what you will say to them in an attempt to convince them of the dangers of weak passwords and the seriousness of the problem, and to inform them about what practical solutions are available. Then approach each friend individually and see whether you can be successful. Make a record of their responses and reactions to stronger passwords.

Record what occurred on the Community Site discussion board. What did you learn from this? How hard or easy is it to challenge users to create strong passwords? What arguments did you hear against it? What helped convince them to create stronger passwords?

References

1. Honan, Mat, "Yes, I was hacked. Hard," *Emptyage*, Aug. 3, 2012, retrieved Apr. 3, 2014, www.emptyage.com/post/28679875595/yes-i-was-hacked-hard.

2. Vu, K.-P., Proctor, R., Bhargav-Spantzel, A., Tai, B.-L., Cook, J., and Schultz, E., "Improving password security and memorability to protect personal and organizational information," *International Journal of Human-Computer Studies, 65*, 744–57.

3. Sasse, M., and Brostoff, S. W., "Transforming the 'weakest link': A human/computer interaction approach to usable and effective security," *BT Technology Journal, 19*(3), 122–31.

4. Schneier, Bruce, *Secrets and lies: Digital security in a networked world* (New York: Wiley Computer Publishing), 2004.

5. Goodin, Dan, "25-GPU cluster cracks every standard Windows password in <6 hours," *ARS Technica*, Dec. 9, 2012, retrieved Apr. 3, 2014, http://arstechnica.com/security/2012/12/25-gpu-cluster-cracks-every-standard-windows-password-in-6-hours/.

6. Schneier, Bruce, "Secure passwords keep you safer," *Security Matters*, Jan. 11, 2007, retrieved Apr. 20, 2011, www.wired.com/politics/security/commentary/securitymatters/2007/01/72458?currentPage=all.

7. Zhao, Ziming, Ahn, Gail-Joon, Seo, Jeong-Jun, and Hu, Hongxin, "On the security of Picture Gesture Authentication," *USENIX Security Symposium, 2013*, retrieved Mar. 22, 2014, www.public.asu.edu/~zzhao30/publication/ZimingUSENIX2013.pdf.

8. "Products," *BioPassword*, 2007, retrieved May 1, 2011, http://stage1.biopassword.com/keystroke-dynamics-history.php.

## part VII

Compliance and Operational Security

Compliance, or conforming to stated requirements, is accomplished by an organization through risk identification and management. In this part, you will learn how to maintain business continuity (Chapter 13), mitigate risk (Chapter 14), and assess vulnerabilities (Chapter 15).

## chapter 13

Business Continuity

After completing this chapter, you should be able to do the following:

- Define business continuity
- List the features of a disaster recovery plan
- Explain different environmental controls
- Describe forensics and incident response procedures

Today's Attacks and Defenses

Superstorm Sandy was the second most costly hurricane in U.S. history, surpassed only by Hurricane Katrina in 2005. When Sandy crashed into the northeastern U.S. in late October 2012, it was the largest Atlantic hurricane ever recorded, covering an area of more than 1100 miles (1800 km). At least 286 people in seven countries were killed, and damage estimates reached more than $68 billion.

Due to the widespread and destructive force of Sandy, most businesses were overwhelmed by the loss of electrical power, cellular telephone service, Internet access, transportation, and even running water. And although the majority of those businesses had business continuity or disaster recovery plans in place, they found that their plans were no match for Sandy. The extreme impact of the storm undermined what once were considered to be the best of plans.

For example, when Lower Manhattan in New York City was flooded by the storm surge, many major media companies saw their websites go dark as water flooded basement floors that contained the electrical equipment that powered their web servers. One business was aware of this risk and planned for this contingency by housing their backup electrical generators on the 17th floor of their building. When the fuel pump in the basement was flooded, however, the diesel fuel could no longer reach the generators. A team of 30 employees lugged buckets of diesel fuel up 17 floors in darkened stairwells for two days in order to keep the generators working.

Other businesses were relying on cloud computing as a major part of their business continuity plans. They had reasoned that by storing their data online, even if a hurricane made their office building inaccessible, the data could still be reached from virtually any other location. What they had not planned on, however, was the widespread cellular telephone and electrical outages. In the 10 states hit by Superstorm Sandy, almost one-quarter of all cell towers and land lines were impacted by the storm. Downtown New York City was without electrical power for nearly one week.

As Sandy was slamming into the Eastern seaboard, almost 3000 miles away a training exercise was taking place to help organizations plan for such catastrophes. This training exercise had a unique twist. Called the "Zombie Apocalypse," it was conducted in San Diego at a 44-acre resort island as a counterterrorism summit attended by hundreds of police, firefighters, and military personnel to prepare them for their worst nightmares.[1] The training scenario consisted of a very important person (VIP) and his personal entourage being trapped in a village, surrounded by zombies (who were actually actors with detailed Hollywood face paint and tattered clothing). When a bomb exploded, the VIP would be wounded and his team had to

(continued)

move through the town, dodging bullets and shooting back at the invading zombies. At one point, several members of the team were bitten by zombies and had to be taken to a field medical facility for decontamination and treatment. The rationale for this zombie scenario was that if an organization was prepared for a zombie attack, it would be ready for virtually any real-life disaster like a hurricane, earthquake, pandemic, or terrorist attack.

Earthquakes, tsunamis, tornados, hurricanes, floods, wildfires—these and other natural disasters can have a major impact on businesses around the world. By some estimates, world economic losses to such disasters can total more than $380 billion annually. Not all disasters, however, are acts of nature. Sabotage, acts of terrorism, and even attacks on information technology also can quickly bring a business to its knees or put it out of operation entirely. The ability of an organization to maintain its operations and services in the face of catastrophe is crucial if it is to survive.

Although preparation for disaster is an essential business element for organizations both large and small, it remains sadly lacking in practice. Many organizations are completely unprepared. It is estimated that one out of every three small businesses impacted by a disaster does not recover.[2] And many organizations that do have plans on paper have never tested those plans to determine whether they would truly bring the business through an unforeseen event.

In this chapter, you will learn about the critical importance of keeping an organization operational in the face of disaster. You will first learn what business continuity is and why it is important. Next, you will investigate how to prevent disruptions through disaster recovery and how to protect resources with environmental controls. Finally, you will see how incident response procedures and forensics are used when an event occurs.

What Is Business Continuity?

2.8 Summarize risk management best practices.

Business continuity can be defined as the ability of an organization to maintain its operations and services in the face of a disruptive event. This event could be as basic as an electrical outage or as catastrophic as a Category 5 hurricane. **Business continuity planning and testing** is the process of identifying exposure to threats, creating preventive and recovery procedures, and then testing them to determine if they are sufficient. In short, business continuity planning and testing is designed to ensure that an organization can continue to function (**continuity of operations**) in the event of a natural (flood, hurricane, earthquake, etc.) or human-made (plane crash, terrorist attack, denial-of-service attack, etc.) disaster. It may also include **succession planning**, or determining in advance who will be authorized to take over in the event of the incapacitation or death of key employees.

13

One important tool in business continuity planning and testing is a **business impact analysis (BIA)**. A BIA identifies mission-critical business functions and quantifies the impact a loss of such functions may have on the organization in terms of its operational and financial position. A BIA typically begins by identifying threats through a **risk assessment**. Then, the impact of having those threats realized is determined. This helps to answer such questions as:

- What would happen if the portion of the building where your department is located were completely destroyed?

- What would you do if all records, data files, technology, and support systems were unavailable?

- What if the four key personnel in your unit were unable to work for two weeks following a disaster?

- What are the primary business processes that would be affected immediately if there was a major disaster such as a flood?

Disaster Recovery

2.1 Explain the importance of risk related concepts.

2.8 Summarize risk management best practices.

Whereas business continuity planning and testing looks at the needs of the business as a whole in recovering from a catastrophe, a subset of it focuses on continuity in the context of information technology (IT). There are two key terms that are used for IT business continuity planning and testing.

A *contingency* is a future event or circumstance that may possibly occur but cannot be predicted with any certainty. **IT contingency planning** is developing an outline of procedures that are to be followed in the event of major IT incident (a denial-of-service attack) or an incident that directly impacts IT (a building fire). The goal of an IT contingency plan is to ensure that the business will continue to function at an acceptable level in the face of a major IT incident or a disaster. Closely related is a **disaster recovery plan (DRP)**, which is involved with restoring the IT functions and services to their former state.

Disaster recovery involves creating, implementing, and testing disaster recovery plans. These plans typically include procedures to address redundancy and fault tolerance as well as data backups.

Disaster Recovery Plan (DRP)

A DRP is a written document that details the process for restoring IT resources following an event that causes a significant disruption in service. Comprehensive in scope, a DRP is intended to be a detailed document that is updated regularly. All disaster recovery plans are different, but most address the common features included in the following typical outline:

Unit 1: Purpose and Scope—The reason for the plan and what it encompasses are clearly outlined. Those incidences that require the plan to be enacted also should be listed. Topics found under Unit 1 include:

- Introduction
- Objectives and constraints
- Assumptions
- Incidents requiring action
- Contingencies
- Physical safeguards
- Types of computer service disruptions
- Insurance considerations

Unit 2: Recovery Team—The team that is responsible for the direction of the disaster recovery plan is clearly defined. It is important that each member knows her role in the plan and be adequately trained. This part of the plan is continually reviewed as employees leave the organization, home telephone or cell phone numbers change, or new members are added to the team. The Unit 2 DRP addresses the following:

- Organization of the disaster/recovery team
- Disaster/recovery team headquarters
- Disaster recovery coordinator
- Recovery team leaders and their responsibilities

Unit 3: Preparing for a Disaster—A DRP lists the entities that could impact an organization and also the procedures and safeguards that should constantly be in force to reduce the risk of the disaster. Topics for Unit 3 include:

- Physical/security risks
- Environmental risks
- Internal risks
- External risks
- Safeguards

Unit 4: Emergency Procedures—The Emergency Procedures unit answers the question, "What should happen when a disaster occurs?" Unit 4 outlines the step-by-step procedures that should occur, including the following:

- Disaster recovery team formation
- Vendor contact list
- Use of alternate sites
- Offsite storage

Unit 5: Restoration Procedures—After the initial response has put in place the procedures that allow the organization to continue functioning, this unit addresses how to fully recover from the disaster and return to normal business operations. This unit should include:

13

- Central facilities recovery plan
- Systems and operations
- Scope of limited operations at central site
- Network communications
- Computer recovery plan

A good DRP will contain sufficient detail. A sample excerpt is shown in Figure 13-1.

COMMUNICATIONS ROOM

The purpose of a communications room is to provide a central point of contact and coordination. The telephone equipment in this room will include the following:

- Three wired telephones
- Four fully charged cellular telephones
- One satellite telephone

Media communications in this room will include the following:

- One television
- One standard radio
- One police radio
- One Citizens' Band radio
- One DVD player/recorder

This room should be isolated from other functional areas and only authorized personnel will be allowed to enter.

Figure 13-1   Sample excerpt from a DRP

 Due to the fluid nature of IT in which new hardware and software are added on a continual basis, a disaster recovery plan itself must be adaptable. Most disaster recovery plans have a backout/contingency option: if the plan is put into place yet it appears to not be working properly, the technology can be "rolled back" to the starting point so that a different approach can be taken.

Disaster exercises are designed to test the effectiveness of the DRP. Plans that may look solid on paper often make assumptions or omit key elements that can be revealed only with a mock disaster. The objectives of these disaster exercises are to:

- Test the efficiency of interdepartmental planning and coordination in managing a disaster
- Test current procedures of the DRP
- Determine the strengths and weaknesses in responses

Disaster exercises are becoming increasingly common in testing different types of DRPs. U.S. federal aviation regulations require all commercial U.S. airports to conduct a full-scale exercise at least once every three years. These exercises are designed to assess the capability of an international airport's emergency management system by testing emergency responders and aid providers in a real-time, stress-filled environment in which personnel and equipment are actually mobilized and deployed.

One way in which DRPs can be tested is by using **tabletop exercises**. Tabletop exercises simulate an emergency situation but in an informal and stress-free environment. Table 13-1 lists the features of a tabletop exercise.

Feature	Description
Participants	Individuals on a decision-making level
Focus	Training and familiarizing roles, procedures, and responsibilities
Setting	Informal
Format	Discussion guided by a facilitator
Purpose	Identify and solve problems as a group
Commitment	Only moderate amount of time, cost, and resources
Advantage	Can acquaint key personnel with emergency responsibilities, procedures, and other members
Disadvantage	Lack of realism; does not provide true test

Table 13-1   Features of tabletop exercises

Redundancy and Fault Tolerance

One of the primary ways to ensure IT business continuity is to remove any **single point of failure**, which is a component or entity in a system which, if it no longer functions, will disable the entire system. This requires the identification of critical systems and their components. Eliminating these single failure points will result in **high availability**, or a system that can function for an extended period of time with little downtime. This availability is often expressed as a percentage of uptime in a year. Table 13-2 lists these percentages and the corresponding downtimes.

Percentage	Name	Weekly downtime	Monthly downtime	Yearly downtime
90	One Nine	16.8 hours	72 hours	36.5 days
99	Two Nines	1.68 hours	7.20 hours	3.65 days
99.9	Three Nines	10.1 minutes	43.2 minutes	8.76 hours
99.99	Four Nines	1.01 minutes	4.32 minutes	52.56 minutes
99.999	Five Nines	6.05 seconds	25.9 seconds	5.26 minutes
99.9999	Six Nines	0.605 second	2.59 seconds	31.5 seconds

Table 13-2   Percentages and downtimes

13

A *service level agreement (SLA)* is a service contract between a vendor and a client that specifies what services will be provided, the responsibilities of each party, and any guarantees of service. Most SLAs are based on percentages of guaranteed uptime.

One way to address a single point of failure is to incorporate redundancy and fault tolerance, which involves building excess capacity in order to protect against failures. The goal of redundancy and fault tolerance is to reduce a variable known as the **mean time to recovery (MTTR)**. This is the average amount of time that it will take a device to recover from a failure that is not a terminal failure. Some systems are designed to have a MTTR of zero, which means they have redundant components that can take over the instant the primary component fails. Redundancy planning can involve redundancy for servers, storage, networks, power, and even sites.

Servers Because servers play such a key role in a network infrastructure, the loss of a single server that supports a critical application can have a significant impact. Some organizations stockpile spare parts to replace one that has failed (such as a server's power supply) or even entire *redundant servers* as standbys. However, the time it takes to install a new part or add a new server to the network and then load software and backup data may be more than the organization can tolerate.

Another approach is for the organization to design the network infrastructure so that multiple servers are incorporated into the network yet appear to users and applications as a single computing resource. One method to do this is by **clustering**, or combining two or more devices to appear as one single unit. A *server cluster* is the combination of two or more servers that are interconnected to appear as one, as shown in Figure 13-2. These servers are connected through both a *public cluster connection* so that clients see them as a single unit as well as a *private cluster connection* so that the servers can exchange data when necessary.

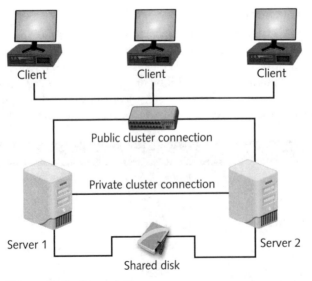

Figure 13-2   Server cluster

There are two types of server clusters. In an *asymmetric server cluster*, a standby server exists only to take over for another server in the event of its failure. The standby server performs no useful work other than to be ready if it is needed. Asymmetric server clusters are used to provide high-availability applications that require a high level of read and write actions, such as databases, messaging systems, and file and print services.

In a *symmetric server cluster*, every server in the cluster performs useful work. If one server fails, the remaining servers continue to perform their normal work as well as that of the failed server. Symmetric clusters are more cost-effective because they take advantage of all of the servers and none sit idle; however, if the servers are not powerful enough in the event of a failure, the additional load on the remaining servers could tax them or even cause them to fail. Symmetric server clusters are typically used in environments in which the primary server is for a particular set of applications. Symmetric clusters are frequently used for web servers, media servers, and VPN servers.

Storage A trend in data storage technologies for computers today is to use *solid-state drives (SSDs)*, which essentially store data on chips instead of magnetic platters. Because SSDs lack spinning platters, actuator arms with read/write heads, and motors, they are more resistant to failure and are considered more reliable than traditional hard disk drives (HDDs). However, traditional HDDs still serve as the backbone of data storage for servers.

Because HDDs are mechanical devices, they often are the first component of a system to fail. Some organizations maintain a stockpile of hard drives as spare parts to replace those that fail. Yet how many spare hard drives should an organization keep on hand?

A statistical value that is used to answer this question is **mean time between failures (MTBF)**. MTBF refers to the average (*mean*) amount of time until a component fails, cannot be repaired, and must be replaced. Calculating the MTBF involves taking the total time measured divided by the total number of failures observed. For example, if 15,400 hard drive units were run for 1000 hours each and that resulted in 11 failures, the MTBF would be (15,400 × 1000) hours/11, or 1.4 million hours. This MTBF rating can be used to determine the number of spare hard drives that should be stored. If an organization had 1000 hard drives operating continuously, it could be expected that one would fail every 58 days, so 19 failures could be expected to occur in three years, which means the number of spare hard drives needed would be 19.

The MTBF does not mean that a single hard drive is expected to last 1.4 million hours (159 years). MTBF is a statistical measure and, as such, cannot predict anything for a single unit.

Instead of waiting for a hard drive to fail, a more proactive approach can be used. A system of hard drives based on redundancy can be achieved through using a technology known as **RAID (Redundant Array of Independent Drives)**, which uses multiple hard disk drives for increased reliability and performance. RAID can be implemented through either software or hardware. Software-based RAID is implemented at the operating system level, while hardware-based RAID requires a specialized hardware controller either on the client computer or on the array that holds the RAID drives.

RAID originally stood for *Redundant Array of Inexpensive Disks.*

Originally there were five standard RAID configurations (called *levels*), and several additional levels have since evolved. These additional levels include "nested" levels and nonstandard levels that are proprietary to specific vendors. Nested RAIDs are usually described by combining the numbers indicating the RAID levels with a "+" in between, such as *RAID Level 0+1*. With nested RAID, the elements can be either individual disks or entire RAIDs.

The most common levels of RAID are:

- *RAID Level 0 (striped disk array without fault tolerance)*—RAID 0 technology is based on *striping*. Striping partitions divides the storage space of each hard drive into smaller sections (*stripes*), which can be as small as 512 bytes or as large as several megabytes. Data written to the stripes is alternated across the drives, as shown in Figure 13-3. Although RAID Level 0 uses multiple drives, it is not fault-tolerant; if one of the drives fails, all of the data on that drive is lost.

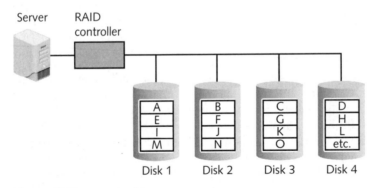

Figure 13-3 RAID Level 0

- *RAID Level 1 (mirroring)*—RAID Level 1 uses *disk mirroring*. Disk mirroring involves connecting multiple drives in the server to the same disk controller card. When a request is made to write data to the drive, the controller sends that request to each drive; when a read action is required, the data is read twice, once from each drive. By "mirroring" the action on the primary drive, the other drives become exact duplicates. In case the primary drive fails, the other drives take over with no loss of data. This is shown in Figure 13-4. A variation of RAID Level 1 is to include *disk duplexing*. Instead of having a single disk controller card that is attached to all hard drives, disk duplexing has separate cards for each disk. A single controller card failure affects only one drive. This additional redundancy protects against controller card failures.

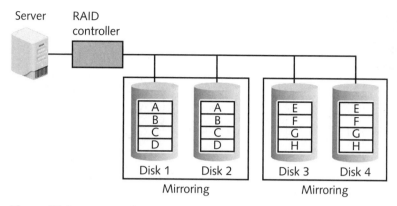

Figure 13-4 RAID Level 1

- *RAID 5 (independent disks with distributed parity)*—RAID Level 5 distributes *parity* data (a type of error checking) across all drives instead of using a separate drive to hold the parity error checking information. Data is always stored on one drive while its parity information is stored on another drive, as shown in Figure 13-5. Distributing parity across other disks provides an additional degree of protection.

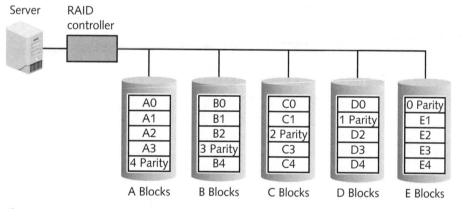

Figure 13-5 RAID Level 5

- *RAID 0+1 (high data transfer)*—RAID 0+1 is a nested-level RAID. It acts as a mirrored array whose segments are RAID 0 arrays. RAID 0+1 can achieve high data transfer rates because there are multiple stripe segments. RAID Level 0+1 is shown in Figure 13-6.

Many operating systems support one or more levels of RAID. Apple's Mac OS X and Mac OS X Server support RAID 0, RAID 1, and RAID 1+0, while FreeBSD Linux supports RAID 0, RAID 1, RAID 3, and RAID 5. Microsoft Windows Server supports RAID 0, RAID 1, and RAID 5.

13

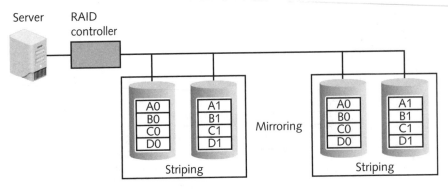

Figure 13-6 RAID Level 0+1

Table 13-3 summarizes the common levels of RAID.

RAID level	Description	Minimum number of drives needed	Typical application	Advantages	Disadvantages
RAID Level 0	Uses a striped disk array so that data is broken down into blocks and each block is written to a separate disk drive	2	Video production and editing	Simple design, easy to implement	Not fault-tolerant
RAID Level 1	Data written twice to separate drives	2	Financial	Simplest RAID to implement	Can slow down system if RAID controlling software is used instead of hardware
RAID Level 5	Each entire data block is written on a data disk and parity for blocks in the same rank is generated and recorded on a separate disk	3	Database	Most versatile RAID	Can be difficult to rebuild if a disk fails
RAID Level 0+1	A mirrored array with segments that are RAID 0 arrays	4	Imaging applications	High input/ output rates	Expensive

Table 13-3   Common RAID levels

Apple's RAID configuration also lists support for JBOD (*Just a Bunch of Disks*). Although this is not a true RAID level, it can be used to combine multiple hard drives into one larger virtual disk.

Networks Due to the critical nature of connectivity today, redundant networks also may be necessary. A redundant network waits in the background during normal operations and uses a replication scheme to keep its copy of the live network information current. If a disaster occurs, the redundant network automatically launches so that it is transparent to users. A redundant network ensures that network services are always accessible.

Virtually all network hardware components can be duplicated to provide a redundant network. Some manufacturers offer switches and routers that have a primary active port as well as a standby failover network port for physical redundancy. If a special packet is not detected in a specific time frame on the primary port, the failover port automatically takes over. Load balancers can provide a degree of network redundancy by blocking traffic to servers that are not functioning. Also, multiple redundant switches and routers can be integrated into the network infrastructure.

Load balancers are covered in Chapter 7.

TIP

Some organizations contract with more than one Internet service provider (ISP) for remote site network connectivity. In case the primary ISP is no longer available, the secondary ISP will be used. If network connectivity is essential, an organization can elect to use redundant fiber-optic lines to the different ISPs, each of which takes a diverse path through an area.

Power Maintaining electrical power is essential when planning for redundancy. An *uninterruptible power supply (UPS)* is a device that maintains power to equipment in case of an interruption in the primary electrical power source.

There are two primary types of UPS. An *off-line UPS* is considered the least expensive and simplest solution. During normal operation, the equipment being protected is served by the standard primary power source. The off-line UPS battery charger is also connected to the primary power source in order to charge its battery. If power is interrupted, the UPS will quickly (usually within a few milliseconds) begin supplying power to the equipment. When the primary power is restored, the UPS automatically switches back into standby mode.

An *on-line UPS* is always running off its battery while the main power runs the battery charger. An advantage of an on-line UPS is that it is not affected by dips or sags in voltage. An on-line UPS can clean the electrical power before it reaches the server to ensure that a correct and constant level of power is delivered to the server. The UPS also can serve as a surge protector, which keeps intense spikes of electrical current, common during thunderstorms, from reaching systems.

A UPS is more than just a big battery, however. UPS systems also can communicate with the network operating system on a server to ensure that an orderly shutdown occurs. Specifically, if the power goes down, a UPS can complete the following tasks:

- Send a message to the network administrator's computer, or page or telephone the network manager, to indicate that the power has failed

- Notify all users that they must finish their work immediately and log off
- Prevent any new users from logging on
- Disconnect users and shut down the server

Because a UPS can supply power for a limited amount of time, some organizations turn to a *backup generator* to create power. Backup generators can be powered by diesel, natural gas, or propane gas to generate electricity. Unlike portable residential backup generators, commercial backup generators are permanently installed as part of the building's power infrastructure. They include automatic transfer switches that can, in less than one second, detect the loss of a building's primary power and switch to the backup generator.

Sites Just as redundancy can be planned for servers, storage, networks, and power, it also can be planned for the entire site. A major disaster such as a flood or hurricane can inflict such extensive damage to a building that the organization will have to temporarily move to another location. Many organizations maintain redundant sites in case this occurs. Three basic types of redundant sites are used: hot sites, cold sites, and warm sites.

- *Hot site.* A **hot site** is generally run by a commercial disaster recovery service that allows a business to continue computer and network operations to maintain business continuity. A hot site is essentially a duplicate of the production site and has all the equipment needed for an organization to continue running, including office space and furniture, telephone jacks, computer equipment, and a live telecommunications link. Data backups of information can be quickly moved to the hot site, and in some instances the production site automatically synchronizes all of its data with the hot site so that all data is immediately accessible. If the organization's data processing center becomes inoperable, typically all data processing operations can be moved to a hot site within an hour.

- *Cold site.* A **cold site** provides office space, but the customer must provide and install all the equipment needed to continue operations. In addition, there are no backups of data immediately available at this site. A cold site is less expensive, but requires more time to get an enterprise in full operation after a disaster.

- *Warm site.* A **warm site** has all the equipment installed but does not have active Internet or telecommunications facilities, and does not have current backups of data. This type of site is much less expensive than constantly maintaining those connections as required for a hot site; however, the amount of time needed to turn on the connections and install the backups can be as much as half a day or more.

Businesses usually have an annual contract with a company that offers hot and cold site services with a monthly service charge. Some services also offer data backup services so that all company data is available regardless of whether a hot site or cold site is used.

A growing trend is to use cloud computing in conjunction with sites. Some organizations back up their applications and data to the cloud and then, if a disaster occurs, restore it to hardware in a hot, cold, or warm site. Other organizations also back up to the cloud but, instead of restoring to hardware at a site, they restore to virtual machines in the cloud, which then can be accessed from almost any location. This approach reduces or even eliminates the need for maintaining sites.

Data Backups

Another essential element in any DRP is **data backups**. A data backup is copying information to a different medium and storing it (preferably at an offsite location) so that it can be used in the event of a disaster. Although RAID is designed to provide protection if a single hard drive fails, RAID is of no help if a system is destroyed in a fire.

When creating a data backup plan or policy, five basic questions should be answered:

1. What information should be backed up?
2. How frequently should it be backed up?
3. What media should be used?
4. Where should the backup be stored?
5. What hardware or software should be used?

One of the keys to backing up files is to know which files need to be backed up. Backup software can internally designate which files have already been backed up by setting an *archive bit* in the properties of the file. A file with the archive bit cleared (set to *0*) indicates that the file has been backed up. Any time the contents of that file are changed, the archive bit is set (to *1*), meaning that this modified file now needs to be backed up. The archive bit is illustrated in Figure 13-7.

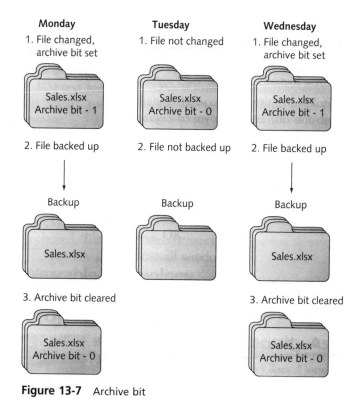

Figure 13-7 Archive bit

There are three basic types of backups: *full backup, differential backup*, and *incremental backup*. These are summarized in Table 13-4. The archive bit is not always cleared after each type of backup; this provides additional flexibility regarding which files should be backed up.

Type of backup	How used	Archive bit after backup	Files needed for recovery
Full backup	Starting point for all backups	Cleared (set to 0)	The full backup is needed
Differential backup	Backs up any data that has changed since last full backup	Not cleared (set to 1)	The full backup and only last differential backup are needed
Incremental backup	Backs up any data that has changed since last full backup or last incremental backup	Cleared (set to 0)	The full backup and all incremental backups are needed

Table 13-4   Types of data backups

Two elements are used in the calculation of when backups should be performed. The first is known as the **recovery point objective (RPO)**, which is defined as the maximum length of time that an organization can tolerate between backups. Simply put, RPO is the "age" of the data that an organization wants the ability to restore in the event of a disaster. For example, if an RPO is six hours, this means that an organization wants to be able to restore systems back to the state they were in no longer than six hours ago. In order to achieve this, it is necessary to make backups at least every six hours; any data created or modified between backups will be lost. Related to the RPO is the **recovery time objective (RTO)**. The RTO is the length of time it will take to recover the data that has been backed up. An RTO of two hours means that data can be restored within that timeframe.

For over 40 years backing up to magnetic tape was the mainstay of data backups. Magnetic tape cartridges can store hundreds of gigabytes of data and are relatively inexpensive. However, due to the disadvantages of magnetic tape backups (such as slow backup speed, high failure rates, and data not encrypted on tape), different alternatives are becoming popular.

 When using magnetic tape, a common strategy for performing backups created three sets of backups: a daily incremental backup performed each Monday through Thursday, a weekly backup done every Friday (instead of the daily backup), and a monthly backup performed the last day of the month.

One popular alternative is *disk to disk (D2D)*. D2D offers better RPO than tape (because recording to hard disks is faster than recording to magnetic tape) and an excellent RTO. However, as with any hard drive, the D2D drive may be subject to failure or data corruption. In addition, some operating system file systems may not be as well-suited for this type of backup because of data fragmentation and operating system limitations on the size and capacity of disk partitions.

A solution that combines the best of magnetic tape and magnetic disk is *disk to disk to tape (D2D2T)*. This technology uses the magnetic disk as a temporary storage area. Data is first written quickly to the magnetic disk system, so that the server does not have to be off-line for an extended period of time (and thus D2D2T has an excellent RTO). Once the copying is completed, this data can be later transferred to magnetic tape. In short, D2D2T provides the convenience of D2D along with the security of writing to removable tape (which also can be stored off the premises).

A more comprehensive backup technology is known as *continuous data protection (CDP)*. As its name implies, CDP performs continuous data backups that can be restored immediately, thus providing excellent RPO and RTO times. CDP maintains a historical record of all changes made to data by constantly monitoring all writes to the hard drive. There are three different types of CDP, as shown in Table 13-5.

Name	Data protected	Comments
Block-level CDP	Entire volumes	All data in volume receives CDP protection, which may not always be necessary
File-level CDP	Individual files	Can select which files to include and exclude
Application-level CDP	Individual application changes	Protects changes to databases, email messages, etc.

Table 13-5   Continuous data protection types

NOTE Some CDP products even let users restore their own documents. A user who accidentally deletes a file can search the CDP system by entering the name of the document and then view the results through an interface that looks like a web search engine. Clicking the desired file will then restore it. For security purposes, users may search only for documents for which they have permissions.

Table 13-6 summarizes the different data backup technologies available. Because one technology does not fit all, it is important that the organization assess its RPO and RTO along with its overall data structure in order to reach the best decision on which technology or technologies to use.

Backup technology	RPO	RTO	Cost	Comments
Magnetic tape	Poor	Poor	Low	Good for high-capacity backups
Disk to disk (D2D)	Good	Excellent	Moderate	Hard drive may be subject to failure
Disk to disk to tape (D2D2T)	Good	Excellent	Moderate	Good compromise of tape and D2D
Continuous data protection (CDP)	Excellent	Excellent	High	For organizations that cannot afford any downtime

Table 13-6   Data backup technologies

Home users should consider using the 3-2-1 backup plan. This plan says that you should always maintain *three* different copies of your backups (that does not count the original data itself) by using at least *two* different types of media on which to store these backups (a separate hard drive, an external hard drive, a USB device, cloud storage, etc.) and store *one* of the backups offsite.

Environmental Controls

2.7 Compare and contrast physical security and environmental controls.

"An ounce of prevention is worth a pound of cure" is an adage that emphasizes taking proactive steps to avoid disruptions rather than just trying to recover from them. Preventing disruptions through environmental controls involves fire suppression, proper shielding, and configuration of HVAC systems.

Video monitoring can be used as an aid to ensure that environmental controls are properly functioning.

Fire Suppression

Damage inflicted as a result of a fire is a constant threat to persons as well as property. In order for a fire to occur, four entities must be present at the same time:

- A type of *fuel* or combustible material
- Sufficient *oxygen* to sustain the combustion
- Enough *heat* to raise the material to its ignition temperature
- A chemical *reaction* that is the fire itself

The first three factors form a fire triangle, which is illustrated in Figure 13-8. To extinguish a fire, any one of these elements must be removed.

Fires are divided into five categories. Table 13-7 lists the types of fires, their typical fuel source, how they can be extinguished, and the types of handheld fire extinguishers that should be used.

Class K fires are actually a subset of Class B. In Europe and Australia, Class K is known as Class F.

In a server closet or room that contains computer equipment, using a handheld fire extinguisher is not recommended because the chemical contents can contaminate electrical equipment.

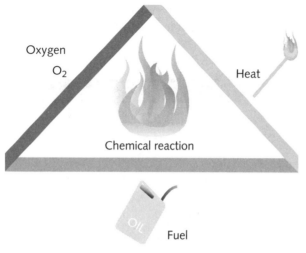

Figure 13-8 Fire triangle

Class of fire	Type of fire	Combustible materials	Methods to extinguish	Type of fire extinguisher needed
Class A	Common combustibles	Wood, paper, textiles, and other ordinary combustibles	Water, water-based chemical, foam, or multipurpose dry chemical	Class A or Class ABC extinguisher
Class B	Combustible liquids	Flammable liquids, oils, solvents, paint, and grease, for example	Foam, dry chemical, or carbon dioxide to put out the fire by smothering it or cutting off the oxygen	Class BC or Class ABC extinguisher
Class C	Electrical	Live or energized electric wires or equipment	Foam, dry chemical, or carbon dioxide to put out the fire by smothering it or cutting off the oxygen	Class BC or Class ABC extinguisher
Class D	Combustible metals	Magnesium, titanium, and potassium, for example	Dry powder or other special sodium extinguishing agents	Class D extinguisher
Class K	Cooking oils	Vegetable oils, animal oils, or fats in cooking appliances	Special extinguisher converts oils to noncombustible soaps	Wet chemical extinguisher

Table 13-7 Fire types

Instead, stationary fire suppression systems are integrated into the building's infrastructure and release fire suppressant in the room. These systems can be classified as *water sprinkler systems* that spray the area with pressurized water; *dry chemical systems* that disperse a fine, dry powder over the fire; and *clean agent systems* that do not harm people, documents, or electrical equipment in the room. Table 13-8 lists the types of stationary fire suppression systems.

Category	Name	Description	Comments
Water sprinkler system	Wet pipe	Water under pressure used in pipes in the ceiling	Used in buildings with no risk of freezing
	Alternate	Pipes filled with water or compressed air	Can be used when environmental conditions dictate
	Dry pipe	Pipes filled with pressurized water and water is held by control valve	Used when water stored in pipes overhead is a risk
	Pre-action	Like dry pipe but requires a preliminary action such as a smoke detector alarm before water is released into pipes	Used in areas that an accidental activation would be catastrophic, such as in a museum or storage area for rare books
Dry chemical system	Dry chemicals	Dry powder is sprayed onto the fire, inhibiting the chain reaction that causes combustion and putting the fire out	Used frequently in industrial settings and in some kitchens
Clean agent system	Low-pressure carbon dioxide (CO_2) systems	Chilled, liquid CO_2 is stored and becomes a vapor when used that displaces oxygen to suppress the fire	Used in areas of high voltage and electronic areas
	High-pressure carbon dioxide systems	Like the low-pressure CO_2 systems, but used for small and localized applications	Used in areas of high voltage and electronic areas
	FM 200 systems (Heptafluoropropane)	Absorbs the heat energy from the surface of the burning material, which lowers its temperature below the ignition point and extinguishes the fire	One of the least toxic vapor extinguishing agents currently used; can be used in computer rooms, vaults, phone rooms, mechanical rooms, museums, and other areas where people may be present
	Inergen systems	A mix of nitrogen, argon, and carbon dioxide	Used to suppress fires in sensitive areas such as telecommunications rooms, control rooms, and kitchens
	FE-13 systems	Developed initially as a chemical refrigerant, FE-13 works like FM 200 systems	Safer and more desirable if the area being protected has people in it

Table 13-8   **Stationary fire suppression systems**

Electromagnetic Interference (EMI) Shielding

Movies and novels often depict a spy aiming a "secret device" at a computer from hundreds of feet away in order to steal the computer's data. As farfetched as this may seem, this capability is actually not far removed from reality.

Computer systems, cathode ray tube monitors, printers, and similar devices all emit electromagnetic fields that are produced by signals or the movement of data. Security researchers have demonstrated that it is possible for attackers to pick up these electromagnetic fields and read the data that is producing them. In one case, researchers placed a cell phone next to a computer and were able to extract the full 4096-bit RSA decryption keys from the computer by using only the sound generated by the computer during the decryption of chosen ciphertexts. This was possible because of the variations in power consumption while the computer was working, electromagnetic noise, timing variations, and even contention for CPU resources such as caches. The vibration of electronic components in the computer, sometimes heard as a faint high-pitched tone or hiss, is caused by voltage regulation circuits and can be correlated with what the CPU is doing and then captured by the cell phone. Since the processor changes its power draw according to the type of operation it performs, such changes can be picked up and used to reveal 4096-bit RSA keys.[3]

A defense for shielding an electromagnetic field is a **Faraday cage**. A Faraday cage is a metallic enclosure that prevents the entry or escape of an electromagnetic field. A Faraday cage, consisting of a grounded, fine-mesh copper screening, as shown in Figure 13-9, is often used for testing in electronic labs. In addition, lightweight and portable *Faraday bags* made of special materials can be used to shield cell phones and portable computing devices like tablets and notebook computers.

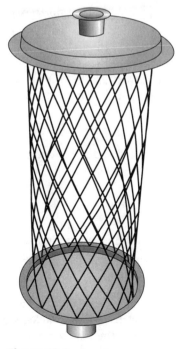

Figure 13-9   Faraday cage

13

Faraday bags are often used in crime scene investigations. Phones, tablets, or laptops found on-scene are placed in Faraday bags, thus eliminating inbound and outbound signals and preventing the devices from being remotely wiped of evidence.

The U.S. government has developed a classified standard intended to prevent attackers from picking up electromagnetic fields from government buildings. Known as *Telecommunications Electronics Material Protected from Emanating Spurious Transmissions*, or *TEMPEST*, the exact details are a secret. What is known is that TEMPEST technologies are intended to "reduce the conducted and radiated emissions from within the sensitive environment to an undetectable level outside the shielded enclosure in uncontrolled areas."[4] TEMPEST uses special protective coatings on network cables and additional shielding in buildings.

HVAC

Data centers, or rooms that house computer systems and network equipment, typically have special cooling requirements. First, additional cooling is necessary due to the number of systems generating heat in a confined area. Second, data centers need more precise cooling. Electronic equipment radiates a drier heat than the human body, so the cooling requires different settings from those used in an office area.

The control and monitoring of **heating, ventilation, and air conditioning (HVAC)** environmental systems that provide and regulate heating and cooling are important for data centers. Temperatures and relative humidity (RH) levels that are too low or high, or that change abruptly, may result in unreliable components or even system failures. Controlling environmental factors also can reduce *electrostatic discharge (ESD)*, the sudden flow of electric current between two objects, which can destroy electronic equipment.

It is important to monitor the environment and then regulate it through the use of temperature and humidity controls.

Because network equipment and servers in a data center generate large amounts of heat, a **hot aisle/cold aisle** layout can be used to reduce the heat by managing air flow. In a data center using a hot aisle/cold aisle layout, the server racks are lined up in alternating rows, with cold air intakes facing one direction and hot air exhausts facing the other direction. The rows composed of the rack fronts are the cold aisles and face air conditioner output ducts. The rows that are the backs of the racks where the heated exhausts exit are the hot aisles and generally face the air conditioner return ducts.

Incident Response

2.4 Given a scenario, implement basic forensic procedures.

2.5 Summarize common incident response procedures.

4.2 Summarize mobile security concepts and technologies.

When an unauthorized incident occurs, an immediate response is required. This response often involves using forensics and following proper incident response procedures.

Forensics

Incident response procedures include using forensic science and properly responding to a computer forensics event by using basic forensics procedures.

What Is Forensics? Forensics, also known as **forensic science**, is the application of science to questions that are of interest to the legal profession. Forensics is not limited to analyzing evidence from a murder scene; it also can be applied to technology. As computers are the foundation for communicating and recording information, a new area known as **computer forensics**, which uses technology to search for computer evidence of a crime, can attempt to retrieve information—even if it has been altered or erased—that can be used in the pursuit of the attacker or criminal. Digital evidence can be retrieved from computers, mobile devices, cell phones, pagers, digital cameras, and virtually any device that has memory or storage.

The importance of computer forensics is due in part to the following:

- *Amount of digital evidence.* According to the Federal Bureau of Investigation (FBI), almost 85 percent of crimes committed today leave behind digital evidence that can be retrieved through computer forensics.[5]

- *Increased scrutiny by the legal profession.* No longer do attorneys and judges freely accept computer evidence. The procedures used in retrieving, transporting, and storing digital evidence are now held up to the same standards as those used with physical evidence.

- *Higher level of computer skill by criminals.* As criminals become increasingly sophisticated in their knowledge of computers and techniques such as encryption, a computer forensics expert is often needed in order to retrieve the evidence.

Basic Forensics Procedures When responding to a criminal event that requires an examination using computer forensics, four basic steps are followed, which are similar to those of standard forensics. The steps are: secure the crime scene, preserve the evidence, establish a chain of custody, and examine the evidence.

Secure the Crime Scene When an illegal or unauthorized incident occurs that involves a computer or other electronic device that contains digital evidence, action must be taken immediately. A delay of even a few minutes can allow the digital evidence to become

13

contaminated by other users or give a person time to destroy the evidence. When an event occurs, those individuals in the immediate vicinity should perform *damage control*, which is the effort to minimize any loss of evidence. The steps in damage control include:

- Report the incident to security or the police.
- Confront any suspects (if the situation allows).
- Neutralize the suspected perpetrator from harming others (if necessary).
- Secure physical security features.
- Quarantine electronic equipment.
- Contact the response team.

Organizations instruct their users that the computer forensics response team must be contacted immediately. This team serves as *first responders* whenever digital evidence needs to be preserved.

TIP If the forensics response team is external to the organization, it is important that they accurately track their hours and expenses from the start of the investigation. This information can be entered into evidence in court to prove that the response team was present from the beginning.

After the response team arrives, the first job is to secure the crime scene, which includes:

- The physical surroundings of the computer should be clearly documented (many forensics experts use a video camera to capture the entire process).
- Photographs of the area should be taken before anything is touched to help document that the computer was working prior to the attack. (Some defense attorneys have argued that a computer was not functioning properly and thus the attacker could not be held responsible for any damages.) The computer should be photographed from several angles, including the images displayed on the screen. Because digital pictures can be altered, some security professionals recommend that photographs be taken with a standard camera using film.
- Cables connected to the computer should be labeled to document the computer's hardware components and how they are connected.
- The team should take custody of the entire computer along with the keyboard and any peripherals. In addition, USB flash drives and any other media must be secured.
- The team must interview witnesses and everyone who had access to the system and document their findings, including what those people were doing with the system, what its intended functions were, and how it has been affected by the unauthorized actions.
- The length of time that has passed since the initial incident should be noted.

Preserve the Evidence Because digital computer evidence is very fragile, it can easily and unintentionally be altered or destroyed through normal use or even by turning on the computer. Only properly trained computer evidence specialists should process computer evidence so that the integrity of the evidence is maintained and can hold up in a court of law.

The computer forensics team first captures any volatile data that would be lost when the computer is turned off. Any data such as contents of RAM, current network connections, logon sessions, network traffic and logs, and any open files must be captured and saved. Because different data sources have different degrees of preservation, an **order of volatility** must be used to preserve the most fragile data first. Table 13-9 lists the order of volatility.

Location of data	Sequence to be retrieved
Register, cache, peripheral memory	First
Random access memory (RAM)	Second
Network state	Third
Running processes	Fourth

Table 13-9   **Order of volatility**

Volatile data is the most difficult type of data to capture. Not only does it have a short "shelf life," but accessing information at a lower level also can destroy data at higher levels. For example, executing a command to retrieve from a running process can destroy the current contents of registers and RAM. Capturing this volatile information can best be performed by capturing the entire **system image**, which is a snapshot of the current state of the computer that contains all current settings and data.

After retrieving the volatile data, the team next focuses on the hard drive. A *mirror image backup*, also called a *bit-stream backup*, is an evidence-grade backup because its accuracy meets evidence standards. A mirror image backup is not the same as a normal copy of the data. Standard file copies or backups include only files. Mirror image backups replicate all sectors of a computer hard drive, including all files and any hidden data storage areas. Using a standard copy procedure can miss significant data and can even taint the evidence. For example, copying a file may change file date information on the source drive, which is information that is often critical in a computer forensic investigation.

 To guarantee accuracy, mirror image backup programs rely upon hashing algorithms as part of the validation process. The digest of the original source data is compared against the digest of the copied data to help create a "snapshot" of the current system based on the contents of the drives. This is done to document that any evidence retrieved came from the system and was not "planted" there.

Mirror image backups are considered a primary key to uncovering evidence because they create exact replicas of the crime scene. Defense teams often focus on mirror image backups; if they can prove that the copy of the data was contaminated or altered in any fashion, then any evidence gathered from the data will likely be dismissed. For this reason, mirror image backup software should be used only by trained professionals and done in a controlled manner, using hardware that does not influence the accuracy of the data it captures.

13

Mirror image backups can be performed using handheld devices that capture through the hard drive, USB, or FireWire connection. The devices are one-way data transfers that can only copy from the external data source to prevent inadvertent corruption. Some devices even use Global Positioning System (GPS) to specify the location of the data capture.

Establish the Chain of Custody As soon as the team begins its work, it must start and maintain a strict chain of custody. The **chain of custody** documents that the evidence was under strict control at all times and no unauthorized person was given the opportunity to corrupt the evidence. A chain of custody includes documenting all of the serial numbers of the systems involved, who handled and had custody of the systems and for what length of time, how the computer was shipped, and any other steps in the process. In short, a chain of custody is a detailed document describing where the evidence was at all times. Gaps in this chain of custody can result in severe legal consequences. Courts have dismissed cases involving computer forensics because a secure chain of custody could not be verified.

The chain of custody is particularly important when documenting the status of the system from the time it is seized as evidence until the time the mirror copies and hashes can be completed.

Examine for Evidence After a computer forensics expert creates a mirror image of a system, the original system is secured and the mirror image examined to reveal evidence. This includes searching word processing documents, email files, spreadsheets, and other documents for evidence. The cache and cookies of the web browser can reveal websites that have been visited. The frequency of emails to particular individuals may be useful. In short, all of the exposed data is examined for clues. Depending on the volume of data, sometimes a big data analysis may be conducted on the data.

Hidden clues also can be mined and exposed. One source of hidden data is called *slack*. Windows computers use two types of slack. The first is RAM slack. Windows stores files on a hard drive in 512-byte blocks called sectors, and multiple sectors are used to make up a cluster. Clusters are made up of blocks of sectors. When a file that is being saved is not long enough to fill up the last sector on a disk (a common occurrence because a file size only rarely matches the sector size), Windows pads the remaining cluster space with data that is currently stored in RAM. This padding creates *RAM slack*, which can contain any information that has been created, viewed, modified, downloaded, or copied since the computer was last booted. Thus, if the computer has not been shut down for several days, the data stored in RAM slack can come from activity that occurred during that time. RAM slack is illustrated in Figure 13-10.

RAM slack pertains only to the last sector of a file. If additional sectors are needed to round out the block size for the last cluster assigned to the file, then a different type of slack is created. This is known as *drive file slack* (sometimes called *drive slack*) because the padded

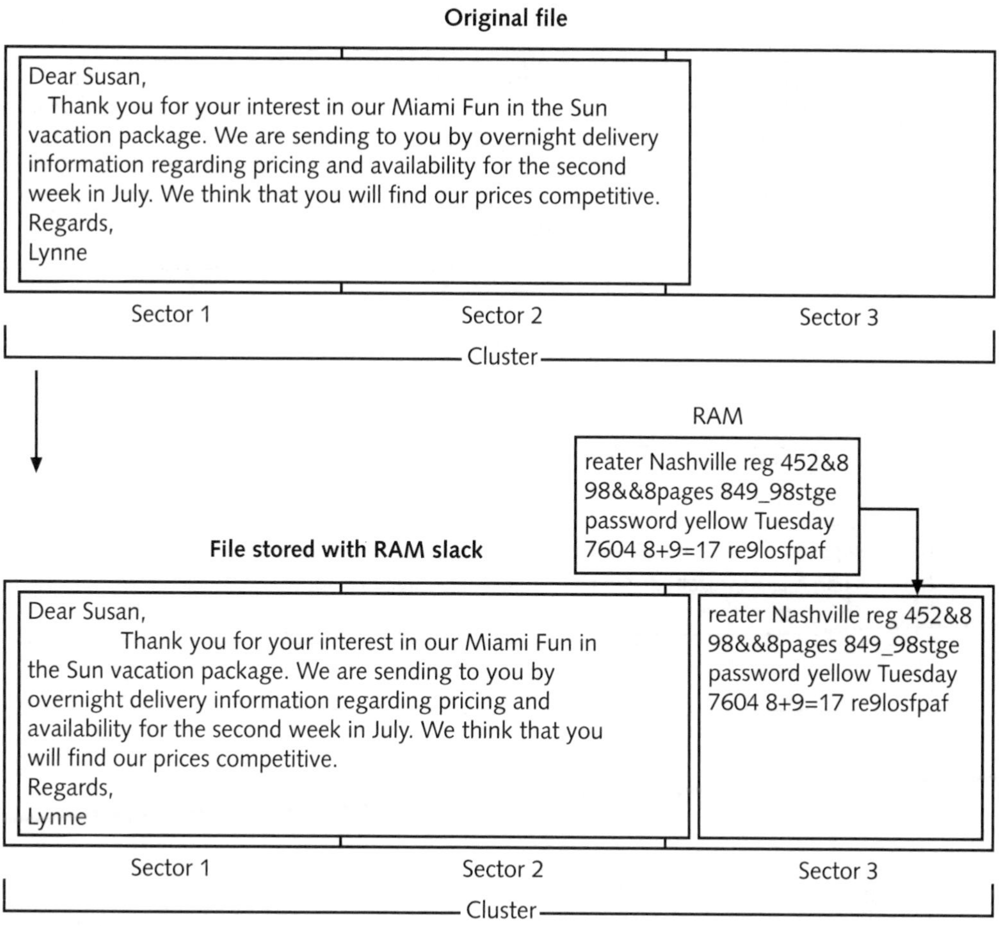

Original file

Figure 13-10   RAM slack

data that Windows uses comes from data stored on the hard drive. Such data could contain remnants of previously deleted files or data from the format pattern associated with disk storage space that has yet to be used by the computer. Drive file slack is illustrated in Figure 13-11. Both RAM slack and drive slack can hold valuable evidence.

An additional source of hidden clues can be gleaned from *metadata*, or data about data. Although some metadata is user-supplied information, most metadata about a file is generated and recorded automatically without the user's knowledge. Examples of metadata include the file type, creation date, authorship, and edit history. Some electronic files may contain hundreds of pieces of such information.

Upon completion of the examination, a detailed report is required that lists the steps that were taken and any evidence that was uncovered in the forensic investigation.

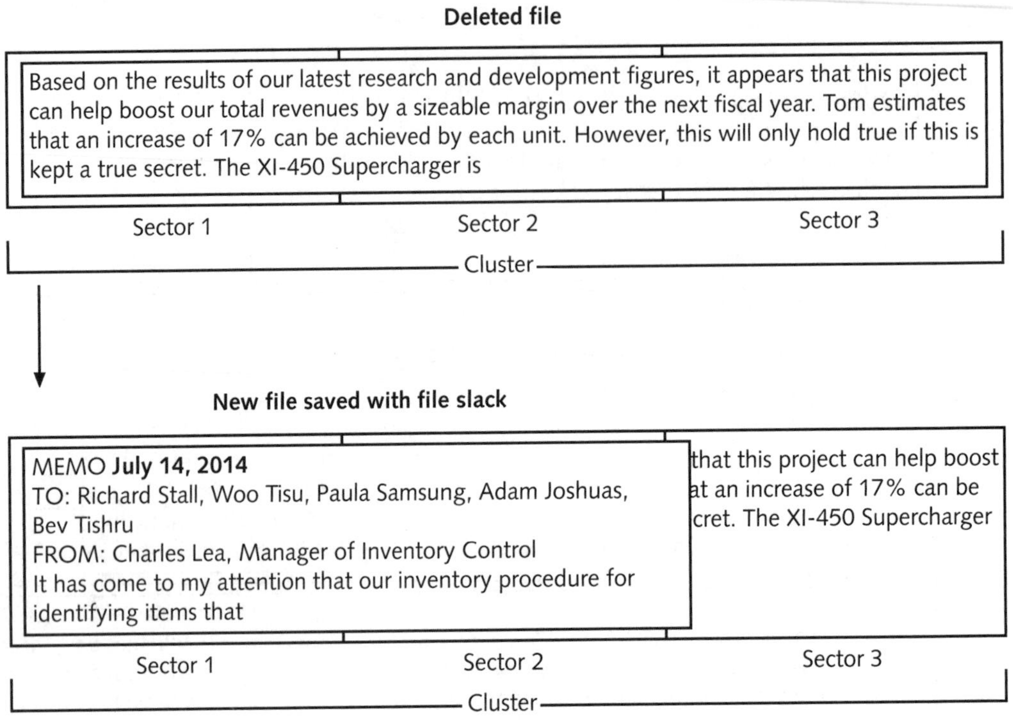

Deleted file

Based on the results of our latest research and development figures, it appears that this project can help boost our total revenues by a sizeable margin over the next fiscal year. Tom estimates that an increase of 17% can be achieved by each unit. However, this will only hold true if this is kept a true secret. The XI-450 Supercharger is

| Sector 1 | Sector 2 | Sector 3 |

Cluster

New file saved with file slack

MEMO **July 14, 2014**
TO: Richard Stall, Woo Tisu, Paula Samsung, Adam Joshuas, Bev Tishru
FROM: Charles Lea, Manager of Inventory Control
It has come to my attention that our inventory procedure for identifying items that

that this project can help boost at an increase of 17% can be cret. The XI-450 Supercharger

| Sector 1 | Sector 2 | Sector 3 |

Cluster

Figure 13-11   Drive file slack

Incident Response Procedures

In an event that requires an incident response, general incident procedures should be followed. These include:

- *Preparation.* The key to properly handling an event is to be prepared in advance by establishing comprehensive policies and procedures.

- *Execution.* Putting the policies and procedures in place involves several crucial steps. The incident first must be properly identified, and then key personnel must be notified and the procedures escalated as necessary. Damage and loss control steps should be taken to mitigate damage, particularly in the event of a data breach. Equipment must be isolated by either quarantine or the entire removal of the device itself. Once secured, the recovery procedures may begin.

- *Analysis.* In the aftermath, proper reporting should document how the event occurred and what actions were taken. In addition, a "lessons learned" analysis should be conducted in order to use the event to build stronger incident response policies and procedures in the future.

Chapter Summary

- Business continuity, which is the ability of an organization to maintain its operations and services in the face of a disruptive event, involves the process of identifying exposure to threats, creating preventive and recovery procedures, and then testing the procedures to determine if they are sufficient. One important tool in business continuity planning and testing is a business impact analysis (BIA), which analyzes the most important mission-critical business functions and then identifies and quantifies the impact a loss of the functions could have on the organization in terms of its operational and financial position.

- Whereas business continuity planning and testing looks at the needs of the business as a whole in recovering from a catastrophe, a subset of it focuses on continuity in the context of IT. In IT contingency planning, an outline of procedures that are to be followed in the event of a major IT incident or an incident that directly impacts IT is developed. Closely related is the disaster recovery plan (DRP), which is the plan for restoring IT functions and services to their former state. Disaster recovery planning involves creating, implementing, and testing disaster recovery plans.

- One of the primary ways to ensure IT business continuity is to remove any single point of failure. This can be done by incorporating redundancy and fault tolerance, which involves building excess capacity in order to protect against failures. Because servers play such a key role in a network infrastructure, the loss of a single server that supports a critical application can have a significant impact. A common approach is for the organization to design the network infrastructure so that multiple servers are incorporated into the network yet appear to users and applications as a single computing resource. One method of doing this is by using a server cluster, which is the combination of two or more servers that are interconnected to appear as one. A system of hard drives based on redundancy can be achieved through using a technology known as RAID (Redundant Array of Independent Drives), which uses multiple hard disk drives for increased reliability and performance.

- Most network hardware components can be duplicated to provide a redundant network. Maintaining electrical power is also essential when planning for redundancy. An uninterruptible power supply (UPS) is a device that maintains power to equipment in the event of an interruption in the primary electrical power source. Just as redundancy can be planned for servers, storage, networks, and power, it also can be planned for the entire site. A major disaster such as a flood or hurricane can inflict such extensive damage to a building that the organization may have to temporarily move to another location. Many organizations maintain redundant sites in case this occurs. Three basic types of redundant sites are used: hot sites, cold sites, and warm sites.

- An essential element in a disaster recovery plan is data backups. A data backup is copying information to a different medium and storing it so that it can be used in the event of a disaster. The storage location is preferably at an offsite facility. There are three basic types of backups: full backup, differential backup, and incremental backup. Different elements are used to determine the frequency of backups. The recovery point objective (RPO) is the maximum length of time that an organization can tolerate

13

between backups. The recovery time objective (RTO) is the length of time it will take to recover data that has been backed up. Due to the disadvantages of magnetic tape backups, alternatives are now available. Disk to disk (D2D) uses magnetic disks, such as a large hard drive or RAID configuration. Another newer backup technology is continuous data protection (CDP), which performs continuous data backups that can be restored immediately, thus providing excellent RPO and RTO times.

- Damage inflicted as a result of a fire is a constant threat, both to persons as well as property. Fires are divided into five categories. In a server closet or room that contains computer equipment, using a handheld fire extinguisher is not recommended because the chemical contents can contaminate electrical equipment. Instead, stationary fire suppression systems are integrated into the building's infrastructure and release the suppressant in the room. These systems can be classified as water sprinkler systems that spray the area with pressurized water; dry chemical systems that disperse a fine, dry powder over the fire; and clean agent systems that do not harm people, documents, or electrical equipment in the room.

- Computer systems and similar devices all emit electromagnetic fields that are produced by signals or the movement of data. A defense for shielding an electromagnetic field is a Faraday cage, which is a metallic enclosure that prevents the entry or escape of an electromagnetic field. Controlling environmental factors also can reduce electrostatic discharge (ESD), the sudden flow of electric current between two objects, which can destroy electronic equipment. The control and maintenance of HVAC systems that provide and regulate heating and cooling are important for data centers. Temperatures and relative humidity levels that are too low or high, or that change abruptly, may result in unreliable components or even system failures.

- Forensic science is the application of science to questions that are of interest to the legal profession. Computer forensics attempts to retrieve information that can be used in the pursuit of the computer crime. Forensics incidence response is carried out in four major steps. First, the crime scene is secured and documented. Next, the data is preserved by capturing any volatile data and then performing a mirror image backup along with hashing the image. A strict chain of custody, or documentation of evidence, must be established at all times. Finally, the mirror image must be examined for evidence and a detailed report made. In an event that requires an incident response, general incident procedures should be followed.

Key Terms

business continuity The ability of an organization to maintain its operations and services in the face of a disruptive event.

business continuity planning and testing The process of identifying exposure to threats, creating preventive and recovery procedures, and then testing them to determine if they are sufficient.

business impact analysis (BIA) An analysis that identifies mission-critical business functions and quantifies the impact a loss of such functions may have on the organization in terms of its operational and financial position.

chain of custody   A process of documentation that shows that the evidence was under strict control at all times and no unauthorized individuals were given the opportunity to corrupt the evidence.

clustering   Combining two or more servers to appear as one single unit.

cold site   A remote site that provides office space; the customer must provide and install all the equipment needed to continue operations.

computer forensics   Using technology to search for computer evidence of a crime.

continuity of operations   The ability of a business to continue to function in the event of a disaster.

data backup   The process of copying information to a different medium and storing it (preferably at an offsite location) so that it can be used in the event of a disaster.

disaster recovery plan (DRP)   A written document that details the process for restoring IT resources following an event that causes a significant disruption in service.

Faraday cage   A metallic enclosure that prevents the entry or escape of an electromagnetic field.

forensics (forensic science)   The application of science to questions that are of interest to the legal profession.

heating, ventilation, and air conditioning (HVAC)   Systems that provide and regulate heating and cooling.

high availability   A system that can function for an extended period of time with little downtime.

hot aisle/cold aisle   A layout in a data center that can be used to reduce heat by managing air flow.

hot site   A duplicate of the production site that has all the equipment needed for an organization to continue running, including office space and furniture, telephone jacks, computer equipment, and a live telecommunications link.

IT contingency planning   The process of developing an outline of procedures to be followed in the event of a major IT incident or an incident that directly impacts IT.

mean time between failures (MTBF)   A statistical value that is the average time until a component fails, cannot be repaired, and must be replaced.

mean time to recovery (MTTR)   The average time for a device to recover from a failure that is not a terminal failure.

order of volatility   The sequence of volatile data that must be preserved in a computer forensic investigation.

RAID (Redundant Array of Independent Drives)   A technology that uses multiple hard disk drives for increased reliability and performance.

recovery point objective (RPO)   The maximum length of time that an organization can tolerate between backups.

recovery time objective (RTO)   The length of time it will take to recover data that has been backed up.

risk assessment   The process of identifying threats.

single point of failure   A component or entity in a system which, if it no longer functions, would adversely affect the entire system.

succession planning   Determining in advance who will be authorized to take over in the event of the incapacitation or death of key employees.

system image   A snapshot of the current state of the computer that contains all settings and data.

tabletop exercises   Exercises that simulate an emergency situation but in an informal and stress-free environment.

warm site   A remote site that contains computer equipment but does not have active Internet or telecommunication facilities, and does not have backups of data.

Review Questions

1. _____ is the process of developing an outline of procedures to be followed in the event of a major IT incident or an incident that directly impacts IT.

    a. Disaster recovery planning

    b. IT contingency planning

    c. Business impact analysis planning

    d. Risk IT planning

2. Who should be involved in a tabletop exercise?

    a. all employees

    b. individuals on a decision-making level

    c. full-time employees

    d. only IT managers

3. The average amount of time that it will take a device to recover from a failure that is not a terminal failure is called the _____.

    a. MTTR

    b. MTBR

    c. MTBF

    d. MTTI

4. Each of these is a category of fire suppression systems EXCEPT a _____.

    a. water sprinkler system

    b. wet chemical system

    c. clean agent system

    d. dry chemical system

5. Which of these is NOT required for a fire to occur?

    a. a chemical reaction that is the fire itself

    b. a type of fuel or combustible material

    c. a spark to start the process

    d. sufficient oxygen to sustain the combustion

6. An electrical fire like that which would be found in a computer data center is known as what type of fire?

    a. Class A

    b. Class B

    c. Class C

    d. Class D

7. Which level of RAID uses disk mirroring and is considered fault-tolerant?

    a. Level 1

    b. Level 2

    c. Level 3

    d. Level 4

8. A standby server that exists only to take over for another server in the event of its failure is known as a(n) _____.

    a. rollover server

    b. asymmetric server cluster

    c. symmetric server cluster

    d. failsafe server

9. What does the abbreviation RAID represent?

    a. Redundant Array of IDE Drives

    b. Resilient Architecture for Interdependent Discs

    c. Redundant Array of Independent Drives

    d. Resistant Architecture of Inter-Related Data Storage

10. Which of these is an example of a nested RAID?

    a. Level 1-0

    b. Level 0-1

    c. Level 0+1

    d. Level 0/1

13

11.   A(n) _____ is always running off its battery while the main power runs the battery charger.

   a.   secure UPS

   b.   backup UPS

   c.   off-line UPS

   d.   on-line UPS

12.   Which type of site is essentially a duplicate of the production site and has all the equipment needed for an organization to continue running?

   a.   cold site

   b.   warm site

   c.   hot site

   d.   replicated site

13.   A UPS can perform each of the following EXCEPT _____.

   a.   prevent certain applications from launching that will consume too much power

   b.   disconnect users and shut down the server

   c.   prevent any new users from logging on

   d.   notify all users that they must finish their work immediately and log off

14.   Which of these is NOT a characteristic of a disaster recovery plan (DRP)?

   a.   It is updated regularly.

   b.   It is a private document used only by top-level administrators for planning.

   c.   It is written.

   d.   It is detailed.

15.   What does an incremental backup do?

   a.   copies all files changed since the last full or incremental backup

   b.   copies selected files

   c.   copies all files

   d.   copies all files since the last full backup

16.   Which question is NOT a basic question to be asked regarding creating a data backup?

   a.   What media should be used?

   b.   How long will it take to finish the backup?

   c.   Where should the backup be stored?

   d.   What information should be backed up?

17. The chain of _____ documents that the evidence was under strict control at all times and no unauthorized person was given the opportunity to corrupt the evidence.

    a. forensics

    b. evidence

    c. custody

    d. control

18. What is the maximum length of time that an organization can tolerate between data backups?

    a. recovery time objective (RTO)

    b. recovery service point (RSP)

    c. recovery point objective (RPO)

    d. optimal recovery timeframe (ORT)

19. What data backup solution uses the magnetic disk as a temporary storage area?

    a. continuous data protection (CDP)

    b. disk to disk to tape (D2D2T)

    c. disk to disk (D2D)

    d. tape to disk (T2D)

20. When an unauthorized event occurs, what is the first duty of the computer forensics response team?

    a. to log off from the server

    b. to secure the crime scene

    c. to back up the hard drive

    d. to reboot the system

13

Hands-On Projects

If you are concerned about installing any of the software in these projects on your regular computer, you can instead install the software in the Windows virtual machine created in the Chapter 1 Hands-On Projects 1-3 and 1-4. Software installed within the virtual machine will not impact the host computer.

Project 13-1: Creating a Disk Image Backup

To back up programs and operating system files in addition to user files, one solution is to create a disk image. A disk image file is created by performing a complete sector-by-sector copy of the hard drive instead of backing up using the drive's file system. In this project, you download Macrium Reflect to create an image backup.

1. Use your web browser to go to **www.macrium.com**.

The location of content on the Internet may change without warning. If you are no longer able to access the program through the above URL, use a search engine and search for "Macrium Reflect".

2. Click **DOWNLOADS** and then click **Download Now**. At the download site, also click **Download Now**.

3. Run the file and then click **Trial software**. Select **Professional** from the drop-down list.

4. Click **Download**.

5. Accept the default settings to download, and install this program onto your computer. Launch the program by double-clicking the icon.

6. When Reflect launches, click **Backup** if necessary.

7. Click **Create an image of the partition(s) required to backup and restore Windows**.

8. Under **Source** select the disk that contains the operating system and data for this computer.

9. Select the location to store the backup. You cannot store the backup on the same hard drive on which you are creating the image; you must store it on another hard drive in that computer or on an external USB hard drive. Under **Destination**, select the appropriate location. Click **Next**.

10. Review the settings that are displayed. Note that, depending on the size of the data to be backed up and the speed of the computer, it will take several minutes to perform the backup. Click **Finish** and then **OK**. Click **OK** and then **Close**.

11. Leave Macrium Reflect open for the next project.

Project 13-2: Restoring a Disk Image Backup

It is important to test the steps necessary to restore a disk image in case a hard drive stops functioning. In this project, you will go through the steps of restoring the Macrium Reflect image backup created in Hands-On Project 13-1, although you will stop short of actually restoring the image.

1. Once the backup in Project 13-1 has finished, you will create a Rescue CD. This CD will allow you to boot your computer if the hard drive becomes corrupt and restore the backup. Click **Other Tasks** and then **Create bootable Rescue media**.

2. Select **Linux – Select this option to create a Linux based recovery media.** Click **Next**.

3. Click **Finish**.

4. When prompted, place a blank CD disk in the tray, and then click **OK**. Reflect will now create a recovery CD.

5. When the recovery CD has been created, close all windows.

6. Now boot from the recovery CD. Be sure the recovery CD is in the disk drive, and restart your computer. If it does not boot from the recovery CD, check the instructions for your computer to boot from a CD.

7. When the Restore Wizard dialog box is displayed, click **Next**.

8. In the left pane, click the location where you stored the image backup.

9. In the right pane, select the backup image that appears.

10. If you were actually restoring your image backup, you would continue to proceed. However, click the **Close** button.

11. Remove the CD.

12. Click **OK** to reboot your computer.

Project 13-3: Entering and Viewing Metadata

Although most file metadata is not accessible to users, with some types of metadata, users can enter and change it. In this project, you will view and enter metadata in a Microsoft Word document.

1. Use Microsoft Word to create a document containing your name. Save the document as **Metadata1.docx**.

2. Click the **FILE** tab on the Ribbon.

3. Click the drop-down arrow next to **Properties** and click **Show Document Panel**.

4. Enter the following information in the Document Panel:

    - Author—The name of your instructor or supervisor
    - Subject—**Metadata**
    - Keywords—**Metadata**
    - Category—**Computer Forensics**
    - Comments—**Viewing metadata in Microsoft Word**

5. Save **Metadata1.docx**.

6. Click the drop-down arrow next to **Document Properties** and then click **Advanced Properties**.

7. Click the **Statistics** tab on the Properties dialog box and view the information it contains. How could a computer forensics specialist use this metadata when examining this file?

8. Click the **Custom** tab. Notice that there are several predefined fields that can contain metadata.

13

9. In the Name box, enter **Reader**.

10. Be sure the Type is set to **Text**.

11. Enter your name in the Value field, and then press **Enter**.

12. Select three predefined fields and enter values for each field. Click **OK**. Save your document when you are finished.

13. Close the Document Properties Information panel and return to **Metadata1.docx**.

14. Erase your name from **Metadata1.docx** so you have a blank document. However, this file still has the metadata. Enter today's date and save this as **Metadata2.docx**.

15. Close **Metadata2.docx**.

16. Reopen **Metadata2.docx**.

17. Click the **FILE** tab on the Ribbon.

18. Click the drop-down arrow next to **Properties** and click **Show Document Panel**.

19. What properties carried over to **Metadata2.docx** from **Metadata1.docx**, even though the content of the file was erased? Why did this happen? Could a computer forensics specialist use this technique to examine metadata, even if the contents of the document were erased?

20. Close all windows.

Project 13-4: Viewing Windows Slack and Hidden Data

RAM slack, drive slack, and other hidden data can be helpful to a computer forensics investigator. In this project, you will download and use a program to search for hidden data.

1. Use your web browser to go to **www.briggsoft.com**.

The location of content on the Internet may change without warning. If you are no longer able to access the program through the above URL, use a search engine and search for "Directory Snoop".

2. Scroll down to the current version of **Directory Snoop** and click **Download** above **Free Trial**.

3. Follow the default installation procedures to install Directory Snoop.

4. Click **Start** and **All Programs**, then click **Directory Snoop 5.0**.

5. Depending on the file system on your computer, click **FAT Module** or **NTFS Module**.

6. Under Select Drive, click **C:** or the drive letter of your hard drive. If the **RawDisk Driver** dialog box appears, click **Install Driver** and then **OK**.

7. Click to select a file and display its contents. Scroll down under **Text data** to view the contents that you can read.

8. Select other files to look for hidden data. Did you discover anything that might be useful to a computer forensics specialist?

9. Create a text document using Notepad. Click the **Start** button, enter **Notepad** in the Search box, and then click the link.

10. Enter the text **Now is the time for all good men to come to the aid of their country.**

11. Save the document on your desktop as **Country.txt**.

12. Exit Notepad.

13. Now delete this file. Right-click **Start**, click **File Explorer**, and then navigate to **Country.txt**.

14. Right-click **Country.txt** and then click **Delete**.

15. Now search for information contained in the file you just deleted. Return to **Directory Snoop**, click the top-level node for the **C:** drive, and then click the **Search** icon.

16. Click **Files**.

17. Enter **country** as the item that you are searching for.

18. Click **Search in slack area also.**

19. Click **Ok**. Was the program able to find this data? Why or why not?

20. Close all windows.

Project 13-5: Viewing and Changing the Backup Archive Bit

One of the keys to backing up files is to know which files need to be backed up. Backup software can internally designate which files have already been backed up by setting an archive bit in the properties of the file. A file with the archive bit cleared (set to 0) indicates that the file has been backed up. However, when the contents of that file are changed, the archive bit is set (to 1), meaning that this modified file now needs to be backed up. In this project, you will view and change the backup archive bit.

1. Start Microsoft Word and create a document that contains your name and today's date.

2. Save this document as **Bittest.docx**, and then close Microsoft Word.

3. Click **Start**, enter **cmd**, and then press **Enter**. The Command Prompt window opens.

4. Navigate to the folder that contains **Bittest.docx**.

5. Type **attrib/?** and then press **Enter** to display the options for this command.

6. Type **attrib Bittest.docx** and then press **Enter**. The attributes for this file are displayed. The A indicates that the bit is set and the file should be backed up.

7. You can clear the archive bit like the backup software does after it copies the file. Type **attrib –a Bittest.docx** and then press **Enter**.

13

8. Now look at the setting of the archive bit. Type **attrib Bittest.docx** and then press **Enter**. Has it been cleared?

9. Close the Command Prompt window.

Case Projects

CASE PROJECTS

Case Project 13-1: Business Continuity Plan

Select four risks that your school or organization may face and develop a brief business continuity plan. Use the steps outlined earlier in the chapter. Share your plan with others and, if possible, test your plan. What did you learn? Modify your plan accordingly.

Case Project 13-2: Continuous Data Protection (CDP)

Use the Internet to research continuous data protection (CDP). Identify three different solutions and compare their features. Create a table of the different features to make a side-by-side comparison. Which product would you consider to be the best solution? Why?

Case Project 13-3: Personal Disaster Recovery Plan

Create a one-page document of a personal disaster recovery procedure for your home computer. Be sure to include what needs to be protected and why. Also include information about where your data backups are stored and how they can be retrieved. Does your DRP show that what you are doing to protect your assets is sufficient? Should any changes be made?

Case Project 13-4: RAID

Use the Internet to research the hardware and costs of adding two levels of hardware RAID. Compare their features as well. Determine which current operating systems support which RAID levels. Create a chart that lists the features, costs, and operating systems supported.

Case Project 13-5: Forensics Tools

Search the Internet for websites that advertise computer forensic tools. Locate reviews of four tools. Create a chart that lists the tool, the type of data that it searches for, its features, the cost, etc. Which would you recommend if you could purchase only one tool and budget were not a concern?

Case Project 13-6: Online Backup Services

Several good online backup services can help make data backup easy for the user. Use a search engine to search for *online backup service reviews*, and select three different services. Research these services and note their features. Create a table that lists each service and compare their features. Be sure to also include costs. Which would you recommend? Why?

Case Project 13-7: Free Synchronization Storage

Although not as full-featured as online backup services, several free synchronization storage tools allow users to back up data by synchronization: when you place a file in a designated folder, it is automatically stored to the remote site. Several of these sites offer free storage from 5 GB to unlimited space. Use a search engine to search for *free cloud synch storage*, and select three different services. Research these services and note their features. Create a table that lists each product and compare their features. Be sure to include storage space limits. How do they compare to online backup services? Which would you recommend? Why?

Case Project 13-8: Bay Pointe Security Consulting

Bay Pointe Security Consulting (BPSC) provides security consulting services to a wide range of businesses, individuals, schools, and organizations. BPSC has hired you as a technology student to help them with a new project and provide real-world experience to students who are interested in the security field.

Miles Comfort Coaches (MCC) is a regional charter bus service. Recently an IT employee was caught using the MCC network servers to store pirated software, yet because there were no incident response procedures in place, he was able to erase the software and destroy the evidence. MCC has approached BPSC to hire them to provide external forensics response services. However, several employees who are aware of the forensic analysis performed on the employee's computer have now raised concern about MCC scanning their computers. MCC has asked BPSC to help educate all employees about computer forensics.

1. Create a PowerPoint presentation that provides an explanation of computer forensics, why it is important, and the basic forensics procedures that should be used. The presentation should be 10 slides in length.

2. Comfort Coaches has asked that you draft a memo to all employees regarding the steps to take when they suspect that an incident has occurred that may require digital evidence to be secured. Write a one-page memo to Comfort Coaches' employees about these steps.

13

Case Project 13-9: Community Site Activity

The Information Security Community Site is an online companion to this textbook. It contains a wide variety of tools, information, discussion boards, and other features to assist learners. Go to **community.cengage.com/infosec**. Click JOIN THE COMMUNITY and use the login name and password that you created in Chapter 1. Visit the **Discussions** section, and then read the following case study.

Use the Internet to locate one incident of a disaster recovery that was successful and one incident that was not successful. Compare and contrast these two accounts. What went right? What went wrong? What type of planning did or did not take place? What would you recommend to improve these disaster recovery plans? Record your answer on the Community Site discussion board.

References

1. Watson, Julie, "'Zombie apocalypse' training drill organized by Halo Corp. for military, police set for Oct. 31 in San Diego," *Huffington Post*, Oct. 27, 2012, retrieved Apr. 7, 2014, www.huffingtonpost.com/2012/10/29/zombie-apocalypse-trainining-military-halo -corp-_n_2036996.html.

2. Hill, Logan, "The workday after tomorrow," *Bloomberg Businessweek*, Nov. 12–18, 2012, pp. 101–103.

3. Genkin, Daniel, Shamir, Adi, and Tromer, Eran, "RSA key extraction via low-bandwidth acoustic cryptanalysis," retrieved Mar. 27, 2014, www.tau.ac.il/~tromer/ papers/acoustic-20131218.pdf.

4. Arik Hesseldahl, "The tempest surrounding Tempest," *Forbes.com*, Aug. 8, 2000, retrieved May 17, 2011, www.forbes.com/2000/08/10/mu9.html.

5. "Digital forensics," *D.63*, Jan. 26, 2011, retrieved May 4, 2011, www.directive63.com/ digital-forensics.

## chapter 14

Risk Mitigation

After completing this chapter, you should be able to do the following:

- Explain how to control risk
- List the ways in which security policies can reduce risk
- Describe how awareness and training can provide increased security

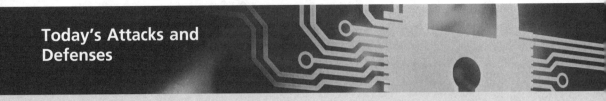

Today's Attacks and Defenses

The life of a high-profile security researcher may sound exciting. Spending time uncovering the latest attacks to expose both the attackers as well as the weak defenses of a company's network has the appeal of exciting "digital detective" undercover work. In addition, being quoted by news media around the world and being in constant demand as a high-profile speaker would only add to the appeal. However, being on the attacker's radar screen as someone who exposes their attacks can actually make the life of a security researcher dangerous.

Consider Brian Krebs, one of the best-known and highly regarded security researchers and cybersecurity blogger. Krebs was one of the first researchers to report on the existence of Stuxnet. This worm, first widely reported in mid-2010, was actively targeting Windows computers that managed large-scale industrial-control systems, which are often referred to as SCADA (Supervisory Control and Data Acquisition). SCADA systems can be found in military installations, oil pipeline control, manufacturing environments, and nuclear power plants. It is speculated that Stuxnet's primary target was the Iranian Bushehr nuclear power plant (almost 6 out of 10 infected Stuxnet computers have been traced back to Iran). This reactor, located in southwestern Iran near the Persian Gulf, had been a source of tension between Iran and the West (including the U.S.) because of fear that spent fuel from the reactor could be reprocessed elsewhere in the country to produce weapons-grade plutonium for use in nuclear warheads. Krebs helped uncover evidence that an unnamed government-sponsored team of programmers—or even teams from multiple opposition governments—created Stuxnet (at a cost exceeding $4 million) to cripple the Bushehr facility. He also was one of the first to bring to light how a credit bureau was tricked into selling consumer data to identity thieves. Krebs even exposed a successful attack on Adobe Systems, which earned him a "Thank you" from Adobe's chief security officer that was posted on the Adobe website.

Krebs's background is not what might be expected for a top-shelf security researcher. He earned a Bachelor of Arts in International Studies from George Mason University in 1994, admitting that "At the time I wasn't much interested in computers," although he had done some programming on an Apple II and spent time visiting online bulletin boards.[1] After graduation he started working in the circulation department of the *Washington Post* and soon worked his way up to being a reporter. A watershed moment for Krebs came in 2001 when his home network was overrun by a group of Chinese attackers who kept locking him out of his network. In defense Krebs started reading everything he could get his hands on about security and how the Internet works. He then began to infiltrate the online forums

(continued)

and chat rooms where attackers often gather. Krebs taught himself Russian and was soon able to persuade others to share with him their tricks. In 2005 he launched the *Post*'s Security Fix blog and maintained it until 2009, when the *Post* merged its online and print newsrooms and Krebs lost his job. He then started his own blog, *krebsonsecurity.com*.

Although Krebs is highly respected in the security community, attackers—obviously—do not hold him in the same high regard. Recently attackers have resorted to trying to make his life miserable. They have routinely planted Krebs's name in the program code of their malware, either as a tribute or in an attempt to convince others that Krebs is behind the code. Krebs has received through the mail 13 packets of heroin (hoping to arouse the suspicion of the local law enforcement) as well as a bag of excrement. Recently attackers called the local police with a fake report of a hostage situation at Krebs's home, which resulted in a police SWAT team storming his house and pointing automatic weapons at his head. Today Krebs has multiple security cameras in his house. He also keeps a 12-gauge shotgun with him in his office.

It is no surprise that the use of technology in the workplace can increase the overall business risk to an organization. At the very heart of information security, therefore, should be the concept of risk. Many different types of risk are encountered in an organization. Although some risks have a small impact and can be easily managed, other risks can threaten the very existence of the business. Because information security risks can be avenues through which an attacker could cripple an organization, they can never be taken lightly.

Many organizations take a multifaceted approach to information security. First, they work to control risk through several different management techniques. Second, they develop a security policy that reflects the organization's philosophy regarding the protection of technology resources. Security policies define what the organization needs to protect and how it should be protected. The third part of the approach is awareness and training. Just as users need to be instructed how to use specific software or hardware, instruction is essential in order to maintain security. Because end-users form one of the most important defenses against attackers, they need to be equipped with the knowledge and skills to ward off attacks.

In this chapter you will learn how organizations can establish and maintain security in the face of risk. First, you will learn about risk and steps to control it. Then, you will study security policies and the different types of policies that are used to reduce risk. Finally, you will explore how training and awareness can help provide the user with the tools to maintain a secure environment within the organization.

Controlling Risk

2.1 Explain the importance of risk related concepts.

2.3 Given a scenario, implement appropriate risk mitigation strategies.

A *risk* is a situation that involves exposure to some type of danger. Yet, not all events that first appear to be a risk may actually result in a risk. An event that, in the beginning, is considered to be a risk yet turns out not to be one is called a **false positive**. A **false negative** is just the opposite: an event that does not appear to be a risk but actually turns out to be one.

False positives and false negatives are often found with anomaly-based monitoring of networks, covered in Chapter 7.

Risks can be divided into several classifications. These are listed in Table 14-1.

Risk category	Description	Example
Strategic	Action that affects the long-term goals of the organization	Theft of intellectual property, not pursuing a new opportunity, loss of a major account, competitor entering the market
Compliance	Following (or not following) a regulation or standard	Breach of contract, not responding to the introduction of new laws
Financial	Impact of financial decisions or market factors	Increase in interest rates, global financial crisis
Operational	Events that impact the daily business of the organization	Fire, hazardous chemical spill, power blackout
Environmental	Actions related to the surroundings	Tornado, flood, hurricane
Technical	Events that affect information technology systems	Denial of service attack, SQL injection attack, virus
Managerial	Actions related to the management of the organization	Long-term illness of company president, key employee resigning

Table 14-1   Risk classifications

How can the impact or seriousness of a risk be reduced? Several different approaches are used to reduce risk. One approach is to modify the *response* to the risk instead of merely accepting the risk. Different risk responses include:

- *Transference.* Risk transference makes a third party responsible for the risk.
- *Risk avoidance.* Risk avoidance involves identifying the risk and making the decision to not engage in the activity.
- *Mitigation.* Risk mitigation is the attempt to address the risk by making it less serious.

Risk is explained in detail in Chapter 1.

Another approach uses the *Simple Risk Model*. Table 14-2 lists the elements of this model.

Element	Description	Example
Preventive	These are controls that prevent the loss or harm from occurring based on the risk.	A preventive control requires the installation of firewalls in a network.
Detective	Detective controls monitor activity to identify instances where practices or procedures were not followed.	A detective control requires a continual review of log files to detect any abnormal activity on a system.
Corrective	Corrective controls restore the system back to its prior state before a malicious event occurred.	A corrective control restores a data backup after a virus infected a system.

Table 14-2   Simple Risk Model

In this model, preventive elements are considered the most effective in reducing risk, since they minimize the possibility of loss by preventing the risk from occurring, and thus should be universally applied. The next most effective are corrective elements, which minimize the impact by restoring the system to its state at a point before the event. However, this may still result in some degree of loss, since the restoration procedure may lead to a system being unavailable, resulting in lost productivity. The least effective—but most often used—are detective elements that identify the event after it has occurred.

A third approach to reducing the impact of risk uses what are called *risk control types*. These types include:

- *Management.* **Management risk control types** are administrative in their nature and are the laws, regulations, policies, practices, and guidelines that govern the overall requirements and controls. For example, almost all states have enacted laws that require businesses to inform residents within a set period of time if the loss of personal information has or is believed to have occurred. In order to comply with this law, the organization would adopt and then enforce as a type of control the policies and procedures to prevent data loss or theft.

- *Technical.* **Technical risk control types** involve enforcing technology to control risk, such as antivirus software, firewalls, and encryption.

- *Operational.* **Operational risk control types** cover operational procedures to limit risk. This may include using video surveillance systems and barricades to limit access to secure sites.

A final approach looks at mitigating risk from a managerial perspective. Three of the most common elements in this approach are privilege management, change management, and incident management. In addition, various methods are used to calculate risk.

Privilege Management

A *privilege* is a subject's access level over an object, such as a user's ability to open a payroll file. *Privilege management* is the process of assigning and revoking privileges to objects; that is, it covers the procedures of managing object authorizations.

14

One element of privilege management is periodic review of a subject's privileges over an object, known as *privilege auditing* (an *audit* is a methodical examination and review that produces a detailed report of its findings). Audits are usually associated with reviewing financial practices, such as an examination of an organization's financial statements and accounting documents to be sure that they follow the generally accepted accounting principles and mandated regulations. Auditing IT functions, particularly security functions, can be equally important. Audits serve to verify that the organization's security protections are being enacted and that corrective actions can be swiftly implemented before an attacker exploits a vulnerability.

 The roles of owners, custodians, and end-users are covered in Chapter 11.

It is important to periodically examine a subject's privilege over an object to ensure that the subject has the correct privileges. The correct privileges should follow the principle of least privilege in which users should be given only the minimal amount of privileges necessary to perform their job functions. This helps to ensure that users do not exceed their intended authorization. Most organizations have a written policy that mandates regular reviews. Figure 14-1 shows a sample review.

Review of User Access Rights

- User access rights will be reviewed on a regular basis by the IT Security Manager. External audits of access rights will be carried out at least once per year.

- The organization will institute a review of all network access rights every six months in order to positively confirm all current users. Any lapsed accounts that are identified will be disabled immediately and deleted within three business days unless they can be positively reconfirmed.

- The organization will institute a review of access to applications once per year. This will be done in cooperation with the application owner and will be designed to positively and deleted within three business days unless they can be positively reconfirmed. This review will be conducted as follows:

  1. The IT Security Manager will generate a list of users, by application.

  2. The appropriate list will be sent to each application owner who will be asked to confirm that all users identifier are authorized to have access to the application.

  3. The IT Security Manager will ensure that a response is received within 10 business days.

  4. Any user not confirmed will have his/her access to the system disabled immediately and deleted within three business days.

  5. The IT Security Manager will maintain a permanent record of list that were distributed to application owners, application owner responses, and a record of any action taken.

Figure 14-1 Sample user access rights review

Change Management

Change management refers to a methodology for making modifications and keeping track of those changes. In some instances, changes to network or system configurations are made haphazardly to alleviate a pressing problem. Without proper documentation, a future change may negate or diminish a previous change or even unknowingly create a security vulnerability. Change management seeks to approach changes systematically and provide the necessary documentation of the changes.

Because change management documentation provides a wealth of information that would be valuable to attackers, it must be secured. Limited copies should be available on a checkout-only basis, with clear markings that they should not be copied, distributed, or removed from the premises.

Although change management involves all types of changes to information systems, two major types of changes regarding security need to be properly documented. The first is any change in system architecture, such as new servers, routers, or other equipment being introduced into the network. These devices may serve as replacements for existing equipment or new equipment that will expand the capability of the network. A detailed list of the attributes of the new equipment should be compiled, including:

- IP and MAC addresses
- Equipment name
- Equipment type
- Function
- Inventory tag number
- Location
- Manufacturer
- Manufacturer serial number
- Model and part number
- Software or firmware version

The second type of change is that of classification, which primarily refers to files or documents. The classification designation of government documents is typically *Top Secret, Secret, Confidential*, and *Unclassified*. Many organizations do not have four levels of documents; they may simply have Standard documents and Confidential documents. Whatever system of classification is used, it is important to clearly label documents that are not intended for public use.

Because the impact of changes can potentially affect all users, and uncoordinated changes can result in security vulnerabilities, many organizations create a *change management team (CMT)* to oversee the changes. Any proposed change (addition, modification, relocation, removal) of the technical infrastructure, or any component, hardware or software, including any interruption of service, must first be approved by the CMT. The team might typically be composed of representatives from all areas of IT, network security, and upper-level management. The duties of the CMT include:

- Review proposed changes
- Ensure that the risk and impact of the planned change is clearly understood

14

- Recommend approval, disapproval, deferral, or withdrawal of a requested change
- Communicate proposed and approved changes to coworkers

Incident Management

When an unauthorized incident occurs, such as an unauthorized employee copying sensitive material, a response is required. *Incident response* may be defined as the components required to identify, analyze, and contain an incident. *Incident handling* is the planning, coordination, and communications functions that are needed to resolve an incident in an efficient manner. **Incident management** can be defined as the "framework" and functions required to enable incident response and incident handling within an organization. The objective of incident management is to restore normal operations as quickly as possible with the least possible impact on either the business or the users.

One part of incident response procedures may include using forensic science and basic forensics procedures to properly respond to a computer forensics event. Computer forensic procedures are covered in Chapter 13.

Risk Calculation

An organization that can accurately calculate risk is better prepared to address the risk. For example, if a customer database is determined to be of high value and also have a high risk, the necessary resources should be used to strengthen the defenses surrounding that database.

There are two approaches to risk calculation. One is **qualitative risk calculation**. This approach uses an "educated guess" based on observation. For example, if it is observed that the customer database contains important information, it would be assigned a high asset value. Also, if it is observed that this database has been frequently the target of attacks, it would be assigned a high risk value as well. Qualitative risk typically assigns a numeric value (*1–10*) or label (*High, Medium,* or *Low*) that represents the risk.

The second approach, **quantitative risk calculation**, is considered more scientific. Instead of arbitrarily assigning a number or label based on observation, the quantitative risk calculation actually attempts to create "hard" numbers associated with the risk of an element in a system by using historical data. In the example, if the customer database has a higher risk calculation than a product database, more resources would be allocated to protecting it.

Quantitative risk calculations can be divided into the *likelihood* of a risk and the *impact* of a risk being successful.

Risk Likelihood Historical data is valuable in providing information on how likely it is that a risk will become a reality within a specific period of time. For example, when considering the risk of equipment failure, several quantitative tools can be used to predict the likelihood of the risk, including:

- *Mean Time Between Failure (MTBF).* MTBF calculates the average (*mean*) amount of time until a component fails, cannot be repaired, and must be replaced. It is a reliability term used to provide the amount of failures. Calculating the MTBF involves taking the total time measured divided by the total number of failures observed.

Although MTBF is sometimes used to advertise the reliability of consumer hardware products like hard disk drives, this value is seldom considered by the purchaser. This is because most consumer purchases are simply price-driven. MTBF is considered more important for industries than for consumers.

- *Mean Time To Recovery (MTTR).* MTTR is the average amount of time that it will take a device to recover from a failure that is not a terminal failure. Although MTTR is sometimes called *Mean Time To Repair* because in most systems this means replacing a failed hardware instead of repairing it, the Mean Time To Recovery is considered a more accurate term.

MTBF and MTTR are covered in Chapter 13.

- *Mean Time To Failure (MTTF).* **Mean Time To Failure (MTTF)** is a basic measure of reliability for systems that cannot be repaired. It is the average amount of time expected until the first failure of a piece of equipment.

- *Failure In Time (FIT).* The *Failure In Time* calculation is another way of reporting MTBF. FIT can report the number of expected failures per one billion hours of operation for a device. This term is used particularly by the semiconductor industry. FIT can be stated as *devices for 1 billion hours, 1 billion devices for 1000 hours each*, or in other combinations.

Other historical data for calculating the likelihood of risk can be acquired through a variety of sources. These are summarized in Table 14-3.

Source	Explanation
Police departments	Crime statistics on the area of facilities to determine the probability of vandalism, break-ins, or dangers potentially encountered by personnel
Insurance companies	Risks faced by other companies and the amounts paid out when these risks became reality
Computer incident monitoring organizations	Data regarding a variety of technology-related risks, failures, and attacks

Table 14-3 Historical data sources

Historical data can be used to determine the likelihood of a risk occurring within a year. This is known as the **Annualized Rate of Occurrence (ARO).**

Risk Impact Once historical data is gathered so that the ARO can be calculated, the next step is to determine the impact of that risk. This can be done by comparing it to the

monetary loss associated with an asset in order to determine the cost that represents how much money would be lost if the risk occurred.

When calculating the loss, it is important to consider all costs. For example, if a network firewall failed, the costs would include the amount needed to purchase a replacement, the hourly wage of the person replacing the equipment, and the pay for employees who could not perform their job functions because they could not use the network while the firewall was not functioning.

Two risk calculation formulas are commonly used to calculate expected losses. The **Single Loss Expectancy (SLE)** is the expected monetary loss every time a risk occurs. The SLE is computed by multiplying the Asset Value (AV) by the Exposure Factor (EF), which is the proportion of an asset's value that is likely to be destroyed by a particular risk (expressed as a percentage). The SLE formula is:

$$SLE = AV \times EF$$

For example, consider a building with a value of $10,000,000 (AV) of which 75 percent of it is likely to be destroyed by a tornado (EF). The SLE would be calculated as follows:

$$\$7,500,000 = \$10,000,000 \times 0.75$$

The **Annualized Loss Expectancy (ALE)** is the expected monetary loss that can be expected for an asset due to a risk over a one-year period. It is calculated by multiplying the SLE by the ARO, which is the probability that a risk will occur in a particular year. The ALE formula is:

$$ALE = SLE \times ARO$$

In the above example, if flood insurance data suggests that a serious flood is likely to occur once in 100 years, then the ARO is 1/100 or 0.01. The ALE would be calculated as follows:

$$\$75,000 = 0.01 \times \$7,500,000$$

Reducing Risk Through Policies

2.1 Explain the importance of risk related concepts.

4.2 Summarize mobile security concepts and technologies.

4.4 Implement the appropriate controls to ensure data security.

Another means of reducing risks is through a security policy. It is important to know what a security policy is, how to balance trust and control, the process for designing a policy, and what the different types of policies are.

What Is a Security Policy?

If the question "What is a security policy?" were posed to both a manager and a security technician, the answers would likely be different. A manager might say that a security policy is as a set of management statements that defines an organization's philosophy of how to safeguard its information. A security technician might respond that a security policy is the rules for computer access and specific information on how these will be carried out. These two responses are not conflicting but are actually complementary and reflect the different views of a security policy.

At its core, a **security policy** is a written document that states how an organization plans to protect the company's information technology assets. The policy outlines the protections that should be enacted to ensure that the organization's assets face minimal risks. A security policy, along with the accompanying procedures, standards, and guidelines, is key to implementing information security in an organization. Having a written security policy empowers an organization to take appropriate action to safeguard its data.

An organization's information security policy can serve several functions:

- It can be an overall intention and direction, formally expressed by the organization's management. A security policy is a vehicle for communicating an organization's information security culture and acceptable information security behavior.

- It details specific risks and how to address them, and so provides controls that executives can use to direct employee behavior.

- It can help to create a security-aware organizational culture.

- It can help to ensure that employee behavior is directed and monitored in compliance with security requirements.

Balancing Trust and Control

An effective security policy must carefully balance two key elements: trust and control. There are three approaches to trust:

- *Trust everyone all of the time.* This is the easiest model to enforce because there are no restrictions. This model, however, is impractical because it leaves systems vulnerable to attack.

- *Trust no one at any time.* This model is the most restrictive, but is also impractical. Few individuals would work for an organization that did not trust its employees.

- *Trust some people some of the time.* This approach exercises caution in the amount of trust given. Access is provided as needed, with technical controls to ensure the trust is not violated.

The approach of trusting no one at any time is mostly found in high-security government organizations.

A security policy attempts to provide the right amount of trust by balancing *no trust* and *too much trust*. It does this by trusting some of the people some of the time and providing the right level of access to resources for the employees to perform their job functions—but no more than that. Deciding on the level of trust may be a delicate matter; too much trust may lead to security problems, while too little trust may make it difficult to find and keep good employees.

Control is the second element that must be balanced. One of the goals of a security policy is to implement control. Deciding on the level of control for a specific policy is not always

14

clear. The security needs and the culture of the organization play a major role when deciding what level of control is appropriate. If policies are too restrictive or too hard to implement and comply with, employees will either ignore them or find a way to circumvent the controls. Management must commit to the proper level of control that a security policy should address.

Because security policies are a balancing act between trust and control, not all employees have positive attitudes toward them. Employees sometimes view security policies as a barrier to their productivity, a way to control their behavior, or as a list of rules that are difficult to follow. This is particularly true if, in the past, policies did not exist or were loosely enforced. Some users simply "give up" and show no concern about security or security policies, maintaining that it is exclusively "IT's job" to provide protection to the organization.

One of the primary challenges is to engage employees to "buy in" and understand the importance of security. Every organization is unique, and a variety of approaches may need to be used in different situations.

Designing a Security Policy

Designing a security policy involves defining what a policy is, understanding the security policy cycle, and knowing the steps in policy development.

Definition of a Policy Several terms are used to describe the "rules" that a user follows in an organization. A *standard* is a collection of requirements specific to the system or procedure that must be met by everyone. For example, a standard might describe how to secure a computer at home that remotely connects to the organization's network. Users must follow this standard if they want to be able to connect. A *guideline* is a collection of suggestions that should be implemented. These are not requirements to be met but are strongly recommended. A *policy* is a document that outlines specific requirements or rules that must be met.

A policy generally has these characteristics:

- Communicates a consensus of judgment
- Defines appropriate behavior for users
- Identifies what tools and procedures are needed
- Provides directives for Human Resources action in response to inappropriate behavior
- May be helpful if it is necessary to prosecute violators

A policy is considered the correct tool for an organization to use when establishing security because a policy applies to a wide range of hardware or software (it is not a standard) and is required (it is not just a guideline).

The Security Policy Cycle Most organizations follow a three-phase cycle in developing and maintaining a security policy. The first phase involves a *vulnerability assessment*, which is a systematic and methodical evaluation of the exposure of assets to attackers, forces of nature, or any other entity that is a potential harm. Vulnerability assessment attempts to identify what needs to be protected (asset identification), what the pressures are against it (threat evaluation), how susceptible the current protection is (vulnerability appraisal), what damages could result from the threats (risk assessment), and what to do about it (risk mitigation). The vulnerability assessment includes:

- *Asset identification.* Asset identification determines the items that have a positive economic value, which may include data, hardware, personnel, physical assets, and software. Along with the assets, the attributes of the assets need to be compiled and their relative value determined.

- *Threat identification.* After the assets have been inventoried and given a relative value, the next step is to determine the threats from threat agents. A threat agent is any person or thing with the power to carry out a threat against an asset.

- *Vulnerability appraisal.* After the assets have been inventoried and prioritized, and the threats have been determined, the next step is to determine what current security weaknesses might expose the assets to those threats. This is known as vulnerability appraisal and in effect takes a snapshot of the security of the organization as it now stands.

- *Risk assessment.* A risk assessment involves determining the damage that would result from an attack and the likelihood that the vulnerability is a risk to the organization.

- *Risk mitigation.* Once the risks are determined and ranked, the final step is to determine what to do about the risks. It is important to recognize that security weaknesses can never be entirely eliminated; some degree of risk must always be assumed.

The second phase of the security policy cycle is to use the information from the risk management study to create the policy. A security policy is a document or series of documents that clearly defines the defense mechanisms an organization will employ to keep information secure. It also outlines how the organization will respond to attacks and the duties and responsibilities of its employees for information security.

The final phase is to review the policy for compliance. Because new assets are continually being added to the organization, and new threats appear against the assets, compliance monitoring and evaluation must be conducted regularly. The results of the monitoring and evaluation (such as revealing that a new asset is unprotected) become identified as risks, and the cycle begins again. The security policy cycle is illustrated in Figure 14-2.

14

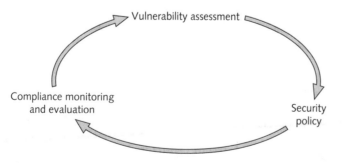

Figure 14-2 Security policy cycle

The security policy cycle is a never-ending process of identifying what needs to be protected, determining how to protect it, and evaluating the protection.

Steps in Development When designing a security policy, many organizations follow a standard set of principles. These principles, which can be divided into what a policy must do and what a policy should do, are summarized in Table 14-4.

Security policy *must*	Security policy *should*
Be implementable and enforceable	State reasons why the policy is necessary
Be concise and easy to understand	Describe what is covered by the policy
Balance protection with productivity	Outline how violations will be handled

Table 14-4   Policy *must* and *should* statements

Security policies do not have to be long in order to be effective. The goal at one major corporation is to limit all policies to two or fewer pages.

It is advisable that the design of a security policy be the work of a team, and not one or two security or IT personnel. The security policy development team should be charged with developing the initial draft of the policy, determining which groups are required to review each part of the policy, completing the required approval process, and determining how the policy will be implemented. Ideally the team should have these representatives:

- Senior-level administrator
- Member of management who can enforce the policy
- Member of the legal staff
- Representative from the user community

The size of the security policy development team depends on the size and scope of the policy. Small-scale policies might require only a few participants, while larger policies might require a team of 10 or more.

The team should first decide on the scope and goals of the policy. The scope should be a statement about who is covered by the policy, while the goals outline what the policy attempts to achieve. The team also must decide on how specific to make the policy (remembering that a security policy is not meant to be a detailed plan regarding how to implement the policy). For example, a statement regarding mandatory vacations could indicate either that vacations must be taken by employees or how frequently vacations must be taken.

In addition to mandatory vacations, specificity in job rotation, separation of duties, and least privilege should be outlined.

Also, statements regarding due care are often included. The term *due care* is used frequently in legal and business settings. It is defined as the obligations that are imposed on owners and operators of assets to exercise reasonable care of the assets and take necessary precautions to protect them. Due care is the care that a reasonable person would exercise under the circumstances. For information security policies, due care is often used to indicate the reasonable treatment that an employee would exercise when using computer equipment. Some examples of due care might include:

- Employees will exercise due care in opening attachments received from unknown sources (a reasonable person should not open an attachment from an unknown source because it may contain malware).

- Technicians will exercise due care when installing a new operating system on an existing computer (a reasonable person would not set up a "Guest" account or leave the new password written down and affixed to the monitor).

- Students will exercise due care when using computers in a lab setting (a reasonable person would be aware that many students in a crowded lab could see a password that is entered).

Because the standard of "reasonable treatment" in a due care clause is open to interpretation, policies often include clear and explicit statements regarding conduct and a statement that due care covers implicit measures that are not enumerated (a "catch-all" statement).

Many organizations follow these additional guidelines while developing a policy:

- Notify users in advance that a new security policy is being developed and explain why the policy is needed.

- Provide a sample of people affected by the policy with an opportunity to review and comment on the policy.

- Prior to deployment, give all users at least two weeks to review the policy and comment on it.

- Allow users given responsibility in a policy the authority to carry out their responsibilities.

Some organizations designate a person who served on the development team to serve as the official policy interpreter in case questions arise.

Types of Security Policies

Because a security policy is so comprehensive and is often detailed, most organizations choose to break the security policy down into smaller "subpolicies" that can be more easily referred to. The term *security policy* then becomes an umbrella term for all the subpolicies included within it.

Many types of security policies exist. Some of these types are listed in Table 14-5.

Name of security policy	Description
Acceptable encryption policy	Defines requirements for using cryptography
Antivirus policy	Establishes guidelines for effectively reducing the threat of computer viruses on the organization's network and computers
Audit vulnerability scanning policy	Outlines the requirements and provides the authority for an information security team to conduct audits and risk assessments, investigate incidents, ensure conformance to security policies, or monitor user activity
Automatically forwarded email policy	Prescribes that no email will be automatically forwarded to an external destination without prior approval from the appropriate manager or director
Database credentials coding policy	Defines requirements for storing and retrieving database usernames and passwords
Demilitarized zone (DMZ) security policy	Defines standards for all networks and equipment located in the DMZ
Email policy	Creates standards for using corporate email
Email retention policy	Helps employees determine what information sent or received by email should be retained and for how long
Extranet policy	Defines the requirements for third-party organizations to access the organization's networks
Information sensitivity policy	Establishes criteria for classifying and securing the organization's information in a manner appropriate to its level of security
Router security policy	Outlines standards for minimal security configuration for routers and switches
Server security policy	Creates standards for minimal security configuration for servers
VPN security policy	Establishes requirements for remote access virtual private network (VPN) connections to the organization's network
Wireless communication policy	Defines standards for wireless systems used to connect to the organization's networks

Table 14-5 Types of security policies

In addition to the security policies listed in Table 14-5, most organizations have security policies that address acceptable use, privacy, data, security-related human resources, ethics, and password management and complexity.

CAUTION

The purpose of security policies is not to serve as a motivational tool to force users to practice safe security techniques. The results from research have indicated that the specific elements of a security policy do not have an impact on user behavior. Relying on a security policy as the exclusive defense mechanism will not provide adequate security for an organization.

Acceptable Use Policy (AUP) An **Acceptable Use Policy** (AUP) is a policy that defines the actions users may perform while accessing systems and networking equipment. The *users* are not limited to employees; the term can also include vendors, contractors, or visitors, each with different privileges. AUPs typically cover all computer use, including mobile devices.

An AUP may have an overview regarding what is covered by the policy, as in the following sample for "Organization A":

> *Internet/intranet/extranet-related systems, including but not limited to computer equipment, software, operating systems, storage media, network accounts providing electronic mail, web browsing, and FTP, are the property of Organization A. These systems are to be used for business purposes in serving the interests of the company, and of our clients and customers, in the course of normal operations.*

The AUP usually provides explicit prohibitions regarding security and proprietary information:

> *Keep passwords secure and do not share accounts. Authorized users are responsible for the security of their passwords and accounts. System-level passwords should be changed every 30 days; user-level passwords should be changed every 45 days.*

> *All computers and laptops should be secured with a password-protected screensaver with the automatic activation feature set at 10 minutes or less, or by logging off when the host is unattended.*

> *Postings by employees from an Organization A on social networking sites should contain a disclaimer stating that the opinions expressed are strictly their own and not necessarily those of Organization A, unless posting is in the course of business duties.*

Unacceptable use may also be outlined by the AUP, as in the following sample:

> *The following actions are not acceptable ways to use the system:*

- *Introduction of malicious programs into the network or server*
- *Revealing your account password to others or allowing use of your account by others, including family and other household members when work is being done at home*
- *Using an Organization A computing asset to actively engage in procuring or transmitting material that is in violation of sexual harassment or hostile workplace laws in the user's local jurisdiction*
- *Any form of harassment via email, telephone, or texting, whether through language, frequency, or size of messages*
- *Unauthorized use, or forging, of email header information*

Acceptable use policies are generally considered to be the most important information security policies. It is recommended that all organizations, particularly educational institutions and government agencies, have an AUP in place.

Privacy Policy Because privacy is of growing concern to today's consumers, many organizations have a **privacy policy**. This policy outlines how the organization uses personal information it collects. A typical privacy policy for consumers is shown in Figure 14-3.

14

In general, you can visit us on the Internet without telling us who you are and without giving any personal information about yourself. There are times, however, when we or our partners may need information from you. You may choose to give us personal information in a variety of situations. For example, you may want to give us information, such as your name and address or e-mail, to correspond with you, to process an order, or to provide you with a subscription. You may give us your credit card details to buy something from us or a description of your education and work experience in connection with a job opening for which you wish to be considered. We intend to let you know how we will use such information before we collect it from you. You may tell us that you do not want us to use this information to make further contact with you beyond fulfilling your request. If you give us personal information about somebody else, such as a spouse or work colleague, we will assume that you have their permission to do so.

Figure 14-3   Sample privacy policy

Data Policies Data policies are important because they address the different aspects of how data should be handled within an organization. These policies are particularly important for mobile devices, since their portable nature more easily exposes data to theft.

One type of data policy is a **data storage policy**. This is a set of procedures designed to control and manage data within the organization by specifying data collection and storage. It provides answers to questions such as, What data can be collected? Who is responsible for maintaining it? Will the data be stored online in a Storage Area Network (SAN) or Network Attached Storage (NAS) or off-line on an optical jukebox or DVD? What about external data collected over the Web? A data storage policy attempts to answer questions about how and where data is stored. Often a data storage policy may contain rules for classification of data within a standardized framework for identifying information assets. Generally, this involves creating classification categories (such as *Level A* or *High Risk*) and then assigning data to these categories.

Another type of a data policy is a **data retention policy**. This policy outlines how to maintain information in the user's possession for a predetermined length of time. Different types of data may require different lengths of retention. In addition to describing how long various types of information must be maintained in the user's possession, retention policies usually describe the procedures for archiving the information and special mechanisms for handling the information when under litigation.

A **data wiping and disposing policy** addresses how and when data will ultimately be erased. Deleting sensitive data has become a problem due to well-intentioned recycling efforts by many organizations. Because of the difficulty in disposing of older computers, often because they contain toxic or environmentally dangerous materials, many organizations recycle older computers by giving them to schools, charities, or selling them online. However, information that should have been deleted from hard drives often is still available on these recycled computers. This is because operating systems do not always completely delete files to make the information irretrievable. For example, when a file is deleted, the file name is removed from a table that stores file information, but the content of the file itself remains on the hard drive until it is overwritten by new files. This results in sensitive data being accessible to an unauthorized party. Even reformatting a drive may not fully erase all of the data on it.

In order to address this problem, a data wiping and disposing policy outlines the disposal of resources that are considered confidential. It typically involves how to dispose of equipment that is no longer used. For example, hard drives should be erased with third-party software that physically "wipes" the disk clean and network devices should have any data stored in memory erased.

TIP

Several companies offer disposal services for IT equipment, guaranteeing the destruction of any data that may have been stored on the system. Such companies will visit the workplace, label the equipment, and then strip it down to the individual component level where it can be sold or given to particular charities on request. If the equipment is faulty and beyond repair, it is then sent for recycling.

Security-Related Human Resource Policy A policy that addresses security as it relates to human resources is known as a *security-related human resource policy*. These policies include statements regarding how an employee's information technology resources will be addressed. Security-related human resource policies typically are presented at an orientation session when the employee is hired, and provide the necessary information about the technology resources of the organization, how they are used, and the acceptable use and security policies that are in force. The penalties for violating policies likewise are clearly outlined.

Security-related human resource policies may contain statements regarding due process. *Due process* is the principle of treating all accused persons in an equal fashion, using established rules and procedures. A due process statement may indicate that any employee accused of a malicious action will be treated equally and not given preferential treatment. The policy also may contain a statement regarding *due diligence*, or that any investigation into suspicious employee conduct will examine all material facts.

The security-related human resource policy typically contains statements regarding actions to be taken when an employee is terminated. For example, the policy may state that:

- When terminating an employee, the employee's access to technology resources will be immediately suspended.

- Once the employee has been informed of the termination, the employee should not be allowed to return to his or her office but should be immediately escorted out of the building.

- The IT department will have a list of all user accounts and suspend the appropriate accounts immediately.

- Log files will be routinely scanned to ensure that all the employee's accounts were suspended.

14

- The supervisor will be responsible for reviewing all employee electronic information and either disposing of it or forwarding it to the employee's replacements.

Termination of an employee calls for close coordination between the supervisor, legal counsel, the Human Resources staff, the IT department, and security.

Ethics Policy The corporate world has been rocked in recent years by a series of high-profile scandals. Once-powerful organizations are bankrupt due to unethical (and illegal) actions. In many instances, the knowledge and approval of such actions went all the way to the top of the organization. The result was billions of dollars lost by investors and shareholders and thousands of employees suddenly unemployed and left without promised pension benefits. These scandals have resulted in new federal legislation in an attempt to force organizations to act in a responsible manner.

Many individuals believe that the only way to reduce the number and magnitude of such scandals is to refocus attention on ethics in the enterprise. *Ethics* can be defined as the study of what a group of people understand to be good and right behavior and how people make those judgments. Ethics are different from *morals*, which are values that are attributed to a system of beliefs that help the individual distinguish right from wrong. Moral values typically derive their authority from something outside the individual, such as a higher spiritual being or an external authority such as the government or society.

An *ethics policy* attempts to establish a culture of openness, trust, and integrity in business practices. Ethics policies often contain such topics as executive commitment to ethics, employee commitment to ethics, how to maintain ethical practices, and penalties for unethical behavior.

Password Management and Complexity Policy Although passwords often form the weakest link in information security, they are still the most widely used form of authentication. A *password management and complexity policy* can clearly address how passwords are created and managed. In addition to implementing controls through technology (such as setting passwords to expire after 60 days and not allowing them to be recycled), organizations should remind users how to select and use passwords. For example, information regarding weak passwords can be included in the security policy, as shown in Figure 14-4.

A Weak Password Has the Following Characteristics

- *Contains fewer than 12 characters.*

- *Is a word found in a dictionary (English or foreign).*

- *Is a common usage word such as names of family, pets, friends, coworkers, fantasy characters, and so on, computer terms and names, commands, sites, companies, hardware, and software.*

- *Contains birthdays and other personal information such as addresses and phone numbers.*

- *Uses word or number patterns like qwerty, 123321, and so on.*

- *Includes any of the preceding spelled backward or preceded or followed by a digit (e.g., secret1, 1secret).*

Figure 14-4   Weak password characteristics

Passwords and authentication are covered in Chapter 12.

Awareness and Training

2.6 Explain the importance of security related awareness and training.

One of the key defenses in information security is to provide security awareness and training to users. All computer users in an organization have a shared responsibility to protect the assets of the organization. It cannot be assumed that all users have the knowledge and skill to protect these assets. Instead, users need training in the importance of securing information, the roles that they play in security, and the steps they need to take to prevent attacks. And because new attacks appear regularly, and new security vulnerabilities are continuously being exposed, user awareness and training must be ongoing. User awareness is an essential element of security.

Awareness and training involves instruction regarding compliance, secure user practices, and an awareness of threats. There are also techniques that should be considered to make the training informative and useful.

Compliance

Users should be made aware of the organization's established security strategy as well as the reasons why it is necessary to adhere to it. In particular, users should be informed regarding the following:

- *Security policy training and procedures.* An understanding of the role that security policies play in the organization, their importance, and the content of those policies as they apply to the user is critical to creating a secure work environment.

- *Personally identifiable information (PII).* Users should be informed regarding the importance of PII and the high risks if it is not properly protected.

- *Information classification.* Training on how to differentiate between the different levels of information and to have sensitivity to critical data is important. Classification levels such as *high, medium, low, confidential, private*, and *public* and how they are used in the organization should be clearly outlined to users.

- *Data labeling, handling, and disposal.* Instruction regarding how to handle and protect different types of data as well as how to properly dispose of equipment that contains that data should be provided.

- *Compliance with laws, best practices, and standards.* Users need to be aware of legislation that affects the organization and its use and protection of customer information. In addition, training regarding security standards and appropriate best practices also should be included.

14

User Practices

Awareness and training also involves helping users understand how their normal practices can impact the security of the organization. Table 14-6 lists categories of user practices and the types of instruction that can be provided to make these practices more secure.

Category	Instruction
Password behaviors	Creating strong passwords that are unique for each account and properly protecting them serve as a first line of defense that all employees must practice.
Data handling	No sensitive data may leave the premises without prior authorization. All data that is temporarily stored on a laptop computer must be encrypted.
Clean desk policy	Employees are required to clear their workspace of all papers at the end of each business day.
Prevent tailgating	Never allow another person to enter a secure area along with you without displaying their ID card.
Personally owned devices	No personally owned devices, such as USB flash drives or portable hard drives, may be connected to any corporate equipment or network.

Table 14-6   User practices

Tailgating is covered in Chapter 2.

Threat Awareness

It is not uncommon for users to be unaware of the security threat that a practice or technology may introduce. Two common examples are the use of peer-to-peer networks and social networking.

In addition to P2P and social networking, users should be made aware of information regarding new viruses, phishing attacks, and zero-day exploits. The Cengage Information Security Community Site contains information on how to stay abreast of new attacks.

Peer-to-Peer (P2P) Networks   Similar to instant messaging (IM) in which users connect directly to each other without using a centralized server, a **peer-to-peer (P2P) network** also uses a direct connection between users. A P2P network does not have servers, so each device simultaneously functions as both a client and a server to all other devices connected to the network. P2P networks are typically used for connecting devices on an ad hoc basis for file sharing of audio, video, and data, or real-time data transmission such as telephony traffic.

P2P networks are often associated with illegal file downloads of movies, software, and music.

The most common type of P2P network is known as BitTorrent. *Torrents* are active Internet connections that download a specific file that is available through a *tracker*, which is a server program operated by the person or organization that wants to share the file. BitTorrent maximizes the transfer speed by gathering pieces of the file and downloading these pieces simultaneously from users who already have them (the collective pieces are called a *swarm*). BitTorrent cannot be used to spread viruses or malware in the same way that traditional P2P networks can, in which spreading a virus can be done by simply copying it to the shared folder for other users to download. Because BitTorrent users only share pieces of well-known files whose integrity is known to the tracker, it is not possible to infect a piece of the file being shared. In addition, BitTorrent users cannot unknowingly share the contents of their hard drive in the way that P2P users have done.

Because P2P networks communicate directly between two devices, they are tempting targets for attackers. Viruses, worms, Trojans, and spyware can be sent using some types of P2P. Most organizations prohibit P2P communications because of the high risk of infection and legal consequences.

Social Networking Grouping individuals and organizations into clusters or groups based on some sort of affiliation is called **social networking**. Although physical social networking is achieved in person at schools or work, social networking is increasingly performed online. The websites that facilitate linking individuals with common interests like hobbies, religion, politics, or school contacts are called *social networking sites* and function as an online community of users. A user who is granted access to a social networking site can read the profile pages of other members and interact with them and can read information posted by others and share documents, photos, and videos. The popularity of these online social networking sites has skyrocketed.

It is estimated that one out of every seven human beings belongs to the popular social networking site Facebook. If Facebook were a country, it would be the third most populous country in the world. The U.S. has the most Facebook users, followed by Brazil, India, Indonesia, and Mexico.

Although using any website has risks associated with it, social networking sites can carry additional risks. These risks include:

- *Personal data can be used maliciously.* Users post personal information on their pages for others to read, such as birthdays, where they live, their plans for the upcoming weekend, and the like. However, attackers can use this information for a variety of malicious purposes. For example, knowing that a person is on vacation could allow a burglar to break into an empty home. Providing too much personal information could be used in identity theft. And even personal information that may appear to be harmless can be very valuable. For example, the challenge password question when resetting a password, such as *What high school did you attend?*, can easily be gathered from a user's social networking page.

- *Users may be too trusting.* Attackers often join a social networking site and pretend to be part of the network of users. After several days or weeks, users begin to feel they know the attackers and may start to provide personal

14

information or click on embedded links provided by the attacker that loads malware onto the user's computer.

- *Accepting friends may have unforeseen consequences.* Some social networking users readily accept any "friend" request they receive, even if they are not familiar with that person. This can result in problems, since whoever is accepted as a friend may then be able to see not only all of that user's personal information but also the personal information of her friends.

- *Social networking security is lax or confusing.* Because social networking sites by design are intended to share information, these sites have often made it too easy for unauthorized users to view other people's information. To combat this problem, many sites change their security options on a haphazard basis, making it difficult for users to keep up with the changes.

Several defenses can be used for social networking sites. First and foremost, users should be instructed to be cautious about what information is posted on these sites. Posting *I'm going to Florida on Friday for two weeks* could indicate that a home or apartment will be vacant for that time, a tempting invitation for a burglar. Other information posted could later prove embarrassing. Asking questions such as *Would my boss approve?* or *What would my mother think of this?* before posting may provide an incentive to rethink the material one more time before posting.

In several court cases, individuals have been ordered by judges to turn over their social networking passwords. For example, a woman who claimed she was seriously injured in an automobile accident was told to turn over her Facebook password to the defense attorneys, who found posts and photographs that indicated she was not seriously injured, including status updates about exercising at a gym.

Second, users should be cautioned regarding who can view their information. Certain types of information could prove to be embarrassing if read by certain parties, such as a prospective employer. Other information should be kept confidential. Users are urged to consider carefully who is accepted as a friend on a social network. Once a person has been accepted as a friend, that person will be able to access any personal information or photographs. Instead, it may be preferable to show "limited friends" a reduced version of a profile. This can be useful for casual acquaintances and business associates.

Finally, the available security settings in social networking sites are often updated frequently by the site with little warning. Users should be instructed to pay close attention to information about new or updated security settings. Also, it is a good idea to disable options and then enable them only as necessary. Users should disable options until it becomes apparent that the options are needed, instead of making everything accessible and restricting access after it is too late.

Table 14-7 lists several Facebook social networking features along with the associated risks.

Feature	Description	Risks
Games and applications	When your Facebook friends use games and applications, these can request information about friends like you, even if you do not use the application.	Information such as your biography, photos, and places where you check in can be exposed.
Social advertisements	A "social ad" pairs an advertisement with an action that a friend has taken, such as "liking" it.	Your Facebook actions could be associated with an ad.
Places	If you use Places, you could be included in a "People Here Now" list once you check in to a location.	Your name and Facebook profile picture appear in the list, which is visible to anyone who checks in to the same location, even if he is not a friend.
Web search	Entering your name in a search engine like Google can display your Facebook profile, profile picture, and information you have designated as public.	Any web user can freely access this information about you.
Photo albums	Photos can be set to be private but that may not include photo albums.	The albums Profile Pictures, Mobile Uploads, and Wall Photos are usually visible to anyone.

Table 14-7   Facebook features and risks

Table 14-8 contains recommendations for contact information settings at Facebook.

Option	Recommended setting	Explanation
Profile	Only my friends	Facebook networks can contain hundreds or thousands of users, and there is no control over who else joins the network to see the information.
Photos or photos tagged of you	Only my friends	Photos and videos have often proven to be embarrassing. Only post material that would be appropriate to appear with a resume or job application.
Status updates	Only my friends	Because changes to status such as "Going to Florida on January 28" can be useful information for thieves, only approved friends should have access to it.
Online status	No one	Any benefits derived by knowing who is online are outweighed by the risks.
Friends	Only my friends (minimum setting)	Giving unknown members of the community access to a list of friends may provide attackers with opportunities to uncover personal information through friends.

Table 14-8   Recommended Facebook profile settings

Training Techniques

All users need continuous training in the new security defenses and to be reminded of company security policies and procedures. Opportunities for security education and training can be at any of the following times:

- When a new employee is hired
- After a computer attack has occurred
- When an employee is promoted or given new responsibilities
- During an annual departmental retreat
- When new user software is installed
- When user hardware is upgraded

TIP

Education in an enterprise is not limited to the average employee. Human resource personnel also need to keep abreast of security issues because in many organizations, it is their role to train new employees on all aspects of the organization, including security. Even upper management needs to be aware of the security threats and attacks that the organization faces, if only to acknowledge the necessity of security in planning, staffing, and budgeting.

One of the challenges of organizational education and training is to understand the traits of learners. Table 14-9 lists general traits of individuals born in the U.S. since 1946.

Year born	Traits	Number in U.S. population
Prior to 1946	Patriotic, loyal, faith in institutions	75 million
1946–1964	Idealistic, competitive, question authority	80 million
1965–1981	Self-reliant, distrustful of institutions, adaptive to technology	46 million
1982–2000	Pragmatic, globally concerned, computer literate, media savvy	76 million

Table 14-9 Traits of learners

In addition to traits of learners, training style also impacts how people learn. The way that one person was taught may not be the best way to teach all others. Most people are taught using a *pedagogical* approach (from a Greek word meaning *to lead a child*). For adult learners, however, an *andragogical* approach (the art of helping an adult learn) is often preferred. Some of the differences between pedagogical and andragogical approaches are summarized in Table 14-10.

In addition to training styles, there are different learning styles. Visual learners learn through taking notes, being at the front of the class, and watching presentations. Auditory learners tend to sit in the middle of the class and learn best through lectures and discussions. The third style is kinesthetic, which many information technology professionals tend to be. These students learn through a lab environment or other hands-on approaches. Most people use a combination of learning styles, with one style being dominant. To aid in knowledge

Subject	Pedagogical approach	Andragogical approach
Desire	Motivated by external pressures to get good grades or pass on to next grade	Motivated by higher self-esteem, more recognition, desire for better quality of life
Student	Dependent on teacher for all learning	Self-directed and responsible for own learning
Subject matter	Defined by what the teacher wants to give	Learning is organized around situations in life or at work
Willingness to learn	Students are informed about what they must learn	A change triggers a readiness to learn or students perceive a gap between where they are and where they want to be

Table 14-10   Approaches to training

retention, trainers should incorporate all three learning styles and present the same information using different techniques. For example, a course could include a lecture, PowerPoint slides, and an opportunity to work directly with software and replicate what is being taught.

Another common approach is to use role-based training. **Role-based training** involves specialized training that is customized to the specific role that an employee holds in the organization. An office associate, for example, should be provided security training that is different from that provided to an upper-level manager, because the duties and tasks of these two employees are significantly different.

All training should include a feedback mechanism by which participants can provide input into the training's effectiveness so that any needed modifications can be made for future training. In addition, such feedback can provide data to validate compliance where training is required.

Chapter Summary

- A risk is a situation that involves exposure to some type of danger. Risks can be divided into several classifications, such as strategic, compliance, financial, operational, environmental, technical, and managerial. There are different strategies for controlling risk: modify the response to the risk; use the Simple Risk Model; reduce the impact of risk using types of risk control; and mitigate risk from a managerial perspective. Privilege management is the process of assigning and revoking privileges to objects; that is, it covers the procedures of managing object authorizations. One element of privilege management involving periodic review of a subject's privileges over an object is known as privilege auditing. Change management refers to a methodology for making changes and keeping track of those changes. Without proper documentation in procedures, a change may negate or diminish a previous change or even unknowingly create a security vulnerability. Change management seeks to approach changes systematically and provide the necessary documentation of them. Incident management is the framework and functions required to enable incident response and incident handling within an organization. The objective of incident management is to restore the normal operations as quickly as possible with the least possible impact on the business.

14

- There are two approaches to risk calculation: qualitative risk calculation, which uses an "educated guess" based on observation; and quantitative risk calculation, which is considered more scientific. Quantitative risk calculations can be divided into the likelihood of a risk and the impact of a risk being successful. The tools used for calculating risk likelihood include Mean Time Between Failure (MTBF), Mean Time To Recovery (MTTR), Mean Time To Failure (MTTF), Failure In Time (FIT), and the Annualized Rate of Occurrence (ARO). Risk impact calculation tools include Single Loss Expectancy (SLE) and Annual Loss Expectancy (ALE).

- A security policy is a written document that states how an organization plans to protect the company's information technology assets. An effective security policy must carefully balance two key elements, trust and control. A security policy attempts to provide a balance between no trust and too much trust. The appropriate level of control is determined by the security needs and the culture of the organization. Most organizations follow a three-phase cycle in developing and maintaining a security policy. The first phase is a risk management study; the second phase is to use the risk management study to develop the policy; and the final phase is to review the policy for compliance. A security policy development team should be formed to handle the task of developing a security policy.

- Because a security policy is comprehensive and often detailed, most organizations choose to break the security policy down into smaller subpolicies. The term "security policy" is a general term for all the subpolicies included within it. An Acceptable Use Policy (AUP) defines the actions users may perform while accessing systems and networking equipment. Because privacy is of growing concern, many organizations have a privacy policy that outlines how the organization uses information it collects. Data policies address the different aspects of how data should be handled within an organization. Policies of the organization that address security as it relates to human resources are known as a security-related human resource policy. An ethics policy is a written code of conduct intended to be a central guide and reference for employees in support of day-to-day decision making. A password management and complexity policy addresses how passwords are created and managed.

- In order to develop the knowledge and skills necessary to support information security, users need to receive ongoing awareness and training, which involves instruction regarding compliance, secure user practices, and an awareness of threats. There are also techniques that should be considered to make the training informative and useful.

Key Terms

Acceptable Use Policy (AUP)   A policy that defines the actions users may perform while accessing systems and networking equipment.

Annualized Loss Expectancy (ALE)   The expected monetary loss that can be anticipated for an asset due to a risk over a one-year period.

Annualized Rate of Occurrence (ARO)   The likelihood of a risk occurring within a year.

change management A methodology for making modifications to a system and keeping track of those changes.

data policy A security policy that addresses the different aspects of how data should be handled within an organization.

data retention policy A security policy that outlines how long to maintain information in the user's possession.

data storage policy A set of procedures designed to control and manage data within the organization by specifying data collection and storage.

data wiping and disposing policy A security policy that addresses how and when data will ultimately be erased.

false negative An event that does not appear to be a risk but actually turns out to be one.

false positive An event that in the beginning is considered to be a risk yet turns out to not be one.

incident management The "framework" and functions required to enable incident response and incident handling within an organization.

management risk control type A type of risk control that is administrative and covers the laws, regulations, policies, practices, and guidelines that govern the overall requirements and controls.

Mean Time To Failure (MTTF) The average amount of time expected until the first failure of a piece of equipment.

operational risk control type Risk control type that covers the operational procedures to limit risk.

peer-to-peer (P2P) network A network that does not have servers, so each device simultaneously functions as both a client and a server to all other devices connected to the network.

privacy policy A security policy that outlines how the organization uses personal information it collects.

qualitative risk calculation An approach to risk calculation that uses an "educated guess" based on observation.

quantitative risk calculation An approach to risk calculation that attempts to create actual numbers of the risk by using historical data.

14

role-based training Specialized training that is customized to the specific role that an employee holds in the organization.

security policy A written document that states how an organization plans to protect the company's information technology assets.

Single Loss Expectancy (SLE) The expected monetary loss every time a risk occurs.

social networking Grouping individuals and organizations into clusters or groups based on a like affiliation.

technical risk control type A risk control type that involves using technology to control risk.

Review Questions

1. An event that appears to be a risk but turns out not to be one is called a _____.
   a. false negative
   b. false positive
   c. negative-positive
   d. risk negative event (RNE)

2. Which of these is NOT a response to risk?
   a. transference
   b. resistance
   c. mitigation
   d. avoidance

3. All of these approaches are part of the Simple Risk Model EXCEPT _____.
   a. regulatory
   b. preventive
   c. detective
   d. corrective

4. A(n) _____ risk control type would use video surveillance systems and barricades to limit access to secure sites.
   a. operational
   b. managerial
   c. technical
   d. strategic

5. A statement regarding due diligence would be found in which security policy?
   a. disposal and destruction policy
   b. security-related human resource policy
   c. acceptable use policy
   d. privacy policy

6. Which risk category addresses events that impact the daily business of the organization?
   a. tactical
   b. strategic
   c. operational
   d. daily

7. _____ management covers the procedures of managing object authorizations.

   a. Asset

   b. Task

   c. Privilege

   d. Threat

8. Which statement does NOT describe a characteristic of a policy?

   a. Policies define appropriate user behavior.

   b. Policies communicate a unanimous agreement of judgment.

   c. Policies may be helpful if it is necessary to prosecute violators.

   d. Policies identify what tools and procedures are needed.

9. _____ is defined as the obligations that are imposed on owners and operators of assets to exercise reasonable care of the assets and take necessary precautions to protect them.

   a. Due process

   b. Due care

   c. Due obligations

   d. Due diligence

10. What is a collection of suggestions that should be implemented?

   a. policy

   b. guideline

   c. standard

   d. code

11. Which statement is NOT a guideline for developing a security policy?

   a. Notify users in advance that a new security policy is being developed and explain why the policy is needed.

   b. Require all users to approve the policy before it is implemented.

   c. Provide a sample of people affected by the policy with an opportunity to review the policy and comment on it.

   d. Prior to deployment, give all users at least two weeks to review the policy and comment on it.

14

12. Which statement is NOT something that a security policy must do?

   a. State reasons why the policy is necessary.

   b. Balance protection with productivity.

   c. Be capable of being implemented and enforced.

   d. Be concise and easy to understand.

13. Which person should NOT serve on a security policy development team?

    a. senior-level administrator

    b. representative from a hardware vendor

    c. member of the legal staff

    d. member of management who can enforce the policy

14. Which policy defines the actions users may perform while accessing systems and networking equipment?

    a. end-user policy

    b. acceptable use policy

    c. Internet use policy

    d. user permission policy

15. _____ may be defined as the study of what people understand to be good and right behavior and how people make those judgments.

    a. Ethics

    b. Morals

    c. Values

    d. Principles

16. Which recommendation would NOT be found in a password management and complexity policy?

    a. Do not use the name of a pet.

    b. Do not use alphabetic characters.

    c. Do not use a password that is a word found in a dictionary.

    d. Do not use personally identifiable information.

17. For adult learners, a(n) _____ approach (the art of helping an adult learn) is often preferred.

    a. pedagogical

    b. andragogical

    c. institutional

    d. proactive

18. Requiring employees to clear their workspace of all papers at the end of each business day is called _____.

    a. empty workspace policy

    b. clean desk policy

    c. disposal and removal policy

    d. sunshine policy

19. What is the security risk of a P2P network?

    a. A virus can be transmitted.

    b. It is issued to spread spam.

    c. It consumes bandwidth.

    d. It allows law enforcement agencies to monitor the user's actions.

20. Which statement is NOT a general security recommendation when using social networking sites?

    a. Consider carefully who is accepted as a friend.

    b. Show "limited friends" a reduced version of your profile.

    c. Only access a social networking site on personal time.

    d. Disable options and then reopen them only as necessary.

Hands-On Projects

HANDS-ON PROJECTS

NOTE   If you are concerned about installing any of the software in these projects on your regular computer, you can instead install the software in the Windows virtual machine created in the Chapter 1 Hands-On Projects 1-3 and 1-4. Software installed within the virtual machine will not impact the host computer.

Project 14-1: Viewing Your Annual Credit Report

Security experts recommend that consumers receive a copy of their credit report at least once per year and check its accuracy to protect their identity. In this project, you will access your free credit report online.

1. Use your web browser to go to **www.annualcreditreport.com**. Although you could send a request individually to one of the three credit agencies, this website acts as a central source for ordering free credit reports. Figure 14-5 shows the website.

2. Click **Request your free credit reports**.

3. Read through the three steps and click **Request your credit reports**.

4. Enter the requested information and click **Continue** and then **Next**.

5. Click **TransUnion**. Click **Next**.

6. After the brief processing completes, click **Continue**.

7. You may then be asked personal information about your transaction history in order to verify your identity. Answer the requested questions and click **Next**.

8. Follow the instructions to print your report.

14

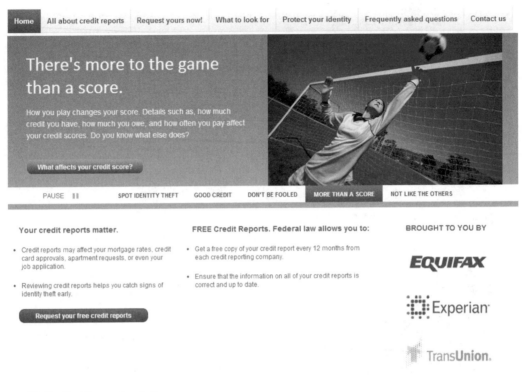

Figure 14-5 *Credit report website*
Source: AnnualCreditReport.com

9. Review it carefully, particularly the sections of "Potentially negative items" and "Requests for your credit history." If you see anything that might be incorrect, follow the instructions on that website to enter a dispute.

10. Follow the instructions to exit from the website.

11. Close all windows.

Project 14-2: Online Ethics Training

One type of training involves online video training. Many state governments have required online video ethics training for state employees and critical stakeholders. In this project, you will view and then comment upon one online ethics training module.

1. Use your web browser to go to **www.mass.gov/ethics**.

The location of content on the Internet may change without warning. If you are no longer able to access the program through the above URL, use a search engine and search for "Massachusetts State Ethics Commission".

2. Click **Education & Training Resources.**

3. Click **Online Training Program.**

4. Read through the requirements for this online ethics training program and make sure that your computer and software is properly configured. Also make sure that your computer's speakers are turned on or you are using a set of headphones.

5. Click **STATE-COUNTY EMPLOYEE ONLINE TRAINING PROGRAM.**

6. Click the **Next** button to begin the presentation. Take notes as you listen to this presentation. It is not necessary to print the certificate at the end of the presentation.

7. What is your assessment of this approach to training? Is it effective? Why or why not?

8. Was the material presented about ethics helpful? What did you learn? Would you recommend this to others? Why or why not?

9. Now compare this online training with that of another state. Use your web browser to go to **ethics.alabama.gov/info-training.aspx.**

10. Click **Click here to go to the online training video.**

11. Click **Continue to video.**

12. Click **Continue to video.**

13. Watch this video and compare it with the previous video. Which contains more information about ethics that you found useful? Why?

14. Close all windows.

Project 14-3: Training Through a Gaming Format

Another type of training involves the use of a gaming format that engages the learner at a higher level of participation. The learner who makes the correct decisions in the game can earn reward points and see the scenario succeed, while making a wrong decision can lose points or cause the gaming scenario to experience a financial loss or other problems. In this project, you will use a gaming format that requires you to respond to privacy and security challenges that can be faced in a small medical practice. Wrong decisions can lead to floods, server outages, fire damage, and other poor outcomes related to a lack of contingency planning.

1. Use your web browser to go to **www.healthit.gov/providers -professionals/privacy-security-training-games.**

The location of content on the Internet may change without warning. If you are no longer able to access the program through the above URL, use a search engine and search for "Healthit.gov privacy and security training games".

2. Under **Cybersecure: Contingency Planning,** click **Play the Game Now.**

3. If a pre-check system window displays, click **Continue.** Click **continue.**

4. Enter your name and click **submit**.

5. Read and listen to the explanation of the game. The opening screen appears as seen in Figure 14-6.

Figure 14-6 Cybersecure Contingency Planning
Source: HealthIT.gov

6. Read and listen to the information, and then click **close**.

7. Click the point icon **+10** at the center top of the screen.

8. Read and listen to the question. Click **make decision**.

9. Select what you think is the appropriate response.

10. If your selection was incorrect, a red "X" is displayed next to that response; if it was correct, a green check mark will display next to the response. Click **continue**.

11. Read the information about the event that is occurring and click the point icon **+10** at the left top of the screen.

12. Read and listen to the question. Click **make decision**.

13. Select what you think is the appropriate response.

14. If your selection was incorrect, a red "X" is displayed next to that response; if it was correct, a green check mark will display to the response. Click **continue**.

15. Continue to work through the game.

16. When completed, close this browser tab to return to the main menu.

17. Under **Cybersecure: Your Medical Practice**, click **Play the Game Now**.

18. Follow the same format to work through this game.

19. What do you think of this type of training format? How does it compare to watching videos as in the previous project? How could it be improved?

20. Close all windows.

Project 14-4: Crossword Puzzle Ethics Training

In this project you look at a more interactive alternative to online ethics training, an online crossword puzzle training tool.

1. Use your web browser to go to **www.ethics.org/resource/values-word -search-puzzle**.

The location of content on the Internet may change without warning. If you are no longer able to access the program through the above URL, use a search engine and search for "Ethics Resource Center".

2. The Values Word Search Puzzle contains 40 words that are related to values and ethical concepts in the scrambled letters. Print this page and identify as many of the words as you can.

3. When completed, click **Click here for the solution**.

4. Compare your results with the solution. How many were you able to find?

5. Would an activity like this be a helpful start in ethics training? Why or why not?

6. Close all windows.

Case Projects

Case Project 14-1: Security Policy Review

Locate the security policy for your school or organization. Based on what you now know about security, do you think it is sufficient? Does it adequately address security for the organization? Is it up-to-date and timely? What changes would you suggest? Write a one-page paper on your findings.

Case Project 14-2: AUP

Create your own Acceptable Use Policy for the computers and network access for your school or organization. Make sure to cover computer use, Internet surfing, email, Web, and password security. Compare your policy with those of other students in the class. Finally, locate the acceptable use policy for your school or organization. How does it compare with yours? Which policy is stricter? Why? What changes would you recommend in the school's or organization's policy? Write a one-page paper on your findings.

Case Project 14-3: Ethics

Defining ethics and determining the ethical standards in an organization can be challenging. Using the Internet, research the definition of *ethics* and how the term is used. Then, find two ethical policies of organizations. What are their good points? What are their bad points? Do they address ethics in the proper way? Finally, create your own ethics policy for your school or organization. Submit a one- to two-page paper with your findings and ethics policy.

Case Project 14-4: Social Network Advice

Select a social network site and research its security features. Are they sufficient? Should they be stronger? What recommendations would you make? Write a one-page summary of your findings.

Case Project 14-5: User Awareness and Training

What user security awareness and training is available at your school or place of business? How frequently is it performed? It is available online or in person? Is it required? Are the topics up-to-date? On a scale of 1–10, how would you rate the training? Write a one-page summary.

Case Project 14-6: Bay Pointe Security Consulting

Bay Pointe Security Consulting (BPSC) provides security consulting services to a wide range of businesses, individuals, schools, and organizations. BPSC has hired you as a technology student to help them with a new project and provide real-world experience to students who are interested in the security field.

Juliet's Desserts is a regional retailer that was recently purchased by new owners, who want to create new security policies. Because they have no experience in this area, they have hired BPSC to help them.

1. Create a PowerPoint presentation that explains what a security policy is, the security policy cycle, and the steps in developing a security policy. The presentation should be 10 slides in length.

2. Juliet's Desserts is ready to start developing security policies and wants to make the security-related human resource policy its first. Create a one-page draft of a policy for them.

Case Project 14-7: Community Site Activity

The Information Security Community Site is an online companion to this textbook. It contains a wide variety of tools, information, discussion boards, and other features to assist learners. Go to **community.cengage.com/infosec**. Sign in with the login name and password that you created in Chapter 1.

What is your reaction to *Today's Attacks and Defenses* regarding security researcher Brian Krebs. How does his nontechnical background help him? How does it hurt him? Would you as a manager hire someone with his background if he were to apply for a security position? Why or why not? And what do you think about the actions that attackers are taking against him? Would this discourage you from being a security researcher? Record your answers on the Community Site discussion board.

Reference

1. Krebs, Brian, "About the author," *Krebs on Security*, retrieved Apr. 1, 2014, http://krebsonsecurity.com/about/.

14

## chapter 15

Vulnerability Assessment

After completing this chapter, you should be able to do the following:

- Define vulnerability assessment and explain why it is important
- Explain the differences between vulnerability scanning and penetration testing
- Describe the security implications of integration with third parties
- List techniques for mitigating and deterring attacks

Today's Attacks and Defenses

A *wild-goose chase* is a figurative term for a lengthy and useless pursuit that ends in frustration. Used as far back as William Shakespeare in his play *Romeo and Juliet*, the phrase rarely comes to mind when thinking about defending against attacks directed at information technology (IT) resources. But one company is now specializing in leading attackers on a wild-goose chase. Mykonos Software offers intrusion *deception* tools. Instead of trying to build a defense against attacks, the Mykonos product is designed to lead attackers down false paths and erect roadblocks. The goal is to make an attack on a website so time-consuming, tedious, and costly that attackers will finally give up. And in a curious spin, Mykonos even makes fun of the attackers in the process.

Mykonos Web Intrusion Deception System Security is a software and hardware product that resides inline in a network and functions as a reverse proxy for web servers. There are four phases to the system: Detect, Track, Profile, and Response. In the Detect phase Mykonos creates what it calls "tar traps," or detection points in the proxy's web server code and website that include fake URLs, forms, and server files. When attackers perform the initial reconnaissance phase of an attack to determine if a web server is vulnerable, the Detect phase of the intrusion deception system can identify attackers as they view and manipulate these tar traps, indicating their malicious intent.

Next, the Track phase seeks to determine who the attacker is. Mykonos captures the attacker's IP address as a starting point. For attackers who are using a web browser, Mykonos injects a persistent token into the attacker's client browser that persists even if the attacker clears her cache and cookies. For attackers who are using automated software and scripts, Mykonos tracks them using a fingerprinting technique to uniquely identify the computer delivering the script. After tracking the attacker, Mykonos builds a smart profile of the attacker in the Profile phase. All attackers are assigned a unique name so they can easily be identified by the IT security team. As the attacker's work is monitored over time, a threat level, based on the intent and skills of the attacker, is created.

Finally, in the Response phase, the Mykonos software flashes a message on the attacker's screen warning that the attacker is being monitored. It also can disrupt attackers' Internet connections to slow down their reconnaissance, block attackers from reaching the target website, and even force a logout on attackers' computers. In addition, Mykonos can plant more fake files and vary the location of the files to confuse intruders. For those attackers using automated reconnaissance systems, Mykonos can display a CAPTCHA to stop the automated reconnaissance and also

(continued)

flood the attacker's automated scanning programs with information about vulnerabilities on the websites that do not exist.

The Response phase also pokes fun at the attackers. Mykonos can display a map on attackers' screens showing the attacker's location, along with a list and map of nearby defense attorneys the attacker may want to hire. Yet another feature delivers a patronizing popup screen that consoles the attackers for getting caught and offers condescending advice on how to attack without being detected.

"Exactly how vulnerable are we?" is a question that too few organizations ask themselves in regard to their IT security. Too often, purchasing expensive security devices, installing the latest antimalware software, conducting employee training sessions, and hiring a staff of security technicians creates a false sense of security and invulnerability. Although each of these defenses is important, they are of limited value unless they are properly used. Security hardware and software must be correctly installed, configured, and maintained. Employee training should be ongoing with a feedback mechanism that determines its effectiveness. Security technicians need continual training on the latest attacks and defenses. Simply having the right security tools does not guarantee a secure system.

It is a fact that *all* computer systems, and the information contained on those systems, are vulnerable to attack; virtually all security experts say that it's not a matter of *if* an attack will penetrate defenses, but only a matter of *when*. Because successful attacks are inevitable, organizations must protect themselves by realistically evaluating their vulnerabilities, assessing how an attacker could penetrate their defenses, and then taking proactive steps to defend against those attacks.

In this chapter, you will study vulnerability assessment. You will first define vulnerability assessment and examine the tools and techniques associated with it. Next, you will explore the differences between vulnerability scanning and penetration testing. The risks associated with third-party integration into a system will also be examined. Finally, you will look at controls to mitigate and deter attacks.

Assessing Vulnerabilities

15

1.2 Given a scenario, use secure network administration principles.

1.4 Given a scenario, implement common protocols and services.

3.2 Summarize various types of attacks.

3.6 Analyze a scenario and select the appropriate type of mitigation and deterrent techniques.

3.7 Given a scenario, use appropriate tools and techniques to discover security threats and vulnerabilities.

The first step in any security protection plan begins with an assessment of vulnerabilities. A variety of techniques and tools can be used in evaluating the levels of vulnerability.

What Is Vulnerability Assessment?

Vulnerability assessment is a systematic and methodical evaluation of the exposure of assets to attackers, forces of nature, and any other entity that could cause potential harm. Vulnerability assessment attempts to identify what needs to be protected (asset identification), what the pressures are against those assets (threat evaluation), how susceptible the current protection is (vulnerability appraisal), and what damages could result from the threats (risk assessment). Once this is completed, an analysis of what to do about it (risk mitigation) can take place.

Asset Identification
The first step in a vulnerability assessment is to determine the assets that need to be protected. An asset is defined as any item that has a positive economic value, and *asset identification* is the process of inventorying these items. An organization has many different types of assets, including people (employees, customers, business partners, contractors, and vendors) and physical assets (buildings, automobiles, and plant equipment). In addition, the elements of IT are also key assets. This includes data (all information used and transmitted by the organization, such as employee databases and inventory records), hardware (computers, servers, networking equipment, and telecommunications connections), and software (application programs, operating systems, and security software).

Asset identification can be a lengthy and complicated process. However, it is one of the most critical steps in vulnerability assessment. If an organization does not know *what* needs to be protected, then how can the organization protect it?

After an inventory of the assets has been taken, it is important to determine each item's relative value. Some assets are of critical value while other assets are of lesser importance. Factors that should be considered in determining the relative value include how critical the asset is to the goals of the organization, how much revenue it generates, how difficult it would be to replace, and the impact to the organization if the asset were unavailable. Some organizations assign a numeric value (such as 5 being extremely valuable and 1 being the least valuable) to each asset. For example, a web application server that receives and processes online orders could be considered a critical asset because without it no orders would be received. For this reason it might be assigned a value of 5. A desktop computer used by an employee might have a lesser value because its loss would not negatively impact the daily workflow of the organization nor prove to be a serious security risk. It might be assigned only a value of 2.

Threat Evaluation
After assets have been inventoried, the next step is to determine the potential threats against the assets that come from threat agents (recall that a *threat agent* is any person or thing with the power to carry out a threat against an asset). Threat agents are not limited to attackers, but also include natural disasters, such as fire or severe weather. Common threat agents are listed in Table 15-1.

Determining threats that could pose a risk to assets can be a complicated process. One way to approach this task is a process known as threat modeling. The goal of *threat modeling* is to better understand who the attackers are, why they attack, and what types of attacks might occur. Threat modeling often constructs scenarios of the types of threats that assets can face. A valuable tool used in threat modeling is the construction of an attack tree. An *attack tree* provides a visual image of the attacks that could occur against an asset. Drawn as an inverted tree structure, an attack tree displays the goal of the attack, the types of attacks that could occur, and the techniques used in the attacks.

Category of threat	Example
Natural disasters	Fire, flood, or earthquake destroys data
Compromise of intellectual property	Software is pirated or copyright infringed
Espionage	Spy steals production schedule
Extortion	Mail clerk is blackmailed into intercepting letters
Hardware failure or errors	Firewall blocks all network traffic
Human error	Employee drops laptop computer in parking lot
Sabotage or vandalism	Attacker implants worm that erases files
Software attacks	Virus, worm, or denial of service compromises hardware or software
Software failure or errors	Bug prevents program from properly loading
Technical obsolescence	Program does not function under new version of operating system
Theft	Desktop system is stolen from unlocked room
Utility interruption	Electrical power is cut off

Table 15-1 Common threat agents

The concept of attack trees was developed by Counterpane Internet Security.[1]

A partial attack tree for stealing a car stereo system is shown in Figure 15-1. At the top of the tree (Level 1) is the goal of the attack, which is to steal a car stereo. The next level, Level 2, lists the ways an attack could occur: someone could break the glass out of a car window and steal the stereo, someone could steal the keys to the car to get to the stereo, or someone could "carjack" the car and drive away. To steal the keys (Level 3), a purse snatcher might grab the purse containing the keys, or someone, such as a parking lot attendant, might make a copy of them. The attendant might copy the keys because of pressure in the form of threats, blackmail, or bribes (Level 4). The attack tree presents a picture of the threats against an asset.

Figure 15-2 shows a partial attack tree for an attacker who is attempting to log into a restricted account. The attacker might attempt to learn the password (Level 2) by looking for one that is written down and stored under a mouse pad in an office (Level 3). He could also try to get the password from the user (Level 3) by installing a keylogger on the computer or by shoulder surfing (Level 4). An alternative approach might be to steal the password digest file to use offline cracking (Level 2). Attack trees help list the types of attacks that can occur and trace how and from where the attacks may originate.

15

These abbreviated examples of attack trees are not intended to show every possible threat, as an actual attack tree would.

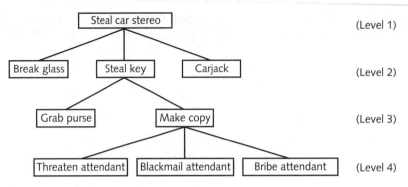

Figure 15-1 Attack tree for stealing a car stereo

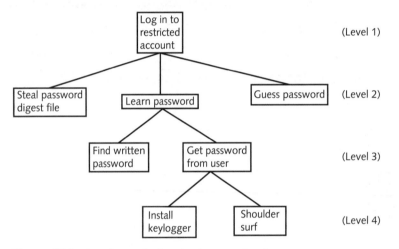

Figure 15-2 Attack tree for logging into restricted account

Vulnerability Appraisal After the assets have been inventoried and the threats have been determined, the next natural question is, "What are our current weaknesses that might expose the assets to these threats?" Known as *vulnerability appraisal*, this process in effect takes a snapshot of the current security of the organization.

Hardware and software assessment tools may be used to assist with determining the vulnerabilities of hardware and software assets. These tools are discussed later in this chapter.

Revealing the vulnerabilities of an asset is not always as easy as it might seem. Every asset must be viewed in light of each threat; it is not sufficient to limit the assessment to only a few of the obvious threats against an asset. Each threat can reveal multiple vulnerabilities, and it is important that each vulnerability be cataloged.

Determining vulnerabilities often depends on the background and experience of the assessor. It is recommended that teams composed of diverse members be responsible for listing vulnerabilities instead of only one person.

Risk Assessment The next step is to perform a risk assessment. A *risk assessment* involves determining the damage that would result from an attack and the likelihood that the vulnerability is a risk to the organization.

Determining the damage from an attack first requires a realistic look at several different types of attacks that might occur. Based upon the vulnerabilities recognized in the vulnerability appraisal, a risk assessment of the impact can then be undertaken. Not all vulnerabilities pose the same risk. One way to determine the severity of a risk is to gauge the impact the vulnerability would have on the organization if it were exploited. A sample scale for ranking vulnerabilities is shown in Table 15-2.

Impact	Description	Example
No impact	This vulnerability would not affect the organization.	The theft of a mouse attached to a desktop computer would not affect the operations of the organization.
Small impact	Small impact vulnerabilities would produce limited periods of inconvenience and possibly result in changes to a procedure.	A specific brand and type of hard disk drive that fails might require that spare drives be made available and that devices with those drives be periodically tested.
Significant	A vulnerability that results in a loss of employee productivity due to downtime or causes a capital outlay to alleviate it could be considered significant.	Malware that is injected into the network could be classified as a significant vulnerability.
Major	Major vulnerabilities are those that have a considerable negative impact on revenue.	The theft of the latest product research and development data through a backdoor could be considered a major vulnerability.
Catastrophic	Vulnerabilities that are ranked as catastrophic are events that would cause the organization to cease functioning or be seriously crippled in its capacity to perform.	A tornado that destroys an office building and all of the company's data could be a catastrophic vulnerability.

Table 15-2 Vulnerability impact scale

NOTE Risk assessment can be done using qualitative or quantitative risk calculation tools to help determine the risk likelihood and risk impact. These tools are covered in Chapter 14.

15

Risk Mitigation Once the risks are determined and ranked, the final step is to determine what to do about the risks, or *risk mitigation*. Realistically, risk can never be entirely eliminated; it would cost too much or take too long. Some risks must simply be accepted by default (war is an example of such a risk that cannot be protected against, and thus most assets cannot be insured against war), that is, some degree of risk must always be assumed. An organization should not ask, "How can we eliminate all risk?" but rather, "How much acceptable risk can we tolerate?" Once the "toleration" level is known, steps can be taken to mitigate the risk.

Chapter 14 covers different ways to mitigate and control risk.

Table 15-3 summarizes the steps in performing vulnerability assessment.

Vulnerability assessment action	Steps
1. Asset identification	a. Inventory the assets b. Determine the assets' relative value
2. Threat identification	a. Classify threats by category b. Design attack tree
3. Vulnerability appraisal	a. Determine current weaknesses in protecting assets b. Use vulnerability assessment tools
4. Risk assessment	a. Estimate impact of vulnerability on organization b. Calculate risk likelihood and impact of the risk
5. Risk mitigation	a. Decide what to do with the risk

Table 15-3   Vulnerability assessment actions and steps

Assessment Techniques

Several different techniques can be used in a vulnerability assessment. These include baseline reporting and techniques associated with software development.

Baseline Reporting A *baseline* is an imaginary line by which an element is measured or compared. It can be seen as the standard. In information security a baseline is a checklist against which systems can be evaluated and audited for their security posture. A baseline outlines the major security considerations for a system and becomes the starting point for solid security.

Sometimes *baseline* is used to refer to an initial value. For example, in medicine a baseline is the initial known data determined at the beginning of a study that is used for later comparison with accumulated data. In information technology the initial value is not the current security state of the system; rather, it is the standard against which that current state is compared.

Baseline reporting is a comparison of the present state of a system to its baseline. Deviations include not only technical issues but also management and operational issues. From a security perspective this can provide valuable information because it indicates something "unusual" is occurring, which could be the result of an attack or a previously unknown vulnerability. Thus any differences from the baseline must be addressed as well as clearly noted, evaluated, and documented.

All deviations from the baseline may not necessarily be harmful.

Software Program Development Because flaws in software can be *threat vectors* for exploiting a vulnerability, it is important that these software vulnerabilities be minimized *while the software is being developed* instead of after it is released. In recent years major software developers have focused their attention on improving their software code in order to provide increased security. These improvements are aimed at reducing the number of design and coding errors in software. From a practical standpoint, however, this software improvement to minimize errors is difficult because of several factors:

- *Size and complexity.* As more features and functions are added to programs, they become very large (up to hundreds of millions of lines of code) and extremely complex.

- *Lack of formal specifications.* Specifications for a program may not always be in written form and formally communicated, so that the work of one programmer may unintentionally open a security vulnerability that was closed by another programmer.

- *Ever-changing attacks.* As attackers continue to create new exploits, it is not possible to foresee all the ways that code written today could be vulnerable tomorrow.

Different assessment techniques can be used in software development to minimize vulnerabilities, shown in Figure 15-3 and described below:

- *Requirements.* In this phase the list of features needed along with the guidelines for maintaining quality are developed. In addition, a review of the **architectural design** is also conducted. This is the process of defining a collection of hardware and software components along with their interfaces in order to create the framework for software development. Understanding the architecture of the hardware and software, and how these interact with each other, can help minimize design flaws and openings for attacks.

- *Design.* As the functional and design specifications are being developed based on the requirements, a **design review** is also conducted. Before the first line of code is written, an analysis of the design of the software program should be conducted by key personnel from different levels of the project. Many software developers are now adding a security consultant who is assigned to the project from its inception in order to assist developers in creating a secure application.

- *Implementation.* While the code is being written it is being analyzed by a **code review**. Presenting the code to multiple reviewers in order to reach agreement about its security can have a significant impact on reducing security vulnerabilities. In addition, the attack surface will also be examined at this time. The **attack surface** for software is the code that can be executed by unauthorized users. Limiting the attack surface includes validating user input, reducing the amount of code that is running to a minimum, and eliminating or restricting services that the software can invoke.

- *Verification.* During this phase of testing, errors or "bugs" can be identified and corrected.

- *Release.* At this phase, the software is shipped.

- *Support.* After the software is released, as vulnerabilities are uncovered, the necessary security updates are created and distributed to users.

15

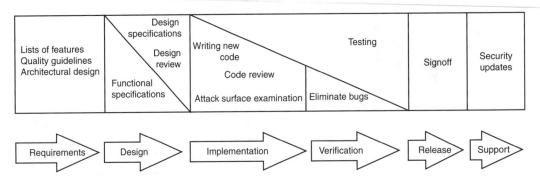

Figure 15-3 Software development process

The developer of the Linux operating system, Linus Torvalds, is said to have advocated that given a large enough pool of tests and developers, almost every problem will be recognized and the fix will become obvious to someone. This is sometimes called *Linus's Law* and is paraphrased as, "Given enough eyeballs, all bugs are shallow."[2]

Assessment Tools

Many tools are available to perform vulnerability assessments. These include port scanners, banner grabbing tools, protocol analyzers, vulnerability scanners, and honeypots and honeynets.

Although the primary purpose of assessment tools is to help security personnel identify security weaknesses, these tools can likewise be used by attackers to uncover vulnerabilities to be exploited in an attack.

Port Scanners Most communication in TCP/IP networks involves the exchange of information between a program running on one system (known as a *process*) and the same, or a corresponding process, running on a remote system. TCP/IP uses a numeric value as an identifier to the applications and services on these systems. This value is known as the *port number*. Each packet/datagram contains the source port and destination port, which identifies both the originating application/service on the local system and the corresponding application/service on the remote system.

The term *port* is also used to refer to a physical outlet on the computer, such as a Universal Serial Bus (USB) port.

Because port numbers are 16 bits in length, they can have a decimal value from 0 to 65535. TCP/IP divides port numbers into three categories:

- *Well-known port numbers (0–1023).* Reserved for the most universal applications
- *Registered port numbers (1024–49151).* Other applications that are not as widely used
- *Dynamic and private port numbers (49152–65535).* Available for use by any application

A list of common protocols, the communication protocol that supports each (TCP and/or UDP), and the service port numbers is provided in Table 15-4.

Protocol name	Communication protocol	Port number
File Transfer Protocol (FTP)—Data	TCP, UDP	20
File Transfer Protocol (FTP)—Commands	TCP	21
Secure Shell (SSH), Secure Shell File Transfer Protocol (SFTP), Secure Copy (SCP)	TCP, UDP	22
Simple Mail Transfer Protocol (SMTP)	TCP	25
Domain Name System (DNS)	TCP, UDP	53
Hypertext Transfer Protocol (HTTP)	TCP	80
Post Office Protocol v3 (POP3)	TCP	110
NetBIOS	TCP, UDP	139
Internet Message Access Protocol (IMAP)	TCP	143
Hypertext Transfer Protocol Secure (HTTPS)	TCP	443
Microsoft Terminal Server	TCP, UDP	3389

Table 15-4   **Common protocols, communication protocols, and ports**

A list of all well-known and registered TCP/IP port numbers can be found at *www.iana.org/assignments/port-numbers.*

Because port numbers are associated with applications and services, if an attacker knows that a specific port is accessible, this could indicate what services are being used. For example, if port 20 is available, an attacker could assume that FTP is being used. With that knowledge he can target his attacks to that service. It is important to implement **port security** by disabling unused application/service ports to reduce the number of threat vectors.

When performing a vulnerability assessment, **port scanner** software can be used to search a system for port vulnerabilities. Port scanners, such as the RADMIN port scanner shown in Figure 15-4, are typically used to determine the state of a port to know what applications/services are running. There are three port states:

- *Open.* An *open port* means that the application or service assigned to that port is listening for any instructions. The host system will send back a reply to the scanner that the service is available and listening; if the operating system receives packets destined for this port, it will give them over to that service process.

- *Closed.* A *closed port* indicates that no process is listening at this port. The host system will send back a reply that this service is unavailable and any connection attempts will be denied.

- *Blocked.* A *blocked port* means that the host system does not reply to any inquiries to this port number.

15

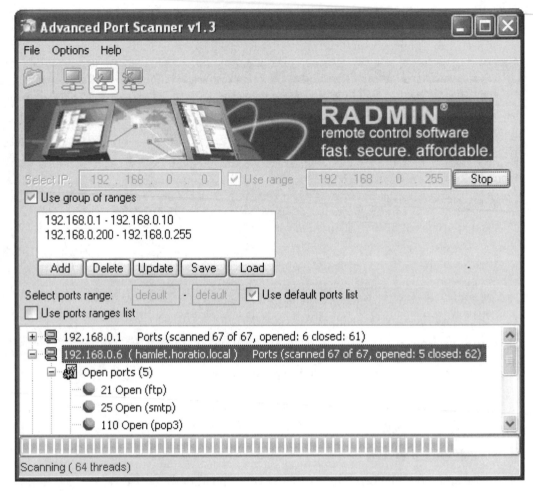

Figure 15-4   Port scanner

There are several types of port scanning processes as shown in Table 15-5.

Banner Grabbing Tools A *banner* is a message that a service transmits when another program connects to it. For example, the banner for a Hypertext Transfer Protocol (HTTP) service will typically show the type of server software, its version number, when it was last modified, and other similar information. When a program is used to intentionally gather this information, the process is called **banner grabbing**.

Banner grabbing can be used as an assessment tool to perform an inventory on the services and systems operating on a server. This can be done by using a tool such as Telnet to create a connection with the host and then querying each port.

Attackers can also make use of banner grabbing when performing reconnaissance on a system.

Name	Scanning process	Comments
TCP connect scanning	This scan attempts to connect to every available port. If a port is open, the operating system completes the TCP three-way "handshake" and the port scanner then closes the connection; otherwise an error code is returned.	There are no special privileges needed to run this scan. However, it is slow and the scanner can be identified.
TCP SYN scanning	Instead of using the operating system's network functions, the port scanner generates IP packets itself and monitors for responses. The port scanner generates a SYN packet, and if the target port is open, that port will respond with a SYN+ACK packet. The scanner host then closes the connection before the "handshake" is completed.	SYN scanning is the most popular form of TCP scanning because most sites do not log these attempts. This scan type is also known as "half-open scanning," because it never actually opens a full TCP connection.
TCP FIN scanning	The port scanner sends a finish (FIN) message without first sending a SYN packet. A closed port will reply but an open port will ignore the packet.	FIN messages as part of the normal negotiation process can pass through firewalls and avoid detection.
Xmas Tree port scan	An Xmas Tree packet is a packet with every option set to *on* for whatever protocol is in use. When used for scanning, the TCP header of an Xmas Tree packet has the flags finish (FIN), urgent (URG), and push (PSH) all set to *on*. By observing how a host responds to this "odd" packet, assumptions can be made about its operating system.	The term comes from the image of each option bit in a header packet being represented by a different-colored "light bulb." When all are turned on, it can be said that the packet "was lit up like a Christmas tree."

Table 15-5   **Port scanning**

Protocol Analyzers   A *protocol analyzer* is hardware or software that captures packets to decode and analyze their contents. Network traffic can be viewed by a stand-alone protocol analyzer device or a computer that runs protocol analyzer software such as the Wireshark software shown in Figure 15-5. Protocol analyzers can fully decode application-layer network protocols such as HTTP or FTP.

Protocol analyzers are covered in Chapter 7.

15

Protocol analyzers are widely used by network administrators for network monitoring. They can assist in network troubleshooting by detecting and diagnosing network problems such as addressing errors and protocol configuration mistakes. They also are used for network traffic characterization. Protocol analyzers can be used to paint a picture of the types and

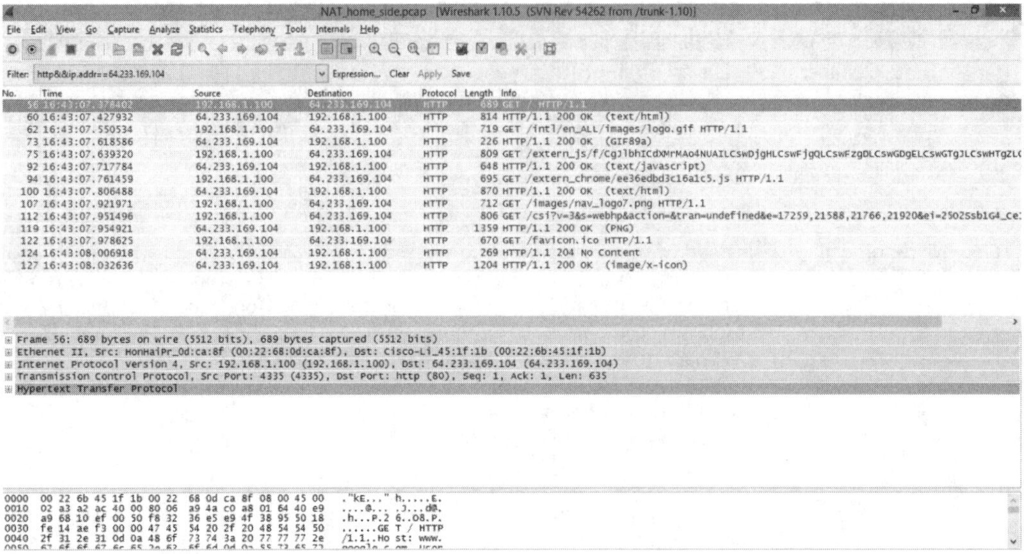

Figure 15-5 Protocol analyzer
Source: Wireshark Software

makeup of network traffic. This representation can be used to fine-tune the network and manage bandwidth in order to provide the highest level of service to users.

In addition, protocol analyzers can be helpful in a security analysis of the network. The types of security-related information available from a protocol analyzer are summarized in Table 15-6.

Security information	Explanation
Unanticipated network traffic	Most network managers know the types of applications that they expect to see utilizing the network. Protocol analyzers can help reveal unexpected traffic and even pinpoint the computers that are involved.
Unnecessary network traffic	Network devices may by default run network protocols that are not required and may pose a security risk. As a precaution, a protocol analyzer can be set to filter traffic so it can help identify unnecessary network traffic and the source of it.
Unauthorized applications/services	Servers can be monitored to determine if they have open port numbers to support unauthorized applications/services. Many protocol analyzers allow filtering on specified port numbers, so it is possible to constantly monitor for specific port number requests.
Virus detection and control	A filter in the protocol analyzer can be set to watch for a known text pattern contained in a virus. The source and destination of the packets can then be used to identify the location of the virus.
Firewall monitoring	A misconfigured firewall can be detected by a protocol analyzer watching for specific inbound and outbound traffic.

Table 15-6 Protocol analyzer security information

Vulnerability Scanners Vulnerability scanner is a generic term for a range of products that look for vulnerabilities in networks or systems. Figure 15-6 shows one such software product, the Acunetix Vulnerability Scanner. Vulnerability scanners for organizations are intended to identify vulnerabilities and alert network administrators to these problems. Most vulnerability scanners maintain a database that categorizes and describes the vulnerabilities that it can detect.

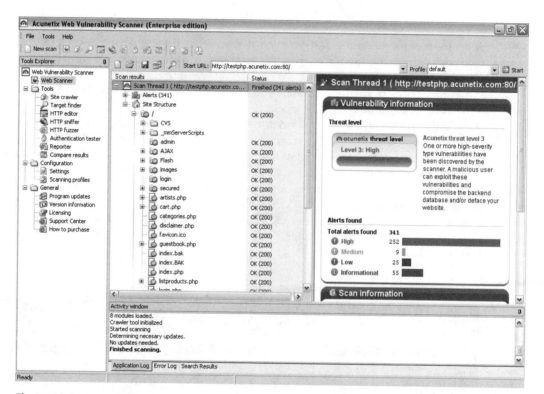

Figure 15-6 Vulnerability scanner
Source: Acunetix Software

A vulnerability scanner can:

- Alert when new systems are added to the network
- Detect when an application is compromised or subverted
- Detect when an internal system begins to port scan other systems
- Detect which ports are served and which ports are browsed for each individual system
- Identify which applications and servers host or transmit sensitive data
- Maintain a log of all interactive network sessions
- Passively determine the type of operating system of each active system
- Track all client and server application vulnerabilities
- Track which systems communicate with other internal systems

15

Some vulnerability scanners also provide built-in remediation steps or links to additional sources for more information on addressing specific vulnerabilities. Other types of vulnerability scanners combine the features of a port scanner and network mapper. These vulnerability scanners begin by searching for IP addresses, open ports, and system applications. Then they examine the operating system patches that have and have not been applied to the system.

A problem with vulnerability assessment tools is that no standard has been established for collecting, analyzing, and reporting vulnerabilities. This means that an organization that installs several assessment tools from different vendors is often forced to read through stacks of information from different sources and then interpret this information to determine if a vulnerability exists, which is a labor-intensive and time-consuming task. To remedy this problem, an international information security standard known as *Open Vulnerability and Assessment Language (OVAL)* has been developed. OVAL is designed to promote open and publicly available security content. It also standardizes the transfer of information across different security tools and services. OVAL is a "common language" for the exchange of information regarding security vulnerabilities. These vulnerabilities are identified using industry-standard tools. OVAL vulnerability definitions are recorded in Extensible Markup Language (XML) and queries are accessed using the database language Structured Query Language (SQL). An example of OVAL output is illustrated in Figure 15-7.

OVAL Results Generator Information					OVAL Definition Generator Information				
Schema Version	Product Name	Product Version	Date	Time	Schema Version	Product Name	Product Version	Date	Time
5.10.1	jOVAL	5.10.1.1_Dev	2012-09-01	18:09:08	5.10	PSIRT OVAL Definition Generator	0.1	2012-09-01	20:26:10

System Information				
Host Name	R1			
Operating System	Cisco IOS			
Operating System Version	15.1(3)T			
Architecture	unknown			
Interfaces	Interface Name	FastEthernet0/0		
	IP Address	172.18.122.246/26		
	MAC Address	001d.a105.9cc8		
	Interface Name	FastEthernet0/1		
	IP Address	14.4.1.126/24		
	MAC Address	001d.a105.9cc9		

OVAL System Characteristics Generator Information				
Schema Version	Product Name	Product Version	Date	Time
5.10.1	jOVAL	5.10.1.1_Dev	2012-09-01	18:09:08

OVAL Definition Results

True		False		Error		Unknown		Not Applicable		Not Evaluated	

ID	Result	Class	Reference ID	Title
oval:cisco.oval:def:13	true	vulnerability	CVE-2012-0381:cisco-sa-20120328-ike	cisco-sa-20120328-ike-CVE-2012-0381

Figure 15-7 OVAL output
Source: jOVAL Open Source Software

Honeypots and Honeynets A honeypot is a computer typically located in an area with limited security and loaded with software and data files that appear to be authentic,

but are actually imitations of real data files. The honeypot is intentionally configured with security vulnerabilities so that it is open to attacks. It is intended to trick attackers into revealing their attack techniques. It can then be determined if actual production systems could thwart such an attack.

A honeypot also can direct an attacker's attention away from legitimate servers by encouraging attackers to spend their time and energy on the decoy server, distracting their attention from the data on the real server.

Similar to a honeypot, a **honeynet** is a network set up with intentional vulnerabilities. Its purpose is also to invite attacks so that the attacker's methods can be studied and that information can be used to increase network security. A honeynet typically contains one or more honeypots.

Vulnerability Scanning vs. Penetration Testing

3.8 Explain the proper use of penetration testing versus vulnerability scanning.

Two important vulnerability assessment procedures are vulnerability scanning and penetration testing. These two activities are similar, and therefore are often confused. Yet, both play an important role in uncovering vulnerabilities.

Vulnerability Scanning

As its name implies, a **vulnerability scan** is an automated software search (*scan*) through a system for any known security weaknesses (*vulnerabilities*) that creates a report of those potential exposures. The results of the scans should be compared against baseline scans so that any changes (such as new open ports or added services) can be investigated.

Vulnerability scanning should be conducted on existing systems and particularly as new technology equipment is deployed; the new equipment should be scanned immediately and then added to the regular schedule of scans for all equipment.

15

A vulnerability scan examines the current security in a passive method of testing security controls. It does not attempt to exploit any weaknesses that it finds; rather, it is intended to only report back what it uncovers. The types of weaknesses that it is searching for include identifying any known vulnerabilities, finding common misconfigurations, and uncovering a lack of security controls. Vulnerability scans are usually performed from inside the security perimeter and are not intended to disrupt the normal operations of the network or devices. These scans are conducted using an automated software package that examines the system for known weaknesses by passively testing the security controls.

There are two methods for performing a vulnerability scan. An **intrusive vulnerability scan** attempts to actually penetrate the system in order to perform a simulated attack, while a **non-intrusive vulnerability scan** uses only available information to hypothesize the status of the vulnerability. These two methods are compared in Table 15-7.

Type of scan	Description	Advantages	Disadvantages
Intrusive vulnerability scanning	Vulnerability assessment tools use intrusive scripts to penetrate and attack.	By attacking a system in the same manner as an attacker would, more accurate results are achieved.	The system may be unavailable for normal use while the scan is being conducted. Also, it may disable security services for the duration of the attack.
Non-intrusive vulnerability scanning	Through social engineering and general reconnaissance efforts, information is gathered regarding the known vulnerabilities and weaknesses of the system.	Organizations can avoid any disruption of service or setting off alerts from IPS, IDS, and firewalls. These scans also mimic the same reconnaissance efforts used by attackers.	Time is needed for all the information to be analyzed so that the security status of the system based on the data can be determined.

Table 15-7   Intrusive and non-intrusive vulnerability scans

Some intrusive vulnerability scanners permit the username and password (*credentials*) of an active account to be stored and used by the scanner, which allows the scanner to test for additional internal vulnerabilities if an attacker were able to successfully penetrate the system. This is called a **credentialed vulnerability scan**, while scanners that do not use credentials conduct what are called **non-credentialed vulnerability scans**.

Vulnerability scans may generate a high number of false positives. A vulnerability scan report should be examined by trained security personnel to identify and correct any problems.

Penetration Testing

Unlike a vulnerability scan, **penetration testing** (*pentesting*) is designed to actually exploit any weaknesses in systems that are vulnerable. Instead of using automated software, penetration testing relies upon the skill, knowledge, and cunning of the tester. The tester herself is usually an independent contractor not associated with the organization. Such testers, known as "white hat hackers" or "ethical attackers," have the organization's permission to exploit vulnerabilities in a system and then privately provide information back to that organization. Testers are typically outside (instead of inside) the security perimeter and may even disrupt the operation of the network or devices (instead of passively probing for a known vulnerability).

White hat hackers are covered in Chapter 1.

The goals of a penetration test are to actively test all security controls and, when possible, bypass those controls, verify that a threat exists, and exploit any vulnerabilities. Whereas vulnerability scan software may uncover a vulnerability, it provides no indication regarding the risk to that specific organization. If a penetration tester uncovers a vulnerability, however, she will continue to exploit it to determine how dangerous it can be to the organization.

The end product of a penetration test is the penetration test report. The report focuses on what data was compromised, how and why it was compromised, and includes details of the actual attack method and the value of the data exploited. If requested, potential solutions can be provided, but often it is the role of the organization to determine how best to solve the problems.

Three different techniques can be used by a penetration tester. Each technique varies in the amount of knowledge the tester has regarding the details of the systems that are being evaluated:

- *Black box.* In a **black box** test, the tester has no prior knowledge of the network infrastructure that is being tested. The tester must determine the location and types of systems and devices before starting the actual tests. This technique most closely mimics an attack from outside the organization.

When using a black box test, many testers use social engineering tricks to learn about the network infrastructure from employees.

- *White box.* The opposite of a black box test is a **white box** test, in which the tester has an in-depth knowledge of the network and systems being tested, including network diagrams, IP addresses, and even the source code of custom applications.

- *Gray box.* Between a black box test and a white box test is a **gray box** test, in which some limited information has been provided to the tester.

15

The Computer Fraud and Abuse Act (18 U.S.C. 1030) states that it is a federal crime if a party "intentionally accesses a computer without authorization or exceeds authorized access." This means that penetration testers should always receive prior approval by the organization before conducting a test.[3]

Vulnerability scanning and penetration testing are important tools in a vulnerability assessment. Table 15-8 compares their features.

Feature	Vulnerability scan	Penetration test
Frequency	When new equipment is installed and at least once per month thereafter	Once per year
Goals	Reveal known vulnerabilities that have not yet been addressed	Discover unknown exposures to the normal business processes
Tester	In-house technician	Independent external consultant
Location	Performed from inside	Performed from outside
Disruption	Passive evaluation with no disruption	Active attack with potential disruption
Tools	Automated software	Knowledge and skills of tester
Cost	Low (approximately $1500 plus staff time)	High (approximately $12,500)
Report	Comprehensive comparison of current vulnerabilities compared to baseline	Short analysis of how the attack was successful and the damage to data
Value	Detects weaknesses in hardware or software	Preventive; reduces the organization's exposure

Table 15-8   **Vulnerability scan and penetration test features**

It is not uncommon for some self-appointed "security experts" to claim they have performed in-depth penetration testing while in reality they have conducted only less-intensive vulnerability scanning.

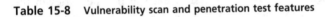

Third-Party Integration

2.2 Summarize the security implications of integrating systems and data with third parties.

In late 2013 attackers penetrated the network of the Target corporation and stole the credit and debit card numbers, expiration dates, and three-digit CVV (*Card Verification Value*) numbers of customers who made purchases during a three-week period. More than 110 million customers were affected. The attack, however, was not the result of a successful penetration by the attackers into the Target network. Instead, the attackers entered through a third-party entity. This particular entity was a refrigeration, heating, and air conditioning subcontractor that had worked at a number of Target stores. Evidently Target provided this third-party subcontractor access to the Target network so that the subcontractor could monitor energy consumption and temperatures in stores that used their equipment. Attackers were able to compromise the subcontractor's computers and steal their login credentials, which then enabled them to access the Target network and craft their attack.

Evidence seems to indicate that the third-party subcontractor was using free antivirus software on its computers that did not continually monitor for malware, and this allowed the attackers to successfully compromise the subcontractor's systems.

As an increasing number of organizations today turn to third-party vendors to create partnerships, the risk of **third-party integration**, or combining systems and data with outside entities, continues to grow. The risks of this integration include:

- *On-boarding and off-boarding.* **On-boarding business partners** refers to the start-up relationship between partners, while **off-boarding business partners** is the termination of such an agreement. Significant consideration must be given to how the entities will combine their services without compromising their existing security defenses. Also, when the relationship ends, particularly if it has been in effect for a significant length of time, work must be done to ensure that as the parties and their IT systems separate, no gaping holes are left open for attackers to exploit.

- *Application and social media network sharing.* How will different applications be shared between the partners? Who will be responsible for support and vulnerability assessments? And as social media becomes more critical for organizations in their interaction with customers, which partner will be responsible for sharing social media information?

- *Privacy and risk awareness.* What happens if the privacy policy of one of the partners is less restrictive than that of the other partner? And how will risk assessment be performed on the combined systems?

- *Data considerations.* All parties must have a clear understanding of who owns data that is generated through the partnership and how that data will be backed up. Restrictions on unauthorized data sharing also must be reached.

One of the means by which the parties can reach an understanding of their relationships and responsibilities is through **interoperability agreements**, particularly as they relate to security policy and procedures. These agreements, which should be regularly reviewed to verify compliance and performance standards, include:

- A **Service Level Agreement (SLA)** is a service contract between a vendor and a client that specifies what services will be provided, the responsibilities of each party, and any guarantees of service.

- A **Blanket Purchase Agreement (BPA)** is a prearranged purchase or sale agreement between a government agency and a business. BPAs are often used by federal agencies to satisfy repetitive needs for products and services.

- A **Memorandum of Understanding (MOU)** describes an agreement between two or more parties. It demonstrates a "convergence of will" between the parties so that they can work together. An MOU generally is not a legally enforceable agreement, but is more formal than an unwritten agreement.

- An **Interconnection Security Agreement (ISA)** is an agreement that is intended to minimize security risks for data transmitted across a network. Examples of network interconnections usually include corporate virtual private network (VPN) tunnels that are used to connect to a network. The ISA ensures the adequate security of both entities as they share data across networks.

15

Mitigating and Deterring Attacks

2.9 Given a scenario, select the appropriate control to meet the goals of security.

3.6 Analyze a scenario and select the appropriate type of mitigation and deterrent techniques.

Although there are a wide variety of attacks, standard techniques should be used in mitigating and deterring attacks. These techniques include creating a security posture, selecting and configuring controls, hardening, and reporting.

Creating a Security Posture

A security posture may be considered as an approach, philosophy, or strategy regarding security. A healthy security posture results from a sound and workable strategy toward managing risks.

Several elements make up a security posture, including:

- *Initial baseline configuration.* A baseline is the standard security checklist against which systems are evaluated for a security posture. A baseline outlines the major security considerations for a system and becomes the starting point for solid security. It is critical that a strong baseline be created when developing a security posture.

- *Continuous security monitoring.* Continual observation of systems and networks through vulnerability scanning and penetration testing can provide valuable information regarding the current state of preparedness. In particular, system logs—including event logs, audit logs, security logs, and access logs—should be closely monitored.

- *Remediation.* As vulnerabilities are exposed through monitoring, a plan must be in place to address the vulnerabilities before they are exploited by attackers.

Selecting Appropriate Controls

Selecting the appropriate controls to use is another key to mitigating and deterring attacks. Although many different controls can be used, there are common controls that are important to meet specific security goals. Table 15-9 summarizes some of these.

Security goal	Common controls
Confidentiality	Encryption, steganography, access controls
Integrity	Hashing, digital signatures, certificates, nonrepudiation tools
Availability	Redundancy, fault tolerance, patching
Safety	Fencing and lighting, locks, CCTV, escape plans and routes, safety drills

Table 15-9 **Appropriate controls for different security goals**

Configuring Controls

Another key to mitigating and deterring attacks is the proper configuration and testing of the controls. One category of controls is those that can either *detect* or *prevent* attacks. For example, a closed-circuit television (CCTV) camera's primary purpose in a remote hallway may be to detect if a criminal is attempting to break into an office. The camera itself, however, cannot prevent the attack; it can only be used to record it for future prosecution or to alert a person monitoring the camera. Other controls can be configured to include prevention as their primary purpose. A security guard whose desk is positioned at the entrance of the hallway has the primary purpose of preventing the criminal from entering the hallway. In the same way, different information security controls can be configured to detect attacks and sound alarms, or to prevent attacks from occurring.

NOTE The difference in detection controls and prevention controls can be seen by comparing an intrusion detection system (IDS), which detects attacks, with an intrusion prevention system (IPS), which attempts to prevent attacks. IDS and IPS are covered in Chapter 7.

One example of configuring controls regards what occurs when a normal function is interrupted by a failure: does safety take priority or does security? For example, consider a school door that is controlled by a special electromagnetic lock requiring the electrical current to be on in order for the door to function properly. If the electricity goes off (fails), should the door automatically be unlocked to allow any occupants to leave the building (safety) or should the door automatically lock to prevent any intruders from entering the building (security)? Which takes precedence, safety or security? In this scenario, a door that automatically unlocks is called a *fail-open* lock, which errs on the side of permissiveness, while one that automatically locks is called a *fail-safe* (or *fail-secure*) lock, which is a control that puts the system on the highest level of security.

The same question should be asked about what occurs when a security hardware device fails or a program aborts: which state should it enter? A firewall device that goes into a fail-safe control state could prevent all traffic from entering or exiting, resulting in no traffic coming into the network. That also means that internal nodes cannot send traffic out, thereby restricting their access to the Internet. If the firewall goes into a fail-open state, then all traffic would be allowed, opening the door for unfiltered attacks to enter the system. If a software program abnormally terminates, a fail-open state could allow an attacker to launch an insecure activity, whereas the fail-safe state would close the program or even stop the entire operating system in order to prevent any malicious activity.

Hardening

The purpose of **hardening** is to eliminate as many security risks as possible and make the system more secure. A variety of techniques can be used to harden systems. Types of hardening techniques include:

- Protecting accounts with passwords
- Disabling any unnecessary accounts
- Disabling all unnecessary services
- Protecting management interfaces and applications

Reporting

It is important to provide information regarding the events that occur so that action can be taken. This reporting can take the form of *alarms* or *alerts* that sound a warning message of

15

a specific situation that is occurring. For example, an alert could signal that someone is trying to guess a user's password by entering several different password attempts. The reporting also can involve providing information on *trends* that may indicate an even more serious impending situation. A trend report may indicate that multiple user accounts are experiencing multiple password attempts.

Because networks play a key role in computer security, network security should be at the forefront of mitigating and deterring attacks. Network security must include MAC limiting and filtering, using IEEE 802.1x, disabling unused interfaces and application service ports, and detecting rogue devices.

Chapter Summary

- Vulnerability assessment is a systematic and methodical evaluation of the exposure of assets to attackers, forces of nature, and any other entity that could cause potential harm. Generally five steps are involved in vulnerability assessment. The first step is to determine the assets that need to be protected. An asset is defined as any item that has a positive economic value, and asset identification is the process of inventorying these items. After an account of the assets has been made, it is important to determine each item's relative value. Once the assets have been inventoried, the next step is to determine the potential threats against the assets that come from threat agents. One tool used to assist in determining potential threats is a process known as threat modeling. The third step is a vulnerability appraisal, which takes a snapshot of the security of the organization as it currently stands. The next step is to perform a risk assessment, which involves determining the damage that would result from an attack and the likelihood that the vulnerability is a risk to the organization. The last step is to determine what to do about the risks. Because risk cannot ever be entirely eliminated, an organization must decide how much acceptable risk can be tolerated.

- Several techniques can be used in a vulnerability assessment. A baseline is the standard or checklist against which systems can be evaluated and audited for their security posture. Baseline reporting is a comparison of the present state of a system compared to its baseline, and any differences need to be properly noted and addressed. Because flaws in software can be points at which an attacker can try to penetrate and launch a successful attack, it is important that software vulnerabilities be minimized while the software is being developed. Reducing these vulnerabilities can be achieved by architectural design reviews, software design reviews, code reviews, and minimizing the attack surface.

- In addition to specific techniques, assessment tools can be used to perform vulnerability assessments. Port scanner software searches a system to determine the state of ports to show what applications are running and to point out port vulnerabilities that could be exploited. Banner grabbing can be used to perform an inventory on the services and systems operating on a server. A protocol analyzer captures each packet to decode and analyze its contents. A vulnerability scanner is a generic term that refers to a range of products that look for vulnerabilities in networks or systems. A honeypot is a computer typically located in an area with limited security and loaded with software and data files that appear to be authentic but are not. The honeypot is intentionally configured with security vulnerabilities to trick attackers into revealing their attack techniques. Similar to a honeypot, a honeynet is a network set up with intentional vulnerabilities.

- A vulnerability scan searches a system for any known security weaknesses and creates a report of those potential exposures. It examines the current security in a passive method and does not attempt to exploit any weaknesses it finds. Vulnerability scans are usually performed from inside the security perimeter and are not intended to disrupt the normal operations of the network or devices. These scans are conducted using an automated software package that examines the system for known weaknesses by passively testing the security controls. Penetration testing is designed to exploit any weaknesses discovered in systems. Penetration testers do not use automated software as with vulnerability scanning. Testers are typically outside the security perimeter and may even disrupt the operation of the network or devices instead of passively probing for a known vulnerability. Penetration testers can use black box (no knowledge of network or systems), white box (full knowledge of systems), or gray box (limited knowledge) techniques in their testing.

- As an increasing number of organizations today are turning to third-party vendors to create partnerships, the risk of third-party integration continues to grow. Some of the risks in third-party integration include on-boarding (the start-up relationship between partners) and off-boarding (the termination of those agreements), application and social media network sharing, privacy and risk awareness, and data considerations. One means by which the parties can reach an understanding of their relationships and responsibilities is through the use of interoperability agreements, particularly as they relate to security policy and procedures. These agreements should be regularly reviewed to verify compliance and performance standards.

- Several standard techniques can be used in mitigating and deterring attacks. A security posture is a philosophy regarding security. A healthy security posture results from a sound and workable strategy toward managing risks. Another key to mitigating and deterring attacks is the selection of appropriate controls and the proper configuration of those controls. One category of controls is those that can either detect attacks or prevent attacks. The purpose of hardening is to eliminate as many security risks as possible and make the system more secure. Reporting can provide information regarding the events that occur so that action can be taken. Reporting also can involve providing information on trends that may indicate an even more serious impending situation.

15

Key Terms

architectural design   In software development, the process of defining a collection of hardware and software components along with their interfaces in order to create the framework for software development.

attack surface   The code that can be executed by unauthorized users in a software program.

banner grabbing   Gathering information from messages that a service transmits when another program connects to it.

baseline reporting   A comparison of the present state of a system to its baseline.

black box   A penetration test in which the tester has no prior knowledge of the network infrastructure that is being tested.

Blanket Purchase Agreement (BPA)   A prearranged purchase or sale agreement between a government agency and a business.

code review   In software development, presenting the code to multiple reviewers in order to reach agreement about its security.

credentialed vulnerability scan   A scan that provides credentials (username and password) to the scanner so that tests for additional internal vulnerabilities can be performed.

design review   An analysis of the design of a software program by key personnel from different levels of the project.

gray box   A penetration test where some limited information has been provided to the tester.

hardening   The process of eliminating as many security risks as possible to make the system more secure.

honeynet   A network set up with intentional vulnerabilities to invite attacks and reveal attackers' methods.

honeypot   A computer typically located in an area with limited security and loaded with software and data files that appear to be authentic, but are actually imitations of real data files, to trick attackers into revealing their attack techniques.

Interconnection Security Agreement (ISA)   An agreement between parties intended to minimize security risks for data transmitted across a network.

interoperability agreement   An agreement through which parties in a relationship can reach an understanding of their relationships and responsibilities.

intrusive vulnerability scan   A scan that attempts to penetrate the system in order to perform a simulated attack.

Memorandum of Understanding (MOU)   An agreement between two or more parties to enable them to work together that is not legally enforceable but is more formal than an unwritten agreement.

non-credentialed vulnerability scan   A scan that does not use credentials (username and password) to conduct an internal vulnerability assessment.

non-intrusive vulnerability scan   A scan that uses only available information to hypothesize the status of the vulnerability.

off-boarding business partners   The termination of an agreement between parties.

On-boarding business partners   The start-up relationship agreement between parties.

penetration testing   A test by an outsider that attempts to actually exploit any weaknesses in systems that are vulnerable.

port scanner   Software to search a system for port vulnerabilities.

port security   Disabling unused application/service ports to reduce the number of threat vectors.

Service Level Agreement (SLA)   A contract between a vendor and a client that specifies what services will be provided, the responsibilities of each party, and any guarantees of service.

third-party integration Combining an organization's systems and data with outside entities.

vulnerability assessment A systematic and methodical evaluation of the exposure of assets to attackers, forces of nature, and any other entity that could cause potential harm.

vulnerability scan An automated software search through a system for any known security weaknesses that creates a report of those potential exposures.

vulnerability scanner Generic term for a range of products that look for vulnerabilities in networks or systems.

white box A penetration test where the tester has an in-depth knowledge of the network and systems being tested, including network diagrams, IP addresses, and even the source code of custom applications.

Xmas Tree port scan Sending a packet with every option set to *on* for whatever protocol is in use to observe how a host responds.

Review Questions

1. At what point in a vulnerability assessment would an attack tree be utilized?

    a. vulnerability appraisal

    b. risk assessment

    c. risk mitigation

    d. threat evaluation

2. In the software development process, when should a design review be conducted?

    a. at the completion of the project

    b. at the same time as the code review

    c. as the functional and design specifications are being developed based on the requirements

    d. during verification

3. A(n) _____ attempts to penetrate a system in order to perform a simulated attack.

    a. intrusive vulnerability scan

    b. vulnerability risk scan

    c. PACK scan

    d. master level scan

4. A(n) _____ is an agreement between two parties that is not legally enforceable.

    a. Service Level Agreement (SLA)

    b. Blanket Purchase Agreement (BPA)

    c. Memorandum of Understanding (MOU)

    d. Interconnection Security Agreement (ISA)

15

5. A _____ is a systematic and methodical evaluation of the exposure of assets to attackers, forces of nature, and any other entity that could cause potential harm.

   a. penetration test

   b. vulnerability scan

   c. vulnerability assessment

   d. risk appraisal (RAP)

6. Each of these can be classified as an asset EXCEPT _____.

   a. business partners

   b. buildings

   c. employee databases

   d. accounts payable

7. Each of these is a step in risk management EXCEPT _____.

   a. attack assessment

   b. vulnerability appraisal

   c. threat evaluation

   d. risk mitigation

8. Which statement regarding vulnerability appraisal is NOT true?

   a. Vulnerability appraisal is always the easiest and quickest step.

   b. Every asset must be viewed in light of each threat.

   c. Each threat could reveal multiple vulnerabilities.

   d. Each vulnerability should be cataloged.

9. _____ constructs scenarios of the types of threats that assets can face in order to learn who the attackers are, why they attack, and what types of attacks may occur.

   a. Vulnerability prototyping

   b. Risk assessment

   c. Attack assessment

   d. Threat modeling

10. What is a current snapshot of the security of an organization?

   a. vulnerability appraisal

   b. risk evaluation

   c. threat mitigation

   d. liability reporting

11. _____ is a comparison of the present security state of a system to a standard established by the organization.

    a. Risk mitigation

    b. Baseline reporting

    c. Comparative Resource Appraisal (CRA)

    d. Horizontal comparables

12. Which of these is NOT a state of a port that can be returned by a port scanner?

    a. open

    b. busy

    c. blocked

    d. closed

13. Which statement regarding TCP SYN port scanning is NOT true?

    a. It uses FIN messages that can pass through firewalls and avoid detection.

    b. Instead of using the operating system's network functions, the port scanner generates IP packets itself and monitors for responses.

    c. The scanner host closes the connection before the handshake is completed.

    d. This scan type is also known as "half-open scanning" because it never actually opens a full TCP connection.

14. The protocol File Transfer Protocol (FTP) uses which two ports?

    a. 19 and 20

    b. 20 and 21

    c. 21 and 22

    d. 22 and 23

15. Each of these is a function of a vulnerability scanner EXCEPT _____.

    a. detects which ports are served and which ports are browsed for each individual system

    b. alerts users when a new patch cannot be found

    c. maintains a log of all interactive network sessions

    d. detects when an application is compromised

16. Which statement about the Open Vulnerability and Assessment Language (OVAL) is true?

    a. It only functions on Linux-based computers.

    b. It attempts to standardize vulnerability assessments.

    c. It has been replaced by XML.

    d. It is a European standard and is not used in the Americas.

15

17. Which statement regarding a honeypot is NOT true?

    a. It is typically located in an area with limited security.

    b. It is intentionally configured with security vulnerabilities.

    c. It cannot be part of a honeynet.

    d. It can direct an attacker's attention away from legitimate servers.

18. Which statement about vulnerability scanning is true?

    a. It uses automated software to scan for vulnerabilities.

    b. The testers are always outside of the security perimeter.

    c. It may disrupt the operation of the network or systems.

    d. It produces a short report of the attack methods and value of the exploited data.

19. If a tester is given the IP addresses, network diagrams, and source code of customer applications, the tester is using which technique?

    a. black box

    b. white box

    c. gray box

    d. blue box

20. If a software application aborts and leaves the program open, which control structure is it using?

    a. fail-safe

    b. fail-secure

    c. fail-open

    d. fail-right

Hands-On Projects

HANDS-ON PROJECTS

NOTE   If you are concerned about installing any of the software in these projects on your regular computer, you can instead install the software in the Windows virtual machine created in the Chapter 1 Hands-On Projects 1-3 and 1-4. Software installed within the virtual machine will not impact the host computer.

Project 15-1: Using Secunia Personal Software Inspector (PSI)

One of the challenges of keeping a system secure is to keep up-to-date on patching software. Although large vendors such as Microsoft and Apple have an established infrastructure to alert users about patches and to install them, few other vendors have such a mechanism. This makes it necessary to regularly visit all the websites of all the installed software on a system to stay current on all software updates. To make the process more manageable, online software vulnerability scanners were created that can compare all applications on a computer with a list of known patches from the different software vendors and then alert the user to any applications that are not properly patched or automatically install the patches when one is detected as missing. In this project, you will use the Secunia Personal Software Inspector (PSI) to determine if your computer is missing any security updates.

The current version of PSI contains several advanced features. It supports applications from more than 3000 different software vendors and encapsulates all of the vendor patches for your computer into one proprietary installer. This installer suppresses any required dialogs so everything can be patched silently without any user intervention. You can even create rules, such as telling PSI to ignore patching a specific application.

1. Open your web browser and enter the URL **secunia.com/vulnerability_scanning/personal/**.

The location of content on the Internet such as this program may change without warning. If you are no longer able to access the program through the above URL, use a search engine and search for "Secunia Personal Software Inspector".

2. Click **PSI 3.0 Walkthrough**, which is a YouTube video about PSI. Click your browser's **Back** button when finished.

3. Click **Download now.**

4. When the download completes, launch the application to install PSI.

5. Select the appropriate language and click **OK.**

6. Click **Next** on the Welcome screen, then click **I accept the terms of the License Agreement**. Click **Next.**

7. Check the box **Update programs automatically (recommended)** if necessary. Click **Next.**

8. Click **Finish** when the installation is complete.

9. When asked **Would you like to launch Secunia PSI now?**, click **Yes.** Depending upon the computer, it may take several minutes to load the program and its modules.

10. If necessary, click **Scan now.**

11. When the scan is finished, the results will appear like those in Figure 15-8.

12. Applications that can be automatically updated will start the download and installation automatically. On any applications that need manual updates, you can go to the application and then update it.

13. Close all windows.

15

Figure 15-8 Secunia PSI
Source: Secunia PSI

The Secunia PSI application will continually run in the background checking for updates. If you do not want this functionality on the computer, you can click Settings and uncheck Start on boot.

Project 15-2: Using HoneyDocs

A honeypot is a computer typically located in an area with limited security and loaded with software and data files that appear to be authentic, but are actually imitations of real data files. The honeypot is intentionally configured with security vulnerabilities so that it is open to attacks. This honeypot concept has been modified to set a trap using fake documents. HoneyDocs is a service designed to let users know when and where someone has opened a file that they have posted online. In this project, you will use HoneyDocs to track when and where a document under your name is being opened.

1.   Use your web browser to go to **www.honeydocs.com**.

The location of content on the Internet, such as this program, may change without warning. If you are no longer able to access the program through the above URL, use a search engine to search for "HoneyDocs".

2. Click **Sign up now.**

3. Enter the required information and follow the steps to create your account. You will also need to access the email account that you entered as part of the information to confirm your account.

4. Click **New Sting.**

5. Under **Sting Name** enter **HoP 15-2.** Click **Save New.**

6. HoneyDocs has now created four documents that look tempting to attackers. At the **Hive** screen, click the link under **Documents.**

7. Click **Passwords.zip** to download this HoneyDoc document to your local computer.

8. Unpack **Passwords.zip.**

9. There are five versions of the same fake password file in five different formats. Double-click **passwords.html** to view the contents.

10. The list of passwords also includes a virtually invisible 1×1 pixel that uniquely identifies the document as belonging to you. Close **passwords.html.**

11. Now copy this file onto different locations, such as a desktop computer in a computer lab, a laptop computer, or on a USB flash drive that is left in a public area for someone to pick up.

12. When **passwords.html** is opened by a nosy intruder, the pixel is used to send back data (called a *buzz*) to HoneyDocs. The buzz is actually an HTTP Get request with a unique identifier sent over Secure Sockets Layer (SSL) on port 443. This returned data includes the time, the IP address of the intruder, and the location of the intruder's Internet Service Provider (ISP).

13. Periodically return to the HoneyDocs site to track your document (users who have the fee-based service will immediately receive an email or text message). Log in to view your **Hive** screen click as seen in Figure 15-9.

Sting Name	Documents	Buzz	Map	Edit	Destroy	Created
HoP 15-2	⬇	0	♀	✎	🗑	2014-04-20 20:17:31 UTC

Figure 15-9 HoneyDocs Hive
Source: HoneyDocs

14. Click **Buzz** to see the access information and **Map** to see the location of the person's ISP.

15. Close all windows.

Project 15-3: Using an Internet Port Scanner

Internet port scanners are available that will probe the ports on a system to determine which ports are open, closed, or blocked. In this project, you will perform a scan using an Internet-based scanner.

1. Use your web browser to go to **www.grc.com**.

The location of content on the Internet, such as this program, may change without warning. If you are no longer able to access the program through the above URL, use a search engine to search for "ShieldsUP!"

2. Point to **Services** and then click **ShieldsUP!**.

3. Click the **Proceed** button.

4. Click the **All Service Ports** button to scan ports on your computer. A grid is displayed indicating which ports are open (red), closed (blue), or blocked (green). When the scan completes, scroll through the report to view the results. Then print the report.

ShieldsUP! refers to blocked ports as "stealth."

5. Scroll down and then click the **File Sharing** button. ShieldsUP! probes your computer to identify basic security vulnerabilities. Print this page when finished.

6. Closing or blocking open ports can be done through either the router or firewall to which the computer is attached or through the software firewall running on the computer. To access the Windows firewall settings to change the configuration of ports go to **Control Panel**, then Click **System and Security**, then **Windows Firewall**.

7. Close all windows.

Project 15-4: Using a Local Port Scanner

In this project, you will download and install the port scanner Nmap on a local computer.

1. Use your web browser to go to **nmap.org/download.html**.

The location of content on the Internet, such as this program, may change without warning. If you are no longer able to access the program through the above URL, use a search engine to search for "Nmap".

2. Under **Microsoft Windows binaries,** click the link next to **Latest release self-installer:**.

3. When the download completes, launch the installation program.

4. Click **I Agree.**

5. Click **Next.**

6. Click **Install.**

7. Click **I Agree.**

8. Click **Next.**

9. Click **Next.**

10. Click **Finish.**

11. Click **Next.**

12. Click **Next.**

13. Click **Finish.**

14. Launch Nmap.

15. Next to **Target:** enter the IP address of a computer on the network to which the computer is connected. Then, click the **Scan** button.

If you do not know the address of any of the devices on the network, click **Start** and enter **cmd** and press **Enter**. At the prompt, enter **arp -a** to view the arp cache of IP addresses and MAC addresses of devices on the network of which the computer is aware. Select one of the IP addresses of the devices on the network to scan.

16. Nmap will scan the ports of that computer and display the results similarly to those shown in Figure 15-10.

17. Scroll down through the results of the port scan. How could this information be valuable to an attacker?

18. For a summary of open ports, click **Topology.**

19. Click **Hosts Viewer.**

20. Click the **Services** tab.

21. Expand each of the entries listed.

22. Close the Hosts Viewer window.

23. Click **Controls.** What information is being provided? How would this be useful to an attacker?

24. Close all windows.

15

```
Zenmap                                                    ☐ ☐ ✕

 Scan  Tools  Profile  Help

 Target:  192.168.1.1          ▼   Profile:  Intense scan       ▼   Scan   Cancel

 Command:  nmap -T4 -A -v 192.168.1.1

  ┌ Hosts ┐ ┌ Services ┐   ┌ Nmap Output ┐ Ports / Hosts │ Topology │ Host Details │ Scans

  Service          ▲  ▲    nmap -T4 -A -v 192.168.1.1               ▼  ≡  Details

  3d-nfsd
                         Starting Nmap 6.40 ( http://nmap.org ) at 2014-04-05
  3exmp                  20:56 Central Daylight Time
  802-11-iapp            NSE: Loaded 110 scripts for scanning.
                         NSE: Script Pre-scanning.
  914c-g                 Initiating ARP Ping Scan at 20:57
  abarsd                 Scanning 192.168.1.1 [1 port]
                         Completed ARP Ping Scan at 20:57, 0.42s elapsed (1
  abyss                  total hosts)
  acc-raid               Initiating Parallel DNS resolution of 1 host. at 20:57
                         Completed Parallel DNS resolution of 1 host. at 20:57,
  accessbuilder          0.02s elapsed
  acmsoda                Initiating SYN Stealth Scan at 20:57
                         Scanning 192.168.1.1 [1000 ports]
  active-net             Discovered open port 80/tcp on 192.168.1.1
  activesync             Discovered open port 53/tcp on 192.168.1.1
                         Discovered open port 23/tcp on 192.168.1.1
  admd                   Discovered open port 3333/tcp on 192.168.1.1
  admdog                 Discovered open port 49153/tcp on 192.168.1.1
                         Discovered open port 5555/tcp on 192.168.1.1
  admeng                 Discovered open port 49152/tcp on 192.168.1.1
  adobeserver-1          Completed SYN Stealth Scan at 20:57, 1.52s elapsed
                         (1000 total ports)
  adobeserver-3          Initiating Service scan at 20:57
  advocentkvm            Scanning 7 services on 192.168.1.1
                         Service scan Timing: About 71.43% done; ETC: 20:59
  aeroflight-ads         (0:00:40 remaining)
  afp                    Completed Service scan at 20:58, 108.82s elapsed (7
                         services on 1 host)
  afrog                  Initiating OS detection (try #1) against 192.168.1.1
  afs3-bos         ▼     NSE: Script scanning 192.168.1.1.
                         Initiating NSE at 20:58
  ┌──── Filter Hosts ────┐ Completed NSE at 20:59, 30.16s elapsed
                         Nmap scan report for 192.168.1.1
                         Host is up (0.0020s latency).
```

Figure 15-10 Nmap
Source: Nmap.org

Case Projects

Case Project 15-1: OVAL

Use the Internet to research OVAL. How is it being used? Who supports it? What are its advantages? What are its disadvantages? How can it help create a more secure posture for an organization? Write a one-page paper on your analysis.

Case Project 15-2: Risk Management Study

Perform an abbreviated risk management study on your personal computer. Conduct an asset identification, threat identification, vulnerability appraisal, risk assessment, and risk mitigation. Under each category, list the elements that pertain to your system. What major vulnerabilities did you uncover? How can you mitigate the risks? Write a one-page paper on your analysis.

Case Project 15-3: Compare Port Scanners

Use the Internet to locate three port scanner applications that you can download to your computer. Install and run each application and examine the results. Based on your study, what are the strengths and weaknesses of each scanner? Which scanner would you recommend? Why?

Case Project 15-4: Interoperability Agreements

Use the Internet to locate three examples of each of the four types of interoperability agreements: Service Level Agreement (SLA), Blanket Purchase Agreement (BPA), Memorandum of Understanding (MOU), and Interconnection Security Agreement (ISA). Compare these examples. Which of the three examples for each type is the strongest? Which is the weakest? Which would serve as the best foundation for an agreement between parties? Why? Write a one-page paper about your research.

Case Project 15-5: Xmas Tree Port Scan

Use the Internet to research the Xmas Tree port scan. How is it used? Why is it popular? What defenses are there to protect against these scans? Write a one-page paper about your research.

Case Project 15-6: Attack Tree

Select an attack, such as "Break into Instructor's Lab Computer" or "Steal Credit Card Number from Online User," and then develop an attack tree for it. The tree should have at least four levels with three boxes on each level. Share your tree with at least two other learners and ask if they can think of other attacks that they would add.

Case Project 15-7: Comparison of Protocol Analyzers

15

Several very good protocol analyzers are available. Two of the most popular are Wireshark (*www.wireshark.org*), which is an open source product, and Colasoft Capsa (*www.colasoft.com/capsa*), which has a free version along with an Enterprise and Professional edition. Research Wireshark and Capsa, and compare their features. Next download and install each product, and perform a basic protocol analysis (there are several free tutorials available regarding how to use these tools). Create a document that lists the features and strengths of each product. Which would you prefer? Why?

Case Project 15-8: Bay Pointe Security Consulting

Bay Pointe Security Consulting (BPSC) provides security consulting services to a wide range of businesses, individuals, schools, and organizations. BPSC has hired you as a technology student to help them with a new project and provide real-world experience to students who are interested in the security field.

Rozenboom Real Estate (RRE) buys and sells high-end residential and commercial real estate across a multistate region. One of the tools that RRE offers is a sophisticated online website that allows potential buyers to take virtual tours of properties. However, RRE's site was recently compromised by attackers who defaced the site with malicious messages, causing several customers to threaten to withdraw their listings. RRE's senior management has demanded a top-to-bottom review of their security by an independent third party. BPSC has been hired to perform the review, and they have contracted with you to work on this project.

1. The first task is to perform a vulnerability assessment of RRE. Create a PowerPoint presentation for the president and his staff about the steps in a vulnerability assessment. List in detail the actions under each step and what RRE should expect in the assessment. Your presentation should contain at least 10 slides.

2. One of the activities recommended by BPSC is to perform a penetration test. However, the IT staff is very resistant to the idea and has tried to convince RRE's senior management that it is too risky and that a vulnerability scan would serve the same purpose. RRE has asked you for your opinion of performing a penetration test or a vulnerability scan. Create a memo that outlines the differences and what your recommendation would be.

Case Project 15-9: Community Site Activity

The Information Security Community Site is an online companion to this textbook. It contains a wide variety of tools, information, discussion boards, and other features to assist learners. Go to **community.cengage.com/infosec**. Sign in with the login name and password that you created in Chapter 1.

Bob is invited to attend a weekly meeting of computer enthusiasts on campus. At the meeting much of the talk centers around the latest attack software and how to bypass weak security settings on the school network. As the meeting starts to break up, Bob is approached by Alice, who strikes up a conversation with him about the latest attack software. Alice soon confides in Bob that she has plans to break into the school's web server that night and deface it (she has a friend who works in the school's IT department and the friend has shared some helpful information with her). Alice goes on to say that she would give Bob the chance to "show he's a man" by helping her break into the server. Bob declines the invitation and leaves.

Later that week Bob receives an email from Alice who says she wasn't successful in breaking into the server that night, but knows that she has the right information now. She asks Bob to meet her at the library that night to watch her.

Bob thinks about it and accepts the invitation. That night Alice shows Bob some of the information she has acquired through her friend in IT and says she's ready to launch her attack. Alice then pauses and gives Bob the chance to make up for being "chicken" earlier in the week. Bob again declines. Alice then tells Bob that she knows he's really stupid because he can't do it and he lacks the nerve. After several minutes of her accusations, Bob finally gives in and uses the information Alice has to break into the web server.

The next day two campus security officers appear at Bob's dorm room. It turns out that Alice is working undercover for campus security and turned Bob in to them. In addition, the web server that Bob thought he was breaking into turned out to be a honeypot the school had set up. Bob was required to go before the school's Office of Judicial Affairs (OJA) to determine if he should be suspended.

When Bob appeared before the OJA he claimed in his defense that he was entrapped in two different ways. First, he was entrapped by Alice to break into the server. Second, he claimed that the honeypot itself was entrapment. He claimed that he should not be suspended from school.

What do you think? Did Alice entrap Bob? Is a honeypot entrapment? (You may want to research *honeypot entrapment* on the Internet.) If you were in Bob's place, what would you say? Enter your answers on the Information Security Community Site discussion board.

References

1. Opel, Alexander, "Design and implementation of a support tool for attack trees," Internship Thesis, Otto-von-Guericke University Magdeburg, Mar. 2005, retrieved Mar. 17, 2011, www.toengel.net/internship/data/internship_thesis.pdf.

2. "Release early, release often," http://catb.org/esr/writings/cathedral-bazaar/cathedral-bazaar/ar01s04.html.

3. "18 U.S. Code §1030—Fraud and related activity in connection with computers," *Legal Information Institute*, retrieved Apr. 20, 2014, www.law.cornell.edu/uscode/text/18/1030.

15

CompTIA SY0-401 Certification Exam Objectives

Security+ Exam Objective Domain	Chapter	Section
1.0 Network Security		
1.1 Implement security configuration parameters on network devices and other technologies.	7	Security Through Network Devices
• Firewalls	7	Network Security Hardware
• Routers		
• Switches		
• Load Balancers		
• Proxies		
• Web security gateways		
• VPN concentrators		
• NIDS and NIPS		
• Behavior based		
• Signature based		
• Anomaly based		
• Heuristic		
• Protocol analyzers		
• Spam filter		
• UTM security appliances		
• URL filter		
• Content inspection		
• Malware inspection		
• Web application firewall vs. network firewall		
• Application aware devices		
• Firewalls		
• IPS		
• IDS		
• Proxies		
1.2 Given a scenario, use secure network administration principles.	7	Security Through Network Devices
• Rule-based management	8	Network Administration Principles
• Firewall rules		

(Continued)

Security+ Exam Objective Domain	Chapter	Section
• VLAN management	11	What Is Access Control?
• Secure router configuration	11	Implementing Access Control
• Access control lists		
• Port Security	15	Assessing Vulnerabilities
• 802.1x		
• Flood guards		
• Loop protection		
• Implicit deny		
• Network separation		
• Log analysis		
• Unified Threat Management		
1.3 Explain network design elements and components.	7	Security Through Network Devices
• DMZ		
• Subnetting	7	Security Through Network Technologies
• VLAN		
• NAT	7	Security Through Network Design Elements
• Remote Access		
• Telephony	8	Securing Network Applications and Platforms
• NAC		
• Virtualization		
• Cloud Computing		
• Platform as a Service		
• Software as a Service		
• Infrastructure as a Service		
• Private		
• Public		
• Hybrid		
• Community		
• Layered security/Defense in depth		
1.4 Given a scenario, implement common protocols and services.	6	Cryptographic Transport Protocols
• Protocols		
• IPSec	7	Security Through Network Devices
• SNMP		
• SSH	8	Common Network Protocols
• DNS	15	Assessing Vulnerabilities
• TLS		
• SSL		
• TCP/IP		
• FTPS		
• HTTPS		
• SCP		
• ICMP		
• IPv4		
• IPv6		
• iSCSI		

A

Security+ Exam Objective Domain	Chapter	Section
• Fibre Channel		
• FCoE		
• FTP		
• SFTP		
• TFTP		
• TELNET		
• HTTP		
• NetBIOS		
• Ports		
• 21		
• 22		
• 25		
• 53		
• 80		
• 110		
• 139		
• 143		
• 443		
• 3389		
• OSI relevance		
1.5 Given a scenario, troubleshoot security issues related to wireless networking.	9	Vulnerabilities of IEEE 802.11 Security
• WPA	9	Wireless Security Solutions
• WPA2		
• WEP		
• EAP		
• PEAP		
• LEAP		
• MAC filter		
• Disable SSID broadcast		
• TKIP		
• CCMP		
• Antenna placement		
• Power level controls		
• Captive portals		
• Antenna types		
• Site surveys		
• VPN (over open wireless)		
2.0 Compliance and Operational Security		
2.1 Explain the importance of risk related concepts.	1	What Is Information Security?
• Control types		
• Technical	8	Securing Network Applications and Platforms
• Management		
• Operational	11	What Is Access Control?

(Continued)

Security+ Exam Objective Domain	Chapter	Section
• False positives	13	Disaster Recovery
• False negatives	14	Controlling Risk
• Importance of policies in reducing risk	14	Reducing Risk Through Policies
• Privacy policy		
• Acceptable use		
• Security policy		
• Mandatory vacations		
• Job rotation		
• Separation of duties		
• Least privilege		
• Risk calculation		
• Likelihood		
• ALE		
• Impact		
• SLE		
• ARO		
• MTTR		
• MTTF		
• MTBF		
• Quantitative vs. qualitative		
• Vulnerabilities		
• Threat vectors		
• Probability/threat likelihood		
• Risk-avoidance, transference, acceptance, mitigation, deterrence		
• Risks associated with Cloud Computing and Virtualization		
• Recovery time objective and recovery point objective		
2.2 Summarize the security implications of integrating systems and data with third parties.	15	Third-Party Integration
• On-boarding/off-boarding business partners		
• Social media networks and/or applications		
• Interoperability agreements		
• SLA		
• BPA		
• MOU		
• ISA		
• Privacy considerations		
• Risk awareness		
• Unauthorized data sharing		
• Data ownership		
• Data backups		
• Follow security policy and procedures		
• Review agreement requirements to verify compliance and performance standards		

A

Security+ Exam Objective Domain	Chapter	Section
2.3 Given a scenario, implement appropriate risk mitigation strategies. • Change management • Incident management • User rights and permissions reviews • Perform routine audits • Enforce policies and procedures to prevent data loss or theft • Enforce technology controls • Data Loss Prevention (DLP)	4 14	Securing Data Controlling Risk
2.4 Given a scenario, implement basic forensic procedures. • Order of volatility • Capture system image • Network traffic and logs • Capture video • Record time offset • Take hashes • Screenshots • Witnesses • Track man hours and expense • Chain of custody • Big Data analysis	13	Incident Response

2.5 Summarize common incident response procedures.
• Preparation
• Incident identification
• Escalation and notification
• Mitigation steps
• Lessons learned
• Reporting
• Recovery/reconstitution procedures
• First responder
• Incident isolation
   • Quarantine
   • Device removal
• Data breach
• Damage and loss control
	13	Incident Response

2.6 Explain the importance of security-related awareness and training.
• Security policy training and procedures
• Role-based training
• Personally identifiable information
• Information classification
   • High
   • Medium
	14	Awareness and Training

(Continued)

Security+ Exam Objective Domain	Chapter	Section

• Confidential
• Private
• Public
• Data labeling, handling, and disposal
• Compliance with laws, best practices, and standards
• User habits
  • Password behaviors
  • Data handling
  • Clean desk policies
  • Prevent tailgating
  • Personally owned devices
• New threats and new security trends/alerts
  • New viruses
  • Phishing attacks
  • Zero-day exploits
• Use of social networking and P2P
• Follow up and gather training metrics to validate compliance and security posture		

2.7 Compare and contrast physical security and environmental controls.
• Environmental controls
  • HVAC
  • Fire suppression
  • EMI shielding
  • Hot and cold aisles
  • Environmental monitoring
  • Temperature and humidity controls
• Physical security
  • Hardware locks
  • Mantraps
  • Video Surveillance
  • Fencing
  • Proximity readers
  • Access list
  • Proper lighting
  • Signs
  • Guards
  • Barricades
  • Biometrics
  • Protected distribution (cabling)
  • Alarms
  • Motion detection
• Control types
  • Deterrent
  • Preventive
	4
	12
	13
		Securing Devices
		Authentication Credentials
		Environmental Controls

A

Security+ Exam Objective Domain	Chapter	Section
• Detective • Compensating • Technical • Administrative		

2.8 Summarize risk management best practices.
• Business continuity concepts
  • Business impact analysis
  • Identification of critical systems and components
  • Removing single points of failure
  • Business continuity planning and testing
  • Risk assessment
  • Continuity of operations
  • Disaster recovery
  • IT contingency planning
  • Succession planning
  • High availability
  • Redundancy
  • Tabletop exercises
• Fault tolerance
  • Hardware
  • RAID
  • Clustering
  • Load balancing
  • Servers
• Disaster recovery concepts
  • Backup plans/policies
  • Backup execution/frequency
  • Cold site
  • Hot site
  • Warm site
	13
	13
		What Is Business Continuity?
		Disaster Recovery

2.9 Given a scenario, select the appropriate control to meet the goals of security.
• Confidentiality
  • Encryption
  • Access controls
  • Steganography
• Integrity
  • Hashing
  • Digital signatures
  • Certificates
  • Non-repudiation
• Availability
  • Redundancy
  • Fault tolerance
  • Patching
	4
	15
		Securing the Host
		Mitigating and Deterring Attacks

(Continued)

Security+ Exam Objective Domain	Chapter	Section

• Safety
   • Fencing
   • Lighting
   • Locks
   • CCTV
   • Escape plans
   • Drills
   • Escape routes
   • Testing controls		

3.0 Threats and Vulnerabilities		
3.1 Explain types of malware. • Adware • Virus • Spyware • Trojan • Rootkits • Backdoors • Logic bomb • Botnets • Ransomware • Polymorphic malware • Armored virus	2	Attacks Using Malware

3.2 Summarize various types of attacks.
• Man-in-the-middle
• DDoS
• DoS
• Replay
• Smurf attack
• Spoofing
• Spam
• Phishing
• Spim
• Vishing
• Spear phishing
• Xmas attack
• Pharming
• Privilege escalation
• Malicious insider threat
• DNS poisoning and ARP poisoning
• Transitive access
• Client-side attacks
• Password attacks
   • Brute force
   • Dictionary attacks
	1
	1
	2
	3
	3
	12
	15
		What Is Information Security?
		Who Are the Attackers?
		Social Engineering Attacks
		Application Attacks
		Networking-Based Attacks
		Authentication Credentials
		Assessing Vulnerabilities

A

Security+ Exam Objective Domain	Chapter	Section
• Hybrid • Birthday attacks • Rainbow tables • Typo squatting/URL hijacking • Watering hole attack		

3.3 Summarize social engineering attacks and the associated effectiveness with each attack.
• Shoulder surfing
• Dumpster diving
• Tailgating
• Impersonation
• Hoaxes
• Whaling
• Vishing
• Principles (reasons for effectiveness)
  • Authority
  • Intimidation
  • Consensus/Social proof
  • Scarcity
  • Urgency
  • Familiarity/liking
  • Trust
	2	Social Engineering Attacks

3.4 Explain types of wireless attacks. • Rogue access points • Jamming/Interference • Evil twin • War driving • Bluejacking • Bluesnarfing • War chalking • IV attack • Packet sniffing • Near field communication • Replay attacks • WEP/WPA attacks • WPS attacks	9 9 9	Wireless Attacks Vulnerabilities of IEEE Wireless Security Wireless Security Solutions
3.5 Explain types of application attacks. • Cross-site scripting • SQL injection • LDAP injection • XML injection • Directory traversal/command injection • Buffer overflow • Integer overflow	3 11	Application Attacks Authentication Services

(Continued)

Security+ Exam Objective Domain	Chapter	Section
<ul><li>Zero day</li><li>Cookies and attachments</li><li>LSO (Locally Shared Objects)</li><li>Flash Cookies</li><li>Malicious add-ons</li><li>Session hijacking</li><li>Header manipulation</li><li>Arbitrary code execution/remote code execution</li></ul>		
3.6 Analyze a scenario and select the appropriate type of mitigation and deterrent techniques. <ul><li>Monitoring system logs</li><ul><li>Event logs</li><li>Audit logs</li><li>Security logs</li><li>Access logs</li></ul><li>Hardening</li><ul><li>Disabling unnecessary services</li><li>Protecting management interfaces and applications</li><li>Password protection</li><li>Disabling unnecessary accounts</li></ul><li>Network security</li><ul><li>MAC limiting and filtering</li><li>802.1x</li><li>Disabling unused interfaces and unused application service ports</li><li>Rogue machine detection</li></ul><li>Security posture</li><ul><li>Initial baseline configuration</li><li>Continuous security monitoring</li><li>Remediation</li></ul><li>Reporting</li><ul><li>Alarms</li><li>Alerts</li><li>Trends</li></ul><li>Detection controls vs. prevention controls</li><ul><li>IDS vs. IPS</li><li>Camera vs. guard</li></ul></ul>	4 7 8 8 15 15	Securing the Host Security Through Network Devices Network Administration Principles Assessment Tools Assessing Vulnerabilities Mitigating and Deterring Attacks
3.7 Given a scenario, use appropriate tools and techniques to discover security threats and vulnerabilities. <ul><li>Interpret results of security assessment tools</li><li>Tools</li><ul><li>Protocol analyzer</li><li>Vulnerability scanner</li><li>Honeypots</li><li>Honeynets</li></ul></ul>	15 15	Assessing Vulnerabilities Assessment Tools

Security+ Exam Objective Domain	Chapter	Section

• Port scanner
• Passive vs. active tools
• Banner grabbing
• Risk calculation
  • Threat vs. likelihood
• Assessment types
  • Risk
  • Threat
  • Vulnerability
• Assessment technique
  • Baseline reporting
  • Code review
  • Determine attack surface
  • Architecture
  • Design reviews		

3.8 Explain the proper use of penetration testing versus vulnerability scanning.
• Penetration testing
  • Verify a threat exists
  • Bypass security controls
  • Actively test security controls
  • Exploiting vulnerabilities
• Vulnerability scanning
  • Passively testing security controls
  • Identify vulnerability
  • Identify lack of security controls
  • Identify common misconfiguration
  • Intrusive vs. non-intrusive
  • Credentialed vs. non-credentialed
  • False positive
• Black box
• White box
• Gray box
	15	Vulnerability Scanning Versus Penetration Testing

4.0 Application, Data, and Host Security		

4.1 Explain the importance of application security controls and techniques.
• Fuzzing
• Secure coding concepts
  • Error and exception handling
  • Input validation
• Cross-site scripting prevention
• Cross-site Request Forgery (XSRF) prevention
• Application configuration baseline (proper settings)
• Application hardening
	4	Application Security

(Continued)

Security+ Exam Objective Domain	Chapter	Section
• Application patch management • NoSQL databases vs. SQL databases • Server-side vs. Client-side validation		

4.2 Summarize mobile security concepts and technologies.
 • Device security
   • Full device encryption
   • Remote wiping
   • Lockout
   • Screen-locks
   • GPS
   • Application control
   • Storage segmentation
   • Asset tracking
   • Inventory control
   • Mobile device management
   • Device access control
   • Removable storage
   • Disabling unused features
 • Application security
   • Key management
   • Credential management
   • Authentication
   • Geo-tagging
   • Encryption
   • Application whitelisting
   • Transitive trust/authentication
 • BYOD concerns
   • Data ownership
   • Support ownership
   • Patch management
   • Antivirus management
   • Forensics
   • Privacy
   • On-boarding/off-boarding
   • Adherence to corporate policies
   • User acceptance
   • Architecture/infrastructure considerations
   • Legal concerns
   • Acceptable use policy
   • On-board camera/video
	10
	10
	10
	10
	12
	13
	14
		Mobile Device Risks
		Securing Mobile Devices
		Mobile Device App Security
		BYOD Security
		Account Management
		Incident Response
		Reducing Risk Through Policies

4.3 Given a scenario, select the appropriate solution to establish host security. • Operating system security and settings • Anti-malware • Antivirus	4 4 4	Securing the Host Securing the Operating System Software Securing with Antimalware

A

Security+ Exam Objective Domain	Chapter	Section

• Anti-spam
• Anti-spyware
• Pop-up blockers
• Patch management
• White listing vs. black listing applications
• Trusted OS
• Host-based firewalls
• Host-based intrusion detection
• Hardware security
   • Cable locks
   • Safe
   • Locking cabinets
• Host software baselining
• Virtualization
   • Snapshots
   • Patch compatibility
   • Host availability/elasticity
   • Security control testing
   • Sandboxing
	7
	
	8
		Security Through Network Devices
		
		Securing Network Applications and Platforms

4.4 Implement the appropriate controls to ensure data security.
• Cloud storage
• SAN
• Handling Big Data
• Data encryption
   • Full disk
   • Database
   • Individual files
   • Removable media
   • Mobile devices
• Hardware based encryption devices
   • TPM
   • HSM
   • USB encryption
   • Hard drive
• Data in-transit, Data at-rest, Data in-use
• Permissions/ACL
• Data policies
   • Wiping
   • Disposing
   • Retention
   • Storage
	4
	5
	8
	8
	
	11
	
	14
		Securing Data
		Using Cryptography
		Common Network Protocols
		Securing Network Applications and Platforms
		Implementing Access Control
		Reducing Risk Through Policies

4.5 Compare and contrast alternative methods to mitigate security risks in static environments. • Environments • SCADA	4 4	Securing Static Environments Application Security

Security+ Exam Objective Domain	Chapter	Section

• Embedded (Printer, Smart TV, HVAC control)
• Android
• iOS
• Mainframe
• Game consoles
• In-vehicle computing systems
• Methods
  • Network segmentation
  • Security layers
  • Application firewalls
  • Manual updates
  • Firmware version control
  • Wrappers
  • Control redundancy and diversity		

5.0 Access Control and Identity Management		
5.1 Compare and contrast the function and purpose of authentication services. • RADIUS • TACACS+ • Kerberos • LDAP • XTACACS • SAML • Secure LDAP	11	Authentication Services

5.2 Given a scenario, select the appropriate authentication, authorization or access control.
• Identification vs. authentication vs. authorization
  • Authorization
  • Least privilege
  • Separation of duties
  • ACLs
  • Mandatory access
  • Discretionary access
  • Rule-based access control
  • Role-based access control
  • Time of day restrictions
• Authentication
  • Tokens
  • Common access card
  • Smart card
  • Multifactor authentication
  • TOTP
  • HOTP
  • CHAP
	9
	11
	11
	
	12
	12
	12
		Wireless Security Solutions
		What Is Access Control?
		Implementing Access Control
		Authentication Credentials
		Single Sign-On
		Account Management

Security+ Exam Objective Domain	Chapter	Section

• PAP
   • Single sign-on
   • Access control
   • Implicit deny
   • Trusted OS
• Authentication factors
   • Something you are
   • Something you have
   • Something you know
   • Somewhere you are
   • Something you do
• Identification
   • Biometrics
   • Personal identification verification card
   • Username
• Federation
• Transitive trust/authentication		

5.3 Install and configure security controls when performing account management, based on best practices.
• Mitigates issues associated with users with multiple account/roles or shared accounts
• Account policy enforcement
   • Credential management
   • Group policy
   • Password complexity
   • Expiration
   • Recovery
   • Disablement
   • Lockout
   • Password history
   • Password reuse
   • Password length
   • Generic account prohibition
• Group based privileges
• User assigned privileges
• User access reviews
• Continuous monitoring
	11
	
	12
		Implementing Access Control
		
		Account Management

6.0 Cryptography		
6.1 Given a scenario, utilize general cryptography concepts. • Symmetric vs. asymmetric • Session keys • In-band vs. out-of-band key exchange • Fundamental differences and encryption methods • Block vs. stream	5 5 6 6	Defining Cryptography Cryptographic Algorithms Digital Certificates Key Management

(*Continued*)

Security+ Exam Objective Domain	Chapter	Section
• Transport encryption • Non-repudiation • Hashing • Key escrow • Steganography • Digital signatures • Use of proven technologies • Elliptic curve and quantum cryptography • Ephemeral key • Perfect forward secrecy		

6.2 Given a scenario, use appropriate cryptographic methods.
• WEP vs. WPA/WPA2 and preshared key
• MD5
• SHA
• RIPEMD
• AES
• DES
• 3DES
• HMAC
• RSA
• Diffie-Hellman
• RC4
• One-time pads
• NTLM
• NTLMv2
• Blowfish
• PGP/GPG
• TwoFish
• DHE
• ECDHE
• CHAP
• PAP
• Comparative strengths and performance of algorithms
• Use of algorithms/protocols with transport encryption
   • SSL
   • TLS
   • IPSec
   • SSH
   • HTTPS
• Cipher suites
   • Strong vs. weak ciphers
• Key stretching
   • PBKDF2
   • Bcrypt
	5
	5
	6
	
	9
		Cryptographic Algorithms
		Using Cryptography
		Cryptographic Transport Protocols
		Wireless Security Solutions

A

Security+ Exam Objective Domain	Chapter	Section
6.3 Given a scenario, use appropriate PKI, certificate management, and associated components.	6	Digital Certificates
• Certificate authorities and digital certificates	6	Public Key Infrastructure (PKI)
• CA	6	Key Management
• CRLs		
• OCSP		
• CSR		
• PKI		
• Recovery agent		
• Public key		
• Private key		
• Registration		
• Key escrow		
• Trust models		

Downloads and Tools for Hands-On Projects

The location of content on the Internet may change without warning. If you are not able to access a program or tool through the URLs listed below, use a search engine to search for the text name of the resource.

- *www.privacyrights.org/data-breach*—Privacy Rights Clearinghouse (Project 1-1)
- *www.microsoft.com/security/scanner/en-us/default.asp*—Microsoft Safety Scanner (Project 1-2)
- *www.virtualbox.org*—Oracle VirtualBox (Project 1-3)
- *www.dreamspark.com*—Microsoft DreamSpark (Project 1-4)
- *www.irongeek.com/i.php?page=security/thumbscrew-software-usb-write-blocker*—Thumbscrew (Project 2-1)
- *support.kaspersky.com/viruses/disinfection/5350*—Kaspersky TDSSKiller (Project 2-2)
- *www.gmer.net*—GMER (Project 2-3)
- *www.spyrix.com*—Spyrix Personal Monitor (Project 2-4)
- *browsercheck.qualys.com*—Qualys BrowserCheck (Project 3-1)
- *www.grc.com/securable*—GRC SecurAble Hardware Support (Project 3-2)
- *www.httpdebugger.com/tools/ViewHttpHeaders.aspx*—MadeForNet HTTP Debugger (Project 3-6)
- *www.macromedia.com/support/documentation/en/flashplayer/help/settings_manager07.html*—Adobe Flash Player Website Storage Settings Panel (Project 3-7)
- *www.eicar.org/86-0-Intended-use.html*—EICAR AntiVirus Test File (Project 4-1)
- *www.virustotal.com*—VirusTotal (Project 4-4)
- *embeddedsw.net/OpenPuff_Steganography_Home.html*—OpenPuff (Project 5-1)
- *people.cs.pitt.edu/~kirk/cs1501/notes/rsademo/*—RSA Cipher Demonstration (Project 5-2)
- *md5deep.sourceforge.net*—MD5DEEP (Project 5-3)
- *implbits.com/Products/HashTab.aspx*—HashTab (Project 5-4)
- *www.truecrypt.org*—TrueCrypt (Project 5-6)

- *www.ssllabs.com/ssltest/index.html*—Qualys SSL Server Test (Project 6-1)
- *www.comodo.com/home/email-security/free-email-certificate.php*—Comodo Free Secure Email Certificate (Project 6-4)
- *www.threatfire.com/download*—ThreatFire (Project 7-2)
- *www1.k9webprotection.com*—K9 Web Protection (Project 7-3)
- *www.sandboxie.com*—Sandboxie (Project 8-1)
- *www.vmware.com/products/converter/*—VMware vCenter Converter (Project 8-2)
- *my.vmware.com/web/vmware/downloads*—VMware Player (Project 8-3)
- *www.mibdepot.com*—MIB Depot (Project 8-4)
- *www.vistumbler.net*—Vistumbler (Project 9-1)
- *www.klcconsulting.net/smac*—KLC Consulting SMAC (Project 9-2)
- *support.dlink.com/emulators/dap1522/*—D-Link Emulator 1522 (Project 9-4)
- *www.qrstuff.com*—QR Stuff (Project 10-1)
- *preyproject.com*—Prey Project (Project 10-2)
- *www.bluestacks.com*—BlueStacks Android Emulator (Project 10-3)
- *www.fileformat.info/tool/hash.htm*—FileFormat (Project 12-1)
- *www.epaymentbiometrics.ensicaen.fr/index.php/app/resources/65*—GreyC-Keystroke Software (Project 12-2)
- *keepass.info*—KeePass (Project 12-3)
- *www.passfaces.com/demo*—Passfaces (Project 12-4)
- *pip.verisignlabs.com*—VeriSign Labs Personal Identity Provider OpenID (Project 12-5)
- *www.livejournal.com/openid*—LiveJournal OpenID (Project 12-6)
- *www.macrium.com*—Macrium Reflect (Project 13-1)
- *www.briggsoft.com*—Directory Snoop (Project 13-4)
- *www.annualcreditreport.com*—Annual Credit Report (Project 14-1)
- *www.mass.gov/ethics*—Massachusetts State Ethics Commission training (Project 14-2)
- *www.ncsl.org/?TabId=15349*—Online ethics training (Project 14-2)
- *www.healthit.gov/providers-professionals/privacy-security-training-games*—HealthIT.gov privacy and security training games (Project 14-3)
- *www.ethics.org/resource/values-word-search-puzzle*—Ethics Resource Center (Project 14-4)
- *secunia.com/vulnerability_scanning/personal*—Secunia Personal Software Inspector (Project 15-1)
- *www.honeydocs.com*—HoneyDocs (Project 15-2)
- *www.grc.com*—ShieldsUP! (Project 15-3)
- *nmap.org/download.html*—Nmap (Project 15-4)

Security Websites

A wealth of security information is available on the Internet in a variety of forms. A sample listing of some of these sites is provided below.

The location of content on the Internet may change without warning. If the URLs below no longer function, open a search engine and search for the item(s) or website(s).

Security Organizations

- *Computer Emergency Response Team Coordination Center (CERT/CC)*—The CERT/CC is part of a federally funded research and development center at Carnegie Mellon University's Software Engineering Institute in Pittsburgh, Pennsylvania. It was created in 1988 to coordinate communication among experts during security emergencies and also to help provide information to prevent future attacks. In addition to responding to security incidents and analyzing vulnerabilities in applications, CERT also develops and promotes secure systems, organizational security, coordinated response systems, and education and training. The CERT website is *www.cert.org*.

- *Institute for Security, Technology, and Society (ISTS)*—Located at Dartmouth College in Hanover, New Hampshire, the ISTS focuses on pursuing research and education for cybersecurity in order to advance information security and privacy. Its website is *www.ists.dartmouth.edu*.

- *Forum of Incident Response and Security Teams (FIRST)*—FIRST is an international security organization composed of more than 170 incident response teams from educational institutions, governments, and business. FIRST's goal is to both prevent and quickly respond to local and international security incidents as well as promote information sharing. Its website is *www.first.org*.

- *SysAdmin, Audit, Network, Security (SANS) Institute*—SANS provides information, training, research, and other resources for security professionals. The SANS Institute website is *www.sans.org*.

- *InfraGard*—The goal of InfraGard is to improve and extend information sharing between private industry and the FBI when dealing with critical national infrastructures. InfraGard provides both formal as well as information channels for exchanging information. Its URL is *www.infragard.net.*

- *Information Systems Security Association (ISSA)*—The ISSA is an international organization of security professionals and practitioners that provides research and education regarding computer security. The ISSA also sponsors advanced security certification programs. Its website is *www.issa.org.*

- *National Security Institute (NSI)*—The NSI provides information about a variety of security vulnerabilities and threats. The website is *www.nsi.org.*

- *Computer Security Resource Center (CSRC)*—The CSRC site is maintained by the National Institute of Standards and Technology and provides guidelines and assistance as security relates to the economic and national security interests of the U.S. The site is located at *csrc.nist.gov.*

- *Common Vulnerabilities and Exposures (CVE)*—Located at *cve.mitre.org*, this site is a dictionary of reported information security vulnerabilities.

Vendor Security Websites

- *McAfee Threat Center*—The Threat Center site provides information about the severity of known global security threats and how they impact the Internet, small office/ home office (SOHO) organizations, and home users' systems. The location of the McAfee Threat Center site is *www.mcafee.com/us/threat-center.aspx.*

- *Microsoft Malware Protection Center*—The Microsoft Malware Protection Center provides a list of the latest desktop threats to Windows computers, the most common adware and spyware, and analysis of these threats. It also contains a searchable encyclopedia of security issues along with tools and other resources. The Microsoft Malware Protection Center is at *www.microsoft.com/security/portal/mmpc/default.aspx.*

- *Norton Security Center*—Operated by Symantec, the Norton Security Center site provides information on active new threats. The website is *us.norton.com/security-center/.*

- *IBM X-Force*—Located at www-935.ibm.com/services/us/iss/xforce, the IBM X-Force Security Research site covers Internet threats and gives information regarding how to respond to these threats.

Threat Analysis

- *SecurityFocus*—SecurityFocus is a technical community for security researchers, developers, and users. It is located online at *www.securityfocus.com/archive/1.*

- *Active Threat Level Analysis System (ATLAS)*—ATLAS is a global threat analysis network maintained by Arbor Networks. Arbor collects and analyzes data that travels through a closed private network of computers used for file sharing known as "darknets." Typically used by attackers, this traffic analysis can be used to identify the latest malware, phishing threats, and botnets and quickly alert users to new types of attacks. The website is *atlas.arbor.net*.

- *Secunia*—Secunia contains information regarding security vulnerabilities, advisories, viruses, and online vulnerability tests. The website is *secunia.com*.

Standards Organizations and Regulatory Agencies

- *Institute of Electrical and Electronics Engineers (IEEE)*—The IEEE website contains a wealth of information about the current activities of working groups and task groups along with the technical IEEE 802 standards that can be freely downloaded. The web address is *www.ieee.org*.

- *Wi-Fi Alliance*—The Wi-Fi Alliance organization has information on Wi-Fi standards, locating a hot spot, as well as technical papers on wireless transmissions and other material. The URL is *www.wi-fi.org*.

- *Federal Communications Commission (FCC)*—Information regarding FCC proposed actions, strategic goals, and consumer issues that relate to wireless transmissions can be found at *www.fcc.gov*.

Laws Protecting Private Information

- *Health Insurance Portability and Accountability Act of 1996 (HIPAA)*—Under HIPAA, healthcare enterprises must guard protected health information and implement policies and procedures to safeguard it, whether it be in paper or electronic format. The official government HIPAA website is *www.hhs.gov/ocr/privacy*.

- *Sarbanes-Oxley Act of 2002 (Sarbox)*—Passed as a reaction to a rash of corporate fraud, Sarbox is an attempt to fight corporate corruption. The act covers the corporate officers, auditors, and attorneys of publicly traded companies. Stringent reporting requirements and internal controls on electronic financial reporting systems are required. Information regarding Sarbox can be obtained at *www.sec.gov/spotlight/sarbanes-oxley.htm*.

- *Gramm-Leach-Bliley Act (GLBA)*—This act, like HIPAA, protects private data. GLBA requires banks and financial institutions to alert customers of their policies and practices in disclosing customer information. All personally identifiable financial information in both paper and electronic formats must be protected. The Cornell University Law School maintains information on GLBA at *www.law.cornell.edu/uscode/text/15/chapter-94/subchapter-I*.

- *USA PATRIOT Act (2001)*—Passed shortly after the terrorist attack of 2001, the USA PATRIOT Act is designed to broaden the surveillance of law enforcement agencies so they can detect and suppress terrorism. Businesses, organizations, and colleges must provide information, including records and documents, to law enforcement agencies under the authority of a valid court order, subpoena, or other authorized agency. The URL for the USA PATRIOT Act is *www.fincen.gov/statutes_regs/patriot/index.html*.

Blogs

- *Windows Security Blog*—This is a blog from Microsoft that covers Windows security vulnerabilities and defenses that can be found at *blogs.windows.com/windows/b/ windowssecurity/*.

- *Apple Security Blog*—The official Apple security blog is at *support.apple.com/kb/ HT1222*.

- *Google Online Security Blog*—This blog from Google covers the latest news items and tips from Google about safely using the Internet. The URL is *googleonlinesecurity. blogspot.com*.

- *Krebs On Security*—Renowned security researcher Brian Krebs maintains a blog at *krebsonsecurity.com*.

- *Microsoft Security Blog*—The security blog by different Microsoft employees contains information about security as it relates to Microsoft. The URL is *blogs.technet.com/ security*.

- *Trend Micro Blog*—The Trend Micro Simply Security blog provides information on the latest attacks and defenses. It can be found at *blog.trendmicro.com*.

- *Mark Russinovich's Technical Blog*—Mark Russinovich is a widely recognized expert in Windows operating system security as well as operating system internals, operating system architecture, and design. The blog is at *blogs.technet.com/b/markrussinovich/*.

- *Schneier on Security*—Bruce Schneier is a well-respected security researcher. His blog is at *www.schneier.com/blog*.

- *Security Research and Defense Blog*—The Microsoft Security Research and Defense blog covers Microsoft vulnerabilities, defenses, and current attacks. It is located at *blogs.technet.com/b/srd/*.

- *SANS Securing the Human Blog*—Hosted by the SANS Institute, this blog can be found at *www.securingthehuman.org/blog*.

- *Microsoft Security Guidance Blog*—This blog contains information regarding advanced security solutions and attacks. It can be found at *blogs.technet.com/b/ secguide/*.

- *Kaspersky Lab Blog*—Maintained by the Kaspersky Lab antivirus software company, this blog is at *www.securelist.com/en/weblog*.

- *VeriSign Blog*—This blog by VeriSign covers topics such as browsers, SSL, malware, and phishing. The URL of the blog is *blogs.verisigninc.com*.

- *Dan Kaminsky's Blog*—Dan Kaminsky is best known as a researcher who uncovers security vulnerabilities within protocols. His blog is at *dankaminsky.com*.

- *Cisco Security Blog*—This blog addresses security from a Cisco perspective. The address is *blogs.cisco.com/security*.

- *FireEye Blog*- This blog, at *www.fireeye.com/blog, looks at threat research and mitigation.*

- *Zscaler Research Security Blog*—The Zscaler security blog covers Internet attacks and defenses. The address is *research.zscaler.com*.

Selected TCP/IP Ports and Their Threats

Although Internet Protocol (IP) addresses are the primary form of address identification on a TCP/IP network and are used to uniquely identify each network device, another level of identification involves the applications that are being accessed through the TCP/IP transmission. Most communication in TCP/IP involves the exchange of information between a program running on one device (a process) and the same or a corresponding process running on another device. It is common to have multiple programs running simultaneously. TCP/IP uses a numeric value as an identifier to applications and services on the systems. These are known as the port number. Each packet contains not only the source and destination IP addresses but also the source port and destination port, which identifies both the originating service on the source system and the corresponding service on the receiving computer.

Because port numbers are 16 bits in length, they can have a decimal value from 0 to 65535. TCP/IP divides port numbers into three categories: the Well Known Ports, the Registered Ports, and the Private Ports. The Well Known Ports are those from 0 through 1023. Ports 255 and below are assigned to public applications such as SMTP, while ports 256–1023 are assigned to companies to identify their network application products. Registered Ports are those from 1024 through 49151, and Private Ports are those from 49152 through 65535. Ports above 1024 are assigned dynamically by the end-user applications that are using the network application. Attackers use port scanners to locate open ports and launch attacks.

A list of all well-known and registered TCP/IP port numbers can be found at *www.iana.org/assignments/port-numbers.*

Table D-1 lists some common TCP ports and their security vulnerability.

Port number	Service	Description	Security risk
0	Commonly used to help determine the operating system	Port 0 is considered invalid and generates a different response from a closed port.	High—Provides attacker knowledge of the OS being used
7	echo	An outdated service that echoes whatever is sent to it	High—Often used in DoS attacks

Table D-1 Select TCP ports (*continues*)

Port number	Service	Description	Security risk
11	sysstat	UNIX service that lists all the running processes on a machine and who started them	Very High
19	chargen	Service that simply displays characters. The UDP version responds with a packet containing garbage characters whenever a UDP packet is received. On a TCP connection, it displays a stream of garbage characters until the connection is closed.	High—Often used in DoS attacks
20	FTP data	File Transfer Protocol	Low
21	FTP	File Transfer Protocol	Very High—Attackers look for open anonymous FTP servers, those with directories that can be written to and read from
22	SSH	Secure Shell (SSH)	Low
23	Telnet	Remote communications	Moderate—Attackers scan for this port to find out what operating system is being used
25	SMTP	Simple Mail Transfer Protocol	Moderate—Attackers are looking for systems to relay spam
53	DNS	Domain Name Service	Moderate—Attackers may attempt to spoof DNS (UDP) or hide other traffic since port 53 is sometimes not filtered or logged by firewalls
67	BOOTP	A network protocol used by a client to obtain an IP address	Low
68	DHCP	Dynamic Host Configuration Protocol	Low
69	tftp	Trivial file transfer protocol	Very High
79	finger	Provides system information	Moderate—Attackers use to determine system information
80	WWW	HTTP standard port	Low
98	linuxconf	Provides administration of Linux servers	High
110	POP3	Used by clients accessing email on servers	Low
113	identd auth	Identifies use of TCP connection	Moderate—Can give attacker information about system

Table D-1 Select TCP ports (*continues*)

Port number	Service	Description	Security risk
119	NNTP	Network News Transfer Protocol	Low—Attackers are looking for open news servers
139	NetBIOS File and Print Sharing	n/a	Low
143	IMAP4	Used by clients accessing email on servers	Low
161	SNMP	Simple Network Management Protocol is used in routers and switches to monitor network.	Low
177	xdmcp	X Display Management Control Protocol for remote connections to X servers	Low
443	HTTPS	Secure WWW protocol	Low
465	SMTP over SSL	n/a	Low
513	rwho	Remote login (rlogin)	High
993	IMAP over SSL	n/a	Low
1024	N/A	The first port number in the dynamic range of ports. Many applications do not specify a port to use for a network connection, but request the next freely available port, which starts with 1024. This means the first application on your system that requests a dynamic port is assigned port 1024.	Low
1080	SOCKS	This protocol tunnels traffic through firewalls, allowing many people behind the firewall to access the Internet through a single IP address.	Very High—In theory, this protocol should only tunnel inside traffic out toward the Internet. However, it is frequently misconfigured and allows attackers to tunnel their attacks into the network.
1433	MS SQL server port	Used by Microsoft Sequel Server	Moderate
6970	RealAudio	Clients receive incoming audio streams from servers on UDP ports in the range 6970–7170. This is set up by the outgoing control connection on TCP port 7070.	Moderate
31337	Back Orifice	n/a	High—Common port for installing Trojans

Table D-1 Select TCP ports

Information Security Community Site

community.cengage.com/infosec

The Information Security Community Site is an online community and information security course enrichment site sponsored by Cengage Learning. It contains a wide variety of tools, information, discussion boards, and other features to assist learners. It contains information that helps users delve more deeply into the world of security as well as interact with other users and security professionals from around the world. And best of all, it's free!

Several kinds of useful material can be found on the Information Security Community Site:

- *Author blog.* You can read blogs from Mark Ciampa, author of *Security+ Guide to Network Security Fundamentals, Fifth Edition*, about the latest trends in information security. New blogs are posted several times each week and contain some of the latest information on attacks, defenses, and developments in the information security community.

- *Security video feed.* Short (1–2 minute) videos of the latest daily information on technology and information security are available.

- *Articles/media.* Additional material is available that supports this textbook. This includes in-depth coverage of security topics, additional assignments, tips on landing a job in information security, lecture videos on chapter material, and more.

- *Author discussion boards.* Have you ever wished you could ask the author of the textbook a question and receive a reply? Here's your chance. There are several discussion boards available in which learners can post questions for the authors of different Cengage Learning security textbooks and have them answered in a timely fashion.

- *Case projects discussion boards.* Each chapter of *Security+ Guide to Network Security Fundamentals, Fifth Edition*, contains a case project that learners read and respond to on the Case Projects Discussion Board. Learners can gain valuable insights from reading the postings from other learners as well as from security experts. Here's the chance to have an online discussion with learners just like you from around the world!

- *Instructor resources.* Links to additional instructor resources for *Security+ Guide to Network Security Fundamentals, Fifth Edition*, are also available.

Table E-1 summarizes many of these features and the benefits to students. To access these features, you must register and join the community as described below the table.

Feature	Description	Use	Benefit to students
One-page articles	4–5 additional articles per chapter on updated information in security or expanded coverage of selected topics	Can be used as additional reading assignments	Helps students explore a security subject more deeply
Chapter lecture video	Approximately 1-hour video lecture on the chapter	Useful for students who miss the lecture on that chapter, or as supplemental lectures, or for online courses that do not have a classroom lecture	Students do not miss content if absent from lecture; can also provide another perspective or explanation to a topic
Demonstration video on a chapter Hands-On Project	5-minute video shows how a project will be conducted	Students can watch prior to performing the actual Hands-On Project by themselves	Will help students see how it's done before they attempt it using the step-by-step instructions in the textbook; also shows additional functions of software not illustrated in textbook
Online labs	Additional Hands-On Project labs in textual form	Can be used as additional extra-credit labs	More hands-on activities to learn security skills
Author's blog	Short posting of current news event 2–3 times per week	Can be used as classroom "openers" to start the classroom lecture discussion	Helps students see the daily challenges of security

Table E-1 Information Security Community Site features

It's easy to get started. Go to *community.cengage.com/infosec*. Click JOIN THE COMMUNITY. On the Register and Join our Community page, enter the requested information. Then visit the Information Security Community Site regularly for the latest information.

Remember, stay secure!

Glossary

Acceptable Use Policy (AUP) A policy that defines the actions users may perform while accessing systems and networking equipment.

acceptance Acknowledging a risk but taking no action to address it.

access control The mechanism used in an information system for granting or denying approval to use specific resources.

access control list (ACL) A set of permissions that is attached to an object.

access control model A predefined framework found in hardware and software that a custodian can use for controlling access.

access list A paper or electronic record of individuals who have permission to enter a secure area, the time that they entered, and the time they left the area.

access log A log that can provide details regarding requests for specific files on a system.

account expiration The process of setting a user's account to expire.

accounting The ability that provides tracking of events.

ActiveX A set of rules for how applications under the Microsoft Windows operating system should share information.

ActiveX control A specific way of implementing ActiveX that runs through the web browser and functions like a miniature application.

activity phase controls Subtypes of security controls, classified as deterrent, preventive, detective, compensation, or corrective.

add-ons Program that provides additional functionality to web browsers. Also called *extension*.

Address Resolution Protocol (ARP) Part of the TCP/IP protocol for determining the MAC address based on the IP address.

administrative control Process for developing and ensuring that policies and procedures are carried out, specifying actions that users may do, must do, or cannot do.

Advanced Encryption Standard (AES) A symmetric cipher that was approved by the NIST in late 2000 as a replacement for DES.

Advanced Persistent Threat (APT) Multiyear intrusion campaign that targets highly sensitive economic, proprietary, or national security information.

adware A software program that delivers advertising content in a manner that is unexpected and unwanted by the user.

alarm An audible sound to warn a guard of an intruder.

algorithm Procedures based on a mathematical formula used to encrypt and decrypt data.

Android The Google operating system for mobile devices that is not proprietary.

Annualized Loss Expectancy (ALE) The expected monetary loss that can be anticipated for an asset due to a risk over a one-year period.

Annualized Rate of Occurrence (ARO) The likelihood of a risk occurring within a year.

anomaly-based monitoring A monitoring technique used by an intrusion detection system (IDS) that creates a baseline of normal activities and compares actions against the baseline. Whenever there is a significant deviation from this baseline, an alarm is raised.

antispyware Software that helps prevent computers from becoming infected by different types of spyware.

antivirus (AV) Software that can examine a computer for any infections as well as monitor computer activity and scan new documents that might contain a virus.

application control See *mobile application management (MAM)*.

application-aware firewall A firewall that can identify the applications that send packets through the firewall and then make decisions about the applications.

application-aware IDS A specialized intrusion detection system (IDS) that is capable of using "contextual knowledge" in real time.

application-aware IPS An intrusion prevention system (IPS) that knows information such as the applications that are running as well as the underlying operating systems.

application-aware proxy A special proxy server that knows the application protocols that it supports.

arbitrary/remote code execution An attack that allows an attacker to run programs and execute commands on a different computer.

architectural design In software development, the process of defining a collection of hardware and software components along with their interfaces in order to create the framework for software development.

armored virus A virus that goes to great lengths in order to avoid detection.

ARP poisoning An attack that corrupts the ARP cache.

asset An item that has value.

asset tracking Maintaining an accurate record of company-owned mobile devices.

asymmetric cryptographic algorithms Cryptography that uses two mathematically related keys.

attachment A file that is coupled to an email message and often carries malware.

attack surface The code that can be executed by unauthorized users in a software program.

audit log A log that is used to record which user performed an action and what that action was.

authentication Proving that a user is genuine, and not an imposter.

authentication factors Five elements that can prove the genuineness of a user: what you know, what you have, what you are, what you do, and where you are.

authorization The act of providing permission or approval to technology resources.

availability Security actions that ensure that data is accessible to authorized users.

backdoor Software code that gives access to a program or a service that circumvents normal security protections.

banner grabbing Gathering information from messages that a service transmits when another program connects to it.

barricade A structure designed to block the passage of traffic.

baseline reporting A comparison of the present state of a system to its baseline.

Bayesian filtering Spam filtering software that analyzes every word in an email and determines how frequently a word occurs in order to determine if it is spam.

bcrypt A popular key stretching password hash algorithm.

behavior-based monitoring A monitoring technique used by an IDS that uses the normal processes and actions as the standard and compares actions against it.

behavioral biometrics Authenticating a user by the unique actions that the user performs.

Big Data A collection of data sets so large and complex that it becomes difficult to process using on-hand database management tools or traditional data processing applications.

birthday attack An attack that searches for any two digests that are the same.

black box A penetration test in which the tester has no prior knowledge of the network infrastructure that is being tested.

blacklist Permitting everything unless it appears on the list; a list of nonapproved senders.

Blanket Purchase Agreement (BPA) A prearranged purchase or sale agreement between a government agency and a business.

block cipher A cipher that manipulates an entire block of plaintext at one time.

Blowfish A block cipher that operates on 64-bit blocks and can have a key length from 32 to 448 bits.

bluejacking An attack that sends unsolicited messages to Bluetooth-enabled devices.

bluesnarfing An attack that accesses unauthorized information from a wireless device through a Bluetooth connection.

Bluetooth A wireless technology that uses short-range radio frequency (RF) transmissions and provides rapid ad hoc device pairings.

bot herder An attacker who controls a botnet.

botnet A logical computer network of zombies under the control of an attacker.

bridge trust model A trust model with one CA that acts as a facilitator to interconnect all other CAs.

broker Attacker who sells knowledge of a vulnerability to other attackers or governments.

brute force attack A password attack in which every possible combination of letters, numbers, and characters is used to create encrypted passwords that are matched against those in a stolen password file.

buffer overflow attack An attack that occurs when a process attempts to store data in RAM beyond the boundaries of a fixed-length storage buffer.

business continuity The ability of an organization to maintain its operations and services in the face of a disruptive event.

business continuity planning and testing The process of identifying exposure to threats, creating preventive and recovery procedures, and then testing them to determine if they are sufficient.

business impact analysis (BIA) An analysis that identifies mission-critical business functions and quantifies the impact a loss of such functions may have on the organization in terms of its operational and financial position.

BYOD (bring your own device) The practice of allowing users to use their own personal devices to connect to an organizational network.

cable lock A device that can be inserted into the security slot of a portable device and rotated so that the cable lock is secured to the device to prevent it from being stolen.

California's Database Security Breach Notification Act The first state electronic privacy law, which covers any state agency, person, or company that does business in California.

captive portal AP An infrastructure that is used on public access WLANs to provide a higher degree of security.

Certificate Authority (CA) A trusted third-party agency that is responsible for issuing digital certificates.

Certificate Repository (CR) A publicly accessible centralized directory of digital certificates that can be used to view the status of a digital certificate.

Certificate Revocation List (CRL) A repository that lists revoked digital certificates.

Certificate Signing Request (CSR) A specially formatted encrypted message that validates the information the CA requires to issue a digital certificate

chain of custody A process of documentation that shows that the evidence was under strict control at all times and no unauthorized individuals were given the opportunity to corrupt the evidence.

Challenge-Handshake Authentication Protocol (CHAP) A weak authentication protocol that has been replaced by the Extensible Authentication Protocol (EAP).

change management A methodology for making modifications to a system and keeping track of those changes.

cipher suite A named combination of the encryption, authentication, and message authentication code (MAC) algorithms that are used with SSL and TLS.

ciphertext Data that has been encrypted.

cleartext Unencrypted data.

client-side attacks An attack that targets vulnerabilities in client applications that interact with a compromised server or process malicious data.

client-side validation Having the client web browser perform all validations and error recovery procedures.

closed circuit television (CCTV) Video cameras and receivers used for surveillance in areas that require security monitoring.

cloud computing A pay-per-use computing model in which customers pay only for the online computing resources that they need, and the resources can be easily scaled.

cloud storage A cloud system that has no computational capabilities but provides remote file storage.

clustering Combining two or more servers to appear as one single unit.

code review In software development, presenting the code to multiple reviewers in order to reach agreement about its security.

cognitive biometrics Authenticating a user through the perception, thought process, and understanding of the user.

cold site A remote site that provides office space; the customer must provide and install all the equipment needed to continue operations.

command and control (C&C or C2) The structure by which a bot herder gives instructions to zombies in a botnet.

command injection Injecting and executing commands to execute on a server.

common access card (CAC) A U.S. Department of Defense (DoD) smart card used for identification of active-duty and reserve military personnel along with civilian employees and special contractors.

community cloud A cloud that is open only to specific organizations that have common concerns.

compensating controls Control that provides an alternative to normal controls that for some reason cannot be used.

computer forensics Using technology to search for computer evidence of a crime.

computer virus (virus) Malicious computer code that, like its biological counterpart, reproduces itself on the same computer.

confidentiality Security actions that ensure that only authorized parties can view the information.

content inspection Searching incoming web content to match keywords.

continuity of operations The ability of a business to continue to function in the event of a disaster.

cookie A file on a local computer in which a web server stores user-specific information.

corrective controls Control that is intended to mitigate or lessen the damage caused by an incident.

Counter Mode with Cipher Block Chaining Message Authentication Code Protocol (CCMP) The encryption protocol used for WPA2 that specifies the use of a general-purpose cipher mode algorithm providing data privacy with AES.

credential management A secure repository for storing valuable authentication information on a mobile device.

credentialed vulnerability scan A scan that provides credentials (username and password) to the scanner so that tests for additional internal vulnerabilities can be performed.

cross-site request forgery (XSRF) An attack that uses the user's web browser settings to impersonate the user.

cross-site scripting (XSS) An attack that injects scripts into a web application server to direct attacks at clients.

cryptography The science of transforming information into a secure form so that unauthorized persons cannot access it.

Cyber Kill Chain® A systematic outline of the steps of a cyberattack, introduced at Lockheed Martin in 2011.

cybercrime Targeted attacks against financial networks, unauthorized access to information, and the theft of personal information.

cybercriminals A network of attackers, identity thieves, spammers, and financial fraudsters.

cyberterrorism A premeditated, politically motivated attack against information, computer systems, computer programs, and data, which often results in violence.

cyberterrorist Attacker whose motivation may be defined as ideological, or attacking for the sake of principles or beliefs.

data at-rest Data that is stored on electronic media.

data backup The process of copying information to a different medium and storing it (preferably at an offsite location) so that it can be used in the event of a disaster.

Data Encryption Standard (DES) A symmetric block cipher that uses a 56-bit key and encrypts data in 64-bit blocks.

data in-transit Data that is in transit across a network, such as an email sent across the Internet.

data in-use A state of data in which actions upon it are being performed by "endpoint devices" such as printers.

data loss prevention (DLP) A system that can identify critical data, monitor how it is being accessed, and protect it from unauthorized users.

data policy A security policy that addresses the different aspects of how data should be handled within an organization.

data retention policy A security policy that outlines how long to maintain information in the user's possession.

data storage policy A set of procedures designed to control and manage data within the organization by specifying data collection and storage.

data wiping and disposing policy A security policy that addresses how and when data will ultimately be erased.

deadbolt lock A door lock that extends a solid metal bar into the door frame for extra security.

decryption The process of changing ciphertext into plaintext.

defense in depth A defense that uses multiple types of security devices to protect a network. Also called *layered security*.

demilitarized zone (DMZ) A separate network that rests outside the secure network perimeter: untrusted outside users can access the DMZ but cannot enter the secure network.

denial of service (DoS) An attack that attempts to prevent a system from performing its normal functions by overwhelming the system with requests.

design review An analysis of the design of a software program by key personnel from different levels of the project.

detective control A control that is designed to identify any threat that has reached the system.

deterrence Understanding the attacker and then informing him of the consequences of the action.

deterrent control A control that attempts to discourage security violations before they occur.

dictionary attack A password attack that creates encrypted versions of common dictionary words and compares them against those in a stolen password file.

Diffie-Hellman (DH) A key exchange that requires all parties to agree upon a large prime number and related integer so that the same key can be separately created.

Diffie-Hellman Ephemeral (DHE) A Diffie-Hellman key exchange that uses different keys.

digest The unique digital fingerprint created by a one-way hash algorithm.

digital certificate A technology used to associate a user's identity to a public key, in which the user's public key is digitally signed by a trusted third party.

digital signature An electronic verification of the sender.

direct trust A type of trust model in which a relationship exists between two individuals because one person knows the other person.

directory traversal An attack that takes advantage of a vulnerability so that a user can move from the root directory to restricted directories.

disabling unused interfaces A security technique to turn off ports on a network device that are not required.

disaster recovery plan (DRP) A written document that details the process for restoring IT resources following an event that causes a significant disruption in service.

Discretionary Access Control (DAC) The least restrictive access control model in which the owner of the object has total control over it.

distributed denial of service (DDoS) An attack that uses many computers to perform a DoS attack.

distributed trust model A trust model that has multiple CAs that sign digital certificates.

DNS poisoning An attack that substitutes DNS addresses so that the computer is automatically redirected to an attacker's device.

Domain Name System (DNS) A hierarchical name system for translating domain names to IP addresses.

dumpster diving The act of digging through trash receptacles to find information that can be useful in an attack.

elliptic curve cryptography (ECC) An algorithm that uses elliptic curves instead of prime numbers to compute keys.

Elliptic Curve Diffie–Hellman (ECDH) A Diffie-Hellman key exchange that uses elliptic curve cryptography instead of prime numbers in its computation.

embedded system A computer system with a dedicated function within a larger electrical or mechanical system.

encryption The process of changing plaintext into ciphertext.

ephemeral keys A temporary key that is used only once before it is discarded.

errors Faults in a program that occur while the application is running. Also called *exceptions*.

event log Log that documents any unsuccessful events and the most significant successful events.

evil twin An access point (AP) set up by an attacker to mimic an authorized AP and capture transmissions, so a user's device will unknowingly connect to this evil twin instead of the authorized AP.

exceptions See *errors*.

exploit kits Automated attack package that can be used without an advanced knowledge of computers.

Extended TACACS (XTACACS) The second version of the Terminal Access Control Access Control System (TACACS) authentication service.

Extensible Authentication Protocol (EAP) A framework for transporting authentication protocols that defines the format of the messages.

extensions Another name for *add-on*.

false negative An event that does not appear to be a risk but actually turns out to be one.

false positive An event that in the beginning is considered to be a risk yet turns out to not be one.

Faraday cage A metallic enclosure that prevents the entry or escape of an electromagnetic field.

federated identity management (FIM or federation) Single sign-on for networks owned by different organizations.

fencing Securing a restricted area by erecting a barrier.

Fibre Channel (FC) A high-speed storage network protocol that can transmit up to 16 gigabits per second.

Fibre Channel over Ethernet (FCoE) A high-speed storage network protocol that encapsulates Fibre Channel frames over Ethernet networks.

File Transfer Protocol (FTP) An unsecure TCP/IP protocol that is commonly used for transferring files.

firewall Hardware or software that is designed to prevent malicious packets from entering or leaving computers. Also called *packet filter*.

firewall rules A set of individual instructions to control the actions of a firewall.

first-party cookie A cookie that is created from the website currently being viewed.

Flash cookie Another name for *locally shared object (LSO)*.

flood guard A feature that controls a device's tolerance for unanswered service requests and helps to prevent a DoS or DDoS attack.

forensics (forensic science) The application of science to questions that are of interest to the legal profession.

FTP Secure (FTPS) A TCP/IP protocol that uses Secure Sockets Layer or Transport Layer Security to encrypt commands sent over the control port (port 21) in an FTP session.

fuzz testing (fuzzing) A software testing technique that deliberately provides invalid, unexpected, or random data as inputs to a computer program.

geo-fencing Using a mobile device's GPS to define geographical boundaries where an app can be used.

geo-tagging Adding or allowing geographical identification data in a mobile app.

geolocation The identification of the location of a person or object using technology.

GNU Privacy Guard (GPG) Free and open-source software that is commonly used to encrypt and decrypt data.

Gramm-Leach-Bliley Act (GLBA) A U.S. law that requires banks and financial institutions to alert customers of their policies and practices in disclosing customer information.

gray box A penetration test where some limited information has been provided to the tester.

Group Policy A Microsoft Windows feature that provides centralized management and configuration of computers and remote users.

guard A human who is an active security element.

hactivist Attacker who attacks for ideological reasons that are generally not as well-defined as a cyberterrorist's motivation.

hardening The process of eliminating as many security risks as possible to make the system more secure.

Hardware Security Module (HSM) A secure cryptographic processor.

hash An algorithm that creates a unique digital fingerprint.

Hashed Message Authentication Code (HMAC) A hash function that is applied to both the key and the message.

Health Insurance Portability and Accountability Act (HIPAA) A U.S. law designed to guard protected health information and implement policies and procedures to safeguard it.

heating, ventilation, and air conditioning (HVAC) Systems that provide and regulate heating and cooling.

heuristic monitoring A monitoring technique used by an intrusion detection system (IDS) that uses an algorithm to determine if a threat exists.

hierarchical trust model A trust model that has a single hierarchy with one master CA.

high availability A system that can function for an extended period of time with little downtime.

HMAC-based one-time password (HOTP) A one-time password that changes when a specific event occurs.

hoax A false warning designed to trick users into changing security settings on their computer.

honeynet A network set up with intentional vulnerabilities to invite attacks and reveal attackers' methods.

honeypot A computer typically located in an area with limited security and loaded with software and data files that appear to be authentic, but are actually imitations of real data files, to trick attackers into revealing their attack techniques.

host availability The ability to quickly make new virtual server machines available.

host elasticity The ability to easily expand or contract resources in a virtualized environment.

host table A list of the mappings of host names to IP addresses.

host virtualization A type of virtualization in which an entire operating system environment is simulated.

host-based application firewall A firewall that runs as a program on a local system.

host-based intrusion detection system (HIDS) A software-based application that runs on a local host computer that can detect an attack as it occurs.

hot aisle/cold aisle A layout in a data center that can be used to reduce heat by managing air flow.

hot site A duplicate of the production site that has all the equipment needed for an organization to continue running, including office space and furniture, telephone jacks, computer equipment, and a live telecommunications link.

hotfix Software that addresses a specific customer situation and often may not be distributed outside that customer's organization.

HTTP header Part of HTTP that is comprised of fields that contain the different characteristics of the data that is being transmitted.

HTTP header manipulation Modifying HTTP headers to create an attack.

hybrid attack A password attack that slightly alters dictionary words by adding numbers to the end of the password, spelling words backward, slightly misspelling words, or including special characters.

hybrid cloud A combination of public and private clouds.

Hypertext Transport Protocol Secure (HTTPS) A secure version of HTTP sent over SSL or TLS.

identity theft Stealing another person's personal information, such as a Social Security number, and then using the information to impersonate the victim, generally for financial gain.

IEEE 802.1x A standard that authenticates users on a per-switch port basis by permitting access to valid users but effectively disabling the port if authentication fails.

impersonation A social engineering attack that involves masquerading as a real or fictitious character and then playing out the role of that person on a victim.

implicit deny Rejecting access unless a condition is explicitly met.

in-band Exchanging secure information within normal communication channels.

incident management The "framework" and functions required to enable incident response and incident handling within an organization.

information security The tasks of protecting the integrity, confidentiality, and availability of information on the devices that store, manipulate, and transmit the information through products, people, and procedures.

Infrastructure as a Service (IaaS) A cloud computing model in which customers have the highest level of control and can deploy and run their own software.

initialization vector (IV) A 24-bit value used in WEP that changes each time a packet is encrypted.

input validation Verifying a user's input to an application.

insiders Employees, contractors, and business partners who can be responsible for an attack.

integer overflow attack An attack that is the result of an attacker changing the value of a variable to something outside the range that the programmer had intended.

integrity Security actions that ensure that the information is correct and no unauthorized person or malicious software has altered the data.

Interconnection Security Agreement (ISA) An agreement between parties intended to minimize security risks for data transmitted across a network.

Internet Control Message Protocol (ICMP) A TCP/IP protocol that is used by devices to communicate updates or error information to other devices.

Internet Protocol Security (IPsec) A set of protocols developed to support the secure exchange of packets between hosts or networks.

Internet Protocol version 6 (IPv6) The next generation of the IP protocol that addresses weaknesses of IPv4 and provides several significant improvements.

interoperability agreement An agreement through which parties in a relationship can reach an understanding of their relationships and responsibilities.

intrusion detection system (IDS) A device that detects an attack as it occurs.

intrusive vulnerability scan A scan that attempts to penetrate the system in order to perform a simulated attack.

inventory control The operation of stockrooms where mobile devices are stored prior to their dispersal.

iOS The operating system for Apple mobile devices that is a closed and proprietary architecture.

IP telephony Using a data-based IP network to add digital voice clients and new voice applications onto the IP network.

iSCSI (Internet Small Computer System Interface) An IP-based storage networking standard for linking data storage facilities.

IT contingency planning The process of developing an outline of procedures to be followed in the event of a major IT incident or an incident that directly impacts IT.

job rotation The act of moving individuals from one job responsibility to another.

Kerberos An authentication system developed by the Massachusetts Institute of Technology (MIT) and used to verify the identity of networked users.

key A mathematical value entered into a cryptographic algorithm to produce encrypted data.

key escrow A process in which keys are managed by a third party, such as a trusted CA.

key exchange The process of sending and receiving secure cryptographic keys.

key recovery agent (KRA) A highly trusted person responsible for recovering lost or damaged digital certificates.

key stretching A password hashing algorithm that requires significantly more time than standard hashing algorithms to create the digest.

keylogger Software or a hardware device that captures and stores each keystroke that a user types on the computer's keyboard.

layered security A defense that uses multiple types of security devices to protect a network. Also called *defense in depth*.

LDAP injection attack An attack that constructs LDAP statements based on user input statements, allowing the attacker to retrieve information from the LDAP database or modify its content.

least privilege Providing only the minimum amount of privileges necessary to perform a job or function.

lighting Lights that illuminate an area so that it can be viewed after dark.

Lightweight Directory Access Protocol (LDAP) A protocol for a client application to access an X.500 directory.

Lightweight EAP (LEAP) A proprietary EAP method developed by Cisco Systems requiring mutual authentication used for WLAN encryption using Cisco client software.

LM (LAN Manager) hash A cryptographic function found in older Microsoft Windows operating systems used to hash data.

load balancer A dedicated network device that can direct requests to different servers based on a variety of factors.

locally shared object (LSO) A cookie that is significantly different in size and location from regular cookies, and can store more complex data. Also called *Flash cookie*.

location services Services that can identify the location of a person carrying a mobile device or a specific store or restaurant.

lock screen A technology that prevents a mobile device from being used until the user enters the correct passcode.

locking cabinet A ruggedized steel box with a lock.

log A record of events that occur.

logic bomb Computer code that lies dormant until it is triggered by a specific logical event.

loop protection Technique to prevent broadcast storms by using the IEEE 802.1d standard spanning-tree algorithm (STA).

MAC limiting and filtering A security technique to limit the number of media access control (MAC) addresses allowed on a single port.

macro A series of instructions that can be grouped together as a single command, often used to automate a complex set of tasks or a repeated series of tasks.

macro virus A computer virus that is written in a script known as a macro.

mainframe A very large computing system that has significant processing capabilities.

malware Software that enters a computer system without the user's knowledge or consent and then performs an unwanted and usually harmful action.

malware inspection Searching for malware in incoming web content.

man-in-the-middle An attack that intercepts legitimate communication and forges a fictitious response to the sender.

management risk control type A type of risk control that is administrative and covers the laws, regulations, policies, practices, and guidelines that govern the overall requirements and controls.

Mandatory Access Control (MAC) The most restrictive access control model, typically found in military settings in which security is of supreme importance.

mandatory vacations Requiring that all employees take vacations.

mantrap A device that monitors and controls two interlocking doors to a small room (a vestibule), designed to separate secure and nonsecure areas.

mean time between failures (MTBF) A statistical value that is the average time until a component fails, cannot be repaired, and must be replaced.

mean time to failure (MTTF) The average amount of time expected until the first failure of a piece of equipment.

mean time to recovery (MTTR) The average time for a device to recover from a failure that is not a terminal failure.

Media Access Control (MAC) address filtering A method for controlling access to a WLAN based on the device's MAC address.

Memorandum of Understanding (MOU) An agreement between two or more parties to enable them to work together that is not legally enforceable but is more formal than an unwritten agreement.

Message Digest (MD) A common hash algorithm with several different versions.

Message Digest 5 (MD5) The current version of MD.

metamorphic malware Malware that rewrites its own code and thus appears different each time it is executed.

mitigation Addressing a risk by making it less serious.

mobile application management (MAM) The tools and services responsible for distributing and controlling access to apps. Also called *application control*.

mobile device management (MDM) Tools that allow a device to be managed remotely.

motion detection Determining an object's change in position in relation to its surroundings.

multifactor authentication Using more than one type of authentication credential.

near field communication (NFC) A set of standards primarily for smartphones and smart cards that can be used to establish communication between devices in close proximity.

NetBIOS (Network Basic Input/Output System) An older transport protocol used by Microsoft Windows systems for allowing applications on separate computers to communicate over a LAN.

network access control (NAC) A technique that examines the current state of a system or network device before it is allowed to connect to the network.

network address translation (NAT) A technique that allows private IP addresses to be used on the public Internet.

network intrusion detection system (NIDS) A technology that watches for attacks on the network and reports back to a central device.

network intrusion prevention system (NIPS) A technology that monitors network traffic to immediately react to block a malicious attack.

non-credentialed vulnerability scans A scan that does not use credentials (username and password) to conduct an internal vulnerability assessment.

non-intrusive vulnerability scan A scan that uses only available information to hypothesize the status of the vulnerability.

non-repudiation The process of proving that a user performed an action.

NoSQL A nonrelational database that is better tuned for accessing large data sets.

NoSQL databases vs. SQL databases An argument regarding which database technology is superior. Also called *SQL vs. NoSQL*.

NTLM (New Technology LAN Manager) hash A hash used by modern Microsoft Windows operating systems for creating password digests.

NTLMv2 The current version of the New Technology LAN Manager hash.

off-boarding The ability to quickly remove devices from the organization's network.

off-boarding business partners The termination of an agreement between parties.

oligomorphic malware Malware that changes its internal code to one of a set number of predefined mutations whenever it is executed.

on-boarding The ability to rapidly enroll new mobile devices.

on-boarding business partners The start-up relationship agreement between parties.

one-time pad (OTP) Combining plaintext with a random key to create ciphertext that cannot be broken mathematically.

one-time password (OTP) An authentication code that can be used only once or for a limited period of time.

Online Certificate Status Protocol (OCSP) A protocol that performs a real-time lookup of a certificate's status.

operational risk control type Risk control type that covers the operational procedures to limit risk.

order of volatility The sequence of volatile data that must be preserved in a computer forensic investigation.

OS hardening Tightening security during the design and coding of the OS.

out-of-band Exchanging secure information outside the normal communication channels.

packet filter Hardware or software that is designed to prevent malicious packets from entering or leaving computers. Also called *firewall*.

password A secret combination of letters, numbers, and/or characters that only the user should have knowledge of.

Password Authentication Protocol (PAP) A weak authentication protocol that has been replaced by the Extensible Authentication Protocol (EAP).

patch A general software security update intended to cover vulnerabilities that have been discovered.

patch compatibility The impact of a patch on other software or even hardware.

Payment Card Industry Data Security Standard (PCI DSS) A set of security standards that all U.S. companies processing, storing, or transmitting credit card information must follow.

PBKDF2 A popular key stretching password hash algorithm.

peer-to-peer (P2P) network A network that does not have servers, so each device simultaneously functions as both a client and a server to all other devices connected to the network.

penetration testing A test by an outsider that attempts to actually exploit any weaknesses in systems that are vulnerable.

perfect forward secrecy Public key systems that generate random public keys that are different for each session.

persistent cookie A cookie that is recorded on the hard drive of the computer and does not expire when the browser closes.

Personal Identity Verification (PIV) A U.S. government standard for smart cards that covers all government employees.

pharming A phishing attack that automatically redirects the user to a fake site.

phishing Sending an email or displaying a web announcement that falsely claims to be from a legitimate enterprise in an attempt to trick the user into surrendering private information.

ping A utility that sends an ICMP echo request message to a host.

ping flood An attack that uses the Internet Control Message Protocol (ICMP) to flood a victim with packets.

plaintext Cleartext data that is to be encrypted and decrypted by a cryptographic algorithm.

Platform as a Service (PaaS) A cloud service in which consumers can install and run their own specialized applications on the cloud computing network.

plug-in A third-party library that attaches to a web browser and can be embedded inside a webpage.

polymorphic malware Malware code that completely changes from its original form whenever it is executed.

popup blocker Either a program or a feature incorporated within a browser that stops popup advertisements from appearing.

port scanner Software to search a system for port vulnerabilities.

port security Disabling unused application/service ports to reduce the number of threat vectors.

pre-image attack An attack in which one known digest is compared to an unknown digest.

preshared key (PSK) The authentication model used in WPA that requires a secret key value to be entered into the AP and all wireless devices prior to communicating.

Pretty Good Privacy (PGP) A commercial product that is commonly used to encrypt files and messages.

preventive controls A control that attempts to prevent the threat from coming in and reaching contact with the vulnerability.

privacy policy A security policy that outlines how the organization uses personal information it collects.

private cloud A cloud that is created and maintained on a private network.

private key An asymmetric encryption key that does have to be protected.

private key cryptography Cryptographic algorithms that use a single key to encrypt and decrypt a message.

privilege escalation An attack that exploits a vulnerability in software to gain access to resources that the user normally would be restricted from accessing.

program virus A computer virus that infects executable program files.

protected distribution system (PDS) A system of cable conduits that is used to protect classified information being transmitted between two secure areas.

Protected EAP (PEAP) An EAP method designed to simplify the deployment of 802.1x by using Microsoft Windows logins and passwords.

protocol analyzer Hardware or software that captures packets to decode and analyze their contents.

proximity reader A device that detects an emitted signal in order to identify the owner.

proxy server A computer or an application program that intercepts user requests from the internal secure network and then processes those requests on behalf of the users.

public cloud A cloud in which the services and infrastructure are offered to all users with access provided remotely through the Internet.

public key An asymmetric encryption key that does not have to be protected.

public key cryptography Cryptography that uses two mathematically related keys.

public key infrastructure (PKI) A framework for managing all of the entities involved in creating, storing, distributing, and revoking digital certificates.

qualitative risk calculation An approach to risk calculation that uses an "educated guess" based on observation.

quantitative risk calculation An approach to risk calculation that attempts to create actual numbers of the risk by using historical data.

quantum cryptography A type of asymmetric cryptography that attempts to use the unusual and unique behavior of microscopic objects to enable users to securely develop and share keys.

RACE Integrity Primitives Evaluation Message Digest (RIPEMD) A hash algorithm that uses two different and independent parallel chains of computation and then combines the result at the end of the process.

RAID (Redundant Array of Independent Drives) A technology that uses multiple hard disk drives for increased reliability and performance.

rainbow tables Large pregenerated data sets of encrypted passwords used in password attacks.

ransomware Malware that prevents a user's device from properly operating until a fee is paid.

RC4 An RC stream cipher that will accept keys up to 128 bits in length.

recovery point objective (RPO) The maximum length of time that an organization can tolerate between backups.

recovery time objective (RTO) The length of time it will take to recover data that has been backed up.

Registration Authority (RA) A subordinate entity designed to handle specific CA tasks such as processing certificate requests and authenticating users.

remote access Any combination of hardware and software that enables remote users to access a local internal network.

Remote Authentication Dial In User Service (RADIUS) An industry standard authentication service with widespread support scross nearly all vendors of networking equipment.

remote wiping The ability to remotely erase sensitive data stored on a mobile device.

replay An attack that makes a copy of the transmission before sending it to the recipient.

reverse proxy A computer or an application program that routes incoming requests to the correct server.

RF jamming Intentionally flooding the radio frequency (RF) spectrum with extraneous RF signal "noise" that creates interference and prevents communications from occurring.

risk A situation that involves exposure to danger.

risk assessment The process of identifying threats.

risk avoidance Identifying the risk but making the decision to not engage in the activity.

rogue access point An unauthorized AP that allows an attacker to bypass many of the network security configurations and opens the network and its users to attacks.

Role Based Access Control (RBAC) A "real-world" access control model in which access is based on a user's job function within the organization.

role-based training Specialized training that is customized to the specific role that an employee holds in the organization.

rootkit A set of software tools used by an attacker to hide the actions or presence of other types of malicious software.

router A device that can forward packets across computer networks.

RSA The most common asymmetric cryptography algorithm.

Rule Based Access Control (RBAC) An access control model that can dynamically assign roles to subjects based on a set of rules defined by a custodian.

rule-based management The process of administration that relies on following procedural and technical rules.

safe A ruggedized steel box with a lock.

salt A random string that is used in hash algorithms.

sandboxing Using a virtual machine to run a suspicious program to determine if it is malware.

Sarbanes-Oxley Act (Sarbox) A U.S. law designed to fight corporate corruption.

SCADA (supervisory control and data acquisition) Large-scale, industrial-control systems.

script kiddie Individual who lacks advanced knowledge of computers and networks and so uses downloaded automated attack software to attack information systems.

Secure Copy Protocol (SCP) A TCP/IP protocol used mainly on UNIX and Linux devices that securely transports files by encrypting files and commands.

Secure Digital (SD) A small form factor storage media of a variety of different types and sizes.

Secure FTP (SFTP) A secure TCP/IP protocol that is used for transporting files by encrypting and compressing all data and commands.

Secure Hash Algorithm (SHA) A secure hash algorithm that creates more secure hash values than Message Digest (MD) algorithms.

Secure LDAP Transporting LDAP traffic over Secure Sockets Layer (SSL) or Transport Layer Security (TLS).

Secure Shell (SSH) A Linux/UNIX-based command interface and protocol for securely accessing a remote computer.

Secure Sockets Layer (SSL) A protocol originally developed by Netscape for securely transmitting data.

Security Assertion Markup Language (SAML) An Extensible Markup Language (XML) standard that allows secure web domains to exchange user authentication and authorization data.

security control Any device or process that is used to reduce risk.

security control testing Testing the existing security configuration.

security log Log that can reveal the types of attacks that are being directed at the network and if any of the attacks were successful.

security policy A written document that states how an organization plans to protect the company's information technology assets.

separation of duties The practice of requiring that processes should be divided between two or more individuals.

server-side validation Having the server perform all validations and error recovery procedures.

Service Level Agreement (SLA) A contract between a vendor and a client that specifies what services will be provided, the responsibilities of each party, and any guarantees of service.

service pack Software that is a cumulative package of all security updates plus additional features.

Service Set Identifier (SSID) The alphanumeric user-supplied network name of a WLAN.

session cookie A cookie that is stored in Random Access Memory (RAM), instead of on the hard drive, and only lasts only for the duration of a visit to a website.

session hijacking An attack in which an attacker attempts to impersonate the user by using the user's session token.

session keys Symmetric keys to encrypt and decrypt information exchanged during a handshake session between a web browser and web server.

session token A form of verification used when accessing a secure web application.

shoulder surfing Watching an authorized user enter a security code on a keypad.

sign A written placard that explains a warning, such as notice that an area is restricted.

signature-based monitoring A monitoring technique used by an intrusion detection system (IDS) that examines network traffic to look for well-known patterns and compares the activities against a predefined signature.

Simple Network Management Protocol (SNMP) A TCP/IP protocol that exchanges management information between networked devices. It allows network administrators to remotely monitor, manage, and configure devices on the network.

Single Loss Expectancy (SLE) The expected monetary loss every time a risk occurs.

single point of failure A component or entity in a system which, if it no longer functions, would adversely affect the entire system.

single sign-on (SSO) Using one authentication credential to access multiple accounts or applications.

single-factor authentication Using one type of authentication credential.

site survey An in-depth examination and analysis of a wireless LAN site.

smart card A card that contains an integrated circuit chip that can hold information used as part of the authentication process.

smartphone A mobile cell phone that has an operating system for running apps and accessing the Internet.

smurf attack An attack that broadcasts a ping request to computers yet changes the address so that all responses are sent to the victim.

snapshot An instance of a particular state of a virtual machine that can be saved for later use.

social engineering A means of gathering information for an attack by relying on the weaknesses of individuals.

social networking Grouping individuals and organizations into clusters or groups based on a like affiliation.

Software as a Service (SaaS) A model of cloud computing in which the vendor provides access to the vendor's software applications running on a cloud infrastructure.

spam Unsolicited email.

spear phishing A phishing attack that targets only specific users.

spim A variation of spam, which targets instant messaging users instead of email users.

sponge function A cryptographic function that applies a process on the input that has been padded with additional characters until all characters are used.

spoofing Impersonating another computer or device.

spyware A general term used to describe software that spies on users by gathering information without consent.

SQL injection An attack that targets SQL servers by injecting commands to be manipulated by the database.

SQL vs. NoSQL An argument regarding which database technology is better. Also called *NoSQL databases vs. SQL databases*.

standard biometrics Using fingerprints or other unique physical characteristics of a person's face, hands, or eyes for authentication.

state-sponsored attackers Attacker commissioned by governments to attack enemies' information systems.

static environment Devices in which additional hardware cannot easily be added or attached.

steganography Hiding the existence of data within another type of file.

storage area network (SAN) A dedicated network storage facility that provides access to data storage over a high-speed network.

stream cipher An algorithm that takes one character and replaces it with one character.

subnetting or **subnet addressing** A technique that uses IP addresses to divide a network into network, subnet, and host.

succession planning Determining in advance who will be authorized to take over in the event of the incapacitation or death of key employees.

switch A device that connects network segments and forwards only frames intended for that specific device or frames sent to all devices.

symmetric cryptographic algorithms Encryption that uses a single key to encrypt and decrypt a message.

SYN flood attack An attack that takes advantage of the procedures for initiating a TCP/IP session.

system image A snapshot of the current state of the computer that contains all settings and data.

tablet Portable computing device that is generally larger than smartphones and smaller than notebooks, and is focused on ease of use.

tabletop exercises Exercises that simulate an emergency situation but in an informal and stress-free environment.

TACACS+ The current version of the Terminal Access Control Access Control System (TACACS) authentication service.

tailgating When an unauthorized individual enters a restricted-access building by following an authorized user.

technical controls Security controls that are carried out or managed by devices.

technical risk control type A risk control type that involves using technology to control risk.

Telnet An older TCP/IP protocol and an application used for text-based communication.

Temporal Key Integrity Protocol (TKIP) The WPA and WPA2 encryption technology.

Terminal Access Control Access Control System (TACACS) An authentication service commonly used on UNIX devices that communicates by forwarding user authentication information to a centralized server. The current version is TACACS+.

third-party cookie A cookie that was created by a third party that is different from the primary website.

third-party integration Combining an organization's systems and data with outside entities.

third-party trust A trust model in which two individuals trust each other because each individually trusts a third party.

threat A type of action that has the potential to cause harm.

threat agent A person or element that has the power to carry out a threat.

threat likelihood The probability that a threat will actually occur.

threat vector The means by which an attack could occur.

time-based one-time password (TOTP) A one-time password that changes after a set period of time.

time-of-day restriction Limitation imposed as to when a user can log in to a system or access resources.

token A small device that can be affixed to a keychain with a window display that shows a code to be used for authentication.

transference Transferring the risk to a third party.

transitive access An attack that exploits the trust relationship between three parties.

transitive trust A two-way relationship that is automatically created between parent and child domains in a Microsoft Active Directory Forest.

Transmission Control Protocol/Internet Protocol (TCP/IP) The most common protocol suite used today for local area networks (LANs) and the Internet.

Transport Layer Security (TLS) A protocol that is more secure than SSL and guarantees privacy and data integrity between applications.

Triple Data Encryption Standard (3DES) A symmetric cipher that was designed to replace DES.

Trivial File Transfer Protocol (TFTP) A light version of FTP that uses a small amount of memory and has limited functionality.

Trojan horse An executable program that is advertised as performing one activity but which actually performs a malicious activity.

trust model The type of trust relationship that can exist between individuals or entities.

trusted OS An operating system that has been designed through OS hardening.

Trusted Platform Module (TPM) A chip on the motherboard of the computer that provides cryptographic services.

Twofish A derivation of the Blowfish algorithm that is considered to be strong.

typo squatting Redirecting a user to a fictitious website based on a misspelling of the URL. Also called *URL hijacking*.

Unified Threat Management (UTM) Network hardware that provides multiple security functions.

URL filtering Restricting access to unapproved websites.

URL hijacking Redirecting a user to a fictitious website based on a misspelling of the URL. Also called *typo squatting*.

username An identifier of a user logging into a system.

video surveillance Monitoring activity that is captured by a video camera.

virtual LAN (VLAN) A technology that allows scattered users to be logically grouped together even though they may be attached to different switches.

virtual private network (VPN) A technology that enables use of an unsecured public network as if it were a secure private network.

virtualization A means of managing and presenting computer resources by function without regard to their physical layout or location.

vishing A phishing attack uses telephone calls instead of emails.

VPN concentrator A device that aggregates VPN connections.

vulnerability A flaw or weakness that allows a threat agent to bypass security.

vulnerability assessment A systematic and methodical evaluation of the exposure of assets to attackers, forces of nature, and any other entity that could cause potential harm.

vulnerability scan An automated software search through a system for any known security weaknesses that creates a report of those potential exposures.

vulnerability scanner Generic term for a range of products that look for vulnerabilities in networks or systems.

war chalking The process of documenting and then advertising the location of WLANs for others to use.

war driving Searching for wireless signals from an automobile or on foot using a portable computing device.

warm site A remote site that contains computer equipment but does not have active Internet or telecommunication facilities, and does not have backups of data.

watering hole attack A malicious attack that is directed toward a small group of specific individuals who visit the same website.

web application firewall A special type of application-aware firewall that looks at the applications using HTTP.

web security gateway A device that can block malicious content in real time as it appears (without first knowing the URL of a dangerous site).

whaling A phishing attack that targets only wealthy individuals.

white box A penetration test where the tester has an in-depth knowledge of the network and systems being tested, including network diagrams, IP addresses, and even the source code of custom applications.

whitelist Permitting nothing unless it appears on the list.

whole disk encryption Cryptography that can be applied to entire disks.

Wi-Fi Protected Access (WPA) The original set of protections from the Wi-Fi Alliance designed to address both encryption and authentication.

Wi-Fi Protected Access 2 (WPA2) The second generation of WPA security from the Wi-Fi Alliance that addresses authentication and encryption on WLANs and is currently the most secure model for Wi-Fi security.

Wi-Fi Protected Setup (WPS) An optional means of configuring security on wireless local area networks primarily intended to help users who have little or no knowledge of security to quickly and easily implement security on their WLANs. Due to design and implementation flaws, WPS is not considered secure.

Wired Equivalent Privacy (WEP) An IEEE 802.11 security protocol designed to ensure that only authorized parties can view transmitted wireless information. WEP has significant vulnerabilities and is not considered secure.

wireless local area network (WLAN) A wireless network designed to replace or supplement a wired local area network (LAN).

wireless replay A passive attack in which the attacker captures transmitted wireless data, records it, and then sends it on to the original recipient without the attacker's presence being detected.

worm A malicious program designed to enter a computer via a network to take advantage of a vulnerability in an application or an operating system.

wrapper functions A substitute for a regular function that is used in testing.

Xmas Tree port scan Sending a packet with every option set to *on* for whatever protocol is in use to observe how a host responds.

XML (Extensible Markup Language) A markup language that is designed to *carry* data, in contrast to HTML, which indicates how to *display* data.

XML injection An attack that injects XML tags and data into a database.

zero-day attack Attack that exploits previously unknown vulnerabilities, so victims have no time (zero days) to prepare for or defend against the attack.

zombie An infected computer that is under the remote control of an attacker.

Index